SECOND ED

REAPPRAISALS IN CANADIAN HISTORY
POST CONFEDERATION

C.M. Wallace

R.M. Bray

A.D. Gilbert

Laurentian University

PRENTICE HALL CANADA INC.,
SCARBOROUGH, ONTARIO

Canadian Cataloguing in Publication Data

Main entry under title:
Reappraisals in Canadian history, post confederation

2nd ed.
Includes index.
ISBN 0-13-454638-5

1. Canada – History – 1867–   . 2. Canada –
History – 1867–   – Historiography. I. Wallace,
C.M. (Carl Murray), 1932–   . II. Bray, R.M.
(Robert Matthew), 1944–   . III. Gilbert, A.D.
(Angus Duncan), 1941–1994.

FC500.R42 1996   971.05   C95-931679-5
F1033.R42 1996

© 1996   Prentice-Hall Canada Inc., Scarborough, Ontario
A Viacom Company

Prentice-Hall, Inc., Englewood Cliffs, New Jersey
Prentice-Hall International (UK) Limited, London
Prentice-Hall of Australia, Pty. Limited, Sydney
Prentice-Hall Hispanoamericana, S.A., Mexico City
Prentice-Hall of India Private Limited, New Delhi
Prentice-Hall of Japan, Inc., Tokyo
Simon & Schuster Asia Private Limited, Singapore
Editora Prentice-Hall do Brasil, Ltda., Rio de Janeiro

ISBN 0-13-454638-5

Acquisitions Editor: Allan Gray
Production Editor: Valerie Adams
Production Coordinator: Deborah Starks
Permissions: Marijke Leupen
Cover Design: Julia Hall
Cover Image: André Bieler, 1938 "Election Day, St. Adèle,"
              Art Gallery of Ontario
Page Layout: Arlene Edgar

  2 3 4 5 RRD 00 99 98 97

Printed and bound in the U.S.A.

Every reasonable effort has been made to obtain permissions for all articles and data used in this edition. If errors or omissions have occurred, they will be corrected in future editions provided written notification has been received by the publisher.

We welcome readers' comments, which can be sent by e-mail to
      collegeinfo_pubcanada@prenhall.com

Table of Contents

Preface

Reappraisals in Canadian History is designed for use in university-level survey courses. It is, however, neither a textbook nor a traditional reader. Each of the units in the two volumes focuses on differing or complementary interpretations of a particular historical problem. A brief introduction to each unit establishes the context for the selected readings, and suggestions for relevant additional sources are included.

The vitality in Canadian historical studies over the past two decades has been outstanding, resulting in a profusion of new periodicals and monographs. Few organizations, groups, or regions are now without a journal. This has created both opportunities and challenges in fashioning a collection such as this. Although much recent historical writing is included, we have not neglected the important contributions of the previous generation of historians. In assembling these volumes we have consciously rejected the popular trend of trying to satisfy every region and province, every interest group, every minority, everybody. Instead we attempted to find common threads pointing to the integration of the exploding body of literature and interests. This topical approach demanded that all interests, including such disparate ones as regions, women, politics, the underclasses, and minorities, be part of the total fabric rather than segregated ghettoes.

In assembling this collection we have incurred a number of obligations. Faye Kennedy, formerly of Prentice Hall Canada, first persuaded us that there was a need for such a collection. We wish also to thank the Dean of the Faculty of Social Science and the Institute of Northern Ontario Research and Development at Laurentian University for financial assistance. Several of our students, including Ross Danaher, Michael Stevenson and James Watson, gave us logistical support. The students in HIST 1406/1407 participated cheerfully as we experimented with the classroom use of these materials in tutorials. Leo Larivière created the maps. Rose-May Demoré, our departmental secretary, responded to every call for help. Finally we must thank the dozens of historians, editors and publishers who have generously given us permission to reprint this material.

Since the publication of the first edition of *Reappraisals*, our co-editor, colleague and friend, Angus Gilbert, has died of cancer. While we have made extensive changes, much of Angus' original contribution remains and we therefore dedicate this edition to his memory.

C.M. WALLACE

R.M. BRAY

Laurentian University
Sudbury, Ontario

Introduction

Canadian History and Historians

History is misunderstood more often than not. At a superficial level it appears to be one of the few immutables in an ever-changing world. That the past itself can never be altered is irrefutable, and students frequently choose history as an option at university believing that at least one subject will provide security when others mystify with unique concepts, vocabulary and content. That cozy view of history never lasts long, for as a discipline history is complex, malleable, and imprecise, subject to changing conditions and perspectives. Far from being set in cement, history is continuously being recast by each generation's need to find its own past. If R.G. Collingwood was correct, then "every new generation must rewrite history in its own way." The past that he, Winston Churchill and others found meaningful differs dramatically from that of today's leaders and their societies.

This characteristic of history causes much confusion for students and academics alike. A psychology professor at lunch with several historians recently declared that, after she had taken world history in grade eight, further study was irrelevant. The subject, like Napoleon, was dead. One of the historians ventured the opinion that history had possibly changed more in the past twenty years than psychology. At that point she threw up her hands and left, unable to entertain such a ludicrous proposition. Yet it may be true.

That dynamic nature of the discipline of history, when compared to the permanence of past events such as the death of Napoleon, is the apparent paradox the psychology professor never unravelled. Over the past three decades a revolution has taken place in historical scholarship. In the era after the Second World War a sort of plateau, encompassing a broad consensus about the nature of the discipline, was reached. The traditional scholar worked for months or years in archives, poring over primary sources, and producing "revisionist" books or articles published in the handful of journals that all historians of Canada read. Triumphs were achieved with the discovery of new source material or a new angle on a known subject. Politics and biography were favoured, though economic, religious, military and international topics found their specialists. The overall nature of history as the study of the activities and ideas of elites, however, was rarely questioned. This view from the "court," or top-down, became the textbook version of the Canadian past, and while there were divisions over some interpretations based on ideology, religion, or even personal hostility, there was no division on what history itself was.

In Canada the small coterie of academics dominating the field included Marcel Trudel, Donald Creighton, A.R.M. Lower, W.L. Morton, Hilda Neatby, C.P. Stacey, W.S. MacNutt, Frank Underhill, Guy Frégault, and Margaret Ormsby. A younger generation of "revisionists" from the same mould was expanding the content without challenging the structures. Among them were J.M.S. Careless, Peter Waite, Margaret Prang, W.J. Eccles, Ramsay Cook, Jean Hamelin, Ken McNaught, Blair Neatby, and Jacques Monet. These people all knew each other personally, frequently comparing notes at the Public Archives of Canada, then located on Sussex Drive beside the Royal Mint in Ottawa. At the annual meetings of the Canadian Historical Association they read papers to each other, and were never short of advice. The *Canadian Historical Review*, published by the University of Toronto Press, was the final authority in English Canada, while Abbé Groulx reigned over French Canada with the *Revue d'histoire de l'Amérique française*. It was from this more or less homogeneous group that the dominant view of Canada, as presented in school textbooks, emerged. The comfortable unity of this well-written version of Canada's past permitted it to survive its generation, which many regard as the "Golden Age" of Canadian historical scholarship.

By the late 1960s, however, several younger scholars reacted against that veneration of the images of a previous generation. To them the historical imagination had been crippled by consistency. More than that, the consensus version of the past, in their view, had no relevance for the current generation. One may admire a Rolls Royce Silver Ghost, a 1955 Chevrolet, or even a Model T, the argument goes, but one must not confuse an abacus with a computer, a museum piece with modern needs.

It is the nature of history that the status quo does not survive long, and in the upheaval that characterized the whole mentality of the 1960s, several academics began to search for a more "usable past," one that abandoned the impressionistic views from the "court," and aimed at the reconstruction of a more meaningful society. The "New Social History" was the umbrella under which most of the innovations may be grouped. The dissatisfaction with a Canadian past dominated by political and economic factors led to a renovation with new methodologies, different approaches and alternate subject matter muscling in on the old-school-tie network. Subjects once ignored moved to centre stage, including work on classes and class relations, demography, literacy, the family, leisure, mobility, immigration, religion and education, though there was little cohesion among the disparate activities. Quantification and the computer found their place in the historian's baggage. *Histoire sociale / Social History*, co-sponsored by the University of Ottawa and Carleton University in 1968, eventually provided a focus and emerged as an alternate journal, though its lack of coherent editorial policy was simply a reflection of the diversity of opinion within the discipline. In a sense each historian could become a different school. The *Annales* of France, for example, were the source of inspiration for many French Canadians, while most English Canadians turned to American sociology for their models. Although there was considerable resentment over this "invasion of the barbarians" among the traditional historians, their own anecdotal approach invited criticism from those who asked different questions of sources and approached the past from new perspectives.

By the 1970s a veritable floodgate had opened. The annual meetings of the Canadian Historical Association became not one but a dozen or more fragments meeting separately. There was the ethnic group, the labour, the Atlantic, the Western, the Arctic, the Native, the women, the urban, the local, the material, the oral—the divisions were endless. Each of these had the capacity to subdivide. Labour quickly separated into the "old-fashioned" and the "New Left," with the latter winning the day and mounting its own journal, *Labour/Le Travailleur*. Each segment, in fact, launched one or more journals, such as *Urban History Review*, *Canadian Ethnic Studies*, *Polyphony*, *Canadian Woman Studies*, *Journal of Canadian Studies*, *B C Studies*, and *The American Review of Canadian Studies*. The range of topics and quality of scholarship were like the rainbow. Some, like *Acadiensis: Journal of the History of the Atlantic Region*, founded in 1971 at the University of New Brunswick, established and maintained an enviable reputation. Others have been less successful.

As a consequence of this fragmentation over recent decades, a student is faced with not one but many versions of Canadian history. This confusion may be considered an unnecessary encumbrance to those who are content with the "good old stuff," but that implies the study of a dead subject. The reappraisal is never-ending, and the challenge for the student is not to learn a few facts and dates but to sample the literature and to recognize what the authors are doing with the subject and trying to do to the reader. This requires an agile and a critical mind.

Reappraisals in Canadian History is intended to reflect this diversity of interpretation in Canadian history and to present it in such a way as to enable a student to make sense of it. This is not a "textbook" history of Canada, and makes no attempt to survey all of the main developments in that history. Nor is it simply a collection of readings, randomly selected and with little or no relationship one to another. Rather, each of the chapters is devoted to a particular historical problem and the different ways in which historians have approached that problem. In some cases their conclusions stand in sharp contradiction to each other; in others they are complementary. In every case students should attempt not merely to grasp the author's conclusions, but, of even greater importance, to understand how they were reached.

In order to do this it is useful to understand the variety of reasons that may lead different historians to reach different conclusions about what appears to be the same historical problem. In one sense, of course, there is nothing new about this. The debate over "historical relativism" is an old one, and it is now a truism that historians are influenced by the context in which they themselves live. It is, after all, hardly surprising that their view of the past is, to some degree at least, relative to their own time and place and circumstance, to their own preferences and prejudices.

This may mean that they view historical evidence in a new light, or that they pose different questions of the past. It has long been accepted, therefore, that there will be differences of emphasis and interpretation, not only between different generations of historians, but also between historians of the same era.

The present fragmentation of the discipline, however, goes far beyond the traditional recognition of the relativity of historical knowledge. Implicit in it is fundamental disagreement over content and methodology, the meaning of history and its purpose. The one point on which historians do agree, however, is that not all historical interpretations are of equal validity. Certainly historians are less inclined than scholars in other disciplines to claim to have discovered any final "truths." This is understandable, given the nature of the evidence with which they deal and the problems with which they are concerned. The readings in this volume are in themselves testimony to the elusiveness of any final answers in history. Despite these limitations, historians do insist that historical scholarship can and must be subjected to critical scrutiny, that historical evidence and the use to which that evidence is put can be evaluated. The study of history at any kind of advanced level requires the development of these analytical skills, and never more so than with its current fragmentation. It is this, rather than the mastery of voluminous detail, that distinguishes the historian from the mere antiquarian. One of the purposes of this collection of readings is to assist students to develop their critical skills. Within each chapter, therefore, students should attempt to identify the interpretative thrust of each author, how the interpretation of one author differs from or complements that of another, what sources and methodologies have been employed, and, finally, how convincingly each author has based his or her interpretation on the historical evidence.

There are a number of fairly obvious points to look for. Has an author found new evidence which calls into question previous work on the subject? Is a new methodology being applied? Is anecdotal evidence, for example, being challenged by statistical analysis? Is a new type of historical evidence being brought to bear on an old problem? Is the historical problem itself being defined in an entirely new way?

For the period in Canadian history since 1867 the student is faced not only with the entirely new nation that was created that year, but with an amalgam of the several histories that were brought together and the complexity of a large nation state in a rapidly changing world. The tensions of the pre-Confederation era survived into the union, many of them being magnified in the new state. These included the regional, linguistic, religious, political and class divisions that were both obvious and divisive. These became even more complicated as Canada emerged from the pre-industrial world of small cities and towns nestled among the dominant rural society that made up over 85 percent of the population. In the decades after 1867 massive technological innovation, combined with rapid urbanization and industrialization, drastically altered the world. Large factory cities emerged in the wilderness and on the prairies, displacing previous inhabitants and creating a dominant urban culture to replace the rural folk. The history of the era, therefore, reflects the reality of a rapidly changing world.

The fourteen chapters in this volume are a selection from that dynamic history. An attempt has been made to strike a balance among the traditional subjects, such as politics, and the several newer fragments. There are three chapters centred directly on politics, though this subject appears in several others. Chapter 1 is somewhat traditional in that it offers two versions of the centralist/regionalist dichotomy that remains a constant throughout Canadian history. The politics of patronage in the Macdonald and Laurier eras are examined in chapter 4, and W.L.M. King is encountered in chapter 10. Not surprisingly King has attracted a diversity of opinion and the three readings in this unit move from a traditional examination of his leadership to psycho-history.

The diversity of Canadian society is examined in several chapters. Chapter 8, "The Immigrant Adjustment in Western Canada," offers the student two very different perspectives on the subject. Women are central to chapter 5 in which there are three positions on women and work, a traditional, a"new left," and a feminist view which emphasizes gender. Class is the focus of the debate in chapter 6. The fumbling unemployment policies of the government in the 1930s are central to chapter 9, while the long shadow of McCarthyism in Canada during the 1940s and 1950s is the problem in chapter 13. The wars of the twentieth century have scarred Canada in a number of ways, and these are discussed in chapter 7, "The Great War," and chapter 11, "World War II: The Dieppe Debacle." Other units look at a variety of subjects, including Riel, Maritime industrialization, Quebec, and the policy of multiculturalism.

Any rigid categorization of the chapters is bound to be misleading since politics, economics, social dynamics and regional aspects pervade most studies about Canada in one way or another. The student must learn to stride through the variety, identifying the interpretations, the mind-sets, the methodologies, and the mythologies. Each chapter in this collection offers a variety of interpretations which are frequently contradictory. At the same time, each chapter has a coherence which explains something about Canada, its history and its historians. Since history is what historians say it is, the student has both the opportunity and the responsibility to identify those views and the objectives of the historians. History will continue to be misunderstood, and the student must know why.

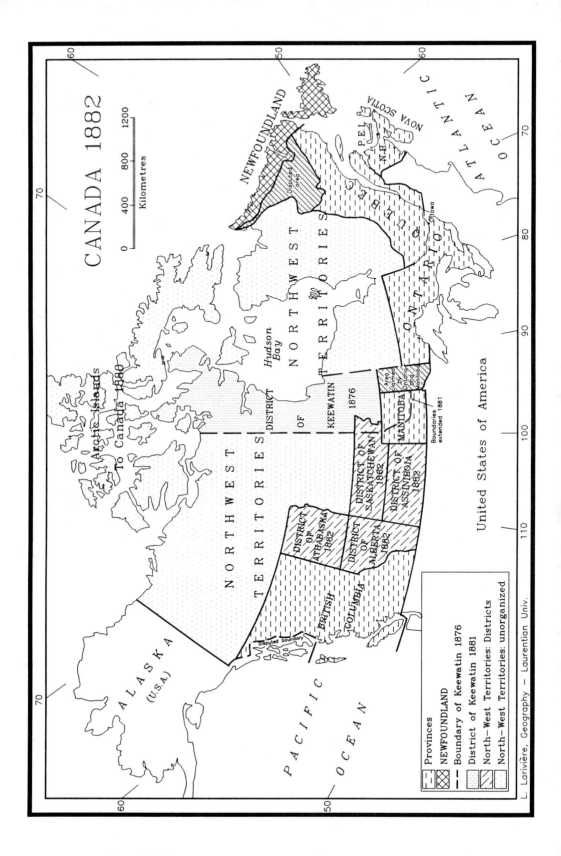

CANADA 1882

ATLANTIC OCEAN

NEWFOUNDLAND

NOVA SCOTIA

P.E.I.

N.B.

QUEBEC

Ottawa

ONTARIO

NORTHWEST TERRITORIES

Hudson Bay

DISTRICT OF KEEWATIN 1876

Area claimed by Ontario and Manitoba

MANITOBA

Boundaries extended 1881

DISTRICT OF SASKATCHEWAN 1882

DISTRICT OF ASSINIBOIA 1882

Arctic Islands

To Canada 1880

NORTHWEST TERRITORIES

DISTRICT OF ATHABASKA 1882

DISTRICT OF ALBERTA 1882

BRITISH COLUMBIA

Disputed boundary

ALASKA (U.S.A.)

United States of America

PACIFIC OCEAN

Kilometres
0   400   800   1200

Disputed area

Provinces
NEWFOUNDLAND
Boundary of Keewatin 1876
District of Keewatin 1881
North–West Territories: Districts
North–West Territories: unorganized

L. Larivière, Geography — Laurentian Univ.

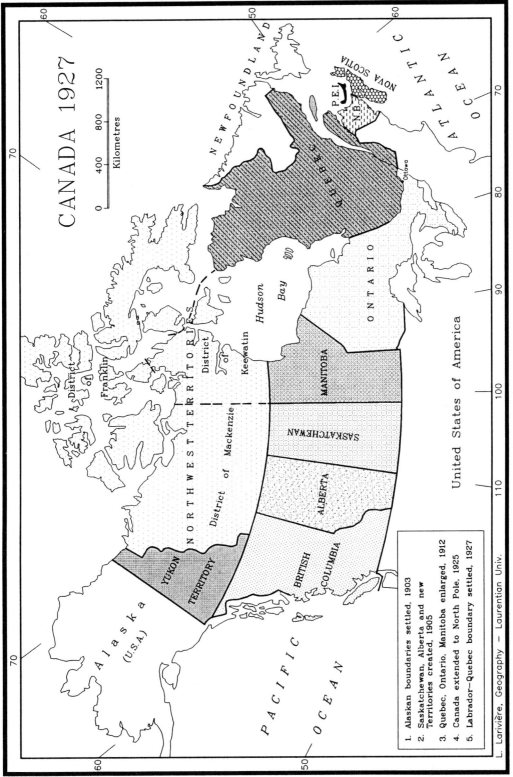

CANADA 1927

Kilometres
0 400 800 1200

1. Alaskan boundaries settled, 1903
2. Saskatchewan, Alberta and new Territories created, 1905
3. Quebec, Ontario, Manitoba enlarged, 1912
4. Canada extended to North Pole, 1925
5. Labrador–Quebec boundary settled, 1927

L. Larivière, Geography – Laurentian Univ.

CHAPTER

1 THE FIRST YEARS AFTER CONFEDERATION: CENTRALISM VS. REGIONALISM

The enthusiasm generated by the July 1, 1867, celebrations had barely subsided when the complexity of governing and nation-building became obvious to the Fathers. "Everyone knows of course," wrote Peter Waite, "that Confederation began badly." Difficulties arose at every turn, especially in matters of power sharing. Every act of the new federal government infringed in one way or another on rights and privileges previously held by the provinces or claimed by them. The national tariff, for example, infuriated Maritimers by imposing the higher rates of the old Province of Canada across the new dominion. Antagonisms over language and religion in both New Brunswick and the West led to armed conflict. Domineering and disdainful Ontario, with its increasingly large population, responded negatively to most federal initiatives while pursuing its own imperial dreams. All the while Sir John A. Macdonald and his government were nation-building with breathless haste. Between 1867 and 1873 they annexed half a continent, a record of expansionism with few parallels in history. They began constructing the Intercolonial Railroad from Quebec to Halifax and agreed to build a line to the Pacific. In the process they certainly overreached the capacity of the fragile new nation, adding to the normal stress of the new relationships.

Donald Creighton, in *Canada's First Century* (1972), elaborated on his centralist view of Canadian history developed over several years, most notably his biography of John A. Macdonald, *The Old Chieftain* (1955). In "Confederation

1

and Expansion," included here, he described the working out of the early kinks in the system and the inevitable expansion of Canada across the continent. The opposition of Joseph Howe and the Nova Scotia "Antis" or of "Provincial Firsters" like Oliver Mowat in Ontario, in Creighton's world view, was the story of small-minded people rejecting the national dream. Despite Creighton's images, there were serious flaws in that landscape. Maritimers, for example, were at a significant disadvantage in the new dominion. The old Canadian civil service administered the new nation with something less than sensitivity to the Atlantic provinces, carrying out what the Halifax *Morning Chronicle* called a "miniature reign of terror." The ineffectual Maritime representatives in the House of Commons failed to protect the interests of their electorate while those from Quebec and Ontario, which permitted its members to sit in both federal and provincial houses, had continuity and numbers in the first Parliament. Quebeckers appeared the most conciliated in the new dominion, while Maritimers came to regard the sacrifices of becoming Canadian as being far greater than the benefits. Ontario, on the other hand, took the offensive and under Oliver Mowat's premiership from 1872 to 1896 went about "Remoulding the Constitution." That is the title and theme of the second article by Christopher Armstrong. The powerful position of Ontario in Canadian history was never more obvious than in those first few years when Macdonald and the centralists encountered their most relentless foe in Ontario. Armstrong examines the origin and vitality of Mowat's alternate view of Canada, the "compact theory."

Suggestions for Further Readings

Bercuson, D.J., ed., *Canada and the Burden of Unity*. Toronto: Macmillan, 1977.

Forbes, E.R., *Aspects of Maritime Regionalism, 1867–1927*. Ottawa: Canadian Historical Association, 1983.

Friesen, Gerald, *The Canadian Prairies: A History*. Toronto: University of Toronto Press, 1984.

Hodgins, Bruce W., Don Wright and W.H. Heick, eds., *Federalism in Canada and Australia: The Early Years*. Waterloo: Wilfrid Laurier Press, 1978.

Hynes, Maureen, "A History of the Rise of Women's Consciousness in Canada and Quebec," in *The Hidden History of the Female*, ed. M. Atkins. Toronto: New Hogtown Press, 1971.

Rawlyk, George, ed., *The Atlantic Provinces and the Problems of Confederation*. St. John's: Breakwater Press, 1979.

Shelton, George, ed., *British Columbia and Confederation*. Victoria: University of Victoria, 1967.

Silver, Arthur, *The French Canadian Idea of Confederation, 1864–1900*. Toronto: University of Toronto, 1982.

Stanley, George, "The Caraquet Riots of 1875," *Acadiensis*, II, No. 1, (Autumn 1972), 21–38.

Waite, P.B., "Becoming Canadian: Ottawa's Relations with Maritimers in the First and Twenty-first Years of Confederation," in *National Politics and Community in Canada*, eds. R. Kenneth Carty and W. Peter Ward. Vancouver: University of British Columbia Press, 1986, 153–168.

CONFEDERATION AND EXPANSION

Donald Creighton

The British North America Act of 1867, the act which laid the constitutional framework for the federal union of four British American provinces, Ontario, Quebec, New Brunswick, and Nova Scotia, was a characteristic expression of their collective political experience. Its authors were the thirty-six delegates, known subsequently as the Fathers of Confederation—though some of them did not deserve the title and would, in fact, have indignantly repudiated it—who had met in conference at Charlottetown, Quebec, and London and framed the bases of the union. They were typical mid-Victorian colonial politicians who were intellectually as remote from the eighteenth-century preoccupation with first political principles as they were from the twentieth-century obsession with ethnic and cultural values. They thought of themselves as British subjects, and assumed that they were legitimate heirs of the British constitutional heritage and full participants in the British political experience. Alone among all the colonies that European nations had founded in the New World, the British American provinces had never sought to separate themselves from the Motherland. They had not followed the path through revolution to republicanism which had been first blazed by the United States and worn smooth and commonplace by a long string of slatternly South and Central American republics.

Constitutional monarchy, parliamentary institutions, and responsible government made up a political tradition which was not only British but also British American. The Fathers of Confederation assumed, without question, that this political tradition must be continued unimpaired in the nation they were creating. The calamities that had overtaken republicanism in the past twenty-five years had simply confirmed and strengthened their belief in the wisdom and efficacy of parliamentary institutions on the British model. In western Europe, the republican and liberal governments which had been born of the revolutions of 1848 had weakened and yielded to much more authoritarian and arbitrary régimes; and, in the United States, a terrible civil war had seemed to cast discredit, not only on American federalism, but also on American democracy. In sharp contrast with this tragic republican record of defeat and dishonour, the British constitution, which Walter Bagehot had just celebrated in a new book, had apparently adapted itself to new, more democratic circumstances, without ever sacrificing the continuity of its development. The Fathers of Confederation had good reason for believing that constitutional monarchy on the British model was the best government for free men that had yet been devised. They regarded the British Empire as the greatest association of free states that had ever existed.

From *Canada's First Century, 1867–1967* (Toronto: Macmillan, 1970), 8–22. Reprinted by permission of the estate of Donald Creighton.

There remained, however, the business of adapting British institutions to a union of British provinces—a union which, it was firmly intended, would ultimately extend from ocean to ocean and over a half of the North American continent. Constitutional monarchy on the British model meant parliamentary sovereignty—the concentration of political power in a single, sovereign legislature; and, if a great many British Americans, including certainly such prominent political leaders as John A. Macdonald and Charles Tupper, could have had their way, they would have preferred to see the whole of British America united in a single Parliament and government. But legislative union, however politically desirable, was not thought to be politically possible. The Fathers of Confederation believed that one legislature would be incapable of coping with the diverse needs of a number of varied and widely separated communities. The French-speaking majority of one of those regions, the future province of Quebec, wished to protect its distinctive culture with a measure of local autonomy; and the provinces of the Atlantic region, which had not developed any system of municipal institutions, would have been left without any local government at all if their provincial legislatures had been taken away.

No, the union could not be legislative. It would have to be federal. But, though the Fathers of Confederation recognized the inevitability of federalism, they could not help regarding it as a suspect and sinister form of government. There had never yet been a federal union in the British Empire; the United States of America was the only federal union in the English-speaking world; and in 1864–7, when the Fathers of Confederation were planning to unite British America, the United States could scarcely be considered a convincing advertisement for federalism. The republic was, in fact, convulsed by a fearful civil war, a war which seemed to prove that a federal union was a divisive form of government which might very readily break up as a result of its own centrifugal pressures. The 'federal principle,' as British Americans called it then, was usually regarded as a highly potent political drug, which might prove efficacious in the cure of certain constitutions, but which must be administered in small doses, with great precautions, and never without a readily available antidote. The obvious corrective to the disruptive forces of 'states rights' was a strong central government; and this the Fathers of Confederation were determined to create. British American union, they admitted, would have to be federal in character; but at the same time it must also be the most strongly centralized union that was possible under federal forms.

This basic principle guided all the planning whose end result was the British North America Act of 1867. The Fathers of Confederation openly declared that they proposed to correct the mistakes and remedy the weaknesses of the American federal union. 'The primary error at the formation of their constitution,' John A. Macdonald said at the Quebec Conference, 'was that each state reserved to itself all sovereign rights, save the small portion delegated. We must reverse this process by strengthening the general government and conferring on the provincial bodies only such powers as may be required for local purposes.' While, in the United States, residuary legislative powers were retained by the State, or by the people, in the new Dominion of Canada they were to be held by the federal Parliament. The Provinces and the Dominion were not to be coordinate in authority, as a purist definition of federalism would have required them to be; on the contrary, as Macdonald frankly explained, the provincial governments were to be subordinate to the central government. Their responsibilities and functions, it was generally expected, would be relatively small and unimportant; and their legislative authority, even within the field of provincial powers, was not to be absolute. The chief provincial executive officer, the lieutenant-governor, who was to be appointed by the federal government, could reserve provincial bills for the federal government's consideration, and the federal government could disallow provincial acts. 'We thereby strengthen the central parliament,' said Macdonald in the Canadian legislature after he had finished describing federal powers, 'and make the Confederation one people and one government, instead of five peoples and five governments with merely a point of authority connecting us to a limited and insufficient extent.'

The primary aim of Confederation was political—the creation of a great 'new nationality'; and the British North America Act was the result of a political agreement among several provinces, not of a cultural compact of two ethnic groups, English and French. Before 1867, British America still remained, and was still regarded, not as a cultural duality but, in the words of George Cartier, as 'a diversity of races.' 'In our own federation,' Cartier declared, 'we should have Catholic and Protestant, English, French, Irish, and Scotch, and each by his efforts and his success would increase the prosperity and glory of the new confederacy.' Language was only one of the many components that made up the curious cultural medley that was British America before Confederation. National origin and national tradition—Irish, Scotch, and English, as well as French—might be equally influential, and religion, so often sharpened by sectarian bitterness, was perhaps the most important of all. The Fathers of Confederation had to take account of these differences; but their great aim was not the perpetuation of cultural diversity but the establishment of a united nation. At the Quebec and London conferences they gave, on the whole, relatively little time to the discussion of ethnic and cultural questions; and the resolutions they adopted on these matters, though important and essential, were few, precise in their wording, and limited in their scope.

The British North America Act contained no general declaration of principle that Canada was to be a bilingual and bicultural nation—or, for that matter, that it would remain 'a diversity of races.' The Fathers of Confederation were as little inclined to lay down the law about the cultural purpose and future of their new nation as they were to issue a general pronouncement on the nature and probable destiny of mankind. The English and French languages were given equal official status in the Parliament and the courts of Canada, and in the legislature and courts of Quebec. Canada was to establish only two federal courts, the Supreme Court and the Exchequer Court, at Ottawa; and all the other courts in the country were to be provincial courts, constituted and maintained by the provinces. The French language had thus no official standing in the courts of any of the provinces except Quebec; and, perhaps even more important, it was given no protected place in any of the nation's schools. The Fathers of Confederation showed a fair amount of interest in education and its legislative control; but it was very characteristic of these typical British Americans, with their strong denominational affiliations and frequent sectarian biases, that what concerned them was not the role of language, but the place of religion, in the schools. The provinces were given the power to legislate in respect of education; but this authority was limited by some rather complicated provisions designed to protect any rights or privileges concerning separate or denominational schools.

In sum, the distinctive cultural features of French Canada—its language, civil code, and educational system—were confirmed in those parts of the new Dominion in which they had already become established by law or custom. They were not extended in their application to Ontario and the Atlantic provinces. They were given no protected position in the nation as a whole.

II

The making and inauguration of the new federal constitution, embodied in the British North America Act, was only the first, theoretical stage in the building of the new nation; the far greater task of its territorial completion and integration still lay ahead. The Canada that celebrated the first Dominion Day on the 1st of July, 1867, was composed of only four provinces, Ontario, Quebec (the two former Canadas), New Brunswick, and Nova Scotia; and, in Nova Scotia, Joseph Howe was leading a popular movement for secession from the Dominion. Beyond the restricted boundaries of the original Dominion, the rest of British America, immense, vulnerable, and largely uninhabited, stretched away, east, west, and north, and far into the distance. In the east, the two island provinces, Newfoundland and Prince Edward Island, still held stubbornly aloof from the union. In the far west, the now united province of British Columbia was a likely candidate for admission to Confederation; but she was separated from Canada by Rupert's Land and the North-West Territories, a vast expanse of almost empty country, still owned or controlled by the Hudson's Bay Company.

A formidable task of national expansion and unification confronted the new federal government, appointed on the 1st of July, 1867. The first cabinet was a coalition of former Confederates, drawn from both parties and all four provinces, and representing every important interest—provincial, ethnic, and religious— in nicely graduated numbers. Its leader, the first Prime Minister of the new

Canada, was John Alexander Macdonald. At fifty-two, he seemed oddly youthful in appearance. His dark, curly hair was thick, his eyes amused and friendly, his smile genially sardonic. The long oval of his face was spare, and almost as unlined as a young man's; and, unlike most of his contemporaries, who followed the mid-Victorian fashion of beards, whiskers, and moustaches, he was invariably clean-shaven. There was no sign of the heaviness of age in his tall, slight figure, and no hint of the pride of position in the easy, rather jaunty fashion in which he carried himself. He had always been something of a dandy, and he wore his clothes well. He seemed to take life very easily and to find it continually entertaining; and for a long time people had refused to take him very seriously. They had admitted his great expertise in all the devices and stratagems of party politics; but they were inclined to write him down as an accomplished political manipulator, with few ideas and even fewer principles. The events of the past ten years had gradually but effectively altered this early impression; and the movement for federal union had enabled him to reveal his exceptional gifts to the full. The success of Confederation was largely the result of his expert leadership. The British North America Act was, in the main, the expression of his political theory.

Macdonald and his cabinet were anxious to complete the work of union—to appease Nova Scotia, bring Newfoundland and Prince Edward Island into Confederation, and acquire Canada's great inheritance in the north-west. As it chanced, the political circumstances, both hostile and friendly, of the first few years that followed 1867 helped to hasten the completion of their design. The native Canadian drive towards continentalism was strengthened by two external forces—the same forces that had aided the union movement of 1864–7: the urgency of Great Britain and the pressure of the United States. Ever since the beginning of the American Civil War, Great Britain had been moving purposefully towards an honourable withdrawal from British America. It was not that she hoped or intended to cut the imperial connection with Canada, certainly not until Canada was fully prepared to accept separation; but she was anxious to recall her isolated military garrisons, and to escape from her remaining territorial obligation in North America—her ultimate responsibility for the future of the Hudson's Bay Company lands. If Canada took over Rupert's Land and the North-West Territories, not only would England be relieved of an unwanted burden, but Canada would also be better able to endure. Great Britain had supported Confederation because it seemed likely to create a colonial nation strong enough to take over imperial responsibilities. But, so long as Canada remained a mere fragment of a still disunited British America, it would remain vulnerable. If it could acquire all remaining British territory and reach its destined continental limits, it would have its best chance to survive.

The anxious encouragement of Great Britain was the first of the two external forces hastening national expansion; the second was the pressure of a resentful and predatory United States. The Civil War was over; but peace had not brought a settlement of those angry wartime grievances that the North had come to nurse against Great Britain and British America. The triumphant republic could not easily forget or forgive the sympathy which both British and colonials had shown for the Southern cause; and the American government insistently demanded enormous reparations for the losses inflicted by the *Alabama* (a Southern cruiser built in a British shipyard) on American shipping during the war. It was seriously proposed that the whole of Rupert's Land and the North-West Territories should be ceded to the United States in satisfaction of the *Alabama* claims; and both the new American President, Ulysses S. Grant, and his Secretary of State, Hamilton Fish, were expansionists who were prepared to use almost any method, short of armed force, to acquire all or part of British America. In the east, where there were established colonies, the danger was less; but, so long as Nova Scotia was dissatisfied and Newfoundland and Prince Edward Island remained outside the union, there was at least a chance of American intervention. The likelihood was much greater in the west where the politicians and journalists of the frontier state of Minnesota were casting covetous glances upon a vast and almost empty territory which seemed as if it might be theirs for the taking. 'It is quite evident to me,' Macdonald wrote in January 1870, '... that the United States government are resolved to do all they can, short of war, to get possession of our western territory, and we must take immediate and vigorous steps to counteract them.'

III

There were dangers everywhere. But the pacification of Nova Scotia was, without any doubt, the immediate and most urgent task. Joseph Howe and the Nova Scotian Anti-Confederates had failed to persuade the British government to exclude their province from the union of 1867; but they refused to believe that this first rebuff was final. In their eyes, the sweeping Anti-Confederate successes in both the federal and provincial elections of 1867 seemed an irrefutable proof, which even the unwilling British government must recognize, of Nova Scotia's unanimous determination to escape from Confederation. Howe led a second delegation to England to ask for repeal of the union; and Charles Tupper, Nova Scotia's leading supporter of Confederation, was dispatched by the Canadian government to counteract his old rival's propaganda. 'Repeal is not even a matter of discussion,' Macdonald declared bluntly; and this was very much the way in which the British government looked at it. Neither Conservatives nor Liberals were willing to undo the work of Confederation. To break up the newly formed union would simply protract and perhaps perpetuate the fragmentation of British America. It might mean the indefinite prolongation of Britain's responsibilities in the region and the indefinite postponement of her military withdrawal from North America.

This second British refusal meant the end of the repeal movement. What were the Nova Scotian Anti-Confederates to do? Two extreme, heroic courses—open rebellion or annexation to the United States—were conceivable; but no Nova Scotian politician, least of all Joseph Howe, could bring himself to advocate such desperate policies. A species of political 'sit-down' strike, in which the Anti-Confederate majority in the provincial legislature would refuse to govern and prevent their opponents from doing so, was perhaps a more feasible plan; but, though Howe suggested this course, his Anti-Confederate associates declined to consider it seriously. The movement had obviously reached a dead end: and Howe came to the conclusion that submission, on the best terms possible, was inevitable. At first he hoped vaguely that he might obtain some amendments of real substance in the British North America Act; but the Canadian and British governments were adamant in their refusal to consider any constitutional changes. Better financial terms—a larger federal subsidy to the provincial government—was all that Macdonald was willing to grant; and in the end this became the basis of an agreement by which Howe renounced repeal and, in January 1869, entered the federal cabinet.

Long before Howe had made his great renunciation and accepted federal office, two of his new colleagues in the Canadian cabinet, Sir George Cartier and William McDougall, had gone to England to make a start on the next and more ambitious phase of the nationalist programme, the acquisition of Rupert's Land and the North-West Territories. With the help of some heavy persuasion from the British government, the Hudson's Bay Company was induced to cede its lands to Canada in return for a payment of £300,000, and a grant of one-twentieth of the western 'fertile belt.' The Canadian government proceeded very cautiously with the political organization of its nearly empty domain. Rupert's Land was to be governed provisionally as a territory with a small nominated council, rather than as a province; representative institutions and responsible government would come later, when they were warranted by the spread of settlement. William McDougall, the Lieutenant-Governor designate, went west early with the intention of familiarizing himself with the country and its people before the transfer of authority actually took place on the 1st of December, 1869. He never reached his future 'capital,' the tiny Red River settlement. On the 30th of October, he was stopped at the Canadian border by a roadblock, held by an armed force of *Métis,* or French-speaking half-breeds.

Undoubtedly, a fair number of people at Red River awaited the coming of the Canadians without enthusiasm, or with doubt and misgiving. But it was the initiative of the *Métis* which alone inspired the resistance and gave it force and direction. They were 'a peculiar people,' conscious of their distinctive corporate identity and grandiloquently styling themselves 'the new nation'; in fact, their slow ascent from nomadism to civilization was far from complete. Reluctant and indifferent farmers, expert horsemen and hunters, born and bred to a long tradition of direct and violent action, they had built up a semi-military organization through the comradeship of the buffalo hunt. Their uniquely gifted son, Louis Riel, was an able but temperamental and dictatorial man, full of delusions of grandeur, quickly infuriated when his will was crossed, and quite without compunction in the use of force. He and his *Métis* seized Fort Garry, the Hudson's Bay Company's fortified post at Red River, and proclaimed a provisional government for the region.

Riel's immediate object was to prevent the automatic and unconditional transfer of the north-west to Canada; he was determined to obtain safeguards which would ensure the survival of his *Métis* against the peril of Protestant and Anglo-Saxon immigration and settlement. His ultimate aim remains uncertain; he may seriously have considered the alternative of annexation to the United States. Certainly, during the first months of the resistance, the principal advisers of his provisional government were a small group of Americans resident at Red River, one of whom was a government agent and the others avowed annexationists. These men joined forces with the annexationist politicians, journalists, and railway men of Minnesota and the American north-west—'the Yankee wire-pullers,' Macdonald called them; and both groups tried, in their various ways, to persuade the American government to exploit Canada's difficulties, to take advantage of the temporary suspension of British and Canadian authority at Red River, and to press forward the territorial aggrandizement of the United States.

This prospect appalled Macdonald. He was determined that 'the United States should not get behind us by right or by force and intercept our route to the Pacific'; and he realized that, as long as the effective acquisition of Rupert's Land was delayed, the whole of his great design for national expansion was in jeopardy. The resistance at Red River must be appeased as quickly as possible. He knew that he would have to make terms for the union of the north-west with Canada; but he was determined that Canada would negotiate, not with Riel's dictatorship, the provisional government with its American and clerical advisers, but with the Red River community as a whole. Donald Smith, sent west as a federal commissioner, succeeded in calling an assembly or 'convention' of elected delegates from all the parishes of the settlement, French and English; and the 'convention,' in its 'list of rights,' drew up reasonable terms for the admission of the north-west, as a territory, into Confederation.

This was a sensible settlement; but it was not to be. Riel was resolved to prevent it. The democratically expressed wishes of the Red River community, where they differed from his private plans for his own people, the *Métis,* meant nothing to him; and the very generosity and goodwill of the settlement gave him his chance of thwarting its intentions. The 'convention,' in a final gesture of conciliation, had confirmed the provisional government and elected Riel as president. Once back in control, Riel took the negotiations with Canada into his own hands. He appointed the delegates who were to go to Ottawa, and he made short work of the 'list of rights' of the 'convention.' Two new 'lists of rights,' drawn up in private by Riel and his clerical advisers, demanded provincial status, which the convention had expressly rejected, and separate or confessional schools, which the convention had not even discussed.

Macdonald was compelled to yield. So long as Riel's provisional government lasted, the threat of American intervention in the north-west remained. A quick settlement was the only solution; but a quick settlement meant, in fact, acceptance of Riel's terms, now strongly backed by French-Canadian influence in the federal government. Macdonald was caught in a squeeze-play with Riel and his clerical and American advisers on the one hand, and Sir George Cartier and the French and Roman Catholic M.P.s at Ottawa on the other. 'The French,' Sir Stafford Northcote, the governor of the Hudson's Bay Company, candidly observed, 'are earnestly bent upon the establishment of a French and Catholic power in the north-west to counteract the great preponderance of Ontario.' 'Manitoba,' the name given to the first political division of the north-west, entered Confederation as a province with a top-heavy bicameral legislature, modelled on that of Quebec, two official languages, and confessional schools.

IV

With the creation of Manitoba, the most serious danger threatening Macdonald's expansionist plans had ended. It was now nearly certain that Canada would acquire the whole of the British north-west and that a new transcontinental nation would come into being in North America. It was also fairly clear that the United States, however reluctantly and disapprovingly, was prepared to accept this situation. In the early spring of 1871 a Joint High Commission met at long last in Washington and proceeded to settle all the wartime grievances and controversies—including the dispute over the *Alabama* claims—which had grown up between Great Britain and the United States.

In the meantime, Canada's onward expansionist march had already been resumed. The acquisition of Rupert's Land and the North-West Territories cleared the way for the union with British Columbia. British Columbia had never seriously considered any other destiny; and a petition, circulated in 1869, for annexation to the United States, collected only a few score signatures. The British Columbia Legislative Council, partly elected and partly appointed, agreed to send a delegation to Canada to negotiate for union on terms proposed by the Executive Council; and the three delegates, R. W. Carrall, J. W. Trutch, and J. S. Helmcken, reached Ottawa in June 1870, just after the passage of the Manitoba Act. Their first request was for provincial status with a fully elected legislative assembly and responsible government; they also wanted a generous debt settlement and lavish federal subsidies. But their most interesting—and, as it turned out, their most controversial—proposals had to do with communications with Canada. They asked for the construction of a coach road between Fort Garry and British Columbia, the commencement of a railway within three years, and thereafter an annual expenditure of $1,000,000 on the British Columbia section of the line. The requests were stiff, almost exorbitant; but to the amazement, almost the incredulity, of the delegates, the terms voluntarily offered by the Dominion government vastly exceeded anything they had ever dreamed of asking. The coach road was dropped; instead, Canada offered to begin a railway within two years, and finish it in ten.

In 1873, two years after the entrance of British Columbia, Prince Edward Island followed and became the seventh province in Confederation. Prince Edward Island had rejected 'better terms' in 1869; she might have gone on almost indefinitely considering and declining 'better terms,' every few years, in the vague hope of getting a superlative bargain; but in the early 1870s a series of events occurred which stopped this temperamental shilly-shallying. An expensive, badly designed, and corruptly managed railway-building programme ended the Island's state of financial innocence and her proud sense of self-sufficiency. In 1864, at the time of the Quebec Conference, she had had a debt of less than $250,000; in 1874, it had risen to a little over $4,000,000. Canada agreed to assume the debt and to buy up the land of the remaining absentee proprietors; and, reluctantly, through sheer necessity, Prince Edward Island overcame her complacent parochialism and entered Confederation. On the 17th of May, the day S. L. Tilley, the new Minister of Finance, presented the terms of union to the Canadian House of Commons, a daughter was born to Lady Dufferin, the Governor General's wife. 'This, with Prince Edward's Island, makes *twins,*' Dufferin wrote to Macdonald.

In the first six years of its existence, the new Dominion had nearly attained its appointed natural limits. Newfoundland, alone of all the British North American territories, remained outside Confederation. The generous terms of union which the Carter government negotiated with Canada in 1869 were rejected in the Newfoundland general election of the autumn of that year; and the defeat was so decisive that all hope of Newfoundland's admission was abandoned for another quarter-century. Apart from this important limitation, the great work of nation building was complete; but the process of expansion had been troubled and hurried, and Canada had incurred costs, the full extent of which could not then be foreseen. In Manitoba the Dominion had been forced to impose an elaborate, highly unsuitable constitution upon an immature province which had not yet developed its real and permanent character. To British Columbia, the Dominion had promised, on its own initiative, to begin a Pacific railway within two years and to finish it within ten. The burden of the railway was to strain Canada's financial resources to their limit; and the enforced and hasty appeasement of the north-west was to provoke a reaction which would seriously divide the Canadian people.

REMOULDING THE CONSTITUTION

Christopher Armstrong

The British North America Act made the Confederation agreement law. In 1867 the compromise arrived at by the colonial politicians during the Quebec Conference of 1864 became a British statute which divided jurisdiction between two levels of government. Surprisingly, the Upper Canadian leaders had agreed to the creation of a highly centralized federation. John A. Macdonald, of course, had long believed in the superiority of a unitary state (or legislative union), but George Brown had for years complained vehemently about the interference of Lower Canadians in local affairs under the unhappy union of the two Canadas formed in 1841. Yet Brown's Reformers, who dominated Upper Canadian politics, consented to the terms of Confederation because they believed that an acceptable balance had been struck by which local interests would be safeguarded while the national government was given power to manage economic development. Moreover, they expected that the new province of Ontario would dominate the federation, owing to its size and wealth.

These expectations were not to be realized; for Sir John A. Macdonald, as first federal prime minister, vigorously exercised the powers of the central government. Before long, the Ontario Reformers, now led by Edward Blake, began to express dissatisfaction at Macdonald's failure to consult the provinces and to demand a provincial veto over important constitutional changes. When Blake retired as Ontario premier in 1872, to be succeeded by Oliver Mowat, the forces of the 'provincial rights' movement acquired a leader of extraordinary longevity and superior political skill. Mowat had much to do with altering the shape of the Canadian federation in the late nineteenth century.

The most contentious issue between Ottawa and Toronto during Mowat's premiership was the dispute over the northwestern boundary of Ontario. Macdonald was eager to whittle down the size and influence of the province by awarding as much of the contested area as possible to the more compliant Manitobans. Mowat was equally determined to retain all the lands and their valuable resources lying west from the Lakehead to the Lake of the Woods. Efforts to secure an agreement between 1873 and 1878 with the more friendly administration of fellow-Liberal Alexander Mackenzie were allowed to drag on until Macdonald regained office in time to block a settlement. Bickering continued throughout the early 1880s until the courts sustained Ontario's claims. Even then the Judicial Committee of the Privy Council had to be appealed to a

From *The Politics of Federalism: Ontario's Relations with the Federal Government, 1867–1942* (Toronto: University of Toronto Press, 1981), 8–32, 243–46. © Queen's Printer of Ontario, 1981. Reproduced with permission.

second time before Macdonald finally gave way in 1889. This dispute was also marked by personal bitterness between the two leaders, each one determined to extract the last ounce of political advantage from the conflict.

Oliver Mowat was determined to widen provincial powers, to raise the province, in fact, to a co-ordinate sovereignty with the central government, each supreme within its own sphere. In the effort to achieve this end he worked to extend the powers of the lieutenant-governor and, in particular, to resist the exercise of the federal cabinet's power to disallow provincial legislation. Here again Mowat's political skills proved an asset as he condemned Macdonald and his ministers for flouting the will of the duly elected representatives of the people. In 1887 he quickly seized on the idea of an interprovincial conference to review the state of the constitution and persuaded those premiers who attended to endorse his position. In this instance, however, Macdonald simply ignored the conference, and no changes were made in the BNA Act. Nonetheless, the interaction of political pressure, institutional change, and legal decisions which often bore little relationship to the intentions of the Fathers of Confederation combined by the end of the century to remould the constitution of Canada. In this process Ontario's influence was of paramount importance.[1]

I

For nearly fifteen years prior to the Quebec Conference George Brown and his Reform supporters from Canada West had been calling for constitutional change to put an end to 'French Canadian domination.' When Brown agreed to enter the 'Great Coalition' of 1864 with the Liberal-Conservatives under John A. Macdonald and George-Etienne Cartier, the new ministry pledged 'to bring in a measure ... for the purpose of removing existing differences by introducing the federal principle into Canada.' At the conferences in Charlottetown and Quebec that same year a general federation of the British North American colonies was agreed upon. With the Civil War in the United States much on their minds, the Fathers of Confederation determined to create a strongly centralized union to avoid any occurrence of a tragedy such as the Americans had suffered. In Macdonald's mind, 'The fatal error which they have committed ... was in making each State a distinct sovereignty, in giving to each a distinct sovereign power except in those instances where they were specially reserved by the constitution and conferred upon the general Government. The true principle of a Confederation lies in giving to the general Government all the principles and powers of sovereignty and in the provision that the subordinate or individual State should have no powers but those expressly bestowed upon them.' Hence section 91 of the BNA Act granted Parliament power 'to make laws for the peace, order, and good government of Canada, in relation to all matters not coming within the classes of subjects by this Act assigned exclusively to the

Provinces,' and sections 92 and 93 of the act enumerated the seventeen areas in which the provinces would possess jurisdiction. The new federal government, however, was also given power to nullify any piece of provincial legislation within one year of its passage by disallowing it or to prevent any bill from becoming law by refusing formal assent. Canada, the Fathers were determined, should never be plagued by a disruptive 'states' rights' movement.[2]

The leading Upper Canadian Reformers heartily approved of these provisions. George Brown thought: 'we have thrown on the localities all the questions which experience has shown lead directly to local jealousy and discord, and we have retained in the hands of the General Government all the powers necessary to secure a strong and efficient administration of public affairs.' To Oliver Mowat fell the task of introducing the resolution setting forth the limited provincial powers at the Quebec Conference. Delegate E.B. Chandler of New Brunswick immediately objected: 'You are adopting a Legislative Union instead of a Federal. The Local Legislatures should not have their powers specified but should have all the powers not reserved to the Federal Government, and only the powers to be given to the Federal Government should be specified. You are now proceeding to destroy the constitutions of the Local Governments and to give them less powers than they have had allowed them from England, and it will make them merely large municipal corporations.' But the Canadian coalition stood firm on the question of where the 'residual' power should rest, although Brown admitted, 'I should agree with Mr. Chandler were it not that we have done all we can to settle the matter with sufficient powers to Local Legislatures.' The conference, therefore, accepted the wishes of the Upper and Lower Canadians.[3]

By section 92 of the British North America Act the provinces were given exclusive jurisdiction over sixteen specified areas, including natural resources, local public works, prisons, charities, the administration of justice, 'property and civil rights in the province,' and 'generally all matters of a merely local or private nature.' To carry out these responsibilities the provinces were permitted to levy direct (but not indirect) taxes, to borrow money, to sell or lease their public lands and resources, and to impose various kinds of licence fees. In addition, the new province of Ontario would receive a fixed annual grant of $80,000 for the support of its government plus a yearly subsidy of 80 cents per head of population for each of its 1,396,091 residents according to the census of 1861 or $1,116,872.80 in all.

The debate at the Quebec Conference revealed that the Upper Canadian Reform leaders accepted Chandler's claim that the provincial governments would be 'merely large municipal corporations.' In the interests of economy and simplicity Brown wanted to abandon parliamentary responsible government and create unicameral legislatures elected for a fixed three-year term. A small executive would be selected to advise the lieutenant-governor, a federal official appointed to 'bring these [provincial] bodies into harmony with the General Government.' This proposal, however, was too radical for the leader of the Lower Canadian *bleus,* George-Etienne Cartier, who thought it smacked of republicanism. Other delegates supported Jonathan McCully on Nova Scotia, who argued, 'We must have miniature responsible Governments.' The BNA Act, therefore, provided that Ontario should have a legislative assembly of eighty-two members with a responsible executive committee (or cabinet) consisting of an attorney general, a provincial treasurer, a provincial secretary, a commissioner of crown lands, and a commissioner of agriculture and public works. Yet there was little in these constitutional debates upon which to base the bold claims of co-ordinate sovereignty for the provinces made subsequently when Oliver Mowat had assumed the premiership.[4]

Why did the Upper Canadian Fathers of Confederation accept such narrowly circumscribed provincial powers? For John A. Macdonald, a believer in legislative union, the outcome was quite satisfactory. Within his lifetime he expected to see the provincial governments 'absorbed in the General Power.' 'My own opinion,' he wrote in 1868, 'is that the General Government or Parliament should pay no more regard to the status or position of the Local Governments than they would to the prospects of the ruling party in the corporation of Quebec or Montreal.' George Brown was equally happy; he wrote jubilantly to his wife from Quebec in 1864, 'all right!!! Conference through at six o'clock this evening—constitution adopted—a most creditable document—a complete reform of all the abuse; and injustice we have complained of!! Is it not wonderful?' Later he would argue that 'the scheme now before us has all the advantages of a legislative union and a federal one as well ... By vesting the appointment of the lieutenant governors in the General Government, and giving a veto for all local measures, we have secured that no injustice shall be done, without appeal, in local legislation ... [A]ll matters of trade and commerce, banking and currency, and all questions common to the whole people, we have vested fully and unrestrictedly in the General Government.'[5] Was this the same George Brown who had spent the past fifteen years railing against Lower Canadian interference in the affairs of his province and demanding 'rep. by pop.'?

Brown, it must be remembered, spoke not only for the farmers of the western peninsula of Upper Canada but also for the ambitious businessmen of Toronto. The latter believed that a strong central government was a prerequisite for economic growth and western expansion, hence Brown's emphasis on the economic authority granted the central government. But the Reform leader was also convinced that the new constitution included safeguards for the vital interests of his locality. The composition of the Senate proved to be the most contentious and time-consuming subject at the Quebec Conference, precisely because that body was to represent regional interests and be selected on a regional basis to balance the House of Commons, where representation by population would rule. Seventy-two senators would be appointed by the federal cabinet, twenty-four from Ontario, twenty-four from Quebec, and twenty-four from Nova Scotia and New Brunswick. Defending himself against charges that he had abandoned the principles of representative government in consenting to this arrangement, Brown argued that 'our Lower Canada friends have agreed to give us representation by population in the Lower House, on the express condition that they shall have equality in the Upper House ... If from this concession of equality in the Upper Chamber we are restrained from forcing through measures which our friends in Lower Canada may consider injurious to their interests, we shall, at any rate, have power, which we never had before to prevent them from forcing through whatever we may deem unjust to us.' The Senate, then, was intended to represent and defend regional interests against outside interference.[6]

Two other factors must have helped to still any fears which Brown may have harboured that a strong central government might use its power to work against the sectional interests of Upper Canada. Ontario would elect 82 members of Parliament in a House of Commons totalling 181. Moreover, the province's population was rising steadily, by almost 225,000 between 1861 and 1871. (Quebec's population, by comparison, rose less than 80,000 in that decade.) In 1867 Brown told a convention of Reformers that in the redistribution following the 1871 census Ontario could expect to have 94 or 95 seats in the Commons, and ten years later, if the rate of population growth were maintained, it would have a majority in that body. (In the event, Ontario was allotted only 88 of 200 seats in 1872 and its representation peaked at 92 of 211 members in 1882.) Brown also naturally assumed that the vast majority of Ontario representatives would be loyal Reformers, ready to rally round whenever the province's interests were at stake. In an age when party lines were fluid, with Brown himself in a coalition including his leading opponents and many independent 'loose fish' among the legislators, he probably assumed that most of the Ontario representatives would respond to a call to protect the rights of the province. In addition, Ontario's twenty-four senators could be relied upon to see that justice was done.[7]

As a result, George Brown and his Reform supporters had no qualms about leading Upper Canadians into a highly centralized federal union, almost a legislative union of the type desired by John A. Macdonald. Ottawa would wield wide authority, especially in the field of economic policy, while exercising close supervision over provincial affairs through the lieutenant-governors and the power of disallowance. Cheap and simple provincial governments would manage local matters such as education, which had caused so much ill-feeling under the union of the Canadas between 1841 and 1867. And there were institutions and individuals who would see to it that Ontario's interests were not neglected at the federal level.

This easy confidence about the terms of Confederation did not survive many years after 1867. The Great Coalition began to fall apart following Brown's withdrawal in 1865, and within a few years an opposition party had coalesced around the Upper Canadian Reform tradition. It was not long before the Reformers began to raise objections to Sir John A. Macdonald's management of national affairs, including his conduct of relations with the provinces.

In 1869 Edward Blake, who had assumed the leadership of the Reformers in the Ontario legislature in opposition to the government of John Sandfield Macdonald, protested strongly against the granting of 'better terms' to Nova Scotia by the Conservative federal cabinet. To pacify the angry Nova Scotians Macdonald had given them a larger subsidy, and Blake promptly introduced in the assembly a series of thirteen resolutions attacking any alteration in the terms of the BNA Act without consultation with the other provinces. These thirteen resolutions articulated a view of provincial rights which Blake's successor, Oliver Mowat, was to elevate to the status of received truth. Reviewing the constitutional history of the Canadas, Blake argued that the union of 1841 had failed because Upper Canada had been unfairly treated. Confederation had remedied that situation, but now the federal government was unilaterally amending the terms of an agreement accepted by the provinces only a few years before 'in full settlement of all future demands on Canada.' Not only was this action unjust to Ontario, but as a result, 'the former evils so far from being removed by Confederation will be intensified, the just expectations of the people will be disappointed, sectional strife will be aroused, the Federal principle will be violated and the Constitution will be shaken to its base.' The consent of all the provinces, Blake insisted, was required for any alteration in the terms of Confederation.

What Blake had provided was the first classic statement of the 'compact theory' of Confederation, the contention that the federal union was the result of a compact or treaty among the provinces and could not be altered without their consent. Sandfield Macdonald's majority turned back Blake's first twelve resolutions but permitted the thirteenth to pass, fearing that many of the government's supporters would desert. This final resolution demanded legislation, presumably by the British parliament, 'to remove all colour for the assumption by the Parliament of Canada of the power to disturb the financial relations established by the Union Act as between Canada and the several provinces.'[8]

In 1871 Blake forced Sandfield Macdonald to resign. Blake explained his government's policy regarding the 'external relations' of the province this way: 'that here should exist no other attitude on the part of the Provincial Government towards the Government of the Dominion than one of neutrality; that each Government should be absolutely independent of the other in the management of its own affairs. As citizens of the Province of Ontario we are called upon to frame our own policy with reference to our Provincial rights and interests and to conduct our own affairs.' Although he pledged non-interference in the affairs of other jurisdictions, he referred specifically to his resolutions attacking the grant of 'better terms' to Nova Scotia as evidence of the fact that 'Occasions may arise ... in which the rights of the Province have been infringed, and upon such occasions, of course, it becomes the duty of the Province to act ... in order to prevent the infringement of the Provincial interests, of which we believe ourselves to be the guardians.'[9]

Blake's statement served notice that the Ontario Reformers had abandoned their previous acquiescence in a highly centralized federal system. This new attitude arose largely from partisanship. The Great Coalition of 1864 had dissolved, and Reformers like Brown, Blake, and Alexander Mackenzie were working to create a competing national party which would take office in Ottawa in 1873. If Macdonald's Conservatives were the party of centralism, then its opponents would become the party of localism and provincialism, recruiting the anti-Confederates of the Maritimes to the Reform cause. In 1872 the decision was taken to abolish dual representation, by which men like Blake, Mackenzie, and Sandfield Macdonald held seats in both the national and the local legislatures. Faced with the choice, Blake and Mackenzie decided to make their careers in Ottawa, and the Reform leaders persuaded Oliver Mowat to leave the judicial post he had held since the end of 1864 and return to active politics. On 25 October 1872 he was sworn in as premier, a post he would hold until 14 July 1896.

Mowat fully accepted the new Reform view of the federal system. Circumstances had changed since 1864 when he had moved the Quebec resolutions setting forth the powers of the general and local governments, content with a system in which the provinces would possess only a narrow range of specified powers. Now he shared the views of Blake, Brown, and Mackenzie, 'that if the province was to be governed from Ottawa, as it had been formerly from Quebec, the chief object of Confederation would be thwarted and provincial autonomy would become a delusion and a sham.' In his first address to the legislature he promised to follow the course already charted by Blake a year earlier. This marked the culmination of a process which had begun even before Confederation when George Brown resigned from the Great Coalition: 'Building on the deep Upper Canadian commitment to self-government and local authority and the developing grass-roots concept of majoritarian populist democracy, he and other Reform leaders began to articulate the relatively alien doctrine of classical federalism.' The compact theory of Confederation was the intellectual link provided by Edward Blake between the well-springs of Reformism and Mowat's day-to-day conduct of relations with Ottawa after 1872.[10]

II

When Oliver Mowat became premier he found the provincial government already embroiled in a serious dispute with Ottawa which had important implications for the future development of Ontario. The issue was the determination of the western boundary of the province.[11] The frontier between the old Province of Canada and the territories of the Hudson's Bay Company had never been clearly defined. In 1869 the new Dominion of Canada purchased all of the company's lands, and in 1870 created the province of Manitoba, a small area surrounding the Red River settlement near the present-day site of Winnipeg.

In July 1871 Sandfield Macdonald and Sir John A. Macdonald agreed to appoint two commissioners to settle the problem, and William McDougall and E.E. Taché were chosen by the respective governments. Nothing had been achieved by the time Edward Blake became premier in December 1871, however, although the importance of reaching an understanding had already been pointed up by applications from private parties for mining licences west of Lake Superior. In the spring of 1872 the Ontario government received a confidential report from McDougall on his preliminary discussions with federal officials. He predicted that Ottawa would try to fix the same boundary as that stipulated in the Quebec Act of 1774, a line drawn due north from the confluence of the Mississippi and Ohio rivers crossing the north shore of Lake Superior in the vicinity of Port Arthur and extending to the height of land around Hudson Bay. However, McDougall argued that a review of the documents had convinced him that the western boundary of the province should be fixed at least as far west as the 'North-West Angle' of the Lake of the Woods, which was about 300 miles beyond the point proposed by the federal government. If Taché stuck to his position, no agreement between the commissioners would be possible, and the likely result would be 'protracted and angry discussion' between the governments.[12]

Within months of taking office, Blake was confronted with a major federal challenge to the rights of Ontario, in his mind an attempt to pare down the size and influence of the province and seize a vast quantity of resources which rightly belonged to it. The accuracy of McDougall's predictions was quickly confirmed when Joseph Howe, the secretary of state for the provinces, forwarded to Toronto his draft instructions to Commissioner Taché. The provincial government promptly ordered McDougall to have nothing further to do with the negotiations and passed an order-in-council, declaring it could not 'consent to the prosecution of the Commission for the purpose of marking on the ground the line so defined.'[13] The government of Sir John A. Macdonald complained that this policy of non-cooperation might mean that crimes committed in the disputed area would go unpunished. However, when Ontario replied by demanding that its boundary should run due north from the source of the Mississippi, slightly west of the Lake of the Woods, Macdonald hastily proposed that the whole matter should be referred to the Judicial Committee of the Privy Council in London, the highest appeal court of the empire, for a final interpretation of the treaties and documents. 'The mineral wealth of the country is likely to attract a large immigration into these parts,' wrote the prime minister; so a speedy settlement was required. Perhaps doubtful of the legal basis of the provincial case, Premier Blake would have nothing to do with a reference to the Privy Council. Instead, he proposed that efforts to settle the matter by negotiation should continue and, in the meantime, that Ontario should be given jurisdiction over the entire disputed territory to avoid confusion over mining and timber licences and law enforcement. The federal government refused to make such concessions, and there the matter rested when Mowat became premier late in 1872.[14]

The new government preferred to do nothing rather than risk losing a case before the courts, and this patience was rewarded in the fall of 1873 when their fellow-Liberals under Alexander Mackenzie took power in Ottawa. Now Mowat could hope for a respectful hearing for the province's claims, and in the spring of 1874 the legislature passed a resolution calling for a settlement by arbitration. In the fall Provincial Treasurer Adam Crooks visited the capital and arranged that Ontario Chief Justice W.B. Richards (selected by the province) and Lemuel A. Wilmot of New Brunswick (chosen by Ottawa) should be appointed arbitrators with power to secure a third party as chairman. Meanwhile, the two administrations arrived at a temporary arrangement by which Ontario would handle all land grants as far west as longitude 91°30', near the headwaters of the Rainy River, at a point roughly half-way between the boundary proposed by Macdonald's government near Port Arthur and the province's claim that the north-west angle of the Lake of the Woods should form the limit. Once a final agreement had been arrived at, all grants could be ratified by legislation, but meanwhile development might proceed.[15]

Both governments placed their faith in negotiation rather than the arbitration, however; for it appears that Richards and Wilmot never bothered to choose a chairman. Mowat relied upon David Mills, a Liberal member of parliament and law teacher, to draw up the provincial brief. Mills suggested that a line drawn due north from the source of the Mississippi (just west of the Lake of the Woods) might form the boundary, but that the province was entitled to demand compensation for a huge area stretching as far west as the forks of the Saskatchewan. This bold claim was too much for even a friendly federal government, and the prime minister wrote privately to the premier in the fall of 1876, 'I think it is likely that we can agree to the western boundary [proposed by Mills], but it is utterly useless to talk of compensation for something upon a suppositious claim west of that. That cannot under any circumstances be even spoken of by us.' All the land within the watershed of Hudson Bay would also have to remain federal property, Mackenzie declared. As a result, the negotiations bogged down because the Ontario government was reluctant to abandon any of its claims without compensation, while Ottawa could not make such concessions without arousing protests in other provinces.[16]

Having arrived at a *modus vivendi* on land granting in 1874, neither government seemed eager to press for a quick settlement. The death of Lemuel Wilmot and the appointment of Chief Justice Richards to the Supreme Court of Canada stalled the arbitration completely. Not until 1878 did the two governments get around to naming their replacements. Chief Justice Robert A. Harrison of Ontario was then appointed by the province and Sir Francis Hincks by the Mackenzie government, and they chose the British minister in Washington, Sir Edward Thornton, as the third member of the board. Both governments committed themselves to accepting the arbitrators' findings as 'final and conclusive' and agreed to implement them by concurrent legislation.

Fear of a Liberal defeat in the forthcoming federal election probably provided the necessary spur to action, and the arbitrators obligingly summoned the two parties for a hearing on 1 August 1878.[17]

Ontario was represented by the premier (and attorney general), Oliver Mowat, while Hugh MacMahon and E.C. Monk were retained by the Dominion. The province argued that its boundaries should be those claimed from the Hudson's Bay Company by the Canadas prior to Confederation and pointed to a statement made by Commissioner of Crown Lands J.E. Cauchon in 1857 that if Canadian territory did not extend all the way to the Pacific then it was bounded by a line due north from the source of the Mississippi to the shores of the Bay. These claims, it was noted, had been reiterated by federal negotiators when Rupert's Land was purchased in 1869. At the very least Mowat argued, Ontario extended to the north-west angle of the Lake of the Woods and perhaps even as far west as the Rocky Mountains. MacMahon stuck by the federal position that historical precedents validated a line running north from the confluence of the Ohio and Mississippi rivers and passing through the Port Arthur area to the height of land around Hudson Bay. The failure of the provincial government to object to the acquisition of Rupert's Land by Ottawa in 1869, he contended, debarred it from claiming additional territory later on. In rebuttal Mowat pointed out that 'there is no evidence that Ontario even knew anything about the matters which are said to estop her before these matters were finally concluded. In fact, they all took place without any reference to the Local Government.'

After three days of hearings the arbitrators produced a unanimous report which accepted almost all the province's claims: the western boundary should run due north from the north-west angle of the Lake of the Woods to the English River, then along the Albany River to the shore of Hudson Bay and follow the shore to a point north of the head of Lake Temiscaming. Ontario, it seemed, would have its way. A report to the government published in 1879 rejoiced that 'this fine region contains within its limits timber lands of great value, rich and varied mineral deposits, rivers and lakes of noble proportions ... the treasure of which, when sought with the ardour and appliances of modern enterprise, may yield a return not even dreamed of by those old explorers who were most sanguine of its resources.'[18]

On 17 October 1878, however, Sir John A. Macdonald once more assumed the prime ministership after a federal election, and when Provincial Secretary Arthur S. Hardy informed the federal authorities of his intention to introduce legislation to take possession of the disputed territory he received no response. The provincial legislature at its 1879 session duly passed 'An Act respecting the Administration of Justice in the Northerly and Westerly parts of Ontario,' but Macdonald continued to ignore requests by the province to bring down concurrent legislation to confirm the award of the arbitrators. The provincial government repeatedly claimed to have accepted the award, 'not because it

was believed to have accorded to this Province all that was claimed on its behalf, or all that the Province might within its strict legal rights have had
awarded to it, but because the tribunal appointed jointly by the two governments was one to whose competency and character no one could take exception,
and because according to the judgement of the people of Ontario neither party
to the arbitration could consistently with good faith refuse to abide by the decisions.' To the Mowat administration it might seem 'embarrassing and
injurious' to have the award ignored, but to Macdonald's Conservatives the
appointment of the arbitrators by Mackenzie and Mowat had been a 'solemn
farce,' since only one of the three men chosen to resolve this complex legal
tangle was a lawyer. The prime minister did not bother to answer the letters
from Toronto calling upon him to act.[19]

In January 1880, however, the federal government at last took the offensive. Justice Minister James McDonald recommended that the recent Ontario
legislation should be disallowed, because it concerned the administration of
justice in territory which had not been recognized as provincial property.
Mowat introduced a series of resolutions in the legislature setting out the
Ontario case and again demanding that the federal government recognize the
award of the arbitrators. Caught in a difficult political situation, provincial
Conservative leader W.R. Meredith felt compelled to support the motion.
Mowat responded to the threat of disallowance with the claim that 'there is far
more reason for maintaining that the award gave us too little, than for main-
taining that it gave us too much; and it gave us considerably less than Dominion
Ministers had claimed before the purchase of the rights of the Hudson's Bay
Company.' In the House of Commons the prime minister defended his actions
by arguing that only the Judicial Committee of the Privy Council could finally
determine the legal boundaries of Ontario, although he did support the appointment of a select committee of the House to look into the whole matter.
Predictably, this committee found that the arbitrators' award did not set forth
the true boundaries of Ontario. Meanwhile, the Ontario legislation was disallowed, and Mowat was able only to persuade Justice Minister McDonald to
introduce a bill to provide for the enforcement of criminal law within the disputed territory. Moreover, in May 1880 Mowat took advantage of a petition
from some businessmen in Rat Portage (Kenora) to create a divisional court
there to administer justice in the area.[20]

The premier continued to press James McDonald to pass further legislation regarding the administration of justice. In February 1881 he wrote, 'I trust
also that authority will be given to the Ontario Government to deal with the land
and timber in the disputed territory, subject to our accounting therefor in case
our right to the territory should not be maintained.' Another series of resolutions
calling upon Ottawa to recognize the award of the arbitrators passed the legislature by a vote of seventy-five to one. The prime minister still paid no
attention. In fact, he deftly countered in March 1881 by placing before the

Senate a bill to extend the boundaries of Manitoba as far east as Port Arthur including the whole of the disputed territory. 'The effect of settling the boundary between these Provinces,' Sir John told the House of Commons, 'will compel, I do not say the Province of Ontario, but the present Government of Ontario, to be reasonable, and not to insist upon a boundary which cannot be supported in any Court or tribunal in the world. They will come to terms quickly enough when they find they must do so. To use an expression which is common in Scotland, it is land hungry they are for that country, and they are resolved to get it rightly or wrongly.' An additional reason for granting the entire territory to Manitoba was that the Dominion would still control all of the valuable lands and minerals. Macdonald frankly admitted that the area 'must be given either to Ontario or to Manitoba, and we cannot afford to give it to Ontario, if it belongs to the Dominion, because the lands would belong to Ontario. Keeping it as a portion of Manitoba, the lands belong to the Dominion.'[21]

The Ontario government immediately registered an 'earnest and vigorous protest' against this move. Dragging Manitoba into the fight between the province and Ottawa was 'an act of direct antagonism and hostility to the interests and rights of the Province of Ontario ... calculated to aggravate all existing difficulties and to prove most prejudicial to the harmony and accord which should prevail between the provinces of the Dominion.' The prime minister paid no more heed to this complaint than to any of the previous ones. He had put himself one up on Oliver Mowat and was confident that once Manitoba confirmed the extension of its boundaries by legislation the matter would be out of his hands. If anyone subsequently challenged the boundary the courts would have to settle the problem. Within a few months the provincial government objected that the federal government was granting land and timber rights to private parties within the disputed area, thus confirming Mowat's worst fears.[22]

In 1881 the premier decided to seek a private meeting with Macdonald in an effort to reach a settlement. But he gave warning beforehand that the province was not prepared to settle for anything less than the full award of the arbitrators, and he rejected the claim that the additional territory would make Ontario too big and give it 'undue weight' within the federation. On the contrary, he argued, with the award added Ontario's area would total about 200,000 square miles as compared with Quebec's 193,355 square miles; without the addition Ontario would occupy only 110,000 square miles. Why, he asked, should Ontario be only a little more than half as big as Quebec or about a quarter the size of British Columbia? The premier lectured Ottawa on how it ought to have behaved: 'It was the duty of the Federal authorities to protect the just rights of all its Provinces; to render unnecessary inter-provincial conflict for the maintenance of such rights: to employ the constitutional powers of the Dominion Parliament and Government respectively in minimizing the evils of a disputed boundary pending the settlement of the dispute; and to take such steps for determining such evils at the earliest possible date.

Unhappily, the present Federal authorities have not chosen to discharge these manifest duties.'[23] Not surprisingly, the negotiations with the prime minister in November 1881 proved fruitless, since he insisted that the whole matter be referred to the Supreme Court for a binding decision on the documents in the case. Ontario would have nothing to do with this idea.

Mowat repeated his attacks on the federal government in the 1882 throne speech, provoking Macdonald to complain that the premier really had no interest in a settlement: 'Mowat is thoroughly hostile. He is the mere jackal to Blake's lion and must be met in the same spirit.' The Ontario legislature discussed the boundary question on several occasions during the assembly's sitting and Mowat went so far as to threaten secession if he did not get his way: 'if they could only maintain Confederation by giving up half of their Province, then Confederation must go, ... and if they could not demand the large amount of property to which they were entitled without forgoing the advantages of Confederation, then it was not worth maintaining.' Before the House rose, however, Mowat introduced a resolution approving the idea of a reference to the British Privy Council, but only on condition that complete control of the disputed territory be handed over to the province in the meantime. Macdonald countered by having Manitoba pass an act incorporating Rat Portage (Kenora) as a Manitoba town during the summer of 1882, ignoring Ontario protests that the area had been under its control since 1871.[24]

The result was the great 'battle' of Rat Portage in the summer of 1883. Both provinces had appointed a number of constables who promptly set about arresting one another, arousing expectations that a general riot would ensue when the citizens released the Manitoban officers from the Ontario jail. In the end the violence petered out, but apparently it convinced the politicians that a settlement was overdue. Mowat, for instance, had called a provincial election in February 1883, and despite the fact that the Liberals had made much of the unjust treatment received by Ontario at the hands of the federal Conservatives, he had seen his majority reduced as the Tories won nine additional seats. Evidently, translating federal-provincial conflict into votes was no simple matter.[25]

In the fall of 1883 negotiations between the provincial governments of Ontario and Manitoba finally produced an agreement to refer the whole matter to the Judicial Committee of the Privy Council; in the meantime the disputed territory would be administered jointly. The Manitobans undertook to try to persuade Macdonald to join in this reference case so that any decision would be binding on all the parties concerned. In the spring of 1884 the prime minister agreed to participate in the reference to fix the boundaries, but at the last moment he withdrew, apparently content to let Manitoba bear the burden of making the federal case. The Judicial Committee undertook to hear the joint reference from the two provinces in the spring of 1884, with Mowat appearing personally for Ontario. The decision, rendered in July, was a satisfying victory for the province, since the Privy Council upheld the award of the arbitrators in 1878 on almost every point, fixing the western limits of Ontario at the north-west angle of the Lake of the Woods.[26]

This decision, however, was not binding until ratified by legislation, and Macdonald steadfastly refused to act. To increase the size of Ontario so greatly would unbalance the union: 'History will repeat itself and posterity will find out that the evils that exist in other federations from the preponderance of one or more members will again happen.' In the end, Mowat was forced to launch a suit against the St Catharines' Milling Company which was cutting timber in the disputed area under a federal licence. The Judicial Committee of the Privy Council found for the province in 1888, holding that the territory had been part of the Province of Canada prior to 1867 and thus had passed into the provincial domain at Confederation. At long last, in 1889, parliament adopted an address requesting the British to pass legislation fixing the western boundary of Ontario at the north-west angle of the Lake of the Woods, extending north-easterly along the English River to Lac Seul and the Albany River flowing into James Bay. The province thus secured not only the huge disputed territory west of the Lakehead but a considerable area north of the height of land separating the Great Lakes from the Hudson Bay watershed, precisely as the arbitrators had recommended over a decade earlier.[27]

The tenacity with which Oliver Mowat prosecuted the Ontario claim to the vast territories west of Port Arthur, including two trips to the Privy Council in London, reflected the value which he placed upon the territory to be gained for the province and its forests, minerals, and waterpowers and the partisan advantage he hoped to extract from the issue. Sir John A. Macdonald may have been right when he argued that the operation of the federal system might be impaired if one province became too big and too powerful, but the premier refused to make any concessions, particularly since his case had been upheld by the arbitrators—which made concessions politically impossible. He remained determined to secure control of all the resources of the province and manage them in the interests of Ontario citizens. Neither he nor the prime minister would give way, with the result that the wrangle lasted for fifteen years and embittered other aspects of the relations between the province and the central government.

III

The bitterness engendered by the Manitoba boundary dispute was most evident in the Mowat government's resistance to federal interference in Ontario affairs through the use of disallowance and the powers of the lieutenant-governor. During the 1880s there occurred a series of acrimonious disputes over the way in which the federal system should operate, disagreements which were settled mainly on Ontario's terms with a consequent diminution of federal powers. As a result, the federal system did not function in the way that the Fathers of Confederation had envisaged, because the provinces through political activity and through the decisions of the courts were gradually recognized as co-ordinate jurisdictions with the central government, fully sovereign within their sphere of authority and not at all like the glorified municipalities originally envisaged.

These disputes involved the authority of the lieutenant-governor, because Mowat perceived that the scope of provincial authority depended in part upon this official's prerogatives and powers. The Fathers of Confederation had intended that the lieutenant-governors should be officials appointed by the federal cabinet, whose function was to keep provincial policies in harmony with national objectives. To do so the governors were given power to nullify any provincial legislation by refusing assent or to reserve any bill for reference to Ottawa where the cabinet could decide whether or not it would come into force. Thus the governors were supposed to act at the bidding of the central government, but Mowat refused to accept this situation. He contended that the governor was the Crown's representative at the local level and hence was possessed of all the prerogative powers of the monarch which fell within the provincial sphere of authority. Not only was this role necessary if the provinces were to enjoy full responsible government, he argued, but it reflected the fact that the provinces were claiming to be co-ordinate sovereignties with the federal power, not subordinate entities.[28]

Thus, much of the debate over the office of the lieutenant-governor was concerned with whether or not he possessed certain prerogative powers of mainly symbolic importance. Should the governor receive royal salutes? Did he have the power to pardon offenders? Could he appoint lawyers as Queen's Counsel? In themselves almost trivial questions, they acquired their significance from their context as a part of Ontario's struggle to achieve wider provincial powers and to create a decentralized federation. In addition, patronage was at stake; in 1872 Oliver Mowat appointed a number of QCs. At that time Macdonald refused to be drawn into a conflict with the province, but in 1886, with relations soured by the conflict over the Manitoba boundary and other issues, a dispute did occur. The administration of justice was a provincial responsibility, and Mowat therefore argued that the governor had full prerogative powers to create QCs: 'The position of my Government is that the Lieutenant-Governor is entitled, *virtue officii* and without express statutory enactments, to exercise all prerogatives incident to Executive authority in matters over which the Provincial Legislatures have jurisdiction.'[29] The federal authorities rejected this contention and the issue was eventually referred to the courts. However, in 1888 Mowat passed legislation giving the lieutenant-governor authority to pardon offenders against the laws of the province. When Justice Minister Sir John Thompson objected to this act, a reference case was also submitted to the courts. Before a final decision could be given in either case, the Privy Council decisively settled these issues in another decision. In the matter of *The Liquidators of the Maritime Bank of Canada v. the Receiver-General of New Brunswick* (1892) the judicial committee upheld the full extent of the provincial claims which Mowat had been making over the past two decades: 'The British North America Act, 1867, has not severed the connection between the Crown and the provinces; the relation between them is the same as that which subsists between the Crown and the Dominion in respect of the powers, executive and legislative, public property and revenue, as are vested in them respectively.' In ringing phrases Lord Watson's decision sustained the notion that the central government and the provinces were co-ordinate sovereignties, separate but equal to one another: 'The object of the Act was neither to weld the provinces into one, nor to subordinate provincial governments to a central authority, but to create a federal government in which they should all be represented, entrusted with the exclusive administration of affairs in which they had a common interest, each province retaining its independence and autonomy.' The Supreme Court of Canada's subsequent decision on the reference case concerning the appointment of QCs reflected this new view of the constitution by upholding Mowat's claims on the grounds 'that the Lieutenant-Governor of a province is as much the representative of Her Majesty the Queen for all purposes of provincial government as the Governor-General is himself for all purposes of the Dominion Government.' With a vital assist from the Privy Council Mowat had gotten his way.[30]

About the power of disallowance there could be no doubt. By sections 56 and 90 of the BNA Act the federal cabinet was given authority to nullify any piece of provincial legislation within one year of the date upon which it was formally received by the secretary of state. This provision had been conceived by the Fathers of Confederation as another means of ensuring that local legislatures acted in harmony with national policies. No restrictions were imposed upon the exercise of this power by the constitution, but disputes soon arose, in which Ontario took a leading part, when the provinces claimed that disallowance violated local autonomy and substituted the will of a small group of federal ministers for that of the elected representatives of the people.

As the first minister of justice it fell to Sir John A. Macdonald to set forth the circumstances in which he would intervene, and in 1868 he reported: 'In deciding whether an Act of a provincial legislature should be allowed or sanctioned, the government must not only consider whether it affects the interest of the whole Dominion or not; but also whether it be unconstitutional, whether it exceeds the jurisdiction conferred on local legislatures, and in cases where jurisdiction is concurrent, whether it clashes with the legislation of the general Parliament,' Macdonald added that there should be as little interference with provincial legislation as possible and suggested that the provincial governments should first be advised of objections and asked to make the necessary changes in their acts.[31]

During the first fifteen years or so after Confederation the federal authorities pursued this relatively cautious policy. Almost all the acts disallowed were believed by successive justice ministers to be *ultra vires,* or beyond the constitutional powers of the provinces, and to interfere with federal policies in a significant way. Edward Blake, minister of justice in Alexander Mackenzie's government, stated the principles which guided him this way:

> I maintain that under our Constitution ... the provinces have the uncontrollable power of passing laws, valid and binding laws, upon all those matters which are exclusively within their competence, except, perhaps, in the rare cases in which such legislation may be shown substantially to affect Dominion interests. If you are to admit the view that the Dominion Cabinet may veto and destroy your legislation on purely local questions, you make your local legislatures a sham, and you had better openly, honestly and above-board ... create one central legislative power and let the parliament at Ottawa do all the business.

The only appeal, Blake added, against clearly valid provincial legislation was to the local electorate rather than the federal cabinet.[32]

Despite this policy of non-interference by the central government, friction over the question of disallowance did arise with some provinces, including Ontario. In 1869 Sir John A. Macdonald nullified two acts passed by the province on the grounds that they were beyond the competence of the legislature. Protests from Attorney-General Sandfield Macdonald were ignored. In 1874 Oliver Mowat's government passed an act by which escheated and forfeited estates would become the property of the provincial treasury. The premier argued that the old Province of Canada had possessed these privileges and that it was 'undeniable that all rights of the provinces as they existed before Confederation have, by the Confederation act, been divided between the Dominion and the provinces, and that whatever has not been given to the former is retained by the latter.' This claim to all residual jurisdiction, quite contrary to the intentions of the Fathers of Confederation, was rejected by the Mackenzie administration and the act was nullified. When Edward Blake was minister of justice he did not hesitate to threaten disallowance of a number of Ontario acts which he believed were ultra vires of the province, and the Mowat government complied with his demands for amendments in each case.[33]

When Sir John A. Macdonald returned to power in 1878 he immediately became embroiled in the dispute over the north-western boundary of Ontario. In 1880 he disallowed an act passed by the province providing for the administration of justice in the disputed territory, pointing out that the boundary was far from settled. This intervention reflected the growing tension between the two levels of government. And the same kind of tensions apparently underlay the disallowance of the Ontario Rivers and Streams Act in 1881.

This legislation originated in a dispute between private parties. In 1879 Boyd, Caldwell and Company began lumbering on the Mississippi River, a tributary of the Ottawa, and floated their logs down that stream. Peter McLaren of Carleton Place attempted to prevent them on the grounds that he alone had financed the dams and improvements which made the river usable for driving logs, and in 1880 McLaren secured an injunction against Boyd, Caldwell and

Company. In 1881 the Mowat administration, doubtless influenced by William C. Caldwell, Liberal member for Lanark North, introduced 'An Act for Protecting the Public Interests in Rivers, Streams and Creeks,' which permitted anyone to drive logs on a waterway upon payment of a fee to those responsible for any improvements. Peter McLaren, a Conservative, promptly appealed to the federal government to protect him by disallowing this legislation, claiming that his rights had been unjustly violated. Macdonald responded instantly; without even consulting the Ontario government he nullified the act. 'I think the power of the local legislatures to take away the rights of one man and vest them in another, as is done by this Act, is exceedingly doubtful,' wrote the prime minister, 'but assuming that such right does, in strictness, exist, I think it devolves upon this government to see that such power is not exercised in flagrant violation of private rights and natural justice.'[34]

Adam Crooks, the acting attorney-general, protested angrily at this swift intervention on behalf of a political ally. He defended the Rivers and Streams Act and denounced the disallowance of a measure clearly within the competence of the provincial legislature. 'The Confederation Act,' he reminded Macdonald, 'was intended to give practical effect to the exercise of the fullest freedom in the administration and control in local matters within each province, which was the main object of Quebec and Ontario, especially, in seeking such union.' Now local self-government was to be overturned 'on the private statement of a private individual.' So strongly did the provincial government feel that it reintroduced the legislation at the 1882 session of the legislature, doubtless with the enthusiastic support of the Caldwell interests.[35]

In disallowing the Rivers and Streams Act Macdonald undoubtedly departed from the principle generally adhered to during the previous fifteen years that only legislation beyond the jurisdiction of the provinces might properly be disallowed. 'Property and civil rights' as well as the natural resources of the province were clearly under the control of the local legislature, but the prime minister was sufficiently angry at Oliver Mowat to interfere. Indeed, he promptly disallowed the Rivers and Streams Act again in 1882 and once more in 1883 when the province persisted in repassing it. In 1884 the act was approved by the legislature for a fourth time, but by then the Judicial Committee of the Privy Council had found in favour of the Caldwell interests in a suit against McLaren. The judges held that the Rivers and Streams Act merely declared to be law certain principles which had been in force even prior to Confederation. Unrepentant, Macdonald continued to defend his action in 'protecting a man from a great wrong, from a great loss and injury, from a course, which if pursued, would destroy the confidence of the whole civilized world in the law of the land.' But he did not disallow the Rivers and Streams Act a fourth time.[36]

The rhetorical violence produced by the repeated disallowances of the Rivers and Streams Act can be explained partly by the pressure from competing private interests and partly by the desire of the politicians to make some capital.

Mowat was happy to have an additional weapon with which to bludgeon Ottawa at the height of the dispute over the north-western boundary. He certainly attempted to capitalize on his role as defender of provincial rights in the provincial election of 1883. Similar considerations of politics and patronage also explained the row over Ontario's new liquor licensing legislation. In 1883 Macdonald passed an act imposing federal liquor licensing, after strongly criticizing Mowat as 'a little tyrant who had attempted to control public opinion by getting hold of every office from that of Division Court bailiff to a tavern-keeper.' Even when the Privy Council upheld provincial authority in this area. Ottawa continued to enforce the new law. Mowat retaliated by bringing in legislation requiring those holding federal licences to pay additional fees to the province—a kind of fine for taking out a federal licence. This act was speedily disallowed by the federal government, but the courts eventually upheld Mowat's contention that the province had exclusive powers in the field of liquor licensing.[37]

After this rash of disagreements in the early 1880s, however, the power of disallowance ceased to be such an important factor in the relations between Ontario and the federal government. In part this change reflected Macdonald's recognition that the political price of such interference in local affairs was too high. Disallowance was a blunt instrument, and its use provoked cries of outrage. Except in the case of provincial legislation which clearly ran contrary to federal policy, it was better to leave the courts to decide upon the constitutionality of provincial statutes. J.S.D. Thompson, who became Macdonald's justice minister in 1885, was inclined to obey Edward Blake's dictum that disallowance could not properly be used on acts clearly within provincial jurisdiction.[38] The partisan bitterness aroused by the boundary dispute was probably more important in creating this conflict between the province and the Dominion than any clash of principles. Sir John A. Macdonald, ever the political pragmatist, used whatever weapon he had to hand to resist Mowat's pretensions, and Mowat, for his part, did all he could to arouse so much antagonism towards Ottawa that the use of disallowance against Ontario came to seem ill-advised.

IV

The combination of these grievances over the north-western boundary, the office of the lieutenant-governor, and the power of disallowance explains Ontario's enthusiastic participation in the interprovincial conference of 1887.[39] The idea that the provinces should meet and discuss changes in the federal system came from the new premier of Quebec, Honoré Mercier. Mercier's primary concern, however, was not so much with federal interference in local affairs but with financial matters. Quebec had not engaged in a series of wrangles with Ottawa of the sort which had embittered Ontario-federal relations, but the province was short of funds, heavily in debt, and constantly pressing Macdonald to concede better financial terms. In the spring of 1887 the Quebec premier suggested to Mowat a meeting to discuss 'the autonomy of the Provinces and their financial arrangements with the Dominion.' Although Mercier mentioned the need for the provinces to organize 'a system of common defence' against 'the centralizing tendencies manifested of late years by the Federal Government,' his real concern was clearly 'the inadequacy and injustice of the financial arrangements' in the BNA Act. In 1867, he pointed out, the provinces had given up customs and excise revenues worth $12,000,000 (which had doubled over the past twenty years) in exchange for subsidies of only $2,750,000 (now increased to $3,340,000).[40]

Better terms had little appeal for Mowat's government. Sandfield Macdonald had accumulated a large surplus while in office, and the Liberals had succeeded in balancing the province's books almost every year thereafter, partly through the sale of timber limits. Ontario did not need financial assistance, and its citizens would have to contribute the lion's share of the funds to provide larger federal transfer payments to the other provinces. Yet Mercier's approach found Mowat in a receptive frame of mind. The dispute over the boundary and the role of the governor was still dragging on, and the dust had barely settled from the row over the repeated disallowance of the Rivers and Streams Act and the liquor licensing legislation. A conference of the provinces, Mowat perceived, might be the perfect body to endorse the compact theory of Confederation and suggest constitutional changes to outflank the centralizing ambitions of Sir John A. Macdonald. Accordingly the Ontario premier replied that 'with regard to the financial arrangements this Province was satisfied with the provisions of the BNA Act and would still prefer them to any change,' but that his cabinet recognized the financial problems of the other provinces and agreed on 'the importance of resisting encroachments on provincial rights.' If new financial terms could be agreed on, this might stop Macdonald from dipping into the federal treasury whenever a province became so importunate as to threaten political damage. To Mowat and his ministers the $2,500,000 in railway subsidies granted to Quebec in 1884, under the threat that MPs from that province would withhold their support for government measures, was only the most flagrant example of a practice against which Edward Blake had protested as early as 1869. In 1885 Commissioner of Public Works Christopher Fraser told the legislature:

> we who have charge of Ontario affairs would be recreant to our trust if in the face of what we see going on, and what is absolutely certain to occur again, we made no sign and did not indicate that Ontario would not continue submitting to these raids by the other Provinces. (Cheers) I say again, let there be any needful readjustment, and when such a readjustment does take place, let it be understood as an absolute and final settlement. That is the attitude of the Province of Ontario. We do not care to get these indirect and unwarranted grants, and that Ontario shall be the milk cow for the whole concern.

Mowat eagerly accepted Mercier's invitation.[41]

The interprovincial conference met in the fall of 1887 after much preliminary manoeuvering. Macdonald had brusquely refused Mercier's invitation to attend, and he succeeded in inducing the premiers of Prince Edward Island and British Columbia to decline as well. Thus, only the Liberal governments of Ontario, Quebec, Nova Scotia, and New Brunswick sent delegates to be joined by representatives from Manitoba's Conservative administration, angered by repeated disallowances of their railway legislation. When the conference opened on 20 October, Honoré Mercier addressed the delegates at length, pointing out the problems which had arisen during the past twenty years. Oliver Mowat was then chosen as chairman and the delegates settled down to a week of closed-door deliberations. On 28 October the meeting broke up after unanimously endorsing a list of twenty-two resolutions.[42]

Most of these resolutions bear the clear stamp of Mowat's influence. In opening the gathering Mercier had placed readjustment of the federal subsidy first among the necessary amendments, but in the final list it was relegated to seventeenth place, coming after changes in the direction of greater provincial autonomy desired by Mowat's government. First on the list, not surprisingly, was a demand for the abolition of the power of disallowance, and second came a proposal for the reference of constitutional issues to the courts for a determination of jurisdiction. Next came the call for Senate reform on the grounds 'that a Senate to which appointments are made by the Federal Government, and for life, affords no adequate security for the provinces.' Half the senators should be chosen by the provinces. In addition, the BNA Act should be amended to give the lieutenant-governor the full prerogative authority of the Crown within the sphere of provincial jurisdiction. This series of constitutional changes was clearly designed to give the provinces a larger role in national affairs of the kind for which Ontario had been contending over the past fifteen years.[43]

The other resolutions agreed to by the provincial delegates also concerned issues over which Ontario had clashed with federal authorities: local works should not be withdrawn from provincial jurisdiction by being declared for the general advantage of Canada without the concurrence of the province concerned; lists of electors should be drawn up solely by provincial enumerators; members of legislative assemblies should have the same privileges and immunities as members of parliament; the provinces should have some authority over bankruptcy and insolvency. Finally, all the delegates approved a demand that the northern and western boundaries of Ontario, as determined by the Privy Council, should be enacted into law by the British parliament. In each case Mowat's interest in these issues was well-known and was endorsed by his fellow premiers.[44]

Their interest, of course, was focused primarily upon the seventeenth resolution of the conference dealing with the revision of the subsidies. Existing payments were declared 'totally inadequate' and a hefty increase was demanded in the scale of grants for the support of government. In addition, the annual sum of 80 cents per capita was to be tied no longer to the population of 1861 but to the most recent census, with provinces receiving 60 cents per head for all population in excess of 2 million. This 'basis for a final and unalterable settlement' would have cost Ottawa almost $1 million more than the $3.2 million it had paid out in 1887 for these purposes, with Ontario alone receiving an additional $580,000. Any reluctance Oliver Mowat may have felt at supporting such large additional subsidies, primarily funded by Ontario taxpayers, was overridden by three considerations: he had the support of the other premiers for the constitutional changes he desired; this act would be a final settlement to the subsidy question; and his government could doubtless put the additional money to good use. The conference concluded by agreeing to submit its resolutions to the provincial legislatures for approval and then to press Britain for appropriate amendment of the BNA Act.[45]

For all the fanfare which surrounded the interprovincial conference of 1887 (Mercier compared it explicitly to the 1864 Quebec Conference which had hammered out the Confederation agreement) its practical results were meagre. Macdonald refused to take any notice of it whatever, insisting it was no more than a Cabal of disgruntled Grits. When Mowat asked him to meet the premiers and formally receive the resolutions of the conference, he refused.[46] Nothing was done. But in a larger sense that was not important; for Macdonald had already abandoned the practice of aggressively disallowing provincial legislation of which he disapproved. In 1884 the Judicial Committee had upheld Ontario's boundary claims and in 1888 it again found for the province in the *St. Catharines Milling Company* case, so that in 1889 Macdonald finally agreed to support legislation to grant the disputed territory to the province. The authority of the lieutenant-governor still remained unclear, but that issue, too, would eventually be settled in favour of the provincial claims by the Privy Council in the *Maritime Bank* case in 1892. Although the BNA Act was formally unaltered, it hardly mattered.

By that time, too, Sir John Thompson had acquired more influence over legal and constitutional affairs at Ottawa. The Nova Scotian seemed more willing than Macdonald to allow the provinces to go their own way, an attitude demonstrated by a less aggressive use of the power of disallowance.[47] In 1890 Edward Blake proposed amendments to the Supreme Court Act to facilitate reference cases so that many jurisdictional disputes could be settled by the courts. Earlier legislation had permitted references to the Supreme Court, but since the judges were not required to give reasons for their decisions they simply gave categorical answers to questions put to them. In 1891 Thompson introduced the necessary amendments, permitting the court to take additional evidence and hear representations from all interested parties before issuing a reasoned decision.[48] The relationship between Mowat and Thompson was not marred by the kind of animosity that existed between Macdonald and Mowat,[49] and the Ontario premier readily agreed to the justice minister's suggestion in mid-1891 that he frame a reference case on the issue of provincial control over the inland fisheries. This proved to be the first of a series of important reference cases on matters such as prohibition and company law which were ultimately dealt with by the Judicial Committee of the Privy Council.[50]

Thus the trend towards greater respect for provincial rights was evident even before Sir John A. Macdonald's death in 1891, and in the words of one historian, 'After 1896 provincial rights and the compact theory attained a position close to motherhood in the scale of Canadian political values. It would be difficult to find a prominent politician who was not willing to pay at least lip-service to the principle of provincial rights and its theoretical underpinning, the compact theory.' Following the *Maritime Bank* decision, the Judicial Committee held in 1895 that 'the exclusive powers of the provincial legislatures may be said to be absolute.' Regarding the duty of the federal government to intervene through the power of disallowance to protect private rights the Privy Council declared, 'The supreme legislative power in relation to any subject-matter is always capable of abuse, but it is not to be assumed that it will be abused; if it is, the only remedy is an appeal to those by whom the legislature is elected.'[51] As we shall see, this doctrine was to assume a vitally important place in the relations between Ontario and the federal government over the succeeding fifteen years.

In bringing about this constitutional revolution, which converted the provinces from glorified municipalities into co-ordinate sovereignties with the federal government, Sir Oliver Mowat had considerable help. In particular, the favourable decisions of the Privy Council provided the legal underpinning for the positions he fought for, yet he was also greatly assisted by his own political canniness. In his conduct of federal-provincial relations he mapped out the methods which his successors would follow up to the Second World War and after.[52] He placed the highest priority on achieving the widest possible independent control over the development of Ontario's resources, and for that reason he fought long and hard with Macdonald over the north-western boundary. He displayed little enthusiasm for increased federal payments from Ottawa to the provinces, preferring to levy and spend his own taxes, but he showed at the interprovincial conference in 1887 that he understood how to rally the other provinces behind him in his constitutional demands by making concessions in the financial field. The key to his defence of provincial rights was the compact theory of confederation, adumbrated by Edward Blake in 1869 but raised to a first principle of federal-provincial relations during Mowat's long tenure of office. It was the compact theory which provided the basis for claiming a veto over any constitutional changes, giving Ontario a strong weapon with which to defend its interests, which Mowat's successors would not hesitate to use. In 1896 Mowat resigned the premiership in response to Wilfrid Laurier's pleas to bolster up the new Liberal government in Ottawa; when the Ontario legislature met in 1897 his roly-poly figure was missing from the leader's chair for the first time in a quarter-century. Andrew Pattullo provided a glowing valedictory: 'In this long series of constitutional victories lies perhaps Oliver Mowat's highest claim to enduring fame and everlasting gratitude of his countrymen. For it was essential to the stability and very existence of Confederation that the rights and privileges of the Provincial and Federal Governments should be clearly and justly defined. Without such just consideration and protection of the rights of the Provinces by the Privy Council, it is quite certain that the Provinces would not have remained in the same union.'[53]

Notes

1. I have benefited greatly from J.C. Morrison's study 'Oliver Mowat and the Development of Provincial Rights in Ontario: A Study in Dominion-Provincial Relations, 1867–1896,' in *Three History Theses* (Toronto: Ontario Department of Public Records and Archives, 1961), on which I have depended for much of the material contained in this chapter.

2. The 'ministerial explanations' made upon the formation of the coalition are quoted in ibid., 28. Macdonald's statement in the Canadian Assembly on 19 April 1861 is quoted in Joseph Pope, *Memoirs of the Right Honourable Sir John Alexander Macdonald, G.C.B.* (Toronto: Musson, n.d.), 242–3.

3. *Parliamentary Debates on the Subject of Confederation of the British North American Provinces, 3rd Session, 8th Provincial Parliament of Canada* (Quebec: Hunter, Rose and Co., 1865) [hereafter Confederation Debates], 108 (Brown's speech); G.P. Browne, comp., *Documents on the Confederation of British North America, A Compilation based on Sir Joseph Pope's Confederation Documents Supplemented by Other Official Material* (Toronto: McClelland and Stewart, 1969), 122–3.

4. Browne, *Documents on Confederation,* 142–3

5. Sir John A. Macdonald to Brown Chamberlin, 26 Oct. 1868, in Joseph Pope. *Correspondence of Sir John Macdonald* (Toronto: Doubleday, 1921), 75; George Brown to Anne Brown, 27 October 1864, quoted in J.M.S. Careless, *Brown of the Globe,* vol. 2, *Statesman of Confederation 1860–1880* (Toronto: Macmillan, 1963), 171; *Confederation Debates,* 108.

6. J.M.S. Careless, 'The Toronto *Globe* and Agrarian Radicalism, 1850–1867.' *Canadian Historical Review,* 29 (1948), 14–39; *Confederation Debates,* 88.

7. M.C. Urquhart and K.A.H. Buckley, eds. *Historical Statistics of Canada* (Toronto: Macmillan, 1965), 14, 614; E.V. Jackson, 'The Organization of the Canadian Liberal Party 1867–1896 with Particular Reference to Ontario,' unpublished MA thesis, University of Toronto, 1962, 95.

8. Morrison, 'Mowat and Provincial Rights,' 250–5 quoting *Globe,* 24 Nov. 1869; Bruce W. Hodgins, *John Sandfield Macdonald 1812–1872* (Toronto: University of Toronto Press, 1971), 103–4.

9. Morrison, 'Mowat and Provincial Rights,' 40, quoting *Globe,* 23 Dec. 1871; Joseph Schull, *Edward Blake, the Man of the Other Way (1833–1881)* (Toronto: Macmillan, 1975), 84–5.

10. Morrison, 'Mowat and Provincial Rights,' 42–5; G. Ramsay Cook, *Provincial Autonomy, Minority Rights and the Compact Theory* (Ottawa: Queen's Printer, 1969), 12–3, 19–20: Jackson. 'Organization of the Liberal Party,' 89–104; Bruce Hodgins, 'Disagreement at the Commencement: Divergent Ontarian Views of Federalism, 1867–1871,' in Swainson, *Oliver Mowat's Ontario, 56.*

11. See Morrison, 'Mowat and Provincial Rights,' 95–176 for an extended account of this dispute and Ontario, *Sessional Papers,* 1882, no. 69, *Correspondence, Papers and Documents of Dates from 1856 to 1882 Inclusive, Relating to the Northerly and Westerly Boundaries of the Province of Ontario, Printed by Order of the Legislative Assembly* (Toronto: C. Blackett Robinson, 1882).

12. Ibid., 1873, no. 44, William McDougall to provincial secretary, 9 March 1872.

13. Ibid., Ontario order-in-council, 25 March 1872.

14. Ibid., Joseph Howe to W.P. Howland, 16 May 1872, enclosing Macdonald's report; Howland to Howe, 31 May 1872; Howe to Howland, 12 Nov. 1872.

15. Morrison, 'Mowat and Provincial Rights,' 114–7; Ontario, *Sessional Papers,* 1882, no. 69, memorandum of agreement for provisional boundary in respect of patents of lands between David Laird and T.B. Pardee, 26 June 1874.

16. Morrison, 'Mowat and Provincial Rights,' 118–26; Mackenzie quoted at 123.

17. Ibid., 126–7.

18. Ontario, *Sessional Papers,* 1879, no. 13, statement of the Ontario case re westerly and northerly boundaries prepared for the arbitrators, 7 Feb. 1879; ibid., 1882, no. 69, statement of the case of the government of the dominion of Canada regarding the boundaries of the province of Ontario, prepared by Hugh MacMahon, QC, counsel for the dominion, 1878; report of the proceedings before the arbitrators in the matter of the boundaries of the province of Ontario, at Ottawa, 1,2,3 Aug. 1878; ibid., 1879, no. 22; *North Western Ontario: Its Boundaries, Resources and Communications, Prepared under Instructions from the Ontario Government* (Toronto: Hunter, Rose and Co., 1879).

19. Ibid., 1879, no. 80. A.S. Hardy to secretary of state, 31 Dec. 1878; ibid., 1880, no. 46, I.R. Eckhart to secretary of state, 23 Sept. 1879; Hardy to J.C. Aikins, 19 Dec. 1879; the quotations are from Eckhart's letter. Morrison, 'Mowat and Provincial Rights,' 133, cites the Conservative Toronto *Mail's* view that the arbitration was a 'farce.'

20. Ontario, *Sessional Papers,* 1881, no. 30, report of Justice Minister James McDonald, 20 Jan. 1880; report of Attorney-General Oliver Mowat, 18 March 1880; report of Justice Minister James McDonald, 17 March 1880; report of Justice Minister James McDonald, 23 April 1880; ibid., 1882, no. 23, Ontario order-in-council, 28 May 1880; Morrison, 'Mowat and Provincial Rights,' 134–5.

21. Ontario, *Sessional Papers,* 1882, no. 23. Mowat to James McDonald, 1 Feb. 1881; Morrison, 'Mowat and Provincial Rights,' Macdonald quoted at 137–9.

22. Ontario, *Sessional Papers,* 1882, no. 23, Lieutenant-Governor John Beverley Robinson to secretary of state, 15 March 1881; Provincial Archives of Ontario [hereafter PAO], provincial secretary's records, series 1-1-D, 1881, no. 1785, Robinson to secretary of state, 30 Sept. 1881.

23. Ontario, *Sessional Papers,* 1882, no. 23, report by Attorney-General Oliver Mowat, 1 Nov. 1881.

24. Morrison, 'Oliver Mowat and Provincial Rights,' 140–51; Macdonald quoted at 145, Mowat at 147–8.

25. See P.B. Waite, *Canada 1874–1896. Arduous Destiny* (Toronto: McClelland and Stewart, 1971), 117–18, for a brief account of the Rat Portage affair; A. Margaret Evans, 'Oliver Mowat and Ontario, 1872–1896; A Study in Political Success,' unpublished PhD thesis, University of Toronto, 1967, 508–20; John Wilson and David Hoffman, 'Ontario, a three-Party System in Transition,' in Martin Robin, ed., *Canadian Provincial Politics* (Scarborough, Ont.: Prentice Hall, 1972), 204.

26. Ontario, *Sessional Papers,* 1884, no. 3. Memorandum of Agreement between governments of Ontario and Manitoba, 18 Dec. 1883; ibid., 1885, no. 8, Lieutenant-Governor John Beverley Robinson to secretary of state, 29 April 1885: Morrison, 'Oliver Mowat and Provincial Rights,' 151–60.

27. Ibid., 160–73; Macdonald is quoted at 171.

28. Ibid., 46–94, contains a full discussion of this dispute. On the powers and responsibilities of the lieutenant-governor, see John T. Saywell, *The Office of the Lieutenant-Governor, a Study in Canadian Government and Politics* (Toronto: University of Toronto Press, 1957) *passim,* and James McL. Hendry, *Memorandum on the Office of Lieutenant-Governor of a Province: Its Constitutional Character and Functions (with Appendices)* (Ottawa: Department of Justice, 1955).

29. Ontario, *Sessional Papers,* 1888, no. 37, Lieutenant-Governor John Beverley Robinson to secretary of state, 22 Jan. 1886.

30. Canada, Senate, *Report Pursuant to Resolution of the Senate to the Honourable Speaker by the Parliamentary Counsel [W.F. O'Connor] Relating to the Enactment of the British North America Act, 1867, Any Lack of Consonance between Its Terms and Judicial Construction of Them and Cognate Matters* (Ottawa: Queen's Printer, 1961) [hereafter *O'Connor Report*], annex 3, case no. to; C.R.W. Biggar, *Sir Oliver Mowat* (Toronto: Warwick Bros and Rutter, 1905), vol. 2, 518.

31. G.V. LaForest, *Disallowance and Reservation of Provincial Legislation* (Ottawa: Queen's Printer, 1955), 24–5, reprints Macdonald's report to council of 8 June 1868.

32. LaForest, *Disallowance and Reservation,* 36–43; Blake quoted at 41.

33. Morrison, Mowat and Provincial Rights,' 177–233, discusses the dispute over disallowance. The disagreement between the two Macdonalds is described at 186–9 and Mowat is quoted at 194.

34. Ibid., 199–203, 206–10; LaForest, *Disallowance and Reservation,* 53–4; Canada, Justice Department, *Correspondence, Reports of the Ministers of Justice and Orders-in-Council upon the Subject of Dominion and Provincial Legislation, 1867–1895* (Ottawa: Government Printing Bureau, 1896), W.E. Hodgins, comp. [hereafter *Provincial Legislation, 1867–1895*], 177, report of minister of justice. James McDonald per J.A.M., 17 May 1881.

35. Ibid., 179, report of acting Attorney-General Adam Crooks, 14 Oct. 1881; Morrison, 'Mowat and Provincial Rights,' 210–13.

36. LaForest, *Disallowance and Reservation,* 54–6; Macdonald quoted at 55; Morrison, 'Mowat and Provincial Rights,' 213–14.

37. Ibid., 223–8; Macdonald quoted at 225.

38. LaForest, *Disallowance and Reservation,* 56–8; John P. Heisler, 'Sir John Thompson, 1844–1894' unpublished PhD thesis, University of Toronto, 1955, 223–4.

39. See Morrison, 'Mowat and Provincial Rights,' 235–85.

40. Ontario, *Sessional Papers,* 1887, no. 51. Mercier to Mowat, 8 March 1887.

41. Ibid., Mowat to Mercier, 15 March 1887: Fraser quoted in Morrison, 'Mowat and Provincial Rights,' 260–1.

42. 'Minutes of the Interprovincial Conference held at the City of Quebec from the 20th to the 28th October, 1887, inclusively,' in *Dominion Provincial and Interprovincial Conferences from 1887 to 1926 / Conférences Fédérales-Provinciales et Conférences Interprovinciales de 1887 à 1926* (Ottawa: King's Printer, 1951) [hereafter *Dominion Provincial Conferences 1887–1926*].

43. Ibid., 20–1.

44. Ibid., 21–4.

45. Ibid., 24–7.

46. Donald Creighton, *John A. Macdonald, the Old Chieftain* (Toronto: Macmillan, 1955), 472–3, 298–500; Pope, *Correspondence of Macdonald,* 431–3, Mowat to Macdonald, 17 Nov. 1888; Macdonald to Mowat, 3 Dec. 1888.

47. See above n. 38 and Public Archives of Canada [hereafter PAC], justice department records, series A2, vol. 65, Mowat to Thompson, 29 June 1886; J.R. Miller, '"As a Politician He Is a Great Enigma": The Social and Political Ideas of D'Alton McCarthy,' *Canadian Historical Review,* 58 (1977), 403–4.

48. Gerald Rubin, 'The Nature, Use and Effect of Reference Cases in Canadian Constitutional Law,' in W.R. Lederman, ed., *The Courts and the Canadian Constitution* (Toronto: McClelland and Stewart, 1964), 223–7; Canada, House of Commons, *Debates* [hereafter Can., H. of C., *Deb.*], 1891, 3586–7.

49. On 29 June 1891, Mowat wrote to Thompson: 'If we are to have a Conservative government, I have great pleasure in saying that there is no Conservative from whom in the common interest I should expect so much good and so little of the contrary as the present Minister of Justice'; quoted in Heisler, 'Thompson,' 274.

50. PAC, justice department records, series A2, vol. 83, Mowat to Thompson 1 April 1891, private. The seemingly interminable negotiations preceding the fisheries reference can be followed in PAO, Aemilius Irving papers, and the decisions may be found in *O'Connor Report,* annex 3, cases no. 13, 16.

51. Cook, *Provincial Autonomy and the Compact Theory,* 44; *Brophy v. Attorney General for Manitoba* (1895) quoted in W.P.M. Kennedy, *The Constitution of Canada* (London: Oxford University Press, 1922), 421, and *Attorney General for Canada v. Attorney General for Ontario (Fisheries Reference)* (1898) in *O'Connor Report,* annex 3, case no. 16.

52. See Armstrong, 'The Mowat Heritage in Federal-Provincial Relations,' in Swainson, ed., *Oliver Mowat's Ontario,* 93–118.

53. *Globe,* 12 Feb. 1897.

CHAPTER
2 LOUIS RIEL

There is no more controversial figure in Canadian history than Louis "David" Riel, who twice led his *Métis* followers in armed resistance against the federal government. Riel has been both lauded and vilified, seen by some as a heroic figure defending a downtrodden people and by others as a traitor who richly deserved his fate. One of the unusual aspects of the large historical literature which exists on this subject is its wide variety of broad interpretative contexts. Thus the Riel agitations can be seen as both resulting from and significantly contributing to divisions between French and English Canada. Alternatively, they may be viewed as the result of a clash between civilization and the frontier. Or they may be placed within the context of regional discontent, the western hinterland protesting against real or prospective exploitation by the east.

The readings which are reprinted in this unit focus on the role of individual participants in the 1885 crisis. The first selection is by Thomas Flanagan who has written widely on Riel. In this reading, a chapter from his book *Riel and the Rebellion: 1885 Reconsidered*, Flanagan places the responsibility for the North West Rebellion on the shoulders of Riel himself. Arguing that the grievances of the *Métis* had been sufficiently remedied, that they could no longer constitute the cause of an armed uprising, Flanagan looks for the answer in Riel's personal—and mistaken—belief that the *Métis* owned the North West by virtue of aboriginal title. This was entirely contrary to Ottawa's position.

In the second reading, D.N. Sprague rejects the view that the Canadian government had moved to remedy *Métis* grievances and presents the provocative thesis that the 1885 uprising was consciously and deliberately provoked by the Canadian prime minister, Sir John A. Macdonald. In his biography of Macdonald, Donald Creighton had linked the 1885 uprising with the successful completion of the Canadian Pacific Railway. The practical demonstration of the railway's usefulness in transporting troops to the North West, so the argument ran, made it possible for the government once again to approach Parliament with a request for further subsidies. Sprague takes this linkage much further, suggesting that circumstantial evidence supports the view that by late August 1884, Macdonald preferred an "angry Riel" and to that end he thereafter followed a policy of "provocative inaction" deliberately designed to bring about an "exploitable crisis"—all in aid of the Canadian Pacific Railway.

ABORIGINAL TITLE

Thomas Flanagan

Why then did the North-West Rebellion occur at all, if the objective grievances of the *Métis* were remedied by the government? In this connection, it must be remembered that many other factors contributed to the *Métis'* sense of alienation. They were still bitter over the events in Manitoba, which, in spite of the seeming success of the movement of 1869–70, had left them a marginal minority in their own homeland. Having moved farther west to escape this status, they could see themselves once again faced with being outnumbered by white settlers. Another long-range consideration was the decline of the *Métis* economy. The buffalo withdrew from the Canadian prairies during the 1870s and vanished altogether after 1878, adversely affecting numerous trades in which the *Métis* had been prominent: buffalo hunting, trading with the Indians for pemmican and robes, and transporting these goods to market. The *Métis* cart trains and boat brigades also suffered from the advent of railways and steamboats in the Canadian West. Deprived of much of the income from traditional occupations, the *Métis* had to rely more on agriculture. As they began to make this transition, they were struck, as were all western farmers, by the economic depression and fall in grain prices which began in 1883. For the *Métis* of St. Laurent, this economic malaise was aggravated by the decision to build the Canadian Pacific Railway along the southern route through Regina instead of along the northern route through Prince Albert. The *Métis* lost out on the jobs and contracts that would have been created by a construction boom in northern Saskatchewan.

All these factors help to explain the prevailing mood in St. Laurent, yet none really accounts for the outbreak of the Rebellion; for similar factors were equally at work in other *Métis* settlements which did not turn to violence. The unique fact about St. Laurent was the presence of Louis Riel. His great prestige made him a prism through which all information from the outside world was refracted to the *Métis*. His interpretation of the government's concessions made them seem like provocations. Any explanation of why the rising occurred must focus on Riel. What motivated him to take up arms? Such questions can never be answered with total certainty, but one can make a reasonable estimation of the forces at work in his mind at this time.

First was Riel's brooding resentment over the aftermath of 1869–70. Thinking himself the natural leader of his people, he had expected a quick amnesty followed by a successful career in politics. Instead he received exile, loss of his Commons seat, and penniless obscurity. His own misfortunes paralleled those of the *Métis* as they were submerged in Manitoba politics and

From *Riel and the Rebellion: 1885 Reconsidered* (Saskatoon: Western Producer Prairie Books), 1983, 75–100, 161–163. Reprinted by permission of Douglas & McIntyre Ltd.

went into voluntary emigration. Riel's bitterness lay behind the efforts he would make in the winter of 1884–85 to obtain a cash payment from the federal government. In his mind, this was fair compensation for the wrongs he had suffered. The failure of these efforts to show any tangible result must have strengthened his readiness to undertake extreme measures.

A second factor was Riel's religious "mission." As I have shown at length in *Louis "David" Riel: "Prophet of the New World,"* he believed himself to be a divinely inspired prophet, even after his "cure" in the insane asylums of Quebec. His mission of religious reform was only in abeyance, awaiting a signal from God to be made public. The longer he stayed with the *Métis,* the more ostentatious became Riel's piety. He began to argue with the Oblate missionaries over points of politics and theology, until the exasperated priests threatened him with excommunication. The notebook of prayers he kept over the winter of 1884–85 shows an ascending curve of spiritual confidence culminating in readiness for action. Riel launched the Rebellion convinced it was the occasion to reveal his new religion to the world. That is why he began his first major speech to the *Métis* with the words, "Rome has fallen."

In spite of this religious dimension, Riel's rising was a political phenomenon whose causes must also be sought at the political level. If the *Métis* grievances over river lots and land scrip do not furnish an adequate explanation, more insight can be found through examining Riel's views on aboriginal rights. For reasons explained below, he held that the *Métis* were the true owners of the North West; that their entry into Confederation had been conditional upon fulfillment of the Manitoba "treaty"; and that they were legally and morally free to secede from Canada since (in his view) the "treaty" had not been kept by Canada. In this sweeping perspective, the grievances of river lots and scrip were petty complaints, useful in mobilizing local support but peripheral to the real issues. Study of the course of the agitation, from July 1884, when Riel arrived at St. Laurent, to February 1885, the eve of the Rebellion, demonstrates that his strategy was built upon his radical view of aboriginal rights. Preexisting local grievances were only pawns in a complex series of maneuvers aimed at vindicating *Métis* ownership of the North West as a whole. To understand this is to explain the apparent paradox that the *Métis* launched an insurrection immediately after the government granted their demands. Under Riel's leadership, they were fighting for stakes which far transcended river lots and scrip. They may have only dimly perceived what the real goals were, but these are plain enough in Riel's writings.

Conflicting Views of Aboriginal Rights

Riel's political views can only be appreciated against the background of the events of 1869–70 and their aftermath. In his interpretation of these events he was quite different from official circles in Ottawa or London. To see the magnitude of this difference, we must first sketch the official view. Here, a word of caution is required.

What I call the "official view" was not articulated until the *St. Catherine's Milling Case,* decided in 1889. But the theory of aboriginal rights developed in this case was, I believe, implicit in the practice of the previous decades, including the acquisition of Rupert's Land by Canada and subsequent dealings with Indians and half-breeds in that territory. Naturally, there is room for debate over the exact contours of an implicit, unarticulated view.

To the rulers of Britain and Canada as well as to the proprietors of the Hudson's Bay Company, the acquisition by Canada of Rupert's Land and the North West Territories was a complicated real estate conveyance. In return for compensation from Canada, the Company surrendered its land to the Crown, which in turn passed it to Canada by Act of Parliament and Royal Proclamation. The transaction was founded on the property rights conferred on the Company by the royal charter of 1670:

> ... the sole trade and commerce of all those seas, straights, bays, rivers, creeks and sounds in whatsoever latitude they shall be that lie within the entrance of the straights commonly called Hudson's Straights together with all the lands and territories upon the countries, coasts, and confines of the seas, bays, lakes, rivers, creeks, and sounds aforesaid that are not already actually possessed by or granted to any of our subjects or possessed by the subjects of any other Christian prince or state.[1]

It is true that Canada had accepted the Company's ownership rights only reluctantly and after years of protest, putting forward the different theory that most of Rupert's Land ought to belong to Canada because of the explorations undertaken from New France. But the Colonial Office refused any measures that might diminish the Company's rights, and in the end the sale went through on the assumption that the Company was the rightful owner of this immense territory.

When the *Métis* of Red River, who had never been consulted about the sale, showed signs of resistance, the Canadian government refused to take possession, much as a purchaser might refuse to take possession of a house which had undergone damage in the period between signing of contract and date of transfer. The Imperial government doubted the legality of Canada's position but did not force the issue. Canada invited the inhabitants of Red River to send a delegation to Ottawa to make their concerns known. Having discussed matters with the three delegates (Father N.-J. Ritchot, Alfred Scott, John Black), the Canadian government drafted the Manitoba Act to respond to the desires of Red River: provincial status, responsible government, official bilingualism, protection of customary land rights, etc. Importantly, the Manitoba Act was a unilateral action of the Canadian Parliament, not a treaty between independent partners (although it was probably *ultra vires* of the Canadian Parliament and had later to be confirmed by Imperial statute). Payment for Rupert's Land was made in London after the Company delivered the Deed of Surrender to the Colonial Office; and the Imperial government, by order-in-council of 23 June 1870, annexed Rupert's Land to Canada, effective 15 July.

It was always assumed by both governments that aboriginal rights of the Indians would be respected. Indeed section 14 of the order-in-council of 23 June 1870 specified that "any claims of Indians to compensation for lands required for purposes of settlement shall be disposed of by the Canadian Government in communication with the Imperial Government."[2] The *Métis* were not explicitly mentioned, but the Canadian government had already recognized their aboriginal rights in the Manitoba Act.

Native title was not seen as sovereignty in the European sense. Only a state could claim sovereignty, and the North American Indian tribes had never been organized as states. Hence the validity of claims to sovereignty made by European states on the basis of discovery, settlement, and conquest. Nor was Indian title understood as ownership in fee simple, for the nomadic tribes of North America had never marked off plots of land in a way compatible with European notions of private property. Indian title was interpreted as an encumbrance upon the underlying title to the land held by the sovereign. Indians had a real and enforceable right to support themselves on this land as they had from time immemorial. This right could be surrendered only to the sovereign, not to private parties; and compensation had to be paid for surrender, according to the ancient principle of common law that there should be no expropriation without compensation.

This understanding was legally articulated in the *St. Catherine's Milling Case,* decided by the Supreme Court of Canada in 1887 and the Judicial Committee of the Privy Council in 1889. There aboriginal title was defined in the context of a dispute between the governments of Ontario and Canada over who owned the lands ceded by the Ojibway in Treaty No. 3: the Crown in right of Canada or the Crown in right of Ontario? We can ignore this aspect of the dispute to concentrate on the issue of aboriginal title. To explain this concept, the judges resorted to the concept of usufruct, which in Roman law was the right to use and enjoy the fruits of property—usually slaves or a landed estate—without actually owning it. The holder of usufructuary rights could enjoy the property undisturbed during the life of those rights, but could not sell or otherwise alienate the property. At the expiration of the usufruct, the property reverted to the owner. The Canadian and British courts, seeking to interpret aboriginal title as it had developed over the centuries, used the concept of usufruct as an analogy. They cast the sovereign in the role of owner and the natives in the role of holders of "a personal and usufructuary right"[3] to occupy the land and support themselves from its produce. This limited right stemmed from the benevolence of the sovereign, who had not yet chosen to make use of the land in other ways. It was an internal concession made by the sovereign as part of Indian policy; it was not a right to be claimed under the law of nations by Indian tribes as if they were sovereign nations.

Title, thus, was vested in the Crown. The aboriginal right to use the land was an encumbrance on that title which had to be extinguished before the Crown could alienate the land to private owners. Extinguishment required compensation, which might take the form of land reserves, money payments, educational or medical services, etc. Logically, the situation was not different from other real estate conveyances where an encumbrance existed upon a title, as from mortgage or other debt. Title had to be cleared before alienation through sale or donation was possible.

The Canadian government acted on this basis to extinguish aboriginal rights in Rupert's Land. The Indians were dealt with in the numbered treaties of the 1870s, and a land grant of 1,400,000 acres was divided among the *Métis* of Manitoba. The only anomaly concerned the *Métis* of the North West Territories, where delay had ensued for various reasons. But on the eve of the Rebellion, the government announced that it would also deal with them, although the precise form that compensation would take was apparently still undecided. This sequence of actions should have wiped the slate clean, according to the official view. All encumbrances to title should have been removed, all aboriginal rights extinguished. Without injustice to Indian or *Métis,* the government could open the land for homesteading, make land grants to railways or colonization companies, and in general act as a landlord with a clear title.

It is crucial to appreciate the intellectual framework within which the government acted. From offer to purchase through taking possession and finally clearing title, everything was based on the validity of the Hudson's Bay Company's charter and on the contemporary understanding of aboriginal rights. The quarrel with Riel arose in large part because he had a view of the situation which diverged at fundamental points. This view was never expressed completely and systematically, but it may be put together from various writings and utterances. Since many of these statements come from the months after the Rebellion was put down, there may be some question as to whether they adequately represent Riel's earlier ideas. We must presume they do; otherwise there is not enough material to analyze Riel's thinking at the pivotal moment of the Rebellion's outbreak. Apart from this one assumption, we will try not to impose an artificial consistency upon the thoughts of a man who was not a political philosopher.

Riel explicitly denied the validity of the Hudson's Bay charter because of its monopolistic provisions. The Company's sole right to trade "unjustly deprived the Northwest of the advantages of international trade and the rest of humanity, especially neighboring peoples, of the benefit of the commercial relations with the North-West to which they were entitled."[4] The result was impoverishment and oppression of the native inhabitants, both Indians and *Métis.* Riel coined the term *haute trahison internationale*[5] to describe the situation, which we might translate into today's idiom as "a crime against humanity." The charter was void, as was any sale based upon it; for the Company could not sell what it did not own. The most Riel would admit was that the Company had an interest in the land which it had sold to Canada;[6] but that transaction did not affect the natives, who were the true owners of the land. Aboriginal rights were clearly in Riel's mind not a mere encumbrance on the title but actual owner-ship—not individual ownership in fee simple, perhaps, but a collective ownership by the *Métis* as a nation and by the Indians as tribes. In effect, he reversed the official view according to which the Hudson's Bay Company was the true owner of lands in which the natives possessed an interest consisting of the usufructuary right of subsistence. Riel made the natives the owners of lands in which the Company possessed the interest of being allowed to trade. They owned their land in the same way as all other nations owned their lands under the law of na-tions; their title was not merely a limited right of occupancy dependent on the grace of the sovereign. He stood in the tradition of *Métis* nationalism which stretched back to the conflict with the Hudson's Bay Company about the Selkirk Settlement. Traders of the Northwest Company had suggested to the *Métis* that the land was theirs, not the Company's, and the idea had persisted across the generations.

Riel had argued in a slightly different way when he established the Provisional Government on 8 December 1869. He issued a Declaration which somewhat grudgingly conceded the legitimacy of the Company's regime while remaining silent about the question of ownership:

> This Company consisting of many persons required a certain constitution. But as there was a question of commerce only their constitution was framed in ref-erence thereto. Yet since there was at that time no government to see to the interests of a people already existing in the country, it became necessary for judicial affairs to have recourse to the officers of the Hudson's Bay Company. Thus inaugurated that species of government which, slightly modified by sub-sequent circumstances, ruled this country up to a recent date.

Although this government "was far from answering to the wants of the peo-ple," the *Métis* "had generously supported" it. But now the Company was abandoning its people by "subjugat[ing] it without its consent to a foreign power"; and according to the law of nations, a people abandoned by its govern-ment "is at liberty to establish any form of government it may consider suitable to its wants."[7] Thus the Provisional Government was legitimate according to the law of nations, and the Hudson's Bay Company had no right to transfer to Canada the land and people it had abandoned. Canada would have to deal with the Provisional Government if it was going to annex Rupert's Land.

Riel's original position of 1869 was that it violated that law of nations (or "international law" as we would say today) to transfer a population without seeking its consent. In 1885 he added the argument that the Company did not own Rupert's Land because its charter was void. Both arguments led to the same conclusions, that the sale to Canada was invalid until the inhabitants of Rupert's Land gave their consent, and that, living in a political vacuum, they certainly had the right to form their own government to negotiate the terms of sale on their behalf.

Riel not only sought to demonstrate the legitimacy of the Provisional Government through abstract reasoning, but also tried to show that the Provisional Government had been recognized by both Britain and Canada. He formulated the facts slightly differently on various occasions, but the main line of argument was always the same: ministers of the Canadian government had invited the insurgents to send delegates to Ottawa and had conducted negotiations with them. An amnesty had been promised by the governor general himself, both directly and through intermediaries. Thus both Canada and Britain had recognized the Provisional Government *de facto,* even if there had not been a formal exchange of ambassadors according to international protocol.[8]

The legitimacy of the Provisional Government was essential to Riel because it determined his interpretation of the Manitoba Act and of the entry of Manitoba into Confederation. His frame of reference was the law of nations (*droit des gens*), because negotiations had been carried out between independent entities, Canada and Red River. Rupert's Land had not been purchased; rather its inhabitants, acting through their government, had decided to join Canada. Union with Canada was not the result of unilateral action in Ottawa; it had required the assent of the Provisional Government, which was formally given after Father Ritchot returned from Ottawa to report on the terms offered by Canada. After the vote, Riel's "secretary of state" wrote to Canada's secretary of state to inform him that

> ... the Provisional Government and the Legislative Assembly, in the name of the people of the North-West, do accept the "Manitoba Act," and consent to enter into Confederation on the terms entered into with our delegates.... The Provisional Government and the Legislative Assembly have consented to enter into Confederation in the belief, and on the understanding, that in the above mentioned terms a general amnesty is contemplated.[9]

The arrangement was a "treaty" in the sense of an international agreement between states. The treaty had two parts: the written text of the Manitoba Act and the oral promise of amnesty for all actions committed over the winter of 1869–70. This explains the final lines of Riel's pamphlet on the amnesty question:

> Ce que nous demandons, c'est l'amnistie: c'est l'exécution loyale de l'acte de Manitoba. Rien de plus, mais aussi rien de moins. [What we demand is amnesty—the fulfillment in good faith of the Manitoba Act—nothing more, but also nothing less.][10]

Riel literally meant that the annexation of Rupert's Land was the result of a "solemn treaty"[11] which, like all treaties, would become void if it were not observed. Ergo the annexation was reversible. The people of Rupert's Land, which had become the Province of Manitoba and the North West Territories, could remove themselves from Canada if the treaty was broken in either of its branches: the amnesty or the Manitoba Act.

In Riel's view, Canada had betrayed its obligations under both headings. We will not go into the amnesty question here. It was certainly never far from Riel's mind, but it would not have sufficed to raise the flag of revolt among the *Métis* in 1885. This purpose was served by Riel's interpretation of the Manitoba Act, particularly of section 31, which authorized the half-breed land grant. At its time of entry into Confederation, Manitoba consisted of approximately 9,500,000 acres. With the 1,400,000 acres set aside by section 31 for the "children of half breed heads of families," the government clearly thought to equip each young *Métis* with enough land to make him economically self-sufficient. It was the same principle as the one by which Indian reserves were calculated at the rate of a quarter-section of land per family of five. The government was thinking in terms of the future needs of a special group among the population.

Riel, on the contrary, viewed the 1,400,000 acres as the sale price of the 9,500,000 acres comprised in Manitoba. This ratio set a precedent for the rest of the land of the North West. As subsequent acres were opened for settlement, the *Métis* of those areas should receive a similar price, in order to extinguish their aboriginal title, namely one-seventh of the land or the financial value of the one-seventh. This would amount to about 176,000,000 acres for the North West outside the original boundaries of Manitoba.[12]

Riel's single best explanation of this theory was given in his final trial speech. It must be read carefully, for his phrasing in English is sometimes awkward, even though the ideas are clear and logically developed:

> But somebody will say, on what grounds do you ask one-seventh of the lands? In England, in France, the French and the English have lands, the first was in England, they were the owners of the soil and they transmitted to generations. Now, by the soil they have had their start as a nation. Who starts the nations? The very one who creates them, God. God is the master of the universe, our planet is his land, and the nation and the tribes are members of His family, and as a good father, he gives a portion of his lands to that nation, to that tribe, to everyone, that is his heritage, that is his share of the inheritance, of the people, or nation or tribe. Now, here is a nation strong as it may be, it has its inheritance from God. When they have crowded their country because they had no room to stay anymore at home, it does not give them the right to come and take the share of all tribes besides them. When they come they ought to say, well, my little sister, the Cree tribe, you have a great territory, but that territory has been given to you as our own land, it has been given to our fathers in England or in France and of course you cannot exist without having that spot of land. This is the principle God cannot create a tribe without locating it. We are not birds. We have to walk on the ground, and that ground is encircled of many things, which besides its own value, increases its value in another manner, and when we cultivate it we still increase that value. Well, on what principle can it be that the Canadian Government have given one-seventh to the half-breeds of Manitoba? I say it must be on this ground, civilization has the means of improving life that Indians or half-breeds

have not. So when they come in our savage country, in our uncultivated land, they come and help us with their civilization, but we helped them with our lands, so the question comes: Your land, you Cree or you half-breed, your land is worth to day one-seventh of what it will be when the civilization will have opened it? Your country unopened is worth to you only one-seventh of what it will be when opened. I think it is a fair share to acknowledge the genius of civilization to such an extent as to give, when I have seven pair of socks, six, to keep one. They made the treaty with us. As they made the treaty, I say they have to observe it, and did they observe the treaty? No.[13]

The statement accepts and justifies the surrender of land by aboriginal peoples in return for compensation. To that extent, it is compatible with the official Indian policy of Britain and Canada. Beyond that, however, lie some marked differences. Riel seems to challenge the unilateral assumption of sovereignty which was the foundation of British rule in North America. (I say "seems to challenge" because his language is ambiguous; he does not distinguish between sovereignty and ownership.) In any case, he certainly does not accept the principle of unilateral extinguishment of aboriginal title through legislation. The land grant of section 31 was valid compensation for surrender of land only inasmuch as it was part of a treaty approved by both sides. Furthermore, the basis of compensation was a *quid pro quo* as in any sale. Because the advantages of civilization could multiply the value of land seven times or more, the *Métis* would be at least as well off by surrendering six-sevenths of their land and adopting civilized ways while retaining one-seventh (or its money equivalent). It was most decidedly not a matter of government allocating a certain amount of land to each *Métis* individual. In another text, Riel derided this approach as a "sophism" designed to let the government "evade its obligations" and "frustrate the *Métis,* as a group or nationality, of their seventh of the lands."[14]

Riel's insistence on the principle of "the seventh" nicely illustrates the theoretical difference between his position and the official view. According to the latter, aboriginal title was only a "personal and usufructuary right" of the natives to gather subsistence from the land. If it was to be extinguished, it was logical to compute compensation on the basis of the number of persons who would now have to subsist in other ways. Riel, however, maintained that the natives were the true proprietors of the soil in the full sense of ownership. Thus compensation for expropriation should be based on the value of the land, not on the number of people affected. To use a modern analogy, if a provincial government has to expropriate land for, say, a hydroelectric transmission line, it would compensate owners according to the fair market value of the asset, not according to the size of their families. Riel's understanding of the nature of aboriginal title drove him to demand analogous treatment for the *Métis.*

The government grudgingly agreed to a new issue of scrip to provide for the relatively few *Métis* who had not participated in the Manitoba land grant.

But in Riel's mind, the whole North West outside Manitoba still belonged to the *Métis*. The Hudson's Bay Company had sold whatever interest it had, and the Indians, at least in the fertile belt, had signed land surrender treaties. It was still necessary to extinguish the *Métis* title, and that could not be done with a few pieces of scrip. It would require payment of the value of one-seventh of the whole North West, following the precedent solemnly established in the "Manitoba Treaty." And if that treaty continued to be broken, the *Métis* would no longer be part of Canada. According to the law of nations, they could once again form a Provisional Government and undertake negotiations with other governments. There might be a new treaty with Canada, or perhaps the North West would become a separate colony within the Empire, or perhaps it would even ask for annexation to the United States, as Riel did after his trial. Everything was possible. It is this train of thought, and only this, which makes the North West Rebellion intelligible.

The Agitation

When Riel came to Saskatchewan on 1 July 1884, it was expected that his work would last only a brief time. The people knew what they wanted; all they needed from Riel was advice on the best way of pressing their demands within constitutional limits. But nothing was sent to the government until 16 December 1884, and that petition was only a preliminary draft. Work on further declarations continued well into February 1885. Why did things drag on for such a long time? Probably because Riel was trying to unite several incompatible points of view:

1. His own radical theory that the North West Territories were free to leave Confederation if Canada continued to refuse large-scale compensation for extinguishment of *Métis* aboriginal rights.

2. The desire of the *Métis* for an issue of scrip and settlement of their disputes with the Department of the Interior. Their aims were moderate; but, as events would show, many of them were willing to resort to arms to achieve their goals.

3. The desire of the English half-breeds for the same goals as the *Métis*. The difference was that the half-breeds were not willing to take up arms.

4. The intention of a group of white businessmen in Prince Albert, mostly allied to the Liberal Party, to win provincial status and responsible government for the North West. Their most active figure, William Henry Jackson, was willing to consider separation from Canada, but it is not known whether there was much support for his extreme position.

5. The demand of the more militant Indians, whose most prominent spokesman was Big Bear, for a renegotiation of treaties on more favourable terms.

Riel tried to coalesce all these groups around his own views, but irreconcilable differences made the coalition unstable. The *Métis* were willing to follow him, except for those, particularly of the merchant class, who disapproved of armed force. The English half-breeds could accept his demand for a massive settlement of aboriginal rights, but they also disapproved of force. William Henry Jackson and perhaps others among the whites were willing to consider a rupture with Canada, but they were put off by Riel's ideas on aboriginal rights, which would have enriched the *Métis,* half-breeds, and Indians at the expense of the white community.

In the nine months between his return to Canada and the outbreak of the Rebellion, Riel grappled with this political problem. He wrote or collaborated on the writing of several documents, but none was completed. Those which expressed his own views could not command universal support among the different groups, while those which could be supported did not express his own radical theory. Thus no single text was produced which adequately expressed all the demands which led to the Rebellion.

Let us now follow the course of the agitation from Riel's return to Canada up to the eve of the Rebellion. This is not a general history of these months, which has been well written by Stanley and others. It is a study of the intellectual difficulties faced by Riel in melding his own views with those of the groups he hoped to organize under his leadership. The analysis is sometimes speculative because very little written by Riel during the period of the agitation has been found. However, there is abundant material in the papers of Riel's collaborator, William Henry Jackson, with which to fill the gaps.[15]

Riel was received at Fish Creek on 1 July. He made public appearances to the *Métis* and half-breeds within the next two weeks, but we do not know what he said. His first major appearance was a speech in Prince Albert, 19 July. His own notes, and the various transcripts of the speech, show that he stressed provincial status and responsible government, themes dear to that audience. "Let the people of Assiniboia, of Alberta, of Saskatchewan petition in the proper manner for immediat[e] admission as provinces in the confederation." Riel also admonished his listeners to insist on provincial control of public lands, which had been denied Manitoba. But they were to strive for all this strictly "within the bonds of constitutional energy."[16] One account reports a brief reference to aboriginal rights;[17] but the reporter garbled what Riel said, and probably its full significance was not apparent to the audience.

Shortly after this meeting Jackson circulated an open letter to residents of Prince Albert and the surrounding area. It began: "We are starting a movement in this settlement with a view to attaining Provincial Legislatures for the North-West Territories and if possible the control of our own resources, that we may build our railroads and other works to aid our own interests rather than those of the Eastern Provinces." Readers were asked to send delegates to the executive committee, "which will be called together in a few days to put our own statement of rights in final shape." The petition would be sent to Ottawa for action by the Canadian government, though Jackson also mentioned a more radical option: "Possibly we may settle up with the East and form a separate Federation of our own in direct connection with the crown." There was no mention of the *Métis,* except to say that Riel had united them "solidly in our favour"; nor was there mention of Riel's special theories.[18]

Jackson's reference to "a few days" shows he was thinking of quick action. This is confirmed by a letter he wrote to Riel the same day: "Today I shall finish up work in town and tomorrow start for the Lower Flat etc. I will try and get out to your place toward end of week. Please be working up the petition into shape and we will get it in neat form before the committee is called to endorse or alter it."[19] This sense of urgency was apparently shared by Riel, for he wrote at this time that he intended to return to Montana around September.

The petition which Jackson expected to finish in a few days has been preserved among his papers. It chided the British government for having permitted the North West Territories to be governed by men "chosen by and responsible to not the people of the said Territories but the people of the Eastern Provinces."[20] A long list of grievances mentioned public works and services, taxation, tariffs, monopolies, and other topics of interest to local businessmen. Homestead regulations got only a few lines, and aboriginal rights were barely mentioned. It was clearly a Prince Albert document, one that would have little appeal to the *Métis* or to Riel, except that he would have been in accord with its closing demand that the Territories "be forthwith formed into Provinces, each Province having full control of its own resources and internal administration, and having power to send a just number of representatives to the Federal legislature."[21]

Another and much more radical draft seems to be connected with Jackson's idea of "settling up with the East." Alleging that the "Government of Eastern Canada hath grossly exceeded and abused" its trusteeship over the North West, it calls upon Great Britain

> to assert its suspended Guardianship and remove the Trusteeship of the said lands from the hands of the Gov't of Eastern Canada and place it in the hands of a council composed partly of members elected by the actual residents to protect interests of actual settlers, and partly of members nominated by Brit. Gov't. to protect interests of future settlers.[22]

August brought two reasons for delay. When a visit from Minister of Public Works Sir Hector Langevin was announced, it was decided to present a list of grievances to him; but he cancelled his trip late in the month. The second reason for delay was a broadening of the movement to include the Indians. In the first ten days of August there was a council of several Cree bands at the Duck Lake reserve. Several speakers denounced the treaties and called for renegotiation. Jackson seems to have been present and taken notes, for the speeches are recorded in his hand. Riel apparently did not attend, but he was in contact with the chiefs through intermediaries. Later in August Riel and Big Bear met at Jackson's house in Prince Albert.[23] These delays caused resentment among the English half-breeds. James Isbister wrote to Riel on 4 September: "I cannot for a moment, understand what is your delay, in not having our Committee meeting, sitting and working.... I must say we the people of the Ridge, Red Deer Hill, Halcro's Settlement, and St. Catherine Parish find you are too slow, or does the delay rest with W. Jackson and his people?"[24] Isbister, one of those who had gone to Montana to fetch Riel, had been the earliest farmer around Prince Albert, and his opinion carried great weight. But even as Riel received this letter, he was off on another tack, this time particularly concerned with the *Métis*.

On 5 September the *Métis* held a large meeting at St. Laurent to discuss their grievances with Bishop Grandin, who was making a pastoral visit. Riel read aloud a memorandum of eleven points. Two days later, as Grandin left for Regina, Riel gave him a slightly abridged written version containing eight items.

It is not clear why the list was reduced from eleven to eight. Perhaps it was only because Riel was writing in haste under awkward conditions. One of the three omitted points was a demand for better rations for the Indians. Riel, complaining that the *Métis* and other settlers were forced to support the Indians, had called on the government to "make the Indians work as Pharaoh had made the Jews work"—a proposal that may lift some eyebrows among those who now regard him as a humanitarian. A second point was a request that the government should pay a thousand dollars to build a convent wherever there were enough *Métis* to justify the nuns in coming to found a school. The third point was a demand for provincial status for the districts of the North West as soon as their populations equalled that of Manitoba in 1870. Provincial status "should be accompanied by all the advantages of responsible government, including the administration of public lands."[25] The first two of the omitted points were rather peripheral to the agitation and to Riel's long-term goals, but the third was absolutely fundamental, so its omission is curious.

Its main idea was, however, partially included in the first item of the eight-point list given to Grandin, which called for "the inauguration of responsible government." Four other points on the list covered long-standing grievances of the local *Métis*. Riel wanted "the same guarantees ... as those accorded to the old settlers of Manitoba," which implied several things such as river lots, hay and wood privilege, and squatter's rights. He demanded patents for the plots of land along the Saskatchewan on which the *Métis* had settled, often in disregard of homestead rules. A land grant similar to that in Manitoba would of course be required. Finally Riel requested that more contracts for public works be let to local inhabitants. These were all old items of complaint, and Riel's document added nothing new to their formulation.

The list did, however, contain three points, stemming directly from Riel, which added a whole new dimension to the *Métis* demands.

5. That two million acres be set apart by the government for the benefit of the half-breeds, both Protestant and Catholic. That the government sell these lands; that it deposit the money in the bank, and that the interest on that money serve for the support of schools, for the construction of orphanages and hospitals, for the support of institutions of this type already constructed, and to obtain carts for poor half-breeds as well as seed for the annual spring planting.

6. That a hundred townships, selected from swampy lands which do not appear habitable at the moment, be set aside by the government and that every eighteen years there take place a distribution of these lands to the half-breed children of the new generation. This to last 120 years.

7. The Province of Manitoba has been enlarged since 1870. The half-breed title to the lands by which it was enlarged has not yet been extinguished. Let that title be extinguished in favour of the half-breed children born in the province since the transfer [i.e. since 15 July 1870] and in favour of the children born there for the next four generations.[26]

Item 5 amounted to a *Métis* trust fund designed to promote their economic and social advancement, while item 6 would have insured the availability of land to several new generations of *Métis*. Item 7, although vague, had the most radical implications, for it hinted at Riel's theory that *Métis* ownership rights to the North West were still alive. All these points flow from his idea of collective ownership of the North West by the *Métis* nation. Riel was asking for a two-million-acre reserve, plus a hundred townships (2,304,000 acres), plus something for the expansion of Manitoba: a considerable amount in all, but far less than one-seventh of the North West. These demands were moderate because they were only a first instalment, as shown by Riel's postscript to the document: "This is what we ask while we wait for Canada to become able to pay us the annual interest on the sum that our land is worth and while we wait for public opinion to agree to recognize our rights to the land in their fullest extent *(dans toute leur étendue)*."[27] Grandin gave a copy of Riel's text to Governor Dewdney, who forwarded an English translation to Sir John A. Macdonald. The bishop stated that he supported the traditional demands of the *Métis* but that he could not speak to the political questions of responsible government and aboriginal title.[28] Macdonald received additional information about Riel's postscript from A.-E. Forget, who had accompanied Grandin. Forget reported that Riel's document

> only purports to contain such requests as need an immediate settlement. In addition to these advantages, they claim that their right to land can only be fully extinguished by the annual payment of the interest on a capital representing the value of land in the Territories estimated to be worth at the time of transfer twenty-five cents an acre for the halfbreeds and fifteen cents for the Indians. This is the claim alluded to in the post-scriptum of Riel's memo to His Lordship.[29]

Forget added that the *Métis* were planning to draw up a memorial on this basis and send it to the House of Commons. He tried to persuade them to direct it to the governor general in council through Governor Dewdney.

A draft of such a memorial exists in Riel's hand, addressed to "Your Excellency in Council." The heading suggests it was written out after the conversation with Forget on 7 September, although earlier drafts must have preceded this neatly written text. Unaccountably long overlooked, this document is an invaluable statement of Riel's true objectives.[30]

The text began by denouncing the Indian treaties as a swindle because they "are not based on a reasonable estimation of the value of their lands." The Indians would not be content until they receive this value. "It is the opinion of your humble petitioners that the land in its uncultivated state, with its natural wealth of game, fish, and berries cannot be worth less to the Indian than twelve and a half cents per acre." The same principle applied to the *Métis,* except that the land was worth twenty-five cents an acre to them because their usage of it was "fairly civilized." Then followed some calculations, based on certain assumptions:

—1,100,000,000 acres of land in the North West
—100,000 Indians
—100,000 *Métis*
—5% interest rate

The result of these assumptions was an annuity of $68.75 for each Indian and $137.50 for each *Métis.* However, not too much importance was attached to these calculations, which were "only approximate." They were offered only to give "a fair idea" of *Métis* rights and to suggest "the profound distress in which the Dominion of Canada plunges us by taking possession of our lands and not giving us the adequate compensation we expect of it."[31]

The line of reasoning embodied in this petition was not a temporary aberration on Riel's part. He reproduced exactly the same argument in his last major piece of writing, published posthumously as "Les Métis du Nord-Ouest," except that he used figures of fifteen cents an acre for the Indians and thirty cents an acre for the *Métis.*[32] Furthermore, the total amounts of money involved were of the same magnitude as the value of the one-seventh of the North West demanded at the trial.[33] The notion of a trust fund based on the value of the land surrendered flowed directly from Riel's conception of aboriginal title as collective ownership, not a mere encumbrance on the sovereign's title, and was in direct contrast to the official policy of calculating compensation proportionally to numbers of individuals rather than to the area of land involved.

Why this petition dropped completely from sight is one of the riddles of the agitation. One may conjecture that its radical theory of aboriginal rights was unacceptable to the white settlers whose support was indispensable to a joint movement. Collaboration with the white settlers and English half-breeds became very active in September. An important meeting was held 10 September at the home of Andrew Spence of Red Deer Hill. A brief minute of that meeting in the hand of Jackson shows the internal strains to which the movement was subject: "Committee met at Red Deer Hill, Andrew Spence's residence Wednesday afternoon, dispute whether Bill of Rights or petition. Committee appointed to prepare samples of both."[34]

As will be shown below, the "petition" was to be a list of grievances submitted to the government for redress. Compiling such a document was a purely constitutional action. The "Bill of Rights" was to be a more sweeping statement of the right of the people of the North West to self-determination. To speak in such terms would at least be to border on sedition, and the committee was still undecided whether to go that far.

Not surprisingly, it was easier to compile the petition than the Bill of Rights. A draft seems to have been completed as early as 22 September,[35] and two days later a copy was sent to Archbishop Taché.[36] Further copies were mailed on 1 October to Father Constantine Scollen, an Oblate missionary in Alberta, and to J. W. Taylor, American Consul in Winnipeg.[37]

Of the three copies sent out, the only one to have been found is Taylor's. Written entirely in Riel's hand, it is very little different from the later draft sent to the secretary of state on 16 December. It was mostly concerned with the redress of specific grievances without challenging the government's authority. But the final paragraph showed a larger strategy:

> Your humble petitioners are of opinion that the shortest and most effectual methods of remedying these grievances would be to grant the N.W.T. responsible government with control of its own resources [sic] and just representation in the federal Parliament and Cabinet. Wherefor[e] your petitioners humbly pray that your excellency in council would be pleased to cause the introduction, at the coming session of Parliament, of a measure providing for the complete organization of the District of Saskatchewan as a province; and that they be allowed, as in 70, to send delegates to Ottawa with their Bill of Rights, whereby an understanding may be arrived at as to their entry into confederation with the constitution of a free Province.[38]

The dispute over whether to prepare a petition or a Bill of Rights had been resolved by deciding to submit the petition first, followed by a Bill of Rights.

The document's meaning is not fully apparent until one recalls Riel's interpretation of the events of 1870. He was not merely calling for the government to hear and act upon complaints; he was proposing a new "treaty" in the international framework of the law of nations. This analysis is confirmed by Riel's covering letter to Taylor, which made the point emphatically:

> The people of the Northwest are poor. They are not happy under the Canadian rule; not only because their public affairs are improperly administered by the federal government, but because they are practically denied by that government the enjoyment *of the right of people.* [Riel's emphasis] That is principally what is ruining them.[39]

Another mystery of the agitation is that nothing further happened for two and a half months after this burst of activity in September. It may be that Riel and the others were waiting for signatures to be gathered. We know little about this, but efforts to obtain signatures in other parts of the Territories seem to have been made.[40] It may also be that they were waiting for reactions to the copies they had sent out.

Taché's reply was not slow in coming, nor was it encouraging. He told Riel to "give up useless agitation, give up certain ambiguities of language whose true meaning would not escape those who reflect."[41] He had obviously divined the implications of allusions to a Bill of Rights. Father Scollen, less politically sophisticated, was more positive. He passed the petition on to Dan Maloney, a political figure of St. Albert who had befriended the *Métis* on other occasions. Maloney promised to do what he could to intercede with the government on their behalf.[42]

The final version of the petition, hardly changed from the text of late September, was sent on 16 December to the secretary of state. There were several odd things about the submission which could not but detract from the impression it made in Ottawa. Although the petition was written out in long-hand by Riel, his name did not appear anywhere. The petition in fact is unsigned, although earlier researchers, confusing the petition with the covering letter, have claimed it bore the names of W. H. Jackson and Andrew Spence.[43] There certainly is no long list of signatures of the kind one would expect to accompany such a petition. It seems that this submission was only preliminary, for Jackson was occupied after the New Year in collecting signatures. Apparently he intended to resubmit the signed petition directly to the governor general. A covering letter, rather bold in tone, was provided by Jackson, who signed himself "Secretary General Committee," without explaining the nature of the committee:

> the petition is an extremely moderate one.... to the Canadian and English wing of the movement a more searching exposition of the situation would have been much more satisfactory. The opinion has been freely expressed that our appeal should be directed to the Privy Council of England and to the general public rather than to the federal authorities.[44]

Jackson's choice of words was deliberately disingenuous. He admitted elsewhere that the petition "was purposely made weak, as a blind," because the agitators were not yet ready to show their hand to the government.[45] The petition gave the impression that it was one last attempt at moderation, which might be followed by more extreme measures if concessions were not made immediately; yet Jackson and Riel were already preparing their next steps even before the petition could have reached its target. On 18 December, Jackson, back in Prince Albert, wrote to Riel that he would be down to see him in ten days or so, adding, "In the meantime please work away at your proclamation," probably a reference to the Bill of Rights.[46]

It cannot be emphasized too strongly that this petition was only secondarily an appeal to the Canadian government for redress of grievances, although it has generally been presented that way in the historical literature. It was primarily a step in a bigger campaign whose objectives, although not absolutely certain, were on a grand scale. Immediate provincial status, control of natural resources, renegotiation of the terms of Confederation, separation from Canada, and a vast settlement of aboriginal claims were all possible outcomes. The concrete grievances of the *Métis* had become merely a means to these ends.

The petition's ulterior purpose helps explain its peculiar structure. It was divided into two parts of roughly equal size: sixteen particular items of complaint, followed by a seventeenth item of great length rehearsing the events of 1870 and the government's subsequent failure to observe the "treaty." The sixteen points corresponded to specific grievances; the seventeenth laid the foundation of a demand for self-determination under the law of nations.

The specific grievances fell into several categories. One demand called for better rations for the Indians. Another called for a half-breed land grant as in Manitoba. Eight items concerned the complicated issues of survey and homestead requirements. The remaining six are readily identifiable as standard tenets of western Liberalism: greater efficiency and economy in public works and buildings, a Hudson's Bay railway, strict liquor laws, secret ballot, and free trade. This part of the petition was truly a comprehensive, if miscellaneous, catalog of local dissatisfactions.

The seventeenth point was in contrast a long, tightly reasoned chain of argument: the people of the North West in 1870 had sent representatives to Ottawa who were recognized "as the Delegates of the North West." Even as Canada negotiated with them, she was preparing a military expedition. Promises of amnesty were made and not fulfilled. The Imperial order-in-council annexing Rupert's Land to Canada was passed before the people of the North West had a chance to ratify the agreement. Since that time Canada had continued to violate the "treaty" by denying provincial status to the North West, by excluding Westerners from the cabinet, and by retaining control of natural resources. Riel did not openly state the conclusion of the argument, namely that the broken "treaty" had released the people of the North West from allegiance to Canada, but he hinted at it obliquely, stating that inhabitants of the North West "are treated neither according to their privileges as British subjects nor according to the rights of people." The implication is clear to anyone familiar with Riel's thinking. The petition closed with virtually the same words as those of the draft of October, calling for delegates to take a Bill of Rights to Ottawa and negotiate entry into Confederation.

Not much came of this petition. A formal acknowledgment was sent to Jackson, while the document was sent to William Pearce for comment. In a point-by-point analysis, he argued that the specific grievances were based on misconceptions or were being dealt with.[47] Indeed the government had already made an inquiry into the homestead problems of St. Laurent and had decided to do something about scrip. Ironically, the petition had arrived after the major problems of the *Métis* were on the way to resolution.

However, the long-range plans of Riel and Jackson were very much alive, as we may deduce from a letter of 27 January. Having received a formal acknowledgment of the petition, Jackson wrote:

> I think with you [Riel] that the mere fact of an answer is a very good sign considering the bold tone of my letter and our audacious assumption that we are not yet in Confederation, an assumption which it seems to me, they have conceded in their letter.[48]

This was surely building on air, for the acknowledgment had only stated that "the matter will receive due consideration." But Jackson was looking for favourable signs for his work. His letter spoke rather confusingly of several documents he had drawn up. There was a reference to a petition for which he was collecting signatures, probably the petition which had already been submitted without signatures to the secretary of state. He may have planned to get it signed and resubmit it with more publicity. Also mentioned were

> a memorial suitable to catch the [Parliamentary] opposition in case the Council [i.e. cabinet] pay no attention—a stronger memorial for the Imperial sec'y of state for the Colonies in case the Federal Parliament pays no attention—and the Declaration of Rights for private circulation, and use if necessary. I will get all these documents signed along with the petition.[49]

The order of the documents suggests a strategy of appeals to cabinet, Parliament, and Great Britain, followed by a unilateral declaration of independence, if necessary. Jackson anticipated quick action as the parliamentary session was about to open, but he was also prepared for delays: "I will have the councillors in good heart for an unlimited period of quietness if found unavoidable. They must learn that quietness does not necessarily mean stagnation."

The description of the strategy was amplified in an undated note by Jackson. The plan was

> to organize every settlement & the N.W.T. convene a central congress in about two months and take our case direct to the throne. In the meantime we will send down a softly worded petition which will leave them under the impression that if they remove some of our present grievances, we will cease to agitate for the power to prevent other grievances. They will therefore ease the present situation by giving us a greater share of grain contract and an order to float cash among us, and we will then have the sinews of war to go for stronger measures. The Bill of Rights is composed so as to cover the whole North West. The various examples of the resolution of those rights will be collected in each settlement, and we will then have a clear case for the Privy Council.[50]

And more radical still:

> Platform
> 1. In regard to Government:
>   Petition Brit. Govt. to appoint Commit. & transfer Govt. to council.
>   In case of refusal declare Independence and appoint Council & assume control.[51]

The most interesting document to recover would be the Bill of Rights, but it was deliberately burnt shortly before the battle of Duck Lake.[52] No one has stated why it was destroyed, but perhaps Riel felt it to be incriminating. His explanation of the revolt was that the *Métis* had taken up arms in self-defence, fearing they were about to be attacked by the Mounted Police.[53] That theory would have been seriously compromised by a Bill of Rights showing that an uprising had long been posited as a possible last step if other measures failed.

Some idea of the Bill of Rights can be gleaned from Jackson's letter of 27 January. As the Bill was an English document, Riel had left the writing to Jackson, who had looked up precedents in law books; but the thought came from Riel. His central principle was that "the world is governed by justice." It was unjust "that the inhabitants of any section of the Globe should possess the right of irresponsible and infallible authority over the inhabitants of some other section of the Globe." Such rule from afar would despoil its subjects, subjecting them to injustice. The aboriginal inhabitants had self-government, and this "consistency between their institutions and natural law ... resulted in fair play & prosperity to each member of the community." But the introduction by the colonial powers of "irresponsible authority" had led to general misery. The declaration concluded "with the assertion of the natural right of self-government thus proven." It was obviously meant not as a theoretical statement but a call to action; Jackson was putting it "into such a simple shape that any ordinary man could catch the main drift of the argument at first reading."[54]

Although Riel and Jackson seemed agreed on strategy, signs of strain were already beginning to show in their alliance. A bizarre episode took place on 14 or 15 January when Riel was having dinner at the Jackson home in Prince Albert. He was served an end cut of roast beef, rather heavily seasoned with salt and pepper. After he tasted it, he ran outside and made himself vomit. Then he went to Father André's residence to fetch Charles Nolin, whom he mysteriously informed that attempts were being made to poison him. The incident, improbable as it sounds, is attested in several independent sources.[55] A few days later, Jackson wrote to the Edmonton newspaperman Frank Oliver: "Efforts are being made to separate Riel and myself, but though we differ on certain theoretical points we have too much confidence in each other's honesty of purpose for such attempts to succeed."[56]

In the first two weeks of February Jackson made the round of the English settlements, collecting signatures for the petition, memorials, and Bill of Rights. According to one report, he also had people sign an authorization for him to be their delegate to Canada.[57] On 14 February, he went upriver to the French parishes to collect more signatures. It was on this trip that he and Riel came into open conflict. According to the subsequent account of T. Eastwood Jackson, William's brother, "[Riel] opposed the petition, attacking it on the basis of Halfbreed ownership, and my brother being equally determined on the other side, the argument lasted all night, and became so fierce that Riel lost his self-control."[58] If Eastwood may be believed, William was kept under house arrest, from which he twice tried unsuccessfully to escape. Whatever the precise details, it was definitely the end of the collaboration between Riel and Jackson as equal partners.

After the Rebellion was over and Jackson had been sent to a lunatic asylum, he briefly explained what had caused the argument. He had maintained his conviction

> that the particles of matter composing the Earth were the property of whosoever first chose to develop them into articles of utility except in case of the express allocation of land as in the case of Canaan, while Mr. Riel was, if I remember, pursuing the argument which I see he advanced on the occasion of his trial of Regina—that *every* nation is allotted its means of existence in the shape of a *land*.[59]

Since it hinges on the idea of uniting one's labour to the land to form property, Jackson's view may loosely be called Lockean. His report of his opinions corresponds substantially to a letter he wrote on 2 February 1885 to Albert Monkman, a leader of the agitation who moved in both the *Métis* and English half-breed communities.

> Let this be our aim. Let us sink all distinctions of race and religion. Let the white man delight in seeing the Indian helped forward to fill his place as a producer of wealth, and let the Indian and Halfbreed scorn to charge a rent for the soil which God has given to man, upon the settler who comes in to help to build up the country.... and let both unite in seeing that the fur country be managed for the benefit of the Indians who live by hunting, not for the good of a grasping company. Direct the attention of the Indian to the H.B.Co. monopoly, and to the necessity of providing schools for those who wish to learn productive arts, and turn them aside from the idea of being landlords. Why should God give a whole continent to 40,000 Indians and coop up 40,000,000 Englishmen in on a little island? The Indians are the same race; they, too, once lived in Europe. America was once without a man in it, why should a part of the human race go into that empty continent, and as soon as they have got there, turn round and forbid any more to come in, unless they pay for the privilege?[60]

It is not hard to see why Riel would have been enraged by such a cogent critique of the very idea of aboriginal title. It contradicted the basis of the agitation as he saw it. The agreement between Jackson and Riel on provincial status and responsible government was superficial compared to this profound disagreement about who really owned the North West.

Riel began to assume a belligerent stance in public from 24 February onwards. Did the recent break with Jackson help steer him in that direction? Perhaps it made him feel that, if he continued the collaboration with the English, he would never be able to make his theory of aboriginal rights prevail.

Absence of documents, particularly on Riel's side, makes it likely that much will always remain obscure about the North West agitation. But we know enough to realize how false is the naive version of events so often found in the contemporary literature. It would be more nearly true to tell the story thus: Riel saw in the grievances of the *Métis* an opportunity to implement his theory that the Manitoba "treaty" had been broken; that the *Métis* were the real owners of the North West; that they could renegotiate entry into Confederation; that they must receive a seventh of the value of the land of the North West as compensation for letting others live there; and that they could seek an independent political destiny if these terms were not met. Collaborating with white agitators like Jackson who were chiefly interested in provincial status and responsible government, he embarked upon a complex and deliberately deceptive strategy of making successively more radical demands. A Bill of Rights amounting to a Declaration of Independence was envisioned almost from the beginning. Finally, when Riel realized there was an unbridgeable gap between himself and Jackson, he determined to go it alone, as he had in 1869. The *Métis* would take the lead, rise in arms, and carry the English half-breeds and white settlers with them.

Notes

1. Cited in Peter A. Cumming and Neil H. Mickenberg, *Native Rights in Canada* (Toronto: General Publishing, 1972; second edition), p. 138. I have modernized the orthography.

2. Ibid., p. 148.

3. See ibid., pp. 13–50.

4. Louis Riel, [Mémoire sur les troubles du Nord-Ouest], *Le Canadien,* 26 December 1885. Ms. missing.

5. Ibid.

6. Interview with C. B. Pitblado, *Winnipeg Sun,* 3 July 1885.

7. Thomas Flanagan, ed., "Political Theory of the Red River Resistance: The Declaration of December 8, 1869," *Canadian Journal of Political Science* 11 (1978): 154.

8. *Le Canadien,* 26 December 1885; and Petition "To His Excellency [Grover] Cleveland ...," [August-September 1885], NARS, Despatches from U.S. Consuls in Winnipeg, No. 441.

9. Cited in Stanley, *Birth of Western Canada,* p. 124.

10. Louis Riel, *L'Amnistie* (Montréal: Bureau du "Nouveau Monde," 1874), p. 22.

11. Ibid.

12. Louis Riel to J. W. Taylor, [2–3 August 1885], NARS, Despatches from U.S. Consuls in Winnipeg, 1869–1906, No. 433; [Manifeste à ses concitoyens américains], [August-November 1885], PAC, MG 27 IC4, 2150–56, 2159–60.

13. Desmond Morton, ed., *The Queen v. Louis Riel* (Toronto: University of Toronto Press, 1974), pp. 358–59.

14. Riel, [Manifeste à ses concitoyens américains], 2150–56, 2159–60.

15. I am indebted to the new research on Jackson carried out by Donald B. Smith and Miriam Carey, although my interpretation differs somewhat from theirs. See Smith, "William Henry Jackson: Riel's Secretary," *The Beaver* 311 (Spring 1981): 10–19; *idem*, "Honoré Joseph Jaxon: A Man Who Lived for Others," *Saskatchewan History* 34 (Autumn 1981): 81–101; Carey, "The Role of W. H. Jackson in the North-West Agitation of 1884–85," Honors Thesis, University of Calgary, Political Science, 1980.

16. [Notes for Speech in Prince Albert], [19 July 1885], PAC, RG 13 B2, 2359, 2345.

17. Prince Albert *Times,* 25 July 1884.

18. W. H. Jackson to "Gentlemen," 23 July 1884, PAC, RG 13 B2, 512–17.

19. W. H. Jackson to Louis Riel, 23 July 1884, PAC, RG 13 B2, 503–9.

20. Louis Riel to Joseph Riel and Louis Lavallée, [25?] [July 1884], PAM, MG 3 D1, No. 418.

21. USL, A. S. Morton Mss. Collection, C555/2/13.9v. Typescript, original missing. Several other typed drafts are in the same collection. None is dated, but the contents match the description of the petition given by Jackson in his letter to "Gentlemen," note 18 *supra*.

22. Ibid., C555/2/13.9q.

23. Sgt. W. A. Brooks to L. N. F. Crozier, 21 August 1884, PAC, RG 13 B2, 522–23. Typed copy.

24. James Isbister to Louis Riel, 4 September 1885, PAM, MG 3 D1, No. 412.

25. A copy of the memorandum in the hand of Louis Schmidt is included in his "Notes: Mouvement des Métis à St-Laurent Sask. TNO en 1884," AASB, T 29799–80. The original has not been found.

26. Louis Riel to J.-V. Grandin, [7 September 1884], ACAE, Correspondence of Vital Grandin.

27. Ibid.

28. Edgar Dewdney to J. A. Macdonald, 19 September 1884, PAC, MG 26 A, 42897–905. The English translations are in ibid., 42935–41.

29. A.E. Forget to Edgar Dewdney, 18 September 1884. Ibid., 42921–34.

30. Gilles Martel, "Le Messianisme de Louis Riel (1844–1885)," Thèse de doctorat, Paris, 1976, p. 393.

31. Pétition à "votre excellence en conseil," [September 1884], PAC, RG 13 B2, 42–43.

32. "Les Métis du Nord-Ouest," Montreal *Daily Star,* 28 November 1885.

33. Riel's petition requested a total compensation to natives of 37 1/2 cents per acre, slightly more than one-seventh of the current preemption price of $2.00 per acre.

34. W. H. Jackson, [Note], [September 1884], PAC, RG 13 B2, 159. The date of the meeting is taken from Jackson to J. Isbister, 8 September 1884, PAC, RG 13 B2, 528.

35. Louis Riel to W. H. Jackson, 22 September 1884. USL, A. S. Morton Mss. Collection, C555/2/13.7d.

36. Enclosed in Louis Riel to A. A. Taché, 24 September 1884. AD, W206.M62F, No. 744, p. 7. Microfilm; the original, once at AASB, is now lost.

37. There are two drafts of a letter from Riel to Scollen, 1 October 1884, PAC, RG 13 B2, 77 and 531–32. The final letter has not been recovered. The letter to Taylor, 1 October 1884, is in DAMMHS, J. W. Taylor Papers. A partial draft, [1 October 1884], is in PAC, RG 13 B2, 74–76.

38. Petition "To His Excellency the Governor General in Council, etc." [1 October 1884]. DAMMHS, J. W. Taylor Papers.

39. Louis Riel to J. W. Taylor, 1 October 1884, DAMMHS, J. W. Taylor Papers.

40. A trip to Battleford is mentioned in Louis Riel to T. E. Jackson, 29 September 1884. USL, A. S. Morton Mss. Collection, C555/2/13.7e.

41. A. A. Taché to Louis Riel, 4 October 1884. AASB, T 29742.

42. Constantine Scollen to Louis Riel, 10 November 1884. PAM, MG 3 D1, No. 415; Dan Maloney to Louis Riel, 17 November 1884, ibid., No. 416.

43. Petition "To His Excellency the Governor General in Council," [16 December 1884]. PAC, RG 15, Dominion Lands Branch Correspondence, File 83808. Assertions that the petition was signed by Andrew Spence and W. H. Jackson are made by Stanley, *Louis Riel,* p. 291; and Lewis H. Thomas, "Louis Riel's Petition of Rights, 1884," *Saskatchewan History* 23 (1970): 16–26.

44. W. H. Jackson to J. A. Chapleau, 16 December 1884. PAC, RG 15, Dominion Lands Branch Correspondence, File 83808.

45. W. H. Jackson to Frank Oliver, 21 January 1885. USL, A. S. Morton Mss. Collection, C555/2/13.9e. Typescript, original not found.

46. W. H. Jackson to Louis Riel, 18 December 1885. PAM, MG 3 D1, No. 417.

47. H. J. Morgan to W. H. Jackson, 5 January 1885; memo by William Pearce, n.d.; PAC, RG 15, Dominion Lands Branch Correspondence, File 83808.

48. W. H. Jackson to Louis Riel, 27 January 1885. PAC, RG 13 B2, 568–79.

49. Ibid.

50. W. H. Jackson, "Summary," n.d. USL, A. S. Morton Mss. Collection, C555/2/13.9o. Typescript, original missing.

51. W. H. Jackson, "Platform," ibid.

52. W. H. Jackson to "Dear Michel," 6 September 1886. AASB, T 53009–11.

53. Louis Riel to Romuald Fiset, 16 June 1885. PAC, RG 13 B2, 1036–43.

54. W. H. Jackson to Louis Riel, 27 January 1885. PAC, RG 13 B2, 568–79.

55. Louis Schmidt "Notes," AASB T 29811. It was described in very similar terms by Cicely Jackson to A. S. Morton, 25 June 1932; USL, A. S. Morton Mss. Collection, C555/2/13.5. W. H. Jackson obliquely refers to it in his letter to Riel, 27 January 1885; PAC, RG 13 B2, 579. It is also mentioned in Louis Riel to Julie Riel, 9 June 1885; PAM, MG 3 D1, No. 420.

56. W. H. Jackson to Frank Oliver, 21 January 1885. USL, A. S. Morton Mss. Collection, C555/2/13.9e.

57. Affidavit of John Slater, 28 July 1885. USL, A. S. Morton Mss. Collection, C555/2/13.9h.

58. T. E. Jackson, Letter to the Editor, Toronto *Globe,* 2 July 1885.

59. W. H. Jackson to "My dear Family," 19 September 1885. PAM, Selkirk Asylum Medical Records, MG 3 C20.

60. Cited in T. E. Jackson to the Toronto *Globe,* 2 July 1885. Original missing.

CONFRONTING RIEL AND COMPLETING THE CPR

D.N. Sprague

As the construction of Stephen's railway proceeded across the Prairies, the largest exodus of Red River *Métis* moved from Manitoba towards Saskatchewan. The most frequent destination was the district of Prince Albert, attractive because of employment by the Hudson's Bay Company (distributing freight to or from nearby Fort Carlton) and because the vacant land fronting the south branch of the Saskatchewan River closely resembled that of the old Red River colony. As positive reports from the first migrants reached discouraged relatives and former neighbours still in the large *Métis* parishes of St. Norbert, St. François Xavier, and Baie St. Paul, one relative followed another with increasing frequency in 1882 and 1883.[1]

In the new colony, called St. Laurent, the many settlers of the early 1880s were careful to avoid trespassing on the claims of their countrymen,[2] but normally they paid little attention to the settlement status of particular parcels as designated by the Department of the Interior. The *Métis* were not concerned with the grid pattern of townships, sections, and ranges, and whether the parcel on which they landed happened to fit into an even-numbered section (potentially open for homesteading) or was odd-numbered (reserved for some system of sale).[3] And even if they had been careful to settle exclusively on even-numbered sections fronting on the river, they would still have encountered difficulty with the Dominion Lands Branch because, although the basic sectional survey had been completed in 1879 (and in the normal course of events would have been open to homestead entry within one year), there was an inexplicable delay in the case of St. Laurent.[4]

Part of the delay is attributable to the effect of Macdonald's land policy: on the south branch of the Saskatchewan, portions of several townships amounting to more than 50,000 acres had been reserved for the Prince Albert Colonization Company in April 1882; and the area underwent an inspection nearly equivalent to resurvey in 1883 before the final reservation occurred in November 1883.[5] Homestead entries became acceptable in February 1884.[6]

From *Canada and the Métis, 1869–1885* (Waterloo: Wilfrid Laurier University Press, 1988), 157–177. Reprinted by permission of Wilfrid Laurier University Press.

In the interim, almost 300 *Métis* families had come into the territory and settled mainly on river lots they laid out for themselves. Periodically, the *Métis* settlers asked George Duck, the Dominion Lands Agent at Prince Albert, to record their claims and to recognize the emerging river-lot pattern. Of course all such requests were frustrated, at first because the land was not open to entry of any kind; then, after February 1884, the *Métis* found their claims were complicated by the distinction between river lots and section land, and whether the land was odd or even-numbered in the sectional survey.[7] A few residents complied with the legal complexities; more than ninety per cent of the population held out for their own pattern of settlement and for the demand for patents immediately. What made claimants all the more persistent was seeing that approximately one-fifth of the area of new settlement had been laid out as river-lots as the *Métis* had wanted (in 1878 to take account of the observed pattern of occupancy at the time of original survey),[8] but even the occupants of the regularly surveyed river lots were deemed to be "squatters" until they made legal entry and completed the settlement duties that would make them eligible for patents.[9]

The Minister of the Interior might have recommended use of the sweeping powers in section 125 of the Dominion Lands Act to cut through the complexities depicted on Map 1. He might have exempted the St. Laurent *Métis* from the odd circumstances that made their case so complicated, but there was no political advantage to be gained by moving boldly on the matter. Sir John A. Macdonald preferred continuing doing nothing, a position he had chosen deliberately in the spring of 1879 after *Métis* land claims first came to his attention as the Minister of the Interior following the Conservatives' return to power in September 1878.

Early in 1878, the North West "half breeds" had petitioned for land, seed grain, and implements to ease their transition to farming as the extinction of the buffalo became more and more evident in the late "1870s."[10] But none of the pleas for assistance had found favour with Macdonald's predecessor, David Mills, who dismissed all such appeals with a peculiar contradiction that was frequently evident in the utterances of officials writing on the subject of "half breeds." On the one hand, they denounced the allegedly inherent aversion of the *Métis* to field agriculture. On the other hand (in response to explicit requests for aid to make the transition to the way of life for which priests and certain government officials seemed to have prayed so fervently), they were told that non-Indians need not apply. In Mills' case, a letter went to the territorial governor explaining that the *Métis* were either Indians or not. If non-Indian, Mills could "not see upon what grounds the half breeds can claim to be treated in this particular differently from the white settlers in the territories."[11]

But the North West Territorial Council (the appointed committee advising the Lieutenant Governor) saw the matter rather differently. In its view, all native people previously dependent on the buffalo were entitled to aid. Council

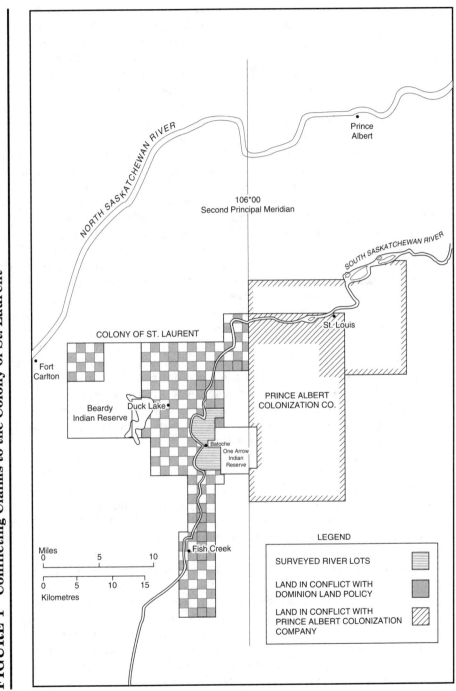

FIGURE 1 Conflicting Claims to the Colony of St. Laurent

members recommended an assistance programme in August 1878 that was remarkably similar to the scheme adopted by the British for the resettlement of Loyalists in Canada after the American Revolution. They proposed that a "nontransferable location ticket" entitling the recipient to 160 acres should be issued to every "half breed" left without land in the North West. Once located on plots of their own choosing, each family could then make free use of government supplied seed-grain and farm implements for up to three years, just as the British had resettled their displaced persons in North America a century before. Then the *Métis* settlements would be carefully monitored in their agricultural development. The council members recommended a ten-year period of probation for each assisted claimant of a free grant. It was not recommended that they should receive their land automatically. The "half breeds" would have to perform settlement duties in their first three years, then continue in residence for seven more years before they would be eligible to claim patents for their farms.[12]

Such was the policy recommended by the persons closest to the scene. Since the North West was a kind of crown colony ruled from Ottawa, one delay followed another. After Sir John A. Macdonald replaced David Mills in the Interior Ministry, he neither accepted nor rejected the advice of the Territorial Council, preferring instead to refer the matter to his Deputy Minister, J.S. Dennis, for more study. Dennis, in his turn, did draft a broader range of alternatives, adding two other possibilities to the council's proposal late in December 1878. One was extending the provisions of the Indian treaties to the *Métis* and native English, to "treat them as wards of the Government ... and look forward to their remaining for many years in their present semi-barbarous state." The other possibility was giving them an issue of scrip as had been done with the Manitoba "half breed heads of families" with the same doubtful benefit to the nominal recipients in the North West. Reluctantly, Dennis recommended the package proposed by the North West Council.[13]

Macdonald still hesitated. He disliked rewarding the *Métis* for what he considered their own improvidence—it was they who spoiled their opportunities in Manitoba, and they as well who killed most of the buffalo.[14] Not worrying about further delay, the Prime Minister instructed Dennis to send his memorandum on the subject to the three bishops most acquainted with the *Métis*. The two Roman Catholic consultants added their endorsements to the Territorial Council's scheme, saying, "the half breed cannot compete with the White man in the discharge of the duties of civilized life unless some steps are taken at the outset to equalize the conditions on which they start." They admitted that the appropriate affirmative action would be expensive, but the first costs were expected to be fully returned by the prosperity of future generations of *Métis*.[15] Later, the Anglican bishop contributed more muted approval to the growing chorus of promoters of aid, saying that he thought that the free land, seed grain, and implements would be "necessary at first." Still, because he believed that fear of starvation was God's way of teaching respect for civilization, Bishop Machray added that "the less of such gifts the better. They are apt to do mischief."[16]

The result of Macdonald's fruitless quest for a cheap and simple alternative to the proposal of the North West Council was the addition of a few phrases to the Dominion Lands Act in the spring of 1879. The new words appeared to recognize that the North West "half breeds" had a claim to a share of the Indian title to the territory and that the Cabinet was empowered to set aside land "to such extent, and on such terms and conditions, as may be deemed expedient" to satisfy such claims.[17] But in 1879, 1880, 1881, 1882, and 1883 nothing was done towards implementing the new authority to deal with the *Métis*. Not surprisingly, Macdonald was no more inclined to respond favourably to the new demands of the *Métis* reinforced in number and resolve by the large migrations from Manitoba. Consequently, the St. Laurent claims underwent the same rigour of evaluation as those of any other group of complaining homesteaders. Of the more than 250 persons demanding patents in 1884, less than 10 were considered legally entitled to what they claimed.[18] Then a new factor suddenly caused Macdonald to reassess his sense of political profit and loss in "half breed" claims. He received an alarming assessment of the situation in June 1884.

Lawrence Clarke, Chief Factor of Fort Carlton, had informed James Grahame (Clarke's superior officer in Winnipeg) that a pattern of escalating discontent was reaching a point of crisis; "repressive measures" were needed. Clarke explained that as "half breeds" in the District of Saskatchewan were losing freighting employment to the railway and steamboats, they were becoming poorer and poorer, and were pressing extravagant claims on the government in the hope of getting something they might readily sell for cash. As their first appeals were failing, they were on the point of taking extreme action—threatening to repeat the events of 1869–70. A delegation had gone to Montana intending to bring Louis Riel back. The repression Clarke proposed was arresting Riel at the border if he accepted the offer of leadership. Otherwise his presence among hundreds of armed *Métis* and native English might involve the Indians and even some of the disgruntled white settlers who resented having been bypassed by the CPR. Clarke admitted that taking Riel prisoner would anger some people, but he said a "strong detachment" of police near St. Laurent could deter the most militant. The others would be calmed by judicious use of the "influence" at Clarke's disposal and that of the Catholic priests in the area.[19]

Receiving the alarm via Grahame,[20] Macdonald reacted immediately by seeking more information. On the one hand, he asked his man on the spot, Edgar Dewdney, for his assessment. The Lieutenant Governor replied in a matter of days that the "half breeds" had been "ventilating their grievances" in secret meetings, and Dewdney also agreed that the principal reason for their discontent was economic because the Hudson's Bay Company had drastically cut both the volume and the rate of pay for overland freighting. But Dewdney added that a little group of Prince Albert speculators (including Clarke) had suffered from the collapse of the recent land boom. They welcomed the idea of a larger police garrison for the money it would bring into the district. Indeed, Lawrence Clarke was playing a double game. Having goaded the "half breeds" to bold protest, his "very sensational" letter now played to his speculator's interest more than to a real crisis.[21]

Dewdney's reassuring letter was not confirmed by the result of the police inquiries that Macdonald requested at the same time. He wanted to know the overall number of "half breeds" in the North West, how many were disaffected Manitobans, where they lived, and their probability of following Riel in the event of his attempting to form a second provisional government. Macdonald had also asked the Deputy Minister in charge of the police, Fred White, to go west for his own firsthand impressions.

Before his departure, Comptroller White ordered Superintendent Crozier and Commissioner Irvine (the field officers in the North West Mounted Police with military ranks of major and colonel, respectively) to collect the statistical data. On June 10, White ordered Irvine to make discreet inquiries while travelling from community to community under some improvised purpose—"with some object ... other than the real one."[22] On the same day, White sent identical instructions to Crozier, ordering him to "visit the settlements and ... form an opinion which you can communicate to me confidentially."[23]

Thus, Macdonald did not ignore Clarke's warning. He moved quickly for a comprehensive view and from diverse sources, even though he rejected the appeal for immediate "repressive measures." Riel and the delegation were not arrested when they reached the Canadian border in late June, but the police did "shadow" the progress of Riel and his entourage closely, and kept the Prime Minister fully informed of what followed.

While Dewdney continued to report that Riel's return was a political nuisance but no threat (not unless the *Métis* leader "tampered" with Indian discontents),[24] White's report was remarkably consistent with the original alarm sounded by Clarke. Canada's most senior policeman was certain that, despite peaceful appearances, Louis Riel did aim for something like a second provisional government. "I am convinced that there is an illegal movement of some kind in contemplation."[25] A detailed statistical report substantiating the danger of such a development suggested that, of the 5,400 "half breeds" in the North West, 4,400 were Manitoba emigrants. Although they were found in twenty-one separate localities, almost half were settled near the forks of the Saskatchewan. There Riel could expect support from an estimated force of 600 men capable of bearing arms in the event of trouble. St. Laurent was the true centre of "disloyalty" because its population was "chiefly from White Horse Plains, Baie St. Paul, etc. in Manitoba. A hard lot, were Riel's supporters in 1869."[26] Other communities were either too small or too far away from St. Laurent to pose any serious difficulty. "They would take no steps unless Riel's party was fairly certain of being successful," or "not ... mixed up, but if Indians were once on the warpath they would likely join them."[27]

On July 10, Macdonald reported the disturbing news to the vacationing Governor General, Lord Lansdowne, saying that the situation was serious but manageable. He believed land was the key. "Some of the Half breeds have land claims which are in the process of adjustment. The claims are for the most part invalid, but they will be liberally treated."[28] Then, as the news continued to be "disquieting," Macdonald outlined a broader programme of conciliation in more correspondence with the absent representative of the Queen. On August 5, the Prime Minister repeated the idea that he was prepared to honour the land claims of Riel's followers, and something special might be offered to Riel himself:

> In his answer to the invitation sent him which was a temperate and unobjectionable paper, he spoke of some claims he had against the Gov't. I presume these refer to his land claims which he forfeited on conviction and banishment, [but] I think we shall deal liberally with him and make him a good subject again.
>
> If I don't mistake his character, he will make a good Moral Agent or Detective for the Gov't and keep the metis in order.[29]

Lansdowne replied the same day with a note stating that the idea of conciliating the leader was the key factor, and urged Macdonald to "make every endeavour to 'obtain touch' " with Riel and offer him a bribe; "it might be intimated to him that you were prepared to deal generously with him in so far as his private requirements seem concerned, and that you were ready to consider in a general conciliatory spirit the demands put forward by the half breeds."[30] In the arrangement envisioned by Lansdowne, the people would get their land, and Riel could receive at least an appointment to the North West Council if not to the Canadian Senate.

In Macdonald's opinion, the contemplated patronage for Riel was excessive. Macdonald protested that Louis Riel had "committed a cold-blooded murder in '69, which will never be forgotten by the whites either in Manitoba or Ontario."[31] A less extravagant offer was more appropriate, but the rest of Macdonald's answer did make clear that he was still committed to conciliation in principle. Emissaries of goodwill would see Riel and his lieutenants as in 1869 and "encourage them to specify their grievances in Memorials and send them with or without delegations to Ottawa." Such a course would "allow time for the present effervescence to subside—and on the approach of winter—the climate will keep things quiet until next spring." Meanwhile officials in the Department of the Interior could use the respite bought by the promise of conciliation to go over the land claims and concede patents to any with "a semblance of foundation."[32]

Lansdowne approved. He appreciated that the problem of Riel and his people was "intricate," and Macdonald's proposed method of handling Riel would make him "understand that he has more to gain, personally and as a public man, by confining himself to the legitimate ventilation of the grievances of his clients, than by leading a disorderly movement."[33]

The first person recruited to have a private word with the *Métis* leader was C.B. Rouleau, a French-Canadian lawyer recently appointed to judicial responsibilities at nearby Battleford, Saskatchewan. A second, more prominent prospective emissary was Sir Hector Langevin, the Minister of Public Works in the federal Cabinet and already committed to tour the West on other errands. Here as well the Governor General gave unqualified approval. On August 13, he agreed that Rouleau could "gauge the situation pretty accurately"[34] and on August 23 Lansdowne expressed special satisfaction that Langevin was going on his errand to "set Riel's head the right way."[35]

All was arranged by the end of August for avoiding the political liability of Riel leading several hundred families into a second provisional government. Macdonald had reliable intelligence from diverse sources that such a development was possible, and he had a plausible plan for undercutting the basis of the "foolish plot"[36] and for buying Riel's loyalty. Should conciliation fail, the safety of the government was still assured by a planned expansion of police power. Macdonald told Lansdowne that he intended to increase the police force in the West by thirty per cent with a flying column of 100 to be garrisoned at Fort Carlton.[37] If there was a second "Riel rebellion," it could be checked quickly by a mounted constabulary already on the scene. Still, timely conciliation was expected to prevent such a development.

The policy Macdonald described to the Governor General in July and August flowed from the obvious calculation that an "outbreak" in the North West was an avoidable political liability. The cost would be land that the *Métis* already occupied and money or patronage to be invested in Riel with the expectation of larger dividends in more general native pacification. In this sense, Macdonald had to agree with Lansdowne that Riel's return was "anything but a misfortune."[38] Yet Macdonald appears to have decided near the end of August 1884 that an angry Riel could be even more useful in the broader field of Canadian politics. For some reason, the Langevin visit was mysteriously[39] cancelled; the land claims were handled more in conformity with the Dominion Lands Act than with what the "half breeds" demanded; and none of Riel's personal claims received favourable consideration. In the context of escalating discontent the *Métis* did become more militant; Riel did lead them into an illegal government; and the Government of Canada did respond with force—with the mobilization of militia from as far away as Halifax, as well as with the police power already on the scene. What were the political advantages of the sequence of events as they actually occurred?

The political problem that made provocative inaction ultimately worthwhile was renewed difficulty with Stephen's railway. At the time that Macdonald was first thinking about his programme of *Métis* conciliation, Stephen had begun to hint that he might need more assistance from Canada.[40] Macdonald's reaction was so swift and completely discouraging on July 18[41] that the railway president promised not to say another word on the subject, then violated his own promise in the same letter: "I will only say here that I cannot under the existing condition of affairs, any longer, look forward to the land grant as affording an available asset ... and our 35 million capital is equally useless...."[42]

Concurrent with Macdonald's corresponding with Lansdowne, Macdonald and Stephen exchanged eight letters[43] (which have survived) and held at least two meetings (mentioned in the correspondence). The Prime Minister fretted about the "many threads" of crisis he had to attend to personally and showed the railway president the papers documenting developments in the North West.[44] Stephen assured Macdonald that the railway construction was proceeding better than expected but continued to complain about a serious deficiency of capital for other needs. Macdonald could not agree to what Stephen thought essential, but he did agree to help in recruiting $5 million from private bankers in London and to accompany the railway president on his Atlantic crossing.

Unfortunately for Stephen, neither a letter of recommendation[45] from Canada's Prime Minister nor Macdonald's presence in London was sufficient to persuade Baring Brothers that the railway was a safe risk, and Stephen's need for the additional $5 million from Parliament matured before anything else to convince Macdonald's colleagues (or the country) that additional legislative assistance was warranted. Then, once Macdonald returned to Ottawa, Sir David Macpherson complained that Langevin had returned from the West as the perfect champion of "dead beats."[46]

Langevin's position even without seeing Riel was that the *Métis* leader was too dangerous to ignore. "We must take care not to make a martyr of him and thus increase his popularity." The solution was "good treatment of the half breeds." Langevin believed even a little would "go a long way to settle matters."[47] Macpherson tried to convince Langevin that every land claim had been "fully considered and equitably disposed of," but Sir David believed Sir Hector remained unconvinced. A meeting with Sir John was needed.[48] That appears to have ended the matter. At least there were no more memoranda advocating concessions such as Langevin had proposed early in November.

Macdonald's greater difficulty was calming Stephen. By mid-January the railway president was insisting that the survival of his company absolutely depended on aid from the government, but Macdonald insisted that the proposition was still "hopeless." A telegram from the Prime Minister on January 20 urged Stephen to "postpone matter to eighteen eight six can carry it in Council."[49] Stephen replied that postponement was "impossible" and begged for a meeting the next day to "decide finally on course am forced to take."[50] They did meet, but the only surviving record of what was apparently agreed to was a letter from Stephen in mid-April alluding to maturing obligations that "three months ago were postponed till now on the faith that by this time we should be in a position to meet them."[51] Further contextual evidence that something had been agreed to in late January was a more optimistic tone and shift in Stephen's correspondence on the subject in February and early March as he devoted most of his letters to the terms of the rescue he was clearly expecting.[52] Conversely, Macdonald seemed more depressed than ever. On January 24 he reported to his old friend Tupper that the situation was nearly as bad as the worst the two had imagined in the previous autumn. "Geo Stephen says the CPR must go down unless sustained," and he enumerated the key personnel in Cabinet who were adamantly opposed to any such additional aid. "How it will end I don't know."[53]

Nothing had happened to change "the thing"[54] in Ottawa. Yet the abandonment of straightforward conciliation had meant that *Métis* discontent was maturing into an exploitable crisis. Riel had spent the entire autumn and early winter writing—and rewriting—the draft of a comprehensive statement of grievances covering claims. The most preliminary statement specified: territorial self-government; land rights similar to the assurances in section 32 of the Manitoba Act; a 2-million-acre trust (the income from which would provide long-term development capital for the *Métis*); 64,000 acres of "swamp lands" to be reserved for the children of *Métis* heads of families (to be distributed every eighteen years over seven generations); reconsideration of the land rights of the Manitoba *Métis*; and preferential consideration of "half breeds" for "works and contracts" in the Territories.[55]

After consulting Bishops Taché and Grandin, Riel dropped some of the demands that the clerical consultants and his own close advisors considered "extravagant."[56] The petition that the St. Laurent *Métis* finally mailed to the Governor General on December 16 was more limited in its focus upon land titles, home rule, and compensation for alleged maladministration of the Manitoba Act. Considering the last point, it was not surprising that the document was addressed to the Governor General with a covering letter requesting that the Queen's representative should forward the document directly to England in the hope that the British would compel Canada to act as in 1870.[57]

Given the direct parallel that the *Métis* drew between their present situation and the events of 1869, the alarms that kept streaming in from the North West might have led Macdonald to expect the formation of a provisional government at almost any moment in January. The police reports of the previous summer had indicated that delay would almost certainly result in some "illegal combination," and six months had passed without meeting any of the agitators' principal demands or taking steps to break up the agitation with police power. But nothing had happened. In late January Riel was still not acting according to prediction even as Stephen's financial crisis reached new, more frightening proportions, and nothing had altered Macdonald's inability to deliver his partner the promised aid.

Here was the context and perhaps also the explanation for the peculiarly provocative content of an important Order in Council that was adopted on January 28. Telegraphed to Dewdney, the news was that Canada would "investigate claims of Half Breeds and with that view [Cabinet] had decided [to make an] enumeration of those who did not participate in Grant under Manitoba Act."[58] The provocation was that only a small minority of the residents of St. Laurent could benefit from awards to non-Manitobans. Moreover, the government already had the figures: 200 of 1,300 potential claimants.[59] Dewdney was so stunned by the news he refused to pass on the information without alteration. Imagining the purpose of the Order in Council was conciliation rather than provocation, he changed the announcement before transmitting the telegram to St. Laurent: "Government has decided to investigate claims of Half Breeds and with that view has already taken preliminary steps." Then Dewdney reminded Macdonald that "the bulk of the French Half Breeds" had "nothing to expect" from the unrevised text. The original news would "start a fresh agitation."[60]

No prime ministerial congratulation came back over the wire thanking Dewdney for his editorial intervention, and Dewdney's text was still far short of the news the *Métis* wanted. They demanded recognition of their aboriginal title demand, not additional consideration of the matter. Equally important, they wanted news that their claims to river lots were recognized. Here too the telegram from Dewdney was silent. Then on February 6, the Dominion Lands Agent at Prince Albert learned from the Deputy Minister of the Department of the Interior that the river-lot question was about to be disposed of. He could expect instructions "in the course of a few days."[61]

The claims reported to Winnipeg in June 1884 had passed from Winnipeg to Ottawa in October, and finally back from headquarters to Prince Albert near the end of February 1885. The news the Lands Agent was to report to the claimants was an enormous disappointment to the vast majority of the families hoping for confirmation of titles.[62] They felt they had done their part. All but a small non-cooperating group of forty-five had compromised their original demand for river lots laid out in the old Manitoba pattern. More than 200 settlers had provided evidence of compliance with the boundaries of subdivisions as laid out in the government survey. Eight such claimants received notification that their periods of settlement, extent of cultivation, and value of improvements entitled them to patents. The others were processed as applications for "entry." Consequently, more than sixty per cent of the settlers expecting patent were confronted with an infuriating contradiction: their claims were allowed; patents were denied. They would not become the owners of their land in the eyes of Canada until paying fees, performing more settlement duties, and going through another process of application, inspection, and consideration by the local agent, by the Winnipeg Lands Board, and by the Dominion Lands Branch in Ottawa. Even then they would have to pay for any acreage in excess of the 160-acre maximum allowable "free grant" (some claimants were told that the pre-emption part of their claim would cost $1 per acre, for others the price was $2). Finally, the question of trespass on the lands of the Prince Albert Colonization Company was unresolved; thirty families were excluded from "entry" as well as from patents.[63]

Canada's handling of the river-lot question was far from conciliatory, but the government could defend itself by saying that the claimants received all the consideration they were entitled to expect under the Dominion Lands Act. Indeed, in one respect—waiving the distinction between odd- and even-numbered sections (except in the vicinity of the Prince Albert Colonization Company)—the government could say that the *Métis* claimants were treated more liberally than the law required.

One last provocation was similarly defensible from the standpoint of rigid adherence to principle. On February 20 the Prime Minister informed Lieutenant Governor Dewdney that the answer to Riel's private claims was a definite no. With uncharacteristic moral outrage Macdonald declared: "We have no money to give Riel. He has a right to remain in Canada and if he conspires we must punish him. That's all."[64]

The last two provocations together—the personal disappointment of Riel and the general frustration of the land claimants—finally broke *Métis* patience the day after Lands Agent Duck sent out the last disturbing notification on March 7. On March 8, Riel announced that he thought that the time had come to form a provisional government.

Three days later, Lieutenant Governor Dewdney telegraphed the latest development to the Prime Minister, saying there was a possibility that the declaration was no more than a "bluff" but "if the Half breeds mean business, the sooner they are put down the better." Dewdney advised taking them by surprise. "They are like Indians. When they gather and get excited it is difficult to handle them, but if they are taken unawares there is little difficulty in arresting the leader."[65]

On the same day, March 11, Stephen demanded bold action for the railway, complaining that his finances were "getting beyond all control." Stephen expressed sympathy for Macdonald's political problems, but the CPR president insisted that the time had come for the Prime Minister to do whatever was necessary to alter the current political impasse. "I know and appreciate fully the reason for delaying consideration of our matters till the proper and most favourable time arrives but I am really concerned about ways and means to carry us along in the meantime.... I hope you will think of this and bring things to a head as soon as possible."[66]

True to his favourite maxim, "He who waits wins,"[67] Macdonald did nothing, but not with any evident comfort. On March 17, he informed Tupper that "Stephen asks a loan for a year of 5 millions (that Tilley [the Minister of Finance] can't face)" and complained that everyone was reaching the limits of endurance. "How it will end God knows—but I wish I were well out of it."[68] No doubt Stephen and Dewdney were equally perplexed. Unable to get a satisfactory answer to his letters and telegrams, Dewdney pursued his own initiative.

On March 12, the Lieutenant Governor convened a meeting to consider the Riel crisis with four other people in Regina: Hayter Reed (the Indian Commissioner),

A.G. Irvine (the Police Commissioner), Hugh Richardson (the Stipendiary Magistrate of the district), and Lawrence Clarke (still Chief Factor at Fort Carlton). The primary concern was Riel's proclamation of intent: whether it was genuine or "a mere matter of bluff ... to frighten the government into making concessions." Clarke suggested that since the total force at Riel's command was probably no more than 350 poorly armed men "with their wives and children, who must be exposed to extreme peril should they be so foolish as to resort to arms," and since the government force "already on the spot" numbered 120 well-armed police backed by artillery, the Hudson's Bay Company officer thought that the "only danger to be apprehended ... would be in the event of Riel attempting to tamper with the loyalty of the Indians." In that event, it was agreed that they should arrest the *Métis* leader "no matter at what risk." And even without Riel's moving towards alliances with the Indians, it was considered that "Mr. Riel and his band of discontents should not be allowed to keep up senseless agitation, destroying all faith in the country and ruining its peaceable inhabitants." Sooner or later they would have to "settle this matter once for all." In Clarke's opinion the question was "whether this was not the time." Under the circumstances of the moment, it was agreed that Clarke should return to Fort Carlton at once, and Irvine would "start for the 'seat of war'" several days later, about the time Clarke reached Fort Carlton from Regina.[69]

Arriving at his destination on the evening of March 17,[70] Clarke reported that Riel's movement had "apparently flattened out" but there was no doubt as to his "tampering with Indians." Clarke did not think Riel would win many over, but advised the immediate arrest of Riel to prevent any further mischief. "No better time to deal with leader and followers."[71] Dewdney responded that he had still "heard nothing from Ottawa" and reported that Irvine was departing for Fort Carlton the next day with 100 reinforcements.[72] Then, as rather an afterthought, Dewdney sent Clarke a second telegram on March 17 advising him to make the government's intentions public. "Put in PA Times that an additional force is being sent.... Get paper to enlarge and state scattered that government intend to have peace in the district."[73]

Clarke passed the instruction on to his new superior officer in Winnipeg, Joseph Wrigley, who responded by telegram that he opposed the newspaper advertisement, at least as a Hudson's Bay Company announcement. Perhaps Wrigley feared that such information would be interpreted as a provocative gesture and lead to criticism of the company later. "Better for you not to act publicly but leave responsibility on Government."[74] As a result, the action that pushed Riel to take the next step was not a printed word, but verbal communication that Clarke subsequently denied he had ever spoken.

The story Lawrence Clarke later denounced as a "tissue of lies"[75] was that he had encountered a group of *Métis* near Fort Carlton some time before March 19 and had given them information resembling the news that Dewdney instructed him to spread through the district on March 17. According to popular legend, the *Métis* asked Clarke if there was any answer yet to their petitions and protest. "His reply was that the only answer they would get would be bullets, and that, indeed, on his way northward, he had passed a camp of 500 policemen who were coming up to capture the Half breed agitators."[76] It is possible that Clarke said only that more police were on the way with the intention of arresting Riel. The rest may have been nothing more than the result of exaggeration in retelling the news at Batoche.

What is certain is that the *Métis* reacted to Clarke's news as the final provocation. The provisional government emerged on March 19 (with eighty-eight per cent support from the inhabitants of the colony of St. Laurent).[77] Despite the risk of police intervention, Riel did not foresee any great danger because the newspapers were full of reports of the possibility of war between England and Russia. With British (and Canadian) forces occupied in a foreign war, surely Canada would dispose of a small domestic crisis peacefully as in 1870. Riel miscalculated. The mobilization for conflict overseas did not occur. Instead, Canada mobilized militia from Halifax to Winnipeg to deal with the *Métis*, even though Dewdney's dispatches indicated that he thought the police were competent to deal with the situation unfolding in late March.

Macdonald did not anticipate a war against the *Métis*. At the time of the mobilization (March 23), he cautioned the Minister of Militia, J.P.R.A. Caron, to "remind General Middleton that the [NWMP] Commissioner and Officers are magistrates and well acquainted with the character of the Half-breeds and Indians and must understand the best mode of dealing with them and inducing them to lay down their arms and submit to legal authority."[78] A massive show of force would compel surrender without a fight. Although Dewdney preferred resolving the problem with local resources ("I would have rather seen the trouble stopped entirely by the police"), the Governor had to concede that the *Métis* were even less likely to resist if thousands of troops suddenly appeared on the scene, especially if the government met Riel's price and whisked him out of the country before the troops arrived. "How far can I go?" Dewdney asked on March 23.[79]

What Macdonald seems to have envisioned was a sudden dash to the Prairies, a mysterious "escape" of Riel back to the United States, conciliatory gestures to the surrendering *Métis*, and aid for the railway after it played such a key role in breaking up the "outbreak" so "speedily and gallantly."[80]

On March 26, however, the situation became unexpectedly complicated by bloodshed. Since the *Métis* believed 500 police were en route to arrest Riel, they prepared to fend off the NWMP in a long siege by sending a force to seize supplies from a store at Duck Lake. Simultaneously, a party of police went to the same place to spoil the attempt. When the two groups came face to face, both sides sent out spokesmen to talk under a flag of truce, but the meeting soon deteriorated into single-champion combat with two men dead, then into general shooting with twelve fallen on the Canadian side and five *Métis* killed.[81]

The confrontation between police and "half breeds" was followed by sporadic Indian action and raised the spectre of war such as the Americans had fought in the 1860s and 1870s. After March 26, greater prospects of danger and longer delays filled Macdonald with increased dread. "This insurrection is a bad business," Macdonald wrote Dewdney on March 29, "but we must face it as best we may."[82]

Since the Americans were almost as worried as some Canadians that the "outbreak" would become a general Indian war, they offered full cooperation in the movement of troops and supplies and their own cavalry for patrolling the border.[83] Macdonald accepted the transport offer for shipping equipment, but he insisted on the CPR as the vehicle for transporting the unfortunate Canadian volunteers, the first contingent of whom left Toronto on March 30 in two separate trains. When the men reached the north shore of Lake Superior in the first week of April, they discovered that there were four gaps in the line that had to be crossed by sleigh or on foot. The worst part, however, was one section of isolated railway where the men had to ride on flat cars in the open, bitter cold.[84] Still, in less than two weeks, more than 3,000 troops did reach the Territories ready to be deployed against the "half breeds" and their few Indian allies.

In the fighting that occurred here and there in late April and early May there were several encounters that could be called battles.[85] For more than fifty Canadians and a similar number of "half breeds" and Indians, death was as final as in any global conflict. And yet Macdonald did not exaggerate later when he dismissed most of the military side of the "North West Rebellion" as a "mere riot."

From Macdonald's point of view, the more important aspects of the affair were showing the flag of British authority and proving that the railway had transformed Canada into a country capable of suppressing challenges to its sovereignty in the most remote sections of habitable territory. To be sure, the Opposition made searing accusations of mismanagement, but Macdonald met their charges that the war could have been avoided with counter-charges that his own "half breed" policy had been far more liberal than his opponents.[86] Indeed, on native affairs in general he claimed to be the epitome of enlightened and progressive action, and he moved to substantiate his claim in April with a diversionary franchise bill that included proposals for nearly universal suffrage for white men and extension of the vote to certain single women and the Six Nations of Loyalist Indians in Ontario.[87]

The Liberals were triply embarrassed. Having denounced Macdonald's handling of North West matters, they seemed sympathetic to natives; then, having posed as friends of the Indians and the *Métis*, they were embarrassed by their own vehement opposition to the inclusion of certain loyal native people in the national franchise because David Mills said they were "savages." Thus, they were set up to be embarrassed the third time when they fought the aid for the railway that had saved the nation from a prolonged war with Canada's native peoples.

The CPR did receive its aid package in July. In the same month, Louis Riel stood trial at Regina where he was held accountable for treason and sentenced to hang. Riel dropped to the end of the hangman's rope in Regina on November 16. The railway reached its official completion almost at the same time in a last-spike ceremony on November 7. Still jubilant over the success of his railway, Stephen wrote Macdonald just before Riel's execution to inform the Prime Minister of his pleasure with the rising value of CPR stock over the preceding week and to tell Sir John how "glad" he was that the "mischievous crank Riel is going to have justice meted out to him."[88] No other correspondent with Macdonald was as quick to link the two events so directly, but few people other than Stephen knew how closely the *Métis* loss had been joined to the railway's gain.

Notes

1. See Mailhot and Sprague, "Persistent Settlers."

2. There were no "Class 16" claims (land disputes) in the detailed report upon St Laurent submitted by the Lands Board to headquarters in the autumn of 1884. See University of Alberta Archives. William Pearce Papers, MG 9/2/4–4, vol. 4, pp. 224–275.

3. For the system of sectional survey adopted by Canada see Chester Martin. *"Dominion Lands" Policy.*

4. Flanagan, *Riel and the Rebellion,* pp. 30–33, 37–40.

5. PAC, RG 15, vol. 277, file 44447, p. 19; and House of Commons Debates, speech by Edward Blake, 6 July 1885, p. 3100.

6. The report of William Pearce, "All Claims to land ... on the South Saskatchewan" (University of Alberta Archives, Pearce Papers, MG 9/2, series 5, vol. 1, file 6 and series 4, vol. 4, pp. 888–901) states that some of the land was open for entry as early as 1881. But in response to a question on the subject in the House of Commons on June 8, 1885, Macdonald admitted that much of the district was not open for homestead entry until February 15, 1884 (House of Commons Debates, 8 June 1885, p. 2358).

7. PAC, Records of the Department of the Interior, RG 15, vol. 336, file 84478, George Duck to Commissioner of Dominion Lands, 15 June 1884.

8. Flanagan, *Riel Reconsidered,* p. 33.

9. Pearce, "All Claims to Land," p. 6–8.

10. PAC, Macdonald Papers, Incoming Correspondence, pp. 42053–42056 42067–42070.

11. Ibid., pp. 42048–42050, Mills to Laird, 18 March 1878. Later, Macdonald told the House of Commons that Mills had given the appropriate response. See House of Commons Debates, 6 July 1885, p. 3112.

12. PAC, Macdonald Papers, Incoming Correspondence, pp. 42067–42070, Minutes of the Council of the North West Territories, 2 August 1878.

13. Ibid., pp. 138984–138987, "Confidential Memorandum: Remarks on the Condition of the Half Breeds of the North West Territories, 20 December 1878."

14. See Macdonald's sketch of the history of Manitoba land claims reported to the Governor General in August 1884 (ibid., Transcripts, vol. 585, Macdonald to Lansdowne, 5 August 1884).

15. Ibid., Incoming Correspondence, pp. 42072–42083, Bishop Grandin to Dennis, 18 January 1879.

16. Ibid., pp. 42084–42091, Bishop Machray to Dennis, 15 February 1879.

17. Statutes of Canada (1879), Chapter 31: "An Act to amend and consolidate the several Acts respecting the Public lands of the Dominion," section 125(e).

18. Pearce, "All Claims to Land," p. 6.

19. PAC, Macdonald Papers, Incoming Correspondence, pp. 42244–42250, Clarke to Grahame, 20 May 1884.

20. Ibid., pp. 42242–42243, Grahame to Macdonald, 29 May 1884.

21. Ibid., pp. 42767–42778, Dewdney to Macdonald, 14 June 1884.

22. Ibid., pp. 42251–42253, White to Irvine, 10 June 1884.

23. Ibid., pp. 42254–42255, White to Crozier, 10 June 1884.

24. See, for example, the letter from André to Dewdney, 7 July 1884, that the Governor forwarded to Macdonald (ibid., pp. 42277–42280).

25. Ibid., pp. 134906–134916, White to Macdonald, 7 July 1884.

26. Other sources tend to corroborate the police report. See "Supplement 2: The Settlers of the Colony of St Laurent," in Mailhot and Sprague, "Persistent Settlers," pp. 18–26.

27. PAC, Macdonald Papers, Incoming Correspondence, p. 148567, "Estimated Number of Half Breeds."

28. Ibid., Transcripts, vol. 585, Macdonald to Lansdowne, 10 July 1884.

29. Ibid., Macdonald to Lansdowne, 5 August 1884.

30. Ibid., Incoming Correspondence, pp. 32872–32879, Lansdowne to Macdonald, 5 August 1884.

31. Ibid., Transcripts, vol. 585, Macdonald to Lansdowne, 12 August 1884.

32. Ibid.

33. Ibid., Incoming Correspondence, pp. 32884–32887, Lansdowne to Macdonald, 13 August 1884.

34. Ibid.

35. Ibid., pp. 32893–32895, Lansdowne to Macdonald, 23 August 1884.

36. Ibid., Letter Books, vol. 23, pp. 33–34, Macdonald to J.C. Aikins, 28 July 1884.

37. Ibid., Transcripts, vol. 585, Macdonald to Lansdowne, 12 August 1884; and Letter Book, vol. 23, pp. 56–57, Macdonald to Donald A. Smith, 5 September 1884.

38. Ibid., Incoming Correspondence, pp. 32872–32879, Lansdowne to Macdonald, 5 August 1884.

39. Why Langevin failed to fulfill the mission is a problem of considerable complexity. The conventional explanation (See Stanley, *Riel,* p. 285; and Bob Beal and Rod Macleod, *Prairie Fire: The 1885 North-West Rebellion* [Edmonton, 1984], pp. 117–118) is that Langevin's change of itinerary represented his own independent alteration of plans. Having arrived at Regina in the last week of August, he is supposed to have been so fatigued by the earlier part of his journey that he could not face travelling 200 miles over muddy cart trails to St. Laurent just to suffer the harangues of political malcontents. Thus he cancelled the trip despite the consequences. Langevin proved later that he was indeed capable of foolish initiatives. But the cancellation of the Riel mission was more than foolhardy. Once Riel had been informed that Langevin was visiting in 1884—in the role Smith had played in 1869–70—and once it became known that Riel regarded the meeting as "marked proof of good will towards the North West" (Riel quoted in Beal and Macleod, *Prairie Fire,* p. 118), cancellation without justification or notification of regret was equivalent to provocation.

The difficulty with assigning sole responsibility to Langevin is evidence of earlier communication with Macdonald. The day of Langevin's departure from his home, August 18, Sir Hector sent a brief note to the Prime Minister inviting last-minute instructions (PAC, Macdonald Papers, Incoming Correspondence, pp. 97438–9743). There is no record of Macdonald's response, but on August 19 a telegram went from Langevin to Judge Rouleau at Battleford informing him that Sir Hector would not be making the digression to Batoche (Stanley, *Riel,* p. 285). Subsequently, Rouleau either forgot or was instructed not to report the news to Riel, with the result that the *Métis* continued an unsatisfying vigil, constantly watching the roadways to Batoche for some face resembling Langevin's.

If the change was Langevin's mistake, Macdonald had an opportunity to correct it on August 29 when his goodwill ambassador sent him a message before leaving Manitoba for Regina (PAC, Macdonald Papers, Incoming Correspondence, pp. 97441–97442). Langevin reported that the train had taken him as far as Brandon. After a brief visit with Dewdney he expected to continue on to the end of the railway: "In a week I will have reached the end of the road and be on the return." Obviously, that itinerary precluded the errand to Batoche. If Macdonald's previous plans were still in effect, it was important to intercept Langevin before his return. No record of attempted interception has been found. Nor did Macdonald complain later about a unilateral upset of his conciliation scheme.

40. PAC, Macdonald Papers, Incoming Correspondence, pp. 122328–122331, Stephen to Macdonald, 17 July 1884.

41. Ibid., Transcripts, vol. 585, Macdonald to Stephen, 18 July 1884.

42. Ibid., Incoming Correspondence, pp. 122340–122347, Stephen to Macdonald, 22 July 1884.

43. Macdonald's letters to Stephen were dated 24 and 30 July 1884 (both in ibid., Transcripts, vol. 585). Stephen's to Macdonald were 27 July, 2 August (two letters), and 13, 16, 19 August (all in ibid., Incoming Correspondence, pp. 122353–122419).

44. Ibid., Transcripts, vol. 585, Macdonald to Stephen, 30 July 1884.

45. Ibid., Letter Book, vol. 23, pp. 59–60, Macdonald to Baring Brothers, 6 September 1884.

46. Ibid., Incoming Correspondence, pp. 112802–112805, Macpherson to Macdonald, 31 December 1884.

47. Ibid., pp. 97452–97456, Langevin to Macdonald, 6 November 1884.

48. Ibid., pp. 112802–112805, Macpherson to Macdonald, 31 December 1884.

49. Ibid., Letter Book, vol. 23, p. 101, Macdonald cypher telegram to Stephen, 20 January 1885.

50. Ibid., Incoming Correspondence, p. 122608, Stephen cypher telegram to Macdonald, 20 January 1885.

51. Ibid., pp. 122818–122821, Stephen to Macdonald, 15 April 1885.

52. See Stephen's letters of 3, 8, 9, 12, 13, 19 February and 2 March in ibid., Incoming Correspondence, pp. 122643–122704.

53. Ibid., Transcripts, vol. 585, Macdonald to Tupper, 24 January 1885.

54. Ibid.

55. Ibid., Incoming Correspondence, pp. 42935–42937, Riel to Bishop Grandin, 7 September 1884.

56. See PAM, Riel Papers, item 414, Taché to Riel, 4 October 1884.

57. Lansdowne did not forward the petition as requested. See Lansdowne to Derby, the Colonial Secretary, 21 April 1885 (PAC, Records of the Governor General, RG 7 G 10, vol. 8).

58. PAC, Macdonald Papers, Incoming Correspondence, pp. 42977–42983, quoted by Dewdney to Macdonald in reply, 4 February 1885.

59. Ibid., p. 148567, "Estimated Number of Half Breeds." Although the document is undated, contextual evidence makes clear that the numbers were determined in the summer of 1884. See also the Governor General's recital of the same figures in PAC, RG 7, G 10 (Drafts to Colonial Secretary, Secret and Confidential), vol. 8, Lansdowne to Derby, 21 April 1885.

60. Ibid., pp. 42977–42983, Dewdney to Macdonald, 4 February 1885.

61. PAC, RG 15, vol. 336, file 84478, A.M. Burgess to Duck, 6 February 1885.

62. See University of Alberta, William Pearce Papers, MG 9/2/4–4, vol. 4, pp. 224–275, 961–962 in relation to Pearce's published report of "All Claims to Land."

63. Their claims were taken up in the autumn of 1885, and accorded the same entry privilege as the others. See University of Alberta Archives, William Pearce Papers, MG 9/2/4–4, vol. 4, pp. 961–962.

64. PAC, Glenbow Dewdney Papers, p. 545, Macdonald to Dewdney, 20 February 1885.

65. PAC, Macdonald Papers, Incoming Correspondence, pp. 43010–43013, Dewdney to Macdonald, 11 March 1885.

66. Ibid., pp. 122735–122742, Stephen to Macdonald, 11 March 1885.

67. See, for example, Macdonald to T. Robertson, in ibid., Letter Book, vol. 23, pp. 85–86.

68. Ibid., Transcripts, vol. 585, Macdonald to Tupper, 17 March 1885.

69. Hudson's Bay Company Archives (hereafter cited as HBCA), D.20/33, fo. 67–74, Lawrence Clarke to Joseph Wrigley, 14 March 1885.

70. HBCA, B332/b/1, vol. 1, fo. 96–121, Clarke to Wrigley, 6 July 1885.

71. Ibid., fo. 87, Clarke cypher telegram to Dewdney, 17 March 1885.

72. Ibid., fo. 82, Dewdney cypher telegram to Clarke, 17 March 1885.

73. Ibid., fo. 81, Dewdney cypher telegram to Clarke, 17 March 1885.

74. Ibid., fo. 44, Wrigley cypher telegram to Clarke, 17 March 1885.

75. Ibid., fo. 96–121, Clarke to Wrigley, 6 July 1885.

76. N.F. Black, *History of Saskatchewan and the Old North West* (Regina, 1913), p. 267. The same story appeared in a contemporary account of Clarke's role by James Isbister. See clipping from Winnipeg *Sun,* 19 June 1885, in PAC, Macdonald Papers, Incoming Correspondence, p. 43861.

77. The opponents of Riel are named in Pearce's manuscript copy of "All Claims to Land" (University of Alberta Archives, Pearce Papers, MG 9/2, series 4, vol. 4, pp. 888–901.

78. PAC, Macdonald Papers, Transcripts, vol. 585, Macdonald to Caron, 23 March 1885.

79. Ibid., Incoming Correspondence, pp. 43020–43023, Dewdney to Macdonald, 23 March 1885.

80. "Speedy" and "gallant" were Macdonald's adjectives in Parliament. See House of Commons Debates, 6 July 1885, p. 3117.

81. A detailed, sensational account of the conflict appears in Beal and Macleod, *Prairie Fire,* pp. 151–159.

82. PAC, Macdonald Papers, Letter Books, vol. 23, p. 140, Macdonald to Dewdney, 29 March 1885.

83. See Blake's questions on the matter, House of Commons Debates, 31 March 1885, p. 838, and 1 April 1885, p. 872.

84. Desmond Morton, *The Last War Drum* (Toronto, 1972), pp. 40–44.

85. On the final siege, in particular, see Walter Hildebrandt, *The Battle of Batoche: British Small Warfare and the Entrenched Métis* (Ottawa, 1985).

86. See Blake's seven-hour speech and Macdonald's shorter reply in the House of Commons Debates, 6 July 1885, pp. 3075–3117.

87. See Malcolm Montgomery, "The Six Nations and the Macdonald Franchise," *Ontario History* 57 (1967), pp. 13–25.

88. PAC, Macdonald Papers, Incoming Correspondence, pp. 123001–123008. Stephen to Macdonald, 14 November 1885.

CHAPTER

3 THE NATIONAL POLICY AND MARITIME INDUSTRIAL-IZATION

Almost from the time of its introduction by Sir John A. Macdonald's Conservative government in 1879, the National Policy has been a subject of controversy among Canadian historians. It has been applauded for establishing the industrial foundations of the country, although admittedly on a somewhat delayed basis (W.T. Easterbrook and H.G.J. Aitken), and damned for impoverishing Canadians individually and collectively (John Dales). It has been praised for creating a 'national,' transcontinental economy and thereby thwarting American economic encroachment (Donald Creighton), and, contrarily, blamed for laying the foundations of the U.S. take-over of the Canadian economy (Michael Bliss).

The regional implications of the National Policy have also been hotly disputed. For many years its impact on western Canada was a topic of discussion, as every dimension of that region's discontent, from the Riel rebellions through the agrarian protest of the Progressive Party to the Social Credit movement of the 1930s was traced to its deleterious effects (W.L. Morton, Daniel Drache, Paul Phillips). On the other side of the coin, historians such as J.M.S. Careless and Kenneth Norrie argued that the West, far from being disadvantaged, had received very tangible benefits from the National Policy.

In the 1970s the focus of the debate on the National Policy shifted to the once largely ignored Maritime provinces. Initially the discussion was not so much about results—historians generally agreed that the introduction of the National Policy stimulated a short period of rapid industrialization in the region, followed by a longer de-industrialization phase—but about timing and cause. Despite significant differences in emphasis, the various contributors to this debate (T.W. Acheson, E.R. Forbes, James Frost) fundamentally agreed that Maritime industrialization had been shaped, in the words of Kris Inwood, by 'a loss of local control over political and economic decision-making' resulting from such developments as the National Policy. Representing this 'structuralist' approach here is T.W. Acheson's now-classic article 'The National Policy and the Industrialization of the Maritimes.'

More recently historians and economists have begun to question the structuralist approach, both in detail and in general. Ken Cruikshank, for example, has challenged E.R. Forbes' conclusions about the importance of Intercolonial freight rates for Maritime industrialization. And in the paper reprinted here, 'Maritime Industrialization from 1870 to 1910: A Review of the Evidence and Its Interpretation,' Kris E. Inwood, while acknowledging the relevance of the structuralist perspective, argues that it alone cannot account for the pattern of Maritime industrialization in the late nineteenth and early twentieth centuries. Instead, Inwood suggests that the more traditional but somewhat out-of-favour 'staple' theory still has much explanatory power with respect to developments in the Maritimes in these decades.

Suggestions for Further Reading

Acheson, T.W., D. Frank and J.D. Frost, *Industrialization and Underdevelopment in the Maritimes, 1830–1930.* Toronto: Garamond Press, 1885.

Bliss, Michael, "Canadianizing American Business: The Roots of the Branch Plant," in *Close the 49th Parallel,* ed. I. Lumsden. Toronto: University of Toronto Press, 1970, 27–42.

Careless, J.M.S., "The Myth of the Downtrodden West," *Saturday Night,* 96 (May 1981), 30–37.

Creighton, Donald, *Canada's First Century.* Toronto: Macmillan of Canada, 1970.

Cruikshank, Ken, "The Intercolonial Railway, Freight Rates and the Maritime Economy," *Acadiensis,* XXII, 1 (Autumn 1992), 87–110.

Dales, John, "The Role of the Tariff in Canadian Development," in *The Protective Tariff in Canada's Development.* Toronto: University of Toronto Press, 1966, 108–139.

Drache, Daniel, "How Nationalist Was the National Policy?," *This Magazine,* XIII (1979), 30–2.

Easterbrook, W.T., and H.G.J. Aitken, *Canadian Economic History.* Toronto: Macmillan, 1956.

Frost, J.D., "The 'Nationalization' of the Bank of Nova Scotia, 1880–1910," *Acadiensis,* XII, 1 (Autumn 1982), 3–38.

Morton, W.L., *The Progressive Party in Canada.* Toronto: University of Toronto Press, 1950.

Norrie, K.H., "The National Policy and the Rate of Prairie Settlement: A Review," *Journal of Canadian Studies,* XIV, 3 (Autumn 1979), 63–76.

Phillips, Paul, "Shafting the Regions," *This Magazine,* XIII (1979), 32–34.

Thornton, Patricia A., "The Problem of Out-Migration from Atlantic Canada, 1871–1921: A New Look," *Acadiensis,* XV, 1 (Autumn 1985), 3–34.

THE NATIONAL POLICY AND THE INDUSTRIALIZATION OF THE MARITIMES

T.W. Acheson

The Maritime provinces of Canada in 1870 probably came the closest of any region to representing the classic ideal of the staple economy. Traditionally shaped by the Atlantic community, the region's industrial sector had been structured to the production and export of timber, lumber products, fish and ships. The last was of crucial significance. In terms of the balance of trade, it accounted for more than one-third of New Brunswick's exports at Confederation. In human terms, the manufacture of ships provided a number of towns with large groups of highly skilled, highly paid craftsmen who were able to contribute significantly to the quality of community life. Against this background, the constricting British market for lumber and ships after 1873 created a serious economic crisis for the area. This was not in itself unusual. Throughout the nineteenth century the region's resource-based economy had suffered a series of periodic recessions as the result of changing imperial policies and world markets. Yet, in one respect, this crisis differed from all earlier: while the lumber markets gradually returned in the late 1870s, the ship market did not. Nova Scotians continued to build their small vessels for the coasting trade, but the large ship-building industry failed to revive.

In the face of this uncertain future the National Policy was embraced by much of the Maritime business community as a new mercantilism which would re-establish that stability which the region had enjoyed under the old British order. In the first years of its operation the Maritimes experienced a dramatic growth in manufacturing potential, a growth often obscured by the stagnation of both the staple industries and population growth. In fact, the decade following 1879 was characterized by a significant transfer of capital and human resources from the traditional staples into a new manufacturing base which was emerging in response to federal tariff policies. This development was so significant that between 1881 and 1891 the industrial growth rate of Nova Scotia outstripped all other provinces in eastern Canada.[1] The comparative growth of the period is perhaps best illustrated in St. John. The relative increase in industrial capital, average wages, and output in this community significantly surpassed that of Hamilton, the Canadian city whose growth was perhaps most directly attributable to the protective tariff.[2]

Within the Atlantic region the growth of the 1880s was most unequally distributed. It centred not so much on areas or sub-regions as upon widely scattered communities.[3] These included the traditional Atlantic ports of St. John, Halifax, and Yarmouth: lumbering and ship-building towns, notably St. Stephen

From *Acadiensis,* I no. 2 (Spring 1972), 3–28. Reprinted by permission *Acadiensis.*

and New Glasgow; and newer railroad centres, such as Moncton and Amherst. The factors which produced this curious distribution of growth centres were human and historical rather than geographic. The one characteristic shared by them all was the existence in each of a group of entrepreneurs possessing the enterprise and the capital resources necessary to initiate the new industries. Strongly community-oriented, these entrepreneurs attempted, during the course of the 1880s, to create viable manufacturing enterprises in their local areas under the aegis of the protective tariff. Lacking the resources to survive the prolonged economic recessions of the period, and without a strong regional metropolis, they acquiesced in the 1890s to the industrial leadership of the Montreal business community. Only at the century's end, with the expansion of the consolidation movement, did a group of Halifax financiers join their Montreal counterparts in asserting an industrial metropolitanism over the communities of the eastern Maritimes. This paper is a study in that transition.

I

The Maritime business community in the 1870s was dominated by three groups: wholesale shippers, lumber and ship manufacturers, and the small scale manufacturers of a variety of commodities for purely local consumption. As a group they were deeply divided on the question of whether the economic salvation of their various communities was to be found in the maintenance of an Atlantic mercantile system, or in a programme of continentalist-oriented industrial diversification. A wedding of the two alternatives appeared to be the ideal situation. While they had warily examined the proposed tariff of 1879, most leading businessmen accepted its philosophy and seriously attempted to adapt it to their community needs.[4]

For a variety of reasons the tariff held the promise of prosperity for the region's traditional commercial activities and, as well, offered the possibilities for the development of new manufacturing industry. For most Nova Scotian business leaders the West Indies market was vital to the successful functioning of the province's commercial economy. It was a major element in the region's carrying trade and also provided the principal market for the Nova Scotia fishing industry. These, in turn, were the foundations of the provincial ship-building industry. The successful prosecution of the West Indies trade, however, depended entirely upon the ability of the Nova Scotia merchants to dispose of the islands' sugar crop. The world depression in the 1870s had resulted in a dramatic decline in the price of refined sugar as French, German, British and American refineries dumped their surplus production on a glutted world market. By 1877 more than nine-tenths of Canadian sugar was obtained from these sources,[5] a fact which threatened the Nova Scotia carrying trade with disaster. A significant tariff on foreign sugar, it was felt, would encourage the development of a Canadian refining industry which would acquire all of its raw sugar from the British West Indies. Through this means,

TABLE I   Industrial Development in Principal Maritime Centres 1880–1890

	Population	Industrial Capital	Employees	Average Annual Wages	Output	Industry Output, 1891
Halifax (1880)	39,886	$2,975,000	3,551	$303	$6,128,000	Sugar**
Dartmouth (1890)	43,132	6,346,000	4,654	280	8,235,000	Rope* Cotton Confectionery Paint Lamps
St. John (1880) (1890)	41,353 39,179	2,143,000 4,838,000	2,690 5,888	278 311	4,123,000 8,131,000	Lumber** Machinery*** Smelting Rope** Cottons Brass* Nails* Electric Light**
New Glasgow (1880) (1890)	2,595 3,777	160,000 1,050,000	360 1,117	255 355	313,000 1,512,000	Primary Steel* Rolling Mills** Glass
St. Stephen (1880)	4,002	136,000	447	314	573,000	Cottons
Milltown (1890)	4,826	1,702,000	1,197	320	1,494,000	Confectionery Fish Canning Soap Lumber
Moncton (1880) (1890)	5,032 8,765	530,000 1,134,000	603 948	418 333	1,719,000 1,973,000	Sugar Cottons Woolens Rolling Stock
Fredericton (1880)	7,218[a]	1,090,000[a]	911[a]	221[a]	1,031,000[a]	Cottons
Marysville (1890)	8,394	2,133,000	1,526	300	1,578,000	Lumber Foundry Products
Yarmouth (1880) (1890)	3,485 6,089	290,000 783,000	211 930	328 312	284,000 1,234,000	Cotton Yarn* Fish Canning Woolens
Amherst (1880) (1890)	2,274 3,781	81,000 457,000	288 683	281 293	283,000 724,000	Foundry Products Shoes Doors

[a] Estimates. Marysville was not an incorporated town in 1880, and totals for that date must be estimated from York County figures.
* Leading Canadian Producer: ** second: *** third.

Source: Canada. *Census* (1891), III, Table I: *Ibid.*, (1901). III, Tables XX. XXI.

most Nova Scotian wholesalers and shippers saw in the new policy an opportunity both to resuscitate the coastal shipping industry of the province and to restore their primacy in the West Indies.

Of the newer industries which the National Policy offered, the future for the Maritimes seemed to lie in textiles and iron and steel products. The optimism concerning the possibilities of the former appears to have emerged out of a hope of emulating the New England experience. This expectation was fostered by the willingness of British and American cotton mill machinery manufacturers to supply on easy terms the necessary duty-free equipment, and by the feeling of local businessmen that the market provided by the tariff and the low quality labour requirements of such an enterprise would guarantee that a profitable business could be erected and maintained by the efforts of a single community. Behind such reasoning lay the general assumption that, despite major transportation problems, the Maritimes, and notably Nova Scotia, would ultimately become the industrial centre of Canada. The assumption was not unfounded. The region contained the only commercially viable coal and iron deposits in the Dominion, and had the potential, under the tariff, of controlling most of the Montreal fuel sources. Under these circumstances the development of textiles and the expansion of most iron and steel industries in the Atlantic area was perhaps not a surprising project.

Despite a cautious enthusiasm for the possibilities offered by the new federal economic dispensation, there was considerable concern about the organizational and financial problems in creating a new industrial structure. The Maritimes was a region of small family firms with limited capital capabilities. Other than chartered banks, it lacked entirely the financial structure to support any large corporate industrial entity. Like the people of Massachusetts, Maritimers were traditionally given to placing their savings in government savings banks at a guaranteed 4 percent interest than in investments on the open market.[6] Regional insurance, mortgage and loan, and private savings corporations were virtually unknown. The result was to throw the whole financial responsibility for undertaking most manufactories upon the resources of individual entrepreneurs.

Since most enterprises were envisioned as being of general benefit to the community at large, and since few businessmen possessed the necessary capital resources to single-handedly finance such an undertaking, most early industrial development occurred as the result of co-operative efforts by groups of community entrepreneurs. These in turn were drawn from a traditional business elite of wholesalers and lumbermen. In Halifax as early as May, 1879, a committee was formed from among the leading West Indies shippers "to solicit capital, select a site and get a manufacturing expert" for the organization of a sugar refinery.[7] Under its leadership $500,000 was raised, in individual subscriptions of $10–20,000, from among members of the Halifax business community. This procedure was repeated during the formation of the Halifax Cotton Company in 1881; more than $300,000 was subscribed in less than two weeks, most of it by thirty-two individuals.[8]

The leadership in the development of these enterprises was taken by young members of traditional mercantile families. The moving spirit in both cases was Thomas Kenny. A graduate of the Jesuit Colleges at Stonyhurst (England) and St. Gervais (Belgium), Kenny had inherited from his father, the Hon. Sir Edward Kenny, M.L.C., one of the largest wholesale shipping firms in the region. In the early 1870s the younger Kenny had invested heavily in shipyards scattered throughout five counties of Nova Scotia, and had even expanded into England with the establishment of a London branch for his firm. Following the opening of the refinery in 1881, he devoted an increasingly large portion of his time to the management of that firm.[9] Kenny was supported in his efforts by a number of leading merchants including the Hon. Robert Boak, Scottish-born president of the Legislative Council, and John F. Stairs, Manager of the Dartmouth Rope Works. Stairs, who had attended Dalhousie University, was a member of the executive council of Nova Scotia, the son of a legislative councillor, and a grandson of the founder of the shipping firm of William Stairs, Son and Morrow Limited.[10]

In contrast to Halifax, St. John had always been much more a manufacturing community and rivalled Ottawa as the principal lumber manufacturing centre in the Dominion. Development in the New Brunswick city occurred as new growth on an existing industrial structure and centred on cotton cloth and iron and steel products. The New Brunswick Cotton Mill had been erected in 1861 by an Ulster-born St. John shipper, William Parks, and his son, John H. Parks. The latter, who had been trained as a civil engineer under the tutelage of the chief engineer of the European and North American Railroad, assumed the sole proprietorship of the mill in 1870.[11] In 1881 he led the movement among the city's dry goods wholesalers to establish a second cotton mill which was incorporated as the St. John Cotton Company.

The principal St. John iron business was the firm of James Harris. Trained as a blacksmith, the Annapolis-born Harris had established a small machine shop in the city in 1828, and had expanded into the foundry business some twenty-three years later. In 1883, in consequence of the new tariff, he determined to develop a completely integrated secondary iron industry including a rolling mill and railway car plant. To provide the resources for the expansion, the firm was reorganized as a joint stock company with a $300,000 capital most of which was raised by St. John businessmen. The New Brunswick Foundry, Rolling Mills and Car Works, with a plant covering some five acres of land, emerged as the largest industrial employer in the Maritimes.[12] The success of the Harris firm induced a group of wholesale hardware manufacturers under the leadership of the Hon. Isaac Burpee, a former member of the Mackenzie Government, to re-establish the Coldbrook Rolling Mills near the city.

Yet, despite the development of sugar and cotton industries and the expansion of iron and rope manufactories, the participation of the St. John and Halifax business communities in the industrial impulse which characterized the early 1880s can only be described as marginal. Each group played the role of participant within its locality but neither provided any positive leadership to its hinterland area. Even in terms of industrial expansion, the performance of many small town manufacturers was more impressive than that of their city counterparts.

At the little railway centre of Moncton, nearly $1,000,000 was raised under the leadership of John and Christopher Harris, John Humphrey, and Josiah Woods, to permit the construction of a sugar refinery, a cotton mill, a gas light and power plant, and several smaller iron and textile enterprises. The Harris brothers, sons of an Annapolis ship builder of Loyalist extraction, had established a ship-building and shipping firm at Moncton in 1856.[13] Under the aegis of their firm they organized the new enterprises with the assistance of their brother-in-law John Humphrey, scion of Yorkshire Methodist settlers of the Tantramar, longtime M.L.A. for Westmorland, and proprietor of the Moncton flour and woolen mills. They were financially assisted in their efforts by Josiah Wood (later Senator) of nearby Sackville. The son of a Loyalist wholesaler, Wood first completed his degrees (B.A., M.A.) at Mount Allison, was later admitted to the New Brunswick bar, and finally entered his father's shipping and private banking business.[14] The leadership of the Moncton group was so effective that the owner of the *Monetary Times,* in a journey through the region in 1882, singled out the community for praise:

> Moncton has industrialized … business people only in moderate circumstances but have united their energies … persons who have always invested their surplus funds in mortgages are now cheerfully subscribing capital for the Moncton Cotton Co. Unfortunately for industrial progress, there are too many persons [in this region] who are quite content with receiving 5 or 6% for their money so long as they know it is safe, rather than risk it in manufactures, even supposing it yielded double the profit.[15]

At St. Stephen the septuagenarian lumber barons and bankers, James Murchie and Freeman Todd, joined the Annapolis-born ship builder, Zechariah Chipman, who was father-in-law to the Minister of Finance, Sir Leonard Tilley, in promoting an immense cotton concern, the St. Croix, second largest in the Dominion at the time. The son of a local farmer, Murchie, whose holdings included more than 200,000 acres of timber lands—half of it in Quebec— also developed a number of smaller local manufactories.[16] At the same time two young brothers, Gilbert and James Ganong, grandsons of a Loyalist farmer from the St. John Valley, began the expansion of their small confectionery firm,[17] and shortly initiated construction of a soap enterprise in the town.

At Yarmouth a group of ship builders and West Indies merchants led by the Hon. Loran Baker, M.L.C., a shipper and private banker, and John Lovitt, a ship-builder and member of the Howland Syndicate, succeeded in promoting the Yarmouth Woolen Mill, the Yarmouth Cotton Manufacturing, the Yarmouth Duck Yarn Company, two major foundries, and a furniture enterprise.[18] The development was entirely an internal community effort—virtually all the leading business figures were third generation Nova Scotians of pre-Loyalist American origins. A similar development was discernible in the founding of the Windsor Cotton Company.[19]

A somewhat different pattern emerged at New Glasgow, the centre of the Nova Scotia coal industry. Attempts at the manufacture of primary iron and steel had been made with indifferent results ever since Confederation.[20] In 1872, a New Glasgow blacksmith, Graham Fraser, founded the Hope Iron Works with an initial capital of $160,000.[21] As the tariff on iron and steel products increased in the 1880s so did the vertical expansion of the firm. In 1889, when it was amalgamated with Fraser's other enterprise, the Nova Scotia Forge Company, more than two-thirds of the $280,000 capital stock of the resulting Nova Scotia Steel and Coal Company was held by the citizens of New Glasgow.[22] Fraser remained as president and managing director of the corporation until 1904,[23] during which time it produced most of the primary steel in the Dominion,[24] and remained one of the largest industrial corporations in the country.[25]

Fraser was seconded in his industrial efforts by James Carmichael of New Glasgow and John F. Stairs of Halifax. Carmichael, son of a prominent New Glasgow merchant and a descendant of the Scottish founders of Pictou, had established one of the largest ship-building and shipping firms in the province.[26] Stairs' investment in the New Glasgow iron and steel enterprise represented one of the few examples of inter-community industrial activity in this period.

The most unusual pattern of manufacturing development in the region was that initiated at Fredericton by Alexander Gibson. Gibson's distinctiveness lay in his ability to impose the tradition and structure of an earlier semi-industrial society onto a changing pattern of development. A St. Stephen native and the son of Ulster immigrants, he had begun his career as a sawyer, and later operated a small lumber firm at Lepreau. In 1865 he bought from the Anti-Confederationist government of A.J. Smith extensive timber reserves on the headwaters of the Nashwaak River,[27] and at the mouth of that river, near Fredericton, built his own mill-town of Marysville. Freed from stumpage fees by his fortunate purchase, the "lumber king of New Brunswick" was producing as much as 100,000,000 feet of lumber annually by the 1880s—about one third of the provincial output. His lumber exports at times comprised half the export commerce of the port of St. John.[28]

One of the wealthiest industrial entrepreneurs in the Dominion, Gibson determined in 1883 to undertake the erection of a major cotton enterprise entirely under his own auspices.[29] He erected one of the largest brickyards in the Dominion and personally supervised the construction of the plant which was opened in 1885.[30] In that same year he employed nearly 2,000 people in his sundry enterprises.[31] By 1888 his sales of cotton cloth totalled nearly $500,000.[32] That same year the Gibson empire, comprising the cotton mill, timber lands, saw mills, lath mills, the town of Marysville and the Northern and Western Railroad, was formed into a joint stock company, its $3,000,000 capital controlled by Gibson, his brother, sons and son-in-law.

Several common characteristics distinguished the men who initiated the industrial expansion of the 1880s. They were, on the whole, men of substance gained in traditional trades and staples. They sought a substantial, more secure future for themselves within the framework of the traditional community through the instrumentality of the new industrial mercantilism. Averaging fifty-four years of age, they were old men to be embarking upon new careers.[33] Coupled with this factor of age was their ignorance of both the technical skills and the complexities of the financial and marketing structures involved in the new enterprises.

The problem of technical skill was overcome largely by the importation of management and skilled labour, mainly from England and Scotland.[34] The problem of finance was more serious. The resources of the community entrepreneurs were limited; the costs of the proposed industry were almost always far greater than had been anticipated. Moreover, most businessmen had only the vaguest idea of the quantity of capital required to operate a large manufacturing corporation. Promoters generally followed the normal mercantile practice and raised only sufficient capital to construct and equip the physical plant, preferring to finance operating costs through bank loans—a costly and inefficient process. The Halifax Sugar Refinery perhaps best illustrated these problems. When first proposed in 1879 it was to have been capitalized at $300,000. Before its completion in 1881 it was re-capitalized twice to a value of $500,000.[35] Even this figure left no operating capital, and the refinery management was forced to secure these funds by loans from the Merchants Bank of Halifax. At the end of its first year of operation the bank debt of the corporation totalled $460,000,[36] which immediately became a fixed charge on the revenues of the infant industry. Fearing bankruptcy, the stockholders increased their subscriptions and kept the business functioning until 1885 when they attempted a solution to the problem by issuing debenture stock to a value of $350,000 of which the bank was to receive $200,000 in stock and $50,000 cash in settlement of debts still owed to it.[37]

While many industries received their initial financing entirely from local capitalists, some projects proved to be such ambitious undertakings that aid had to be sought from other sources. The St. Croix Cotton Company at St. Stephen, for example, was forced to borrow $300,000 from Rhode Island interests to complete their huge plant.[38] Some industries came to rely so heavily on small community banks for perpetual loans for operating expenses that any general economic crisis toppled both the industries and the banks simultaneously. The financing of James Domville's enterprises, including the Coldbrook Rolling Mills, was a contributing factor in the temporary suspension of the Maritime Bank of Saint John in 1880,[39] while such industrial loans ultimately brought down the Bank of Yarmouth in 1905.[40]

II

The problem of industrial finance was intricately tied to a whole crisis of confidence in the new order which began to develop as the first enthusiastic flush of industrial expansion paled in the face of the general business downturn which wracked the Canadian economy in the mid-1880s. At the heart of this problem was a gradual deterioration of the British lumber market, and the continued shift from sea borne to railroad commerce. Under the influence of an increasingly prohibitive tariff and an extended railroad building programme a two cycle inter-regional trading pattern was gradually emerging. The westward cycle, by rail into the St. Lawrence basin, left the region with a heavy trade imbalance as the central Canadians rapidly replaced British and American produce in the Maritime market with their own flour and manufactured materials.[41] In return, the region shipped to Montreal quantities of primary and primary manufactured products of both local and imported origins. The secretaries of the Montreal and Saint John boards of trade estimated the extent of this inter-regional commerce at about $15,711,000 in 1885, more than 70 percent of which represented central Canadian exports to the Maritimes.[42] By contrast the external trade cycle moved in traditional fashion by ship from the principal Maritime ports to Great Britain and the West Indies. Heavily balanced in favour of the Maritimes, it consumed most of the output of the region's resource industries. The two cycles were crucially interdependent: the Maritime business community used the credits earned in the external cycle to meet the gaping deficits incurred in the central Canadian trade. The system worked as long as the equilibrium between the two could be maintained. Unfortunately, as the decade progressed, this balance was seriously threatened by a declining English lumber market.[43]

In the face of this increasingly serious trade imbalance, the Maritime business community became more and more critical of what they regarded as the subversion of the National Policy by central Canadian interests. Their argument was based upon two propositions. If Canadian transportation policy was dedicated to creating an all-Canadian commercial system, then this system should extend not from the Pacific to Montreal, but from the Pacific to the Atlantic. How, in all justice, could the Montreal interests insist on the construction, at a staggering cost, of an all-Canadian route west of that city and then demand the right to export through Portland or Boston rather than using the Maritime route? This argument was implicit in almost every resolution of the Halifax and Saint John boards of trade from 1880 onward.[44]

The second proposition maintained that, as vehicles of nationhood, the railways must be considered as a means of promoting national economic integration rather than as commercial institutions. The timing of this doctrine is significant.

Before 1885 most Maritime manufacturers were competitive both with Canadian and foreign producers. Nails, confectionery, woolens, leather, glass, steel and machinery manufactured in the Maritimes normally had large markets in both central Canada and the West.[45] The recession of 1885 reached a trough in 1886.[46] Diminishing demand coupled with over-production, particularly in the cotton cloth and sugar industries, resulted in falling prices, and made it increasingly difficult for many Maritime manufacturers to retain their central Canadian markets. The *bête noir* was seen as the relatively high freight rates charged by the Intercolonial Railway. The issue came to a head late in 1885 with the closing of the Moncton and the two Halifax sugar refineries. The response of the Halifax manufacturers was immediate and decisive. Writing to the Minister of Railways, John F. Stairs enunciated the Maritime interpretation of the National Policy:

> Four refineries have been set in operation in the Lower Provinces by the policy of the Government. This was right; but trade having changed so that it is now impossible for them to work prosperously it is the duty of the Government to accommodate its policy to the change. The reduction in freight rates asked for is necessary to this .... If in answer to this you plead that you must manage so that no loss occur running the I.C.R., we will reply, we do not, and will not accept this as a valid plea from the Government ... and to it we say that the people of Nova Scotia, nor should those of Ontario and Quebec, for they are as much interested, even admit it is essential to make both ends meet in the finance of the railroad, when it can only be done at the expense of inter-provincial trade, and the manufacturers of Nova Scotia .... How can the National Policy succeed in Canada where such great distances exist between the provinces unless the Government who control the National Railway meet the requirements of trade ....[47]

At stake, as Stairs later pointed out in a confidential memorandum to Macdonald, was the whole West Indies trade of Nova Scotia.[48] Equally as important and also at stake was the entire industrial structure which had been created in the region under the aegis of the National Policy.

The Maritimes by 1885 provided a striking illustration of the success of that policy. With less than one-fifth of the population of the Dominion, the region contained eight of the twenty-three Canadian cotton mills—including seven of the nineteen erected after 1879[49]— three of five sugar refineries, two of seven rope factories, one of three glass works, both of the Canadian steel mills, and six of the nation's twelve rolling mills.

Although Stairs succeeded in his efforts to have the I.C.R. sugar freight rates reduced,[50] the problem facing the Maritime entrepreneur was not one which could be solved simply by easier access to the larger central Canadian market; its cause was much more complex. In the cotton industry, for example, the Canadian business community had created industrial units with a production potential sufficient to supply the entire national market. In periods of recession many American cloth manufacturers were prepared to cut prices on exports to a level which vitiated the Canadian tariff: this enabled them to gain control of a considerable portion of the Canadian market. The problems of the cotton cloth manufacturers could have been solved by a further increase in the tariff—a politically undesirable answer— by control of railway rates, or by a regulated industrial output.

From a Maritime regional viewpoint the second of these alternatives appeared to be the most advantageous; the limitations of the tariff could then be accepted and, having attained geographic equality with Montreal through a regulated freight rate, the more efficient Maritime mills would soon control the Montreal market. Such was the hope: there was little possibility of its realization. Such a general alteration in railway policy would have required subsidization of certain geographic areas—districts constituting political minorities—at the expense of the dominant political areas of the country, a prospect which the business community of Montreal and environs could hardly be expected to view with equanimity. Apart from the political difficulties of the situation, most Maritime manufactories suffered from two major organizational problems: the continued difficulty faced by community corporations in securing financing in the frequent periods of marginal business activity,[51] and the fact that most firms depended upon Montreal wholesale houses to dispose of their extra-regional exports.[52] Short of a major shift in government railway or tariff policy, the only solution to the problem of markets which seemed to have any chance for success appeared to be the regulation of industrial production, a technique which was to bring into the Maritimes the Montreal interests which already controlled the major part of the distributive function in eastern Canada.

III

The entry of Montreal into the Maritime region was not a new phenomenon. With the completion of the Intercolonial Railway and the imposition of coal duties in 1879, Montreal railway entrepreneurs moved to control both the major rail systems of New Brunswick and the Nova Scotia coal fields. A syndicate headed by George Stephen and Donald Smith had purchased the New Brunswick Railroad from Alexander Gibson and the Hon. Isaac Burpee in 1880,[53] with the intention of extending it to Rivière du Loup. This system was expanded two years later by the purchase of the New Brunswick and Canada Railroad with the ultimate view of making Saint John the winter port for Montreal.

In the same year, another Montreal group headed by John McDougall, David Morrice and L.-A. Sénécal acquired from fifteen Saint John bondholders, four-fifths of the bonds of the Springhill and Parrsboro Railroad and Mining Company,[54] and followed this up in 1883 with the purchase of the Springhill Mining Company, the largest coal producer in Canada.[55] The following year another syndicate acquired the International Mine at Sydney.[56] The coal mine take-overs were designed to control and expand the output of this fuel source, partially in an effort to free the Canadian Pacific Railways from dependence upon the strike-prone American coal industry. By contrast, the entry of Montreal interests into the manufacturing life of the Maritimes aimed to restrict output and limit expansion.

The first serious attempts to regulate production occurred in the cotton industry. Although informal meetings of manufacturers had been held throughout the mid-1880s, the business depression of 1886 and the threatened failure of several mills resulted in the organization of the first formal national trade association. Meeting in Montreal in the summer of 1886, representatives of sixteen mills, including four from the Maritimes, agreed to regulate production and to set standard minimum prices for commodities. The agreement was to be renegotiated yearly and each mill provided a bond as proof of good faith.[57] The arrangement at least stabilized the industry and the agreement was renewed in 1887.

The collapse of the association the following year was precipitated by a standing feud between the two largest Maritime mills, the St. Croix at St. Stephen and the Gibson at Marysville. Alexander Gibson had long been the maverick of the organization, having refused to subscribe to the agreement in 1886 and 1887. During this period he had severely injured his larger St. Stephen competitor in the Maritime market. By the time Gibson agreed to enter the association in 1888, the St. Croix mill, faced with bankruptcy, dropped out and reduced prices in an effort to dispose of its huge inventory. The Gibson mill followed suit. With two of the largest coloured cotton mills in the Dominion selling without regulation, the controlled market system dissolved into chaos, and the association, both coloured and grey sections, disintegrated.[58] The return to an unregulated market in the cotton industry continued for more than two years. A business upswing in 1889 mercifully saved the industry from what many manufacturers feared would be a general financial collapse. Even so, only the mills with the largest production potential, regardless of geographic location, escaped unscathed; most of the smaller plants were forced to close temporarily.

In the summer of 1890 a Montreal group headed by A. F. Gault and David Morrice prepared the second attempt to regulate the cotton market. The technique was to be the corporate monopoly. The Dominion Cotton Mills Company, with a $5,000,000 authorized capital, was to bring all of the grey cotton producers under the control of a single directorate. In January 1891, David Morrice set out on a tour of Maritime cotton centres. On his first stop, at Halifax, he accepted transfer of the Nova Scotia Cotton Mill to the syndicate, the shareholders receiving $101,000 cash and $101,000 in bonds in the new corporation, a return of 25 cents on the dollar of their initial investment.[59] The following day Morrice proceeded to Windsor, "to consummate the transfer of the factory there,"[60] and from there moved on to repeat the performance at Moncton.

Fearful of total bankruptcy and hopeful that this stronger organization would provide the stability that earlier efforts had failed to achieve, stockholders of the smaller community-oriented mills readily acquiesced to the new order. Although they lost heavily on their original investment, most owners accepted bonds in the new corporation in partial payment for their old stock.

The first determined opposition to the cotton consolidation movement appeared in Saint John. Here, John H. Parks, founder and operator of the thirty-year old New Brunswick Cotton Mill, had bought the bankrupt Saint John Cotton firm in 1886 and had proceeded to operate both mills. Despite the perennial problem of financing, the Parks Mills represented one of the most efficient industrial operations in the Dominion, one which had won an international reputation for the quality of its product. The company's major markets were found in western Ontario, a fact which made the continued independence of the firm a particular menace to the combination. The firm's major weakness was its financial structure. Dependent upon the Bank of Montreal for his operating capital, Parks had found it necessary to borrow more heavily than usual during the winter of 1889–90. By mid-1890 his debts totalled $122,000.[61]

At this point two events occurred almost simultaneously: Parks refused to consider sale of the Saint John Mills to the new corporation, and the Bank of Montreal having ascertained that the Montreal syndicate would buy the mills from any seller, demanded immediate payment in full of the outstanding debts of the company[62]—a most unusual procedure. Claiming a Montreal conspiracy to seize the company, Parks replied with an open letter to the dry goods merchants of greater Saint John.

> ... I have made arrangements by which the mills of our company will be run to their fullest extent.
>
> These arrangements have been made in the face of the most determined efforts to have our business stopped, and our property sold out to the Montreal syndicate which is endeavouring to control the Cotton Trade of Canada .... I now propose to continue to keep our mills in operation as a Saint John industry, free from all outside control. I would therefore ask you gentlemen, as far as your power, to support me in this undertaking—
>
> It remains with you to assist the Wholesale Houses in distributing the goods made in Saint John in preference to those of outside manufacture so long as the quality and price of the home goods is satisfactory.
>
> The closing of our mills ... would be a serious calamity to the community, and you, by your support can assist materially in preventing it. I believe you will.[63]

Parks' appeal to community loyalty saved his firm. When the bank foreclosed the mortgage which it held as security for its loans, Mr. Justice A. L. Palmer of the New Brunswick Supreme Court placed the firm in receivership under his control until the case was resolved. Over the strongest objections of the bank, and on one legal pretext after another, the judge kept the mill in receivership for nearly two years.[64] In the meantime he forced the bank to continue the provision of operating capital for the mill's operations, and in conjunction with the receiver, a young Fredericton lawyer, H. H. McLean, proceeded to run an efficient and highly profitable business. When the decision was finally rendered in December 1892, the firm was found to have cleared profits of $150,000 during the period of the receivership. Parks was able to use the funds to repay the bank debts and the mill continued under local control.[65]

The Saint John experience was unique. Gault and Morrice organized the Canadian Coloured Cotton Company, sister consolidation to the Dominion Cotton Mills, in 1891. The St. Croix Mill entered the new organization without protest early in 1892,[66] and even the Gibson Mill, while retaining its separate corporate structure, agreed to market its entire output through the new consolidation. By 1893 only the Saint John Mills and the small Yarmouth plant remained in the hands of regional entrepreneurs.

The fate of the Maritime cotton mills was paralleled in the sugar industry. In 1890 a syndicate of Scottish merchants, incorporated under English laws as the Halifax Sugar Refinery Ltd., bought up the English-owned Woodside Refinery of Halifax.[67] The ultimate aim of the Scottish group was to consolidate the sugar industry into a single corporate entity similar to Dominion Cotton. Failing in this effort because of the parliamentary outcry against combines, they turned their efforts to regional consolidation. With the assistance of John F. Stairs, M.P., they were able, in 1894, to secure an act of incorporation as the Acadia Sugar Refineries which was to amalgamate the three Maritime firms. Unlike the Cotton Union, the new consolidation worked in the interests of the regional entrepreneurs, the stock holders of all three refineries receiving full value for their holdings. Equally important, the management of the new concern remained in the hands of Thomas Kenny, M.P.

The consolidation movement of the early 1890s swept most of the other major Maritime manufactories. In some cases local entrepreneurs managed to retain a voice in the direction of the new mergers—John Stairs, for example, played a prominent role on the directorate of the Consumers Cordage Company which swept the Halifax and Saint John rope concerns into a new seven-company amalgamation in 1890.[68] On the other hand, the Nova Scotia Glass Company of New Glasgow disappeared entirely in the Diamond Glass consolidation of that same year.[69] On the whole, saving only the iron and steel products, the confectionery and the staple export industries, control of all mass consumption industries in the Maritimes had passed to outside interests by 1895. Thus, in large measure the community manufactory which had dominated the industrial growth of the 1880s ceased to exist in the 1890s. Given the nature of the market of the period, some degree of central control probably was inevitable. The only question at stake was whether it would be a control effected by political or financial means, and if the latter, from which centre it would emanate.

The failure of any Maritime metropolis to achieve this control was partly a result of geography and partly a failure of entrepreneurial leadership. The fear of being left on the fringes of a national marketing system had been amply illustrated by the frenetic efforts of the Saint John and Halifax business communities to promote political policies which would link the Canadian marketing system to an Atlantic structure with the Maritime ports serving as the connecting points.[70]

The question of entrepreneurial failure is more difficult to document. In part the great burst of industrial activity which marked the early 1880s was the last flowering of an older generation of lumbermen and wholesale shippers. Having failed to achieve their position as the link between central Canada and Europe, and faced with the dominant marketing and financial apparatus of the Montreal community, they drew back and even participated in the transfer of control. This failure is understandable in the smaller communities: it is more difficult to explain in the larger. In the latter case it may well be attributable to the perennial failure of most Maritime communities to maintain a continuity of industrial elites. The manufacturing experience of most families was limited to a single generation: Thomas Kenny's father was a wholesale merchant, his son a stockbroker. John F. Stairs was the son of a merchant and the father of a lawyer. Even in such a distinguished industrial family as that of John Parks, a second generation manufacturer, the son attended the Royal Military College and then entered the Imperial service. Commerce and the professions provided a much more stable milieu, and while many participants in both of these activities were prepared to make the occasional excursion into manufacturing, usually as part of a dual role, few were willing to make a permanent and sole commitment to an industrial vocation.

IV

The lesson brought home to the Maritime entrepreneur by the industrial experience between 1879 and 1895 was that geography would defeat any attempt to compete at parity with a central Canadian enterprise. In response to this lesson, the truncated industrial community of the region turned increasingly to those resource industries in which geography gave them a natural advantage over their central Canadian counterparts. In the 1890s the thrust of Maritime industrial growth was directed toward the processing and manufacturing of primary steel and of iron and steel products. In part, since these enterprises constituted much of the industrial machinery remaining in the hands of regional entrepreneurs, there was little choice in this development. At the same time, Nova Scotia contained most of the active coal and iron deposits in the Dominion and had easy access to the rich iron ore deposits at Belle Isle. In any event, most competition in these industries came from western Ontario rather than Montreal, and the latter was thus a potential market.

Iron and steel development was not new to the region. Efforts at primary steel making had been undertaken successfully at New Glasgow since 1882. Yet production there was limited and would continue so until a more favourable tariff policy guaranteed a stable market for potential output. Such a policy was begun in 1887 with the passage of the "iron" tariff. Generally labeled as a Nova Scotia tariff designed to make that province "the Pennsylvania of Canada"[71] and New Glasgow "the Birmingham of the country",[72] the act provided an effective protection of $3.50 a ton for Canadian-made iron, and imposed heavy duties on a variety of iron and steel products.[73] Protection for the industry was completed in 1894 when the duty on scrap iron, considered a raw material by secondary iron manufacturers, was raised from $2 to $4 a ton, and most rolling mills were forced to use Nova Scotia-made bar iron rather than imported scrap.[74]

The growth of the New Glasgow industries paralleled this tariff development. In 1889 the Nova Scotia Steel Company was united with the Nova Scotia Forge Company to form a corporation capable of manufacturing both primary steel and iron and steel products. In the same year, to provide the community with its own source of pig iron, a group of Nova Scotia Steel shareholders organized the New Glasgow Iron, Coal and Railroad Company with a capital of $1,000,000.[75] Five years later, following the enactment of the scrap iron duty, New Glasgow acquired the rich Wabana iron ore deposits at Belle Isle—some eighty-three acres covered with ore deposits so thick they could be cut from the surface. This was followed the next year by the union of the Nova Scotia Steel and Forge and the New Glasgow Iron companies into a $2,060,000 corporation, the Nova Scotia Steel Company. Containing its own blast and open hearth furnaces, rolling mills, forges, foundries, and machine shops, the firm represented the most fully integrated industrial complex in the country. The process was completed in 1900 when the company acquired the Sydney Coal Mines on Cape Breton Island, developed new steel mills in that area and re-organized as the Nova Scotia Steel and Coal Company with a $7,000,000 capital.[76]

The development of the Nova Scotia Steel and Coal corporation had begun under the direction of a cabal of Pictou County Scottish Nova Scotians, a group which was later enlarged to include a few prominent Halifax businessmen. Aside from Graham Fraser, its leading members included James D. McGregor, James C. MacGregor, Colonel Thomas Cantley, and John F. Stairs. All four were third-generation Nova Scotians, the first three from New Glasgow. Saving only Cantley, all were members of old mercantile families. Senator McGregor, a merchant, was a grandson of the Rev. Dr. James McGregor, one of the founders of the Presbyterian Church in Nova Scotia; MacGregor was a partner in the large ship-building concern of Senator J. W. Carmichael, a prominent promoter of Nova Scotia Steel. Cantley was the only member of the group of proletarian origins. Like Graham Fraser, he spent a lifetime in the active service of the company, having entered the newly established Nova Scotia Forge Company in 1873 at the age of sixteen. Promoted to sales manager of the amalgamated

Nova Scotia Steel Company in 1885, he had been responsible for the introduction of Wabana ore into England and Germany. In 1902 he succeeded Graham Fraser as general manager of the corporation.[77]

Aside from its value to the New Glasgow area, the Nova Scotia Steel Company was of even greater significance as a supplier of iron and steel to a variety of foundries, car works and machine mills in the region. Because of its unique ability to provide primary, secondary and tertiary steel and iron manufactures, it was supplying most of the Maritime iron and steel needs by 1892.[78] In this respect, the industrial experience of the 1890s differed considerably from that of the previous decade. It was not characterized by the development of new industrial structures, but rather by the expansion of older firms which had served purely local markets for some time and expanded in response to the demand created by the tariff changes of the period.[79]

The centres of the movement were at New Glasgow, Amherst and Saint John, all on the main lines of the Intercolonial or Canadian Pacific railroads. At New Glasgow, the forge and foundry facilities of the Nova Scotia Steel Company consumed half the company's iron and steel output. At Amherst, Nathaniel Curry (later Senator) and his brother-in-law, John Rhodes, continued the expansion of the small woodworking firm they had established in 1877, gradually adding a door factory, a rolling mill, a railroad car plant and an axle factory, and in 1893 bought out the Harris Car Works and Foundry of Saint John.[80] At the time of its incorporation in 1902, Rhodes, Curry & Company was one of the largest secondary iron manufacturing complexes in the Dominion.[81] Curry's industrial neighbour at Amherst was David Robb. Son of an Amherst foundry owner, Robb had been trained in engineering at the Stevens Institute of New Jersey and then had entered his father's foundry. Specializing in the development of precision machinery, he expanded his activities into Massachusetts in the 1890s and finally merged his firm into the International Engineering Works of South Framingham of which he remained managing director.[82]

If under the aegis of a protective government policy the iron and steel industry of the Maritimes was rapidly becoming a viable proposition for local entrepreneurs, it was also increasingly attracting the interest of both Boston and Montreal business interests. There was a growing feeling that, once a reciprocal coal agreement was made between Canada and the United States, Nova Scotia coal would replace the more expensive Pennsylvania product in the New England market. Added to this inducement was the fact that Nova Scotia provided the major fuel source on the Montreal market—the city actually consumed most of the coal produced in the Cape Breton fields.[83] With its almost unlimited access routes and its strategic water position midway between Boston and Montreal, Nova Scotia seemed an excellent area for investment.

In 1893 a syndicate headed by H. M. Whitney of Boston and composed of Boston, New York and Montreal businessmen, including Donald Smith, W. C. Van Horne and Hugh McLennan, negotiated a 119-year lease with the

Nova Scotia government for most of the existing coal fields on Cape Breton Island.[84] The new Dominion Coal Company came into formal being in March of that year, with David MacKeen (later Senator) as director and general manager, and John S. McLennan (later Senator) as director and treasurer. The son of a Scottish-born mine owner and member of the legislative council, MacKeen had been an official and principal stockholder in the Caledonia Coal Company which had been absorbed in the new consolidation.[85] McLennan was the second son of Hugh McLennan of Montreal, a graduate of Trinity College, Cambridge, and one of the very few entrepreneurs who made the inter-regional transfer in this period.[86] The success of the Dominion Coal syndicate and the growing feeling that the Canadian government was determined to create a major Canadian primary steel industry led Whitney in 1899 to organize the Dominion Iron & Steel Company. The date was significant. Less than two years earlier the government had announced its intention to extend bounty payments to steel made from imported ores.[87] The $15,000,000 capital of the new company was easily raised, largely on the Canadian stock market,[88] and by 1902 the company was employing 4,000 men in its four blast and ten steel furnace works.[89] Graham Fraser was induced to leave Nova Scotia Steel to become general manager of the new corporation,[90] and J. H. Plummer, assistant general manager of the Bank of Commerce, was brought from Toronto as president.

The primacy of American interests in both the Dominion Steel and Dominion Coal companies was rapidly replaced by those of Montreal and Toronto after 1900. The sale of stocks added a strong Toronto delegation to the directorate of the steel company in 1901.[91] In that same year James Ross, the Montreal street railway magnate, bought heavily into the coal corporation, reorganized its management and retained control of the firm until 1910.[92]

V

The increasing reliance on the stock market as a technique for promoting and securing the necessary financial support to develop the massive Nova Scotia steel corporations emphasized the growing shift from industrial to financial capitalism. Centred on the Montreal stock market, the new movement brought to the control of industrial corporations men who had neither a communal nor a vocational interest in the concern.

In emulation of, and possibly in reaction to the Montreal experience, a group within the Halifax business and professional communities scrambled to erect the financial structure necessary to this undertaking. The city already possessed some of the elements of this structure. The Halifax stock exchange had existed on an informal basis since before Confederation.[93] The city's four major banking institutions—the Nova Scotia, the Union, the Merchants (which subsequently became the Royal Bank of Canada) and the Peoples—were among the soundest in the Dominion. The development of Halifax as a major centre for industrial finance began in 1894, at the height of the first Montreal-based merger movement, when a syndicate headed by J. F. Stairs founded the Eastern Trust Company.[94] The membership of this group was indicative of the change that was occurring in the Halifax business elite. Although it contained representatives of the older mercantile group, such as Stairs, T. E. Kenny and Adam Burns, it also included manufacturers and coalmen, notably J. W. Allison and David McKeen, a stockbroker, J. C. MacKintosh, and lawyers such as Robert L. Borden and Robert E. Harris.

Until his death in 1904, the personification of the new Halifax finance capitalism was John Stairs. It was Stairs who arranged the organization of Acadia Sugar in 1894, who initiated the merger of the Union bank of Halifax with the Bank of Windsor in 1899, and who led the Halifax business community back into its traditional imperium in the Caribbean with the organization of the Trinidad Electric and Demerara Electric corporations.[95] After 1900, it was Stairs who demonstrated to this same group the possibilities for industrial finance existing within the Maritimes. With the assistance of his young secretary, Max Aitken, and through the medium of his own holding company, Royal Securities, he undertook the reorganization of a number of firms in the region, most notably the Alexander Gibson Railroad and Manufacturing Company which was recapitalized at $6,000,000.[96] The scope of his interests, and the changes which had been wrought in the Maritime business community in the previous twenty-five years, were perhaps best illustrated in the six corporation presidencies which Stairs held in his lifetime, five of them at his death in 1904: Consumers Cordage, Nova Scotia Steel, Eastern Trust, Trinidad Electric, Royal Securities, and Dalhousie University.

Yet, while promotion of firms such as Stanfields Woollens of Truro constituted a fertile field of endeavour,[97] the major industrial interest of the Halifax finance capitalists was the Nova Scotia Steel Company. In its search for additional capital resources after 1900, the entrepreneurial strength of this firm was rapidly broadened from its New Glasgow base. The principal new promoters of the company were Halifaxmen, notably James Allison, George Campbell and Robert Harris. The New Brunswick-born nephew of the founder of Mount Allison University, Allison had entered the chocolate and spice manufactory of John Mott & Company of Halifax in 1871, and had eventually been admitted to a partnership in the firm. He had invested heavily in several Nova Scotia industries and sat on the directorates of Stanfields Woollens, the Eastern Trust, and the Bank of Nova Scotia in addition to Nova Scotia Steel.[98] George Campbell, the son of a Scottish gentleman, had entered the service of a Halifax steamship agency as a young man and ultimately became its head. Like Allison he was deeply involved in a number of Nova Scotian firms including Stanfields, the Silliker Car of Amherst, the Eastern Trust and the Bank of Nova Scotia.[99]

By far the most significant figure in the Nova Scotia Steel Corporation after Stairs' death was Mr. Justice Robert Harris. The Annapolis-born scion of a Loyalist family, Harris shared the same antecedents as the Moncton and Saint John entrepreneurs of the same name. After reading law with Sir John Thompson, he was called to the Nova Scotia bar in 1882 and rapidly became one of the leading legal figures in the province. In 1892 he moved his practice to Halifax and there became intimately involved in the corporate promotions of the period, ultimately serving on the directorates of thirteen major corporations including the Eastern Trust, Eastern Car, Bank of Nova Scotia, Maritime Telegraph and Telephone, Acadia Sugar, Robb Engineering, Brandram-Henderson Paint, and held the presidencies of Nova Scotia Steel, Eastern Trust, Demerara Electric, and Trinidad Electric.[100]

Despite the continuing need for additional capital, the Nova Scotia Steel Company found little difficulty obtaining most of this support from the Halifax business community.[101] In turn, the corporation remained one of the most efficiently organized industrial firms in the country. In striking contrast to the larger Dominion Steel enterprise, Nova Scotia Steel's financial position remained strong, its performance solid and its earnings continuous. It was generally credited with being the only major steel company which could have maintained its dividend payments without the aid of federal bounties.[102]

As the first decade of the twentieth century wore to a close, the Halifax business elite appeared to have succeeded in establishing a financial hegemony in the industrial life of an area centred in eastern Nova Scotia and extending outward into both southern New Brunswick and peninsular Nova Scotia. Yet, increasingly, that hegemony was being challenged by the burgeoning consolidation movement emanating from Montreal. The most serious threat was posed in 1909 when Max Aitken, with Montreal now as the centre for his Royal Securities Corporation, arranged the amalgamation of the Rhodes, Curry Company of Amherst with the Canada Car, and the Dominion Car and Foundry companies of Montreal to form the Canadian Car and Foundry Company. The union marked a triumph as much for Nathaniel Curry as for Aitken—he emerged with the presidency and with nearly $3,000,000 of the $8,500,000 capital stock of the new corporation.[103] The move was a blow to the Halifax capitalists, however, as it placed the largest car manufactory in the country, an Amherst plant employing 1,300 men and annually producing $5,000,000 in iron and steel products,[104] firmly in the Montreal orbit of the Drummonds and the Dominion Steel and Coal Corporation. Tension was heightened by the feeling that this manoeuvre was a prelude to the creation of a railroad car monopoly. The reaction was swift. To prevent the take-over of the other Amherst car works, the Silliker Company, a Halifax-based syndicate bought up most of the Silliker stock and organized a greatly expanded company, Nova Scotia Car Works, with a $2,625,000 capital.[105] The following year Nova Scotia Steel organized its own $2,000,000 car subsidiary, the Eastern Car Company.

The contest between Montreal and Halifax finance capitalism reached its climax at the annual meeting of the Nova Scotia Steel Company of New Glasgow in April, 1910. Fresh from the triumph of the Dominion Coal and Steel merger, Montreal stockbrokers Rudolphe Forget and Max Aitken determined to extend the union to include the smaller steel firm, a proposal which the Scotia Steel president, Robert Harris, flatly refused to consider. Arguing that the firm was stagnating and that a more dynamic leadership in a reorganized corporation would yield greater returns, Forget launched a major effort to acquire proxies with a view to taking control from the Nova Scotia directors. Using the facilities of the Montreal Stock Exchange, he bought large quantities of Scotia stock at increasingly higher prices, an example followed by Robert Harris and his associates at Halifax. At the April meeting, Harris offered Forget a minority of the seats on the directorate; Forget refused. In the voting which followed, the Montreal interests were narrowly beaten. The *Monetary Times,* in a masterpiece of distortion, described this victory as the triumph of "the law ... over the market place,"[106] and proclaimed that "New Glasgow prefers coal dust to that of the stock exchange floor."[107] In fact, it marked a victory, albeit a temporary one, for New Glasgow industrial capitalism and Halifax financial capitalism. More important, it marked the high point of a late-developing effort on the part of the Halifax business community to create an industrial region structured on that Atlantic metropolis. It was a short-lived triumph. By 1920 the Halifax group made common cause with their Montreal and London Counterparts in the organization of the British Empire Steel Corporation, a gigantic consolidation containing both the Dominion and the Nova Scotia Steel companies. This event marked both the final nationalization of the region's major industrial potential and the failure of its entrepreneurs to maintain control of any significant element in the industrial section of the regional economy.

VI

The Maritimes had entered Canada very much as a foreign colony. As the least integrated part of the Canadian economy, it was the region most dependent upon and most influenced by those policies designated to create an integrated national state. The entrepreneurs of the 1880s were capable men, vividly aware of the problems involved in the transition from an Atlantic to a continental economy. The tragedy of the industrial experiment in the Maritimes was that the transportation lines which linked the region to its new metropolis altered the communal arrangement of the entire area; they did not merely establish a new external frame of reference, they re-cast the entire internal structure. The Maritimes had never been a single integrated organic unit; it was, in fact, not a "region" at all, but a number of British communities clustered on the Atlantic fringe, each with its separate lines of communication and its several metropolises—lines that were water-borne, flexible and changing. In this sense the railroad with its implications of organic unity, its inflexibility, and its assumption that there was a metropolitan point at which it could end, provided an experience entirely alien to the Maritime tradition. The magnitude of this problem was demonstrated in the initial attempts at industrialization; they all occurred in traditional communities ideally located for the Atlantic market, but in the most disadvantaged positions possible for a continental one.

Central to the experience was the failure of a viable regional metropolis to arise to provide the financial leadership and market alternative. With its powerful mercantile interests and its impressive banking institutions Halifax could most easily have adopted to this role, but its merchants preferred, like their Boston counterparts, to invest their large fortunes in banks and American railroad stocks than to venture them on building a new order. Only later, with the advent of regional resource industries, did that city play the role of financial metropolis.

Lacking any strong regional economic centre, the Maritime entrepreneur inevitably sought political solutions to the structural problems created by the National Policy; he consistently looked to the federal government for aid against all external threats and to his local governments for aid against Canadians. Since the regional politician was more able to influence a hostile environment than was the regional businessman, the latter frequently became both. In many respects the National Policy simply represented to the entrepreneur a transfer from a British to a Canadian commercial empire. Inherent in most of his activities was the colonial assumption that he could not really control his own destiny, that, of necessity, he would be manipulated by forces beyond his control. Thus he produced cotton cloth for the central Canadian metropolis in precisely the same manner as he had produced timber and ships for the British. In so doing he demonstrated considerable initiative and considerable courage, for the truly surprising aspect of the whole performance was that he was able, using his limited community resources, to produce such a complex and diversified industrial potential during the last two decades of the nineteenth century. The inability of the Canadian market to consume his output was as much a failure of the system as of the entrepreneur; the spectacle of a metropolis which devoured its own children had been alien to the Maritime colonial experience. Ultimately, perhaps inevitably, the regional entrepreneur lost control to external forces which he could rarely comprehend, much less master.

Notes

1. Nova Scotia's industrial output increased 66 percent between 1880 and 1890; that of Ontario and Quebec by 51 percent each. Canada, *Census* (1901), III, pp. 272, 283. Bertram estimates that the per capita value of Nova Scotia's industrial output rose from 57.8 percent to 68.9 percent of the national average during the period. Gordon Bertram, "Historical Statistics on Growth and Structure of Manufacturing in Canada 1870–1957," Canadian Political Science Association Conference on Statistics 1962 and 1963, *Report,* p. 122.

2. Canada, *Census* (1901), III, pp. 326–9. The increase between 1880 and 1890 was as follows:

	Saint John	Hamilton
Population	–3%	34%
Industrial Capital	125%	69%
Industrial Workers	118%	48%
Average Annual Wage	12%	2%
Value of Output	98%	71%

3. See Table I.

4. For a sampling of business opinion on the National Policy see K. P. Burn's reply to Peter Mitchell in the tariff debate of 1883, Canada, House of Commons, *Debates,* 1883, pp. 551–2; the opinion of Josiah Wood, *ibid.,* pp. 446–8; and the view of John F. Stairs, *ibid.,* 1885, pp. 641–9.

5. Quoted by J. F. Stairs in the tariff debate of 1886, Canada, House of Commons, *Debates,* 1886, p. 775.

6. *Monetary Times,* 4 June, 6 September 1886. Forty-five of the fifty savings banks in the Dominion were located in the Maritimes.

7. *Monetary Times,* 16 May 1879.

8. *Monetary Times,* 20 May 1881.

9. George M. Rose, ed., *Cyclopedia of Canadian Biography* (Toronto, 1886–8), II, pp. 729–31 (henceforth cited as *CCB*).

10. *Encyclopedia of Canadian Biography* (Montreal, 1904–7), I. p. 86: *CCB,* II, p. 155; W. J. Stairs. *History of Stairs Morrow* (Halifax, 1906), pp. 5–6.

11. *Canadian Biographical Dictionary* (Montreal, 1880–1), II, pp. 684–5 (henceforth cited as *CBD*); Parks Family Papers, F, no. 1. New Brunswick Museum.

12. *CBD,* II, pp. 684–5: *Monetary Times,* 27 April 1883, 22 June 1888.

13. *CCB,* II, pp. 186–7, 86.

14. *CCB,* II, pp. 354–5; *CBD,* II, p. 693: Henry J. Morgan, ed., *Canadian Men and Women of the Time* (Toronto, 1898), p. 1000.

15. *Monetary Times,* 16 December 1882.

16. *CCB,* II, pp. 221–2; *CBD,* II, pp. 674–5; Harold Davis, *An International Community on the St. Croix (1604–1930)* (Orono, 1950), chapter 18: *Monetary Times,* 1 August 1890.

17. Canada, *Sessional Papers,* 1885, no. 37, pp. 174–97.

18. *Monetary Times,* 11 December 1885; *Canadian Journal of Commerce,* 3 June 1881; *CBD,* II, pp. 409–10, 510; *Canadian Men and Women of the Time* (1898), p. 44.

19. *Canadian Journal of Commerce,* 10 June 1881.

20. W. J. A. Donald. *The Canadian Iron and Steel Industry* (Boston, 1915), chapter 3.

21. *Monetary Times,* 28 April 1882.

22. *The Canadian Manufacturer and Industrial World.* 3 May 1889 (henceforth cited as *Canadian Manufacturer*).

23. Henry J. Morgan, ed., *Canadian Men and Women of the Time* (Toronto, 1912), p. 419; C. W. Parker, ed., *Who's Who and Why* (Vancouver, 1916), VI & VII, p. 259 (hereafter cited as *WWW*).

24. *Canadian Manufacturer,* 1 April 1892.

25. *Ibid.,* 7 March 1890.

26. *CBD,* II, pp. 534–5.

27. A. G. Bailey, "The Basis and Persistence of Opposition to Confederation in New Brunswick." *Canadian Historical Review,* XXIII (1942), p. 394.

28. *Monetary Times,* 9 January 1885.

29. *Ibid.,* 11 May 1883.

30. *Our Dominion, Historical and Other Sketches of the Mercantile Interests of Fredericton. Marysville, Woodstock, Moncton, Yarmouth, etc.* (Toronto, 1889), pp. 48–54.

31. Canada, *Sessional Papers,* 1885, no. 37, pp. 174–97.

32. Canada, Royal Commission on the Relations of Labour and Capital (1889), *Evidence,* II, p. 448.

33. American industrial leaders of the same period averaged 45 years. See W. F. Gregory and I. D. New. "The American Industrial Elite in the 1870s: Their Social Origins", in William Miller, ed., *Men in Business* (Cambridge, 1952), p. 197.

34. Canada, Royal Commission of the Relations of Labour and Capital, *Evidence,* II, pp. 256, 458 and III, pp. 78, 238, 249; *Canadian Manufacturer,* 24 August 1883; *Monetary Times,* 17 June 1887.

35. *Monetary Times,* 18 March 1881.

36. *Ibid.,* 17 February 1882.

37. *Ibid.,* 19 March 1886.

38. *Canadian Journal of Commerce,* 26 October 1883.

39. *Monetary Times,* 18 October 1880.

40. *Ibid.,* 10 May 1905.

41. *Ibid.,* 8 January 1886.

42. *Monetary Times,* 30 January 1885. Principal Maritime imports from Central Canada included flour, shoes, clothing, textiles, alcoholic beverages and hardware; exports to Quebec and Ontario centred on sugar, coal, cotton cloth, iron and fish.

43. Exports of New Brunswick lumber declined from 404,000,000 board feet in 1883 to 250,000,000 feet in 1887, *Monetary Times,* 9 January 1885, 2 and 7 January 1887, 21 January 1898.

44. See particularly, *Proceedings of the Ninth Annual Meeting* of the Dominion Board of Trade (1879), pp. 65–73: *Monetary Times,* 27 January 1882; Minute Book of the Saint John Board of Trade (1879–87), 14 October 1887, New Brunswick Museum.

45. Canada, *Sessional Papers,* 1885, no. 34, pp. 86–125.

46. Bertram, p. 131.

47. J. F. Stairs to J. M. Pope, 10 September 1885, Macdonald Papers, 50080–5, Public Archives of Canada.

48. J. F. Stairs to Macdonald, 5 February 1886, *ibid.,* volume 155.

49. *Monetary Times,* 5 October 1888.

50. *Ibid.,* 12 February 1886.

51. See the problems faced by John Parks and the N. B. Cotton Mills, Parks Family Papers, F. New Brunswick Museum.

52. Montreal *Herald,* 15 October 1883.

53. *Monetary Times,* 8 October 1880.

54. *Ibid.,* 15 December 1882.

55. *Ibid.,* 8 June 1883.

56. *Ibid.,* 16 November 1884.

57. *Ibid.,* 13 August 1886; *Canadian Manufacturer,* 20 August 1887.

58. *Canadian Journal of Commerce,* 7 September 1888.

59. Thomas Kenny in Canada, House of Commons, *Debates,* 1893. p. 2522.

60. *Monetary Times,* 16 January 1891.

61. Saint John *Globe,* 1 May 1891.

62. E. S. Clouston to Jones, 25 April 1891. Bank of Montreal, General Managers Letterbooks, vol. 8. Public Archives of Canada.

63. 15 December 1890, Parks Papers, Scrapbook 2, New Brunswick Museum.

64. Clouston to Jones, 13, 22 April, 23 May 1891. Bank of Montreal, General Managers Letterbooks, vol. 8, Public Archives of Canada.

65. Saint John *Sun,* 28 December 1892.

66. *Monetary Times,* 18 March 1892.

67. *Ibid.,* 24 October 1890.

68. *Canadian Journal of Commerce,* 22 March 1895.

69. *Monetary Times,* 24 October 1890.

70. *Ibid.,* 12 June 1885, 22 April 1887, 22 August 1902; Minutes of the St. John Board of Trade 1 December 1879, 8 November 1886, New Brunswick Museum.

71. *Monetary Times,* 20 May 1887.

72. *The Canadian Journal of Commerce,* 29 April 1887.

73. Canada, Statutes, 50–1 Victoria C. 39.

74. Simon J. MacLean, *The Tariff History of Canada* (Toronto, 1895), p. 37.

75. *Nova Scotia's Industrial Centre: New Glasgow, Stellarton, Westville, Trenton. The Birthplace of Steel in Canada* (n.p., 1916), pp. 45–6.

76. *Monetary Times,* 9 March 1900; *Industrial Canada,* 20 July 1901.

77. *WWW, VI & VII,* pp. 927, 1075–6.

78. R. M. Guy, "Industrial Development and Urbanization of Pictou Co., N. S. to 1900" (unpublished M.A. thesis, Acadia University, 1962). pp. 120–3.

79. *Canadian Manufacturer,* 20 April 1894.

80. *Monetary Times,* 30 June 1893.

81. *Industrial Canada,* March, 1910; *Canadian Men and Women of the Time* (1912), p. 290.

82. *CCB,* II, p. 183; *CBD,* II, pp. 506–7; *WWW,* VI & VII, p. 997; *Canadian Men and Women of the Time* (1912), p. 947.

83. *Monetary Times,* 26 November 1896. The St. Lawrence ports imported 88,000 tons of British and American coal in 1896, and 706,000 tons of Nova Scotia coal. The transport of this commodity provided the basis for the Nova Scotia merchant marine of the period.

84. *Ibid.,* 3 February 1893.

85. *Canadian Men and Women of the Time* (1912), pp. 698–9; *WWW,* VI & VII, p. 1118.

86. *WWW,* VI & VII, p. 1322.

87. Donald, however, argues that Whitney had been determined to go into steel production even if no bounty had been granted. See Donald, *The Canadian Iron and Steel Industry,* p. 203.

88. Partly, the *Canadian Journal of Commerce* (15 March 1901) suggested, on the promise of the promoters that the Company would receive bonuses of $8,000,000 in its first six years of operation.

89. *Industrial Canada,* May, 1902.

90. J. H. Plummer to B. E. Walker, 3 December 1903. Walker Papers, University of Toronto Archives.

91. *Annual Financial Review,* I (1901), p. 92; III (1903), pp. 158–160.

92. *Monetary Times,* 3 August 1907.

93. *Ibid.,* 17 April 1903.

94. *Ibid.,* 23 February 1894.

95. *Annual Financial Review,* XXIII (1923), pp. 682, 736.

96. *Monetary Times,* 5 December 1902.

97. *Ibid.,* 22 April 1911.

98. *Canadian Men and Women of the Time* (1912), p. 19; *WWW,* VI & VII, p. 762; *Annual Financial Review,* III (1903), pp. 174–6.

99. *Canadian Men and Women of the Time* (1912), p. 192; *WWW,* VI & VII, p. 803.

100. *Canadian Men and Women of the Time* (1912), p. 505; *WWW,* VI & VII, p. 1107; *Annual Financial Review,* III (1903), pp. 174–6.

101. Most of the stock in this concern was held by Nova Scotians who also bought up two-thirds of the $1,500,000 bond which the company put out in 1904. L. M. Jones to B. E. Walker, 5 August 1904, Walker Papers; *Monetary Times,* 15 August 1902.

102. *Monetary Times,* 9 March 1907.

103. *Ibid.,* 8 January 1910.

104. *Industrial Canada,* August, 1913.

105. *Monetary Times,* 29 October 1910.

106. *Ibid.,* 2 April 1910.

107. *Ibid.,* 9 April 1910.

MARITIME INDUSTRIALIZATION FROM 1870 TO 1910: A REVIEW OF THE EVIDENCE AND ITS INTERPRETATION

Kris E. Inwood

Regional differences in Canadian manufacturing have attracted a good deal of attention in a literature dominated by two conceptual perspectives. The "staple" theory popular during the middle decades of this century recognizes the influence of location, resource and technology on the growth of manufacturing. "Structuralism," which became influential during the 1970s and 1980s, associates Maritime development with a loss of local control over political and economic decision-making. Still missing from the discussion is a careful documentation of the nature and extent of provincial manufacturing differences before the First World War.

This paper presents census data describing early industrial progress in Eastern Canada. A brief consideration of this information sharpens our understanding of the terrain contested by staple and structuralist interpretations. It is clear that important differences existed between Central Canadian and Maritime industry, between New Brunswick and Nova Scotia, and among the various industries. The degree of heterogeneity suggests that no single explanation is likely to account for all facets of the regional industrial experience. The second part of the paper argues that the data do not inspire confidence in the new orthodoxy of structuralism and that themes broadly consistent with a staple approach invite further consideration. Elements from both analytic traditions are likely to figure in an improved explanation for arrested industrialization in Canada's eastern periphery.[1]

It is useful to begin with a recognition that industrial production in any society inevitably reflects the local pattern of settlement. In the nineteenth century New Brunswick and Nova Scotia were thinly settled even by Canadian standards. Only 8 per cent of Maritimers lived in census districts with a population density exceeding 25 persons per square mile in 1851, against 53 per cent in Quebec and 75 per cent in Ontario.[2] In 1881 the population density of settled areas in the Maritimes was one-third that in Quebec and Ontario.[3] By 1891, only 20 per cent of the Maritime population lived in urban areas against 29 per cent in Quebec and 35 per cent in Ontario.[4]

The rural nature of society undoubtedly contributed to the less centralized pattern of production in the Maritimes. The available evidence for cloth and dairy products reported in Table One confirms that on-farm processing was more important in the Maritime provinces than in Ontario. Although farm households everywhere gradually abandoned manufacturing in order to specialize in agricultural production, this change came more slowly in New Brunswick and Nova Scotia.[5]

From *Acadiensis*, XXI, 1, 1991 (Autumn 1991), 132–155. Reprinted by permission *Acadiensis*.

TABLE 1   The Farm Share (%) of All Processing

	BUTTER AND CHEESE				WOOLENS AND LINENS			
	NS	*NB*	*PQ*	*ONT*	*NS*	*NB*	*PQ*	*ONT*
1870	100	99	98	84	98	98	69	60
1890	62	49	47	17	28	19	27	5

SOURCES: Sources are Canada, *Census, 1870,* volume 3, Tables XXIV, XXXIV and XXXVI and 1891, Tables III and IV; J. Snell, "The Cost of Living in Canada in 1870," *Histoire sociale / Social History* 12 (1979), pp. 186–189; R.H. Coats, *Wholesale Prices in Canada* (Ottawa, 1910), pp. 84–85, 132–34, 136, 290 and 146–47. In 1870 the price of ticking is used for linen, and the price of tweed for woolens. For 1890 Coats supplies the butter and cheese prices; the linen price is obtained by scaling the 1870 price with the DBS textile index J38; and the woolen price is obtained by scaling an 1897 price with Coats' textile index.

NOTE: Unless otherwise noted all data underlying this and the following tables are taken from volume III of the Canadian censuses of 1870–71, 1890–91 and 1910–11. The industry groups are those of the 1948 Standard Industrial Classification used to organize Canada's early national accounts. I have ignored certain industries such as dentistry and painting which were not manufacturing activities in any sense. The consumer, durable and intermediate goods sectors are my own constructions. Output is calculated as value of production less raw materials. All values are in nominal terms; available price indices do not permit satisfactory adjustment for regional price differentials or price change over time. Note that these data do not support a measure of productivity change from 1870 to 1910 because (i) there is no adjustment for price change, (ii) the 1910 data exclude firms with fewer than five employees which were included in 1870, and (iii) capital in 1870 is restricted to fixed capital whereas 1910 encompasses both fixed and working capital. The 1910 data at the level of individual industries reflect the suppression of information by census authorities concerned with preserving confidentiality in districts where fewer than three firms comprised the entire industry.

A belated arrival of the factory system in the Maritimes parallels important provincial differences within the factory system. The typical industrial establishment in 1870 was smaller in Nova Scotia and New Brunswick than in Ontario (Table Two). Moreover, the size difference increased during the first four decades of Confederation. In Nova Scotia, for example, the average factory was only two-thirds that of one in Ontario in 1870 and one-half in 1910. The average New Brunswick factory was 10 per cent smaller in 1870 and 60 per cent smaller in 1910. There were exceptions; several industry groups in 1870 New Brunswick exceeded their Ontario counterparts in size. On average, however, Maritime factories were relatively small in 1870 and even smaller in 1910 particularly in the consumer goods sector.

Maritime mills and shops also tended to be less efficient. New Brunswick and Nova Scotia labour productivity averaged only three-quarters of the Ontario level in 1870 (Table Three). By 1910 relative labour productivity in Nova Scotia had changed little while in New Brunswick it had declined dramatically. Capital productivity in Nova Scotia was four-fifths of the Ontario level in 1870 and even lower in 1900 (Table Four). Capital productivity in New Brunswick, by

TABLE 2   Average Output of Industrial Establishments (relative to Ontario)

	1870			1910		
	NS	*NB*	*PQ*	*NS*	*NB*	*PQ*
all firms	0.65	0.90	0.94	0.51	0.41	0.72
consumer goods	0.71	0.75	1.19	0.26	0.21	0.54
durable goods	0.65	0.78	0.81	0.34	0.56	1.21
intermediate goods	0.66	1.07	0.84	0.80	0.65	0.96
chemical products	0.47	2.30	1.61	0.52	0.20	1.32
clothing	0.88	1.54	1.51	0.41	0.27	1.22
coal & petroleum products	0.97	0.29	0.91	0.65	0.91	0.69
electrical goods	na	na	na	na	na	1.79
food & beverages	0.51	0.43	1.08	0.25	0.19	0.19
iron & steel products	0.48	0.80	0.71	0.74	0.58	0.80
leather & fur products	0.92	0.99	1.95	0.63	0.72	1.09
nonferric metal products	0.92	1.20	2.38	0.29	0.15	1.14
nonmetallic mineral products	2.19	1.59	1.51	0.54	0.52	1.17
printing	1.16	0.72	1.32	0.36	0.48	1.02
paper products	0.23	0.98	1.74	na	0.21	3.11
rubber goods	na	na	10.49	0.01	na	0.20
transport equipment	1.14	1.17	1.38	0.22	0.72	2.13
tobacco products	4.94	0.51	4.78	0.16	na	2.06
textiles	0.23	0.41	0.35	1.05	2.31	3.36
wood products	0.47	0.95	0.62	0.35	0.72	0.67

contrast, was comparable to that in Ontario throughout the period. The productivity gap tended to be smaller for capital because Maritime firms were more efficient in using capital than labour. Maritime productivity was weakest in the consumer goods industries which in 1910 experienced capital and labour productivity less than half that in Ontario.

Because regions differed in their capital/labour ratio, a comparison of efficiency requires the combination of labour and capital in an index of total factor productivity (TFP) reported in Table Five. In 1870 Nova Scotia industry appears to have been seriously inefficient while the productivity handicap of Quebec and New Brunswick was modest. Indeed, certain industry groups in New Brunswick rivalled or bettered Ontario efficiency; these tended to be the same industry groups in which the average size of establishment exceeded that in Ontario (chemicals, clothing, non-ferric metals, paper and transportation equipment).

The relative position of efficiency among the various provinces changed during the following decades. By 1910 Quebec had caught up with Ontario in terms of relative provincial efficiency. Maritime chemicals, coal, transportation

TABLE 3   **Labour Productivity ($ value added/worker), 1870 and 1910**

	1870				1910			
	NS	NB	PQ	ONT	NS	NB	PQ	ONT
all firms	419	432	487	574	925	683	1053	1182
consumer goods	490	408	503	572	570	535	1014	1292
durable goods	437	468	463	558	831	908	1063	1056
intermediate goods	363	424	487	591	1102	700	1087	1182
chemical products	569	1496	1403	986	654	765	1437	1739
clothing	368	333	430	350	644	597	809	779
coal & petrol products	2196	1018	1472	3226	3662	2279	3789	2962
electrical goods	na	na	na	na	na	na	1704	1156
food & bev	589	479	1092	1443	498	441	1110	1980
iron & steel products	447	561	504	598	1039	1011	1230	1177
leather & fur products	513	488	523	497	981	1119	985	1427
nonferric metal products	550	769	524	631	946	492	842	1112
nonmetallic min. products	397	307	407	326	662	555	1127	1153
printing	755	591	553	641	878	862	1001	1073
paper products	609	774	646	730	na	474	1178	1017
rubber goods	na	na	285	2250	237	na	1512	2125
transport equipment	462	487	403	559	859	988	876	983
tobacco products	727	205	647	380	1024	na	1351	1523
textiles	371	434	487	486	611	670	938	812
wood products	274	373	368	429	629	590	730	932

equipment (New Brunswick) and non-ferric metals (Nova Scotia) were relatively efficient in 1910 although production was small. On the other hand, inefficiency in the large wood and food processing sectors contributed to an overall level of total factor productivity only three-quarters of the level in Ontario and Quebec. The first forty years of Confederation apparently produced the unhappy result that New Brunswick factories fell to a level of relative inefficiency experienced by Nova Scotia in 1870, and that Nova Scotia unlike Quebec failed to improve its relative position.

TABLE 4   Capital Productivity ($ value added/$ capital), 1870 and 1910

	1870				*1910*			
	NS	*NB*	*PQ*	*ONT*	*NS*	*NB*	*PQ*	*ONT*
all firms	1.08	1.32	1.15	1.31	0.33	0.47	0.51	0.47
consumer goods	1.56	2.55	1.48	1.65	0.50	0.73	0.52	0.67
durable goods	1.67	2.34	1.37	1.66	0.42	1.06	0.78	0.46
intermediate goods	0.67	0.95	0.88	0.96	0.30	0.37	0.41	0.36
chemical products	0.71	1.25	0.91	1.07	1.01	1.11	0.51	0.46
clothing	1.69	5.00	1.41	2.18	0.44	1.50	1.06	0.89
coal & petroleum products	0.24	0.14	0.25	1.18	0.20	0.27	0.11	0.15
electrical goods	na	na	na	na	na	na	0.71	0.39
food & beverages	0.79	0.87	0.77	1.15	0.53	0.65	0.45	0.67
iron & steel products	1.07	1.66	1.34	1.66	0.55	0.55	0.57	0.38
leather & fur products	1.61	1.85	2.07	2.00	0.60	0.63	0.57	0.58
nonferric metal products	1.13	2.35	0.92	1.54	1.32	0.59	0.45	0.50
nonmetallic mineral products	0.55	1.22	2.00	2.42	0.30	0.73	0.59	0.65
printing	1.09	1.37	0.77	1.24	0.47	0.67	0.43	0.59
paper products	0.70	1.46	1.06	0.70	na	0.49	0.34	0.45
rubber goods	na	na	0.31	7.50	0.99	na	1.23	0.65
transport equipment	2.39	3.35	1.24	1.64	0.29	4.16	1.17	0.61
tobacco products	3.58	4.76	1.95	2.15	2.16	na	0.48	1.14
textiles	0.61	0.71	0.78	0.75	0.23	0.29	0.39	0.35
wood products	0.88	1.07	1.09	1.04	0.56	0.37	0.39	0.46

Low labour productivity typically brings with it low wages. For this reason we are not surprised to learn that the average factory worker in 1870 earned 14 per cent and 17 per cent less in New Brunswick and Nova Scotia than in Ontario. By 1910 these differences had jumped to 32 per cent and 25 per cent.[6] There are obvious difficulties with these data because of possible variation in the cost of living, payments in kind, composition of workforce, length of working week and occupational pluralism. Nevertheless, the general pattern is confirmed by information about mill hands and general labourers gathered by immigration agents in 1890 and by Department of Labour information on carpenters, electricians, plumbers and labourers (1901), female cotton spinners (1911) and pulp grinders (1913).[7]

TABLE 5   Total Factor Productivity Relative to Ontario, 1870 and 1910

	Relative TFP 1870			Relative TFP 1910		
	NS	NB	PQ	NS	NB	PQ
all firms	0.78	0.88	0.86	0.74	0.77	0.99
consumer goods	0.90	1.09	0.89	0.59	0.71	0.78
durable goods	0.87	1.05	0.83	0.83	1.27	1.23
intermediate goods	0.66	0.86	0.88	0.88	0.77	1.02
chemical products	0.61	1.35	1.13	1.14	1.28	0.99
clothing	0.90	1.50	0.88	0.68	1.04	1.09
coal & petroleum products	0.25	0.14	0.24	1.30	1.41	0.86
electrical goods	na	na	na	na	na	1.55
food & beverages	0.61	0.62	0.69	0.57	0.64	0.64
iron & steel products	0.70	0.97	0.83	1.09	1.09	1.03
leather & fur products	0.91	0.95	1.04	0.86	0.94	0.84
nonferric metal products	0.81	1.35	0.72	1.61	0.77	0.83
nonmetallic mineral products	0.56	0.70	1.03	0.51	0.77	0.94
printing	1.04	0.99	0.75	0.81	0.91	0.86
paper products	0.92	1.55	1.19	na	0.71	0.94
rubber goods	na	na	0.07	0.67	na	1.39
transport equipment	1.06	1.26	0.74	0.71	1.93	1.16
tobacco products	1.86	0.70	1.52	0.88	na	0.73
textiles	0.79	0.92	1.02	0.70	0.83	1.13
wood products	0.73	0.94	0.95	0.88	0.71	0.81

NOTE: Total factor productivity (TFP) is a weighted average of labour and capital productivity. I define relative TFP as labour productivity in one province relative to that in Ontario and raised to the power of the labour share of factor costs, multiplied by capital productivity in one province relative to that in Ontario and raised to the power of the capital share of factor costs; see W.E. Diewert, "Exact and Superlative Index Numbers," *Journal of Econometrics,* 4 (May 1976), pp. 115–145. Factor costs are computed as total value of production less raw material costs and imputed miscellaneous costs. The latter are assumed to be the same ratio to total product for each industry group in 1870 and 1910 as they were in 1900, in which year the census report on manufacturing was particularly detailed. Shares are calculated by industry group. The labour share derives from reported wages and salaries; the capital share is a residual derived from total factor costs less labour. The residual capital share may be overestimated because miscellaneous costs are likely to be underestimated. This would imply a bias to portray Maritime factories as being more efficient than they actually were, since Maritime factories tended to make more productive use of capital than labour. I follow the published census in using fixed capital in 1870 and both fixed and working capital in 1910.

TABLE 6   Estimated Profitability in Manufacturing

	NS	NB	PQ	ONT
1870				
production	12338	17368	77205	114707
return to capital	1881	2589	14153	18735
capital	11159	9439	56813	81725
profitability	0.17	0.27	0.25	0.23
1890				
production	30968	23850	147460	239242
return to capital	4569	3018	17111	40002
capital	19823	15823	118292	175972
profitability	0.23	0.19	0.14	0.23
1910				
production	52706	35422	350902	579810
return to capital	9020	5179	57709	109784
capital	79596	36125	326947	595395
profitability	0.11	0.14	0.18	0.18

NOTE: Profitability is estimated as the ratio of profit (the value of production less labour, material, depreciation and miscellaneous costs) to capital invested. All values are reported by the census except depreciation which is calculated at 10 per cent of physical capital, miscellaneous costs which are taken to be same share of product value in 1870 and 1910 as they had been in 1900, 1870 working capital which is taken to be the same share of total capital as in 1890 and salaries are imputed in 1870 and 1890 in the same proportion to wages as they were reported in 1910. This method of estimating profitability is described in more detail elsewhere; see F. Bateman and T. Weiss, *A Deplorable Scarcity: The Failure of Industrialization in the Slave Economy* (Chapel Hill, 1981), Appendix C.

It appears that Maritime workers worked for relatively low wages before the First World War and perhaps as early as 1870.[8] But what about their employers? Did investments in manufacturing pay as well in the Maritimes as they did in Ontario? The estimates of profitability reported in Table Six indicate a steady decline in the rate of profit in New Brunswick from 1870 to 1910, absolutely and relative to Ontario and Quebec. Manufacturing in Nova Scotia follows a more interesting pattern; profitability was low in 1870 but it had largely recovered by 1890 after a decade of National Policy expansion. Between 1890 and 1910, however, the rate of profit in Nova Scotia as in New Brunswick fell absolutely and relative to both Central Canadian provinces.

The data describing factory size, efficiency and profitability suggest a pattern in which *intra*-regional differences diminished while *inter*-regional differences became more pronounced between 1870 and 1910. The indicators for New Brunswick in 1870 are not unlike those for Central Canada while Nova

Scotia industry was noticeably less robust. Nevertheless, Nova Scotia did relatively well during the following forty years in contrast to the disastrous experience of New Brunswick industry. By 1910 the two provinces had converged toward the pattern of industrial weakness familiar in the twentieth century.

Provincial differences in the level and growth of output reported in Tables Seven, Eight and Nine follow a similar pattern.[9] New Brunswick's level of manufacturing activity was within ten per cent of Ontario's in 1870 (Table Nine) but it fell increasingly behind in both subsequent sub-periods (Tables Seven and Eight). By contrast, the Nova Scotia manufacturing sector started out remarkably small but it grew quickly from 1870 to 1890 in the consumer and intermediate goods industries. Even in Nova Scotia, however, consumer goods production decelerated at a tremendous rate after 1890 while durable goods production declined absolutely.

TABLE 7 Percentage Change in Manufacturing Output, 1870–1890

	NS	*NB*	*PQ*	*ONT*
all factories	128	42	104	116
farm production	60	67	50	34
all manufacturing	120	44	101	113
consumer goods	160	95	100	119
durable goods	30	−10	83	61
intermediate goods	214	50	120	162
chemical products	210	03	149	410
clothing	224	49	125	277
coal & petroleum products	164	321	365	−5
electrical goods	na	na	na	na
food & beverages	361	292	122	82
iron & steel products	142	21	92	90
leather & fur products	−1	−12	50	41
nonferric metal products	348	204	191	854
nonmetallic mineral products	114	121	186	215
printing	54	111	86	177
paper products	48	−52	313	254
rubber goods	na	na	202	4311
transport equipment	3	−38	154	26
tobacco products	−78	64	162	265
textiles	505	443	406	150
wood products	213	21	64	143

NOTE: Farm output includes butter, cheese and cloth only. I have adjusted the 1870 data for missing data on railway workshops; see P. Craven and T. Traves, "Canadian Railways as Manufacturers, 1850–1880," *Communications historiques / Historical Papers* (1983), pp. 254–281. In order to make the adjustment I assume that the capital/labour ratio was the same for unreported as for reported firms and that labour productivity in the Great Western's Hamilton shop was identical with that of the Grand Trunk in its Brantford shop.

TABLE 8   Percentage Change in Output of Factories Employing Five or More Workers, 1890–1910

	NS	*NB*	*PQ*	*ONT*
factories with more than 5 employees	129	78	187	214
consumer goods	26	48	184	277
durable goods	-4	68	214	260
intermediate goods	248	92	171	142
chemical products	−11	−71	227	319
clothing	−45	26	237	165
coal & petroleum products	224	377	139	615
electrical goods	−100	na	2435	1288
food & beverages	16	39	64	228
iron & steel products	101	65	132	279
leather & fur products	47	86	103	315
nonferric metal products	6	−65	173	373
nonmetallic mineral products	−56	−19	33	196
printing	99	73	163	193
paper products	−100	150	478	309
rubber goods	na	na	18	1332
transport equipment	−33	172	162	340
tobacco products	−7	−100	315	351
textiles	−2	29	202	30
wood products	38	72	134	93

SOURCE: K. Inwood and J. Chamard, "Regional Industrial Growth in the 1890s: The Case of the Missing Artisans," *Acadiensis,* XVI, 1 (Autumn 1986), pp. 101–117.

One point of similarity between New Brunswick and Nova Scotia was the slow growth of durable goods production. Over the entire four decades durable goods output eked out an increase of 25 per cent in Nova Scotia and 50 per cent in New Brunswick; in contrast durable goods output quadrupled in Quebec and Ontario. Overall, Ontario increased its strength in consumer goods and durable goods while the Maritimes tended to specialize in intermediate goods industries. These tendencies were so pronounced that by 1910 Maritime output per capita of consumer and durable goods was less than one-quarter that in Ontario.

Perhaps the most important regional contrast is that Maritime manufacturing expanded with equal vigour in the two sub-periods (1870–1890 and 1890–1910) whereas Ontario and Quebec manufacturing expanded much more quickly in the second interval. Most scholars attribute the acceleration in Canadian economic growth to the effect of the wheat boom, a dramatic quickening in the pace of Prairie settlement during the 1890s.[10] One popular view is that the wheat boom influenced the pace of extensive growth but did not bring structural change

**TABLE 9   Per Capita Manufacturing Output ($),
1870 and 1910**

	1870				1910			
	NS	NB	PQ	ONT	NS	NB	PQ	ONT
all factories	16.76	27.66	27.48	31.41	54.13	48.04	83.02	111.67
farm production	2.01	2.00	1.93	1.33				
total	18.77	29.66	29.41	32.74				
consumer goods	4.25	5.27	10.31	9.76	9.18	9.67	31.51	43.67
durable goods	6.61	7.56	6.31	10.11	5.40	7.82	19.55	31.30
intermediate goods	5.90	14.83	10.85	11.54	39.54	30.55	31.96	36.69
chemical products	0.19	0.63	0.57	0.22	0.30	0.10	2.30	2.45
clothing	0.83	1.62	2.08	1.98	0.82	1.57	7.41	9.31
coal & petroleum products	0.23	0.12	0.21	1.09	1.52	1.98	1.39	4.24
electrical goods	0.00	0.00	0.00	0.00	0.00	0.00	2.23	1.66
food & beverages	1.34	1.38	3.47	6.32	5.88	5.44	6.58	21.03
iron & steel products	2.47	3.90	3.63	5.72	6.52	4.64	7.46	20.90
leather & fur products	2.65	2.88	5.37	2.99	1.29	1.94	8.20	6.06
nonferric metal products	0.12	0.31	0.44	0.19	0.17	0.17	1.52	2.79
nonmetallic mineral products	0.87	0.64	0.85	0.83	0.59	0.89	1.85	4.53
printing	0.51	0.50	0.72	0.89	0.94	1.45	2.01	4.19
paper products	0.01	0.14	0.24	0.16	0.00	0.13	3.46	1.43
rubber goods	0.00	0.00	0.12	0.00	0.04	0.00	0.25	1.06
transport equipment	3.28	3.41	1.80	2.52	1.50	3.93	6.42	6.44
tobacco products	0.49	0.05	0.64	0.17	0.08	0.00	4.12	1.66
textiles	0.36	0.66	0.58	1.40	1.37	3.55	4.87	2.71
wood products	3.41	11.35	6.31	6.79	9.78	18.09	12.77	18.19

in the sense of an industrial recomposition.[11] Nevertheless, the inability of Maritime factories to benefit from the wheat boom created structural change of a different kind involving a locational shift of production within Eastern Canada.

The importance of the wheat boom depends somewhat upon one's choice of conceptual framework. Scholars influenced by the staple perspective view the wheat boom as a prime example of the importance of natural resources and location. Structuralists, on the other hand, have tended to ignore the direct impact of the wheat boom on the Canadian market for manufactures.[12] The structuralist literature combines the tradition of regional economic grievance with the social science ideology of dependency to argue that political and financial control by outsiders undermined regional interests.[13] Although diverse, the literature tends to focus on the loss of local control over public policy and private enterprise following Confederation, which is viewed as a "critical turning point" for the region.[14]

Evidence supporting or contradicting the 'turning point' hypothesis is elusive since the first good census in British North America was not undertaken until three years after the alleged turning point. Nevertheless, there is some evidence that the manufacturing lag antedates Confederation; Inwood and Chamard have reported that Maritime industrial employment lagged in six large industries during the 1850s and 1860s even after adjusting for differing provincial rates of population growth.[15]

Confidence in the turning point hypothesis is further undermined by evidence reported above that as early as 1870 Maritime factories were small, unproductive in their use of capital and labour, paid low wages and, at least in Nova Scotia, relatively unprofitable. New Brunswick manufacturing was more robust in 1870 but even its per capita output was noticeably less than that in Ontario.

Obviously, the political union cannot be blamed for something which preceded it. It remains possible, however, that the policies of the new Canadian government may have made matters worse than they otherwise would have been. According to this line of argument, an inward-looking or continentalist Central Canada dominated the political union and established policies unsuitable for an outward-looking Maritime region. But what policies? During the first few years of Confederation the national government spent heavily in the Maritimes in order to construct the Intercolonial Railway. It is difficult to discern a spending bias against the Maritimes in this period, although a careful regional accounting of expenditures by various government departments might alter this judgement.

A more persistent controversy surrounds changes in the tax or tariff on manufactured imports. The tariff acts as a subsidy to manufacturing and hence to any region in which manufacturing predominates or has the potential to grow. The first effect of political union in 1867 was to abolish tariffs on trade between the Maritimes and the Canadas. Although it is at least possible that Maritime factories suffered through a Confederation-related change in protection, any effect along these lines cannot have been large since tariffs were relatively low before and immediately after 1867.[16]

Much has been made of the 1879 shift in Canadian government policy which systematically increased the Canadian tariff on manufactured imports as part of a new "National Policy." Canadian historians commonly assume that tariff changes allowed the domestic price of manufactured goods to rise and that domestic firms substituted their output for imported goods. This view credits the National Policy with responsibility for a manufacturing boom during the early

1880s and perhaps a permanently faster rate of industrial growth. Maritime firms contributed some of the extra output in the short term. It would not be surprising that Maritime interests benefited from the tariff since powerful Maritime politicians dominated the finance ministry during the 1880s and 1890s and gave regional interests a voice in the delicate negotiations over tariff structure. In the longer run, however, increases in domestic production came disproportionately from Central Canada.

Why did Ontario manufacturing come to dominate the tariff-bound Canadian market? One answer might be that Ontario was more industrialized and hence enjoyed the advantages of a more developed industrial infrastructure. Support for this answer is undermined, however, by the evidence of Table Ten that Ontario was no more industrialized than the Maritimes in 1870. Another answer suggested by the structuralist literature is that Canadian manufacturing over-expanded as a short term response to the National Policy tariffs. Subsequent rationalization of capacity provided an opportunity for ownership to concentrate. As part of this process Central Canadians acquired control of Maritime plants and shut them down. The regional economy suffered unfairly in the rationalization because Central Canadian owners trimmed their excess capacity with a regional bias.[17]

This argument comes in two parts—that tariffs were responsible for output growth and that ownership changes caused industry to relocate. The first part suffers from a difficulty that characterizes almost all discussion of the nineteenth century tariff. Economic historians have been remarkably unsuccessful in identifying Canadian industries which were significantly affected

TABLE 10   The Manufacturing Share of Commodity Production

	Inwood-Irwin		Green	
	1870	*1890*	*1890*	*1910*
Nova Scotia	.29	.39	.36	.34
New Brunswick	.37	.46	.35	.42
Quebec	.38	.52	.47	.55
Ontario	.32	.45	.40	.49

SOURCE: Kris Inwood and Jim Irwin, "Inter-regional Differences in Canadian Commodity Output in 1870: Preliminary Estimates," paper presented to the 17th Conference on the Use of Quantitative Methods in Canadian Economic History, October 1990 and Alan Green, *Regional Aspects of Canada's Economic Growth* (Toronto, 1971), Appendix B. The Inwood-Irwin estimates are based on a regional decomposition of M.C. Urquhart's new national income estimates for Canada; see M.C. Urquhart, "New Estimates of Gross National Product, Canada, 1870 to 1926," in S. Engerman and R. Gallman, eds., *Long-Term Factors in American Economic Growth* (Chicago, 1986), pp. 9–88. Green follows an earlier estimating methodology used by O. J. Firestone, *Canada's Economic Development, 1867–1953* (London, 1958).

by the tariff.[18] The fundamental problem is a lack of evidence indicating that the tariff really mattered. Maritime manufacturing provides a useful example here. We might be tempted to credit the tariff with Nova Scotia's fast manufacturing growth from 1870 to 1890. It is equally plausible, however, that Nova Scotia was experiencing a kind of "catch-up" from a low level of activity in 1870 because of improved railway services, because the coal trade was growing so quickly or because 1870 was an unusually bad year for Nova Scotia business. Without a careful study of individual industries, it is difficult to make firm conclusions about the impact of the tariff.[19]

Another line of argument might draw upon the economics of international trade for an analysis of regional welfare effects.[20] Unfortunately, these techniques are of doubtful relevance to our problem since capital and labour were mobile among sectors and regions, factor endowment in 1870 does not appear to have differed markedly between Ontario and the Maritimes, and there is no evidence of sectoral differences in factor proportions. Use of traditional trade analysis is further limited by the common structure shared by Ontario and the Maritimes; both regions exported primary products, imported manufactures and shortly after Confederation had a manufacturing sector accounting for approximately one-third of all commodity production (Table Ten).

The second part of the argument suggests that there may be some connection between ownership change and industrial relocation. This is difficult to sustain in part because we know so little about ownership. No systematic evidence is available to support the presumption of an ownership shift at the end of the nineteenth century. Indeed, evidence of capital outflow and the career patterns of Maritime promoters suggest that local capital may have increased its influence over firms outside the region during the late nineteenth century, rather than the reverse.[21] The presumed shift in ownership might have been linked to an apparent decline in Maritime output during the 1890s, but the linkage would be spurious since the appearance of output decline (relative and absolute) during the 1890s is an artifact created by enumeration changes which introduced a regional bias into census data.[22]

The argument is flawed more fundamentally by its implied portrait of capitalists and capital markets. The pursuit of profit led Canadians in this period to invest in a wide variety of enterprise throughout Canada, in Latin America and Europe.[23] There seems little reason to think that they would have avoided investment in Maritime factories if there had been some reasonable anticipation of profit. But how profitable were these factories? Evidence reported in Table Four suggests that Nova Scotia factories were less profitable in 1870, and that throughout the region relative profitability deteriorated after 1890. It is difficult to resist the conclusion that poor profitability undermined the willingness of Maritime business to borrow at rates acceptable to Ontario business and thereby directed Maritime savings into extra-regional investments.[24] If this is correct, then the well-documented capital outflow simply reflects a dearth of good investment opportunities within the region.

Of course, we might seek to explain the poor profitability in the Maritimes in other ways. Structuralists suggest that the Canadian government increased freight rates on the Intercolonial Railway in 1912 and 1917, and in so doing hurt Maritime manufacturing.[25] Unfortunately, little is known about Intercolonial costs and pricing. By nineteenth-century standards the Intercolonial carried relatively few passengers and less freight. The low density of traffic possibly made it difficult to implement technological advances enjoyed by other North American railways, in which case shipping from Maritime factories to the Ontario market would have been costly.[26] But a dearth of relevant evidence makes it difficult to evaluate the contribution of other influences such as pricing by competing carriers (water and rail) and government policy. Although further research is needed, one point already is clear. The changes alleged to have handicapped Maritime manufacturers came too late to explain a regional lag that originated in the nineteenth century. The 1912 and 1917 policy decisions may have aggravated an already difficult situation for local manufacturing, but they could not have been the sole cause.

The influence of transportation, tariff and other factors is easier to discern for individual industries than for the manufacturing sector as a whole. Advocates of the structuralist perspective have pioneered consideration of an important case study, the steel and coal industry. In this industry Nova Scotia companies participated in a tariff-assisted expansion of Canadian capacity between 1890 and 1910. In the latter year the local owners of a profitable regional firm successfully thwarted a hostile take-over bid by Central Canadian promoters. Ten years later a second take-over bid by British interests was successful. Almost immediately the Nova Scotia steel industry plunged into a disastrous period of contraction and wage reduction. The drain of capital out of the region allegedly was facilitated by the watering of stock during the early 1920s.[27]

The story of Maritime steel and coal has been interpreted as an example of de-industrialization on the periphery resulting from the loss of local control. From this perspective, the regional industry was a casualty in the international concentration and centralization of capital. However, an alternate interpretation of the industry is available. In this view corporate re-organization in the Nova Scotia steel industry was a belated and largely unsuccessful effort to salvage firms already facing bankruptcy.[28] A small scale of operations, diminishing resources and distance to market undermined profits and contributed to a declining share of national output long before the first take-over bid. Capital drain via stock-watering was impossible since there seldom was sufficient profit to pay dividends. The Nova Scotia firms faced much more fundamental problems as mining costs rose in a time of excess capacity worldwide and decreased domestic demand.[29]

International market conditions and a rising cost of extraction would have brought hard times to the Nova Scotia coal fields regardless of ownership and organizational arrangements. It is possible of course that the industry would have adapted more effectively to its difficult circumstances under local ownership. However, this conjecture has not yet been investigated. Careful examination of other industries one day may provide stronger support for the structuralist perspective, but the case will have to be made.

The structuralist failure to account for many aspects of Maritime manufacturing before the First World War redirects attention to the staple theory, an older explanatory tradition emphasizing the adverse effect of resource characteristics and technological developments.[30] Several key developments figure in most staple accounts of Maritime development.[31] Thin soil, a short growing season and lack of a nearby urban market hampered agricultural adjustment in the Maritimes during the nineteenth century.[32] Technological change in ocean shipping undermined local wooden ship-building and shipping industries.[33] The eclipse of cane by beet sugar doomed the West Indies trade.[34] Limited waterpower and hydroelectric potential impeded the diffusion of new industrial technologies,[35] as did the small size of local market. The decline of the fishing industry during the early twentieth century in spite of increased prices suggests either a reduction in accessible stocks or the withdrawal of labour for some other reason.[36] Diminishing returns and rising costs undermined the region's coal and steel industries.[37] The Maritimes had no natural hinterland; a location south of the St. Lawrence River and north of the great east-west rail routes brought little stimulus from the booming trade between the North American interior and Europe.[38] Finally, it is argued that the major primary products in the Maritimes did not sustain as much processing as in Central Canada, either because of the intrinsic characteristics of a product or because it could not be produced locally at a competitive cost.[39]

A systematic evaluation of these arguments is not possible with summary information of the sort available in this paper. Nevertheless, the impact of resource availability is visible in the data reported in Table Nine. New Brunswick's per capita output among wood-using industries was very high in 1870 because of local timber availability, just as Ontario's strength in food and beverage manufacturing reflected that province's excellent supply of farm products. Maritime industrial growth after 1870 was strongest in the Nova Scotia coal belt in part because of a strong demand for coal originating in the substitution of coal and steel in a wide variety of industrial applications.[40] Another development reflected in these data was the replacement of Great Britain by the United States as the source of fuel, machinery and semi-finished iron used by Canadian industries. Manufacturers in Montreal and the Maritimes were favoured as long as these imports originated in Britain. When American supplies displaced the British late in the century southwestern Ontario acquired the locational advantage.[41]

A full evaluation of these suggestions will require precise information about regional price differentials that is not yet available. It is also suggested that resource availability limited the size and population density of the region, which in turn prevented Maritime factories from adopting new technologies requiring a large scale of production. Research using American data permit a preliminary consideration of this point. Jeremy Atack has used census data to identify the scale of production needed to minimize production cost in 1870 American factories.[42] In a wide range of industries the minimum efficient size identified by Atack was considerably larger than the average Maritime factory.[43] This comparison recommends further consideration of the possibility that Maritime factories were inefficient *because* they were small.

Smallness may have handicapped regional transportation systems as well. With the possible exception of coal, regional commodities were not shipped in sufficient volume to support bulk transportation technology of the kind used on the Great Lakes.[44] The geography of the continent made it difficult for Halifax and Saint John to attract the large volume of freight needed to justify the modern material handling equipment or to become a home base for oceanliners.[45] A similar point might be made about land transportation. Railways such as the Intercolonial carried surprisingly small volumes of freight, and this must have made it difficult to reduce costs using the new railway technology of large cars and long trains.[46]

Another hypothesis entertained by staple theorists is that the small size and slow growth of primary sector income undermined the local demand for manufactures and hence the growth of industry. Census-based estimates confirm that farm family income was lower in the Maritimes; this affected the demand for manufactures in a variety of ways.[47] Limited income-earning opportunities in the primary sector undoubtedly spurred out-migration by young Maritime men and women. The local demand for durable goods would have been stronger if the level of primary production had supported greater capital formation in primary production and transportation. Moreover, income earned by rural families was an important potential market for factory-made consumer goods.[48]

The various links between the primary sector and industrial demand complement input price and scale considerations in the analysis of slow Maritime industrial growth beginning in the pre-Confederation era. By 1870 New Brunswick was relatively industrialized but, as we have seen, its manufacturing grew slowly in subsequent decades. Nova Scotia industry was quite anaemic in 1870 but it expanded quickly during the following twenty years. Neither Maritime province was able to match the dramatic acceleration experienced elsewhere in Canada after 1890. The pattern of growth presumably reflected the distinctive characteristics of Maritime industry. By and large factories were smaller and operated at a lower capital-labour ratio in the Maritimes. Household production survived much later. Factor productivity and wages were lower. Relative profitability also declined in New Brunswick between 1870 and 1910 and in Nova Scotia between 1890 and 1910.

These distinctive characteristics of Maritime manufacturing became more pronounced between 1870 and 1910. Their early visibility in 1870, however, adds to the evidence of slow pre-Confederation growth and undermines the idea that Confederation marked a major turning point in regional development. Indeed, a more significant turning point may have been the onset of the wheat boom during the late 1890s. Maritime manufacturing continued to grow at a steady pace during this period but in so doing it missed out on the biggest boom in Canadian history.

The staple theory provides a simple locational explanation for the Maritime failure to capture linkages from western settlement. Among other factors, transportation costs to the west were lower from southern Ontario than from the Maritimes. Structuralists, on the other hand, might cite the influence of Central Canadian control over capital markets, tariffs and transportation. A comprehensive explanation for the salient characteristics of Maritime industrial development is likely to require some consideration of hypotheses drawn from the staple tradition as well as influences associated with political and financial control.

It may be helpful to view Maritime industry in the context of American and British industrialization. European industrial success in the nineteenth century involved the intensive use of craft labour. This model was difficult to adopt in the high-wage North American environment, and especially so in a corner of the continent relatively remote from the larger centres of innovation and fashion. The literature on North American growth, on the other hand, has tended to emphasize the effect of abundant natural resources and an expanding frontier; Gavin Wright argues that natural resources were the key to success even in the manufacturing sector.[49] The American model was difficult to adopt in regions such as the Maritimes with a weak resource endowment. Was there a third alternative, a distinctive Maritime strategy for industrial success? It would seem not, or at any rate if some alternative existed, history has not revealed it to us.

One final question concerns the relative importance of manufacturing within the wider economy. Manufacturing largely was ignored by an earlier generation of Maritime historians working in the staple theory tradition. One important contribution of the structuralist literature has been to correct this imbalance and draw attention to the phenomenon of arrested industrialization east of Montreal. We are now aware that manufacturing evolved along distinctive lines in Canada's thinly settled eastern periphery. Nevertheless, the modern fascination with industrial growth should not lead us to equate industrialization with economic development, or at least not without careful thought. It is not obvious that manufacturing growth is essential for satisfactory social and economic development.[50] Some economies manage to support a growing population at higher and higher incomes through the judicious exploitation of natural resources and the efficient supply of services. Recent discussions of the nineteenth century rural household have reminded us that regional development ultimately depends upon individual and family struggles for survival and betterment.[51] For an individual household, the nearby presence of factory employment provided a useful alternative, but it was not the only option. Income earned in primary production or the service sector was for many families as helpful as the same level of income earned in manufacturing. The manifest ability of Maritime families to survive and in some cases to prosper in the absence of industrialization provides a useful caution to the modern scholarly passion for smokestacks.

Notes

1. In this paper I consider Canada's original four provinces; data are unavailable for other provinces during the early part of the period under consideration. I use "industrialization" in the sense of a rise in manufacturing share of all commodity production. I thank the many people who have influenced the writing of this paper. The most recent draft has benefited from the constructive criticism of Morris Altman, Phyllis Wagg, participants in the Economic History Workshop at the University of Toronto and the editors and referees of this journal. The Social Sciences and Humanities Research Council of Canada funded much of the research on which this paper is based.

2. Canada, *Census, 1931,* vol. 1, Table 6.

3. O. Sitwell and N. Seifried, *The Regional Structure of the Canadian Economy* (Toronto, 1984), p. 46.

4. Bill Marr and Don Paterson, *Canada: An Economic History* (Toronto, 1980), p. 429.

5. Further discussion of regional differences in domestic textile production is provided by Janine Grant and Kris Inwood, "Gender and Organization in the Canadian Cloth Industry," *Canadian Papers in Business and Economic History,* 1 (1989), pp. 17–32.

6. Canada, *Census, 1870–71,* vol. 3, Table LIV and *Census, 1911,* vol. 3, Table I. Here I divide the total wage bill by the number of workers to obtain a measure of average labour earnings.

7. M.C. Urquhart and K.A.H. Buckley, *Historical Statistics of Canada* (Toronto, 1965), D40–43, D48–51, D90, D96, D117, D127, D204–205 and D206–207. Here the information is a wage per worker per unit of time.

8. Phillip Wood reads the evidence differently; see his "Barriers to Capitalist Development in Maritime Canada, 1870–1930: A Comparative Perspective," *Canadian Papers in Business History,* 1 (1989), pp. 33–58 and "Marxism and the Maritimes: On the Determinants of Region: Capitalist Development," *Studies in Political Economy,* 29 (Summer 1989), pp. 123–53.

9. Growth is examined from 1870 to 1890 and from 1890 to 1910 because the Canadian census changed its basis of enumeration after 1890; see Kris Inwood and John Chamard, "Regional Industrial Growth in the 1890s: The Case of the Missing Artisans," *Acadiensis,* XVI, 1 (Autumn 1986), pp. 101–17.

10. M.C. Urquhart, "New Estimates of Gross National Product, Canada, 1870 to 1926," in S. Engerman and R. Gallman, eds., *Long-Term Factors in American Economic Growth* (Chicago, 1986), p. 9–88; M. Altman, "A Revision of Canadian Economic Growth: 1870–1910 (a challenge to the gradualist interpretation)," *Canadian Journal of Economics,* XX, 1 (February 1987), pp. 86–113; Kris Inwood and Thanasis Stengos, "Discontinuities in Canadian Economic Growth, 1870–1985," *Explorations in Economic History,* Vol. 28, no. 3 (July 1991), pp. 274–286.

11. Alan Green and M.C. Urquhart, "New Estimates of Output Growth in Canada: Measurement and Interpretation", in Douglas McCalla, ed., *Perspectives on Canadian Economic History* (Toronto, 1987), pp. 182–199; Gordon Bertram, "Economic Growth and Canadian Industry, 1870–1915: The Staple Model and the Takeoff Hypothesis," *Canadian Journal of Economics and Political Science,* XXIX (1963), pp. 159–84.

Morris Altman has argued that adjustments for price change provide greater evidence of structural change; see his "A Revision of Canadian Economic Growth." Useful perspective is brought to bear on the debate by Ken Norrie and Doug Owram, *A History of the Canadian Economy* (Toronto, 1991), pp. 293–298, 329–333 and 359–368.

12. Influential contributions by historians include T.W. Acheson, "The National Policy and the Industrialization of the Maritimes," *Acadiensis*, 1, 2 (Spring 1972), pp. 1–28 and "The Maritimes and Empire Canada" in David Bercuson, ed., *Canada and the Burden of Unity* (Toronto, 1977), pp. 87–114; E.R. Forbes, *The Maritimes Rights Movement* (Toronto, 1977) and "Misguided Symmetry: The Destruction of Regional Transportation Policy for the Maritimes," pp. 60–86 in Bercuson, ed., *Canada and the Burden;* David Frank, "The Cape Breton Coal Industry and the Rise and Fall of the British Empire Steel Corporation," *Acadiensis*, VII, 1 (Autumn 1977), pp. 3–34; James Frost, "The Nationalization of The Bank of Nova Scotia," *Acadiensis*, XII, 1 (Autumn 1982), pp. 3–38; Greg Kealey, Ian McKay and Nolan Reilly, "Canada's 'Eastern Question': A Reader's Guide to Regional Underdevelopment," *Canadian Dimension*, Vol. 13, No. 2 (1978), pp. 37–40. Contributions from social science include R. J. Brym and J. Sacouman, eds., *Underdevelopment and Social Movements in Atlantic Canada* (Toronto, 1979); Michael Clow, "Politics and Uneven Development: The Maritime Challenge to the Study of Canadian Political Economy," *Studies in Political Economy*, 14 (Fall 1984), pp. 117–40 and his "Situating a Classic: Saunders Revisited," *Acadiensis*, XV, 1 (Autumn 1985), pp. 145–52; Ralph Matthews, *The Creation of Regional Dependency* (Toronto, 1983).

13. Keith Griffin and John Gurley, "Radical Analyses of Imperialism, the Third World and the Transition to Socialism, *Journal of Economic Literature*, XXIII, 3 (September 1988), pp. 1089–1143; Cristobal Kay, *Latin American Theories of Development and Underdevelopment* (New York, 1989); S. Lall, "Is Dependency a Useful Concept in Analyzing Underdevelopment?," *World Development*, 3, nos. 11–12 (1975), pp. 799–810; Patrick O'Brien, "A Critique of Latin American Theories of Dependency," in I. Oxaal, et al, eds., *Beyond the Sociology of Development* (London, 1975), pp. 7–27; Alec Nove, "On Reading Andre Gunder Frank," *Journal of Development Studies*, 10, nos. 3–4 (April-July 1974), pp. 445–55 and Eric Sager, "Dependency, Underdevelopment and the Economic History of the Atlantic Provinces," *Acadiensis*, XVII, 1 (Autumn 1987), pp. 117–37. I borrow the term "structuralism" from the Latin American literature; see Joseph Love, "The Origins of Dependency Analysis," *Journal of Latin American Studies*, 22, no. 1 (February 1990), pp. 143–68.

14. David Alexander, "Economic Growth in the Atlantic Region, 1880–1940," *Acadiensis*, VIII, 1 (Autumn 1978), p. 47. See also Canada, *House of Commons Debates*, 1879, pp. 1306–8 and Phillip Buckner, P. B. Waite and William Baker, "The Maritimes and Confederation: A Reassessment," *Canadian Historical Review*, LXXI, 1 (March 1990), pp. 1–45.

15. Inwood and Chamard, "Regional Growth during the 1890s," Table 4. The industries are tanning, foundries and machine shops, brewing and various mills (carding, fulling, weaving, saw, flour and grist). Regrettably, ship building is not represented.

16. S.A. Saunders, *The Economic History of the Maritime Provinces* (Fredericton, 1984, [1939]). p. 25.

17. Acheson, "The Maritimes and Empire Canada" and Henry Veltmeyer, "The Capitalist Underdevelopment of Atlantic Canada" in Brym and Sacouman, eds., *Underdevelopment and Social Movements in Atlantic Canada,* pp. 37–58.

18. John Dales, *The Protective Tariff in Canada's Economic Development* (Toronto, 1966) and "'National Policy' Myths, Past and Present," *Journal of Canadian Studies,* 14 (Fall 1979), pp. 39–50; Ian Drummond, *Progress without Planning* (Toronto 1987), pp. 112–14; Kris Inwood, *The Canadian Charcoal Iron Industry* (New York, 1986), pp. 46–51.

19. Lou Cain, "Ontario's Industrial Revolution," *Canadian Historical Review,* LXIX, 3 (1988), pp. 300–307.

20. James Markusen and James Melvin, *The Theory of International Trade and its Canadian Applications* (Toronto, 1984), pp. 384–90.

21. Chris Armstrong, "Making a Market: Selling Securities in Atlantic Canada before World War I," *Canadian Journal of Economics,* XIII, 3 (August 1980), pp. 438–54; Neil Quigley, "Bank Credit and the Structure of the Canadian Space Economy, 1890–1935," Ph.D. thesis, University of Toronto, 1986.

22. Inwood and Chamard, "Regional Industrial Growth." I circumvent this problem in the present paper by reporting data for 1870–1890 and 1890–1910.

23. Armstrong, "Making a Market," Greg Marchildon, "Promotion, Finance and Merger in the Canadian Manufacturing Industry, 1885–1918," Ph.D. thesis, The London School of Economics and Political Science, 1990.

24. Armstrong, "Making a Market," Quigley, "Bank Credit."

25. Forbes, *Maritime Rights* and "Misguided Symmetry."

26. Ken Cruikshank, "The Transportation Revolution and its Consequences," *Communications historiques / Historical Papers* (1987), pp. 112–37.

27. Acheson, "The National Policy," Frank, "The Cape Breton Coal Industry."

28. Kris Inwood, "Local Control, Resources and the Nova Scotia Steel and Coal Company," *Communications historiques / Historical Papers* (1986), pp. 254–82.

29. Barry Supple, "The Political Economy of Demoralization: The State and the Coal-mining Industry in America and Britain between the Wars," *Economic History Review,* XLI, 4 (November 1988), pp. 566–91.

30. Douglas North, "Location Theory and Regional Economic Growth," *Journal of Political Economy,* LXIII (February-December 1955), pp. 243–58 and *The Economic Growth of the United States, 1790–1860* (New York, 1966); A. D. Scott, "Policy for Declining Regions: A Theoretical Approach," in W.D. Wood and R.S. Thoman, eds., *Areas of Economic Stress in Canada* (Kingston, 1965), pp. 73–93; R. Caves and R. Holton, *The Canadian Economy: Prospect and Retrospect* (Cambridge, 1961), pp. 141–95; Boris Schedvin, "Staples and Regions of Pax Britannica", *Economic History Review,* XLIII, 4 (November 1990), pp. 533–59.

31. A. Blackbourn and R. Putnam, *The Industrial Geography of Canada* (London, 1984), Chapter 7; Caves and Holton, *The Canadian Economy,* p. 145; A.W. Currie, *Canadian Economic Development,* (Toronto, 1942), p. 131; C.R. Fay and H.A. Innis, "The

Economic Development of Canada 1867–1921: The Maritime Provinces," in *The Cambridge History of the British Empire,* Volume VI (Cambridge, 1929), pp. 657–71; Harold Innis, *Essays in Canadian Economic History* (Toronto, 1956), pp. 148, 226 and 349; R.C. Harris and J. Warkentin, *Canada Before Confederation* (New York, 1974), pp. 208–10; L.D. McCann, "Staples and the New Industrialism," *Acadiensis,* VIII, 2 (Spring 1979), pp. 47–79; S. A. Saunders, *The Economic History* and *The Economic Welfare of the Maritime Provinces* (Wolfville, 1932).

32. Currie, *Canadian Economic Development,* p. 123.

33. Eric Sager and Lewis R. Fischer, "Atlantic Canada and the Age of Sail Revisited," *Canadian Historical Review,* LXIII, 2 (June 1982), pp. 126–150; Eric Sager and Gerald Panting, *Maritime Capital: The Shipping Industry in Atlantic Canada, 1820–1914* (Kingston and Montreal, 1990).

34. W.A. Mackintosh, *The Economic Background to Dominion-Provincial Relations* (Ottawa, 1939), p. 34.

35. Peter Wylie, "When Markets Fail: Electrification and Maritime Industrial Decline," *Acadiensis,* XVII, 1 (Autumn 1987), pp. 74–96.

36. Canada, Dominion Bureau of Statistics, *The Maritime Provinces since Confederation* (Ottawa, 1929), p. 56.

37. Inwood, "Local Control".

38. Saunders, *The Economic History,* p. 24.

39. Caves and Holton, *Canada,* p. 180.

40. Inwood and Chamard, "Regional Industrial Growth."

41. Kris Inwood, "Transportation, Tariffs and the Canadian Iron Industry," University of Guelph Economics Working Paper 89–3 (1989). The point is more often made in the literature on Quebec; see A. Faucher and M. Lamontagne, "History of Industrial Development," in C. Falardeau, ed., *Essays on Contemporary Quebec* (Quebec, 1953), p. 23–37 and Morris Altman, "Resource Endowments and Location Theory: A Case Study of Quebec and Ontario at the Turn of the Twentieth Century," *Journal of Economic History,* XLVI, 4 (December 1986), pp. 999–1009.

42. Jeremy Atack, "Returns to Scale in Antebellum United States Manufacturing," *Explorations in Economic History,* 14, 4 (October, 1977), pp. 337–59.

43. Using Atack's Table 2, the industries are meat packing, distilleries, cotton textiles, woolen goods, men's clothing, millinery, furniture, tanneries, boots and shoes, sheet metal, agricultural implements, wagons and carriages. The exceptions appear to be bakeries, flour milling, saw milling, tobacco manufacture and engine building.

44. J. Laurent, "Trade, Transportation and Technology: The American Great Lakes, 1866–1910", *Journal of Transport History,* 4 (March 1983), pp. 1–24; Sam H. Williamson, "The Growth of the Great Lakes as a Major Transportation Resource", *Research in Economic History,* 2 (1977), pp. 103–183.

45. Saunders, *The Economic History,* pp. 21, 27.

46. Cruikshank, "The Transportation Revolution."

47. Inwood and Irwin, "Inter-regional Differences."

48. Higher primary sector incomes also would have made available greater savings for investment in manufacturing. I do not dwell on this mechanism because capital, like entrepreneurship, was relatively mobile between regions. There is no evidence of a failure to undertake sound business opportunities within the region because of scarce capital or entrepreneurship.

49. Gavin Wright, "The Origins of American Industrial Success, 1879–1940," *American Economic Review,* LXXX, 4 (September 1990), pp. 651–68.

50. Indeed, some would argue that fast industrialization breeds increased income inequality and poverty. For an introduction to this literature see Cynthia Taft Morris and Irma Adelman, *Comparative Patterns of Economic Development,* 1850–1914 (Baltimore, 1988) and Ben Polak and Jeffrey G. Williamson, "Poverty, Policy and Industrialization: Lessons from the Distant Past," World Bank Working Paper WPS 645, April 1991.

51. Rusty Bittermann, "The Hierarchy of the Soil: Land and Labour in a 19th Century Cape Breton Community," *Acadiensis,* XVIII, 1 (Autumn 1988), pp. 33–55; Rosemary Ommer, "The Truck System in Gaspé, 1822–77," *Acadiensis,* XIX, 1 (Autumn 1989), pp. 91–114.

CHAPTER

4 POLITICS, PATRONAGE AND POWER UNDER MACDONALD AND LAURIER

"Canada is a difficult country to govern" is an often-repeated lament of those who have tried, and the shattered reputations of most of our prime ministers is a stark reminder of that dilemma. Macdonald and Laurier are usually considered to have been successful, though Macdonald has had several detractors. Laurier, on the other hand, consistently received the best press, and until as recently as the 1960s was considered, in the uncritical prose of Frank Underhill, "the greatest of all Canadians" (*Image of Confederation,* 47). His natural purity of spirit sparkled more brilliantly when viewed beside Macdonald's fraudulence. "The Macdonald system," Underhill wrote, " ... involved a tremendous amount of corruption, which lowered the standards of our public life and has remained one of the heavy costs of this kind of nationalism ever since." It was that image of Macdonald wallowing in patronage and corruption that pervaded the literature, while Laurier gallantly saved Canada as Sir Galahad on his white horse.

Such a simplistic and partisan interpretation eventually lost favour as modern academics and journalists turned from ideology to evidence for their answers. One of the areas of investigation has been the critical bonding role of patronage for the national parties and the country itself. Laurier certainly understood its central function. "Reforms are for the opposition," Laurier once snapped at John Willison who dared to criticize Laurier's use of patronage; "It is the business of Government to stay in office." Laurier has the record of fifteen uninterrupted years as prime minister.

Both Macdonald and Laurier understood the intimate relationship between patronage and power, as the readings included here demonstrate. Historian Gordon Stewart examines the details of the systems of "Political Patronage under Macdonald and Laurier," providing a rationale for their evolution. While not condemning either Macdonald or Laurier, Stewart concludes that "Canadians of the twentieth century are reaping the harvest of patronage politics during the 1867 to 1911 period," a harvest of failure and possible disintegration. Jeffrey Simpson is a journalist and in *Spoils of Power: The Politics of Patronage* comes to a somewhat different conclusion. If Stewart looks at the details, Simpson takes a broader view. He also concludes that patronage was both essential and beneficial. The problems of the later twentieth century, in Simpson's view, do not derive from the flaws of the system of the earlier era but from the special interests of the modern era which lack a national perspective but have specific agendas which they attempt to impose on political parties and the nation itself. "In recent years," Simpson writes, "the traditional reflections in the patronage mirror—partisan, religious, linguistic and regional interests—are no longer sufficient proof of the broadness of a political party. Now the mirror must also reflect the interests of women, native people, young Canadians, old Canadians and various multicultural groups. Their understandable desire for recognition accentuates a political leader's frustration at the gap between the demands for reward or recognition and the supply of positions and preferment."

Suggestions for Further Reading

"Le Patronage/Patronage," A special Issue of the *Journal of Canadian Studies,* Vol. 22, No. 2, Summer 1987.

Beavan, Brian, "Partisanship, Patronage and the Press in Ontario, 1880–1914, Myths and Realities," *Canadian Historical Review,* Vol. 64, No. 3, 1983.

Brown, Robert Craig, and Ramsay Cook, *Canada 1896–1921 A Nation Transformed.* Toronto: McClelland and Stewart, 1974.

Creighton, Donald G., *John A. Macdonald: The Old Chieftain.* Toronto: Macmillan, 1955.

Neatby, Blair, *Laurier and a Liberal Quebec: A Study in Political Management.* Toronto: McClelland and Stewart, 1973.

Schull, Joseph, *Laurier: The First Canadian.* Toronto: Macmillan, 1965.

Simpson, Jeffrey, *Spoils of Power: The Politics of Patronage.* Toronto: Collins, 1988.

Stevens, Paul, "Wilfrid Laurier: Politician," in *The Political Ideas of the Prime Ministers of Canada*, ed. Marcel Hamelin. Ottawa: University of Ottawa Press, 1969.

Underhill, Frank H., *The Image of Confederation.* Toronto: Canadian Broadcasting Corporation, 1964.

Waite, Peter, *Canada 1874–1896 Arduous Destiny.* Toronto: McClelland and Stewart, 1971.

POLITICAL PATRONAGE UNDER MACDONALD AND LAURIER

Gordon Stewart

It is standard knowledge that patronage was endemic to Canadian politics in the 1867–1911 period. Source-books for undergraduate students contain sections on patronage and the major historians who have written about these years refer to the ubiquitous nature of patronage, describing it as the natural currency of public life.[1] Professor W. L. Morton has pointed out that the cabinet minister of the time, "a beneficiary of patronage himself ... was well disposed towards being a dispenser of patronage. Indeed it was the power to distribute patronage that in the main gave his office meaning and substance." [2] In his authoritative account of this period Professor Peter B. Waite remarks of Mackenzie Bowell, minister of customs throughout the entire span of Macdonald's administrations from 1878 to 1891, that his "principal pre-occupation was patronage." [3] As well as these reminders from respected modern scholars, the official records of the period offer testimony to the pervasiveness of patronage. Commissions to investigate the civil service were established in 1880–81, 1891–92, 1907–08, and 1911–12 and all drew attention to the "patronage evil." [4] In 1909 the Department of Marine and Fisheries had the doubtful honor of being the object of a separate investigation and it failed to disappoint its critics, revealing widespread practices not only of patronage but also of corruption.[5] Newspapers, periodicals and parliamentary debates are full of dramatic stories, charges and counter-charges concerning patronage. Major political scandals of the time, involving national figures such as Charles Rykert and Hector-Louis Langevin, revolved round issues of patronage.[6] Because of this kind of evidence it is now common knowledge that patronage was of central importance to Canadian political life. Yet there has been no study made of the workings and significance of patronage. Professor Hodgetts has noted this odd gap in Canadian historical studies. "It is somewhat curious," he writes, "that the practice of patronage has never been the subject of sustained analysis on the part of Canadian social scientists and historians." [7] This article is an attempt at such an analysis.

I

A useful and informative starting point for examining the mechanics of the patronage system is to look at John A. Macdonald's own constituency of Kingston. The picture that emerges from the Kingston patronage evidence shows that patronage was distributed by the party on a bureaucratic-like basis. Appointments

From *The American Review of Canadian Studies,* X, no. 1 (Spring 1980), 3–26. Reprinted by permission of the Association for Canadian Studies in the United States.

and contracts were not distributed hurriedly but invariably followed discussion between local party leaders in Kingston and the Member of Parliament (in this case Macdonald) in Ottawa. Those party activists seeking posts in the public service or public contracts made application, usually in writing, to the executive committee of the local Conservative Association. The committee considered all the applications, weighed the contributions of each applicant to the party's electoral campaigns and then passed on a recommendation to Macdonald who in turn would pass on the name to the appropriate cabinet minister for formal action. In no case in the correspondence was consideration given to the applicants' qualifications—the sole criterion was service to the party.[8]

Within the executive committee there was formal discussion over each piece of patronage. The local party, through its executive committee, functioned almost as an employment agency for party workers. In 1889, for example, Edward Smythe, a barrister and president of the Liberal-Conservative Association, discussed with Macdonald various jobs in the Kingston Post Office. Smythe informed Macdonald that the committee had now filled all but one of the current vacancies. "That will leave," he noted, "a vacancy among the letter carriers that we will subsequently fill up." [9] Two months earlier Macdonald had written to the executive committee to inform the local party leaders of changes in the Kingston post office that would open up new jobs. These developments, Smythe replied, "received the hearty recommendation of our Executive Committee." [10] When the committee discussed the distribution of such posts, the merits of the candidates were discussed exclusively in terms of their work in the local party organization. Writing in January 1891 in connection with the application of William A. Newlands for a clerkship in the post office, J. A. Metcalfe explained that "his [Newland's] father and brother are active workers in the Conservative interest and William A. is a good Conservative." Metcalfe added that Newlands had followed the proper procedure, having "applied through the Executive Committee." [11] Once Macdonald received the recommendation from the committee, he passed it on to the cabinet minister in charge of the appropriate department. In response to one such recommendation to the Customs Department, the minister, Mackenzie Bowell, sent a note to Macdonald explaining he had signed the necessary papers implementing the requested appointments. Mackenzie Bowell pointed out that neither of the two individuals recommended had "passed the 'qualifying' examinations" and therefore could not be employed as landing-waiters or clerks. But they still received posts in the customs service.[12] Local party considerations took precedence over questions of qualifications.

Because party considerations were paramount it was essential for any applicant to show a solid record of work in local electoral campaigns. An example of these values occurred over the position of second engineer at the federal dry dock facility in Kingston. Thomas McGuire, a local party notable, had been told "the Conservative Association have recommended" Joseph Levitt for the post.

McGuire wrote in support of Levitt and warned Macdonald about two other aspirants for the job who should be rejected because they had made contract with the Liberal "enemy." Those other two, wrote McGuire, "are Heretics while Levitt is one of the Faithful as that term is understood by the archbishop." [13] In another case the importance of long, faithful and uncontaminated party service was emphasized. In this instance the record of the family as a whole was considered. A "claim of patronage has been brought before the Executive Committee," wrote J. H. Metcalfe to Macdonald. "I do not admire the tone of the letter yet as the old man and his sons have never gone grit I feel kindly disposed toward them." [14] During the winter of 1890–91 similar considerations dominated discussion of a vacancy for a staff officer in the militia. In December 1890 S. M. Conger, president of the Prince Edward County Liberal-Conservative Association, pressed the claims of his candidate, Colonel Graveley. Conger wrote of Graveley that he was not only "a most efficient military officer ... he is more ... he is a staunch Conservative and has made many sacrifices for the party." [15] Another endorsement of Graveley came from R. R. Pringle of Cobourg who reminded Macdonald that "as far as this riding is concerned he [Graveley] has always worked well and he certainly sacrificed himself when he ran for the local [elections] when nothing but defeat stared him in the face." [16] Writing from Port Hope another correspondent addressed himself to the essential point—Graveley deserved the appointment because of "his service to the party." [17]

The fact that service to the party was the most important element in appointments did not make Macdonald's or the committee's task any easier for in many cases there were several suitable party workers seeking a post. In such cases it was difficult to make a recommendation without causing dissent and factionalism in the local organization. In other cases local party notables might either try to dominate the executive committee or try to by-pass the committee and deal directly with Macdonald on patronage issues. All these factors appeared over the appointments of a landing-waiter in the customs service at Kingston, a case that well illustrates some of the local complexities involved in distribution of patronage. In this instance John Gaskill of the Montreal Transport Company and a prominent local Conservative had ignored the work of the executive committee and had pressed his own candidate on Macdonald. On January 8, 1891 Macdonald was warned by George Fitzpatrick of the consequent trouble—"Gaskill is raising a row and I hear that the Executive Committee had a real lively time yesterday. The Kilkenny Election was nothing to it."[18] Fitzpatrick sent a telegram to Macdonald asking that the appointment be held up until a local solution to the conflict was found. The situation was more tangled because Gaskill's candidate had been "insulting" to the executive committee. The committee's viewpoint was put by John McIntyre who explained to the Prime Minister that "we are all anxious to do what we can for the party ... but I know the majority of the Committee will feel greatly humiliated if Gaskill is allowed to reverse every recommendation that is made."[19]

The Kingston patronage letters also reveal that Macdonald and local party leaders did not deal simply with appointments but also were actively involved in promotions within the public service and even in the creation of new posts to satisfy the patronage demands within the party. In September 1889, for example, John Haggart, Postmaster General in Ottawa, replied to the Prime Minister concerning the promotion of a clerk within the postal service. Macdonald himself had requested the promotion after hearing from the executive committee and Haggart was willing to comply except there was no vacancy to which the clerk could be promoted. Haggart, however, went on to suggest a solution. He could do what Macdonald requested by "providing in the Estimates for the coming year a first-class clerkship in the Inspectors office at Kingston."[20] There was no discussion about the necessity of a clerkship; it was simply to be created in the interests of the local party.

From this Kingston evidence we begin to get an idea of the workings of patronage, particularly the relationship between Ottawa and the localities. The Member of Parliament, in this case Macdonald, made the formal and final decision about appointments from the Kingston area as he passed on names to other cabinet ministers. Usually the MP received the nomination from the local executive committee. It was assumed that the local party organization, by its executive committee, was the normal channel through which patronage business flowed. When acting on patronage matters the committee did so in a formal way, receiving and reviewing applications, weighing credentials, passing resolutions and forwarding the recommendation to the MP at Ottawa. One final point to emerge is that the structure of the patronage system, as revealed in the Kingston evidence, excluded outsiders from sharing in contracts and appointments. The patronage was given only to local figures who could prove their loyalty to the local party organization.

II

The Kingston evidence while informative may not be typical because of Macdonald's position as Prime Minister. This may have led him to leave much of the daily patronage business in the hands of the local leaders. It is therefore essential to examine other evidence to assess whether this pattern was representative.

One report during the period revealed a good deal about the day-to-day workings of the patronage system. This was the investigation in 1909 by Judge Cassels into the Department of Marine and Fisheries. A basic point made in the report was that since 1867 the department had been used by both the Conservatives and Liberals, when they were in power, for partisan purposes. Positions and contracts were given to reward party activists. Regular "patronage lists" drawn up by the MP and local party leaders were kept on file so business could be directed to party faithful. "The system," noted the report,

> seems to have been handed down from one administration to another since Confederation.... It is apparently based on the old maxim of 'to the victor belong the spoils' utterly ignoring the fact that the money to be disbursed is mainly contributed by the people generally and not the money of the political followers of the party at the time being in power.[21]

During the course of the investigation the activities of the department's office in Halifax provided detailed evidence on how the system worked. In the case of Halifax the MPs were active in the regular distribution of jobs and contracts. The report explained that

> patronage in Halifax extended beyond the mere naming of the merchants and others who should comprise the patronage list. It extended to the nomination by the Members of Parliament representing the constituency of individuals or an individual to whom orders were to be given.[22]

The questioning of witnesses showed the way things were managed. When work needed to be done or supplies furnished "then the members would recommend ... that the orders should be given to A, B, C, or D as the case may be." Mr. Jonathan Parsons, the Department's chief agent in Halifax, explained that this was done "under the rules of patronage." He further explained that these rules applied "from year to year and from month to month every year." On every occasion a contract was to be placed the MPs "would designate ... which merchant or manufacturer or dealer particular orders should be given to." The questioning concluded:

Q: That has been the cause?
A: Yes
Q: Each time?
A: Yes
Q: So it is not your independent judgment that was exercised from time to time as to where the work should be done or by whom material should be furnished; that was done upon the recommendations?
A: By the member of parliament having the patronage.[23]

The evidence also showed that aside from this regular management of patronage the MPs authorized "taking on an employee" because they "had the patronage." [24]

The 1909 Report on the Department of Marine and Fisheries confirmed the assessment made the previous year by a civil service inquiry that the organization of the department, comprehensively influenced by patronage, had "few redeeming features." The Commission of 1908 had made a broad investigation of the public service outside the home departments in Ottawa and had concluded that these outside agencies were entirely at the disposal of the party in power. "As a rule," the commissioners explained,

> in the outside service ... politics enter into every appointment and politicians on the spot interest themselves not only in the appointments but in the subsequent promotion of the officers ... in the outside service the politics of the party is of greater importance in making appointments and promotions than the public interests of the Dominion.[25]

In each locality the MP and the party leaders regarded appointments and contracts as their exclusive right to be used to reward local party workers. "In practically no case," the commissioners discovered, "is it possible to fill a vacancy in one locality by a transfer from another." [26] In the Inland Revenue Department, for example, "political appointments as in other branches of the public service, prevail and as a rule the officers in one district are confined to that one district." In Montreal all the appointments in the customs service were made "at the insistance of the members of parliament for the district." Indeed throughout the entire customs service the commissioners concluded that each riding was "looked upon as local patronage" and that posts were awarded to local people only.[27] In his evidence Dr. Barrett, inspector of Inland Revenue at Winnipeg, explained the active role MPs took in preserving local patronage exclusively for local party use. Barrett described how when a post became available "the member for the constituency says, 'No, I will not allow any one outside my constituency to go in there.' " In Winnipeg as in Kingston, the names for appointments were "generally given by the Liberal Association of Winnipeg." Barrett emphasized that "when the Conservatives were in power they did the same thing." [28] In their general observations on this kind of evidence, the commissioners concluded that "each locality was separately guarded."[29] Even the national party leader could not interfere with this local exclusivity. Writing to a party worker who had asked for a position outside his own constituency, Wilfrid Laurier pointed out how hard this would be to arrange. "I need not tell you," wrote the Prime Minister, "that it is always difficult to bring an outsider into a locality." [30]

It is important to note that this type of patronage distribution exclusively to party activists was not confined to minor posts in the customs or postal services and other such branches of the federal bureaucracy but operated at all levels. This can be demonstrated by looking at Macdonald's policies in making appointments to the bench and the bar. County judgeships and the earning of the title of Queen's Counsel (QC) were sought-after plums in the legal profession and were at the disposal of the party in power. As with the customs service workers and post office employees the positions in the judiciary were given by the party in power primarily on the basis of the candidate's service to the party. An example of the essential relationship between party service and advancement in the legal profession is contained in correspondence from 1887 between John

Small and John A. Macdonald. Small wrote a confidential memorandum to the Prime Minister with a list of barristers eligible for a QC and set out against each name the reasons for his recommendation:

> Michael Murphy: defeated candidate 1882 ... attended meetings in recent elections ... Roman Catholic;
>
> Daniel Defoe: strong supporter, always took a prominent part in political movements;
>
> James Reeve: did good work in the last election;
>
> James Fullerton: takes the platform in the interests of the party;
>
> George Blackstock: has contested elections;
>
> Emerson Coalsworth: rising young barrister, pillar of the Methodist Church, a strong Temperance advocate, President of the Liberal Conservative Association for his ward, was my agent in the last election.[31]

These candidates for QC had varied characteristics—some Roman Catholic, others Methodist, some with long legal experience, others just beginning to become noted in the profession—yet each shared one necessary qualification without which any other would be useless. In one way or another all had worked for their local Conservative parties either by running as candidates, being speakers or canvassers, or drawing up and scrutinizing the voters lists. It was this kind of information on good hard party work that Macdonald looked for when creating a new batch of QCs. And these criteria were well understood throughout the party. In October 1889 Robert Birmingham, the Secretary-Treasurer of the Liberal Conservative Union of Ontario, sent Macdonald "the names of a few legal friends who rendered us special service in the recent campaign in the hope that you might be able to repay them with the much sought after QC." [32]

The next step up beyond QC were county judgeships and these too were distributed with the party's interest in mind. The context in which the awarding of judgeship was discussed can be seen from a case involving the Prime Minister, Frank Smith, the Senator who was the most important Ontario Catholic in the party, and B. L. Doyle, a party worker seeking a promotion to the bench. Doyle set forth his qualifications which rested on the premise that his "services to the Party for the last 15 years entitled me to something." He then proceeded to recount the details of this party work, emphasizing that he had "stood by the party in the darkest hours of its severest trials [and] fought for it when it was down and persevered in the desperate struggle on behalf of our principles till the victory again crowned our efforts." Doyle then went on to describe the election campaigns, particularly the one of 1878, in which he had done a great deal to get out the Catholic vote. He concluded his letter with the blunt request—"I want a County Judgeship." [33] This request was endorsed by Senator Frank Smith, who confirmed that Doyle had indeed done all the party work he claimed to have done over the years. Smith wrote of Doyle that he was "a plucky, active man whom I know to have worked hard for his party." Therefore, concluded the Senator, "he deserves to get what he asks." [34] Macdonald was unable to satisfy Doyle immediately because of some rival candidates but he did promise to do what he could and in January 1880 Doyle was appointed junior judge of Huron county.[35]

Other evidence from the Macdonald papers confirms this pattern of judicial appointments being related to partisan activity. In November 1883 Robert Smith QC was recommended for a vacant judgeship in Huron. He was considered deserving of such honor because he was "ever willing to go where duty to his party called him." In April 1885 H. C. Gwyn applied to the Prime Minister for a vacant judgeship on the grounds that he had been:

> actively identified with the party ... and up to a year ago and for seven or eight years previously [was] the Secretary of the Liberal-Conservative Association of North Wentworth ...[36]

In May 1884 a Conservative MP recommended J. M. Hamilton of Sault Sainte Marie for a judgeship, explaining that Hamilton was "very much esteemed throughout Algoma and it is of some political importance that he should be appointed." [37] About a year later another Conservative MP, N. C. Wallace, in recommending Edward Morgan, a barrister for a junior county judgeship in York, explained that Morgan had "fought, bled and almost died for the Party and has very much stronger claims than anyone else that has been proposed for the position." [38] In the summer of 1887 A. M. Boswell, a party leader in Toronto, after reporting to Macdonald about party fundraising turned to judicial patronage and recommended N. C. Stewart for a junior judgeship in that city. Stewart, explained Boswell, was "an out and out Conservative and as steady as a rock. At one time he was not a cold water man but now he is all right." [39]

This evidence concerning the legal profession confirms that at all levels of public employment, from judgeships down to landing-waiters in the customs service, the party in power distributed patronage only to those who had worked for the party. It was not enough simply to be a contributor to party funds or an occasional canvasser but necessary to prove a long period of active, dedicated work in the ridings. The immutability of this standard was well illustrated by a case from London, Ontario that developed in that spring of 1900. It concerned the family of John A. Donegan who had volunteered to fight in the Canadian contingent in the Boer War. Donegan had been killed in South Africa, leaving a widow and two sons in London. There were some efforts to find jobs for the two boys to help support the family and James Sutherland, a Liberal MP, had written to local party leaders in London asking their views of the proposal to find posts for the Donegan boys. It might be expected that in this part of Ontario the sons of war-dead in South Africa would receive sympathetic treatment but the local party balked and refused to consider them for any posts. In response to Sutherland's inquiries, George Reid, a local party leader, explained that

> as for making a position for either of the Donegans in this locality, it would be very unpopular, they have never been Friends of ours in any particular and [it] would never do to appoint any one who has not been identified with the work of the party.... To appoint him for any position purely [and] simply because his father was killed in Africa would be to my mind very absurd.[40]

Reid also pointed out that the man who was doing most to find jobs for the Donegans was not a party supporter. If he had been, that might have been a reason to give the Donegans something to reward a party worker but, warned Reid, there was no point in helping the Donegans' backer for "he is a strong supporter of the enemy and of no use to us whatsoever." [41]

A comprehensive example of the normalcy of these expectations is contained in some private correspondence between Laurier and Roy Choquette concerning the Liberal party in the district of Quebec. Following the Liberal victory in 1896 Laurier had asked Choquette to report on the patronage requirements of the local party in the Quebec area. Choquette was to sound out party notables and send Laurier "une liste des nominations ... sur lesquels nos amis insistent le plus pour le moment."[c] On September 12 Choquette sent Laurier a detailed list of demands by Quebec Liberals:

> Voici ce qui en est: L'Hon. M. Joly [controller of Inland Revenue] devrait immédiatement remplacer le Dr. Fiset de St. Sauveur par le Dr. Coté, et ce, pour faire plaisir à nos jeunes amis de Québec M. l'Orateur, devrait remercier de ses services M. Fournier, pour satisfaire M. Talbot, et en même temps le Ministre des Chemins de fer devrait faire l'échange des stations de l'Intercolonial entre Castonguay de St. Charles et M. Roy de St. Moise. M. l'Orateur devrait encore destituer un nommé Gagnon, messager sessional pour donner satisfaction à M. LaForest, notre candidat contre Costigan. M. Paterson [minister of customs] ou Joly devrait remplacer Philéas Dubé, de Fraserville, officier du Douane, part M. Amédé Gagan de St. Arseire, comte de Temiscouta....[d] [42]

Choquette then continued, in the same matter-of-fact manner, to list further patronage requirements of other important local Liberals, each of whom,

---

[c] a list of nominations...that our friends insist upon most at present.

[d] Here is what they are: the Honourable Mr. Joly (controller at Inland Revenue) should immediately replace Dr. Fiset of St. Saveur with Dr. Coté in order to please our young friends in Quebec City. Mr. Speaker should thank Mr. Fournier for his services and thus satisfy Mr. Talbot, and at the same time, the Minister of Railways should switch Castonguay from St. Charles and Mr. Roy from St. Moïse in their positions on the Intercolonial. In order to please Mr. LaForest, our candidate running against Costigan, Mr. Speaker should also let go a certain Gagnon who was a messenger during the session. Mr. Paterson (Minister of Customs) or Joly should replace Philéas Dubé from Fraserville as the customs officer with Mr. Amédé Gagan from St. Arseire in the riding of Temiscouta...."

typically enough, had specific rewards in mind for himself and his fellow-workers:

> Pour faire plaisir à l'ami Lemieux, un nommé Baudin, gardien de phare de la Grande Rivière, et qui a voulu le battre à son arrivée à cet endroit, devrait être remercié de ses services et remplacé par M. William Bisson.
>
> L'ami Fisset attend avec impatience ce qui lui est promis depuis longtemps, la nomination du Dr. Ross de Ste. Flavie, à la place du Dr. Gauvreau, partisan bleu enragé, comme médecin du port à la Pointe au Père; et la nomination du Dr. Boullion, de Matane, à la place du Dr. Pelletier comme médecin du port à cet endroit.
>
> L'ami Angers aimerait avoir la reinstallation immédiate de M. Joseph Gaudreau, comme maître de poste à Grands Fonds, Malbaie.[e] [43]

Choquette ended this list of patronage requirements by briskly noting his own demands, "Quant à moi," he wrote, "si l'ami Fisher [minister of Agriculture] pouvait me nommer Desiré Vezina à la place de Zephiron Danceuse comme homme de police à la Grosse Ile, et l'ami Mulock [postmaster-general] me nommer M. Georges Gagné, maître de poste à Ste. Pierre, à la place de madame C. Dienne, j'en serais bien content." [f] [44]

The working of the patronage system as revealed by these examples continued right down to the eve of World War I. The Royal Commission that investigated the civil service in 1911–1912 uncovered the same practices that their predecessors have [sic] described in the 1880's and 1890's. One particular interchange between the commissioners and a witness laid out clearly the mechanics of the patronage system. The witness was Robert G. MacPherson, post-master at Vancouver. He was asked how appointments were made to the staff and the following exchange took place:

> A: Appointments are made through recommendations by the patronage committee or the members supporting the government
> Q: Do they communicate directly with you when vacancies occur
> A: No. I will apply for one or two men to the department at Ottawa who authorize the appointment of men who shall be recommended by the member of parliament or the patronage committee as the case may be.[45]

---

[e] To please our friend Lemieux, a certain Baudin, who is lighthouse keeper on the Grand River and who wished to fight with him when he arrived there should be thanked for his services and replaced by Mr. William Bisson. Our friend Fisset is still waiting impatiently for what he was promised long ago: the appointment of Dr. Ross of Ste. Flavie to the post of harbour doctor at Pointe au Père instead of Dr. Gauvreau, who is a strong Conservative supporter; and the nomination of Dr. Boullion of Matane instead of Dr. Pelletier as harbour doctor at this location.

[f] As for me, if our friend Fisher (Minister of Agriculture) could appoint Desiré Vezina as head of police on Grosse Île to replace Zephiron Danceuse, and if our friend Mulock (Postmaster General) would appoint Mr. Georges Gagné as postmaster at St. Pierre to replace Mrs. C. Dienne, I would be very happy.

From the other side of Canada, on Prince Edward Island, came evidence of how the system worked there. Thomas Mann, agent at Charlottetown for the Department of Marine and Fisheries, explained that appointment and purchasing worked "by patronage." If a position fell vacant, "the members supply a list of men they want put on and if they are suitable I put them on...." In the matter of buying supplies these were purchased "from the patronage people." The questioning continued:

Q: You have a list
A: It is not a list from the government, just from the local members. They do the same as when the other government was in power. They have their friends to go and so have these
Q: You have a patronage list
A: A patronage list of friends to go to the same as before.[46]

The evidence in this section has provided an overview of the workings of the patronage system in the years between 1878 and 1911. There emerges a remarkable similarity in how the system worked under Macdonald and Laurier and a remarkable stability in a system that had the same structure in 1912 as it did in the 1880's. From Vancouver to Halifax, from London to Quebec, from Winnipeg to Prince Edward Island, Conservative and Liberal administrations of the period used their power in the same way. Federal posts and contracts were given to local party activists in a regular, time-honored manner. Although the actual decisions on patronage were made by the cabinet ministers in Ottawa, the evidence shows that much of the work in terms of identifying applicants and proposing candidates was done by the local party organization, usually working through a committee. It is also clear that the patronage system applied to all levels of the public service from judgeships down to temporary positions in the post office. The system had become so rooted a part of Canadian political culture that it was considered legitimate and normal. It was only late in the period with the Royal Commission of 1911–1912 that serious questions were raised about the impact of so extensive a system of patronage on Canadian governments and their effectiveness in dealing with the needs of society.[47]

III

To understand all the ramifications of the patronage system it is essential to relate it to the structure of Canadian society during this period. The first and most fundamental point to make here is that Canada was a small-town, rural society which was only beginning to be changed by the consequences of industrialization and urbanization. Professor Waite has reminded us of this basic fact in his authoritative study of the period between 1873 and 1896. The rural nature of Canada, he writes, "must be kept continually in mind when considering the character and setting of Canadian life. The conservativeness of the French-Canadian countryside is well known, its resistance to social change is as strong as its political allegiances, but so much of Canada was similar ... Canada was rural." [48] In 1881 the census classified 81% of the population as rural. By 1911 it was down to 56%, still over half the population. But even that figure does not tell the whole story. The census for 1911 shows that out of a total population of 7,206,643 there were 5,507,214 Canadians living in rural areas or in towns with less than 30,000. As late as 1911 about 76% of the Canadian population was living in small-town or rural conditions.[49]

One characteristic related to these conditions is that Canadian society was localistic. Professor Gibson has remarked on this quality of Canadian society, pointing out that "at Confederation and for many years afterwards, the Canadian people, a small and widely dispersed population, formed a simple and individualistic society, exhibiting strong local loyalties." [50] The evidence on patronage cited above shows again and again how social and political leaders in each locality were anxious to keep "outsiders" from moving in to their traditional sphere of influence. An insight into the isolation and localism of Canadian society in this period is provided by the memoirs of the historian A. R. M. Lower. He was born and raised in Barrie, Ontario, and recalled that in 1907 when he was eighteen years old he "had not been more than sixty or seventy miles away from home." Lower wondered whether he was "exceptional" in being thus rooted. "It is remarkable," he then added, "how local everyone was in those days." [51]

Another basically important fact to be borne in mind was that there was limited economic growth during this period and that in contrast to the United States, for example, there was no dramatic advance of industrial capitalism. Even the Laurier "boom years" after 1900 rested on the development of agriculture in the West and well into the first decade of the twentieth century contemporaries still regarded Canada's economy as essentially an agricultural one.[52] In 1896 Bryon Walker wrote in the *Monetary Times* that agriculture was "the substratum of our well-being." [53] Two years later D. R. Wilkie in a speech before the Canadian Bankers Association explained that Canada "was essentially an agricultural country" [54] and in 1907 this characteristic was again referred to, that "the real backbone of Canada is its agricultural and its dairy and pastoral interests." [55] A 1906 piece in *Industrial Canada* pointed out that "Canada is and always will be a great agricultural country ... [the farmer] is the very foundation stone of our social economy." [56]

A natural consequence of this reality was the relative insignificance of the industrial, manufacturing sector of the Canadian economy in moulding the social structure and value system of Canada. Some caution is required in broaching this topic for there is some disagreement among scholars about the nature and performance of the Canadian economy during this period. It used to be a conventional enough statement that there was little economic development between 1867 and 1900, at which point there was a take-off based on the wheat boom in the West. The picture of unrelieved gloom for the pre-1896 years can no longer be sustained, as Professor Waite has recently explained in his assessment of the new evidence.[57]

There was steady growth in some manufactures; the GNP rose from $710,000,000 in 1873 to $1,800,000,000 in 1896. Clearly the economy did grow and the transportation and banking structures developed before 1900 proved a solid base from which the more rapid, diversified growth of the twentieth century could develop. Yet while acknowledging the reality of this economic growth its limitations must be kept in mind. The manufacturing firms in Canada were small, employed tiny work forces and had a very restricted impact on the social structure.[58] In 1870 the average number of persons employed in each manufacturing establishment was 4.6; in 1890 it had risen to only 5.5.[59] Manufacturing was still small-scale, decentralized and geographically dispersed.

These economic circumstances were important for sustaining such a flourishing patronage system. The key point is that there were limited job opportunities available in the private manufacturing sector and that as a consequence federal contracts and positions in the federal public service were important areas of career opportunities.[60] In a system in which there was dynamic capitalist growth as in the United States, employment opportunities at the disposal of the federal government assumed a minor place but in the case of Canada such opportunities were a foremost feature in the job market. The way in which the Donegan family immediately turned to political patronage for jobs is a good example of the role federal posts played in this respect. When it is further remembered that the major capitalist activity of the period—the Canadian Pacific Railroad—was also controlled by the state, it is clear that federal patronage played a dominant role in job distribution in post-Confederation Canada. It is revealing to note that patronage started to decline once the economy began to develop and diversify. There were several reasons for the decline of patronage after the 1914–18 war but one of the basic ones was that the advance of manufacturing reduced the heavy dependence on the federal government (and therefore the federal political parties) for jobs and contracts.[61]

The slow development of industry in Canada had another social consequence that intensified the central significance of the patronage system. Again in contrast to contemporary United States, where capitalists and businessmen formed he dominant social class, these groups were numerically small and socially insignificant in Canada. In a society where industrial development was in its infancy and where manufacturing was small-scale, the professional middle classes flourished.[62] The prestige occupations in Canada lay in this area—barristers, solicitors, clergy, civil servants. In the case of Quebec the pre-eminence of these groups is accepted readily enough. Jean-Charles Falardeau has provided a good summary of the situation in Quebec, pointing out that by the mid-nineteenth century the professional middle-classes had succeeded the traditional elites. "La noblesse professionelle," Falardeau notes, "constituent effectivement, jusqu'à l'époque contemporaine, l'élite Canadienne-Française—c'est cette élite que l'on est tenté d'appeler et que l'on appelle souvent notre bourgeoisie." [g][63] But while this social phenomenon of a "bourgeois" class composed mostly of professionals rather than businessmen is normally associated with Quebec, it was equally a hallmark of English-Canadian society before the industrialization of the twentieth-century. Because there was no rapid capitalist and industrial development in Canada, there failed to develop a large and powerful middle class whose members could earn a living in ways that were open to trained and educated men in the United States and Britain. Opportunities for upward mobility through business corporations or by selling technical skills were very limited in Canada. This weakened "the development within Canadian society of capitalist, urban middle-class social values and forms of social structure." [64] In these circumstances there was little choice for each generation between 1867 and 1911 but to earn a living and gain social status by entering the legal profession or gaining a position in the public service.

A nice example of the social prestige a professional man could achieve in this small-town society was given by the Civil Service Commission in their 1908 report. Looking back to the 1880's for an overview of the reasons why public service was so attractive to Canadians the commissioners pointed out the advantages:

> Owing to the small mileage of railways and to the lack of communications most of the necessities of life raised in the different localities were consumed locally. Butter, eggs, meats, foodstuffs and articles entering into daily consumption were produced in the locality in which they were consumed. The same characteristic feature was applicable to domestic servants employed in the households of officials in the public service. A generation ago there was no means by which the farmers' daughters could remove easily from the locality in which they were born, and as the supply of domestic servants was greater than the demand the wages were comparatively small.... The civil servant in these days, although not in receipt of a large income, had his wants satisfied cheaply and without stint.[65]

Not all public employees could afford servants. Nevertheless it is a valid proposition that for most of the 1867–1911 period, bearing in mind prevailing economic conditions, the public service was the biggest single area of attractive, secure and prestigious employment. Even as late as 1911 employees in the public service still talked in terms of the "dignity" and "respectability" of their position in society.[66] The only way to get one of these jobs was to have some claim on one of the two political parties. It was these basic social and economic realities that enabled the political parties to make the patronage system such a powerful organizing force in Canadian society and politics.

---

[g] Up to the present time, the professional elite basically made up the French-Canadian elite and it is to this elite that we tend to and indeed often do refer to as our middle class.

IV

These final two sections will put forward some general conclusions about the significance of the patronage system and its long-term consequences in Canadian political development. The first point to make is that the pervasive patronage system that lasted throughout these years confirmed the power and prestige of professional middle classes who ran the two federal parties. In Canada these middle class groups—barristers, solicitors, doctors, notaries— which controlled the political parties did not, as in Europe, face serious social or economic competition. There was no aristocratic or traditional landed class that still had an influence in public affairs; there was no lingering peasant presence upon which a political movement could be based; there was no rapidly expanding capitalist class deriving wealth and power from industrialization; there was no mass labour movement seeking to form its own party. In these conditions the federal political parties, representing the dominant middle class and particularly the professionals, were extraordinarily influential in Canadian society. To understand the ramifications of these circumstances it is useful to consider the observations made by Hans Daalder in his analysis of political development in Western Europe.[67] Daalder, in tackling the question of how political elites relate to other elite groups in society, has suggested that one method of assessing the relative power of elites is to gauge the extent to which important positions within society could be obtained without reference to the political elite, without going through party channels.[68] In Canada nearly every important position in society was available only through the two political parties. Judges were appointed on the basis of partisan loyalty; QCs were distributed to lawyers who had been active in party work; senators were purely political appointments; posts throughout the public service, from the most senior down to the temporary and from Halifax to Vancouver, were disposed of by the parties to those who had worked for them. Even men with technical qualifications, such as civil engineers seeking work on the railroads, thought it wise to let their party credentials be known.[69] And in filling these positions the party leaders were approached in a supplicating manner by archbishops, bishops, deacons, priests, ministers, university principals, manufacturers and individuals from their prominent social groups. In Daalder's terms the political elite in Canada was the top power elite, no other group approaching it in terms of power and influence.[70]

The course of Canada's economy during these years helped sustain the dominant role of the parties and their patronage system. Again it is helpful to compare Canada with Europe and the United States. Jacques Ellul has written that "the nation-state is the most important reality of our days.... Nowadays it is the state that directs the economy.... The state is not just a superstructure. Marxist analysis is only valid in the nineteenth century when the emergence of uncontrolled, explosive economic power relegated a weak, liberal and unclearly delineated state to the shadows and subjugated it." [71] In Canada things did not happen this way. There was no explosive economic growth and the state was not relegated to a position of insignificance by the powerful forces of industrial capitalism. On the contrary, the state in Canada, the federal government, was the single most important energizing agency as it took the lead in stimulating economic growth, protecting infant industries, building a national transportation network as well as constructing its own physical presence in hundreds of public work projects across the country in the form of harbours, bridges, railways, post offices, customs houses and other buildings to house its bureaucracy. Upon entering office, each political party fell heir to this extensive sphere of government activity. In the United States the party in power had similar room for maneuver but in that country the party's scope for activity was circumscribed by other powerful interests in the expanding capitalist economy whereas in Canada the parties faced no rivals. Quite simply in Canada the parties were dominant and pervasive. A contemporary observer in the 1880's caught this development in the new Confederation. There was in Canada, he wrote, "an overgrowth of partyism." [72] In these circumstances the patronage system was like water finding its own level as it permeated post-Confederation Canadian society.

Another important point to emerge from the ramifications of the patronage system is that in the 1867 to 1911 period English- and French-Canadians were more alike in their social and political behavior than has commonly been accepted. Scholars have drawn attention to the fact that a major reason for the French-Canadian attachment to the Union (1840–1867) was that the Québécois professional middle class received, through patronage, opportunities for social advancement. Jacques Monet has well described this phenomenon in the twenty years before Confederation. "For two generations since 1800," explains Monet,

> The Canadian professional class had been struggling to secure an outlet for its ambitions: so now with a kind of bacterial thoroughness it began to invade every vital organ of government, and divide up among its members hundreds of posts as Judges, Queen's Counsels, Justices of the Peace, Medical Examiners, school inspectors, militia captains, postal clerks, mail conductors, census commissioners. And as the flatteries and salaries of office percolated down to other classes of society—from merchants who wanted seats on the Legislative Council down to impoverished habitants on the crowded seigneuries—the Canadians came to realize how parliamentary democracy could be more than a lovely ideal. It was also a profitable fact. And henceforth ... there could be guaranteed for all French-Canadians the possibility of room at the top.[73]

This process continued after 1867. Jean-Charles Bonenfant has described a typical pattern of upward mobility through politics—"l'homme politique était bourgeois d'une certaine aisance, ayant de préférence une formation juridique, se faisant élire à la chambre basse pour mourir plus tard conseiller legislatif, senateur ou juge." [h] [74] Jean Falardeau in his analysis of nineteenth century Quebec society also draws attention to the relationships among politics, patronage and social status. Falardeau makes distinctions between professionals and politicians, suggesting that the political bourgeoisie represented by such leaders as La Fontaine and Laurier and the members elected to Ottawa were more susceptible to English values, while within the localities of Quebec the "pure" professionals such as doctors, advocates, notaries, derived office and rewards from political patronage but remained rooted in Quebec language and culture. By the middle of the nineteenth century these professional and political elements, flourishing off the patronage system and all its ramifications, had replaced the ailing seigneurs as "la class dirigeante" in Quebec. Falardeau describes them in that perceptive phrase already noted as "la noblesse professionelle." [i] [75]

All this may be familiar enough but such historical social analysis should not stop short at the Ottawa river. Most of the preceding observations about the mobility patterns, values and social aspirations of the Quebec middle classes apply almost as well to English Canada between 1867 and 1911. Of course conditions were not identical in English Canada and Quebec. In the English provinces there were more varied responses to business, finance and commerce; there were more opportunities in these fields and more social credit attached to them. Also in English-Canada there was no one dominant church to which all successful men had to defer or relate in some manner. Yet recent research has downplayed some of these conventional distinctions and shown that Quebec's response to economic change was not as reactionary as was once supposed.[76] Whatever the final verdict of scholars on these distinctions it is essential to point out the similarities that did exist. Before industrialization developed in a dynamic manner in the decade after 1900, English-Canada was a rural, small-town and churched society with limited contacts with the secular and transforming world of industrial capitalism. The opportunities for posts and social advancement through businesses and companies were restricted. It was a society in which the most prestigious and important groups were the professional middle classes; a society in which patronage was normal, legitimate and pervasive; a society in which patronage was the single most important route of upward mobility to sought-after positions that gave security and status. English-speaking Canadians like their counterparts in Quebec turned to the patronage of the parties to become judges, senators, QCs, post office officials, customs service officials, collectors of inland revenue, medical examiners and a multitude

---

[h] the man of politics was from the middle class and possessed some personal fortune, preferably had some legal background and got himself elected to the lower house in order to later die as a legislative assistant, senator or judge.

[i] the ruling class...the professional class

of other positions in the public service. The operation of these social processes in English-Canada may have been less intense than in Quebec, more directly linked to business and commercial goals, but the profound similarities between French- and English-Canadians remain. There was then a fundamental convergence in how English- and French-Canadians regarded politics and political parties and the social ramifications of politics. In particular both major ethnic groups in Canada shared the same expectations and derived the same kind of rewards from the system of political patronage. On patronage English- and French-Canadians spoke the same language.

V

In the turning to the long-term consequences of the patronage system a paradox appears. On the one hand patronage helped to create and maintain political stability, an essential condition if Confederation were to succeed, but on the other hand it helped to entrench a political culture which because of its nature pushed problems concerning the nature of Confederation to the background. On the positive side the ability of the parties to utilize patronage on so grand a scale over so long a period helped them to attract and retain supporters and thereby establish a solid base in the population. The process of establishing political stability has been analyzed by many scholars studying new nations in the modern world and one conclusion they have come to is that political stability usually requires political parties to have an extensive and influential reach in society. The political parties must be able to show that they can effectively reward supporters and so encourage loyalty to the party. Often some form of patronage or corruption is the means by which a party establishes its position. As Joseph Palombara puts it, "corruption or its functional equivalent may be critically important to a developing nation." [77] For example, in such a new nation if merit alone were the criterion for appointment to the public service then there would be a growth of bureaucratic power which would push the parties to the sidelines and thus lead to political instability as the parties became unable to attract and reward supporters. In the Canadian case patronage functioned in this manner. Patronage cemented the support of both federal parties, enabled them to exert extensive influence throughout society, and thus helped create a stable party system.

Such an achievement should not be underestimated in a country as fragmented ethnically and regionally as Canada. But for the achievement of political stability there was a price to pay. One of the adverse consequences of the patronage system was that it encouraged the persistence of localism in Canadian politics. The way in which patronage was dispersed made every local party organization across Canada jealous of its own territory and suspicious of outsiders. Local exclusivity was sanctioned by the national party leaders. Indeed, this was a deliberate object of policy in order to create strong local organizations to fight election campaigns. This tendency must be kept in perspective. Localism, given the social, economic and geographic setting of Canada at the time, was bound to be a natural characteristic of Canadian politics.[78] The parties were moulded by the type of society in which they functioned. It is therefore a question of degree. Localism was bound to exist and the parties could either simply live with this reality or try to lessen its impact or encourage its persistence. They did the last. The patronage system of the two parties encouraged Canadian political culture to remain localized. From a party viewpoint this was a good thing since it created strong, loyal, hard-working local associations that could be managed by skilled leadership in Ottawa from the center of the patronage web. But it also restricted the vision of those in politics: MPs and local party notables were not encouraged by the system to interest themselves in affairs outside their own areas. The system worked in the direction of local inwardness. Because of this the Canadian House of Commons was in a metaphorical sense "la maison sans fenêtres." [j] [79] The MP's vision was narrowly focussed back into his locality and the windows on national issues were closed or obscured. The long reign of the patronage system contributed to a persistent parochialism in Canadian politics.

The great paradox lying at the center of Canadian political culture in this period was that this emphasis on localism and avoidance of debate on the relationships between the two racial groups were the very reasons for the success of the party system in maintaining stability prior to 1911. To explain this paradox it is useful to relate the case advanced in this article to recent work done by Arend Lijphart on elite accommodation and consociational democracy.[80] Lijphart's model seems a fruitful one to apply to Canada. He argues that European countries which have an ethnically segmented population have developed a peculiar form of democracy. In these systems each major ethnic group supports its own political party and the leaders of these parties, the representative elites, negotiate and mediate to form governments and maintain stability without sacrificing the interests of one particular group. Thus while there may be little communication and even great tension between the various linguistic blocs the elites of each group compromise in an attempt to reach solutions to national problems. The system then is characterized by elite accommodation. In a stimulating and thoughtful study Kenneth McCrea has applied the consociational democracy model to the Canadian case.[81] McCrea points out that the model can be useful for Canada only if it is modified to account for the fact that the two major ethnic blocs have never been represented by separate political parties at the national level. If accommodation does take place between the elites of each society, it must take place within the parties rather than between ethnically based parties. Having made this adjustment to the model McCrea analyzed how the system has worked in Canada and concluded that "even by the

---

[j] the house with no windows

most charitable interpretation, the political system's capacity to learn and adapt to linguistic-cultural diversity has not been high." [82] The federal parties have not been able to work out solutions to national problems but have instead created a situation of "immobilism and stalemate" in which the federal government seems weak and ineffective. Accommodation within the parties which should have been going on since 1867 has not taken place. On the contrary the gulf between English- and French-Canadians has widened to the point where the continued survival of the nation is in doubt. McCrea concludes that the Canadian political system has a low learning capacity.[83]

This is a complex topic which requires multi-factor analysis. Yet one of the principal reasons for the apparent ineffectiveness of the federal party system lies in the structure of parties as they developed between 1878 and 1911. The cardinal point here is that both parties relied on patronage so heavily that they reduced the need for any genuine accommodation on such issues, for example, as language in the public service. As Brown and Cook have recently pointed out, communication between the two races hardly existed except in the realm of politics. In 1902 Lord Minto remarked that he found "the leaders of society of both races unacquainted with each other. " [84] In these conditions much depended on the intercourse among the politicians of each race within the two federal parties and they found it easier and more congenial to deal with patronage and localized politics rather than "questions of race." [85]

The impact of patronage limited accommodation in the whole system of appointments and promotions in the public service. As far back as 1877 William Le Sueur drew attention to the fact that in the Canadian public service no heed was paid to whether or not an employee or candidate was bilingual and no recognition or reward was given to those who happened to be bilingual. Le Sueur pointed out that:

> in a service where two languages are used it is obviously unfair that a man who brings to the Service a knowledge of both, and whose knowledge of both is made use of by the Department in which he serves, should derive no advantage whatever from the fact. Such, however, is the fact. In the Department in which I serve a man who knows both French and English is made to do work requiring a knowledge of both those languages and to do it for his seniors. A senior clerk may send to a junior clerk that portion of his work which requires knowledge of a second language and the junior gets nothing at all in the way of promotion for this special qualification.[86]

It is important to emphasize that both English- and French-speaking politicians were responsible for this non-recognition of the value of two-language people in the public service—it was not a policy concocted by bigoted Anglo-Canadian politicians. The fact that a contemporary like Le Sueur could put his finger on a fundamental issue like this shows that it is not anachronistic to suggest that more could have been done by the parties to incorporate linguistic duality more securely and formally into the structure of the federal administration. The parties did not do so because it did not occur to them to do so.

Whether they came from the Gaspé or western Ontario or Halifax or Vancouver the politicians of the day were interested in the public service from the viewpoint, above all, of patronage. Their interest lay in placing party workers in the service, not trying to make the civil service a setting for reasonable accommodation of French- and English-Canadian interests.[87] In such ways the patronage system, while satisfying the immediate needs of local party associations in Quebec and the rest of Canada, constricted any incipient structural accommodation between the two racial blocs.

Canadians of the twentieth century are reaping the harvest of patronage politics during the 1867 to 1911 period. Parties relied heavily on patronage to satisfy ethnic groups within each party and so avoided the need to think about genuine accommodation in terms of the relationship of English- and French-Canadians in Confederation. Patronage was a great strength yet also a great weakness in the Canadian party system. It enabled the parties to flourish and maintain political stability as long as social and economic conditions were fertile ground for patronage and as long as society placed no major demands upon the parties. But once conditions changed, as Canada became an industrialized, urbanized society, as the provinces became more powerful and, above all, as Quebec modernized and began demanding that attention be paid to the basic meaning and structure of Confederation, then the parties which had been successful before 1911 began to become less effective. Their historical development had not prepared them for finding solutions to national problems.[88]

Notes

1. W.L. Morton, "The Cabinet of 1867," in F. W. Gibson, ed., *Cabinet Formation and Bicultural Relations* (Ottawa, 1970), p. 3; an example of a source Book treatment of the topic is J. H. Stewart Reid, Kenneth McNaught, Harry S. Crowe, *A Source Book of Canadian History* (Toronto, 1964), pp. 331–346.

2. Morton, "The Cabinet of 1867," p. 2. Political reminiscences of the period are full of references, charges and counter-charges to patronage and corruption. Richard Cartwright, *Reminiscences* (Toronto, 1912), is particularly rich in this regard. So too is W.T.R. Preston, *My Generation of Politics and Politicians* (Toronto, 1927).

3. Peter B. Waite, *Canada 1874–1896* (Toronto, 1971), p. 96.

4. Commission to Inquire into the Present State and Probable Requirements of the Civil Service (1868–1870), 1st and 2nd Reports in Sessional Papers, #19 (1869), 3rd Report in Sessional Papers, #64 (1870); Royal Commission to Inquire into the Organization of the Civil Service Commission (1880–81), 1st Report in Sessional Papers, #113 (1 80–81), 2nd Report in Sessional Papers #32 (1882); Royal Commission to Inquire into the Present State of the Civil Service at Ottawa (1891–92), Report in Sessional Papers, #16C (1892); Report of the Civil Service Commission (1907–08), Sessional Papers, #29A (1907–08); Commission to Inquire into the Public Service (1911–12), Sessional Papers, #57 (1913).

5. Report of Investigation into the Department of Marine and Fisheries, Sessional Papers, #38 (1909).

6. Waite, *Canada 1874–1896*, pp. 218–221, 230.

7. J.E. Hodgetts, William McClockey, Reginald Whitaker, V. Seymour Wilson, *The Biography of an Institution. The Civil Service Commission of Canada 1908–1967* (Montreal, 1972), p. 8.

8. The evidence is taken from the John A. Macdonald Papers, Public Archives of Canada [hereafter P.A.C.], Vol. 14, Kingston Patronage. On the formalities of the process see John McIntyre to John A. Macdonald, October 11, 1891.

9. Edward Smythe to John A. Macdonald, Kingston, November 13, 1889, Private, Macdonald Papers, Vol. 14, P.A.C

10. Smythe to Macdonald, Kingston, September 17, 1889, Private, Macdonald Papers, Vol. 14, P.A.C.

11. J.A. Metcalfe to John A. Macdonald, Kingston, January 18, 1890, Macdonald Papers, Vol. 14, P.A.C.

12. Mackenzie Bowell to John A. Macdonald, Ottawa, January 8, 1891, Macdonald Papers, Vol. 14, P.A.C.

13. Thomas H. McGuire to John A. Macdonald, Kingston, January 9, 1891, Macdonald Papers, Vol. 14, P.A.C.

14. J.A. Metcalfe to John A. Macdonald, Kingston, November 29, 1890, Private Macdonald Papers, Vol. 14, P.A.C.

15. M. Conger to John A. Macdonald, Picton, December 26, 1890, Macdonald Papers, Vol. 14, P.A.C. The militia appointment involved the interests of several ridings in southeast Ontario.

16. R.R. Pringle to John A. Macdonald, Cobourg, December 28, 1890, Macdonald Papers, Vol. 14, P.A.C.

17. H. Ward to John A. Macdonald, Port Hope, December 23, 1890, Private. On the relationship of this piece of patronage to local party "strength" see also Sam Hughes to Charles Tupper, Jr., Lindsay, Ontario, December 25, 1890, Macdonald Papers, Vol. 14, P.A.C.

18. George Fitzpatrick to John A. Macdonald, Kingston, January 8, 1891, Private, Macdonald Papers, Vol. 14, P.A.C.

19. John McIntyre to John A. Macdonald, January 10, 1891, Private.

20. John Haggart to John A. Macdonald, Ottawa, September 19, 1889. In another case Edward Smythe discussed with the Prime Minister the plight of "our old friend B. McConville," a party activist who had been given a contract for carrying the mail and now wished the amount to be increased. See Smythe to Macdonald, Kingston, September 17, 1889. Private, Macdonald Papers, Vol. 14, P.A.C.

21. Report of Investigation into Department of Marine and Fisheries (1909), p. 10.

22. *Ibid.,* p. 41.

23. *Ibid.,* p. 44.

24. *Ibid.,* p. 42–43.

25. Report of the Civil Service Commission (1907–08), pp. 37, 27.

26. *Ibid.,* p. 28.

27. *Ibid.,* p. 89–90.

28. *Ibid.,* pps. 7, 28, 440–443.

29. *Ibid.,* p. 28.

30. Hugh Falconer to Wilfrid Laurier, Shelburne, Ontario, January 13, 1908; Laurier to Falconer, Ottawa, January 15, 1908, Private Laurier Papers, P.A.C. Vol. 950.

31. John Small to John A. Macdonald, Toronto, April 5, 1887, Confidential, Macdonald Papers, P.A.C., Vol. 24.

32. Robert Birmingham to John A. Macdonald, Toronto, October 10, 1889, Macdonald Papers, P.A.C., Vol. 24. Macdonald kept a list of all the barristers in Toronto and noted opposite each name the party affiliation. He also estimated the composition of the Ontario bar as a whole according to party membership. The Toronto bar had 150 barristers eligible for the QC—95 were Conservatives, 55 were "Reformers." See List of in Toronto, Macdonald Papers, P.A.C., Vol. 24.

33. B.L. Doyle to Frank Smith, Goderich, November 28, 1879, Private, Macdonald Papers, P.A.C., Vol. 25 II.

34. Frank Smith to John A. Macdonald, [?], December 1, 1879, Macdonald Papers, P.A.C., Vol. 25 II.

35. N.O., Cote, *Political Appointments, Parliaments and the Judicial Bench in Canada 1890–1903* (Ottawa, 1903), pp. 571–72.

36. H.C. Gwyn to John A. Macdonald, Dundas, April 22, 1885, Macdonald Papers, P.A.C., Vol. 26.

37. S. Dawson to John A. Macdonald, Ottawa, May 13, 1884, Macdonald Papers, P.A.C., Vol. 26.

38. N.C. Wallace to John A. Macdonald, Ottawa, July 15, 1885, Private, Macdonald Papers, P.A.C., Vol. 26.

39. A.M. Boswell to John A. Macdonald, Toronto, July 7, 1887, Macdonald Papers, P.A.C., Vol. 27 II.

40. George Reid to James Sutherland, London, May 4, 1900, Laurier Papers, P.A.C., Vol. 873.

41. *Ibid.*

42. Roy Choquette to Wilfrid Laurier, Ottawa, September 12, 1896, Personelle, Laurier Papers, P.A.C., Vol. 833.

43. *Ibid.*

44. *Ibid.* Laurier himself would act on these patronage requests, even down to the most minor, by notifying (as Macdonald had done) the appropriate minister of the necessary appointments. For example, in response to one request for Liberal appointees to the International railroad Laurier made out a memorandum naming those employees to be dismissed and indicating their replacements. See H.G. Carroll to Wilfrid Laurier, Quebec, December 29, 1896; Memorandum by Laurier in Reply, n.d., Laurier Papers, P.A.C., Vol. 833.

45. Royal Commission on the Public Service (1911–12), p. 1292. Macpherson's evidence was given on July 30 and 31, 1912.

46. *Ibid.*, pp. 1416–1417.

47. With the changes wrought by industrialization and urbanization the Canadian government was forced to acknowledge that the patronage-ridden public service system was inefficient and ineffective in the new conditions. This was a basic factor pushing for change. Public opinion was also increasingly critical of patronage after 1900, and an increasing sense of professionalism within the service were additional factors. Public employees in the western provinces were particularly critical in their appearance and representation to the Royal Commission of 1911–12. See R.C. Brown and R. Cook, *Canada 1896–1921. A Nation Transformed* (Toronto, 1974), pp. 192–194, 321; Norman Ward, *The Canadian House of Commons* (Toronto, 1950), pp. 275–281; Royal Commission on the Public Service (1911–1912), pp. 16–20, 337–338; Civil Service Commission (1908–09), p. 13. The latter report noted that "it was the universal feeling amongst the officials who gave evidence ... that this patronage evil was the curse of the public service."

48. P.B. White, *Canada 1873–1896* (Toronto, 1971), pp. 8–9.

49. M.C. Urquhart and K.A.H. Buckley, eds., *Historical Statistics of Canada* (Toronto, 1965), pp. 5, 14–15, Series A 15–19 and A 20–24. On pp. 5–7 Urquhart and Buckley discuss the problems of "urban" and "rural" classification in this period.

50. F. Gibson, ed., *Cabinet Formation and Bicultural Relations* (Ottawa, 1970), p. 171.

51. A.R.M. Lower, *My First Seventy-five Years* (Toronto, 1967), p. 33. Some examples of suspicion of "outsiders" appear in this article. The patronage papers of both Macdonald and Laurier are full of other instances. For example a lawyer looking for work in London, Ontario was regarded with deep antipathy because he had no roots in the area. Another individual who was not known locally was described as an "unscrupulous professional man" —i.e., with no base in the local church or community, simply interested in pursuing a career wherever he could get a job. See John Barwick to John A. Macdonald, Woodstock, February 10, 1879, Macdonald Papers, P.A.C., Vol. 251; A. McKean to John A. Macdonald, Bothwell, Ontario, September 19, 1887, Macdonald Papers, P.A.C., Vol. 271. Also see note 30 above for an example in the Laurier Papers.

52. Michael Bliss, "A Living Profit: Studies in the Social History of Canadian Business 1883–1911," Ph.D. Thesis, University of Toronto, p. 331.

53. *Monetary Times,* June 21, 1896, quoted in Bliss, "A Living Profit," p. 331.

54. *Journal of Commerce,* November 4, 1898, pp. 634–635; Byron Walker to G.F. Little, October 10, 1907, both quoted in Bliss, "A Living Profit," p. 331.

55. Byron Walker to G.F. Little, October 10, 1907, quoted in Bliss, "A Living Profit," p. 331.

56. *Industrial Canada,* March 1906, p. 484, quoted in Bliss, "A Living Profit," p. 332.

57. Waite, *Canada 1893–1896,* pp. 74–78.

58. S. D. Clark, "The Canadian Manufacturers Association," *Canadian Journal of Economics and Political Science,* Vol. IV (1938), pp. 506–508. R. T. Naylor, *The History of Canadian Business 1867–1914,* 2 Vols., Toronto, 1975), Vol. 2, pp. 276–284 argues Canadian industrial development was stultified during these decades.

59. Urquhart and Buckley, eds., *Canadian Historical Statistics,* p. 463, Series Q 1–11.

60. Naylor, *History of Canadian Business 1867–1914,* Vol. 2, pp. 276–284. Contemporaries talked of the very recent growth of industrial capitalism in Canada and referred to the fact that there was not as yet a class of entrepreneurs who could sit back and enjoy their profits. W. T. R. Preston in *My Generation of Politics* (Toronto, 1927), pp. 204, 487 described the 1880's and 1890's as "the twenty years [which witnessed] the creation and establishment of a capitalist system." Robert Laird Borden in his *Memoirs* (Toronto, 1938), p. 151, pointed out that "we have no men of leisure or of means." Goldwin Smith in his *Reminiscences* (New York, 1910) pp. 456–457, 487 remarked that "Toronto wealth is not munificent. It certainly is not compared with the United States." All these points reflect the fact that Canadian industry was as yet only a struggling part of the social and economic structure.

61. The Report of the Civil Service Commission (1907–08), pp. 14, 17, pointed out that public service positions while still sought after were becoming less attractive as opportunities expanded in the economy. They pointed to the significance of the fact that the lower levels of the public service were being increasingly filled by women. Norman Ward in his study of Canadian MPs emphasizes that many of them went on to important patronage positions. "The evidence is fairly strong," he writes, "that politics in Canada is by no means the precarious occupation it is often assumed to be. Until very recently, only a small number of private businesses were in a position to provide positions for 30% of their employees." See Ward, *House of Commons,* p. 98–101, 103, 146.

62. Bliss, "A Living Profit," pp. 1, 321, 341; S. D. Clark, *The Developing Canadian Community* (Toronto, 1968), pp. 227, 234. Clark argued that "in a way scarcely true of any other Western nation, the middle class in Canada has been the Establishment."

63. J. C. Falardeau, "Evolution des structures sociales et des élites au Canada francais Quebec," (1960), pp. 10–11.

64. Clark, *The Developing Canadian Community,* pp. 243–252.

65. Report of the Civil Service Commission (1907–08), pp. 14–17.

66. Royal Commission on the Public Service (1911–12), p. 1213.

67. Hans Daalder, "Parties, Elites and Political Development in Western Europe," in Joseph Palombara and Myron Weiner, eds., *Political Parties and Political Revolution* (Princeton, 1966).

68. *Ibid.,* p. 75. Daalder talks of the "reach" or "permeation" in society of political parties.

69. For example, George Grant to John A. Macdonald, Kingston, November 26, 1883, Macdonald Papers, P.A.C., Vol. 26, Bishop of Hamilton to Macdonald, Hamilton, October 15, 1880, Macdonald Papers, P.A.C., Vol. 25 II, Bishop of Peterborough to Macdonald, Peterborough, November 23, 1887, Macdonald Papers, P.A.C., Vol. 27 I,

Reverend A. McKean to Macdonald, Bothwell, September 19, 1887, Macdonald Papers, P.A.C., Vol 27 I, Byron Nicholson to William Gibson, Quebec, November 28, 1908 (Nicholson was a newspaper editor and "literateur"), Laurier Papers, P.A.C., Vol. 950, Thomas Swan to John A. Macdonald, Mount Forest, Ontario, March 17, 1883, Macdonald Papers, P.A.C., Vol. 5 (Swan owned a carriage works business), R. McKechnie to Macdonald, Dundas, March 11, 1891, Macdonald Papers, P.A.C., Vol. 22 (McKechnie was head of a manufacturing company and former President of the Canadian Manufacturers Association). On railroad patronage see N. A. Belcourt to Laurier, Ottawa. August 31, 1904, Laurier Papers P.A.C., Vol. 950. Also, Waite, *Canada 1873–96*, pp. 136–137, Brown and Cook, *Canada 1896–1921,* pp. 147–153.

70. Alexander Tillock Galt caught the essence of this condition in the new confederation when he wrote that "politics form the only short cut from the middle to the upper ranks." See O. D. Skelton, *The Life and Times of Alexander Tillock Galt* (Toronto, 1920), pp. 377–379. In 1880 an observer noted the dominance of fashionable society in Ottawa by politicians, civil servants and associated professionals. See J. E. Collins, *Canada Under Lord Lorne,* p. 309. See also Lady Aberdeen's comments in Saywell, ed., *The Canadian Journal of Lady Aberdeen* (Toronto, 1960), p. 42. J. W. Dafoe, "Canadian Problems of Government," *CJEPS,* Vol. V (1939), p. 288, pointed out that a career in politics in pre-1914 Canada carried more "personal distinction" than since that time and that to be an MP "meant a good deal more than it does now; and to be a member was a very general, if not all but universal desire among ambitious men."

71. Jacques Ellul, *The Political Illusion* (New York, 1967), p. 9.

72. Hans Muller, *Canada. Past, Present and Future* (Montreal, 1880), p. 7. J. D. McClokie back in 1948 described a new state form, "the party state" in which the political party was the most dominant power. See McClokie, "The Modern Party State," *CJEPS,* vol. XIV (1948), p. 143.

73. Jacques Monet, "Les Idées politiques de Baldwin and LaFontaine," in Hamelin, ed., *The Political Ideas of the Prime Ministers of Canada* (Ottawa, 1969), pp. 16–17. See also l'Hon. Charles Langelier, *Souvenirs Politiques* (Quebec, 1912), pp. 25–26.

74. Jean-Charles Bonenfant, "L'evolution du statut de l'homme politique Canadien-Français," in Fernand Dumont et Jean-Paul Montmigny, eds., *Le Pouvoir dans la société Canadienne-Française* (Quebec, 1966), pp. 117–118.

75. Falardeau, "Evolution des structures," op. cit., p. 11. The phrase "La noblesse professionelle" comes from P. J. O. Chauveau, *Charles Guerin. Roman de moeurs canadiennes* (Montreal, 1853), pp. 55–56.

76. For example, William F. Ryan, *The Clergy and Economic Growth in Quebec 1896–1914* (Quebec, 1966). Two other studies put Quebec economic development in a much clearer light than traditional works. See Albert Faucher, *Quebec en Amérique au XIX siècle* (Montreal, 1973) and Jean Hamelin and Yves Roby, *Histoire Economique du Québec 1851–1896* (Montreal, 1971). Faucher, for example, deals with the economic divergence between Quebec and Ontario in terms of technical development, regional pulls and so on rather than in terms of differences in value systems. See too the assessment in Brown and Cook, *Canada 1896–1921,* pp. 127–143.

77. Joseph Palombara, ed., *Bureaucracy and Political Development* (Princeton, 1963), p. 11; Hodgetts, et al., *Biography of an Institution,* pp. 14–16.

78. Gibson, ed., *Cabinet Formation,* p. 171. See note 51.

79. Daalder, "Parties, Elites and Political Development," op. cit., pp. 64–65.

80. Arend Lijphart, *The Politics of Accommodation: Pluralism and Democracy in the Netherlands* (Berkeley, 1968), "Typologies of Democratic Systems, *Comparative Political Studies,*" Vol. I (1968), pp. 17–35, "Consociational Democracy," *World Politics,* Vol. 21 (1969), pp. 207–225.

81. Kenneth D. McRae, *Consociational Democracy: Political Accommodation in Segmented Societies* (Toronto, 1974).

82. *Ibid.,* pp. 250, 259–260.

83. *Ibid.,* pp. 254, 261.

84. Brown and Cook, *Canada 1896–1921,* pp. 164–165.

85. In a letter written shortly before his death Macdonald complained, almost in a tone of surprise, that such issues should arise in Canada, that it was "a great pity that these questions of race should arise so frequently." John A. Macdonald to Alphonse Desjardins, Ottawa, January 6, 1891, Alphonse Desjardins Papers, P.A.C., MG 271, E22.

86. Notes on Civil Service Reform by William D. LeSueur Select Committee on Present Conditions of the Civil Service (1877), p. 106.

87. McRae's comments are pertinent here. "In retrospect," he writes, "the quest to accommodate linguistic diversity in Canada may be viewed as a series of lost opportunities ... and it seems likely that this low capacity of the system to devise effective solutions has helped to increase the intensity of linguistic and cultural cleavage in recent decades." McRae, *Consociational Democracy,* p. 259.

88. It is necessary not to press this case too far lest the tone become anachronistic. Professor Creighton has warned against placing politicians of post-Confederation Canada in an alien context. They were not eighteenth century politicians interested in ethnic and cultural issues. They were Victorian politicians who were successful in building a viable Canada in arduous circumstances. D. G. Creighton, *Canada's First Century 1867–1967* (Toronto, 1970), p. 8. These are weighty reminders of the dangers of anachronistic analysis. Yet, as the 1877 evidence of LeSueur shows, there were alternatives even in the context of the times. Macdonald and Laurier then can be characterized as limited in their responses to the basic problem of Confederation—and these limitations took root and flourished because the patronage system enabled the political leaders to close their minds to structural responses to the "question of race."

SIR WILFRID LAURIER
GRITS ON HIGH

Jeffrey Simpson

> *Remember this, that in politics, the question seldom arises to do the ideal right. The best that is generally to be expected, is to attain a certain object, and for the accomplishment of this object, many things have to be done which are questionable, and many things have to be submitted to which, if rigorously investigated, could not be approved of.*

> Sir Wilfrid Laurier, 1904, writing to a friend.

When the Frenchman André Siegfried visited Canada in the first decade of the twentieth century, the precarious, testy relations between English and French Canadians struck him as the key to understanding the country, including its politics. "A land of fears and jealousies and conflicts," he wrote of Canada in 1907.[1] Wise politicians understood that fierce ethnic and religious rivalries lurked just below the surface of Canadian life, capable of bubbling up at a moment's notice. "They exert themselves, therefore, to prevent the formation of homogeneous parties, divided according to creed or race or class," Siegfried thought. "The purity of political life suffers from this, but perhaps the very existence of the Federation is the price."

Political parties tried, said Siegfried, to keep these rivalries under control by removing "ideas and doctrines" from the political arena. "The consequence is that rival candidates commit themselves to identical promises moved by an identical determination to win," he wrote. "Whichever side succeeds, the country it is well known will be governed in just the same way: the only difference will be in the *personnel* of the government." Parties tended "to become mere associations for the securing of power, their doctrines serving merely as weapons, dulled or sharpened, grasped as the occasion arises for use in the fight." Parties made "extraordinary compromises" within themselves to keep together "heterogeneous elements," and by these internal compromises the parties "have come to regard each other without alarm; they know each other too well, and resemble each other too closely."

To a shrewd outsider, it may have appeared that nothing distinguished Conservatives and Liberals, but to the members of the two parties, their differences provided the stuff of daily political combat. Election campaigns remained raw-boned affairs, replete with widespread chicanery, flaming rhetoric, and elaborate promises. "There [can] be few countries in the world in which elections rouse more fury and enthusiasm than in Canada," Siegfried thought, echoing observations made by a variety of nineteenth-century British governors. Siegfried also noted that "public works are what Colonials demand most of all ... thus provinces, *communes* and individuals are all united in soliciting from the Government as much in the way of public works as possible." In the House of Commons, debates rumbled into the wee hours of the morning, and committee meetings often featured one side attempting to pin charges of corruption, waste or extravagance on the other. In the Commons public accounts committee from 1896 to 1905, for example, thirty-seven of the forty substantive reports were "frank attempts by one political party to unearth and publicize evidence that would embarrass the other."[2] At the turn of the century, the Liberals and Conservatives were like two rival tribes, membership in which was often fixed at birth, although alterable by appeals to ethnicity, policy or personal self-interest, facilitated by the judicious application of patronage.

When Siegfried's book appeared in 1907, the Liberals had been in office for eleven years under the leadership of Prime Minister Wilfrid Laurier. By 1907, the first French-Canadian leader of a national party had broadened the coalition of the Liberal party. He had succeeded in turning Quebec from its Conservative traditions into a Liberal bastion. Using the advantages of office, he had created Liberal strongholds in the new provinces of Saskatchewan and Alberta, while retaining sufficient strength in the other western provinces, Ontario and the Maritimes to produce the election victories that had allowed the Liberals to supplant the Conservatives as the dominant party of Canada. In the process, Laurier had weaned the Liberals from some of the Clear Grit traditions that had inspired and plagued his predecessors, Edward Blake and Alexander Mackenzie. He had also transformed—and this was perhaps his most lasting contribution—the Liberals in Quebec from a collection of anti-clerical *rouges* into a broadly based coalition. Laurier made the Liberal party acceptable to the clergy, welcoming to Conservatives repelled by intolerant ultramontanism, open to all French-speaking Quebeckers resentful of the Conservatives' handling of the Riel and Manitoba Schools questions, and prepared to extend the helping hand of government to the English-speaking capitalists of Montreal.[3] This transformation changed the dynamics of Canadian politics for nearly a century. Laurier had adopted Macdonald's formula for political success, both its transcending vision and particular tactics, and demonstrated again that imitation in politics, as in life, can be the highest form of flattery.

Laurier has come down to us as one of our most virtuous prime ministers, and indeed he did not lack for virtues. Kindly of spirit, benevolent by disposition, Laurier made friends easily. He forged loyalties that withstood lacerating linguistic and ethnic divisions, until the fiercest ethnic division of Canada's history—conscription—shattered his party. Even then, a rump of English-speaking Liberals remained faithful to this extraordinary man, despite the self-evident political risks they ran in their inflamed constituencies. Like Macdonald, Laurier had an uncanny ability to let men down easily, to remember that the game of politics never stops, and that today's foe might become tomorrow's ally. He had principles, and strong ones at that, but principles that could always be tempered for partisan advantage or national unity. In matters of patronage—still embedded in the heart and soul of Canadian politics—Laurier displayed a finesse and an attention to detail that would have done Macdonald proud. Laurier had no choice because, as his biographer Oscar Douglas Skelton wrote, "the distribution of patronage was the most important single function of the government."[4] Laurier appreciated the importance of patronage and meticulously attended its demands. In the words of Sir John Willison, editor of *The Globe* and a long-time friend, Laurier displayed "a large toleration for patronage."[5]

Laurier's toleration arose partly from his background. In Quebec, political patronage was woven deeply into the texture of society. But his Quebec upbringing alone could not have shaped his views, for patronage suffused the politics of other parts of Canada. Laurier's ambition played a part. Like Lester Pearson half a century later, Laurier cloaked his driving ambition with self-effacement, combining the charade of Sir Galahad with the cunning of Prince Machiavelli, as newspaper editor John Dafoe wrote. The requiting of political ambition required paying due heed to patronage. Successful party management demanded it and the country expected it. Laurier, after all, had been vanquished by John A. Macdonald, and the lessons of the master were not lost on him. Laurier's personality also made for "toleration." Like Macdonald, he took men as they were, and left their moral perfection to churchmen. He was a politician, and to be a successful politician in the political culture of the period meant to dispense favours so as to ally the interests of ambitious men with the interests of the Liberal party.

In many ways, the Laurier years marked a continuation of the electoral and patronage practices during the Macdonald years. Most, if not all, of the campaign irregularities and illegalities that had sullied elections in the Macdonald era resurfaced in Laurier's. Nearly ninety controverted election cases were heard from 1897 to 1911. This number represented a decline from an earlier period—over eighty constituencies were contested in the 1891 election alone!—not because electoral conduct had improved, but because politicians on both sides increasingly used that old device, the "saw-off." In other matters as well, the Laurier Liberals preferred to imitate the dubious morality of Sir John A. rather than the dismal rectitude of previous Liberal leaders, Alexander Mackenzie and Edward Blake. They had been men of high moral principle, but they also projected a more stunted vision of the nation than had Macdonald. Heirs of Ontario's Clear Grit ethic, they had preached expenditure restraint, attacked waste in government, questioned massive outlays for such public works as the Canadian Pacific Railway, flailed at the cozy relations between the Conservative party and powerful capitalists, and generally lamented the decline in political morality. Neither one had understood Quebec politics and had not found anyone to interpret its intricacies correctly. They were admirable men in their ways, but prickly and rigid, more inclined than others to believe in their own special gifts. Goldwin Smith may have been too harsh, but he came close to the truth: If Mackenzie's virtue as prime minister resided in once having been a stone mason, his liability lay in remaining one.[6]

Clever politicians learn from their opponents' virtues; unwise ones concentrate on their opponents' faults. To Mackenzie, Macdonald had perverted sound government through his profligate spending and had debased political morality through his flagrant favouritism. The mobs of Conservative office-seekers, contractors and partisan hangers-on of the first Macdonald governments appalled Mackenzie, who never tired of furiously denouncing their apparent influence on the Conservative government. The Pacific Scandal confirmed Mackenzie's beliefs: Macdonald ran a government whose partisanship, corruption and brazen illegalities shocked a nation which he felt cried out for higher standards at the top. In this refrain, Mackenzie echoed the Clear Grits, and if he doubted for a moment that the country agreed, he needed only to glance through the Liberal bible, *The Globe,* whose editorial on the eve of the 1874 election proclaimed: "The poll tomorrow is the Thermopylae of Canadian political virtue."[7]

Prime Minister Mackenzie made himself minister of public works, the portfolio with the most obvious opportunities for porkbarrelling and one of the most alluring for patronage. Mackenzie reckoned that by controlling this portfolio, he could bring his own standards to bear on the principle repository of waste and corruption. Instead, the portfolio controlled him. It crushed his spirit, burdened him with a thousand details, and made him the lightning rod for complaints from the Liberals' own mob of office-seekers, contractors and partisan hangers-on. Smith's crack about Mackenzie the stone mason captured his essence in office: Mackenzie chiselled dutifully away, trying to shape each piece of the political edifice according to his own exacting standards, but forgetting about the grand design of broadening the base of his political party. He could not take men as he found them. He insisted upon trying to remake them, and when he repeatedly failed, his isolation and frustration increased. Nor could he effectively delegate responsibility, as Macdonald did and as Laurier would do. Of course, prime ministers in the nineteenth century were expected to immerse themselves in a myriad of patronage details later generations of political leaders could leave to trusted lieutenants. But there came a point, even then, when prime ministers had no choice but to delegate responsibility or be submerged by the avalanche of requests that poured across their desks. Mackenzie, however, never grasped that point, perhaps because he knew he could not trust his colleagues to live by the same standards he set for himself.

The clash between political reality and Mackenzie's values bedevilled his government. In practice, Mackenzie turned out to be less virtuous in matters of patronage than he might like to have been. Having set high standards, he suffered the humiliation of being unable to meet them. His "toleration" for patronage and porkbarrelling never came naturally, but from an always grudging acquiescence to irresistible pressures from party members.

Mackenzie's Scottish sense of economy recoiled as demands for spending poured into Ottawa. He soon discovered that keeping the promises he made while Opposition leader was earning his administration rampant disfavour and probable defeat. The business interests, in particular, counted on government contracts to flow from a robust program of public works. They favoured restraint all right, except when it involved their own commercial interests. And in the constituencies, the clamour for improvements never abated, especially in the far-flung reaches of the Dominion, where grievances had already accumulated against the insensitivity and greed of Central Canada. Coastal communities demanded better harbours. Cities screamed for new federal buildings, especially post offices. Every hamlet desired if not a main railway then at least a branch line.

The pressures for federal spending—and for preferment and place—rained down upon Mackenzie from within his own political formation, itself an uncongealed coalition of interests, not yet a national party. "I have no sinecure," he wrote to his brother, his pen rushing past the required points of punctuation, "in trying to keep together a crowd of French Liberals Irish Catholics Methodists Free Traders Protectionists Eastern Province men Western men Central Canada men Columbians Manitobans all jealous of each other and striving to obtain some advantage or concession. I always knew it was very hard to keep liberals together but my experience has been far in excess of my utmost belief."[8]

Mackenzie arrived in office to find the civil service packed with Conservatives and the Senate with a lopsided Conservative majority. Even in defeat, Macdonald had tried to shoehorn a few more Conservatives into office. In the three weeks before the Mackenzie government took office, Macdonald appointed dozens of his supporters to various positions. On the day John A. resigned, he announced appointments for four former MPs and ministers. The Liberals, naturally enough, cried foul and cancelled most of the last-minute Macdonald appointments.[9] But Mackenzie would not go further, despite his supporters' howls that he dismiss Conservatives from the public service.

Wholesale dismissals marked changes of government in the United States, where the spoils system had been accepted in politics since the presidency of Andrew Jackson. Mackenzie's Liberals, however, had attracted many Conservative voters; a wholesale purge might alienate some recent converts. A purge would also have offended Mackenzie's own sense of fair play and the higher standards of political conduct he set for his government. Despite his cryptic comment that "all the offices are crammed with hostile people so that we can trust no one," Mackenzie retained the vast majority of public servants. "We have not superannuated one man," he wrote, "except where it was urgently sought, and ample reasons were given—and these cases were three in all, I think."[10] Despite what he called "hordes" of spies around him, Mackenzie stood firm. "My object will be … justice for all, let the consequences be what they may."[11]

The consequences for internal party harmony were entirely baleful. Mackenzie's government represented the first chance since Confederation for Liberals, or Reformers as some still called themselves, to seize the spoils of power. Mackenzie's rectitude immediately confronted political reality. Office-seekers camped in his waiting rooms. Liberal MPs demanded positions for their supporters. A walk from his office to the Commons chamber often meant listening to importuning advice from a host who had been waiting for a chance to fill his ear. And the mail! Dozens of letters arrived daily, some burdening his conscience, all demanding his personal attention. Several weeks into the job, he wrote to his daughter: "I devote an hour of this peaceful, beautiful Sabbath morning to the pleasant duty [of letter-writing]. Today, the great army of contractors and office-seekers are shut out and the very office has a Sabbath look."[12] He tried to reward Liberals, as he explained in his bulky correspondence, where everything else was equal. But therein lay the problem, because for almost every Liberal nothing else equalled partisanship. To be a Liberal was to be qualified.

Alfred Jones, Liberal MP from Halifax, whom Mackenzie frequently consulted on patronage, insisted that an insufficient number of Liberals had found jobs on the railway. "It is impossible to fill the Railway offices on political grounds," Mackenzie fumed. "They must have experience, and if we cannot get experienced men among our friends we must take them elsewhere just as you would in a private company or in your own office … Don't ask me to do a thing you would not freely do in my place."[13] Mackenzie utterly missed the point: Jones spoke as a politician, not a businessman. Mackenzie poured his special frustrations about the patronage deluge from the Maritimes into another letter to Jones, "I am in receipt of your extraordinary letter about railway and other appointments, and I confess nothing has been written to me for months that has astonished me more. It is really too bad. Half my time is taken up with this question of patronage in Nova Scotia and Prince Edward Island. My life has become a torment to me about it."[14]

Mackenzie, unlike Macdonald and Laurier, could not let disappointed supplicants down gracefully. He made supplicants feel insignificant, angry or rejected. As a device for weeding out the unqualified, he took to administering impromptu examinations for competence to everyone who entered his office looking for a job, hoping to make supplicants realize their unsuitability. He also instructed his secretary to administer the same examinations, and to send in only those who had passed. He wrote George Brown of *The Globe:* "At this point there is a little soreness in several quarters at me simply because the public interest forced me to stand between them and some cherished but improper object."[15] As a wag put it, Macdonald could say no with more grace than Mackenzie could say yes.

The onset of recession heightened Mackenzie's frustration because it threw up more office-seekers and forced the government to curtail expenditures. In 1875, he wrote to a fellow Liberal: "Friends expect to be benefited by offices they are unfit for, by contracts they are not entitled to, by advances they have not earned. Enemies ally themselves with friends and push friends to the front. Some dig trenches at a distance and approach in regular seige form. A weak Minister would ruin the party in a month and the country very soon …"[16] A resolute prime minister, as things turned out, was ruining his party. The country survived.

If Mackenzie could do little about the patronage of appointments and contracts, apart from setting his face against it wherever possible, his government did reflect the Liberals' reforming spirit by changing the laws governing elections. One bill replaced staggered polling days—which had been spaced over six weeks in the 1867 election and over eleven weeks in the 1872 election—with a single polling period in a few far-flung constituencies. Another statute gave the courts a role in determining controverted elections, although this reform looked better on paper than in application since the Commons often failed to act on judicial findings.[17]

Mackenzie, for all his moral outrage, saw nothing wrong in rewarding senior party stalwarts, because it neither compromised government efficiency nor wasted money. A long list of ministers received appointments, including Justice Minister Antoine-Aimé Dorion, chief justice of the court of Queen's Bench for Quebec; Minister of the Interior David Laird, lieutenant-governor of the North-West Territory; and Secretary of State David Christie, Speaker of the Senate.

Recession, however, laid its dead hand upon the country during Mackenzie's government and as economic conditions worsened, internal party bickering increased. Liberals seemed disgruntled, every region discontented with its slice of the spoils. An allegation that his brother's company unfairly won a government contract—an allegation he successfully rebuffed—wounded him personally and sent critics snickering about his holier-than-thou double standard. His habitual dourness mirrored the country's mood; perhaps the majority of Canadians did prefer John A. drunk to Mackenzie sober.

Defeated at the polls, Mackenzie underlined his difference from Macdonald. He refused, despite the strongest pleas from Liberal colleagues, to appoint more than a handful of people. "I can quite understand," he wrote to a supplicant, "you have considered me omnipotent in such matters. There could not be a greater mistake. It's all over now. I have no power to make appointments." To another, he explained his motives, "As the election went against us, I could not do in the matter as I intended. It would be creating a new office, and this would be contrary to our own avowal of principle and our convictions. My doctrine was that I was bound as the trustee and guardian of the Liberal party to do nothing that could be held up as a reproach against us, in short, to go out clean."[18] He left, if not necessarily clean, then cleaner certainly than John A. and, for that matter, cleaner than most subsequent prime ministers. He remained to the end a Clear Grit, admirable in his way, standing for important principles, but a prisoner of a limited view of government and a poor practitioner of the arts of patronage. He never shared Macdonald's understanding of patronage as a tool for widening coalitions, meeting the party's financial needs, buying off the disaffected, rewarding the contented. Patronage was a burden, nothing more. That it could also be an opportunity apparently never occurred to him.

It certainly did occur to Laurier. He had been leader of the Opposition for nine years and a member of Parliament for twenty-two years before becoming prime minister in 1896, so he was steeped in the political culture of his time. If he only observed the pressures for patronage before 1896, he felt them directly as soon as he moved into the Prime Minister's Office. They bore down with the arrival of every mailbag, each letter staking out a claim on preferment.

Prime Minister Charles Tupper, following the path blazed by Macdonald, had attempted after his defeat in 1896, but before the Liberals took power, to pad the civil service with Conservatives and to pay off some prominent party stalwarts. The governor-general, Lord Aberdeen, blocked the outgoing prime minister's designs on the grounds of constitutional impropriety. But the padding of the public service had actually begun months before the election call, which rendered Laurier's patronage problems more acute since the Liberals, as was their wont, had campaigned on economy in government. Whatever the merits of economy, Liberal MPs and ministers soon grated against its constraints. "This policy of economy, of being penny-wise and pound-foolish," complained MP Albert Malouin, "is a policy from which the government does not benefit and which hurts the party."[19] Laurier, pestered by Montreal Liberals about why an insufficient number of partisans (including a certain Mr. Nugent) had been not appointed to the main city post office—one of Montreal's patronage plums since the days of Cartier—received this revealing explanation from Postmaster-General William Mulock: "The late Government in the last year or so of their tenure of office appointed a large number of persons temporarily to the service, the Montreal post-office having been specially favoured in this respect, and when I came to look into the condition of affairs there I found the staff vastly in excess of the needs of the service, and there were a large number of temporaries drawing pay without the knowledge of Parliament, and for whose pay Parliament had voted no money, they having been paid illegally out of the appropriation for the succeeding year ... If I could get the number reduced to what is required, then when vacancies arise appointments could be made, and that would afford an opportunity for Mr. Nugent's appointment if he were recommended by our friends having the patronage."[20]

Never tortured by the exigencies of patronage, Laurier did occasionally give vent to a weary frustration. "If you were sitting in the chair from which I now write," he confided to John Willison, "being besieged from all sides and having to determine in every case for the best interest of the party, to conciliate, to appreciate, and to smooth difficulties, you would realize how difficult a task it is, though how much more agreeable it would be to follow one's own inclinations in all such matters."[21] Like Macdonald, Laurier could "smooth difficulties" in matters of policy and patronage. He clothed his negative replies in velvet, never making the supplicant feel guilty or inadequate for having bothered the prime minister. He often replied briefly, using a form letter to brush aside requests, but even this letter contained graceful turns of phrase.

Under Laurier a formal system for handling patronage soon developed, the same one, with a notable variation, that Macdonald had successfully employed. Each Liberal constituency association, or regional association, established a patronage committee, sometimes comprising just the MP or defeated candidate and a handful of local notables. These committees' recommendations were heeded by ministers and the prime minister. As Laurier wrote in 1898 to an office-seeker, "Government patronage in each locality is distributed on the recommendation of the member for that locality."[22] Local patronage constituted a government MP's principal tool of political discretion. Proper use of this tool could maintain harmony within the local association, or tear it apart. Appointments of a city-wide or regional nature were made on the basis of recommendations from MPs and ministers, a practice that endures today. Departmental patronage lists for the ordering of supplies and services also followed recommendations of Liberal MPs and defeated candidates. So did the lists of authorized local newspapers receiving government advertising and printing contracts, although ministers kept an alert eye on the major metropolitan dailies. Appointments of province-wide or national importance could be made only after advice from the appropriate regional ministers, except in Quebec where Laurier decided. Laurier replied to a senior member of the Ontario cabinet who wrote recommending the appointment of an organizer, "I have made it a rule not to dispose of any patronage in any Province, except after previous consultation with my colleagues from that Province. You know, as well as I do, that this is the only safe course to follow, and any deviation from it, would be bad tactics."[23]

Macdonald, an Upper Canadian, had delegated Quebec patronage to lieutenants, since his own grasp of politics in that province could never equal his detailed knowledge of conditions in Ontario. Laurier turned Macdonald's formula on its head. He needed lieutenants elsewhere; in Quebec, Laurier would be supreme. It was, after all, Laurier's abiding preoccupation and singular accomplishment to secure Quebec for the Liberal party. This accomplishment, which subsequent generations of federal Liberals took for granted, ranks as among the most important in the political history of Canada. It altered fundamentally the dynamics of Canadian politics, making Quebec a "sheet anchor," to use Macdonald's phrase, for the Liberals rather than for the Conservatives.[24] The political transformation of Quebec, which took the better part of two decades, required the establishment of a *modus vivendi* between the Catholic

Church and the Liberal party. Laurier, having played a critical role in establishing that *modus vivendi,* naturally paid careful attention to the views of bishops, as Macdonald had done, hoping at least to win from them political neutrality if not overt support. He took care, therefore, not to appoint prominent anti-clerical *rouges* to any positions that might rile the bishops, induced the Vatican to admit publicly the difference between political liberalism and religious deviance, and tried, wherever possible as prime minister, to keep the bishops out of politics by giving them no cause for complaint.

Laurier's relations with the Catholic Church formed part of a broader plan to extend the Liberal coalition in Quebec. In this, the Conservatives immeasurably assisted Laurier, for in the 1890s they presented an increasingly sorry spectacle of factionalism. The ultramontane group, nicknamed Castors—the pseudonym of a pamphleteer who brilliantly expressed their views—attacked Conservative party members suspected of deviation from church views on politics. Personal rivalries aggravated the divisions; splits over the Manitoba Schools question and railway policies exacerbated them. The precarious state of Quebec's provincial finances, Premier Honoré Mercier's nationalist attacks on Ottawa, the aftermath of the Riel affair—all these factors ate away at the Conservatives' standing in Quebec. In Ottawa, none of the Conservative leaders who succeeded Macdonald used sufficient finesse in dealing with the Quebec wing of the party. Laurier—a French Canadian, a champion of provincial rights, a Liberal acceptable to, if not the first choice of, many clerics—began exploiting the developing fissures within the Conservative ranks, gradually gathering up prominent Conservatives, persuading others to remain neutral, and slowly reducing the Conservative party to what the Liberal party had once been: a doctrinal rump representing only a minority of Quebec opinion.

This transformation, however, spread over many years. By Laurier's second term Quebec was a solidly Liberal province, a bastion that testified to Laurier's skilful party management during his first term, a shift accomplished partly by his use of patronage. In selecting cabinet ministers from Quebec, Laurier all but ignored the *rouge* faction, also known as the "old Liberals," appointing instead Liberals of more recent standing. "No man who had hitherto filled the post of first minister has cared so little for those who were his colleagues in Opposition," grumbled a frustrated aspirant.[25] That statement did not amount to much, there having been only six previous prime ministers, but it did reflect a potential danger. The *rouge* elements could reasonably have demanded more. Laurier smothered their incipient objections with patronage. One with a substantial claim became Speaker of the Senate, another received a written assurance that he would become lieutenant-governor of Quebec, and still another wound up a judge.

The flip side of forestalling trouble from the "old Liberals" was wooing disaffected Conservatives, the "school of Cartier." Laurier's handling of J.A. Chapleau, symbol for the disaffected Conservatives, exemplified the prime minister's sure touch. Chapleau, a lieutenant-governor appointed by the

Conservatives, had nonetheless subtly favoured the Liberals in the 1896 election. Chapleau's term was coming to an end in December 1897, and the possibility arose in correspondence between Laurier and Chapleau that he might be appointed for a second term. That possibility outraged the "old Liberals," especially François Langelier, who had been promised the position in writing by Laurier. From this predicament Laurier extracted himself with customary aplomb. He carefully explained his problem to an understanding Chapleau, but allowed Chapleau to serve out his term. He then appointed a Liberal acceptable to the clergy as lieutenant-governor and sent Langelier to the bench, where he continued to receive promotions until Laurier appointed him lieutenant-governor in 1911.

Arthur "Boss" Dansereau was another disaffected Conservative, the nickname appropriately awarded for his control of patronage while the Conservatives dominated Quebec. Dansereau reigned as postmaster of Montreal, a position with considerable patronage possibilities. He had gradually fallen out of favour with elements of the Conservative party and, like Chapleau, yearned for a Quebec united behind a French-speaking leader. Powerful in politics, Dansereau cared little for administration, a weakness that so appalled Postmaster-General William Mulock that he put Dansereau on a leave of absence "pending final action."[26] When Laurier heard of Mulock's action, he immediately restrained his stern colleague and ordered him to write a letter of apology. "For reasons which I deem paramount, knowing the situation in Quebec perfectly, I expect that you will at once re-instate Dansereau in his position." Laurier's treatment of Dansereau paid off handsomely. Dansereau subsequently became editor of *La Presse* and dismayed the Conservatives by turning the paper into a sympathetic organ for Laurier and the Liberal party.

The winning over of newspaperman and Conservative politician Joseph Israel Tarte, however, was Laurier's most stunning coup. Here was a man, more mercurial than any, more dogged than most, who had excoriated the Liberal party during an earlier, ultramontane phase of his career. For him to be enlisted in the Liberal cause, let alone to receive such a prominent portfolio as public works, struck some "old Liberals" as certainly dangerous and possibly politically traitorous. Throughout Tarte's six years as a Laurier minister, elements in the Liberal party waged a relentless campaign against him. But they gained nothing, apart from a higher level of personal frustration, since Laurier always stood behind his sometimes impetuous ally.[27]

Tarte's appointment as minister of public works carried a certain irony. After all, as a newspaper editor and member of Parliament Tarte had been responsible for breaking the McGreevy Scandal which disgraced the Conservative minister of public works, Hector Langevin. That scandal exposed the brazen kickbacks from contractors and the ceaseless application of favouritism that characterized the Conservatives' fund-raising and other political activities in Quebec. Now Tarte entered the temple from which he had chased a previous gang of money-changers and replaced them with another. He used the public works portfolio in the traditional manner, as an extensive slush fund for the Liberal party and its friends, relentlessly spending public funds in a systematic porkbarrelling campaign. Temporary employees on public works projects were preferred to employees on full-time contracts, since their loyalty would be to their political boss rather than their business boss. He had no patience with ministers who did not pay sufficient attention to patronage, and sometimes infuriated them by intervening in their departments. Tarte's constant efforts to secure public works for Montreal, especially the city's port, irritated fellow ministers, and his disregard for the sacred Liberal principle of economy in government scandalized party greybeards such as Richard Cartwright and William Mulock. "We are entering a new era; it is no use being afraid to spend more money," Tarte told the House, speaking as much to his colleagues as to the Conservative Opposition.[28] He did draw the line at wholesale firings of public servants after the 1896 election, a decision that merely incurred the wrath of some "old Liberals" in Quebec, who accused him of shielding his Conservative friends.[29]

Tarte, having once been deeply involved in political organization for the Conservative party, knew how to win elections. In 1893, he spoke some of the most famous words in the history of Canadian patronage, "I was treasurer of the Conservative party for three elections and I must say that we didn't win elections with prayers." Those words, slightly amended (*les élections ne se font pas avec des prières,* or, elections are not won by prayers), became a telltale phrase for critics of the corruption and patronage that characterized Quebec's political life. But the words rang true. Elections in Quebec, including those involving Laurier, remained struggles of lofty rhetoric and lined pockets.

Tarte transferred his organizational talents to the Liberals when Laurier made him chief organizer in Quebec. He became to Laurier what André Ouellet would later become to Trudeau, a political fixer in the prime minister's backyard, especially in Montreal. (Agriculture minister Sydney Fisher looked after the Eastern Townships; Laurier and minister without portfolio R.R. Dobell, a former Conservative recruited by Laurier, oversaw the Quebec City region.) With Laurier's blessing, Tarte organized constituencies for elections, selected candidates, paid the right people, stayed in close touch with local notables, passed on political gossip, steered contracts in the proper political direction, and recommended patronage appointees. He often ran afoul of fellow Liberals, since tact did not figure prominently in his character, nor did modesty disturb his soul. Yet Laurier stood behind him while always reserving the right to mediate disputes caused or left unresolved by Tarte. If Tarte occasionally required a harness, Laurier would apply it in private. "Don't forget," Laurier wrote a prominent Quebec Liberal, "Tarte is my colleague, and as much through friendship as tactics, my intention is not only to prevent him being attacked, but even to defend him in all times and in all places, without examining whether he is wrong or right."[30]

While Tarte looked after the particulars of federal organization and patronage, Laurier kept up close, friendly relations with the provincial Liberal governments. The federal and provincial Liberals shared workers, sources of money, and a common foe. Laurier is thought to have played an important behind-the-scenes role in the selection of S.N. Parent as leader of the Liberals and premier of Quebec. A strict acknowledgement of each other's patronage terrain, however, characterized relations between the federal and provincial parties, not only in Quebec but across the country. "Provincial patronage is distributed upon the recommendation of supporters of the provincial government in the Legislative Assembly, or of its friends in the riding where it has to be exercised," Laurier wrote a supplicant for a provincial position. "Their full knowledge of all the local circumstances and of what would there serve the best interest of the party, gives to their recommendations a preponderance to which mine was and never will be entitled."[31]

By the time Tarte resigned in 1902, over a dispute about the tariff, he and Laurier had built a mighty political machine in Quebec. Of course, the skilful use of political patronage was only one reason for the Liberal's success, but without it Liberal gains would have come more slowly. Laurier used patronage in Quebec, as Macdonald had across the country, as a tool for enticing political opponents into the fold, rather than exclusively as a system of rewards for the faithful.

Laurier assembled in 1896 one of the most impressive cabinets in Canadian history; friendly commentators called it the "ministry of all the talents." Nova Scotia's W.S. Fielding and Ontario's Oliver Mowat had been lured to federal politics after highly successful careers as premiers. Andrew Blair of New Brunswick, Richard Cartwright and William Mulock of Ontario, and Clifford Sifton of Manitoba were among the other cabinet heavyweights. In English Canada, patronage necessarily flowed through these regional chieftains. Laurier could occasionally intervene to mediate factional disputes in English-Canadian provinces, but wherever possible he gave ministers the discretion of patronage. After 1901, Ontario ministers set up a patronage committee to review appointments for the Senate and judiciary, thus initiating a strategy that became a fixture in federal cabinets. First Mowat, then Mulock, and finally Allan Aylesworth were Laurier's Ontario lieutenants, the main conduits through whom federal Liberals maintained links with their provincial cousins.[32] When Laurier in 1907 wrote suggesting the name of a possible Senator from Ontario, Cartwright, never one to mince words, harrumphed that the prime minister was being "highly impolitic."[33]

Nowhere was the decentralization of patronage authority under Laurier clearer than in Clifford Sifton's empire as federal minister of the interior. Sifton had displayed his talents as an administrator and partisan brawler in the provincial government of Manitoba, where he served as attorney general during the Greenway Administration. He had organized constituencies and election campaigns with eyes deliberately averted from pervasive bribery, chicanery and skulduggery. He had slipped through changes to the *Election Act* to benefit the Manitoba Liberal government by changing the appointed hour for debate without informing the Opposition.[34]

There were, to be sure, the pious—Mulock, Cartwright and Mowat—in the federal Liberal party. Touched by that sanctimony special to Upper Canadian Reformers, they looked askance at the more brazen partisan activities of their cabinet colleagues, occasionally even troubling the prime minister with their views on ethical conduct. The Ontario Liberal party, over which Mowat presided and to which they were all linked, had evolved into one of the country's most effective political machines, with all its implications for patronage, favouritism, electoral irregularities and occasional corruption. Yet, as O.D. Skelton wryly remarked, "Ontario ... was frequently too busy saving the souls of the other eight provinces to have time for its own."[35] Sifton, however, remained untouched by the Ontario brand of piety. For him, "politics was a continuous war. The Conservative party was, simply, 'the enemy.' Each battle or squirmish required serious preparation. Independence and idealism therefore had little place among the troops."[36] As minister of the interior and Liberal party organizer for the entire Canadian West, Sifton held sway over a territory stretching from the Ontario border to the Pacific Ocean, and from the American border to the northernmost outposts of civilization in North America. His ministry's regulation of the North-West Territory and the Yukon included homesteading and settlement, immigration, schools, forestry, mineral rights, grazing, railways and national parks. No Canadian politician, before or since, ever ruled such a vast geographic territory.

Sifton harboured equally vast ambitions, for the territory, the Liberal party and himself. Crude though his methods may often have been, Sifton fulfilled almost all of those ambitions, as testified by the territory's population expansion, the Liberal preference of the majority of its inhabitants, and his own personal fortune. Like the Conservatives, Sifton used the authority of the interior ministry for partisan purposes. But what made the political consequences of his tenure so durable was the coincident rapid expansion of the prairies and the subsequent grant of provincial status to Alberta and Saskatchewan, so that for several decades thereafter the Liberal party's imprint remained fixed on the new provinces. Within a year of assuming office, he had placed his own men in positions of authority within the immigration section of the ministry. When the Klondike gold rush opened up the Yukon, most of the officials sent to bring a semblance of order to the unruly territory were Liberals. The homestead agents who fanned out across the prairies—spear carriers in "Sifton's army"—were often the first personal contacts immigrants systematically experienced with Canadians. Immigrants tended to remember that they had arrived under a Liberal government, and government officials constantly refreshed their memory. Similarly, newspapers published in their native languages were subsidized by Liberal governments or owned by Liberal proprietors. By 1904, thirty-five papers in Manitoba, twenty-two in the North-West Territory, and sixteen in British Columbia were on the Liberal government's patronage list.[37] Once again, patronage was being used to integrate newcomers to a political party, in the same way municipal political machines in the United States secured the loyalties of ethnic groups who huddled in the great American cities of the Northeast and Midwest.

The civil service, padded with Conservatives, quickly felt the Sifton whip. Civil servants who had worked actively for the Conservative party received their dismissal notices; others of suspect political sympathies found themselves superannuated, demoted, transferred, denied salary increases, and otherwise made sufficiently miserable that departure seemed preferable to endurance. The deputy minister of the interior and the deputy superintendent-general of Indian affairs both got the chop.[38]

The North-West Territory had its own council, on which the conventional wisdom suggested that non-partisanship could maximize the Territory's leverage on the federal government. (This attitude changed in 1905 when the Laurier government ensured a Liberal cast to the first provincial administrations.) But Ottawa directly administered the Yukon through a commissioner and other officials appointed by the minister of the interior, Clifford Sifton. Once installed in a place so far removed from Ottawa, officials sometimes got too big for their britches, or at least too independent for Sifton. When Commissioner William Ogilvie appointed several known Conservatives, Sifton upbraided him with a lesson in Canadian political reality, "Under our system of government we cannot appoint our opponents to office, and while you are an Administrator under a party government you will have to be guided by that rule."[39] Superintendent Sam Steele, the popular officer in charge of the Yukon constabulary, also resisted the patronage system by appointing several officers without due regard to partisanship. Sifton transferred him to Fort MacLeod. Mining permits were issued with an eye to party affiliation; liquor permits went to party supporters; civil servants held their jobs through patronage; the whole governance of this raw Territory exhibited the full panoply of corruption, from kickbacks to all sorts of under-the-table deals.

Governor-General Lord Minto, a stern critic of Sifton, wrote after returning from a Yukon tour, "The Dominion government seem to have looked upon the Yukon as a source of revenue, as a place to make as much out of as they could, and have used the proceeds largely for political corruption instead of the development of the country, and in so doing are in a fair way to kill the goose that laid the golden egg."[40] Sifton's biographer noted that elections featured attempts to rig the voting lists and also enormous government slush funds, "possibly as much as $10 for every voter in the Yukon. There was a corps of prostitutes and dance-hall girls, paid to keep Opposition voters occupied on election day, but otherwise usually in tow to government officials and businessmen. A small army of unemployed miners was paid just before elections for constructing roads and other works which they never saw. There was a reserve force of aliens (mostly American) who were paid and voted illegally at distant polling stations on the creeks."[41] Perhaps Sifton and Laurier were unaware of all the sordid details of these campaigns, but to suggest their total innocence is to accept that piano players in whorehouses are ignorant of what transpires upstairs.

Sifton scored a major commercial and political coup in securing control of *The Manitoba Free Press* in 1898. The paper, formerly a Conservative organ, immediately became the principal propagator of the Liberal gospel in Western Canada—and an eloquent and skilful one when John Dafoe assumed the editor's chair. Sifton's ownership of the paper, and the attention he paid to its commercial success and editorial slant, reflected the continuing interest leading politicians of the Laurier era took in the newspaper business. Sifton and the Liberal premiers of Alberta and Saskatchewan after 1905 encouraged the creation and commercial profitability of numerous papers throughout Western Canada in the mother tongues of the newly arrived ethnic groups. This they accomplished by the then-conventional methods of steering government advertising and letting printing contracts to friendly papers capable of handling the work, taking out a large number of subscriptions and paying for them with government funds, and, if necessary, finding financial resources among party supporters to keep marginal enterprises alive.

Laurier, too, had always keenly appreciated the need for party organs. As early as 1882, he had written to Edward Blake about the situation in Quebec, "It stands to reason that as our adversaries have 21 papers to our 5, we must forever remain in the minority, no matter what may take place in the political world."[42] Laurier's prime ministerial instructions to Mulock about withdrawing a dismissal notice to Arthur "Boss" Dansereau arose, in part, because Laurier knew Dansereau had been offered the editorship at *La Presse*. Laurier remained in close touch with leading editors of Liberal papers, especially John Willison at *The Globe* and Ernest Pacaud at *Le Soleil* in Quebec City. And he expected Liberal organs to follow the party line closely, since he applied to them his first commandment of politics—loyalty. Laurier owned shares in *Le Soleil* which he sold to Premier Jean-Lomer Gouin in 1907 to satisfy Gouin's gripes that supporters of his old provincial Liberal rival, Simon-Napolean Parent, had infiltrated the paper. The agreement stipulated that Laurier would continue to oversee the reselling of the shares and to control completely the paper's editorial approach to federal politics.[43] The Liberals, like the Conservatives under Macdonald, drew up a list of newspapers authorized to receive federal advertising and printing contracts. No sooner had the Liberals won in 1896, for example, than *The Mail* in Toronto ceased receiving government advertising (to be fair, *The Mail* received five dollars of advertising in 1898–1899 and five more in 1899–1900), whereas *The Globe,* which had been all but shut out by the Conservatives, began receiving several thousand dollars a year.[44]

That Sifton bent his part of the civil service for partisan purposes simply reflected the well-established practices of his time. Some firings usually attended a change of government. After the Laurier government took office in 1896, four hundred and seventy-three employees lost their jobs, of whom one hundred and ninety-six—only two percent of the entire federal civil service—were fired for "offensive political partisanship."[45] New civil servants, especially field workers in the so-called "outside service," were hired for partisan reasons, competence being a desirable but not necessary side benefit. The civil service remained small, since Laurier's economic views were those of a nineteenth-century British laissez-faire liberal, and the demands for social-policy reforms from isolated groups and nascent trade unions had not yet gained sufficient public support to warrant a government response. To a large extent, the civil service represented an extension of the party in power.

The federal government had essentially borrowed elements from colonial civil services existing at the time of Confederation to create the new federal civil service. One year into the Confederation experiment, a royal commission began investigating the state of the civil service. Its report heralded a series of subsequent investigations—by royal commissions in 1880–81 and 1891–92, as well as by special committees—all of which underlined the deleterious effects of patronage on internal morale and efficiency. The Liberals, with dreary predictability, had attacked the Conservatives for larding up the civil service with their political friends, but once elected in 1896, the Liberals found patronage in the civil service too enticing a means of consolidating power to act on their previous criticisms. The outside service, in particular, offered a range of part-time or seasonal positions which, allocated by the proper MPs, brought political benefits in the constituencies, notwithstanding periodic headaches caused by the inevitable small-supply, large-demand dilemma. Reforms measures had been implemented, in particular, a board of examiners to administer tests and screen prospective candidates. But the dictates of patronage frequently overrode such fine intentions. Positions were simply listed as not requiring entrance by examination, or the results of examinations were disregarded by politicians more interested in satisfying the needs of supporters than in bowing to the merit principle.

Yet, as the Laurier years stretched on, the prime minister confronted a series of pressures for civil-service reforms which he found difficult to ignore. His predilection had always been to short-circuit critics of civil-service patronage. He wrote his friend John Willison, one such critic of pervasive patronage, "Reforms are for Oppositions. It is the business of Governments to stay in office."[46] Reflecting years later on Laurier's attitude, Willison wrote:

> When eager civil service reformers confessed their desire to relieve him of the "incubus of patronage" there crept into his eyes a look of humorous wisdom which would have cooled their ardour if they had understood its significance. He believed there was far more of gain than of loss to governments

and parties through control over appointments to office and distribution of government contracts. He knew that "friends" were necessary to organize constituencies and carry elections and seldom was anxious to discover the sources of their contributions.[47]

If, as O.D. Skelton justly wrote of Laurier and patronage, "no other subject bulked so large in correspondence; no other purpose brought so many visitors to Ottawa," then in Laurier's eyes, so be it. This was the political system he understood, the one with which he felt comfortable and from which he believed indispensable political benefits flowed. But by the turn of the century, American critics had begun to flail at the spoils system in their country. Some of that criticism influenced assorted social reformers, academics and writers in Canada, who urged, often in highly moralistic tones, improvements in various walks of life, including the elimination of patronage from the civil service. The British example continued to inspire those who defined Canada as part of the glorious Empire.[48] All the speeches from Canadian politicians pledging undying fidelity to things British, especially to the traditions of the Mother of Parliaments, rang hollow when critics compared the extent of patronage in the British public service with that in the Canadian. In Quebec, nationalist critics such as Henri Bourassa chastised Laurier for a variety of sins, including the abuse of patronage.

More important still in the growing pressures for reform were the scandals, real and alleged, that beset the Laurier Government in 1906, 1907 and 1908, many of them involving Sifton's previous administration of the Interior department. The Conservatives charged—and they presented compelling evidence—that the advertising of timber limits had been manipulated to favour Liberal friends, and that the system of sealed bids for timber rights had been corrupted.[49] The Commons expended enormous energies debating a series of charges and countercharges about malpractices in government. The battles raged with special ferocity in the public accounts committee, wherein Conservatives charged Liberals with favouritism, disregard for due process in awarding contracts, and other forms of costly patronage, to which the Liberals frequently replied by dredging up similar practices by Conservatives.[50] Serious charges were also brought against Minister of Militia and Defence Sir Frederick Borden and against Minister of Railways Henry R. Emmerson, forcing him to resign. Minister of Public Works Charles Hyman left the cabinet over charges of electoral corruption, including bribery in his London constituency. Allegations against the administration of the department of marine and fisheries sparked so much controversy that Laurier ordered a judicial inquiry, whose report led to the suspension of three civil servants and the resignation of the deputy minister. He also agreed to yet another royal commission into the civil service.

The commissioners picked up where their predecessors of 1892 had left off, lamenting widespread patronage. True, the commissioners acknowledged, the *Civil Service Act* remained on the statute books, but "the Act has been so amended, re-amended, and whittled down, that the public service, the Commissioners believe, not only at Ottawa but elsewhere throughout the Dominion, has fallen back the last fifteen years."[51] Some genuflections towards the merit principle accompanied appointments to the "inside service," but "as a rule your Commissioners found in the outside service that politics enter into every appointment, and politicians on the spot interest themselves not only in the appointments but in subsequent promotions of officers." The results of examinations were easily circumvented by creating new classifications for prospective appointees other than those listed in the *Civil Service Act,* or by hiring people who failed the exams as temporary staff, then indefinitely extending their term of service. The commissioners recommended a civil service commission, a revamped system of classification, examinations for civil service posts, and respect for the merit system.

Even Clifford Sifton, of all people, welcomed the recommendations. By now a private member—he had left the cabinet in 1905 in a dispute over state funding for Catholic schools—Sifton called patronage "the greatest nuisance in public life" and asked that the civil service be placed on a "higher plane." Across the aisle, Conservatives sat dumbfounded by Sifton's gall, but he repeated his support for civil service reform so frequently that even some skeptics admitted that maybe, just maybe, he believed his own words. As for the Conservatives, their leader Robert Borden was nudging his party towards civil service reform. So Laurier, with no evident enthusiasm, presented the *Civil Service Amendment Act* which, among other changes, established the civil service commission. The reform looked impressive on paper, but in reality the mere existence of a commission could not shake politicians from their old habits, especially the use of patronage to fill positions in the "outside service."[52] Laurier, then, left the system of patronage in the civil service he had inherited fundamentally intact. Circumstances forced him to make cosmetic reforms, but the Laurier era represented the continuation of the old ways of patronage rather than the beginning of a new approach.

Laurier also carried forward the Macdonald tradition in dealing with the private sector, transforming his own party in the process. The Grits of Ontario, who formed the largest group in the Liberal coalition when Laurier became leader, had always been Jeffersonians in the Canadian context, suspicious of expanding government, spokesmen for small farmers and merchants. The tariff, indeed Macdonald's entire National Policy, vexed them, because to leading Liberals such as Richard Cartwright it meant the triumph of economically inefficient but politically powerful manufacturing interests over economically efficient but politically weak agrarian and small-business interests. The tariff question periodically gnawed at the party—Tarte left over it, eighteen prominent Toronto Liberals bolted over the issue of reciprocity in 1911, an issue that contributed to the Party's defeat in the election of that year. Until 1911, despite his own free-trade inclinations, Laurier always bore in mind the protectionist preferences of the large commercial interests. In Quebec, peace with those interests dove-tailed with his own long game of expanding the base of the Liberal party, especially forging stronger ties with the English-speaking community of Montreal, which had largely supported the Conservatives under Macdonald. The Liberals, once so critical of the Canadian Pacific's links with the Conservative party, even entered the railway sweepstakes themselves, autho-rizing a second transcontinental line and riding the turn-of-the-century railway boom to establish bonds with the banks and the construction companies that were actively promoting this development. Although flickers of the old Jeffersonian values occasionally disturbed the party, Laurier's Liberals became almost as Hamiltonian in their approach to economic policy as the Macdonald Conservatives.[53]

Laurier's tenure coincided with Canada's first prolonged economic boom since Confederation, a boom that populated the prairies, fleshed out the cities, created the first stirrings of organized labour, galvanized the efforts of social re-formers, and set the Laurier government afloat on a sea of buoyant revenues. In such circumstances, money sloshed back and forth between the political and commercial worlds. Some of the uproar that plagued Laurier's governments arose from comfortable relationships of favouritism, which none of the institu-tions of Parliament—including the auditor-general and the public accounts committee—could control, even if occasionally they could shed light on the darker corners of political practice.

The royal commission into the civil service of 1908, to take just one exam-ple, highlighted the widespread practice of padding purchase prices to include payments for patronage. The looseness of control procedures and the preva-lence of the assumption that political favouritism should count in government were fixtures of the Laurier period, just as they had been through Macdonald's long years of power.

The need for a physical infrastructure to unify so vast an expanse of terri-tory, the habitual clamour for public works improvements, and limited size of the Canadian market continued to make business heavily dependent upon gov-ernment. Even before Confederation, but certainly during the Macdonald and Laurier eras, the symbiotic relationship between the governing party and com-mercial interests politicized economic decision-making, and tempted both entities into using such leverage as they could muster to extract benefits from one an-other. Thus, during the Laurier years, corporations and their wealthy owners continued to be the politicians' major sources of money for campaigns.

Elections still drained cash from the pockets of candidates and wealthy supporters in part because election days still featured widespread treating and bribery. Party propaganda was also costly, since Liberal party organizers such as Tarte believed in saturating a constituency with political pamphlets during the campaign. As one member of Parliament told the House in 1903, "So long as the candidates agree to suspend all ideas of morality during an election and go in for a general picnic, we shall continue to have all the expenditure of money that we have at the present time. Down in my part of the country we have the most moral people to be found in the world; but when an election comes around, they regard it as a splendid holiday.... They size up each candidate for what they can get out of him, and they generally run it up to the limit." Under these circumstances, any party needed hooks into the business community for funds.

Canada remained a rural country despite the economic boom of the Laurier period. When Laurier left office in 1911, slightly more than three-quarters of the population still lived in small-town or rural conditions, a slight percentage decline from 1881, when the figure was eighty-one percent. Manufacturing and banking grew apace in some of the large urban centres of Ontario and Quebec, but much of the Laurier boom resulted from the opening of Western Canada, an opening that confirmed the essentially rural nature of Canadian society. Localism pervaded politics, and conditions were rife for the politics of patronage.[54] Parties pitched for the loyalty of voters through partisan media outlets; they built competing networks of local notables in hundreds of communities across the country through the granting of favours, preferment and place. Invariably, these advantages went to local businessmen or members of the professional middle classes, lawyers especially, so the patronage that glued parties together also contributed to the middle-class essence of political leadership. James Bryce, the acute if snobbish British observer of American democracy, wrote of Canada a decade after Laurier's defeat that politics was "a game played over material interest between ministers, constituencies and their representatives, railway companies and private speculators [which] is not only demoralizing to all concerned, but interferes with the consideration of the great issues of policy."[55] The words belonged to Bryce, the echoes to André Siegfried.

And yet, perhaps these foreign observers had missed what the politics of patronage and the economics of porkbarrelling had achieved. They were the tools that had allowed Laurier to expand the base of his party, making it fully competitive with the Conservative party—as Canadian political history unfolded, more than competitive. If the twentieth century did not belong to Canada, as Laurier had predicted, most of the twentieth century in Canadian politics belonged to the Liberals. Adopting the Macdonald model, Laurier knit together disparate ethnic and linguistic groups, diverse regions, men of different religions, and proponents of varying economic ideas into a political blanket that covered the country.

There could have been other models, based on region or religion or language or class—a French party and an English one; a Catholic party and a Protestant one; a Western Canada party and a Maritimers' Rights party and so on—all sending representatives to Ottawa, there to form ever-shifting coalitions in unstable governments of the kind known in pre-Confederation Canada. Instead the two national parties, the Conservatives under Macdonald and the Liberals under Laurier, held out the hope of rewards to all regions and all electors, whatever their race, religion, or class. In so doing, they brought stability to the governance of the country and legitimacy to its political institutions, both so sorely lacking during the tumultuous decades before Confederation. And patronage, around which so many things political turned, encouraged loyalties to national causes as well as national parties, and helped Canadians conceptualize the national interest.

The centrality of patronage to Canada's developing political culture could not endure throughout the twentieth century in the face of new social and economic pressures, especially pressures stemming from the emergence of the mass media and welfare state. But rather than disappearing, patronage took on new and more subtle forms because patrons and clients continued to feel it satisfied not only certain conditions crucial to effective political management in Canada, but also, as Laurier once observed, a basic human need.

Canadian prime ministers have always understood that, properly applied, patronage helps to build and maintain broadly based national parties, turning Canada away from the patchwork coalitions of religious, ethnic or regional parties in some Western European countries. Patronage provided a mirror the party in power could hold up for the whole country, beckoning individuals, groups and regions to see some of their own reflected in it and be reassured or dismayed, depending upon the effectiveness of patronage, about the accuracy of the party's claim to represent the whole damnable complexity of Canada. In recent years the traditional reflections in the patronage mirror—partisan, religious, linguistic and regional interests—are no longer sufficient proof of the broadness of a political party. Now the mirror must also reflect the interests of women, native peoples, young Canadians, old Canadians and various multicultural groups. Their understandable desire for recognition accentuates a political leader's frustration at the gap between the demands for reward or recognition and the supply of positions or preferment.

Notes

1. These and subsequent quotations are taken from André Siegfried, *The Race Question in Canada* (London, 1907), pp. 142–143, 173.

2. Norman Ward, *The Public Purse: A Study in Canadian Democracy* (Toronto, 1962), pp. 103–104.

3. Hilda Blair Neatby, *Laurier and a Liberal Quebec* (Toronto, 1973).

4. O.D. Skelton, *Life and Letters of Sir Wilfrid Laurier,* vol. 2 (Toronto, 1921), p. 270.

5. Sir John Willison, *Sir Wilfrid Laurier* (Toronto, 1926), p. 468.

6. Quoted in Frank Underhill, "The development of national political parties in Canada," *CHR*, vol. 16, no. 4, 1935, p. 384.

7. Ibid., p. 383.

8. Quoted in T.A. Burke, "Mackenzie and His Cabinet, 1873–1878," *CHR*, vol. 41, June 1960, p. 128.

9. P.B. Waite, *Arduous Destiny* (Toronto, 1971), p. 19. Waite notes that Leonard Tilley's appointment as lieutenant-governor of New Brunswick Mackenzie found impossible to cancel.

10. Quoted in William Buckingham and George Ross, *The Honourable Alexander Mackenzie, His Life and Times* (Toronto, 1892), p. 525.

11. Dale Thomson, *Alexander Mackenzie: Clear Grit* (Toronto, 1960), p. 174.

12. Ibid., p. 179.

13. Ibid., p. 219.

14. Underhill, op. cit., p. 385.

15. Mackenzie to Brown, October 8, 1874, PAC, call no. M–197.

16. Thomson, op. cit., pp. 232–233.

17. Norman Ward, "Money and Politics: The Costs of Democracy in Canada," *CJPS*, vol. 5, no. 3, September 1972, p. 335. See also Ward, "Electoral Corruption and Controverted Elections," *CJEPS*, vol. 40, 1949, pp. 79–80.

18. Buckingham and Ross, op. cit., pp. 525–526.

19. Albert Malouin to Laurier, November 24, 1896, PAC file 850.

20. Mulock to Laurier, May 12, 1898, PAC file 850.

21. Laurier to Willison, November 10, 1896, quoted in A.H.U. Colquhoun, *Laurier* (Toronto, 1935), p. 59.

22. Laurier to Edouard Nadeau, June 28, 1898, PAC file 850.

23. Laurier to A.S. Hardy, July 23, 1898, call no. C–758.

24. The fascinating story of how Quebec changed is beyond the scope of this book, and anyway the story has been captured by Neatby, in *Laurier*, op. cit., and by the early volumes of Robert Rumilly's massive *Histoire de la Province de Québec*. Rumilly, of course, offered only grudging admiration for Laurier, preferring his heroes to be nationalist politicians.

25. F. Landon, "A Canadian Cabinet Episode, 1897," in *Transactions of the Royal Society of Canada*, 1938, p. 52, quoted in Neatby, *Laurier*, op. cit., p. 125. See also Paul Stevens, "Wilfrid Laurier, Politician," in Marcel Hamelin (ed.), *The Political Ideas of the Prime Ministers of Canada* (Ottawa, 1969).

26. The handling of Dansereau is recounted in Neatby, op. cit., p. 128.

27. Laurier Lapierre, "Politics, Race and Religion in French Canada: Joseph Israel Tarte," Ph.D. Thesis, University of Toronto, 1962, p. 357.

28. House of Commons debates, March 28, 1899.

29. Lapierre, op. cit., pp. 523–524.

30. Laurier to E. Pacaud, December 13, 1900, quoted in Neatby, op. cit., p. 136.

31. Laurier to S. Springer, January 22, 1900, file 873.

32. Paul Stevens, "Laurier and the Liberal Party in Ontario, 1887–1911," Ph.D. Thesis, University of Toronto, 1966, p. 308.

33. Quoted in Stevens, "Wilfrid Laurier, Politician," op. cit., p. 80.

34. D.J. Hall, *Clifford Sifton, The Young Napoleon*, vol. 1 (Vancovuer, 1981), p. 57.

35. Skelton, op. cit., p. 269.

36. Hall, op. cit., p. 133.

37. Hall, vol. 2, op. cit., p. 150

38. Hall, vol. 1, op. cit., pp. 125–126.

39. Hall, vol. 2, op. cit., p. 3.

40. Quoted in Hall, vol. w, op. cit., p. 129.

41. Ibid., p. 141.

42. Quoted in P.G. Shea, "Electoral Practices in the Province of Quebec, 1861–1882," M.A. Thesis, McGill University, 1968, p. 196.

43. J.A.A. Lovink, "The politics of Quebec: provincial political parties, 1897–1936," Ph.D. Thesis, Duke University, pp. 158–159.

44. Norman Ward, "The press and the patronage: an exploratory operation," in J.H. Atkinson (ed.), *The Political Process in Canada* (Toronto, 1963), p. 9.

45. These figures are supplied by R. MacGregor Dawson, *The Civil Service of Canada* (London, 1929), p. 72.

46. Quoted in Hall, vol. 2, op. cit., p. 86.

47. Sir John Willison, op. cit., p. 468.

48. See Carl Berger, *A Sense of Power: Studies in the Ideas of Canadian Imperialism, 1867–1914* (Toronto, 1971), especially chapter 8. Berger quotes critics of political chicanery as disparate as Goldwin Smith, Henri Bourassa and Sir Sandford Fleming. A less likely trio with a common interest can scarcely be imagined.

49. Hall, vol. 2, op. cit., p. 189.

50. Ward, *A Public Purse*, op. cit., pp. 130–133.

51. These and subsequent quotations are taken from *Royal Commission into the Civil Service Commission*, 1908, sessional papers 29a.

52. See J.E. Hodgetts et al., *The Biography of an Institution: The Civil Service Commission of Canada, 1980–1967* (Montreal, 1972), ch. 2.

53. Years later, this shift still dismayed some Ontario Liberals of the Grit tradition. See Underhill, op. cit., pp. 384–386.

54. Gordon Stewart, "Political Patronage under Macdonald and Laurier," *The American Review of Canadian Studies,* vol. 10, no. 1, pp. 12–14.

55. Quoted in Berger, op. cit., p. 203.

CHAPTER
5 WOMEN AND WORK

The virtue of hard work traditionally was taken for granted in our society, and a body of homilies justified it. For example, there was "pride in one's work," all work was "noble," "work is love made visible," and, above all, "a woman's work is never done." These pre-industrial ideas were carried into the modern period when the idealization of the solitary artisan completing his task became even more powerful when placed in relief against those in mindless factory jobs. As the twentieth century wore on laments over the "tyranny of work" replaced the hymns celebrating its virtue. Historians of the "New Left," in particular, have raged against the indecency of the workplace and the inevitable class conflict starkly manifest in industrial strikes. They reinvented the history of the early industrial era, making the working class and its culture the centrepiece, not only of their studies, but of Canadian history as well. The journal *Labour/Le Travailleur*, which was begun by the Committee on Canadian Labour History in 1976, became the catalyst for many innovative studies, though it stumbled at the beginning. The title *Le Travailleur* and the very first article "Most Uncommon Common Men" were inadvertent indications of a male world view of work. The title was changed to *Labour/Le Travail* with issue number 13 in 1983. Numerous articles on women and work, the subject of this chapter, appeared in the journal, including one of the readings reprinted here.

The reformulation of Canadian history from a woman's perspective has been extensive, with the nature of both paid and unpaid work being of special interest. During the past twenty years studies have ranged widely, including house and farm work, industrial and clerical employment, teaching, the sweat shops, and the streets. In the process the nature of analysis has diverged as well, from maternal feminist views which sought a place for women in the past, through marxist and radical views with agendas, to an emphasis on gender itself. The readings offered here represent different views from that literature. The first, by Sara Brooks Sundberg, on "Farm Women on the Canadian Prairie Frontier: The Helpmate Image" is the more traditional and places women solidly within the farm structure "as homemakers, home manufacturers, field hands and wage earners" as well as nurses. From her analysis of reminiscences Sunberg concludes: "Although women's responsibilities on the farm meant hard work, prairie women did not unanimously agree that their work on the farm was drudgery."

In the second reading in this chapter, Star Rosenthal's "Union Maids: Organized Women Workers in Vancouver 1900–1915," the relationship of women and work is placed within the union structure in which women faced injustice not just from employers but from male unionists, who practised "overt discrimination" against both non-white and female workers. While the prejudice against non-whites has been acknowledged, trade unions today "refuse by and large to see the parallels to their attitudes towards women workers." Rosenthal's "union maids" struggled in a hostile environment. The third selection, "Feminization of the Labour Process in the Communication Industry: The Case of the Telephone Operators, 1876–1904" by Michèle Martin, is solidly within the "New Social History" with its emphasis on concepts and methodology. Martin reviews the evolution of studies on women's work and offers her analysis of a "female job ghetto" with low pay based on "sexually stereotyped requirements."

Suggestions for Further Reading

Acton, Janice, Penny Goldsmith and Bonnie Shepard eds., *Women at Work. Ontario, 1850–1930*. Toronto: Canadian Women's Educational Press, 1974.

Bourne, Paula, *Women's Paid and Unpaid Work: Historical and Contemporary Perspectives*. Toronto: New Hogtown Press, 1985.

Bradbury, Bettina, "Women's History and Working Class History," *Labour / Le Travail*, 19 (Spring 1987), 23–43.

Briskin, Linda and Lynda Yanz, eds., *Union Sisters: Women in the Labour Movement*. Toronto: The Women's Press, 1983.

Carroll, William K. and Rennie Warburton, "Feminism, Class Consciousness and Household-Work Linkages among Registered Nurses in Victoria," *Labour / Le Travail*, 24 (Fall 1989), 131–145.

Kealey, Linda, "Canadian Socialism and the Woman Question, 1900–1914," *Labour / Le Travail*, 13 (Fall 1984), 77–100.

Kinnear, Mary, " 'Do you Want your Daughter to Marry a Farmer?': Women's Work on the Farm, 1922," in *Canadian Papers in Rural History*, ed. Donald H. Akenson. Vol. VI. Gananoque: Langdale Press, 1988, 137–153.

Lindstron-Best, Varpu, " 'I Won't be a Slave!' - Finnish Domestics in Canada, 1911–30," in *Looking into My Sister's Eyes: An Exploration in Women's History*, ed. Jean Burnet. Toronto: Multicultural History Society of Ontario, 1986, 33–53.

Parr, Joy, *The Gender of Bread Winners: Women, Men, and Change in Two Industrial Towns 1880–1950*. Toronto: University of Toronto Press, 1990.

Roberts, Wayne, *Honest Womanhood: Feminism, Femininity and Class Consciousness Among Toronto Working Women, 1893 to 1914*. Toronto: New Hogtown Press, 1976.

Sangster, Joan, "The 1907 Bell Telephone Strike: Organizing Women Workers," *Labour / Le Travailleur*, 3 (1978), 109–130.

Strong-Boag, Veronica, "Keeping House in God's Country: Canadian Women at Work in the Home," in *On the Job: Confronting the Labour Process in Canada*, ed. Craig Heron and Robert Storey. Montreal: McGill-Queen's, 1986, 124–151.

_____, "Pulling in Double Harness or Hauling a Double Load: Women, Work and Feminism on the Canadian Prairie," *Journal of Canadian Studies*, XXI, no. 3 (Fall 1986), 32–52.

Tillotson, Shirley, "'We May all Soon be First-Class Men': Gender and Skill in Canada's Early Twentieth Century Urban Telegraph Industry," *Labour/Le Travail*, 27 (Spring 1991), 97–125.

Trofimenkoff, Susan, "One Hundred and Two Muffled Voices: Canada's Industrial Women in the 1880s," *Atlantis*, III, no. 1 (Fall 1977), 66–82.

FARM WOMEN ON THE CANADIAN FRONTIER: THE HELPMATE IMAGE

Sara Brooks Sundberg

'Poor girl!' say the kind friends. 'She went West and married a farmer'—and forthwith a picture of the farmer's wife rises up before their eyes; the poor, faded woman ... hair the color of last year's grass, and teeth gone in front.[1]

In the case of farm life on the grassland frontiers of western Canada there is little argument that life was difficult for women. Nevertheless, women were part of the earliest efforts to establish agricultural settlements on the prairie and plains of the western interior of Canada. What were the experiences of these women, and how did they respond to pioneer life in the grasslands?

Previous attempts to answer these questions have not revealed women's experiences in all their variety. Instead what has emerged are images that obscure differences between individual women's experiences. Responding to these images, this study examines, from the perspective of women themselves, one image of pioneer farm women on the Canadian prairies—that of pioneer farm women as helpmates.

In her analysis of the helpmate image for frontiers-women in the United States, Beverly Stoeltje writes, "the primary defining feature of [helpmates] was their ability to fulfill their duties which enabled their men to succeed, and to handle crises with competence and without complaint."[2] Carl Dawson and Eva R. Younge, in *Pioneering in the Prairie Provinces: The Social Side of the Settlement Process,* expresses this image when they use this description to depict the experiences of pioneer farm women in Canada:

As for the pioneer woman, what shall we say? When her man was at home she stood shoulder to shoulder with him in the conduct of the day's affairs. When he was absent ... she cared for the family, she looked after the stock, she took upon her lone shoulders burdens which were none too light for husband and wife to bear.[3]

Because a pioneer woman's experiences were tied to the needs of her husband and family she, as June Sochen explains in her study of frontier women, "is not the prime mover in her life. She does not determine her own individual destiny."[4] This image is taken to its gloomy extreme in the following interpretation of prairie women's lives:

A prairie woman's life was defined by the needs of her family. When her children left, the habit of working remained. Tasks which once were necessary for survival now had no point, yet they had become so much a part of her that only death could bring release.[5]

Another dimension of the image of pioneer women as helpmates is the notion that farm work for pioneer women was drudgery. A recent study of Canadian prairie women describes farm life for pioneer women in dreary terms:

For the typical pioneer woman, life was a hectic chorus of mend, weed, pump, chop, churn, bake and scrub. If she had children—and families tended to be large in those days—they added their giggles and howls.[6]

The monotony of pioneer life was intensified by the isolation of the prairie frontier. Women stoically endured these hardships because, as prairie pioneer Nellie McClung explained, they were just too busy to complain.[7]

But Nellie McClung also observed "that people love to generalize; to fit cases to their theory, they love to find ... farmers' wives shabby, discouraged and sad."[8] Women's writings challenge these images and generalizations. Autobiographies, letters, journals, and reminiscences recount the experiences of women as wives, mothers, daughters, and single women on the frontier. They are some of the sources used in this essay. These women are not representative of pioneer farm woman as a whole. Instead they are a small group of women who had the ability and the inclination to record their experiences and attitudes. In some cases women wrote contemporary accounts, in others they relied upon memory. Regardless of these distinctions and limitations, women's writing still clearly reveal a rich variety of experiences which are useful in examining images of pioneer farm women in the grasslands.

Most Canadian pioneer women came to the grasslands in one of two migrations. The first wave began about 1870 and lasted until the late 1890s. Prior to 1870 the grasslands were part of Rupert's Land, a broad expanse of territory, controlled by the Hudson Bay Company. Its boundaries lay between the Red River in the east and the Rocky Mountains in the west. In 1870, the Canadian government acquired Rupert's Land from the Hudson Bay Company and the grasslands began to be recognized for its agricultural potential. Settlers from various parts of Ontario, the United States, and Europe trickled into the grasslands.

By the late 1890s, a second, larger migration began. Promising free homesteads and assisted passages, the Canadian government and the Canadian Pacific Railway launched vigorous advertising campaigns to encourage agricultural settlement within the grasslands. Partially as a result of these campaigns, significant numbers of settlers from the United States, Great Britain, the Balkans, the Ukraine, and Russia immigrated to the grasslands of Canada. The rapid influx of settlers during this second migration lasted until about World War I. The pioneer experiences of most women cited in this study fall between 1870 and 1914.

The beginnings of the first migration to Canada coincided with the passage of Homestead legislation in 1872, which provided settlers with 160 acres of land for a ten-dollar fee, providing they plowed the land, built a shelter, and lived on the property for six months out of a year for three years. The lure of cheap land, the chance for economic independence, captured the imaginations of women as well as men. Sarah Roberts, an early twentieth-century Alberta pioneer, remembered that land was a major factor influencing her family's decision to move from Illinois to Canada, "We had lived for years in Illinois where land is priced at one hundred dollars per acre. No doubt the thought of receiving 480 acres 'free' made more of an appeal to us than was justified."[9] It is important to note that Sarah Roberts included herself as part of the decision-making process to move west. Her participation in this process is contrary to the notion that women did not affect decisions concerning their futures and the futures of their families.

In fact, women were sometimes the first to recognize the opportunities inherent in western land. In 1880 Letitia McCurdy Mooney persuaded her husband that the future of their children depended upon their opportunity to acquire fertile land. Letitia's daughter, Nellie Mooney McClung, recalled her mother's persuasive argument to move west:

> "We'll have to go some place, John," she said one night to my father. "There's nothing here for our three boys. What can we do with one-hundred-and-fifty stony acres? The boys will be hired-men all their lives, or clerks in a store. That's not good enough!"
>
> Father was fearful! There were Indians to consider, not only Indians, but mosquitoes. He had seen on the Ottawa what mosquitoes could do to horses; and to people too. No! It was better to leave well enough alone.[10]

Clara Goodwin, another late nineteenth-century Manitoba pioneer, remembered "my mother had visited Winnipeg the year before and was very much taken with the West. I remember quite distinctly her saying to my father, 'Richard, you MUST go to that country! That's the place to live!' "[11]

Sometimes it was not just the economic opportunities that persuaded women to suggest moving their families to the west. Letters from friends and family exerted a strong influence. Lulu Beatrice Wilken recalled that her mother was persuaded to go west to Saskatchewan by her brother Edward:

> So he wrote to her to try to persuade Father to move his family West and to take up land also.
>
> I am sure that it did not take long to convince Father of the advantages to be obtained in such a move, and, in the spring of 1891, Mother took her three small children and joined her brother.[12]

For Muriel Parsloe it was not enticements from family members, but a sense of adventure that caused her to initiate her family's move to Swan Lake, Manitoba. After reading an advertisement for western Canadian land she said, "We've tried Australia, let's take a trip to Canada and see how we get on there."[13]

A more conventional reason brought Kathleen Strange to the grasslands. It was because of their doctor's recommendation that Kathleen Strange and her husband purchased a farm in the remote area of Fenn, Alberta, in 1920. The active outdoor life of a farm in the west was their doctor's prescription for an injury received by Kathleen's husband in World War I.[14]

Unmarried women also came to farms in the grasslands. Western farmland offered these women a means for achieving economic independence. Land was not "free" for these women. Women could not obtain "free" homesteads unless they were the sole support for their families. Qualified women took advantage of this opportunity. A women's column in a 1914 issue of the *Grain Grower's Guide* carried this appeal:

> Dear Miss Beynon: I am writing to ask for a great favor for a very deserving widow with children. She wants to homestead and has not the wherewithal to look about.... perhaps some of the kind sisters know of one suitable for mixed farming....[Intending Homesteader][15]

A notable example of a successful woman homesteader during this period is Georgina Binnie-Clark. For a period of about five years between 1909 and 1914, Binnie-Clark owned and operated her own wheat farm in the Qu'Appelle Valley in Saskatchewan. In her book *Wheat and Woman,* Binnie-Clark detailed her farming experiences and argued the case for farming as a means of achieving economic independence for women.[16]

Unmarried women came to farms in the grasslands for other purposes as well. In 1886 the Canadian Pacific Railway issued a questionnaire asking women about their lives in the Northwest Territories. One of the questions read, "Can hard-working honest girls easily obtain situations at good wages on farms or [in] households in the North-West...." A concise reply came from Mrs. T. D. Elliott in Alexandria. She answers, "1. Good girls can get plenty of good places at good wages then marry good young men with good farms."[17] Opportunities for women in farm homes as domestics or home-helps promised gains for women in other ways besides wages. The shortage of females on the frontier was a prominent theme in appeals for female immigrants to the west.

This theme was evident in the *MacLeod Gazette* of May 15, 1896:

> "Do you know" remarked W. D. Scott to a Toronto newspaper reporter, "one of the greatest needs in the North West at the present time? It is women, simply women. Married men with their wives are contented enough out there, but single men on farms are apt to get lonely. If girls could only be persuaded to go out there they would be sure of good situations, and I tell you it would not be long before they would get married."[18]

Educated middle-class women from the British Isles were prime targets for these appeals. At the turn-of-the-century the British Isles found itself saddled with an over-supply of single, middle-class women unable to find suitable jobs. Employment and marriage opportunities in the Canadian west offered relief to these women. In her book *West-Nor'-West,* published in 1890, Jessie Saxby, herself a middle-class British widow, expressed this concern:

> In Britain one of the most urgent social difficulties is what to do with our surplus women—how to provide for them, how to find remunerative employment for them. In Canada one of the most urgent social difficulties is how to persuade women to come there.... In Quebec, in Winnipeg, in Regina, everywhere, I was told the same thing. "Oh, if respectable women from the old country would come out West!"[19]

To assure the successful adaptation of British emigrant gentlewomen to the west, emigration societies and training schools were established to provide information about the west and to instruct women in necessary domestic skills.

Women did not always have a choice of whether to stay in their present circumstances or to take a chance in a new land. Edna Jaques' family migrated from Ontario to Moose Jaw, Saskatchewan, in 1902. She remembered her father announcing they would leave for Moose Jaw:

> His name was Robert Jaques. He came to visit dad one day in January 1902. They were in the parlor talking and laughing together.... Suddenly the folding doors between the two rooms opened and dad stood in the doorway (I can see him yet) and loudly announced to my mother, "We're leaving Collingwood." Taking a long breath he said, "We're going homesteading in the Northwest Territories...."
> My mother fainted.[20]

Nevertheless, after the initial shock some women adapted to the idea, as did Jessie Raber's mother. Jessie Raber remembered that even though it was her father's idea to take up a homestead near Lacombe, Alberta, in 1895, her mother soon recognized the economic and social advantages of the move.

> Mother said perhaps she had been selfish in not being anxious to move to a farm in Canada before, for she knew that a growing family did need plenty of room. The milk, fresh eggs and the wonderful vegetables one could grow in Canada: for she did want us all to grow up into strong and healthy men and women, with good educations.[21]

Other women remained unconvinced of the advantages of a westward move. Clara Middleton "had no urge to go adventuring," but went along because "Homer was bent on it [and] that was enough for me."[22] Laura Salverson simply resigned herself to the inevitable, "And now George had the grand vision of the independent life of a landowner.... There was nothing to be done about it, except to let the disease run a swift unhindered course."[23]

Without the satisfaction that comes from participation in an important decision and without the confidence that comes from belief in the promise of a new land, women's journeys to Canada could be painful experiences. Maria Adamowska's family emigrated from the Ukraine to Alberta in 1899. She recalled her mother's sad experience:

> Mother, on the other hand, was tenderhearted. Of all the trials that had been her lot in life, this one was the most bitter. Whenever father had mentioned going to Canada, she had started to cry. And she cried all the way on the train and missed seeing the lovely sights in God's good world.[24]

The experience of this unhappy emigrant woman fits one aspect of the helpmate image. That is, in this instance, Maria Adamowska's mother did not determine her own future. However, clearly this is not true for all women on the frontier. Women came to the grassland frontiers for themselves, as well as for others, and when they did come for others, they were energetic, as well as reluctant, pioneers.

Whatever their reasons for coming to the grasslands, women worked when they arrived. As prairie homesteader Georginia Binnie-Clark observed "On a prairie settlement the women work ... I owe one debt to my life on the prairie and that is a fair appreciation of my own sex."[25] For married women, the home was the hub of pioneer farm women's work. In her study of frontier women's work, Susan Armitage identifies two categories of household work. The first category, household maintenance, involves routine activities, such as cooking and cleaning.[26] The lack of mechanical aids made their chores time consuming. The experience of Laura Salverson's mother, an Icelandic immigrant, illustrated this fact, "Mama was forever busy. She had a passion for keeping things scoured and scrubbed.... When you carried water from a pump half a block away or melted snow after the winter set in, all this washing and cleaning consumed a lot of time."[27] In another example, Kathleen Strange remembered a dreaded chore, wash day:

> Washing! What a job that always was. Usually it took me the entire day. In summer I washed outside; in winter, down in the basement. The boiling, sudsy water had to be carried in pails from the stove to wherever my tubs were set. More than once I burned myself severely, spilling water on unprotected hands and legs.[28]

Nevertheless, some women found satisfaction in these routine chores. Edna Jaques recalled the "glow" on her mother's face as the wash emerged "whiter than white."[29] Lulu Beatrice Wilken remembered the pride her mother felt in the polished appearance of the floor in their sod shack. Years of washing with hot sudsy water made it smooth and white.[30]

It was not just the lack of conveniences that made chores time consuming. It was also the number of people requiring women's care. Because children were potential laborers, large families were an asset. Women often had several children to tend, in addition to housekeeping chores. Jessie Raber, daughter of immigrant parents who homesteaded in Alberta during the early 1900s, remarked on her mother's experience, "Mother often wished she could bundle us all off to school or somewhere. Just think, seven [children] under her feet all day and every day. Such patience she must have had."[31]

The number of people in a household was enlarged in other ways as well. Hospitality was an integral part of frontier life and an important social custom. Saskatchewan pioneer Harriet Neville remembered "No stranger was ever refused meals or shelter night or day at our home."[32] Sometimes women turned this custom to profit by taking boarders and earning a wage.

It should be noted here that daughters, like their mothers, worked on the family farm. Often they assumed their mother's chores, thereby reducing their mother's overall workload. For example, as a teenager, Jessie Raber assumed responsibility for much of the cooking and for care of the younger children.[33] In some cases daughters' chores as surrogate mothers came at an early age. Because both her parents worked outside the home, Veronica Kokotailo, even though she was only five years old at the time, took care of the younger children![34] Daughters also worked as field hands. Nellie McClung recalled overseeing the cattle rather than going to school.[35]

Daughters contributed to the family's economic well-being in other ways. In some cases they worked as home-helps, a term applied to domestic help, to earn wages to assist their parents. Ukrainian immigrant Anna Farion remembered her work as a home-help. "My work was harder than the year before as there were four children, and four or five hired men to look after. But I stuck it out, as I wanted to help my parents as much as I could."[36] In another way Anna's experience illustrates the hardships some immigrant girls and women experienced. Earning only a few dollars a month, Anna requested a raise. Her employer "brushed me off with the rejoinder that she had trained me for the job and, besides, she had paid Kolessar $5.00 for me. Her words hurt me deeply. Evidently, I had been sold...."[37]

Not all immigrant girls and women working as home-helps encountered discriminatory treatment of this kind. In an effort to evaluate employment opportunities for British women, Elizabeth Keith Morris travelled throughout western Canada during the early part of the twentieth century. She considered the position of home-help suitable employment for capable British women:

> The position of home help is a safe, cheap and sure way of earning capital to start in other work, of learning Canadian methods and requirements, and of feeling one's feet in a new country; but the work is hard and heavy including washing, ironing, baking, scrubbing, ... therefore, only to be undertaken by the robust.[38]

The second category of frontier women's work was household sustenance. Armitage defines household sustenance as "work which contributed directly to family economy by making cash expenditure unnecessary."[39] Farm women were manufacturers in their own homes. Harriet Neville used skins to make "hoods, mittens, muffs and necks" as well as spinning wool to make clothing, bed mattresses and quilts.[40] The daily entries of Mrs. Seward St. John revealed she made butter and raised chickens to use in trade for other goods.[41] Lulu Wilken remembered "Soap making is an art, ... The fat and lye water had to be boiled to the right stage, and the proper proportions of water and grease maintained or they would separate and it became a failure."[42] Mrs. Emma Phair remembered that her mother manufactured the fuel necessary for their cooking stove. "She knew just how many twists of straw it took to heat the oven for baking.... It took one hundred and twenty five twists to heat the oven; four bags altogether to heat the oven and bake the bread."[43]

Women's contributions to sustenance reached beyond the domestic sphere. They worked as field hands. Late nineteenth-century homesteader Harriet Neville drove the oxen while her husband pitched hay.[44] Another Saskatchewan pioneer, Mrs. Edward Watson, noted that she and her children built their sod barn,[45] and Sarah Roberts helped to brand cattle.[46] Some women, like Georgina Binnie-Clark preferred outdoor work. She wrote:

> I worked hard through June at the stoning, and started to harrow ... From the beginning I was perfectly happy working on the land, only I wished it was someone else's turn to get those tiresome three meals a day.[47]

Sarah Roberts, on the other hand, said of her branding job: "I stayed with my job until it was done, and I am glad that I never had to do it again. I think that it is not a woman's work except that it is everyone's work to do the thing he needs to do."[48] Veronica Kokotailo's mother must have agreed. For two weeks she worked for a neighbor plastering his barn. Her payment was a pail of potatoes.[49]

Aside from their responsibilities as homemakers, home manufacturers, field hands, and wage earners, women performed other important functions. They were nurses and doctors for their families and neighbors. In a letter written to her grandmother from her family's Saskatchewan homestead, Maryanne Caswell described picking herbs for medicinal purposes.[50] Ukrainian immigrant, Maria Adamowska remembered, "As I was reaping with a sickle, I cut my finger. The gash was so deep that the finger dangled, just barely held on by the skin. Mother managed to splice it somehow, and the wound healed."[51] Even in the prairie town a woman's medical skills were relied upon. As late as 1930, Fredelle Maynard, a young resident of the town of Birch Hills, Saskatchewan, recalled that a doctor's responsibilities were limited to declaring quarantine and delivering babies.[52] In more isolated areas women acted as midwives, even if they were inexperienced. Clara Middleton described such an experience:

We got home about midnight and at one o'clock came Mr. Barnes. His wife was in labour, and would I come? I protested that I wouldn't be any good, that I knew nothing.... No; his wife wanted me.

"It's up to you," said my husband, but I knew by his tone that he had no doubts. I could almost hear him thinking, "You're a woman and you're needed."[53]

The thoughts of Clara's husband are a fitting description of women's work on the prairie. Women performed whatever work was needed. Regardless of training or experience women were expected to be self-reliant. Sometimes the responsibilities of self-reliance could soften women's adjustment to the isolation of the frontier. For example, Clara Middleton remembered that women acted as morticians as well as doctors. The ritual of preparing a body for burial provided women the opportunity to support and comfort one another.[54] In another example, Harriet Neville, finding herself isolated from nearby schools during the winter of 1884–1885, ordered textbooks from Toronto and kept regular school hours for her children. Of this experience she said, "One thing these things did for me. I never had a moment to be lonely to feel the lack of neighbors. I slept well and did not dream so much about old friends."[55]

Nevertheless, the challenge of self reliance proved too great for some women. On their way to their homestead in Manitoba, Nellie McClung remembered encountering a family returning from the prairie. The wife, dressed in a silk dress and flimsy shoes, was sobbing. She tearfully explained, "She hated the country ... it was only fit for Indians and squaws...." In an effort to comfort the woman, Nellie's mother suggested that perhaps the woman would be more comfortable travelling in simple clothes. The roads were muddy, sturdy shoes and gingham dresses were more practical. The woman did not sew, her mother had always done her sewing. "Mother's zeal began to flag, 'Take her back,' she said to Willard, 'she's not the type that makes a pioneer.'"[56]

The confining nature of women's work was a different source of discontent for women. Peace River pioneer Ida Scharf Hopkins articulated this frustration:

> Much as the woman becomes completely involved in the homestead life many of the challenges become repetitive....
>
> We women were never unhappy, but sometimes life was a bit dull. There was so little variety in the day-by-day routine. So much necessary work to be done there was little time or energy left for anything else. We had to keep the homefires burning.[57]

But women did appreciate their vigorous lives on the frontier prairie. Saskatchewan pioneer Alice Rendell illustrated this when she wrote to a friend in 1904:

> I would never advise anyone to come out here who is the least afraid of work. They are better off at home. There is plenty of room to breathe in this country and if the work is hard the freedom, which is the indispensable attribute of life here, makes one far less susceptible to physical fatigue.... Here one feels that each week's work is a step onward whilst in the old country oftentimes a year's toil brought nothing but disappointment and additional anxiety.[58]

Kathleen Strange, like Alice Rendell, appreciated freedom. For Kathleen, pioneer life offered a new opportunity to work as a full partner with her husband. She missed this partnership in her later, less rigorous role of a city wife:

My own life, on the other hand, is almost completely changed. And, most important of all, I am deprived of one particularly vital thing. On the farm I was a *real* partner with my husband, sharing with him in almost every detail of his daily work. Now his work is carried on in a downtown office, with professional help. There is little I can do to assist him.[59]

Prairie farm women like Kathleen Strange were, indeed partners with their husbands, not only because they shared in their husbands' day-to-day work, but also because of their own day-to-day responsibilities. Farm women's roles as homemakers, home manufacturers, field hands, wage earners, doctors, morticians, and teachers meant that women made substantial contributions to the business of farming. These contributions receive inadequate recognition when interpreted from the perspective of women as helpmates. Viewed as ancillary to the work of farm men, our conception of prairie farm women's work loses equality within the economic structure of the farm, an equality which is justified given women's roles as providers of valuable goods and services.

In a similar way the diversity of prairie farm women's experiences is lost when they are assigned the blanket role of helpmate. Women in this study reveal that it is a mistake to assume that all women on farms were wives and mothers. Single women were farmers in their own right, and they worked on farms as home-helps or domestics. Women's experiences also reveal that contrary to the image of women as obedient helpmates, some women did affect the decision-making process which led to their pioneer experiences in the grasslands. Some women actively participated in the decision-making process, others made the decision solely on their own.

Women's experiences differed in other important ways as well. Although women's responsibilities on the farm meant hard work, prairie women did not unanimously agree that their work on the farm was drudgery. The notion of universal drudgery, more than any other aspect of the helpmate image, deprives women of any possibility of joy or fulfillment in the process of pioneering. Prairie women's experiences reveal that although some women found their chores monotonous and confining, others felt obvious pride in their accomplishments. Some even found their responsibilities to be useful buffers between themselves and the loneliness of the frontier. Others appreciated the freedom and opportunity resulting from their work. As Kathleen Strange perceptively observed, "Drudgery! That is a word with many connotations. What is drudgery to one person may not be drudgery at all to another."[60]

The image of the stoic, hardworking helpmate not only homogenizes prairie women's experiences, it leaves some experiences out altogether. What about the women who could not cope with frontier life on the prairie? What factors made the difference between success and failure? We lose part of the story of women who stayed, when we ignore those who left.

The experiences of women in this study raise more questions than they provide answers. Yet the diversity of experiences revealed in women's writings admonish us to look more closely at our images of pioneer farm women on the Canadian prairie.

Notes

1. Nellie McClung, *In Times Like These* (1915; reprint ed. Toronto: University of Toronto Press, 1972), p. 109.

2. Beverly Stoeltje, " 'A Helpmate for Man Indeed': The Image of the Frontier Woman," *Journal of American Folklore* 88 (January-March 1975): 32.

3. Gerald Willoughby, *Retracing the Old Trail* (Saskatoon, 1933) quoted in C. Dawson and E. R. Younge, *Pioneering in the Prairie Provinces: The Social Side of the Settlement Process,* Canadian Frontiers of Settlement Series, Vol. 8 (Toronto: The Macmillan Co. of Canada Ltd., 1934), p. 19.

4. June Sochen, "Frontier Women: A Model for All Women?" *South Dakota History* 7 (1), 1976: 36.

5. The Corrective Collective, *Never Done: Three Centuries of Women's Work in Canada* (Toronto: Canadian Women's Educational Press, 1974), p. 54.

6. Linda Rasmussen, et al., *A Harvest Yet to Reap: A History of Prairie Women* (Toronto: The Women's Press, 1976), p. 42.

7. Ibid., pp. 42–43.

8. McClung, p. 109.

9. Sarah Ellen Roberts, *Alberta Homestead: Chronicle of a Pioneer Family,* Lathrope E. Roberts, ed. (Austin: University of Texas Press, 1971), p. 4.

10. Nellie McClung, *Clearing in the West* (New York: Fleming H. Revell Company, 1936), p. 32.

11. Audrey Peterkin and Margaret Shaw, *Mrs. Doctor: Reminiscences of Manitoba Doctors' Wives* (Winnipeg: The Prairie Publishing Company, 1976), p. 2.

12. Lulu Beatrice Wilken, "Homesteading in Saskatchewan," *Canada West Magazine* 7 (Spring 1977): 27.

13. Muriel Jardine Parsloe, *A Parson's Daughter* (London: Faber and Faber Ltd., 1935), p. 220.

14. Kathleen Strange, *With the West in Her Eyes* (Toronto: George J. McLeod, Ltd., 1937), p. 8.

15. "Sunshine," *The Grain Grower's Guide,* 11 March 1914, p. 20.

16. Georgina Binnie-Clark, *Wheat and Woman* (1914; reprint ed. Toronto: University of Toronto Press, 1979).

17. Canadian Pacific Railway, *What Women Say of the Canadian Northwest* (n.p. 1886), p. 32.

18. *MacLeod Gazette,* 15 May 1896 quoted in Rasmussen, et al., p. 14.

19. Jessie M. E. Saxby, *West-Nor'-West* (London: James Nisbet and Company, 1890), p. 100.

20. Edna Jaques, *Uphill All the Way: The Autobiography of Edna Jaques* (Saskatoon, Saskatchewan: Western Producer Prairie Books, 1977), p. 14.

21. Jessie Browne Raber, *Pioneering in Alberta* (New York: Exposition Press, Inc., 1951), p. 10.

22. Clara and J. E. Middleton, *Green Fields Afar* (Toronto: The Ryerson Press, 1947), p. 12.

23. Laura Salverson, *Confessions of an Immigrant's Daughter* (London: Faber and Faber Ltd., 1939), p. 480.

24. Maria Adamowska, "Beginnings in Canada," in *Land of Pain; Land of Promise: First Person Accounts by Ukrainian Pioneers 1891–1914,* trans. Harry Piniuta (Saskatoon, Saskatchewan: Western Producer Prairie Books, 1978), p. 54.

25. Georgina Binnie-Clark, *A Summer on the Canadian Prairie* (London: Edward Arnold, 1910), p. 278.

26. Susan Armitage, "Household Work and Childrearing on the Frontier: The Oral History Record,"*Sociology and Social Research* 63 (3): 469.

27. Salverson, p. 37.

28. Strange, p. 220.

29. Jaques, p. 105.

30. Wilken, p. 28.

31. Raber, p. 67.

32. Harriet Johnson Neville, "Pioneering in the North-West Territories," Harriet Purdy and David Gagan, eds. *Canada: An Historical Magazine* 2 (June 1975): 42.

33. Raber, pp. 136–137 and 140–141.

34. Anne B. Woywitka, "A Roumanian Pioneer," *Alberta History* 21 (4) 1973: 22–23.

35. McClung, *Clearing in the West,* p. 116.

36. Anna Farion, "Homestead Girlhood," in *Land of Pain; Land of Promise,* p. 92.

37. Ibid., p. 91.

38. Elizabeth Keith Morris, *An Englishwoman in the Canadian West* (Bristol: J. W. Arrowsmith or London: Simpkin Marshall, 1913), p. 188.

39. Armitage, p. 469.

40. Neville, pp. 48–51.

41. Seward T. St. John, "Mrs. St. John's Diary," *Saskatchewan History* 2 (Autumn 1949): 25 and 29.

42. Wilken, p. 29.

43. Isabel M. Reekie, *Along the Old Melita Trail* (Saskatoon, Saskatchewan: Modern Press, 1965), p. 49.

44. Neville, p. 20.

45. Mrs. Edward Watson, "Reminiscences of Mrs. Edward Watson," *Saskatchewan History* 5 (Spring 1952): 67.

46. Roberts, p. 226.

47. Binnie-Clark, *Wheat and Woman,* p. 151.

48. Roberts, p. 226.

49. Woywitka, p. 22.

50. Maryanne Caswell, *Pioneer Girl* (McGraw-Hill Co. of Canada Ltd., 1964), 10th letter.

51. Adamowska, p. 67.

52. Fredelle Bruser Maynard, *Raisins and Almonds* (Toronto: Doubleday Canada, Ltd., 1972), p. 16.

53. Middleton, p. 48.

54. Ibid., p. 51.

55. Neville, p. 30.

56. McClung, *Clearing in the West,* p. 58.

57. Ida Scharf Hopkins, *To the Peace River Country and On* (Richmond, British Columbia: The Author, 1973), pp. 118–119.

58. Alice Rendell, "Letters from a Barr Colonist," *Alberta Historical Review* (Winter 1963): 24–25.

59. Strange, p. 292.

60. Ibid., p. 276.

UNION MAIDS: ORGANIZED WOMEN WORKERS IN VANCOUVER, 1900–1915

Star Rosenthal

The history of women in the labour force is by and large a neglected area of study, especially with regard to trade unionism. For British Columbia in the early years of this century, while there are various accounts of men's union struggles, there does not exist at present any published secondary material on the union activity of women. This article will attempt to give a preliminary account of the organization of some women workers in Vancouver during the period from 1900 to 1915.

Research on such a topic is full of problems. Women's organizing efforts are recorded in scattered fashion throughout old labour newspapers and minutes of meetings, but the records are fragmentary and often ambiguous. It is extremely rare to find accounts by the women themselves, so their motivations are often a matter of speculation. The failure of historians and trade unionists of the time to record women's activities has contributed to a present lack

From *BC Studies,* no. 41 (Spring 1979), 36–55. Reprinted by permission of *BC Studies.*

of knowledge of this area. The main chronicles of labour history in B.C. and Canada ignore the very existence of women workers, let alone their union activity.[1] The earlier failure to record information probably stemmed from a belief that women's struggles were unimportant or insignificant in a historical context. The failure of later historians to retrieve what data exist seems to reflect this same belief.

As a consequence of this ignorance of the role of women in the labour movement, various myths have arisen. One, of course, is that women have not attempted to organize in the past. Another, which was also prevalent in the earlier period, is that women are in fact unorganizable. This latter myth was in the past based simply on prejudice against women, but nowadays uses the erroneous historical myth as a rationale.

The trade union movement has both shared in and propagated these assumptions. Then and now a male-dominated movement, it has a tendency to view women as reactionary, materialistic and non-class-conscious. Their supposed non-participation in trade unionism is blamed on "false consciousness" and "femininity," and because of this, female workers, especially in white-collar occupations, tend to be ignored when unions conduct organizing drives. Thus the myth of unorganizability is perpetuated. For example, until very recently mainstream trade unions did not make any significant effort to organize bank workers, who are mostly female. It took a small, independent and feminist union in B.C., the Service, Office and Retail Workers' Union of Canada, to change this situation. They conducted a drive to organize these workers, received a good response, took their case to the Labour Relations Board, and won the right for bank workers to be unionized. As soon as SORWUC's success became apparent, the labour movement jumped on the bandwagon and allocated funds and a female organizer to start its own drive for a bank workers' union.

The labour movement in the early part of this century had much the same attitude towards women as the modern trade unionists. Women were often seen as a threat to male job security, and instead of the unions trying to organize them, the response to this "threat" was to admonish women to remain in the home. Also, the medical misconceptions of the day led people to believe, for example, that work in factories wasn't healthy for women specifically, rather than leading them to push for improved health and safety standards for all workers. These factors contributed to resolutions such as the following put forward by the Dominion Trades and Labor Council in their 1903 platform of principles. They called for "abolition of child labor by children under 14 years of age; and of female labor in all branches of industrial life, such as mines, workshops, factories, etc."[2]

Ten years later attitudes had not changed. At a meeting of the Vancouver Trades and Labor Council (VTLC) in 1913, a delegate from the Moulders' Union presented a motion that women not be employed in foundries, as "we consider such labor for women is physically, mentally and in every way detrimental to the sex and consequently to the race."[3] This motion was endorsed by the Council.

By 1915, however, some change was made in official policy, at least. The annual convention of the Trades and Labour Congress of Canada discussed amending the 1903 principle cited above to read: "Abolition of child labour by children under sixteen years of age and the establishing of the principle of equal pay for equal work for men and women."[4] It is unclear if this amendment passed.

In looking at the history of women in the labour movement, it is interesting to note that there are some obvious parallels to the history of non-white workers. Overt discrimination was practised especially against Chinese, Japanese and East Indians by the society at large, and this was reflected in the union movement. The same kinds of myths grew up about these workers as grew up about female workers, that they were potential scabs rather than potential union comrades.

In every labour newspaper of the period, there are repeated calls for bans on immigration, boycotts of businesses owned by Asian people or businesses which employed them, and general racist comments, such as by the Press Agent for the Waiters and Waitresses Union, who termed Orientals "yellow objects."[5] Instead of trying to establish a feeling of solidarity with immigrant and female workers, the labour movement fell back on the rhetoric of "unorganizability," and its solution to all of these low-wage workers was to send them back where they came from, either across the seas or to the kitchen. The outstanding exception appears to have been the Industrial Workers of the World, who interestingly enough advocated both the organization of Asiatics[6] and the active participation of women (such as Elizabeth Gurley Flynn) as leaders and members.

Both Japanese and native Indian workers attempted to organize at times during these years, but were subject to sabotage by the racist attitudes of the other workers. In 1893, for example, Japanese fishermen were asked to support a strike by the Fraser River Fishermen's Protective and Benevolent Association, but were turned down when they wanted to join the Association. An offer of $500 to the Association, to help them set up their own Japanese Fishermen's union, was also rejected. In 1900 they did set up their own Japanese Fishermen's Benevolent Society, with 1,250 members, which took a leading part in the strike of Fraser River Fishermen in 1900. Native Indians took part in this, as they had in the 1893 strike. Native Indians were also organizing in the lumber industry, and formed the main part of the IWW Lumber Handlers' Union, around 1906.[7]

Nowadays, trade unions have changed their line on the unorganizability of non-white workers, and generally look back on this period of their history with shame. They acknowledge that their past attitudes and policies in this respect stemmed from prejudice.[8] Strangely, though, they refuse by and large to see the parallels to their attitudes towards women workers.

Women, however, *did* organize, despite the lack of support from their union brothers. They joined male unions, formed their own locals, and even their own separate unions in many of the main occupations in which they were employed. In addition to this, they gave active support to men's union struggles, and organized campaigns to buy only union-made goods in what they called "Label" campaigns. Their organizations during this period were generally short-lived, but their failure seems to be due more to objective conditions such as economic depression, lack of labour movement support, lack of legislative protection and political power, than to what historian Wayne Roberts, criticizing recent historical studies, refers to as the "allegedly warped personality structure of their femininity."[9]

This article aims, through a compilation of primary source materials, to recover for the reader a general outline of Vancouver women's early trade union activities. Hopefully, with the presentation of factual data, it will be seen that, just as the history of non-white workers has been distorted by prejudice, so has the history of women workers.

At the turn of the century, women's place in the labour force was changing. While the majority of wage-earning female workers remained in such occupations as domestic service, positions such as sales clerk were becoming "women's work" and still others, such as telephone operators, used female labour more or less from their inception. Between 1891 and 1911, the percentage of working women in Canada engaged in domestic and personal service work dropped from 51.9 percent to 38.1 percent. The percentage of women in trade and merchandising rose from 4 percent to 11.6 percent, and the percentage of professional women rose from 10.2 percent in 1891 to 16.1 percent in 1901, and then dropped slightly to 15.9 percent in 1911. The percentage of women in manufacturing remained steady throughout these years, at around 25 to 27 percent of all women in the labour force.[10]

In 1911, women made up only 13.4 percent of the total workforce in Canada, and of these women 23.8 percent were immigrants.[11] The highest proportion of immigrant women were in domestic and personal service (55.2 percent), with manufacturing claiming almost 20 percent of the immigrant women. For women born in Canada the situation was different. Only 32.7 percent of them were in domestic and personal service, and 29.23 percent were in manufacturing.[12] The statistics for domestic service are easily explainable by the fact that many women were imported specifically to be domestic servants by organizations such as the Salvation Army.

One of the most interesting statistics is that of the ages of workers. In 1911 51.5 percent of female workers were under the age of 25. Approximately 49 percent of these were from 15 to 24 years old, and 2 percent were between 10 and 14 years old. Most of the female children under 15 in the workforce were in domestic and personal service (56 percent) or manufacturing (35.5 percent).[13]

Between 1891 and 1911, B.C.'s workforce underwent a significant change. The percentage of workers who were female went from 4.4 percent in 1891 to 5.86 percent in 1901, and had almost doubled the 1891 figure by 1911, when 8.07 percent of the workforce was female. These figures are much below the Canadian average, which went from 12.2 percent in 1891 to 13.39 percent in 1911. Alberta and Saskatchewan had even lower percentages of women workers in 1911 than did B.C. The Canada Census Report attributes these low rates to the pioneer nature of the western provinces at this time, and the fact that there were simply more men than women living there.[14]

In B.C. in 1911, the occupational distribution was somewhat different from the national averages, although the same general trends are shown. Forty-two percent of B.C. working women were domestic and personal service workers, slightly higher than the national figure; manufacturing claimed 19.6 percent, lower than nationally; and professionals comprised 19.5 percent of the female workforce, higher than the national average.[15]

To narrow it down even further, in Vancouver women were 14.6 percent of the workforce, about one percentage point more than nationally. In actual numbers, this meant that in 1911 there were only 6,452 women (and 44,176 men) employed in the city of Vancouver. Of this number (6,452), the largest group were in domestic service (2,720 women), followed by 1,484 in the professions and 1,075 in trade and merchandising. Here, however, the census figures become clearer. Of "professional" women, 604 turn out to be stenographers and typists, 357 teachers (a very low-paid, low-status job at this time), and 242 nurses. In trade and merchandising 548 were saleswomen and 292 were office employees.[16]

In looking at these figures, Wayne Roberts' statement that working women before 1914 were "politically and socially isolated"[17] takes on a new dimension. In Vancouver, at least, they were also numerically isolated. Not only were there very few of them, but the nature of their occupations meant that they were scattered and fragmented, in offices, stores and homes all over the city. Their hours of work were long, and they did not have access to the resources of middle- and upper-class women, such as club rooms and adequate, affordable transportation, not to mention childcare and servants.

Given all this, it is not hard to see the difficulties which women and girls faced in trying to unionize. That women did organize argues either a large degree of class-consciousness, or a large degree of desperation, or both. Union activity took place in many of the main occupations in which women were engaged. Only some of these occupations will be touched on here, and it must be emphasized that the accounts that will be given by no means pretend to be definitive.

One of the better known, if only recently, of the organizing efforts of women of this period is that of the female telephone operators. Employees of what was originally the New Westminster and Burrard Inlet Telephone Company, later B.C. Telephone Company, organized a Vancouver local, No. 213, of the International Brotherhood of Electrical Workers (IBEW), in October 1901. (The parent body had been formed in 1891.)[18] They held two major strikes, one in 1902 and one in 1906.

On 26 November 1902 telephone operators, and male linemen, inspectors, trouble men and repairers all went out on strike for higher pay, shorter hours, and recognition of the union. The operators were asking for a wage increase of $2.50 per month, and the male employees wanted increases of from $5.00 to $10.00 per month. Two days after the start of the strike, on November 28, New Westminster employees went out in sympathy, as did Victoria employees on November 29.[19]

The strike lasted until 12 December 1902.[20] The telephone company was forced to suspend service temporarily, and the general Vancouver business community went up in arms against the phone company, supporting the strikers and offering to send volunteers to run the service. The telephone company then, as now, was not a popular institution in the city, as they tended to behave as a law unto themselves, and of course had a monopoly on an essential (for businesses) service. One incident serves to illustrate this: in June of 1905 a B.C. Telephone superintendent and five workmen were arrested for destroying public property—they had been tearing up a city street, presumably to lay cables, without city permission.[21]

Either during or just after the strike, the telephone operators decided to form their own organization, a branch of the local called Auxiliary #1 of Local 213. They had their own officers: Miss J. Hunter of 812 Homer St., president; Miss F. Livingstone, 660 Granville St., vice-president; Miss J. Browne, 827 Richards St., recording secretary; and Miss E. Bentley, 1121 Seymour Street, treasurer.[22] A local labour newspaper reported of Auxiliary #1 that they "control their own business, local 213 being represented by two delegates at their meetings."[23]

The Telephone Company appears to have given in to all of the strikers' demands. IBEW Local 213 was recognized, and the eight-hour day granted to the operators, although the company reserved the right to request that they work Sundays. A half-holiday every sixth Saturday was given, and three days per month sick leave. An immediate advance of $2.50 per month was to be given every operator who had been six months in receipt of her present salary, and scheduled increases every six months after until the top limit was reached. For city operators this meant a ten-day probationary period at the start, then $20 per month for the first six months, increasing to $30 per month after two and a half years. For long distance operators and "assistant chiefs," $32.50 per month was to be paid the first year and $35.00 per month thereafter. In contrast the linemen were to receive a new starting salary of $3 per day, approximately $66 per month for a five and a half day work week, assistant foremen $3.25 per day, and so on.[24]

A month and a half after the conclusion of the strike the operators celebrated by getting together a committee of five women and five men to organize a dance at the O'Brien Hall, which was frequently used for various union social events. Eighty couples came and appeared to enjoy themselves; according to *The Independent*, "One of these affairs which go to make life worth the living was held Wednesday night in the O'Brien Hall. The telephone operators entertained themselves and their friends at dancing, games, luncheon, etc."[25]

The gaiety had totally died down, however, by 1906. On February 22, the telephone operators struck to protest the company's refusal to hire only members of what the *Labour Gazette* called the "Telephone Operators Union," the auxiliary branch of Local 213. The next morning, all the IBEW members employed there also walked off the job. Thirty-four female operators and twenty male workers were involved. This time, though, there was no service interruption, as by a day after the start of the strike, the company had twenty-one operators working.

The operators said that the cause of the strike was

> that the officers of their union had been discriminated against, and an attempt had been made by the management of the company to induce them to disband. It was on this account that the operators asked for recognition of their auxiliary, in the form in which the men's union was recognized.[26]

The company claimed that their agreement to give hiring preference to IBEW members was made only with the men, and that the female operators had expressed no desire for such an agreement. They also said that on 9 January 1906 thirty-one out of thirty-seven operators had signed a declaration that they did not wish to belong to the union. Since then many had joined it (possibly out of indignation at being coerced to sign the declaration!) and had asked that only members of the union should be employed. The company said they could not grant this demand, as it would mean dismissing the other operators. They also used a technicality to claim that the men had broken their agreement by striking. Finally, the dispute was referred to the Vice-President of the International.[27]

The strike dragged on for months, with claims and counter-claims being made by the company and the strikers. Finally, in May, B.C. Telephone broke off all negotiations. No settlement was made, and the places of all the strikers were filled.[28] Local 213 of the IBEW still exists in Vancouver today, but the power of the Telephone Operators Union appears to have been permanently broken by their defeat in this strike.

Various other unions had women among their membership, where women were a small or large part of the industry. One of these was the Retail Clerks International Protective Association, which was formed in August 1899 and chartered in January 1900. The Vancouver union was apparently the first of its kind in Canada. It tried to affiliate with the American National Association of Retail Clerks, which became the International so as to include "Canadian subordinates."[29]

Female clerks are mentioned as active members as early as 1902, when they were reported as attending a meeting in Victoria. By mid-1903, the total membership was seventy-two and enlarging. They campaigned for shorter hours, closing on Sundays and legal holidays, and met with some success in getting stores that stayed open until 9 or 10 o'clock at night to close earlier. They also asked union members and the public to demand to see a clerk's union card, and if it could not be produced, not to buy from that clerk.[30]

By late 1904 or 1905 the union had disbanded.[31] In May 1913 reorganizing had started, with women and men joining together to form a union.[32] In February 1914 the VTLC received a communication from the Retail Clerks Protective Association about organizing a local of the union in Vancouver.[33] In April 1913 it was reported that women clerks made from $3 to $25 per week, the average wage being $10 per week. At the same time, the local Women's Council estimated that the bare minimum for survival for a woman was $7.50 per week: $5 for room and board (a very conservative estimate); $.50 for carfare: $.50 for laundry; $1.50 for all clothing necessary. Girls of fourteen and under were employed by the stores at $3 a week, working for at least two years before gradually rising to a living wage.[34]

Other unions with female workers in them included the Bookbinders' and the Tailors' unions. The Bookbinders Union was established about 1901, as Local 105 of the International Bookbinders Union. In 1903 they are reported as having a full membership of "workmen," and no mention is made of female members at this time, although they could well have been there.[35] In Toronto, women had formed the Women's Bindery Union in 1901, and by 1902 had 350 members.[36] By 1913, there must have been a significant female membership in Local 105, as it is one of the few unions mentioned, in the monthly report of the Vancouver Women's Correspondent to the *Labour Gazette,* as having women members.[37] In 1914 the total membership of the union was thirty-one.[38]

Data on tailoresses are somewhat more accessible, as prominent trade unionist and suffragist Helena Gutteridge was a member of the Tailors' Union. She represented the union as a delegate to the VTLC, became the recording secretary of the council, led the British Columbia Women's Suffrage Society, and later became a Vancouver alderwoman.[39] The Tailors' Union began in the early 1890s, but dissolved in the depression of 1893–5. In 1898 it was reorganized, with a Miss McRae serving as the treasurer.[40] She was still active in the union in late 1913, when she is mentioned as attending VTLC meetings to report on garment workers.[41] Sometime during these years, the union became the United Garment Workers of America (UGWA).

The 1911 census lists 86 tailoresses and 484 tailors in the city of Vancouver. There were also 388 dressmakers, all female, 7 male milliners, plus 26 female and 46 male "other clothing makers." These women workers appear to have been older than in many other trades—424 of them were in the 25–65 years old bracket, and only 248 were under 25.[42]

Although there were obviously women in the union from its 1898 inception, reports on the extent of early female participation could not be found for this study. In April 1913, however, it was reported that tailors were trying to organize tailoresses, despite "opposition" from the IWW.[43] In June of that year, tailoresses in conjunction with tailors decided to organize to get the forty-eight hour week, and in August there was a strike of twenty garment workers, ten men and ten women, in a joint effort to reduce the work week from fifty-four hours to forty-eight. It had been estimated that garment workers received from $6 to $15 a week on a nine-hour day basis.[44]

The UGWA and the IWW appear to have had a jurisdictional dispute in B.C. as well as in other places in North America. In November 1913 Miss McRae brought to the attention of the VTLC meeting the fact that at Turner Beeton Company in Victoria an IWW label was being used. In March 1914 a warning was given at another meeting that the Turner Beeton Company label was "not that of a bona fide international union. It was known as a Pacific Coast union, using a yellow label, and was only a local organization." Later in the year the UGWA sent circulars to the VTLC explaining the dispute between them and the Industrial Tailors Union International (formerly Journeymen Tailors International). Apparently delegates from the latter union had been attending VTLC meetings.[45]

The Shirt, Waist and Laundry Workers International Union established a local in Vancouver on 12 March 1902. Local 105 originally included among its officers three women: vice-president Mrs. Henderson, financial secretary Miss M. Whitmar, and treasurer Miss Jealouse. A year and a half later, Miss Whitmar (or Whitmore) was listed as the vice-president, and the other women were no longer officers. A Miss Lomie had replaced Miss Jealouse as the treasurer.[46]

Laundry Workers in Vancouver struck at least once or twice around 1902–1903, but the data on this are rather confusing, and the extent of women's participation not clear. One strike is reported to have occurred when the Excelsior Laundry declined to put work schedules into effect.[47] A benefit was given for striking laundry workers on 30 April 1903 in the form of a dance and social at O'Brien Hall.[48] The *Labour Gazette* mentions another strike on 12 June 1903 that lasted until June 29. It involved fifteen workers at two laundries who struck in a refusal to work with non-unionists, and was settled by arbitration. A slight increase in wages is the only reported outcome.[49]

The SWLWIU established a local in Victoria as well, in November 1903.[50] On 19 June 1905 a strike was held by thirty employees, of whom twenty-two were girls and women, to recover backwages owed them. They were not paid as usual on Saturday night, and some of the women did not have enough money to last until Monday, so were given assistance by the other workers. One woman with three small children was evicted by her landlord, and the children's breakfast on Monday "came from the lunchpails of the striking laundrymen and laundrywomen."[51]

By the end of 1902, the Vancouver local had 70 members,[52] but in 1904 the union sent a letter to the VTLC expressing their intention to withdraw delegates from the Council.[53] Sometime after this they disbanded. In early 1914 they re-formed as Local 37 of the Laundry Workers and re-affiliated with the VTLC.[54] By April they had one place willing to sign up with them, and were working on two others. One business, Pioneer Laundry, responded by firing four or five employees who joined the union.

Over 700 women were said to be working in laundries in Vancouver in 1914, and women on heavy machines received only $9 a week.[55] The report of the first female inspector for the Civic Health Department stated that the work in laundries was done standing, in buildings which were generally hot, and about three days of the week the women worked nine-hour days.[56]

An early women's union to which only one reference was found was the Factory Workers Union, in existence in 1903. It was composed of women who worked in candy factories and confectionery shops, and had, according to *The Independent,* "a fair membership." The paper also reported that "J. B. Williams enjoys the proud distinction of being the only male member of this progressive union. And the girls *[sic]* have made him president."[57] In 1911 there were only thirty-one female workers in biscuit and confectionery making.[58] Figures could not be found for the earlier period.

One union in which women first formed part of the membership, and later launched their own autonomous local, was the union which incorporated hotel and restaurant employees. It was called, variously, Local 28 of the Waiters and Cooks Union, the Waiters and Waitresses, the Cooks, Waiters and Bartenders, and so on. The women's local suffered from the same confusion when established, being termed usually the Waitresses Union, but also the Waitresses and Lady Cooks Union, or the Hotel and Restaurant Employees Union, Local 766.

The original union started as a Knights of Labour local in 1898 or earlier.[59] Women were probably involved in it from the beginning. Waitresses are mentioned frequently in reports of the union's activities, and in 1903 at least one of the officers was female, a Miss A. Scuitto, the recording secretary.[60] The union was rabidly anti-Oriental, and one of its main concerns during this whole period was lobbying for restrictions on immigration, asking union members and the public not to patronize establishments owned by or employing Orientals, and trying to prevent white women from being employed by Orientals or even working along-side them.

This bias was present in the Waitresses Union as well, which was organized in June or July 1910, with thirteen women present at the meeting. They sent delegates to the VTLC regular meetings, and seem to have maintained an active presence there. An estimate at this time shows 300 women employed in hotels and restaurants in the city.[61] This appears to have been fairly accurate, as in 1911 the census lists 232 female restaurant employees and 155 female hotel and boarding house employees.[62]

By August 1910 five hotels and cafes employed union waitresses. Mrs. Rose Gardiner, who reported this fact to a VTLC meeting, also "discussed the proposition confronting the waitresses and the necessity of doing something to assist the girls in their battle to improve conditions."[63] In September an agreement for hotel and restaurant owners to sign was drawn up and sanctioned by the VTLC. It read:

We, the undersigned, do hereby agree to employ union waitresses and to apply to the secretary of the waitresses' union when there is a vacancy in my place ... [to take effect] for a term of one year, from September 1, 1910. The waitresses' union, in consideration of the signature herein contained, do promise the support of the local unions and the central bodies in Vancouver to support houses displaying the card of the Waitresses Union, Local 766, Vancouver.[64]

By October membership was increasing, but the demand by employers had outstripped the supply of union waitresses. Delegate Gardiner told the VTLC that the union was going to hold a dance at German Hall, on the corner of Robson and Granville, and a note of annoyance can be heard as she continued "that they would expect the delegates to the council and the members of organized labour generally to assist them as they had promised repeatedly to." At subsequent meetings she took the floor to make racist comments on Chinese cooks, and she specifically complained about one restaurant where the Chinese owner had a white wife who waited on the tables.[65]

In 1913 the Women's Correspondent of the *Labour Gazette* reported that waitresses received $10 per week for an eight-hour day, and $12 per week for a ten-hour day with board. The Waitresses Union was still going strong and maintaining their close relationship with the mainstream trade union movement. Their headquarters was located in the Labour Temple,[66] and their delegate to the VTLC, Miss Polly Brisbane, was elected Statistician of that body, a position she held until her resignation in May 1914. In 1913, when Helena Gutteridge asked the VTLC to appoint a female delegate to appear before the Minister of Labour (along with delegates from women's societies), Polly Brisbane was chosen, and accepted.[67]

In January 1914 Miss Brisbane reported the membership of her union as thirty-five, with two members being unemployed. But in June of that year her report to the VTLC was that the charter of the Waitresses Union had been sent back. The waitresses were merging back with the men, into one union. Miss Brisbane continued to attend meetings as a delegate for a while, and filled in as Statistician occasionally, but eventually dropped out of sight.[68]

Possibly the most interesting union of the period was the Home and Domestic Employees Union of British Columbia. This organization was made up entirely of women and was not connected with any male union. The aims and policies of the union were expressly radical and feminist, and the president of the HDEU wrote shortly after its formation that "[the HDEU] bids fair to be one of the most important organizations of women ever formed."[69]

The HDEU was started on 19 March 1913 at a meeting at the Labor Temple to which about thirty-five women came. They were governesses, housemaids, nursemaids, cooks and other domestic workers. Their aims were ambitious. Aside from the three main objectives of the union—the nine-hour day, a minimum wage, and recognition as a body of industrial workers— they hoped eventually to establish a union hiring hall where employers would directly contract workers, to keep records on every place where members had worked or were at present employed, and to someday lease a building for a co-operative rooming house where they could live in healthy surroundings and enjoy a social life.[70]

Within a month they had fifty members,[71] and by August 1913 there were sixty-five women in the union.[72] At this point they applied for affiliation with the VTLC, and were accepted. Two delegates were sent to the VTLC meetings, a Miss K. McCall and a Miss M. E. Priest. Later a Miss A. M. Evans and the president of the union, Lillian L. M. Coote, also attended these meetings.[73] Applications for membership were to be sent to the union secretary, Miss E. Plaister, at 1537 Fifth Avenue East. Their office was in the Labor Temple, where the reading room had been divided in half and rented to them.[74]

Like the Waitresses Union, and possibly despite their belief in industrial unionism, they appear to have had a close relationship with the main labour movement. At one VTLC meeting, Miss Evans "requested the delegates to do all they could to make known the objects of her organization, and asked union men to urge women to join." Miss Evans also joined an organizing committee, together with Miss Coote, Helena Gutteridge and a male business agent, to look into organizing laundry workers in December 1913.[75] In January 1914, the B.C. Federation of Labour held its Fourth Annual Convention, and resolutions passed included one "Endorsing the Domestic Employees Union, pledging hearty co-operation and demanding that any eight-hour law enacted shall include domestic employees in its scope."[76]

The union was sensitive to the problems of organizing women in domestic service. The long hours worked and the tiring nature of the work meant that it was difficult for women to attend meetings or even to go to the office to register. To deal with this, the HDEU planned to establish what they called a "walking bureau,"[77] presumably to go house-to-house as had been done earlier by a woman in Toronto.[78] They also dealt with the fear that single women might get married and leave the union by pointing out that many married women continued to do domestic work in the daytime, and left their children at the city creche. When this question arose at their first meeting, the reply was that "no woman of the working classes who gets married need be afraid that she may have to leave the union because she is not out working. And anyhow, does a woman work less hours, or get more wages, when she gets married than she did before? Well then."[79]

The HDEU rejected the low status of their work, and the idea that they were "service" workers. They saw themselves, according to Miss Coote, as industrial workers under the capitalist system. Their Membership Creed, a copy of which was framed to hang on the wall of their club room in the Labor Temple, stated: "Believing that the home has a greater influence on the community than the community has on the home, we pledge ourselves as members of the union, to do all in our power to dignify the labour pertaining thereto."[80]

President Lillian Coote wrote a series of articles for the *B.C. Federationist* on the theories of the union and their goals. These form some of the only documents written by the women workers themselves that exist from this period, and in them she dealt with a variety of topics.

On working conditions for domestic employees, she stated that fourteen-hour days were common, and that even when not working, the women were almost totally at the disposal of their employers. Although the women came from differing social stations, their position in society was "a relic of feudalism."[81]

Upper- and middle-class women came in for some heavy criticism. On the same day that the HDEU was formed, 200 club women sold a women's edition of a daily paper on Vancouver streets, to raise money for a Women's Building. Miss Coote commented sarcastically that "they were filled with enthusiasm at what they appeared to think was their own original idea, namely the *awakening of women to the power of combination*" (her emphasis).[82] In a later article she went on to say:

> One cannot help wondering whether the many philanthropically inclined women of this province have seen fit to practically ignore the domestic problem question owing to the fact that the remedy would affect them—that they ... fall short when it is a problem of touching their own pockets.... [83]

But she also understood the nature of these women's position and the nature of women's work:

> Work must be clearly defined. Some women call afternoon teas, entertaining their husbands' friends, dressing to pay calls, etc., work and to a certain extent they are justified, because their object is mental and social advancement, which cannot be obtained without work of some sort or other. But after all, they have a free will in regard to their affairs, and if in the pursuit of their own advancement they work, it is they who reap the benefits of so doing.
>   There is another class of women, namely, the wives of working men.... Their husbands take it for granted that their wives work because they like it. Some men are foolish enough to say that it is not really work—it is just "keeping at it." These women, however, do not need our sympathy—the remedy is in their own hands.[84]

Lillian Coote was certainly not a revolutionary, although she talked about the employees' "relationship with labor and capital,"[85] and the "degradation of a system which bartered for practically the ownership of an individual." She, and the union, hoped to force legislation to be enacted to carry out their main objects. To this end, they determined to hold public meetings once a month "to show to the public the necessity of what they are asking."[86] In 1914, a bill was introduced in the provincial legislature, an "Act Relating to the Employment of Domestic Employees." It contained provisions for a nine-hour day and a fifty-four-hour week; it would have ended wage deductions for breakage of goods; and it stated that "wages" should mean lawful money of Canada, and should not include recompense by way of room and/or board. It did not get past committee.[87]

At the time of the union's formation in 1913, it was reported that the average wage for domestics was $30 per month with room and board. By the end of 1915 this had fallen to from $10 to $15 per month.[88] Vancouver was in a deep depression and unemployment was extremely high. Women who lost their jobs in other trades turned to domestic service in large numbers, which further contributed to the lowering of wages. Skilled domestic workers apparently were continually leaving the city, some to go south, in search of better wages and conditions. In 1915, the Home and Domestic Employees Union, faced with such heavy odds against them, appears to have dissolved.[89]

By now it should have become clear that, far from showing a "lack of interest in her economic future ... [and] lack of interest in trade unions,"[90] women attempted to organize persistently in most of the major occupations they were engaged in, during the 1900–1915 period. Although the forms of this organization varied, and women were not necessarily interested in forming their own autonomous or semi-autonomous unions, their belief in trade unionism was clearly demonstrated.

Since statistics on the make-up of union membership, in unions composed of both men and women, probably do not exist, it is even possible that unions thought of as mostly male may have been largely female in composition. Though the leadership of these unions tended to be largely male, this does not necessarily reflect the proportions of the membership. In turn, the male domination of leadership positions does not mean that women were not interested in or did not have a permanent commitment to trade unions. Many other factors could have been responsible for the largely male leadership, not the least of which would have been children, for married women, and the burden of housework for all women, cares which would have reduced to almost nothing the time available to them for attending meetings and conventions. Another factor was probably the negative attitudes of many male unionists towards women working for wages at all, let alone their holding leadership positions in trade unions.

The problem remains of how many women participated in these unions; in other words, were they only a small percentage of working women and, if so, why? The first question may be unanswerable, although further enquiry may turn up more data. At this point, though, it appears that their numbers were indeed small in relation to the total female working population.

This leaves the second question, of why this was so. When the nature of women's work and of their lives at this period in time is looked at, it is not justifiable to assume simply that their own psychology was to blame. Undoubtedly psychology had something to do with it—most women at this time probably assumed that they would at some point marry; and given the kind of work available to women—work performed for long hours, under oppressive and unhealthy conditions, at incredibly low wages, they also probably hoped not to have to work outside their homes as well as in them. Given this hope of temporary status as a worker, and the economic marginality of many women's survival (and therefore the need to cling to what jobs they had), some women would not have been willing to risk joining or starting a union in an age where no protective legislation existed ensuring union rights.

The objective difficulties surrounding unionization must have been enormous for them, in any case. Most women were separated from each other both at their workplace and when they returned home; they lacked places to meet each other where they could realize their common problems; and they did not have media avenues wherein to discuss their grievances. Their long hours of work, combined with the housework they returned to, meant not only that it would have been hard to find time to meet, but also indicates that many women must have spent their lives in a state of mental and physical exhaustion. Lillian Coote stated one of the objectives of the Home and Domestic Employees Union to be "help other women to realize that there is something more in life than work and sleep."[91]

The fact that the unions formed did not last for long can be partly attributed to just such difficulties. The lack of permanent and measurable improvements in wages and working conditions, due to employer intransigence and the anti-union policies of government, must also have been a discouraging factor. In the later years from 1911 on, and especially from 1913 to 1915, Vancouver, in common with the rest of the country, was suffering from a severe economic depression. Under these conditions, resulting in an employer's labour market, the situation for trade unions and workers in general was hardly favourable.

In sum, it seems rather amazing that women were able to organize at all. But organize they did, despite the overwhelming odds against them, and in large enough numbers to justify re-evaluating their place in the history books.

Notes

1. To test the truth of this assertion, see for example: Paul Phillips, *No Power Greater;* Ross McCormack, *Reformers, Rebels and Revolutionaries;* Charles Lipton, *The Trade Union Movement of Canada 1827–1959;* Stuart Jamieson, *Times of Trouble: Labour Unrest and Industrial Conflict in Canada 1906–1966.*

2. *The Independent,* 29 August 1903.

3. *Vancouver Trades and Labour Council,* General Meetings minute (hereinafter *VTLCg*), 21 August 1913.

4. *Labour Gazette,* (hereinafter *LG*), Ottawa, Canada, Vol. XVI, October 1915, p. 405.

5. *Independent,* 3 January 1903.

6. A. Ross McCormack, *Reformers, Rebels and Revolutionaries: The Western Canadian Radical Movement 1899–1919* (Toronto and Buffalo: University of Toronto Press, 1977), p. 102.

7. Paul Phillips, *No Power Greater: A Century of Labour in British Columbia* (Vancouver: B.C. Federation of Labour and Boag Foundation, 1967), pp. 25, 35–37, and 46.

8. See, for example, Edward S. Seymour, *An Illustrated History of Canadian Labour 1800–1974* Ottawa: Canadian Labour Congress, 1976, p. 10, where he calls a 1906 resolution to stop the immigration of Asiatics and East Indians "a tragic testimony in labour history by trade unionists."

9. Wayne Roberts, *Honest Womanhood: Feminism, Femininity, and Class Consciousness Among Toronto Working Women 1893 to 1914* Toronto: New Hogtown.

10. *Census of Canada,* 1911, Vol. VI, Table 11, p. xx.

11. *Ibid.,* Table 13, p. xxi.

12. *Ibid.,* Table 14, p. xxii.

13. *Ibid.,* Tables 20 and 21, pp. xxvii, xxviii.

14. *Ibid.,* Table 7, p. xvii.

15. *Ibid.,* Table 15, p. xxiii.

16. *Ibid.,* Table VI, pp. 286–96.

17. Roberts, *Honest Womanhood,* pp. 10–11.

18. *Independent,* 5 September 1903.

19. *LG,* Vol. III, December 1902, pp. 477 and 479.

20. *Ibid.,* Vol. III, January 1903, p. 566.

21. *Victoria Daily Times,* 23 June 1905 and 26 June 1905.

22. *Independent,* 31 January 1903. Directory of Unions.

23. *Ibid.,* 31 January 1903.

24. *LG,* Vol. III, January 1903, p. 517.

25. *Independent,* 31 January 1903.

26. *LG,* Vol. VI, March 1906, pp. 1030–31.

27. *Loc. cit.*

28. *LG,* Vol. VI, April 1906, p. 1153, and June 1906, p. 1383.

29. *Ibid.,* 5 September 1903.

30. *Ibid.,* 17 May 1902; 5 September 1903; 27 December 1902.

31. *B.C. Federationist,* 27 December 1912, p. 25.

32. *LG,* Vol. XIII, June 1913, p. 1380.

33. *VTLCg,* 19 February 1914.

34. *LG,* Vol. XIII, April 1913, p. 1080.

35. *Independent,* 5 September 1903.

36. Roberts, *Honest Womanhood,* p. 23.

37. *LG,* Vol. XIII, April 1913, p. 1079.

38. *VTLCg,* 15 January 1914. Report by the delegate of the union named Mowatt, to the VTLC.

39. Doreen Madge Weppler, *Early Forms of Political Activity Among White Women in British Columbia 1880–1925* (Burnaby, B.C.: Simon Fraser University, unpublished M.A. Thesis, 1971), pp. 33 and 84, footnotes.

40. *Independent,* 5 September 1903.

41. *VTLCg,* 16 October 1913 and 6 November 1913.

42. *Census of Canada,* 1911, Vol. VI, Table VI, pp. 288–89.

43. *VTLCg,* 17 April 1913.

44. *LG,* Vol. XIV, July 1913, p. 42, and September 1913, p. 266: Vol. XIII, April 1913, p. 1080.

45. *VTLCg,* 6 November 1913; 5 March and 19 November 1914.

46. *Ibid.,* 5 September and 7 November 1903.

47. Weppler, *Political Activity,* pp. 32–33.

48. *B.C. Federationist,* 27 December 1912, p. 19.

49. *LG,* Vol. IV, July 1903, p. 88.

50. *Ibid.,* Vol. IV, December 1903, pp. 591 and 679.

51. *Victoria Daily Times,* 19 June 1915, p. 4.

52. Weppler, *Political Activity,* p. 32.

53. *VTLCg,* 18 November 1904.

54. *Ibid.,* 5 February 1914.

55. *Ibid.,* 2 April 1914.

56. *LG,* Vol. XV, August 1914, pp. 189–90.

57. *Independent,* 5 September 1903.

58. *Census of Canada,* 1911. Vol. VI, Table VI, p. 288.

59. Weppler, *Political Activity,* p. 35.

60. *Independent,* 5 September 1903.

61. *Western Wage Earner,* July 1910, p. 11.

62. *Census of Canada,* 1911, Vol. VI, pp. 286–88.

63. *VTLCg,* 18 August 1910.

64. *LG,* Vol. XI, October 1910, p. 421.

65. *VTLCg,* 6 October 1910; 3 November 1910; 17 November 1910.

66. *LG,* Vol. XIII, April 1913, pp. 1079–80.

67. *VTLCg,* 21 May 1914; 3 July 1913.

68. *Ibid.,* 15 January 1914; 4 June 1914, and various dates to end of 1914.

69. *B.C. Federationist,* 28 March 1913, p. 3.

70. *Ibid.,* 28 March 1913, pp. 1 and 4.

71. *Ibid.,* 18 April 1913, p. 1.

72. *LG,* Vol. XIV, August 1913, p. 152.

73. *VTLCg,* 7 August and 21 August 1913; 6 November 1913; 8 January 1914.

74. *B.C. Federationist,* 28 March 1913, p. 4; *VTLC,* Board of Directors, meetings minutes, 11 July 1913.

75. *VTLCg,* 20 November and 18 December 1913.

76. *LG,* Vol. XIV, February 1914, p. 954.

77. *B.C. Federationist,* 18 April 1913, p. 1.

78. Roberts, *Honest Womanhood,* p. 15.

79. *B.C. Federationist,* 28 March 1913, p. 4.

80. *LG,* Vol. XIV, September 1913, p. 266.

81. *B.C. Federationist,* 28 March 1913, p. 3.

82. *Loc. cit.*

83. *Ibid.,* 11 April 1913, p. 2.

84. *Ibid.,* 4 April 1913, p. 2.

85. *Loc. cit.*

86. *Ibid.,* 28 March 1913, p. 3; 18 April 1913, p. 1.

87. *LG,* Vol. XIV, April 1914, p. 1163.

88. *Ibid.,* Vol. XIII, April 1913, p. 1079; Vol. XVI, November 1915, pp. 569–70.

89. Genevieve Leslie. "Domestic Service in Canada, 1880–1920." in *Women at Work: Ontario 1850–1930* (Toronto: Canadian Women's Educational Press, 1974), p. 123.

90. *LG,* Vol. XIII, April 1913, p. 1079.

91. *B.C. Federationist,* 11 April 1913, p. 2.

FEMINIZATION OF THE LABOUR PROCESS IN THE COMMUNICATION INDUSTRY: THE CASE OF THE TELEPHONE OPERATORS, 1876–1904

Michèle Martin

In early 1880, the first woman was hired by Bell Telephone Co. as an operator in the Main Exchange in Montreal, and soon after the company's managers in Toronto also hired a woman. Thus began the replacement of an all-male operating labour force by one that was entirely female. At the time, the use of "boys" as operators was said to be a total failure. A Bell Telephone Company manager stated that if the company continued with boys as operators, "it was virtually facing bankruptcy."[1]

This article examines the process of feminization in the telephone industry. It especially focuses on the Bell Telephone Company[2] in Ontario and Quebec, with particular emphasis on Montreal and Toronto.

From *Labour/Le Travail,* XXII (Fall 1988), 139–162. Reprinted by permission of the Canadian Committee on Labour History.

I

During the last decade, the issue of feminization has occasioned a growing debate among social scientists, especially feminist writers. Much has been said, about the feminization of teaching,[3] of office work,[4] and of domestic labour.[5]

Prentice's "The Feminization of Teaching in British North America and Canada, 1845–1875," presents a largely economic analysis of the phenomenon. She argues that the creation of a public school system promoting the grading of school children "led to the feminization of the teaching labour force." The feminization of teaching brought cheap and effective teachers to a section of the system which was considered unattractive by men. Low wages for women allowed school boards to give higher wages to male, career-oriented teachers. However, the social acceptance of women as teachers was essential,[6] and contemporary beliefs such as the degrading of the profession by its feminization, the ineptitude of women at discipline, and the identification of women with truncated career paths had to be overcome.[7] Moreover, the willingness of women to take badly paid teaching jobs with difficult working conditions, where they were in a position of subordination, was due, according to Prentice, to a crowded female labour market coupled with women's personal choice to work outside the home.[8] In short, Prentice argues that a change in educational organization due to the building of a public school system, the existence of a large female reserve army of labour, and the changing social role of women are the main factors which influenced the feminization of teaching in the mid-nineteenth century.

Danylewycz, *et al.,* also recognised economic factors as central in the feminization of teaching. Yet, in "The Evolution of the Sexual Division of Labour in Teaching: A Nineteenth Ontario and Quebec Case Study," they suggest that other elements have also influenced the evolution of the feminization of teaching, especially in Ontario and Quebec. In Ontario, for instance, age structure, ethnicity, and the household status of teachers were also responsible for the change in elementary school teaching, while in Quebec alternatives in terms of job openings for men, and male under-schooling in comparison to women, encouraged the feminization of teaching in elementary school.[9]

Lowe's "Women, Work and the Office" supports these arguments as well. Lowe argues that the transition from small entrepreneurial capitalism to corporate capitalism led to the feminization of office work. He identifies four models used to account for feminization: the "consumer choice" model; the "reserve army of labour" model; the "demand" model; and the "segmentation" model.[10] However, none of these presents a satisfactory explanation for the feminization of telephone operators.

The "consumer" choice model is "based on the concept of rational economic choice" made subjectively upon a family consensus in view of economic necessities of the household. Women are assumed to exercise free choice and the model explains work rates in terms of subjective processes rather than socio-economic variables.[11] The second model uses the Marxist concept of "reserve army of labour" to explain the place of women in the labour force. This model, developed by Braverman, emphasizes the ways in which capital has created a supply of cheap female labour related to the decreasing or increasing demand on the labour market made by the requirements of capitalists.[12] It is helpful in explaining the position of women after they have been integrated into the labour market, and in shedding light on the process of their exploitation by capitalist industry. The "demand" model is concerned with the occupational segregation of women through the manipulation of job requirements. This model argues that an increased supply of female labour is caused by the growing demand for women in certain occupations. Gender discrimination in terms of specific occupations is "reinforced by the process of sex-labelling." The labour supply is manipulated by capital in terms of job requirements and wages.[13] Finally, the "segmentation" model, proposed by Edwards, gives the "structural properties" as the basic elements of the process of feminization of an occupation. It suggests that sex-based dimensions of power and inequality can be related to the fragmentation of the labour force in the labour process developed by corporate capitalism. Sex differentiation would be due to changes in productive process, mostly brought about by the technologisation of the work place. This would create "sub-markets" constituted of new occupations with different characteristics and working conditions.[14]

While each model identifies some factors influencing the process of the feminization of occupations, none of them furnishes an adequate explanation. While the "consumer choice" model suggests a weak concept of rational and conscious choice subjectively made by women, the "reserve army of labour market" model, although it explains women's inferior position within the labour force in capitalist production, does not give the essential elements to understand the process through which women are hired in the first place. The "demand" and the "segmentation" models furnish more concrete conceptions. For the case with which I am concerned—telephone operating—the former model suggests that operating work became a female occupation because of changes made by the telephone industry in terms of job requirements. Sexually stereotyped requirements were assigned to the occupation, and with these came low wages. On the other hand, the "segmentation" model would emphasize that this new assignment of requirements was due to the fact that operator's work was segmented from other occupations and did not require high skills. Moreover, the level of stability did not have to be high because it was easy to train new operators. Training time for that occupation correspond to the time necessary to subject the operators to the switchboard.

However, according to Lowe, the segmentation model largely explains the feminization of office work. Fragmentation of the work rendered the job unattractive to skilled workers. This opened the occupation to women through a "secondary labour market of female clerks."[15] In effect the manipulation of sex-labelled job characteristics by the employers resulted in the appropriation by men of the most interesting and rewarding positions in the office and left the "minor tasks" to women. Those were at the bottom of the hierarchy of occupations in bureaucratic organizations and required qualifications usually attributed to women in a patriarchal society: obedience and submissiveness.[16]

Finally, another debate on the process of feminization is concerned with domestic work. In "Capital, the State and the Origins of the Working-Class Household," B. Curtis investigates how domestic labour became women's work. This is a result, he says, of the separation of household and industry under capitalism, and was sustained by state activity. "It is the state that reproduces labour power in the commodity form and that reproduces the oppression [or subordination] to which the unemployed domestic worker is subject."[17] From the struggle of the working-class against exploitative working conditions, and for a domestic life, emerged the working-class household with women in the subordinated position of full-time houseworkers without economic power:[18] in periods of high labour demand, women participated in certain sectors of the labour market, and when unemployed, they were dependent on their husbands. "Their condition as housewives structure[d] their participation in production in capitalist industries [and] ... *discipline[d] them in relations of subordination and dependence* ...."[19] Thus, women's subordination was not simply the result of sexist attitudes, says L. Briskin in "Domestic Labour," "rather, it [was] *firmly rooted in the material conditions of women's lives,* primarily in the institution of the family."[20] A definite split occurred between domestic labour and capitalist production which forced women into labour consisting mainly of the reproduction of the labour force.

In their respective analyses of the feminization of the domestic labour, Briskin and Curtis argue the centrality of women's subordination for understanding the expansion of the capitalist economy. It is an essential element of the manipulation of women as domestic workers and as wage labourers. Indeed, the concept of subordination, which is also discussed in Luxton's *More than a Labour of Love,*[21] but which is absent from the previously reviewed studies, is indispensible to understanding not only women's acceptance of second rate and low-waged jobs, but their willingness to take occupations whose demands include patience, obedience and submissiveness. Women's subordination, institutionalized in the family and the workplace, is central to the moral regulation of women in the public realm. Here it works to incite women to consider their work as a "labour of love." Telephone operating had many of the characteristics of a labour of love.

The degree of feminization of an occupation is affected by the state of the labour market, and the financial structure of the organization within which the process occurs. Moreover, the traditional attitudes towards women in the society in which the process occurs influence the characteristics attached to the job.[22] Other factors such as age structure, ethnicity, household status, job openings, and level of education have also to be taken into consideration to account for the timing of the phenomenon. Finally, there seems to be a general consensus among researchers that the feminization of an occupation results in a decrease of its social status and in a reduction in its pay.

These assumptions suggested in the debate on job feminization do not satisfactorily explain the process of feminization of the operating labour force in the telephone industry. Indeed, although the latter passed from an entirely male to an entirely female force, the telephone company's administrators who organized the hiring of women seemed to imply that the job had never been suitable to the male personality, although the work was directly related to the handling and repairing of technical apparatuses, a domain commonly reserved to men.[23] Moreover, the feminization of the operating occupation did not undermine its economic status and was not due to a new fragmentation of work within the operating workplace. Rather, it appears that the job of operator acquired a higher social status after its feminization and, although the job was low-waged, the wages did not decrease, at least in absolute terms, after the feminization of the labour force. Wages for female workers stayed relatively the same as for male workers. Finally, unlike the case of teaching and office work, operators were not confined to inferior position, but had access to the highest degrees of a hierarchical scale, created within the operating labour force.[24]

This article investigates how the occupation of telephone operator came to be a female job ghetto. Its main theme is that the process of feminization of operating work was central to the rapid development of the telephone industry in late nineteenth and early twentieth centuries. The particular characteristics of the women operators facilitated the telephone industry's transition from a small-scale enterprise to a modern corporate capitalist monopoly. In effect, the telephone system represented a general, public system producing individual, private telephone calls. The work of the operators as mediators in the production of telephone calls placed them in a paradoxical situation in which their intervention was essential in the connection of subscribers on telephone lines and, at the same time, was resented as an obstruction to the privacy of these calls. This situation in which the operators were a necessity and a nuisance at the same time created contradictions which the telephone business attempted to resolve in developing a set of moral regulations to be applied to the female operators. In fact, the feminization of the operating work occurred during the mid-Victorian period, in a context of intense moral regulation for those women working in the public sphere. As mediators between subscribers, the operators had to imitate the "moral values" conveyed by those with whom they were regularly in contact. Rules and regulations coming from the company gradually covered not only the technical aspects of their formation but their "moral education" as well. Thus, feminization brought no decline to the job's social status, that is, honour, but rather created some moral barriers intended to improve the public "image" of the telephone system and, thus to activate the development of the enterprise. The features of the female operating labour force in question were its adaptability first to the "military" discipline necessary to work on increasingly mechanized switchboards in huge central offices, then to the growing administrative control and moral regulation, finally to the wide variety of customers' demands. The definition of the operating work was dramatically altered during the period from its creation in 1876 to its near elimination in the early 1920s, with the coming of automatic switchboards.

This study is concerned with the characteristics of the operating work which were used in its definition as "women's work." What factors motivated the telephone industry to shift very early towards women operators, despite the technical nature of the job, the "risky" night shifts, and patriarchal attitudes about women's work outside the home?

II

The development of the telephone system coincided with a wave of capitalist concentration in Canadian industry. Small entrepreneurial businesses were becoming large capitalist firms. In this competition, the development of technical means of communication, through which capitalists could rapidly get relevant information on national and international markets, played a central role.[25] A network of telegraphic communication already existed which had considerably shortened the circulation time of invested capital. However, the telegraph was relatively slow and access to it was limited by the mastery of specific skills. When the telephone came on the market, it represented the "ideal" means through which business transactions could be made from person to person. Bell Telephone Company's management was quick to understand the utility of the telephone for businessmen and oriented its development from the outset to please that group of subscribers. Before direct-dial systems, telephone operators mediated between subscribers.

In order to understand the extension of the telephone system (with particular attention to the Bell Company's development in the provinces of Quebec and Ontario), it is useful to divide its expansion into two stages based partly on the improvement of the technical means, partly on the economic and political climate. The first period, 1876 to 1889, was that of the establishment of Bell Telephone Company. During the first years, from 1876 to 1880, a certain number of independent companies had started in the business, some using A.G. Bell's invention, others employing Edison's. However, in 1880 Bell's company, represented by C.F. Sise, an American businessman, bought most of these businesses in Montreal and Toronto, as well as in the other towns and cities of Quebec and Ontario. Bell's company began to feel its way towards the realization of what would become one of the biggest private monopolies in Canada. The technical means of the telephone were still in an experimental stage and their performance, although advertised as "wonderful" in the newspapers of that time, created much frustration and despair for both management and subscribers. The switchboards had a capacity of fifty lines and were operated manually. When there were more than fifty subscribers in an exchange, two or more sections of the switchboard, which were interconnected by conducting strips known as "trunk," were necessary. If a subscriber was calling someone on a different section of the switchboard, the two sections had to be plugged or switched together. This job was done by "switch-boys" under the operators' command. Unlike the operators, the switch-boys did not have any direct contact with the subscribers.[26] In this type of telephone system, the operating work actually constituted the most reliable part of the telephone business.

The second stage, from 1890 to 1904, was the period of confirmation. It involved some major developments of the technical means of telephoning which attracted a larger number of subscribers. One major development was the enlargement of the switchboards and the elimination of the switch-boy's job. Operators could then carry out the whole process of connecting two subscribers' calls. This was a period of continual, although not spectacular growth, which was accompanied by a more formal organization of the operating labour force. The company began to impose a hierarchical structure on operators based on formal rules and regulations. In this period women replaced men as operators.[27]

At the beginning of its expansion, the telephone system was operated by a male labour force. As the telephone industry developed, however, the telephone companies started to hire women for the operating work, asserting that their personalities were "better suited" to the work. By the end of the 1880s, almost all telephone operators were women. Indeed, the job of operator became a prototypical job ghetto from which the male labour force was almost entirely barred. Nonetheless, during the first years of the telephone's development, telephone companies, including Bell Exchange, had hired "boys" as operators. According to a manager who worked as a male operator in 1878, "it was most natural to use boys as operators in the first telephone exchanges. Boys and young men had served as telegraph operators from the beginning. Then, too, it was unthinkable in the early eighties that a girl should be out after 10 o'clock so that the operating staff on the night shift was of necessity male."[28]

In the mid-Victorian era, the period of the early development of the telephone, official discourse presented men as assertive and aggressive and women as submissive and passive. A woman was expected to be patient, tactful, prudent, as well as forceful and courageous within her family in order to "use to the advantage the limitless and indivisible affection she *owe[d]* her husband." At the same time, she was required to be intelligent, discerning, firm, and energetic with her children to "properly direct their education." This difference in social expectations for men and women was based on the distinct role to which each gender was subordinated:

> A young lady, unlike a young man, is not in the least required to be present in the public sphere; on the contrary, it is in the interior of the family, under the eyes of her parents, that she ought to reveal all the treasures of purity, modesty, humility, and piety, which her heart possesses. These are the best qualities, the most beautiful ornaments of the young girl.[29]

This image of modest, pure and submissive women was particularly widespread in the dominant and middle classes which attempted to convey their "ideal" moral virtues to the other classes through magazines and newspapers. An article entitled "The Family," in *Le monde illustré,* a newspaper written by philanthropically minded bourgeois and middle class ladies but intended for lower-middle and working classes,[30] made it clear that a woman

> ... ought never to seek other than the pure pleasures which the interior of the family offers to her. Woman's life, that life full of love, self-denial, and sacrifice, should only be lived there; so that the obscurity of her surroundings might make her virtues shine forth more brightly.[31]

Furthermore, since woman's place was in the interior of her family, she was not allowed to go outside of it alone, particularly not in the evening. According to the Catholic church, these "feeble creatures ought never to be left ... without effective control and supervision."[32] This constant supervision was to be performed by their husbands, parents or by a responsible person, approved by the parents, to protect women against "a liberal current of ideas" and against "pronounced tendencies towards excessive liberty."[33] This protective attitude towards women's "fragility" and "vulnerability" applied to their social rights as well. Because women had to be protected, their guardians needed the power necessary to subdue the "dangers." In as much as men were to be the protectors, they required control of the means of protection. Since one of them was the material means provided by labour, men's power was extended to women's right to have a job as well. Hence, women's work was socially ill-regarded, and that which was available usually was in the form of low-status and low-paid jobs. As the Archbishop of Montreal stated,

> The ignorance of some and the ill-will of others work to produce an unfortunate situation in which people come to believe that equality [between men and women] involves identical rights, and women are urged to enter into a ridiculous and odious revolt with men on a field of combat where neither the conditions of the struggle nor the chances of success could possibly be equal. The realization of such theories would be obnoxious to women and the family, and would shortly lead to the fall of one and the ruin of the other.[34]

Equal opportunity at work would cause family breakdown and women's "fall." This was a common patriarchal discourse during the first periods of development of the telephone industry and one which guided its employment policies. Joan Sangster stresses that Mackenzie King's "perceptions of the operators reflect[ed] a Victorian image of woman," and that the Ontario press sustained that view as well. In the press reports of the 1907 telephone operators' strike, "it was the moral, rather than the economic, question of woman labour which was emphasized." This Victorian view of woman was not restricted to the dominant class, however. According to Sangster, trade unionists held similar opinions. "The views of many craft unionists were dominated by their belief that woman's role was primarily a maternal and domestic one." Moreover, "it was woman's contribution to the home rather than her status as a worker, which was most often stressed in the labour press. In fact, concern that woman's wage labour would destroy the family was very strong."[35] This concern was general. The telephone industry recruited its first operators among a group of "boys" who were already employed as telegraph messengers and who knew a little about electrical communication, although they were by no means skilled labourers. Besides, young men were "cheaper" than mature and married men.[36] These young telegraph messengers were paid only by the message, and very poorly so.

The Operators' Work

In the early 1880s, when the telephone industry started hiring operators, the labour process was largely unstructured. It consisted mainly of improvised work on an unsophisticated technical instrument which provided an irregular production in quality and quantity. No specific conditions were required. In fact, the only requirements attached to the job of operator were to be male and young: "They were boys 16 or 17 years old, and young imps, immune to all discipline."[37] Nevertheless, the telephone company pioneers and managers had not "envisioned the fact, later proved by experience, that *men and boys were temperamentally unsuited* to the exacting duties of switchboard operation, and that this work was *destined to be performed by members of the opposite sex.*"[38] The larger the operating rooms, the more undisciplined were the "boys." John J. Carty, an operator during this period, remembered that male operators were very "wild." William J. Clarke related the "fondness for clowning and practical jokes of the boys and young men employed in the operating room" when he was one of them. These jokes were "often at the expense of the subscriber." Moreover, male operators were not submissive and when "subscribers were rude the boys did not always turn the other cheek but matched insult for insult and curse for curse." Furthermore, according to Clarke, the boys were inclined to "wrestling on the floor," failing to answer incoming calls. Their training was very casual. They would "drop into the office during a slack period on Saturday and Sunday to learn how to operate the switchboard at which [they were] to start on Monday." The majority of the male operators were doing operating work on a part-time basis and were employed for other work either within the telephone companies or for other industries. In spite of that, some men who were operating asserted that there was the prospect of advancement within the telephone business, especially with Bell Telephone Company after its incorporation in 1880, and that since "most of them were ambitious," this "tended to keep them trying to do a good job in spite of the natural tendencies."[39]

Even after Bell Telephone Company started to hire women as day operators,[40] men continued to be hired during the day in order "to connect the calling lines with the trunk line to office called," or, in other words, to do the technical work necessary within the exchange. Besides, male operators continued to work on the evening and night shifts, some starting at 6:00 p.m., others at 10:00 p.m., according to the size of the exchange in which they were working. In big and busy offices, male operators were used as little as possible, and only during the period of the day where the business was quiet. However, company managers concluded that "... boys as operators were proved complete and consistent failures. They were noisy, rude, impatient and talked back to subscribers, played tricks with wires, and on one another."[41] The company's response to such undisciplined behaviour was an attempt to enforce control over the male operators in order to meet the subscribers' complaints. In a letter to the local managers in Montreal, in response to a complaint he received against a male operator, L.B. McFarlane assessed Bell Telephone Company's expectations towards the operators' attitude with the subscribers: "He as well as other operators should know they have no business to talk back to a subscriber, and you can inform him that if we have any further complaint of this nature his services will be dispense with."[42] Nonetheless, disciplining male operators did not transform their "unsuitable characteristics" into suitable qualities for the operation of the telephone system.

The operator's work did not represent a sub-market created by the telephone industry for women, however. The particularity of that job was that it involved both "masculine" and "feminine" tasks. It implied a technical knowledge of electricity to cope with frequent repairs; as a mediating job, it entailed a direct contact with subscribers, a sort of "labour of love."[43] It seems that, in 1876, the telephone business gave more importance to the technical aspect, and hired young men for the work. Undoubtedly, patriarchal attitudes were mainly responsible for that first decision. However, bad experiences with men made Bell Telephone Company managers realize that, to keep their few customers, they had to emphasize the characteristics attached to the mediating aspect of the occupation. The position of operator came to be seen as "naturally" women's work.

In 1880, Bell Telephone Company hired the first female operator to work in the Main Exchange in Montreal.[44] The early experience of the industry had already pointed to a few specific requirements for the operator's work which appeared essential to the expansion of the telephone system. The telephone company concentrated on matching poor wages with adequate characteristics for its operators. The particularity of the product—an instantaneous telephone call—and the essential role of the operators as mediators to produce it, created a situation in which users and operators were constantly interacting. Since the subscribers were mostly businessmen from the dominant and middle classes, the company's managers decided that "courtesy" and "discipline" were the most important qualities to "perform successfully the duties of ... [such] subordinate places" as telephone operators.[45] K.J. Dunstan, general manager for the Ontario district, insisted that "rules and discipline" were to be "strictly enforced" to insure operators' courtesy with users: "Mistakes may be overlooked, but lack of courtesy is an unpardonable offence. Subscribers will forgive a great deal if the operator is invariably pleasant and polite [and submissive], and the necessity of only employing educated and refined operators is very apparent."[46] The solution to that problem appeared to be hiring women as operators: "A woman would give better service and be a better agent," said C.F. Sise, general-manager of Bell Telephone Company.[47] It was suggested to employ "young women at salary not greater than commission amounts to commission men," the telegraph messengers, who treated the telephone as secondary to their own business, and acted very independently. "The young women would be *directly under the company's control,* would attend promptly to calls and are as a rule more honest and careful than men."[48] Hence, the company's attempt at structuring the labour force by starting a process of subjection of its male operators through enforcement of control and work discipline led to a process of feminization of the occupation. The unresponsive behaviour of the male operators to the process of subjection forced the company's management to adopt a policy of hiring female operators.

The first woman was hired soon after "a conference between Mr. Forbes, president of the American company, Mr. Sise, Mr. Baker and myself [K.J. Dunstan] re. girls as telephone operators. Mr. Forbes said he believed they were used somewhere, did not know where and had heard nothing against them."[49] Sometime later, Mr. Dunstan in the Toronto exchange hired the "Misses Howell" as telephone operators.[50] These women and most female operators were mainly coming from lower-middle and respectable working classes. They were "girls"[51] who needed to earn some money and, at the same time, could meet the moral standard of subscribers coming from the dominant and upper-middle classes. On the other hand, subscribers had also some duties vis-à-vis the female operators, as a message in the telephone directories indicated: "Ladies are employed as operators; we ask for their courteous treatment."[52] The occupation of telephone operator was a new opening for the large female reserve army of labour. An operator described the place of women on the labour market at that time: "Few jobs were open to women then; even most stenographers were male."[53] Another operator of the 1880s reinforced that statement: "Employment for women back in the 80's was limited to teaching school, factory work, restaurant and domestic work."[54] Some women preferred telephone operating to teaching: "Teaching was prosaic, poorly paid and the profession was overcrowded."[55] It appears, though, that female teachers and telephone operators were from the same classes. Moreover, some of the requirements for getting the jobs were similar. For instance, for both occupations, women had to present recommendations from three persons, including their clergymen.[56] Age limits were also imposed, and although Bell Telephone Company accepted women as young as fourteen years old as operators in the 1880s,[57] when the schools for operators started in 1900, the age limit increased to seventeen. Finally, women needed to have "good memories," "be tall enough so that their arms would reach all lines on the switchboard and be slim enough so that they could fit into the narrow spaces allotted to the #1 standard switchboard positions."[58] L.B. McFarlane, Bell Telephone Company's manager for Canada East, declared in the *Daily Witness* that "in their selection the greatest care is exercised. They must be girls of irreproachable character, recommended by their clergymen."[59] With such requirements as recommendations from a clergyman, doctor and property owner, it is clear that these women could only be from "respectable" backgrounds.

However, the feminization of the occupation of operator entailed some difficulties for the company. Indeed, although the telephone operating work required no particular skills, some technical knowledge in the field of electricity was useful. The telephone system in its early development constantly required minor repairs and adjustments which were effected by the "boys."[60] Since Bell Company's managers thought women incapable of doing electrical work, for a few years after the hiring of the first woman as operator, boys continued to be hired to do the technical aspect of the job. While women answered the subscribers, the young men were connecting the busy lines with the trunk. However, this was inconvenient, said a female operator at that time, as the boys were playing tricks on the female operators whom they did not like.[61] The problem was resolved by the company's managers who provided all female operators with a "small book on telephone troubles and how to remove them," a book which helped the female operators to be "more self-reliant and to fix small troubles that will come up."[62] Thus, for equal wages, women provided the telephone industry with new labour power, furnishing not only the "feminine" qualities of submission and courtesy, but the "masculine" characteristics of technical and mechanical skills as well. In spite of changes applied to the job definition and its labelling as a "female" occupation, some essential aspects of the work remained traditional male domains to which the hired women had to adapt, at least until the end of the 1890s, when the improved technology eliminated the need for such interventions. It seems, then, that women had succeeded in adapting to the "male" characteristics of the work, while men had failed to adjust to its "female" features. For the telephone company, this represented a value which even its most chauvinist managers could not ignore.[63]

Yet, the process of feminization of the operator's occupation did not happen instantly. As an operator remarked: "Elimination of the masculine touch ... was not made with one gesture. It covered a long period of years."[64] On the one hand, in that mid-Victorian society so very protective of "ladies' virtues," "some people thought that it was pretty hazardous to allow women to be at work at night alone."[65] Since the "traffic load" was much lighter at night than during the day, the company continued to hire male operators for the evening and night duties for many years after women had started as day operators. The first hiring of a woman as night operator occurred in 1888.[66] On the other hand, even male day operators were not eliminated all at once. Rather, women gradually replaced the "boys" as they were promoted to higher wage jobs, as they quit, as they were dismissed for bad conduct, or as jobs were opened.

Still, the job, by then, was seen as a female occupation which, as B. Lalonde, a female operator in Ottawa put it: "requires a lot of *devotion* and brings very little gratitude from the public." The operators were "women who have *put their femininity to the service of the community.* Very few men would be patient enough to perform the duties of a telephone operator."[67] An Ontario newspaper, *The Watchman,* gave a very accurate summary of the sex-labelled characteristics defining the operator work as a female job:

> In the first place the clear feminine quality of voice suits best the delicate instrument. Then girls are usually more alert than boys, and always more patient. Women are more sensitive, *more amendable to discipline,* far gentler and more forebearing then men.... Boys and men are less patient. They have always an element of fight in them. When spoken to roughly and rudely they are not going to give the soft answer. Not they. And every man is a crank when he gets on a phone. The personal equation stands for naught. He is looking into the blank wooden receiver and it doesn't inspire him with respectful politeness.[68]

Apparently, then, woman's upbringing in Victorian society gave her all the necessary qualities to be a perfect operator. She was said to be "gifted" with "courtesy," "patience," "skillful hands." In addition, she possessed a "good voice" and a "quick ear," and was "alert," "active," "even-tempered," "adaptable," and "amendable."[69] As such, the female operator was considered "the heart of the place,"[70] "the most valuable asset that a telephone company possesses," "the stock in trade" of that company.[71] One of her major assets was her "voice." The "feminine" voice was considered "limitless" in terms of possibilities in the operation of the telephone.[72] The perfect operator had a "gentle voice; musical as the woodsy voices of a summer day," "sweetly distinct to the subscribers ... yet ... carefully articulated."[73] This voice was supposed to play "a big part in moulding the temper of the time. Irascible, petulant, hurried, the subscriber cannot help but feel the influence of that something which appeals to him as quiet, dignified, soothing, until his temper melts away as the mountain snows before the compelling chinook of the south west."[74] The operator's voice was transforming the technical work into a "labour of love."

Thus, the female operator was a great asset to the telephone business. Telephone companies's managers did not hesitate to say that she was instrumental in the growth of the telephone industry. As L.I. McMahon, a Bell Telephone Company's official, pointed out: "If ever the rush of girls into the business world was a blessing it was when they took possession of the telephone exchanges."[75] Yet, she was very poorly paid, and her working conditions were difficult, in spite of the improvement of her physical environment by Bell Telephone Company, with the addition of rest rooms, comfortable cafeterias, modern bathrooms, etc.[76] For that reason, this soothing effect that the operators exerted on the subscribers (who were still mostly male) and which was considered a "feminine" quality, was not to be found in all of them. Indeed, with the technical improvement of the telephone system, the task of operating was becoming increasingly exacting and the subscribers more and more demanding, so that only "girls with steady nerves and a phlegmatic constitution" could stand the constant pressure. Moreover, a hierarchy had been created within the operating labour force. In 1884, a female chief-operator had been appointed in Montreal, creating the first rank in a hierarchy that was to grow over the years, with the addition of female supervisors and assistant chief-operators. In fact, all these appointments were given to women, although men were still working as night operators.[77] These women's task was to exercise a tight control over the regular operators. The discipline imposed on the operators for the subscribers' satisfaction and the company's development was "unfriendly to relaxation." "You can't make an operator out of a nervous girl. That has been tried ... she produces a species of emotion which borders on hysteria," said McFarlane.[78] Hence, since the work was so demanding and nerve racking, the operators occasionally would lose their tempers and surprise the subscribers who were used to more consideration, especially from women. An operator describes some ways of dealing with "arrogant" subscribers: "There are plenty of ways one finds to avenge one's self upon the telephone bogs. You can give them the click of the 'busy back,' you can ring the bell in their ears, or you can simply let them wait and rattle their hooks."[79]

In general, however, the operator's job was seen as a "respectable" occupation for women. Mary Rosetta Warren, an operator in Montreal from 1880 to 1891, clearly summarizes the "spirit" of the operators of that period: "I doubt whether the modern operator ever felt the *thrill and glamour* that we did in being part of the early telephone development ... It was a daily occurrence to be asked by a subscriber to say a few words to a gentleman who had never used a telephone before—*which made me feel very important.*"[80] In short, the company's decision to sex-label telephone operating as a female position did not, as generally suggested in the literature on feminization, decrease its economic and social status but, rather, increased the qualitative requirements of the job, and made it possible for the company to obtain better educated and better qualified applicants. The feminization of the operating work transformed a job which was considered at the outset as a part-time occupation of male operators into a "labour of love" for female operators. Although the female operators doing such work were considered to be finding their reward more in the "love" they received from the subscribers than in the wages they were given by the company, it gave women opportunities to be upwardly mobile, within the operator force. In fact, while the true operator was invaluable to the company, the occupation offered by the telephone industry constituted one of the few opportunities of "decent" job for young women despite low wages attached to it.

IV

It is impossible to find a pay-roll book for the first period of expansion of the telephone business, as wages were based on arbitrary criteria such as age, discipline, quality of voice, etc., which manager McFarlane called the operator's "ability and experience."[81] However, operators' life stories give a fair account of the wages they earned when working for Bell Telephone Company. For example, during the 1880s, an operator earned $8.00 per month for 12 hours—and sometimes 16 hours—of work per day.[82] Overtime was not paid and, often, operators worked two or three years without an increase. In addition, night operators, who were men, were better paid than day operators. Frank A. Field, for instance, who was a night operator in 1889 was paid $25 per month.[83] L.I. McMahon stated that "girls came in not because they were cheaper, but because they were better."[84] In a way, he was right. A male day operator was paid $8 per month in 1879, the same as a female operator in 1880. The difference, however, lay in the fact that the occupation of operator represented, for men, a job "secondary to their own business"[85] while, for women, it constituted a full-time job. It seems that operators' wages varied according to other obscure criteria as well. For example, in 1880, Lillian W. Camp earned $12 per month (soon raised to $17.50) in Montreal while eleven years later, in the same city, Florence Hendry earned $12 per month.[86] Moreover, Margaret E. Helsby, who was also working in the Montreal Exchange, earned $20 per month in 1889, while Ethel V. Hannaford earned $12 per month in 1908 in Hamilton, both working nine hours per day.[87] These few examples show the arbitrariness of the operators' wages during the period studied. The common denominator, however, was that most of them were paid very little. Indeed, in a sample of seven operators working during the period from 1880 to 1902, five earned $12 or less per month[88,] which certainly did not constitute living wages. As an operator pointed out: "We were just unsophisticated school girls who lived at home with our parents—but where else could we live on ten dollars a month?"[89] Even L.B. McFarlane said, in 1905, during hearings of the Select Committee on the Telephone, that operators' wages "were probably insufficient to get along with respectability."[90] Yet, the job was considered "steady work ... which [gave] one a sense of security in case of illness ... and [provided] pension plans."[91] Besides, other female jobs were not much better paid. For instance, in 1901, in the clothing industry, female factory workers earned about $16 per month while female workers in the book binding and publishing industry earned between $15 and $18 per month.[92] On the other hand, a 1879 *Montreal Daily Witness* reported that "the girls who can use the new typewriter machine ... are earning from $10.00 to $36.00 a week."[93] As for teachers, their wages varied greatly according to their classification and the place where they were teaching. In 1870, a third class female teacher earned between $13 and $20 per month while a first class teacher could earn as much as $34 per month.[94] Finally, in 1889, women caretakers in school institutions earned around $30 per month.[95] Perhaps women did not en-gage in the operator occupation for the pay alone which compared unfavourably with other jobs, but rather for the job status. The direct contact with the sub-scribers and the role of community agent rendered their job "glamorous" in comparison with teaching in obscure places or cleaning a building. Moreover, be-cause of the "spirit of family" developed by Bell Telephone Company's patriarchal attitude, operators stated that they were "proud" to work for the telephone in-dustry "which has contributed so much to the needs and comfort and convenience of civilization."[96] The telephone company seemed to be, for the young women, "a new door ... toward the economic independence for which they were striving,"[97] and a way to obtain some social recognition as useful members of the society. This seems to support Prentice's claim that women accepted poorly paid job outside the household in order to be provided with "respectable independence,"[98] even if the wages would not support them independently.

V

The feminization of the occupation of operator in the telephone industry brought new opportunities to women on the labour market. However, although this gave Bell Telephone Company the appearance of being a progressive employer, it is clear that the company started the process of feminization of its operating labour force as a response to an acute problem of production which it had en-countered with its male operators. After a few years of craftwork development, the telephone business started to expand more systematically, especially after the Bell Telephone Company was chartered in 1880. It is not a coincidence that the feminization of the operator's occupation started with the incorpora-tion of Bell Company. The high quality work produced by women contributed to the expansion of the telephone industry. Finally, the feminization of the job of operator constituted, for the telephone industry, more efficient ex-ploitation of its employees as it was paying equal wages for higher and better quality production by female operators. The process of feminization of the op-erator's occupation supports some of the assumptions suggested in the different perspectives attempting to explain the process of feminization of the labour force. The telephone industry manipulated the job requirements and applied stereotyped female qualities to the job of operator. Moreover, due to the tech-nical segmentation of the labour process, the job was a low-skill occupation requiring low level of stability which corresponded to the sex-labelling assig-nation of low stability given to women. As it was, the level of turnover at the switchboard was very high as most operators left after one or two years ei-ther to marry, or because of physical or nervous breakdown due to the constant pressure exercised on them. Finally, women were forced, in some ways, to take that low-paid job, as the female reserve army of labour was large and the jobs open to women were few.

The operator occupation, however, did not represent a sub-market job involving a low social status. The job was a very important part of the production process of the telephone industry, and acquired a higher social status after being labelled as a "female" occupation, although its wages did not improve. This higher status was partly due to the fact that barriers of "respectability" were placed before prospective employers, and because certain behavioural demands were imposed on actual employees. Moreover, when the process of feminization began, the job was not entirely defined as a female occupation. Some of its characteristics (for example, repairing electrical breakdown) were "male," and women had to adapt their socially recognized skills to these job demands. Thus, although the case of the telephone operators supports several conceptions of the reviewed researches on feminization, there exist some differences at the level of its location in the structure of the organization, as well as in term of social status and social mobility.

Notes

I would like to thank Bruce Curtis and anonymous readers for their helpful comments on a first draft of this article. This study would not have been possible without the generous access to the archives of Bell Canada and the Archdiocese of Montreal which I was allowed. Of course, all errors are my own responsibility.

1. Early operators' file, Bell Company's Historical Collection (hereafter called BCHC).

2. This decision is based on the fact that most data are from Bell Telephone Co. However, some data from other telephone companies in the United States and Canada show that competitive businesses were using more or less identical hiring policies. Hence, examples from other companies will also be employed when relevant.

3. See, for example, Alison Prentice, "The Feminization of Teaching in British North America and Canada, 1845–1875," *Social History,* 3(1975), 5–20; and M. Danylewycz and A. Prentice, "Teachers' Work," *Labour/Le Travail,* 17 (1986), 58–80; M. Grumet, "Pedagogy for Patriarchy: The Feminization of Teaching," *Interchange,* 12 (1981), 165–84.

4. See G.B. Lowe, "Women, Work and the Office: The Feminization of Clerical Occupations in Canada, 1901–1931," *Canadian Journal of Sociology,* 5 (1980), 361–81; "Class, Job and Gender in the Canadian Office," *Labour/Le Travail* 10 (1982), 11–37.

5. See B. Curtis, "Capital, the State, and the Origins of the Working-Class Household" and L. Briskin, "Domestic Labour: A Methodological Discussion," in B. Fox, ed., *Hidden in the Household* (Toronto 1980), 101–34, 135–72.

6. Prentice, "Feminization," 6–7.

7. *Ibid.,* 19.

8. *Ibid.,* 16–7.

9. M. Danylewycz, *et al.,* "The Evolution of the Sexual Division of Labour in Teaching: A Nineteenth Century Ontario and Quebec Case Study," *Social History,* 16 (1983), 81–109.

10. Lowe, "Women, Work, and the Office."

11. *Ibid.,* 367.

12. H. Braverman, *Labor and Monopoly Capitalism* (New York 1974), 385.

13. Lowe, "Women, Work, and the Office," 368.

14. *Ibid.,* 369–70.

15. *Ibid.,* 371.

16. *Ibid.,* 375–6.

17. B. Curtis, "Capital," 131. Note that B. Fox shows that women are not simply a labour reserve as Curtis implies, but continually occupy certain sectors of the paid labour force. See Fox, *Hidden in the Household.* On the debate on domestic labour, see also M. Barrett and R. Hamilton, eds., *Politics of Diversity* (London 1986). B. Taylor's *Eve and the New Jerusalem,* (New York 1983) outlines changing domestic politics in nineteenth-century England.

18. *Ibid.,* 121.

19. *Ibid.,* 113–4, emphasis added.

20. L. Briskin, "Domestic Labour," 137, emphasis added.

21. M. Luxton, *More than a Labour of Love* (Toronto 1980).

22. Women's subordination resulting from economic structures caused them to accept occupations characterized by low-wages, low-status jobs, and requiring such characteristics as obedience and submissiveness.

23. Although a few occupations needing some technical skill, for example bookbinders, were given to women, it is a fact that these jobs were mainly attributed to men.

24. Here the phenomenon may be compared to that examined by R. Edwards in *Contested Terrain* (London 1979). In "bureaucratic control," Edwards points out, a hierarchy is created within each occupation, giving the illusion of advancement in the general hierarchy of the enterprise. However, although it is relatively easy to climb the hierarchical scale within a specific occupation, it is very difficult to have access to other "job families" rated at a higher level of the general hierarchy of the enterprise. For the operators, for instance, it was near to impossible to become local managers, except in very small rural exchanges and, then, they were paid as supervisors.

25. I analyze the role of communication in the process of accumulation in "Communication as Circulation: A Political Economic Analysis," paper presented at the meeting of the International Association of Communication Studies, Montreal, 25 May 1987. See also my "Communication and Social Forms: A Historical Study of the Development of the Telephone, 1876–1920," unpublished Ph.D. thesis, University of Toronto, 1987.

26. " 'Bread Toaster' to Common Battery: Mostly about Boy Telephone Operators and Operating Conditions in the Nineteenth-Century," unpublished manuscript, 1943, Operators-Boy file, BCHC.

27. The job of operator was labelled "female only" long before it actually became an entirely female job. Indeed, it had been recognized as a woman's occupation while there are still male operators working on the night shifts. This will be discussed later.

28. " 'Bread Toaster' to Common Battery," Operators-Boy file, BCHC.

29. *Mandements, lettres pastorales, circulaires, et autres documents,* 9 (1882), 439, Diocese of Montreal Historical Collection (hereafter DMHC).

30. The periodical gave advice on how to economize, low budget recipes, etc.

31. "The Family," *Le Monde Illustré,* 1884. This is not to say that all working-class women followed this advice.

32. *Mandements, Lettres Pastorales, Circulaires et autres Documents,* 13 (1901), 453, DMHC.

33. *Ibid.,* 9 (1887), 66.

34. *Ibid.,* 14 (1909), 577.

35. Joan Sangster, "The 1907 Bell Telephone Strike: Organizing workers," *Labour / Le Travail* 3 (Fall 1978), 122–3, 126–7. Although Sangster's study is concerned with a period not covered by this paper, it is safe to state that these social prejudices expressed in 1907 must have been even stronger earlier.

36. This was also true for other occupations. See Danylewycz, "Evolution," 101.

37. K.M. Schmith, "I Was Your Old 'Hello Girl'," *The Saturday Post,* 12 July 1930.

38. F.B. Jewett, "The Social Implication of Scientific Research in Electrical Communication," *Bell Telephone Quarterly,* 14 (1936), 205–18. Emphasis added.

39. " 'Bread Toasters' to Common Battery," 2, 3, 4, BCHC. In contrast to female operators, the prospect of advancement for male operators was not limited to that occupation. It involved other job families such as technicians and, even, managers.

40. Shortly after Bell Telephone Co. started to hire women as operators, other independent telephone companies followed their example.

41. K.M. Schmitt, "I was." These "unsuitable" characteristics, however, might have been intensified by the poor wages given to the operators. According to C.F. Sise, males would apply as operators only "as spare-time job as the income was too low." (C.F. Sise's Letter, 21 February 1887, BCHC). Since males had other possibilities of income—even within the telephone industry—they were not particularly attracted by the operator's work.

42. Letter from L.B. McFarlane to C.E. Cutz, 7 July 1887, document #27144–44, BCHC. This worker was probably a night operator as the day operators were already women, especially in big cities.

43. Other occupations involved one or the other of these two characteristics. However, the case of the operators was unique in that the job become a female occupation *uniting* those two aspects.

44. "Telephone History—Montreal," no date, BCHC.

45. H.S. Coyle, "The Operating Forces of Modern Telephone Exchange," Telephony, 2 (1901), 218.

46. K.J. Dunstan, "Office Management," no date, BCHC.

47. Report of Meeting of C.F. Sise with Local-managers, 16–17 May 1887, document #26606, BCHC, 9.

48. Questionnaire from C.F. Sise to Local-managers, 16 May 1887, document #27344, BCHC, 3, emphasis added.

49. K.J. Dunstan's Life Story, BCHC. Mrs. Dunstan and Baker were local-managers respectively in Toronto and Hamilton, and Mr. Sise was general manager of Bell Telephone Co.

50. K.J. Dunstan's payroll, October 1880, document #2405b, BCHC.

51. I use the word "girl" despite its sexist connotation, because it was the way the female operators were referred to by most people, including themselves.

52. Telephone Directory, Halifax, N.S., March 1886, BCHC.

53. K.M. Schmitt, 1930, *op. cit.*

54. "60 Years at the Switchboard," *Michigan Bell Magazine,* October 1940, BCHC. At that period, women could also be hired to work on typewriter machines, taking the place of male copyists and shorthand writers. See "New Industry," *Montreal Daily Witness,* 4 January 1879.

55. K.M. Schmitt, "I was."

56. Later, Bell Telephone Co. required five letters of recommendation. In addition to the three formers, one letter was required from a physician and one from a property owner.

57. "60 Years at the Switchboard."

58. Quotations and Anecdotes file, BCHC.

59. "Across the Wires," *The Daily Witness,* 21 March, no date, in *McFarlane's Scrapbook,* document #12016, BCHC. Although there is no date on the article, the clipping was glued in McFarlane's scrapbook among other newspaper clippings dated of the end of the 1890s.

60. Actually, several of these young men later became technicians, linemen, and, even, managers for Bell Telephone Co.

61. K.M. Schmitt, "I was."

62. Document #27344, BCHC, 7.

63. Since women were considered useless and inefficient in technical and mechanical work, some companies' managers had serious reservations. (Document 27344, BCHC, 5) These, however, faded when confronted with some female operators, especially in small towns, who had effected—with the aid of the instructions in the small book— all the work necessary to maintain the telephone exchange in working condition.

64. K.M. Schmitt, "I was."

65. "Use of Women Operators at Night," *Quebec City Letters,* 1888, BCHC.

66. K.M. Schmitt, "I was."

67. B. Lalonde's Life Story, 1906, BCHC. Emphasis added.

68. "Who Wouldn't Be a Telephone Girl?" *Watchman,* 12 June 1898.

69. *Ibid.*

70. "Héros inconnus et méconnus: la téléphoniste," *La Patrie,* 14 July 1908.

71. "Treatment of Telephone Operators," *Telephony,* 8 (August 1904), 124–5.

72. "Voice Culture," *Mail,* 2 August 1916.

73. "A Study of the Telephone Girl," *Telephony,* 9 (1905), 388–90.

74. *Ibid.*

75. "Girls Were Never Greater Blessing than When They Entered Phone Exchanges," *News,* 4 November 1916.

76. Here I do not completely agree with Sangster who stated that the 1907 strike of the operators in Toronto was the significant event which brought more comfortable surroundings to the operators. (Sangster, "1907.") Indeed, already in 1896, the biggest exchanges were provided with an "early form of air conditioning, recreational and lunch rooms, steel locker for each worker, drying room (even for clothing), bathrooms where last fashion baths were available for operators if necessary." (H.G. Owen, *One Hundred Years,* Bell Canada Publication, 1980, BCHC, 12.) A telephone company's manager stressed that these improvements in the physical environment were not primarily for the operator's well-being, but "I suppose the plan has its humanitarian side, but it is also a good business investment. Give your employees a pleasant and comfortable place in which to work, treat them with consideration and the results will more than repay for the trouble." ("Treatment of Telephone Operators.") This shows that many years before the Toronto strike, telephone companies had already understood some psychological principles at the basis of the employees' productivity.

77. However, there were no opportunities for women to get a promotion outside the operating labour force. They could not, for instance, be appointed as local-managers, the most lucrative position. Actually, the promotion of women as chief-operators and supervisors was due to patriarchal attitudes, since the managers felt that women would be more protective towards the young operators, like good mothers!

78. "Across the Wires."

79. "The Diary of a Telephone Girl," *The Saturday Evening Post,* 19 October 1907.

80. M.R. Warren's Life Story, 1880–1891. Emphasis added. The story was told in 1937, which sheds more light on what she meant by "modern operator."

81. "Across the Wires."

82. Mary Ann Burnett's Life Story, 1887, BCHC.

83. F.A. Field's Life Story, 1889, BCHC.

84. "Girls Were Never Greater Blessing...."

85. Document #27344, 3.

86. L.W. Camp's Life Story, 1880–95; F. Hendry's Life Story, 1891–1931, BCHC.

87. M.E. Helsby's Life Story, 1888–96; E.V. Hannaford's Life Story, 1908–17, BCHC.

88. Life Stories of M. Hill, 1900; F. Hendry, 1891–1931; M.E. Helsby, 1888–96; M.A. Burnett, 1887–1916; M.I. Phillips, 1889–93; W. Chevalier, 1896.

89. K.M. Schmitt, "I was."

90. "Telephone Inquiry on Wages and Living Expenses," *Montreal Gazette,* 11 February 1906. Another inquiry occurred, started by the 1907 Bell Telephone strike. However, it does not contain relevant data related to the subject of this article, as its target was limited to the Toronto operators working in 1907.

91. C.M. Cline's Life Story, 1907, BCHC.

92. *Census of Canada,* III (Ottawa 1901).

93. "A New Industry," *Montreal Daily Witness,* 4 January 1879.

94. Prentice, "Feminization," 14.

95. Danylewycz and Prentice, "Teachers' Work," 75.

96. Olive Geach's Life Story, 1918–20, BCHC.

97. "60 Years at the Switchboard," 1940.

98. Prentice, "Feminization," 17.

CHAPTER

6 RADICALISM AND THE CANADIAN WORKING CLASS, 1900–1919

In the course of the 1980s, the study of the history of Canadian workers came to be dominated by a generation of self-styled "New Left" historians such as Greg Kealey and Brian Palmer, to name only the two most prominent. Ideologically committed and intellectually indebted to the revisionist Marxist analyses of men such as E.P. Thompson of Great Britain and the American Herbert Gutman, this school set out in the early 1970s to cast what until then had been known in Canada as "labour history" in a new mould, "working class history."

For New Left historians, the concept of working-class history was an urgently needed new departure in Canadian historiography, for in their view the old labour history left much to be desired. The traditional, pre- and immediate post-World War II institutional studies by trail-blazers such as Harold A. Logan, which focussed on formal trade union organizational structures, were considered too elitist and too consensus-oriented. The latter criticism was levelled as well against the more modern "social democratic scholars" of the 1950s to the 1970s such as Eugene Forsey, Stuart Jamieson and Ken McNaught. The "Old Left" tradition in Canada, as represented by Charles Lipton, was also deemed unsatisfactory. It was not so much rejected by the New Left as dismissed as feeble and unsophisticated in its application of Marxist principles to the study of the Canadian working class.

The main wrath of the New Left, however, was reserved for another group of Canadian historians, the product of the expanding university world of the 1960s, which eschewed Marxist theory for a supposedly non-ideological, realist approach to the study of working-class history. The leading spokesman for this group, which came to the fore in the 1970s, was David Bercuson, but it also included individuals such as Irving Abella and Ross McCormack. For New Leftists, the deliberate rejection of Marxist theory meant this group could never come to a genuine understanding of the history of Canadian workers.

In particular, New Left historians stressed that the study of working class history must explain the development in Canada of what it called a "working class culture." The imperatives of the capitalist system, they argued, had elicited a common response from workers across the country, both in the workplace and in their everyday lives, and thereby produced a distinct and identifiable class culture. The Bercuson approach disputed the very existence of such a culture, arguing that the history of Canadian workers was marked more by factors which divided them—region, ethnicity, gender—than by those which united them.

The essence of the debate between these two poles of interpretation is to be found in the two articles presented here with respect to the development of radicalism within the Canadian labour movement in the first two decades of the twentieth century, culminating in the year of labour revolt, 1919. David Bercuson's "Labour Radicalism and the Western Industrial Frontier, 1897–1919" presents the view that western Canadian workers were more radical than their eastern Canadian and Maritime counterparts, a fact attributable in large part to their immigrant origins. In "1919: The Canadian Labour Revolt," on the other hand, Greg Kealey rejects the west/east distinction, arguing that by 1919 labour revolt was endemic across Canada and not limited by regional or other boundaries. Students should also carefully assess the implications for the Bercuson/Kealey debate of recent feminist articles such as Mary Horodyski's "Women and the Winnipeg General Strike of 1919."

Suggestions for Further Reading

Abella, Irving, *Nationalism, Communism and Canadian Labour: The CIO, the Communist Party and the Canadian Congress of Labour, 1935–1956*. Toronto: University of Toronto Press, 1973.

Bercuson, David. J., "Through the Looking Glass of Culture: An Essay on the New Labour History and Working-Class Culture in Recent Canadian Historical Writing," *Labour/Le Travail*, VII (Spring, 1981), 95–112.

Bradbury, Bettina, "Women's History and Working-Class History," *Labour/Le Travail*, XIX (Spring, 1987), 23–43.

Conley, J.R., "Frontier Labourers, Crafts in Crisis and the Western Labour Revolt," *Labour/Le Travail*, 23 (Spring 1989), 9–37.

Forsey, Eugene, *The Canadian Labour Movement, 1812–1902*. Ottawa: The Canadian Historical Association, 1974.

Horodyski, Mary, "Women and the Winnipeg General Strike of 1919," *Manitoba History* (Spring, 1986), 28–37.

Jamieson, S., *Times of Trouble: Labour Unrest and Industrial Conflict in Canada, 1900–1966*. Ottawa: Privy Council Office, 1971.

Kealey, Greg, "Labour and Working-Class History in Canada: Prospects in the 1980s," *Labour / Le Travail*, VII (Spring, 1981), 67–94.

Lipton, Charles, *The Trade Union Movement in Canada*. (3rd ed.), Toronto: NC Press, 1967.

Logan, Harold, *Trade Unions in Canada*. Toronto: Macmillan, 1948.

McCormack, A.R., *Reformers, Rebels, and Revolutionaries: The Western Canadian Radical Movement, 1899–1919*. Toronto: University of Toronto Press, 1977.

McInnis, Peter, "All Solid Along the Line: The Reid Newfoundland Strike of 1918," *Labour / Le Travail*, XXVI (Fall, 1990), 61–84.

McNaught, Kenneth, *A Prophet in Politics*. Toronto: University of Toronto Press, 1959.

Naylor, J., "Toronto 1919," Canadian Historical Association, *Historical Papers*, 1986, 33–55.

Palmer, B., *A Culture in Conflict: Skilled Workers and Industrial Capitalism in Hamilton, Ontario, 1860–1914*. Montreal: McGill-Queen's University Press, 1979.

Reilly, N., "The General Strike in Amherst, Nova Scotia, 1919," *Acadiensis*, IX, (1980), 56–77.

LABOUR RADICALISM AND THE WESTERN INDUSTRIAL FRONTIER, 1897–1919

David Bercuson

The rapid growth of the Canadian west from the mid-1890s to the start of World War I was based upon the arrival and settlement of millions of immigrants. [Throughout this essay the term is applied generally to all those who migrated to the frontier including central and eastern Canadians.] The agricultural frontier attracted prospective farmers from every corner of the globe and their settlement saga has held the attention of a generation of Canadians. The frontier has been called a great leveller which broke down class distinctions because men were equal, free and far from the traditional bonds and constraints of civilization.[1] On the frontier every 'Jack' was as good as his master. But the settlement of the agricultural frontier was only part of the total picture of western development. An urban-industrial and a hinterland-extractive frontier was being opened at the same time which underwent spectacular productive expansion and attracted many thousands of pioneer workers. Most of these men had gone to the frontier pushed by the same ambitions and seeking the same opportunities as other immigrants. But once in western Canada most entered into closed and polarized communities

From *The Canadian Historical Review*, LVIII, no. 2 (June 1977), 154–175. Reprinted by permission of the University of Toronto Press.

and were forced to work in dangerous or unrewarding occupations. For these men there was little upward mobility, little opportunity for improvement. They were not free and were not as good as their masters.

The pioneer workers had come a long way to improve themselves. Most lost the inhibitions and inertia which usually characterized those who stayed behind. They were ready to work hard and live frugally, to sacrifice, to do what was necessary to win the rewards they had come to seek.[2] But their way was usually blocked, their efforts thwarted not because of their failures but by a system. They usually faced a big difference between what they had sought and what could be achieved. Some immigrants came from such poverty and desperation that anything was an improvement and they were satisfied. But most eventually decided to break out of the closed systems which bound them or, if they could not break out, to smash them. The system thus lost its claim to their hearts and minds and labour radicalism emerged.

Were western workers really more radical than those in central Canada and the maritime provinces? The answer depends upon the definition of radicalism because major, prolonged, and violent strikes, as well as political insurgency, can be found in all regions of Canada during this period.[3] The dictionary is precise: Radicalism is 'the quality or state of being radical' while radical is 'favoring fundamental or extreme change: specifically, favoring such change of the social structure; very leftist.' Militancy is 'the state or quality of being militant' while militant is 'ready and willing to fight; warlike; combative.'[4] These definitions allow the conclusion that up to 1919 western workers were more radical than those of other regions though they were, perhaps, no more militant. Their radicalism emerged in several ways, which involved efforts to effect radical change. For example, the Socialist Party of Canada, which called for the elimination of capitalism and its replacement by the dictatorship of the proletariat, had its headquarters in Vancouver, the bulk of its membership in the west, and, after 1914, the official endorsation of District 18 of the United Mine Workers of America. Major Socialist party supporters could be found in the leading ranks of western unions—George Armstrong, Robert B. Russell, Richard Johns in Winnipeg, Joseph Sanbrooke in Regina, Joseph Knight and Carl Berg in Edmonton, William Pritchard, Jack Kavanagh, Victor Midgley, A.S. Wells in Vancouver. Support for other left-wing socialist parties, such as the Social Democratic party, was also centred primarily in western Canada. Though union members in other parts of the country engaged in independent political action, only in the west was their politics so definitely and unmistakable Marxian. Radical industrial unionism and syndicalism also flourished in the west. The Industrial Workers of the World [IWW], the United Brotherhood of Railway Employees, the American Labour Union, and the One Big Union all attained varying degrees of success in western Canada but almost none in Ontario, Quebec, or the maritimes. The west's attraction to these forms of unionism was also reflected in its experiments with general strikes.[5]

Western radicalism reached the peak of its influence in 1919. Conventions of the British Columbia Federation of Labor, the Alberta Federation of Labor, and District 18 of the United Mine Workers passed resolutions advocating worker control of industry, the formation of syndicalist-oriented unions, and general strikes to achieve political change. The workers pointedly expressed sympathy and support for Russian and German revolutionaries.[6] These three gatherings were prelude to the now famous Western Labor Conference held in March 1919 at Calgary and to the emergence of the One Big Union.[7] In each case large and representative bodies of western workers declared that their unions must be instruments for social change. This was the essence of western labour radicalism.

There were, to be sure, radicals in central Canada and the maritimes. The coal miners of Cape Breton were susceptible to radical ideas, particularly after 1917 when the Provincial Workmen's Association [PWA] was disbanded. In 1919 there was some experimentation with general strikes on a limited scale and some scattered sympathy for the One Big Union idea.[8] But, for the most part, Nova Scotia miners responded to the exigencies of militancy, not political radicalism. Syndicalism, with its rejection of electoral politics, went against the grain of a group of workers 'content to remain within the rules.'[9] When the Nova Scotia Independent Labour party was formed in 1919, it advocated traditional progressive reform such as the initiative, referendum, recall, and proportional representation.[10] J.B. McLachlan, a radical Scottish miner who led the drive to destroy the PWA in the coal fields, tried to lead District 26 of the United Mine Workers into the Red International of Labor Unions in the early twenties.[11] He was personally popular but stood outside the mainstream and his views alienated others and eventually undermined his own support.[12] There was a tradition of independent political activism amongst island miners but it tended towards labour-oriented reform, not socialist or marxist radicalism. Outside the coal fields even this tradition was almost non-existent.

In a 1966 article, and later in his history of the IWW, Melvyn Dubofsky sought to explain labour radicalism in the American west particularly amongst miners. He asserted that rapid industrialization, the introduction of technological innovations, ethnic homogeneity of the workforce, and other factors created class polarization in the mining industry. Polarization led to class war which, in turn, led to the development of class ideology. Dubofsky did not agree with the idea that western American radicalism was 'the response of pioneer individualists to frontier conditions.'[13]

The validity of this argument is something which American labour historians are more competent to judge but its applicability to Canada should be seriously questioned. There was certainly rapid industrialization in the Canadian west but there was no technological revolution in mining because most coal and hardrock mining began *after* the major technological changes in the western United States had occurred. Americans were mining for metals on a large scale in the 1870s and when Canadian hardrock mining did begin in the 1890s it was initially financed and directed largely by Americans who generally applied what they had already learned.[14] Most western Canadian coal mines were too small to benefit from the major advances of the day and mechanization was not widespread prior to 1919. The ethnic homogeneity pointed to by Dubofsky did not exist in western Canada. In the Kootenay region, for example, 34 per cent of the male population in 1911 were Canadian, 24 per cent British, 25 per cent European, 10 per cent American, and 4 per cent Asian.[15] In Vancouver 28 per cent were Canadian, 33 per cent British, 9 per cent European, 7 per cent Asian, and 9 per cent American. If Dubofsky's ideas are to be applied to the Canadian west, they will have to be significantly altered because the opening of the western Canadian mining frontier and the settlement, growth, and industrialization of western Canadian cities occurred at least two decades later than in the United States.

Paul Phillips has put forward arguments rooted in Canadian experience. He asserted that the character of western labour developed in response to the nature of the resource-based economy.[16] The National Policy of tariff protection to manufacturers raised the costs of primary production, encouraged investment in commerce and transportation but provided 'little or no scope for industrial expansion in the west ...' Employers developed 'a short-term rather than a long-term view toward labour issues' and were not greatly interested in 'developing a permanent and peaceful relation with the labour force.' Phillips believed these factors, combined with regional isolation, created 'greater insecurity of employment and wages ...' primarily because 'frontier employers ... wanted to shift as much of the entrepreneurial risk onto the employees as possible.' In this way the resource-based economic structure of the region created 'a very much more militant and class-conscious type of union.'

If Phillips' thesis is to hold it must apply to the miners because they were clearly the vanguard of radicalism. The National Policy may have forced an inordinate concentration on resource extraction in the west and pressured employers into 'short-term' attitudes but resource extraction was also significant in Nova Scotia which, in this period, produced more coal than Alberta and British Columbia combined.[17] The mine workforce in Nova Scotia in 1910 was slightly more than 17,000 out of a total labour force of just over 173,000. This was a far larger proportion of the workforce than in either Alberta or British Columbia or even the two together.[18] The miners of Nova Scotia should have been under the same constraints and difficulties as those of the west because if the National Policy put difficulties in the path of western resource extraction industries, it also created problems for maritime resource extraction industries. Indeed, Nova Scotia coal operators, even the giant Dominion Coal (and British Empire Steel and Coal which succeeded it), could not compete in the lucrative markets of Ontario against Pennsylvania and West Virginia coal because of insufficient tariff protection.[19] If the National Policy was responsible for labour radicalism in western Canada, why not Nova Scotia? Nova Scotia miners were often very militant but prior to 1919 showed little radicalism.

The capital structure of mining in western Canada was actually far from being unsophisticated or 'frontier-like.' Andy den Otter observed that 'although Alberta's coal deposits were vast, mining ventures did not realize quick, high returns but required very careful planning and large scale, long-term financing.' Thus the federal government granted Sir Alexander Tilloch Galt large tracts of land to subsidize his combined railway and coal mining operations in the Coal Banks (Lethbridge) area and enabled him to attract the British investment capital needed for expansion in the 1890s.[20] Investors such as Barings and Glyn and Company, the Grand Trunk Railroad, the Industrial and General Trust, and other like concerns could hardly have held short-term, quick return, expectations. Similarly, railway companies such as the CPR could not have acted the role of 'frontier employers' in their ownership of, or investment in, large mining properties. Canadian Pacific took over F. Augustus Heinze's smelter at Trail (and the railways and land grants that went with them) in 1897.[21] This was the beginning of Consolidated Mining and Smelting (Cominco), which combined Heinze's operation with large Canadian Pacific investments and acquired valuable properties such as the Sullivan mine at Kimberly, British Columbia.[22] Cominco soon became the largest employer of miners and smeltermen in the region and was clearly intended to be a long-term capital venture. The Crows Nest Pass Coal Company, with a capitalization in 1911 of $3.5 million, had an agreement with Canadian Pacific, concluded in 1897, to provide coal for smelting and other purposes.[23] This mining concern earned large profits[24] selling coal and coke to smelters in the west Kootenay and Boundary regions and was typical of many mines in the area.

The mineral economy of the British Columbia interior quickly developed a complex inter-related structure. Coal mines supplied coal and coke to the smelters while hardrock mines supplied ores.[25] As long as the smelters operated profits were made. The smelter concerns may have had to sell their products in an unprotected world market but there were few uncertainties associated with this phenomenon in the period under examination. The mines in the region were prosperous and went through phenomenal growth up to the end of World War I. New smelters were opened, rail lines laid, mines dug, and camps, towns, and cities expanded.[26] The key to the region's success was the low cost of extraction and the high grades of ore. Even world depressions had little impact in the region's hot house economic atmosphere. One observer commented: 'During the past summer [1897] the rapid decline in the value of silver, that proved so disastrous to other silver countries, had little effect on our silver mines, other than to check investment, as the ores were usually of such high grade, as to leave, even at the lowest price, a good margin of profit.'[27] What was true of silver was also true of copper. The size of the deposits and the heavily mechanized nature of the industry, combined with cheap railway charges, kept profits high. Another observer claimed that 'nowhere on the continent can smelting be carried on more cheaply given fair railroad rates and fuel at a reasonable cost.'[28] Both conditions existed and business boomed except for a brief period just after the turn of the century. Some of the mine owners blamed the downturn on restrictive mining legislation and labour agitators (there was a major strike at Rossland that year) but the *British Columbia Mining Record,* leading journal of the industry, attributed the condition to swindling, mismanagement, and over-taxation.[29] Stagnation there was—for a few years—but the factor which most often closed down the smelters and caused a back-up of ore and production cuts in the hardrock mines was strikes in the coal fields supplying fuel to the area.[30]

The collieries of Vancouver Island do not easily fit a general picture of struggling and uncertain resource extractors. The largest operator was the Dunsmuir family who sold out to Canadian Collieries in 1911. The Dunsmuirs enjoyed steady markets in the United States at the turn of the century and were able to sell as much as 75 per cent of their production in San Francisco. This was true for all the collieries on the island.[31] During these years 30 to 40 per cent of the coal consumed in California was mined in British Columbia—the largest amount from any one source.[32] Profits to the Dunsmuirs from coal were enhanced by land grants and subsidies acquired from the British Columbia government to build the Esquimalt and Nanaimo Railway.[33] When the Dunsmuirs sold out to a syndicate headed by Sir William Mackenzie, co-owner of the Canadian Northern Railway, the new company, Canadian Collieries (Dunsmuir) Limited, was capitalized at $15 million.[34] Mackenzie's interest in coal was not confined to Canadian Collieries. He and Sir Donald Mann, his partner in the Canadian Northern, provided half the capital to develop the Nordegg Field in Alberta through Mackenzie, Mann and Company Limited. The other half of the money came from the German Development Company, which was sole owner of the Brazeau Collieries in the same area.[35] These mines, like many that were opened in western Canada, were 'steam' coal operations which sold everything they could produce to the railways. The greatest market problem facing most of these mines prior to World War I was the increased use, particularly in California but also in Canadian coastal areas, of California fuel oil to replace coal.[36] This problem was, however, seriously aggravated by the serious production cuts in the island collieries resulting from the 1913 coal strike.[37] Up to this point island coal production showed a slow but steady increase.[38]

The mining industry may not have been protected by National Policy tariffs but it was frequently given generous subsidies by provincial and federal governments. It also had little trouble attracting capital from Britain and the United States as well as major Canadian companies such as Canadian Pacific. Some of the region's most intransigent employers were the largest. Canadian Collieries and Granby Consolidated Mining and Smelting were probably the most 'hard nosed' operators in western Canada and yet were large, heavily capitalized, and secure. Their attitude to industrial relations may have been short-sighted but could hardly have been prompted by insecurity. They shifted risks to their workers because they, like most employers, wanted to and, unlike some employers, were able to. The National Policy had little to do with it.

The argument could be made that the National Policy was the culprit behind most labour problems in the area because it had produced a resource-based economy in the west and such economies are riddled with labour problems. This is clearly so simplified that it explains nothing. Industry in the west was primarily resource-based because that was where the resources were (and still are). In this period there had been no appreciable industry established in urban areas but the west was still very young and industrial output was expanding at tremendous rates.[39] It is an interesting but fruitless exercise to speculate if, in this period, the economy would have been resource-based anyway or whether the National Policy was already suppressing the growth of secondary industry. The key problem here is whether western manufacturing had yet reached the point where it was large enough to be restricted by the National Policy. So far, there is no answer to the question.

What about the 'domestic' coal operators—those smaller mines producing coal for heating purposes? These mines in the east Kootenays and Alberta had more limited markets.[40] They could not compete with Pennsylvania anthracite in Winnipeg or points east because American coal, though usually slightly higher in price, was better quality.[41] They were also unable to compete in the coastal trade, in Canada or the United States, and had no entry to the northern California market. The prairies, northern Idaho, and eastern Washington were their domain. These operators sold in a less certain market than the steam coal producers or the Vancouver Island collieries and their uncertainty *was* at least partly due to the absence of sufficient tariff protection. However, they were the most reasonable for their employees to deal with and were less reluctant to sign agreements recognizing unions.[42] Perhaps the very uncertainty of their markets prompted them to avoid serious labour troubles, unlike a powerful giant such as Canadian Collieries.

Phillips asserts that western employers tended to take short-run, commercial views of their relations with their workers primarily because they purchased capital goods in a high-priced, protected market and sold their raw materials in unprotected world markets,[43] like the prairie grain farmers. But the parallel was superficial in reality whatever it may be in theory. Perhaps Phillips has explained why there were some uncertainties amongst western resource extraction employers at certain times, but even this tells little. There was no necessary connection between these uncertainties (when they did occur) and the rise of labour radicalism. There is, in fact, no real evidence that mine owners or smelter operators, with large capital investments in their enterprises, acted any differently from industrial capitalists anywhere. Conversely, there is no evidence that manufacturers in central Canada, when faced with the inevitable uncertainties of business, acted any differently from the resource extractors. Unions were fought and demands resisted by most businessmen when the cost of the struggle fell within economically acceptable limits. Unions were tolerated and their demands considered when the cost of resisting was greater than the price of capitulation. When mine owners in the Crowsnest Pass area faced a strong union (organized before the scattered operators had a chance to unite against it) in the reality of a limited labour supply and uncertain markets, they chose to deal with their workers. But the large operators of Vancouver Island, with a ready surplus of Chinese labour, assured markets, and facing a struggling union, dug in their heels.

The men who worked the mines of western Canada were mostly immigrants. This is in sharp contrast to the mine workforce in Canada's other major mining area—Nova Scotia. The 1911 federal census revealed that almost three-quarters of the mine employees in Nova Scotia were Canadian born compared to 12 per cent in Alberta and 16 per cent in British Columbia mine workers.[44] This picture is reflected in the male population of two Nova Scotia coal counties, Cumberland and Inverness. Eighty-one per cent of Cumberland men and 92 per cent of Inverness men were Nova Scotia born. In British Columbia 22 per cent of the men in Nanaimo District and 11 per cent in Kootenay District were native to the province. Conversely, only 19 per cent of Cumberland and 8 per cent of Inverness men were immigrants, while immigrants accounted for 78 per cent of the males of Nanaimo District and 89 per cent in Kootenay District. The western mines and mining communities were almost exactly opposite in composition to the mines and mining communities of the east. In addition, as Donald MacGillivray has pointed out, the strong presence of the Roman Catholic church in Cape Breton, with its belief in an organic, structured society, was important. Conservative religious traditions added to the influence of conservative metropolitan centres such as Halifax and Antigonish. His picture is one of an essentially conservative community with a 'thread of radicalism.'[45]

The pioneer immigrant nature of western mining society is reflected in other statistics. In the two Nova Scotia counties the ratio of men to women was 1.04:1. In Nanaimo District the ratio was 1.7:1 and in Kootenay District 1.9:1 The average age of mine employees in the west was higher than in Nova Scotia. Eighty per cent of British Columbia mine employees were between twenty-five and sixty-four years of age, while 70 per cent of Alberta and 65 per cent of Nova Scotia mine employees were in the same range. Literacy rates were also higher in the western mining regions for Canadian- and British-born miners. A composite emerges: in Nova Scotia young men born in the mining communities, or living in towns or on farms close by, went into the collieries at the earliest opportunity. They had travelled little, were younger, and less educated than western miners. They probably worked for the company their fathers had served before them and had few expectations about improving their immediate environment. In western Canada the miners had come from Ontario or Idaho or Wales or Italy or Austria to make their fortune. Perhaps they simply sought more cash to send back to the village. Troper and Harney have pointed to a crisis in rural village life in late nineteenth-century Europe as a factor causing young men to seek opportunities elsewhere[46] and many were clearly refugees from economic hardship.[47]

The British and Americans who came to the mining communities were usually skilled miners as were some Canadians from Nova Scotia.[48] The vast majority of European miners had been peasants and had no experience in mining. One result was that better paying jobs—miners in the hardrock mining industry, contract miners in the coal fields—usually went to Anglo-Saxons while the lower paying positions—muckers (ore loaders) in hardrock mining and 'day men' in the collieries—were taken up by the Europeans.[49] Contract mining was an especially skilled occupation in the coal fields since a miner had to know the best way to work a seam, shoring and bucking, safety techniques, coal quality, and other factors in order to earn an above standard wage. In hardrock mining the use of machinery such as air drills rendered many old skills unnecessary but certain semi-skilled procedures and techniques were still required for the use of air drills, blasting, and other jobs.

The urban workforce was also mostly immigrant during this period. The composition of western cities contrasted sharply with those of the east and more closely reflected the ethnic and demographic profile of the western mining regions. The 1911 census showed that only slightly more than 12 per cent of Vancouver men and 18 per cent of the women were British Columbians.[50] In Halifax about 88 per cent of the men and 89 per cent of the women were born in Nova Scotia. Hamilton, one of the county's most heavily industrialized cities, contained a larger proportion of immigrants than Halifax—about 41 per cent of the men and 33 per cent of the women (primarily from the British Isles), but most of the population was born in Ontario. Calgary closely matched Vancouver in that 90 per cent of the men and 84 per cent of the women were immigrants, most from Great Britain but with a very large number of Canadians. Here, about 12 per cent of the men and 14 per cent of the women were from the United States and approximately 12 per cent of the men and 8 per cent of the women were from Europe. Though Winnipeg was the oldest, largest, and most industrialized western city its profile closely followed the other western urban areas. Seventy-nine per cent of the men and 73 per cent of the women were immigrants. The British were the largest group—32 per cent of the men, 26 per cent of the women—followed by Canadians and Europeans. The ratio of men to women was also disproportionately high in the two most western cities, reflecting their frontier character: 1.5:1 in Vancouver, 1.6:1 in Calgary. In Winnipeg the ratio was 1.2:1. The ratios were more normal in the east: 1.1:1 in Hamilton, 1:1 in Halifax.

Immigrants responded differently to the industrial frontier. Those who came from deplorable conditions of poverty, powerlessness, and oppression sometimes found the new cities and mining communities of the west considerably better than whatever they had left behind. Most of the Italians in British Columbia were from southern Italy, an area of grinding rural poverty.[51] They probably felt a distinct improvement in their situation simply because of the steady wages. Many never intended to remain in Canada and only stayed as long as necessary to earn cash to bring home. Donald Avery has called them sojourners.[52] They constituted a conservative element: in the radical and tumultuous environment of the Kootenay country, Trail, with a heavy Italian immigrant population, was an island of labour tranquillity.[53] Managers welcomed Italians to the mining communities because of their excellent (or infamous?) reputation as strikebreakers.[54] The Chinese were in much the same position. They too found Canada to be a heaven compared to what they had left. It is impossible to tell whether their strikebreaking activities resulted from exclusion from unions by white workers or vice versa but their conservative temper and exclusiveness mirrored the attitudes of many Italians.

At the other end of the scale were the British, Canadians, and Americans who had been reared in liberal democratic societies, were used to a democratic franchise, and might well have been involved in trade union or radical activities. These workers enjoyed an additional advantage over Europeans since they knew English and were familiar with the methods and mores of the political system. They were usually the most radical in their response to hardships and inequities and always provided the leadership for the socialist and syndicalist movements that vied for the allegiance of western workers. When the Social Democratic party was formed in 1911 a large majority of its membership was European but every one of its public leaders was Anglo-Saxon.[55]

British and American workers brought well-developed traditions of trade unionism and radicalism to western Canada. The British labour movement had been undergoing continuous change, growth, and increased militancy and radicalism since the London dock strike of 1889. Amalgamation and industrial unionism vied with socialism, syndicalism, and anarchism as theories and ideas were adopted, discarded, re-examined and adopted again. Leaders such as Keir Hardie, Tom Mann, James Connolly, and other worker-philosophers kept British labour in ideological turmoil.[56] The British labour movement, from which thousands of western workers had graduated, was in constant search for new directions and more effective means of bringing the organized power of the workers to bear.

Much the same sort of thing was happening in the United States, particularly the western mining states which sent the bulk of the American hardrock miners to the British Columbia interior. These men had no use for the business unionism and conservative moderation of Samuel Gompers and formed radical industrial unions such as the Western Federation of Miners and the United Brotherhood of Railway Employees. They founded the American Labor Union to challenge the AFL and supported socialist and syndicalist causes.[57]

These British and American workers drew on a rich heritage of trade unionism and radicalism developed in industrial and/or urban contexts. When they found themselves closed in by their adopted society, their unions beset upon by courts and governments, their employers using police, spies, dismissals, evictions from company towns, and alliances with governments against most efforts to organize, they responded with all the fury of the militancy and the radicalism they brought with them.

The new societies of the western mining camps were totally polarized as were the economic regions in which mining was carried out. Company towns were a feature of the region because most of the coal and ore deposits were far from normal settlement areas. It was not possible for miners to live in Lethbridge or Victoria and work in the collieries nearby, even when they were close. The company camps grew immediately adjacent to the collieries and the miners were forced to spend most of their lives in these controlled towns. The company town could be a wretched place, with stinking outhouses, no fresh water supply, dilapidated shacks, and cold, damp bunkhouses. There may have been no medical facilities, no schools, bad food, lice-ridden blankets, and frequent attacks of typhoid.[58] Or a company town could have been the epitome of paternalism. Nordegg, in the Coal Branch area of Alberta, was planned as 'a modern and pretty town' with the best equipped hospital west of Edmonton, bathrooms in the larger cottages, a poolroom, a miners club, and several company stores.[59] Martin Nordegg, who laid out the town, decided to paint the miners' cottages in different pastel shades.[60] In the British Columbia interior the Granby Consolidated Mining and Smelting Company offered cottages with electric lights, running water, and sanitary facilities. Their town had a recreation hall, meeting hall, tennis court, reading room, baseball diamond, and moving pictures.[61] All the towns and camps scattered throughout Alberta and British Columbia had one thing in common—they were closed societies, highly polarized, which isolated the workers and made them as dependent on each other above the ground as they were below. In Nordegg, for example, it was not long before company officials and their families occupied the cottages on the heights and refused to mix with the miners.[62] In the Granby camp the velvet glove concealed a company policy of ejecting 'agitators.'[63] On Vancouver Island the Dunsmuirs' favourite tactic for dealing with labour unrest was to eject miners from the company towns.[64] There was never any question about who owned and controlled. The miners faced this reality every time they went to the company store, used company scrip (which was still circulating in Nordegg as late as 1915), or availed themselves of any company facility.

The polarization of the camps was enhanced by the newness of society on the mining frontiers. The only important social institutions were the companies and the unions. That which the company did not provide the union did. The unions built their own halls, which served as the major recreation area for the men—a place where they could bitch and drink away from company ears. The union provided compensation, helped with legal fees in suits brought by accident victims, or provided burial funds. In the BC interior the only hospital for miles was apt to be owned and financed by the union as was the case in Sandon.[65] The unions, whether the Western Federation of Miners or the United Mine Workers, were organized on the basis of a lodge for each colliery, mine, or smelter. The lodge was, therefore, locally organized and supported. The men were the local and the local was the men-identification was complete. When the United Mine

Workers fought wage reductions in Alberta and the Crowsnest Pass in the years 1924–5, the miners who disagreed with this policy did not leave their unions, they withdrew their locals and established 'home locals'[66] which survived to be reunited in a rejuvenated District 18 in the early 1930s.

Mining society was raw. There was no established tradition of servitude or corporate paternalism handed from generation to generation such as existed in many Nova Scotia coal communities. In most company-owned towns and camps the presence of church and other moderating social institutions was weak while the class structure of the community reflected its totally mine-oriented existence. There were miners and their families and the managers. There were no teachers, clerks, merchants, priests, salesmen, artisans, doctors, or other professionals. And if there were they too were company employees. Mining was the only industry and the entire social and economic structure of the region depended upon the labour of the miners or the smeltermen. In southern Alberta mining communities were often located near agricultural districts but this did not lessen the polarity of the camps because the professional miners resented the farmers who came looking for work after the harvest, found employment in the mine, and undercut the earnings of the permanent miners.[67] Some mining towns—Rossland and Sandon in the British Columbia interior, Drumheller in south central Alberta—were open communities not under direct company control. A handful of tailors, drygoods merchants, tobacconists, hoteliers, barmen, and preachers set up shop to service the miners' needs. Well-stocked bars in small frame hotels and enterprising prostitutes provided 'recreation'[68] as did miners' day parades and, in the hardrock country, July Fourth celebrations. Relay races, rock drilling contests, and union band concerts drew large crowds and eager participants. These towns offered more individual freedom—the men could come and go if they were single and debt-free—and more class diversity than closed company camps. But they were always isolated, by miles of open prairie or by the high mountains and thick forests of the rainy Kootenays. And though not owned, they were dominated by the mining companies whose managers formed a close bond with the handful of local independent businessmen. Costs to the miners in these towns were high—for room, board, or recreation[69]—and the everpresent closeness and isolation helped make them pressure-cookers of discontent.

The polarization of these communities was also reflected in the limited opportunities for improvement available to the workers. Day men (paid a flat daily wage) might become contract miners (paid by the amount of coal dug, graded as suitable and weighed at the pit head) but this was as far as they could go. In the hardrock mines a mucker might become a miner, an even less important promotion that that from day man to contract miner in the coal fields.

Working conditions were uniformly poor. Death rates in western coal mines were more than twice those of Nova Scotia (see Table I). The mines were newer than those in Nova Scotia and the men and their managers had less expertise

TABLE 1   Fatalities per Million Tons of Coal Mined over One Decade

	1907	*1908*	*1909*	*1910*	*1911*	*1912*	*1913*	*1914*	*1915*	*1916*	*Avg*
BC	13.96	8.53	23.75	8.92	7.30	9.25	10.5	9.39	26.36	11.26	12.92
ALTA	10.35	5.96	4.14	20.08	4.13	6.09	6.50	54.68	5.24	4.30	12.15
NS	5.61	6.09	5.82	5.05	5.18	4.46	5.95	4.72	5.74	3.99	5.26
US	na	5.97	5.73	5.62	5.35	4.53	4.89	4.78	4.27	3.77	4.99

SOURCES: Nova Scotia, *Annual Report on Mines 1940* (Halifax 1941), 114; ibid. (1944), 186; Alberta, *Annual Report of the Department of Public Works of Alberta 1916* (Edmonton 1917), 110; British Columbia, *Annual Report of the Bureau of Mines 1910* (Victoria 1911), 230; ibid. (1920), 358.

in how to extract the mineral.[70] It was not discovered until after several major disasters, in which hundreds of miners were killed, that the coal of the east Kootenay region was fifteen times more gaseous and therefore much more likely to cause explosions than comparably-graded bituminous in Pennsylvania.[71] In the hardrock mines heat, unstable explosives, faulty machinery, unguarded shafts, flooded sumps, cave-ins, and mining related diseases took a constant toll of lives.[72] Here conditions were about the same as those of the American hardrock mines.

When conditions in mining camps and in the mines themselves were intolerable, there were few places to escape. The skilled miners were tied to their occupations (if not to the company store) and faced lower wages as unskilled workers in cities or as agricultural labour. American hardrock miners could always migrate back across the border, and many appear to have done so, but mines there were just as dangerous and the communities just as polarized as in Canada. Those miners with families had little mobility to begin with. The unskilled single miners did have options, but very restricted ones.

Southern Alberta coal mines were located near agricultural areas and even those not so near were a short train ride away. But agricultural labour, when available, was twenty-four hour a day work at low wages. Farmers gained unsavoury reputations amongst migratory agricultural workers from both sides of the border because of the treatment meted out to their employees. Added to this was competition from small farmers needing additional cash[73] and immigrants who wanted to learn homesteading before filing on a piece of their own land.[74] Every fall thousands of men were brought west by the railways to help bring in the harvest. Even if work was available under decent circumstances it would rarely be steady since farms were still small and extra labour requirements were seasonal. For the single miners of the BC interior or Vancouver Island, however, even this was not an option.

The other escapes were railway construction work and migration to the cities. Railway construction workers—navvies or 'bunkhousemen'—were just above slaves in the general scheme of things. Under the direction of brutish foremen, navvies worked from dawn past dusk clearing rights of way, laying track, hauling rock and gravel. The work was gruelling and the pay negligible. The food was usually bad—though a charge was always deducted for it, the sleeping conditions fit for animals: bunks rigged up in old box cars with almost no heat, proper ventilation, or space to move. Sanitary facilities were nonexistent. The workers on these construction jobs were closely watched to assure that 'agitators' would not get close to them.[75] It was a wise policy. When the IWW managed to get a foothold in the construction camps in the Fraser River canyon in 1912 two long strikes of navvies, one on the Grand Trunk Pacific, the other on the Canadian Northern, gave these wretched men an opportunity to protest their deplorably bad working and living conditions.[76]

The cities offered the greatest chance to escape. Here, at least, there was recreation, companionship, freedom to roam about, and, during this period, usually plentiful work. But if the city offered good opportunities for advancement and the chance to forge a decent life for the skilled worker, it offered barely enough to get by for the unskilled. Urban slums blighted the new cities of the west and in times of depression, when there was no work to be had, primitive and patchwork welfare schemes offered little hope.[77] In truth, western cities were also closed and polarized societies for many thousands of industrial workers.

Every western city had an 'across the tracks.' In Calgary there were tent towns in Hillhurst or near the Centre Street Bridge. In Edmonton frame shacks were thrown up along the Grand Trunk Pacific main line, near the Calder Yards, or east of Mill Creek. In Vancouver tenements scarred the urban landscape along the waterfront to the southeast of Stanley Park. In Winnipeg there were the tenements and broken down hovels of the 'North End' where overcrowding, lack of sanitary facilities, and a near absence of fresh water created one of the highest infant mortality and death rates per thousand persons on the continent.[78] For the unskilled these slums were a dead end.

The skilled fared better. They built modest homes in Calgary's Mount Pleasant or Winnipeg's Ward 4 near the Point Douglas Yards. Many eventually went into business on their own and started printing shops, contracting firms, and other small enterprises. A few became successful in politics. The skilled workers quickly formed themselves into an aristocracy of labour, their exclusive and conservative craft unions presiding over respectable Trades and Labor Councils.

For the unskilled there were no unions since the crafts would not stoop to attempting mass organization. They had no political voice because of restrictive franchises. Many of the Europeans sought out ethnic-based socialist clubs and in Winnipeg Jews and Ukrainians organized vigorous and active left-wing parties[79] but they had no real power. This was a common frustration which affected both the skilled and the unskilled: the cities of western Canada were tightly controlled by commercial élites who ran them like closed corporations.[80] Winnipeg offers the best though certainly not the only example and this was reflected in the restricted franchise, based upon property qualification. In 1906, when Winnipeg contained over 100,000 persons, only 7,784 were listed as municipal voters.[81]

This situation was particularly hard for workers. The city government was reluctant to spend money to improve facilities in the North End. It provided little impetus for the privately owned but municipally chartered street railway system to operate adequate services in working-class areas. It was not receptive to requests for improved health and building bylaws or minimum wage schedules from the local labour movement. The imbalance of electoral power also assured the election to office of men such as Thomas Russell Deacon who, in the midst of the depression of 1913–15, opposed giving his policemen a day's rest in seven and told his city's unemployed to 'hit the trail' but struggled hard to obtain a municipal vote for property-owning corporations.[82] Men like Deacon were representative of and supported by a commercial élite which constantly stymied and frustrated the working people's attempts to make their jobs safer, their homes more secure, their lives better.

Nevertheless, the cities were clearly the best places to be on the industrial frontier, especially for skilled workers. They could find the jobs and build the homes and families they had come to the west for. Unless and until they were thwarted in their own drives for improvement they remained moderate, though reform minded. The unskilled were better off in the cities but just barely. They were still powerless, living in bad conditions, earning low wages, and living in fear of unemployment. The cities were significantly different from the mining communities in that they offered some middle ground between polarized extremes. Here there were churches, religious and social clubs, city missions, ethnic self help societies, socialist and free thought clubs, and libraries.[83] Here, also, there appeared to be a middle class—clerks, salesmen, priests, professionals—lacking in the mining communities. The mix was not as volatile, the chances for improvement better, the edges not so rough. Perhaps this is why radicalism took longer to dominate the cities.

All western workers were not radicals. Those who were did not become radical at once. The coal miners of Vancouver Island, the Crowsnest Pass, and Alberta and the hardrock miners of the British Columbia interior were the vanguard of radicalism in the west, founding it, nurturing it, and lending its spirit of revolt to other western workers. These miners early rejected reformism and swung behind Marxist political organizations, particularly the Socialist Party of Canada. They also provided the most fertile ground in the west for doctrines of radical industrial unionism and syndicalism and were amongst the strongest supporters of the Industrial Workers of the World. The miners formed a large and cohesive group in British Columbia and they quickly overwhelmed, dominated, and greatly influenced the urban crafts and railroad lodges. Radicals were more influential in Vancouver prior to 1914 than other western urban centres. In Alberta the urban crafts formed the Alberta Federation of Labor partly to offset the radical influence of the coal miners who dominated the labour movement in the south,[84] but by 1918 the miners had become undisputed masters of the provincial labour movement. Radicalism, therefore, emerged first and was strongest in the highly polarized and closed mining communities. In these camps workers with a common employer and common interests were grouped into a single community. Their struggle with their bosses did not begin with the morning whistle and end when the shift was over because the entire area was controlled by their employer and they were forced to cope with the company on a twenty-four hour basis. Since they were grouped into one place a little radical propaganda went a long way.

The situation in the cities was, as we have seen, different and radicalism took much longer to dominate, even though it was always present. Prior to the war urban workers were ready to defend the rights of groups such as the IWW but, for the most part, refused to endorse their aims. Urban workers even elected radicals to important positions, particularly in Vancouver, but would not support radical objectives. Though a socialist such as R.P. Pettipiece was editor of the *B.C. Federationist,* a moderate such as W.R. Trotter (a trades congress organizer), was a regular contributor. In part this was the result of indecisiveness and ideological uncertainty. Christian Sivertz, socialist and a leader of the British Columbia Federation of Labor, demonstrated this lack of clarity when he wrote that a general strike (contemplated to support the Vancouver Island coal miners in 1913) would make employers aware that such a weapon existed and they would then be 'more amenable to reasonable consideration of the demands of organized labor.'[85] This one radical leader only supported a general strike to force the bosses to be more reasonable. Clearly the pressures of polarization and limited opportunities were not yet great enough or had not yet been perceived by enough workers to have thoroughly radicalized the Vancouver labour movement. Radical strength existed in that radicals had achieved important positions, but there was no concerted radical purpose. In the other major urban centres— Calgary, Edmonton, and Winnipeg—radicals played second fiddle to men such as Alex Ross, Alfred Farmilo, and Arthur W. Puttee. All this changed after 1914.

The emergence of radicalism as the dominant factor in the urban labour movement was primarily due to the war. The domestic industrial and political situation convinced many urban workers that opportunity and mobility were illusions. Inflation and manpower shortages prompted moves to increased organization, union recognition, and higher wages but these drives were usually stymied by court injunctions, federal orders in council, and the indifference or hostility of the Imperial Munitions Board. Many otherwise economic and industrial issues, such as higher wages for railway shopcraft workers, became politicized as worker hostility towards the war itself became the major issue. Western urban labour turned increasingly against the war and, conversely, more supportive of radical alternatives.[86] Urban labour leaders were also immigrants and now reacted in a fashion similar to their brothers in the mines. By September 1918 the urban-industrial and the extractive-hinterland labour movement was united behind radical leadership.

Western labour radicalism was born when immigrant industrial pioneers entered into the closed, polarized societies of the mining communities and the western cities. Once settled there was little chance for improvement. Many of these individuals could not accept their change in status from free immigrants, some of them from a rural background, to regulated and enclosed industrial workers.[87] In Nova Scotia and in central Canada, by contrast, radicalism was slow to develop. Its signs were not apparent in Nova Scotia until sixty years after mining began in earnest and at least two generations had worked in the mines. Young men growing up in the closed communities of the Nova Scotia coal towns knew little else and expected little better. They too would go down in the mines and would live in the company towns as did their fathers before them. If not, they would themselves emigrate. In central Canadian cities radicalism was never a dominant factor though it was always present. But in the west most workers did expect better. Those who had worked the land in Europe, who had survived the mining wars of the American frontier, who escaped the turbulence, insecurity, restrictiveness, and polarization of British society, or the falling wages and lower productivity of the Welsh coal fields, had come to the Canadian frontier for a new start and better opportunities. But they soon found themselves victims of a new oppression. This was the frontier; but the mining communities were pockets of industrial feudalism denying the opportunity of the frontier to those who sought it while the cities were only slightly better. This deep frustration provided fertile soil for the socialists and syndicalists who offered radical change and abolition of 'wage slavery.' The freedom which was sought, but not found, could be found yet in the commonwealth of toil. It became apparent to those with little patience that the traditional methods of business unionism—organization, negotiation, strike, arbitration, and so on—won no battles. Even the few victories that were achieved changed little; perhaps a slightly higher wage or shorter hours, but the company town, the slum, the whole polarized and closed environment continued to exist. In one sense the entire labour system in the west was a closed environment. Thus the one apparent hope—the unions—offered little real hope.

For many who sought improvement the only answer lay with those who attacked the basic structure of the system that held immigrant workers in thrall: the political socialists who preached the dictatorship of the proletariat and scorned reformism; the syndicalists who advocated use of the trade unions as instruments for radical change; the radical industrial unionists who advocated general strikes to overcome the combined power of employers and state. These solutions offered hope to men who refused to wait for gradual, evolutionary improvement. Far from becoming a leveler, the Canadian industrial frontier was the chief stimulus to the development of class consciousness and radical working-class attitudes in the Canadian west.

Notes

1. The classic statement is 'The Significance of the Frontier in American History' in Frederick Jackson Turner, *The Frontier in American History* (New York 1920). A Canadian discussion is included in M.S. Cross, ed., *The Frontier Thesis in the Canadas: The Debate on the Impact of the Canadian Environment* (Toronto 1970), 104–25.

2. Some immigrant attitudes can be found in H. Palmer, ed., *Immigration and the Rise of Multiculturalism* (Toronto 1975), 82–111. A good account of a Ukrainian pioneer worker is A.B. Woywitka, 'Recollections of a Union Man,' *Alberta History*, autumn 1975, 6–20.

3. See S.M. Jamieson, *Times of Trouble: Labour Unrest and Industrial Conflict, 1900–1966* (Ottawa 1968), 62–151.

4. Taken from *Webster's New World Dictionary of the American Language, College Edition* (Cleveland and New York 1968)

5. For examples see P. Phillips, *No Power Greater* (Vancouver 1967), 60, 72–3: M. Robin, *Radical Politics and Canadian Labour* (Kingston 1968), 127–32: E. Taraska, 'The Calgary Craft Union Movement, 1900–1920' (unpublished MA thesis, University of Calgary, 1975), 69–70; D.J. Bercuson, *Confrontation at Winnipeg* (Montreal 1974), 58–65, 83.

6. See British Columbia Federation of Labour, *Proceedings of the Ninth Annual Convention* (Calgary 1919), 2, 4, 5, 7; Alberta Federation of Labor, *Proceedings of the Sixth Annual Convention* (Medicine Hat 1919), 41; 'Sixteenth Annual Convention District 18 United Mine Workers of America' (typewritten), 133.

7. One Big Union, *The Origin of the One Big Union: A Verbatim Report of the Calgary Conference, 1919* (Winnipeg nd), 10–12.

8. I am grateful to E.R. Forbes for bringing these events to my attention. See his 'The Maritime Rights Movement, 1919–1927: A Study in Canadian Regionalism' (unpublished PhD thesis, Queen's University, 1975), 88–9.

9. D. MacGillivray, 'Industrial Unrest in Cape Breton 1919–1925' (unpublished MA thesis. University of New Brunswick, 1971), 35, 44.

10. Ibid., 33.

11. H.A. Logan, *Trade Unions in Canada* (Toronto 1948), 334–5.

12. MacGillivray, 'Industrial Unrest,' 226.

13. M. Dubofsky, 'The Origins of Western Working Class Radicalism, 1890–1905,' *Labor History*, spring 1966, 131–54.

14. R.M. Longo, ed., *Historical Highlights of Canadian Mining* (Toronto 1973), 21–3; M. Robin, *The Rush for Spoils* (Toronto 1972), 25–6.

15. Canada, *Census of Canada* 1911, II. 377–8 [hereafter *Census*].

16. P. Phillips, 'The National Policy and the Development of the Western Canadian Labour Movement,' in A.W. Rasporich and H.C. Klassen, eds., *Prairie Perspectives 2* (Toronto 1973), 41–61.

17. *Census,* v, 106–9, 118–19.

18. Ibid., 10–11.

19. E.S. Moore, *The Mineral Resources of Canada* (Toronto 1933), 188–92.

20. A.A. den Otter, 'Sir Alexander Tilloch Galt, the Canadian Government and Alberta's Coal,' *Historical Papers* 1973, 38.

21. R. Chodos, *The CPR: A Century of Corporate Welfare* (Toronto 1973), 63–5.

22. J.L. McDougall, *Canadian Pacific* (Montreal 1968), 143–8.

23. Chodos, *The CPR,* 63–4.

24. Public Archives of Canada, Sir Thomas Shaughnessy Papers, Canadian Pacific Railway Letterbooks, Shaughnessy to Elias Rogers, 4 March 1903. I am grateful to Donald Avery for bringing this source to my attention.

25. Ibid., Shaughnessy to W. Whyte, 27 March 1907.

26. H.A. Innis, *Settlement and the Mining Frontier* (Toronto 1936), 282–320, contains the best description of the region's growth.

27. Ibid., 280.

28. Ibid., 284.

29. Robin, *Spoils,* 76.

30. This emerges constantly in Innis. See, for example, pages 284, 285, 288, 289. He notes that the 1911 Crowsnest Pass coal strike necessitated the importation of 41,000 tons of coke from Pennsylvania (285).

31. British Columbia, *Annual Report of the Minister of Mines* (for the year ending 31 December 1914) (Victoria 1915), 333 [hereafter *Mines Reports*).

32. *Mines Reports* 1902, 1202.

33. Robin, *Spoils,* 79–80.

34. *Mines Reports* 1915, 348.

35. A.A. Den Otter, 'Railways and Alberta's Coal Problem, 1880–1960,' in A.W. Rasporich, ed., *Western Canada Past and Present* (Calgary 1975), 89–90.

36. C.J. McMillan, 'Trade Unionism in District 18, 1900–1925: A Case Study' (unpublished MA thesis, University of Alberta, 1968), 23.

37. *Mines Report* 1914, 329.

38. Ibid., 1915, 426.

39. *Census,* III, XI–XIII.

40. den Otter, 'Railways,' 84.

41. Canada, 'Evidence Presented to the Royal Commission on Industrial Relations, 1919' (typewritten). Testimony of Jesse Gough, 690–2, and C.G. Sheldon, 1003–6 [hereafter 'Royal Commission Evidence'].

42. Jamieson, *Times of Trouble,* 99, 126–32.

43. Phillips, 'National Policy,' especially 41–3.

44. *Census,* II. All these statistics were compiled from Table xv. Literacy rates were obtained from Table xxxv.

45. MacGillivray, 'Industrial Unrest,' 23–4.

46. H. Troper and R. Harney, *Immigrants* (Toronto 1975), 8.

47. See, for example, H. Palmer, *Land of the Second Chance* (Lethbridge 1972), 29–30, 71–2, 194; Woywitka, 'Recollections,' 6.

48. For American examples see A.R. McCormack, 'The Emergence of the Socialist Movement in British Columbia,' *B.C. Studies,* spring 1974, 6; A.R. McCormack, 'The Origins and Extent of Western Labour Radicalism: 1896–1919' (unpublished PhD thesis, University of Western Ontario, 1973), 24, 104.

49. D. Avery, 'Foreign Workers and Labour Radicalism in the Western Canadian Mining Industry, 1900–1919' (paper presented to the Western Canadian Urban History Conference, Winnipeg, October 1974), 4–5, 8–9.

50. *Census,* II, Table xv.

51. Palmer, *Chance,* 174; J.S. Woodsworth, *Strangers within our Gates* (Rep. ed., Toronto 1972), 133.

52. Avery, 'Foreign Workers,' 7, discusses this and the 'padrone' system.

53. I am grateful to Professor S.H. Scott for his impressions of the role of the immigrants in the Trail labour movement.

54. Avery, 'Foreign Workers,' 8.

55. Robin, *Radical Politics,* 104–15, tells of the birth of the SDP.

56. H. Pelling, *A History of British Trade Unionism* (London 1963), 94–100; McCormack, 'Emergence,' 6.

57. V.H. Jensen, *Heritage of Conflict: Labor Relations in the Non Ferrous Metals Industry up to 1930* (New York 1950), 61–2, 64–70.

58. Glenbow Alberta Institute [GAI], United Mine Workers of America, District 18 Papers. 'Report of Alberta Coal Mining Industry Commission, Dec. 23, 1919' contains valuable information concerning the state of Alberta coal towns.

59. M. Nordegg, *The Possibilities of Canada are Truly Great* (Rep. ed., Toronto 1971), 176–7.

60. Ibid., 184

61. 'Royal Commission Evidence,' 393–5, 405–7.

62. Nordegg, *Possibilities,* 196–8.

63. 'Royal Commission Evidence,' 396–7.

64. Phillips *No Power,* 5–9.

65. University of British Columbia Special Collections [UBC], *By Laws and Sketch of Sandon Miners' Union Hospital* (Sandon, nd).

66. F.P. Karas, 'Labour and Coal in the Crowsnest Pass' (unpublished MA thesis, University of Calgary, 1972), 36–51, 129–33.

67. GAI, United Mine Workers of America, District 18 Papers, 'Special Convention held at Calgary, June 14–16, 1921' 101–5, 108.

68. James Gray discusses prostitution in Drumheller in *Red Lights on the Prairies* (Toronto 1971). See also Provincial Archives of British Columbia, Cominco Papers, Add. MS 15/8/3, 'St. Eugene Arbitration.'

69. For Kootenay town living costs see 'St. Eugene Arbitration,' and Cominco Papers, Add. MS 15 9/2.

70. McMillan, 78–82, summarizes some of the dangers and the evolution of safety legislation.

71. British Columbia, *Special Report on Coal Mine Explosions, 1918* (Victoria 1918), 529–30.

72. R.E. Lingenfelter, *The Hardrock Miners* (Los Angeles 1974), 12–26, tells of conditions in American hardrock mines in the period prior to 1896. For evidence that many of these conditions existed in British Columbia mines see UBC, Orchard Interviews. Interview of William Byers, 7–10. Byers worked in the Phoenix and Rossland area. See also *By Laws and Sketch of Sandon Miners' Union Hospital.*

73. D.P. McGinnis, 'Labour in Transition: Occupational Structure and Economic Dependency in Alberta, 1921–1951' (paper read to the Western Canadian Studies Conference, Calgary, Alberta, March 1975), 4–6.

74. This was a close to universal experience. See G. Shepherd, *West of Yesterday* (Toronto 1965), 17–18, for one example.

75. E. Bradwin, *The Bunkhouse Man* (Rep. ed., Toronto 1972), 63–90

76. Jamieson, *Times of Trouble,* 143–6.

77. J. Taylor, 'The Urban West: Public Welfare and a Theory of Urban Development,' in A.R. McCormack and I. Macpherson, eds., *Cities in the West* (Ottawa 1975), 298–301.

78. A.F.J. Arbitise, *Winnipeg: A Social History of Urban Growth, 1874–1914* (Montreal 1975), 223–45.

79. Ibid., 163–5.

80. J.M.S. Careless, 'Aspects of Urban Life in the West, 1870–1914,' in A.W. Rasporich and H.C. Klassen, eds., *Prairie Perspectives* 2, 32–5.

81. Artibise, *Winnipeg,* 38.

82. *The Voice* (Winnipeg), 9 and 16 Jan. and 9 Oct. 1914.

83. Artibise, *Winnipeg,* 113–65.

84. Taraska, 'Calgary Craft Union Movement,' 38–40.

85. *B.C. Federationist,* 'Wage Workers' Forum,' 12 Sept. 1913.

86. See Phillips, *No Power,* 61–77; Bercuson, *Confrontation,* 32–77.

87. This phenomenon has been explored in Herbert G. Gutman, 'Work, Culture, and Society in Industrializing America, 1815–1919,' *American Historical Review,* June 1973, 531–87.

1919: THE CANADIAN LABOUR REVOLT

Gregory Kealey

In late March 1919 a worried Union government appointed a Royal Commission to "enquire into Industrial Relations in Canada." From 26 April to 13 June, the Commissioners toured industrial Canada visiting 28 cities from Victoria to Sydney and examining a total of 486 witnesses. Their travels coincided with the greatest period of industrial unrest in Canadian history. Their report, published in July 1919, and the subsequent September National Industrial Conference held to discuss their recommendations, appear now only as minor footnotes to the turbulence of the year. Like many Royal Commissions, the Mathers investigation proved far more important than the lack of tangible results.

The Royal Commission on Industrial Relations had two recent and prominent predecessors in its field of inquiry: the 1914 United States Commission on Industrial Relations and the 1917 British Whitley Committee on Industrial Conciliation. It also had one earlier Canadian predecessor, although one suspects it was but dimly remembered in 1919. The Royal Commission on the Relations of Capital and Labor had been appointed by a previous Conservative prime minister, Sir John A. Macdonald, at a similar moment of crisis in class relations in 1886. That inquiry had also included trade unionists as commissioners, had toured the industrial sections of the nation, and had interviewed hundreds of Canadian workers. Its report also received little attention and resulted only in the establishment of Labour Day as a national holiday—a considerable accomplishment compared to the complete legislative failure of the Mathers Commission.

The Royal Commission on the Relations of Capital and Labor, a testament to the turmoil of the "Great Upheaval," has been extensively studied by historians interested in the social history of Canadian workers in the late nineteenth century. The Industrial Relations Commission, however, has received far less attention. Yet the evidence it heard is an equally rich source for the post-war upsurge of working-class militancy. The very titles of the two Royal Commissions convey much about the transformation which had taken place in Canadian industrial capitalist society in the approximately thirty intervening years. The rather quaint, Victorian "Relations between Labor and Capital" with its echo of classical political economy gives way to the modern sounding "Industrial Relations," hinting now not at conflicting classes but at a system of mutual interests. If the titles suggest something of transformed bourgeois and state attitudes, then the contents of the two collections of testimony tell us much about the development of the Canadian working class. The specific material complaints enumerated by Canadian workers vary little

From *Labour/Le Travail*, XIII (Spring 1984), 90–114. Reprinted by permission of the Canadian Committee on Labour History.

from 1886 to 1919—unemployment, low wages, high prices, long hours, unsafe and unsanitary working conditions, abysmal housing, the super-exploitation of women workers, employer blacklists, non-recognition of unions, refusal of collective bargaining—all remain a constant in the working-class bill of grievances. What differs, however, is the workers' attitude. The cautious note of respectability and, in some cases, of near deference present in 1886 was transformed into a clarion cry for change. From Victoria to Sydney, Canadian workers appeared before the 1919 Commission and defiantly challenged it. From Socialist Party of Canada (SPC) soap-boxer Charles Lestor in Vancouver to the Nova Scotia leaders of newly-organized District 26, United Mine Workers of America (UMWA), the message the Commission received was the same across the country. The capitalist system could not be reformed, it must be transformed. Production for profit must cease; production for use must begin.

British Columbia MLA J.H. Hawthornthwaite, a former SPC stalwart and then Federated Labour Party leader, asserted in his appearance before the Commission:

> Working men today understand these matters ... and if you go into any socialistic bodies and listen to the discussion you would understand the grasp that these men have. I do not know any college man or university man who can for ten minutes hold their own in an argument among these people.[1]

Workers across the country more than lived up to Hawthornthwaite's boast. In city after city, the Commissioners were regaled with Marxist-influenced histories of the development of industrial capitalism. A few of these lectures came from middle-class proponents of the workers' movement such as Edmonton Mayor Joseph Clarke or social gospel ministers William Irvine, A.E. Smith, William Ivens, Ernest Thomas, and Salem Bland. But more impressive were the many workers—some well-known leaders, but many not—who appeared to explain patiently to the Commissioners, in the words of Edmonton Grand Trunk Railway machinist E.J. Thompson, "We are the producers and we are not getting what we produce." Like most other workers who appeared, Thompson was uninterested in the Commission's extensive plans for Industrial Councils; only "complete ownership of the machines of production by the working class" would suffice, he asserted. When pushed by hostile Commissioners who claimed that the new Canadian National Railway represented the nationalization he sought, Thompson responded in kind, reminding the Commissioners that workers saw their investigation as nothing but "a talkfest" and as "camouflage" for the anti-labour Union government.[2]

Thompson's evidence is of interest for two reasons: first, he was not a front-line leader of western labour; second, he came directly out of the railway machine shops. In city after city, metal trades workers from the shipyards, from the railway shops, and from the more diversified contract shops came forward and talked socialism. Even James Somerville, the International Association of Machinists' (IAM) Western representative, who predictably chose to distinguish himself from the radicals in his testimony, and who worried about the workers having "gone so far that they do not recognize the authority even in their own organization," explained:

> One of the things they want first is nothing short of a transfer of the means of production, wealth production, from that of private control to that of collective ownership, for they know that is the only solution.[3]

Lest there be any notion that this was a regional manifestation of class unrest, let us travel east to Sudbury, Ontario. There Frederick Eldridge, a machinist and secretary of the local Trades and Labour Council, received "considerable handclapping, stamping of feet, and vocal enthusiasm" from the Commission's working-class audience, when he asserted:

> The workers do not get enough of that which they produce.... I advocate government ownership of everything: mills, mines, factories, smelters, railroads, etc. That is the only solution of the problem and I am only one of hundreds of workmen in Sudbury that think the same thing.[4]

In Toronto, machinist James Ballantyne called for the nationalization of all industry.[5] In Hamilton, IAM District 24 representative Richard Riley more cautiously noted that "although a great many workers have not given the matter much thought, they are beginning to think that there must be a change of the system, that is to say the present competitive system."[6] When the Commission reached Montreal, John D. Houston of IAM District 82 presented a prepared brief on the economic system, arguing in part:

> I believe that in the system of ownership lies all our social problems.... For 300 years or over, while the businessman was consolidating his position as captain of industry, the institutions of autocracy provided, through the law, the machinery of force and fraud which was rigorously applied, to make the worker a proletarian with no means of livelihood except to work for wages or a salary....

He closed with the familiar call for production for use, not for profit.[7]

By the time the Commission arrived in the Maritimes, the Commissioners' impatience was showing, no doubt increased by the mounting industrial crisis which was sweeping the nation. While the evidence of their sessions in Amherst, Nova Scotia, at the height of the General Strike there, has unfortunately been lost, evidence from New Glasgow and Sydney demonstrates the eastern manifestation of the workers' revolt.[8] While UMWA District 26 leaders such as Dan Livingstone, Robert Baxter, and Silby Barrett provided much of the fire, Alex T. Mackay, representing carmen and steelworkers, infuriated the Commissioners by warning of an intensification of the struggle:

> The way the fight in Winnipeg will be terminated, will very largely influence the attitude throughout Canada. I think if matters are allowed to run their course there will be no interference in this part of Canada, but if there is any attempt at coercion, the first shot fired in Winnipeg, will hit every labouring man in eastern and western Canada, and the result will be confusion from the Atlantic to the Pacific.[9]

A day earlier, in Halifax, Nova Scotia Federation of Labour organizer C.C. Dane had threatened a province-wide General Strike for the eight-hour day and had added almost gratuitously: "Industrial unrest? Why, gentlemen, we have none to what we are going to have. I am a Bolshevist and I will warn these two governments that trouble is coming and the men will have what belongs to them."[10] Dane, a boilermaker from Australia, had played a major role in the March 1919 establishment of the Federation.

Machinists were not the only group of workers who testified in these terms. Indeed most workers who appeared made similar points, although not always couched in a socialist framework. An additional important group of witnesses who echoed much of the above but who also added a new dimension to the workers' revolt were women witnesses. Unlike the young women workers paraded before the 1886 Commission, who testified only to oppressive conditions and often answering in monosyllables, the women appearing in 1919 included representatives of retail clerks' unions, women's labour leagues, local councils of women, and consumer groups. Among them were then-prominent figures such as Montreal's Rose Henderson or later leading Communist militant Bella Hall, but also many women who enjoy no such historical fame. These women universally complained of bad housing, runaway inflation, high food prices, and the low wages paid to working women. Calgary's Mrs. Jean MacWilliams, who had organized laundry workers, asked rhetorically, "Are we in favour of a bloody revolution?" and answered, "Why any kind of revolution would be better than conditions as they are now."[11] In Saskatoon, Miss Francis, representing the local TLC, demanded that "plundering must cease, profiteering must go, commercialized industries and institutions must give way to the larger hopes of the people" and "production for use" must replace "production for profit."[12] Mrs. Resina Asals of the Regina Women's Labour League told the Commission:

> There is only one thing that the workers have to thank the capitalists for, and that is that they have tightened the screw up so much that they are awakening the worker up to the fact that he is the most important factor and that until we produce for use instead of profit this unrest will still prevail. Let the workingman, the one who produced, have control and then we shall see the light of a new dawn.[13]

Rose Henderson simply advanced the proposition that "the real revolutionist is the mother—not the man. She says openly that there is nothing but Revolution."[14] Working-class women, both wage workers and unpaid domestic workers, also had started to view the world in new ways in 1919.

These examples are intended simply to demonstrate that the revolt was national in character and that its seeds were not rooted in any unique regional fermentation. The "radical" west and the conservative east have become sorry shibboleths of Canadian historiography. The foundations of our understanding of 1919 must be built on national and international conjunctures. While the local and regional pictures are not identical, as we come to know the history of eastern and central Canadian workers as well as we know that of western workers, the similarities of struggle begin to outweigh the initial impression of regional particularism. World War I, a profoundly national experience for Canadians, helped provide part of the cement for this nascent national working-class response.[15] Moreover, we should also remind ourselves at the outset that, as David Montgomery has argued, "Strikes can only be understood in the context of the changing totality of class conflicts, of which they are a part."[16] In 1919 Canada, that totality was increasingly national in scope.

Yet World War I, while providing specific sparks to light the flame of working-class struggle in 1919, should not be viewed as its cause. Underlying structural changes in capitalist organization, both on a national and international scale, must be viewed as providing the necessary fuel for this fire.

Indeed, although the early war years 1914 to 1916 had seen little overt class conflict in Canada, the changes in the capitalist organization of production and the consequent "remaking" or reconstitution of the working class was well advanced before the outbreak of war. The years 1912 and 1913 should be seen as a prelude to the 1917 to 1920 conflagration. Table I demonstrates this continuity with pre-war class conflict.[17] This argument is not unique to this paper as various community studies, including Bercuson's on Winnipeg and Reilly's on Amherst, have perceived the continuity of class struggle between the pre- and post-war period.[18] This continuity extended, however, throughout the entire country. Craig Heron and Bryan Palmer's perceptive study of strikes in southern Ontario from 1901 to 1914 demonstrates a pattern that held for the other cities whose labour history has been chronicled, including Winnipeg.[19] Lest there be any doubt about this, note the provincial distribution figures in Table II for the pre- and post-war peak strike years. The one striking anomaly on

TABLE I   Strike Activity in Canada, 1912–1922

Year	Number of Strikes	Number of Workers Involved	Striker Days Lost
1912	242	43 104	1 136 345
1913	234	41 004	1 037 254
1914	99	9 911	491 358
1915	86	11 480	95 242
1916	168	26 971	241 306
1917	222	50 327	1 123 916
1918	305	82 573	657 152
1919	428	149 309	3 401 843
1920	459	76 624	814 457
1921	208	28 398	1 049 719

Table II, namely the especially high British Columbia figures, are largely accounted for by loggers' strikes as shown in Table III. When we turn from regional variation to the industrial pattern for these years, some other important common ingredients emerge, especially the ongoing importance of mining and the metal trades. Yet our attention is also drawn to new developments apparent only in the later period such as the importance of wartime shipbuilding, and the rise of logging and "service strikes."

A more specific look at 1919 and especially at the months of May, June, and July helps to clarify some of these points. While these months generally figure high in the calendar of industrial conflict, clearly summer 1919 was not

TABLE II   Number of Disputes by Province

	1912	*1913*	*1917*	*1918*	*1919*	*1920*
N.S.	9	12	8	18	19	39
P.E.I.	1	–	2	–	–	1
N.B.	21	20	5	11	19	15
Que.	32	31	31	28	100	79
Ont.	100	114	68	112	158	122
Man.	13	6	18	20	16	5
Sask.	19	10	6	10	13	4
Alta.	23	15	24	53	29	39
B.C.	22	25	55	46	73	124
Interprov.	2	1	5	7	2	1
Total	242	234	222	305	428	459

TABLE III   Number of Disputes by Selected Industry

	1912	*1913*	*1917*	*1918*	*1919*	*1920*
Logging	1	–	1	–	32	66
Coal Mining	6	5	22	49	22	48
Other Mining	6	6	6	3	10	14
Metal Mfrg.	27	30	44	43	46	61
Shipbuilding	2	3	13	16	25	12
Steam Railway	16	8	12	16	6	2
Electric Railway	2	7	5	11	12	5
Service	12	18	11	30	39	38
General	–	–	–	1	12	–
Total	72	77	114	169	204	246
N	242	234	222	305	428	459
% Total	29.8	32.9	51.4	55.4	47.7	53.4

simply any year. Table IV shows both the geographic and industrial range of the strikes and Table V highlights the central role of coal, the metal trades, shipbuilding, and, of course, the general strikes themselves in the wave of unrest.

The summer strike wave consisted of three main types of strikes: first, local strikes contesting the normal range of issues; second, general strikes called in support of such local strikes as in Winnipeg, Amherst, and Toronto; and, third, general sympathy strikes called either in support of the Winnipeg General Strike or to protest its repression. Variants two and three have received some attention, although even here the focus on Winnipeg has tended to obscure these less well-known struggles. Local strikes, however, have received little study.

Table V, while describing all industrial action in these three months of 1919, suggests how important the local or category one conflicts were to the strike wave. Clearly these strikes cannot be described in this paper in any detail but I will highlight a few to suggest the range of activity. Let us reverse the historiographic trend and travel across the country from east to west.[20] In Moncton, N.B., and Amherst, N.S., moulders won victories over iron founders. A lockout of 350 quarry workers in Sweet's Corner, N.S., lasted 55 working

TABLE IV   Strikes: May, June, and July 1919[1]

A. By Month:	Number of Strikes (total)	Number of Strikes (complete data)	Number of Workers Involved[2]	Duration in Worker Days[3]
May	110	96	68 606	742 506
June	101	89	84 054	1 274 998
July	84	75	71 121	555 802
Total	210[4]	178[4]	114 423[4]	2 573 306
B. By Province:				
Nova Scotia	11	9	3 461	85 135
New Brunswick	6	6	128	631
Quebec	57	50	25 988	395 285
Ontario	90	78	34 544	632 409
Manitoba	6	5	21,756	817 686
Saskatchewan	9	7	2 041	31,833
Alberta	9	8	9 271[5]	304 967[5]
British Columbia	23	16	17 234[5]	305 360[5]
Total	210[6]	178[6]	114 423	2 573 306

[1] Strikes in progress.

[2] Figures for strikes beginning before May or extending beyond the end of a month are not adjusted to account for strikers returning to work.

[3] Figures are adjusted to account for strikers returning to work.

[4] Totals are for strikes in progress over the three-month period.

[5] Includes provincial estimates for the District 18 coal mining strike.

[6] District 18, UMWA strike counted once.

FIGURE 1 **Striker Days: May, June, July 1919**

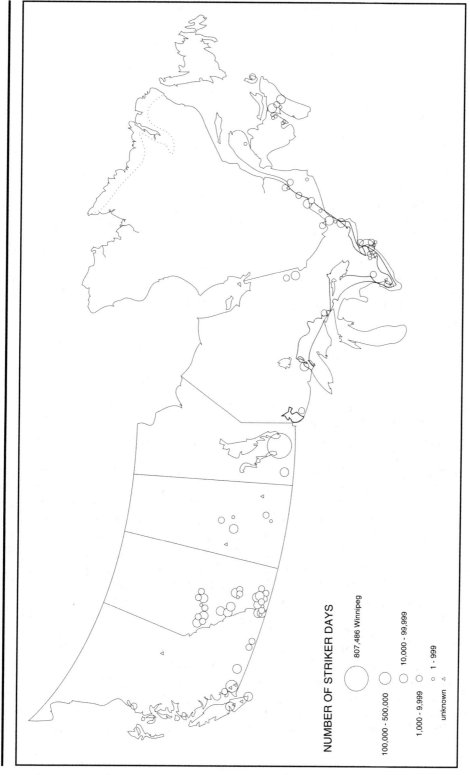

NUMBER OF STRIKER DAYS

807,486 Winnipeg

100,000 - 500,000

10,000 - 99,999

1,000 - 9,999

1 - 999

unknown

TABLE V   Strikes: May–July 1919, by Industry

	Number	%	Number of Workers Involved	%	Duration in Strikes Days	%
Mining	11	5.2	10 216	8.9	340 216	13.2
Manufacturing Total	101	48.1	43 495	38.0	922 117	35.8
Mfrg. Leather & Textile	(20)	(9.5)	(9 505)	(8.3)	(204 897)	(8.0)
Mfrg. Metal & Shipbldg.	(43)	(20.5)	(24 590)	(21.5)	(623 577)	(24.2)
Construction	32	15.2	9 829	8.6	185 488	7.2
Transportation & Public Utilities	21	10.0	4 772	4.2	68 964	2.7
Service & Public Administration	19	9.1	1 137	1.0	4 799	.2
Other Industries	14	6.7	607	5	18 036	.7
General	12	5.7	44 367	38.8	1 033 686	40.2
Total	210	100.0	114 423	100.0	2 573 306	100.0

days and resulted in higher wages. Brief walkouts on the street railway systems in Halifax and Moncton also occurred. The most significant story in the Maritimes, however, focused on Amherst and we will return to it in our discussion of general strikes.

Quebec's 57 strikes were highly concentrated in Montreal which accounted for 47 of them (82 per cent). Outside Montreal, the major strikes occurred in the shipbuilding industry at Lauzon and Trois Rivières, and in the metal trades at Lachine and Sherbrooke. The brief metal strikes were both successful for the workers, and the Trois Rivières shipyard strike won union recognition for the strikers. Montreal, however, was the centre of activity in Quebec. Indeed, the Borden government was sufficiently alarmed about the conflicts in Montreal that the city was included on their emergency daily briefing list. Over 22,000 workers in Montreal struck during the three-month period, logging nearly 380,000 striker days lost. Again the metal trades and shipbuilding figured prominently. A metal trades strike at Canadian Car and Foundry in early May involving 4,000 workers ended in victory after only three days. In the shipyards, however, it took a one-day strike to force negotiations and then a five-week strike before the employers conceded to some of the demands of their 3,500 workers. This strike was led by a General Strike Committee, not by the union officials of the Marine Trades Federation. A major strike of 2,000 wire workers failed after three weeks. A series of skirmishes in the garment trades led to a

FIGURE 2 General Strikes, 1919

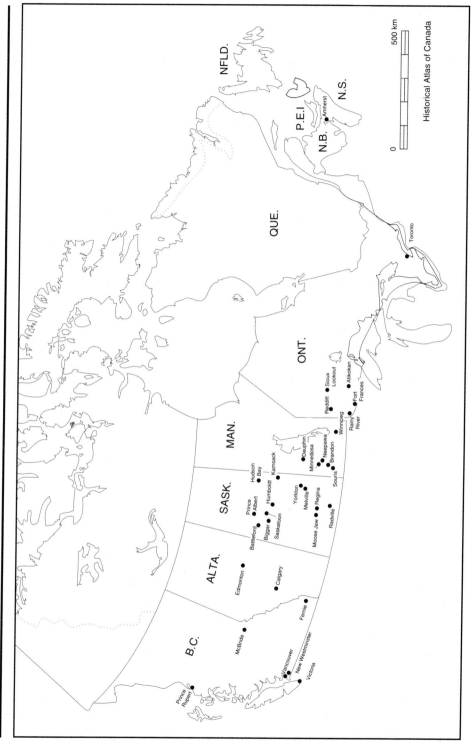

Historical Atlas of Canada

number of worker victories, and a major battle involving over 3,500 workers at Dominion Textiles gained some employer concessions after nearly three months of struggle. This strike was marked by a successful sympathetic strike at Montmorency Falls where 1,100 workers stayed out for ten days in support of their Montreal comrades and returned to work with a wage increase. Other industrial workers showed a new ability to organize as well. Over 1,400 rubber workers, for example, won a compromise settlement after a strike of three weeks, as did 350 sugar refinery employees, while 700 meat packers won a quick victory to match a settlement won earlier by Toronto workers. This militant activity on the part of industrial workers represented a new departure for Montreal's working class, as did the willingness of Montmorency textile workers to resort to a sympathy strike.[21] While the majority of the Montreal Trades and Labour Council (MTLC) opposed a general sympathetic strike, the tactic had proponents in Montreal. The machinists (IAM) and the engineers (ASE), true to national form, held a massive support rally in late May which was addressed by Winnipeg strike leader R.J. Johns, who was in Montreal representing Division #4, railroad shop craft workers, at Railroad Board arbitration meetings. Those attending, identified as workers from the Canadian Vickers Shipyard, heard speeches from A.H. McNamee, president of the ASE, and radical machinists Richard Kerrigan and William Turnbull, as well as from Montreal "reds" such as Beckie Buhay and Albert St. Martin.[22] In early June the MTLC endorsed the 44-hour week and called for the reinstatement of the postal workers who had been dismissed in Winnipeg.[23] At their subsequent meeting in mid-June the arrests of the Winnipeg strike leaders were roundly condemned and Richard Kerrigan led a debate in which the Canadian Vickers General Strike Committee sought to gain the endorsation of the Council for a general sympathetic strike. In this, they failed.[24]

Ontario's 90 strikes involving 34,122 workers were not as concentrated as Quebec's, although Toronto did account for 22 (24 per cent) in addition to its General Sympathetic Strike, which I will deal with later. Ottawa had eleven strikes, London seven, Hamilton six, St. Catharines and Windsor, five each. Major mining strikes took place in Cobalt and Kirkland Lake where 2,200 and 525 miners respectively struck for eight and 21 weeks. In both cases the miners were defeated by intransigent mining companies, although not before there had been discussions of a Northern Ontario-wide general strike.[25]

In Toronto, newly-organized workers in the meat packing industry, organized on an industrial basis, took on the giants of the industry, including Swift Canada, as over 3,000 workers struck in the stockyards area after the companies refused to negotiate with the union. In addition to union recognition, they sought the eight-hour day and 44-hour week, and guaranteed minimum levels of employment. After just over a week on the picket line in early May, an IDIA board was agreed to by both sides and reported unanimously on 29 May mainly in favour of the workers, granting a 48-hour week, a weekly guarantee of 40 hours, overtime pay, a formal grievance procedure, and seniority provisions. This settlement became the model for the industry and workers in Montreal, Ottawa, Hamilton, and Peterborough fought for it in summer 1919 and spring 1920.[26] Beginning in July almost 2,000 Toronto garment workers led by the International Ladies Garment Workers Union (ILGWU) struck over 40 shops for twelve weeks before winning wage and hour concessions. Both of these industries involved high proportions of ethnic workers and their successful strikes suggest the expansion of both trade union organization and class struggle to new and difficult terrain.

Ontario's shipyard workers, who in 1918 had organized a Marine Trades and Labour Federation of Canada, engaged in a series of seven strikes covering almost all the province's shipbuilding centres. Bridgeburg, Collingwood, Fort William-Port Arthur, Midland, Welland, and Toronto each witnessed strikes involving workforces ranging from 100 to 1,300. Most of these strikes were fought for wage increases and the 44-hour week, and resulted in significant worker gains. In Collingwood, however, 900 workers failed in a three-week strike in July demanding the rehiring of Orange fellow-workers who had been fired for refusing to work on the glorious twelfth.

In the metal trades, which included many of the same trades as shipbuilding, 1919 saw the machinists attempt to gain Ontario-wide uniformity of wages and conditions. The first provincial convention of Ontario machinists held in Toronto in July 1918 had decided to force this issue. Their major aim was to gain the eight-hour day and 44-hour week and in spring 1919 metal trades meetings were organized province-wide to prepare for that struggle. IAM Vice-President John McClelland reported that "the largest halls in many of the towns" were "too small to accommodate the crowds." Moving beyond IAM exclusivism, McLelland worked for "complete affiliation of the metal trades," and "in the meantime" organized metal trades councils as the basis for a strike which would "completely close down the industry until a settlement is reached."

The Toronto campaign became the central battle for the war for recognition of the metal trades councils as bargaining agents and for the eight-hour day. The demands were sent to the employers on 1 April and tools were dropped on 1 May by some 5,000 metal trades workers. Meanwhile in Peterborough, approximately 100 moulders struck on 1 May and were followed by their fellow workers in Brampton (thirty) and Hamilton (250) on 5 May. Four days later the Kingston Metal Trades Council struck the Canadian Locomotive Company, pulling out 650 workers. On 12 May the Ottawa Metal Trades Council called some 200 machinists and patternmakers out of fifteen small shops. The following day Brantford moulders struck. St. Catharines moulders and machinists left work on 23 May.[27]

The results of these strikes varied but by and large they were defeated. In Toronto the metal trades council ended its strike on 28 July, although 750 moulders refused to end their strike which was still continuing at year's end.

In Peterborough the moulders won a victory after a 22-week strike. Their fellow craftsworkers in Brampton returned after eight weeks but 250 striking moulders in Hamilton remained out for the rest of the year. In Kingston a compromise ended the metal trades strike after almost 26 weeks, while Ottawa machinists and patternmakers admitted defeat after almost thirteen weeks on the lines. Brantford moulders remained out the entire year. Clearly the metal trades workers' optimism as they approached May Day 1919 had turned out to be illusory.

In the west, Manitoba's strikes revolved totally around the epic struggle in Winnipeg and the General Sympathy Strike in Brandon which we will turn to later. In Saskatchewan, the pattern was similar involving primarily sympathetic strikes. In Alberta, however, a successful Calgary metal trades strike in April and May won shorter hours and higher wages for machinists, moulders, and other metal workers. In addition, UMWA District 18's over 6,200 coal miners left the pits at the end of May and stayed out until 1 September when they returned on the advice of OBU leaders.[28] This General Strike was exceptional in that as a "100 per cent" strike involving the maintenance people, it transgressed UMWA custom and in the fact that some of the firebosses, the foremen in the mines, also took part. By July what had started partially as a sympathy strike with Winnipeg had been transformed into a major struggle for recognition of the OBU which would play itself out over the next few years.

In British Columbia the District 18 strike spread into the southeastern coal field and a series of small logging strikes under the leadership of the new, later OBU, B.C. Loggers Union took place. The major activity in B.C., however, also revolved around the June sympathy strikes.

The three General Sympathetic Strikes generated by local industrial struggles were in Amherst, N.S., Toronto, and Winnipeg. The sensitive work of Nolan Reilly has provided us with a model study of the community background to the Amherst General Strike, an event which had gone almost unnoticed. In Amherst, the local Federation of Labour, under the rubric of One Big Union, led a general strike which spread out from the Canadian Car and Foundry workers' demands that they receive pay equal to that which their 4,000 Montreal co-workers had won in a three-day strike in early May. The company's intransigence led to a city-wide walkout involving all of Amherst's major employers. While proceeding from local causes and representing the culmination of a decade of industrial conflict in Amherst, the strikers identified themselves with the national struggle, as their enthusiastic correspondence with the OBU suggests.[29]

Events in Toronto in 1919, while less dramatic than those in Amherst, nevertheless caused Prime Minister Borden and his government considerable consternation.[30] As elsewhere, the metal trades were central in the crisis. Toronto's extensive foundries, machine shops, and metal factories had been at the core of war production. The city's metal trades workers, who had organized a joint council in 1901 and who had endorsed a call for industrial unionism in 1913, led the battle to enforce collective bargaining and a "fair-wage schedule" on the Imperial Munitions Board (IMB).[31] This struggle first came to a head in spring 1916 when Toronto machinists tried to extend gains they had made in some shops in December 1915 to the entire city. In addition, Hamilton machinists also demanded parity with their Toronto comrades. The joint threat of a general metal trades strike in Toronto issued by IAM District 46 in March, and a machinists' strike in Hamilton, combined with McClelland's public worry that he could no longer retain control of his people, led to the appointment of a three-member government commission to investigate the munitions plants in Toronto and Hamilton and the general extension of the Industrial Disputes Investigation Act (IDIA) to all war industry. This commission, however, which the Trades and Labour Congress (TLC) regarded as a victory, eventually proved meaningless when Hamilton employers refused to abide by its recommendation of the nine-hour day and wage increases. The subsequent Hamilton-wide strike of some 2,000 workers which included a coalition of machinists (IAM), engineers (ASE), and unorganized, unskilled workers ended in a major defeat for Hamilton workers at the hands of Canadian Westinghouse, National Steel Car, the Steel Company of Canada, Otis Elevators, and Dominion Steel Foundry. Although Toronto IAM members, for the second time in only a few months, threatened a general strike in sympathy with the Hamilton workers, the IAM international leadership managed to prevent it. The Metal Trades Council did manage, however, to help move the Toronto Trades and Labour Council (TTLC) significantly to the left during these developments. In March and April TTLC condemnation of the Borden government and of the IMB for failure to implement a fair-wage schedule had been shelved by a worried TLC executive in Ottawa. Both Secretary Draper and President Watters apparently hoped their cap-in-hand lobbying would result in a breakthrough. In this they were to be sadly disappointed. The late March extension of the IDIA to cover shipbuilding and munitions led to a furious response from the TTLC which "emphatically denounced this uncalled for and unwarranted action" and accused the TLC executive "of not fulfilling their obligation to the workers of Canada."[32] Thus Toronto and Hamilton metal trades workers as early as summer 1916 found themselves moving in opposition to state labour policy and already identifying their differences with both the TLC leadership and to some degree with their own international officers such as McClelland and James Somerville, all of whom were continually promoting patience and industrial peace. These latter strategies looked increasingly problematic. Thus, as Myer Siemiatycki has noted with considerable irony, "the war-induced epidemic of general strikes, which one prominent unionist subsequently dubbed 'Winnipegitis,' found its earliest germination in Toronto."[33]

By the time of the next major metal trades struggle which came in May 1919, the metal workers exercised considerable control over the TTLC. In a May Day meeting, the TTLC voted to contact all Canadian Trades and Labour

Councils to get support for the metal trades fight for the eight-hour day. Moreover, they "requested sympathetic action to bring about the result desired." A 13 May meeting demanded that metal trades employers negotiate and then issued a call for a general strike convention for one week hence. While this motion noted western strikes in Winnipeg and Calgary and other Ontario strikes, its major interest was in the Toronto Strike.[34]

The vote in favour of a general strike by 44 unions representing 12,000 workers led to hurried correspondence between Toronto politicians and Ottawa. Newton Rowell, president of the Privy Council, sought permission from his cabinet colleagues to pressure the employers to concede to the demand for collective bargaining. If they refused, he proposed to embarrass them publicly. Not surprisingly, a hurried negative response came from Minister of Finance Thomas White who had consulted Minister of Labour Gideon Robertson.[35] The following day Toronto Mayor Tommy Church wrote directly to Prime Minister Borden seeking government legislation on shorter hours, explaining that his offer of mediation had won a brief delay in the planned walkout, and seeking Borden's personal intervention in the talks if necessary. Borden's agreement provided Church with an important talking point in a 27 May conference at City Hall which brought together the strike leaders and some of the major metal employers such as Findlay of Massey-Harris and White of Canadian Allis-Chalmers. Although the employers made no major concessions, the workers were placed in an embarrassing situation and finally agreed to Church's proposal that a joint delegation visit Ottawa and talk to Borden. Subsequently the union "convention" authorized this trip, while reaffirming that the General Strike would commence on Friday, 30 May, unless the right of collective bargaining and the 44-hour week were granted to the Metal Trades Council.[36]

Borden's intervention led only to an offer of arbitration, which the workers scornfully declined, but again the employers scored a minor publicity coup by offering a compromise 48-hour week, although not agreeing to Metal Trades Council recognition.[37]

The sympathetic strike commenced on 30 May and from 5–15,000 workers left their jobs. The strike's strength predictably lay in the metal trades, in shipbuilding, among some groups of building trades workers, especially carpenters, and among garment workers. Its major failing was the decision by civic employees and especially the street railway workers to stay on the job until their contract expired on 16 June. The strike lasted until 4 June when it was called off by the Central Strike Committee at the request of the Metal Trades Council. The Committee of fifteen which ran the strike included nine metal trades workers, four building trades workers, and two garment trades workers.[38]

Although the left in Toronto had suffered a defeat in this struggle, they were not repudiated. Instead they took control of the TTLC in its subsequent July election. Left-wing revelations that prominent right-wingers on the Council's executive had received $5,000 from the Toronto Employers' Association to support a new labour paper in Toronto which had worked to divide metal trades workers during the strike, helped them gain control. These charges were sustained by a Council investigation.[39]

The Winnipeg General Strike we will simply pass over in order to discuss the rather less well-known wave of general sympathy strikes. Compilation of these is somewhat risky since the Department of Labour's official version and even their manuscript materials do not necessarily conform to all strikes mentioned in the labour press or even in the various security reports which crop up in the Borden Papers and elsewhere. Table VI lists those identified in Department of Labour data (A) and then adds a list compiled from other sources (B).[40]

In Manitoba many small railroad junction towns such as Dauphin supported Winnipeg as did workers in Brandon. The strike in Brandon, the longest of all the sympathy strikes, was extremely solid and orderly. It eventually involved civic workers who had fought and won their own strike in April but who still came out in solidarity as repression mounted in Winnipeg. Controlled throughout by the Brandon Trades and Labor Council, the strike extended to unorganized workers who were guaranteed "full protection" from the labour council.[41]

TABLE VI General Strikes in Sympathy with Winnipeg, May–July 1919

	Location	Dates	Number of Workers Involved	Duration in Strike Days
A.	Brandon	20 May–2 July	450	10 200
	Calgary	26 May–25 June	1 500	31 700
	Edmonton	26 May–25 June	2 000	24 000
	Saskatoon	27 May–26 June	1 200	24 000
	Prince Albert	28 May–23 June	300	5 000
	Regina	29 May–26 June	350	1 500
	Vancouver	3 June–4 July	8 000	160 000
	New Westminster	13 June–23 June	537	3 400
	Victoria	23 June–7 July	5 000	28 000

B.	Atikokan, Ont.	Neepawa, Man.	Melville, Sask.
	Fort Frances, Ont.	Souris, Man.	Moose Jaw, Sask.
	Rainy River, Ont.	Battleford, Sask.	Radville, Sask.
	Redditt, Ont.	Biggar, Sask.	Yorkton, Sask.
	Sioux Lookout, Ont.	Hudson Bay Jct., Sask.	Prince Rupert, B.C.
	Dauphin, Man.	Humboldt, Sask.	McBride, B.C.
	Minnedosa, Man.	Kamsack, Sask.	Fernie, B.C.

The list of small Saskatchewan railway junction towns makes clear the support of railroad shop workers and of some running trades workers, although the Brotherhoods exerted all the pressure they were capable of to prevent this. Prince Albert's sympathy strike involved mainly Canadian Northern workers.[42] In Saskatchewan's larger urban centres a similar pattern prevailed. Regina workers initially supported a general strike but only a minority eventually struck, mainly from the railroad shops. In Moose Jaw, shopcraft workers, street railway workers, civic employees, and some building trades workers provided the strike's backbone. Saskatoon's sympathy strike was the most successful in the province and included the Sutherland CPR shop workers, street railway workers, freight handlers, postal workers, teamsters, and at least eleven other local unions.

In Alberta, as elsewhere in the west, both Edmonton and Calgary workers had flirted with general strikes earlier. In Edmonton, the Trades and Labour Council had endorsed a general sympathy strike in October 1918 to aid the Canadian Brotherhood of Railway Employees. Events in 1919 led to a vigorous left-right struggle for control of the Edmonton TLC which culminated in late April in the expulsion of the Carpenters, led by SPC militant Joe Knight, Federated Labour Union, No. 49, which included Carl Berg and Sarah Johnson Knight, and the UMWA, Local 4070. As a result of the expulsions, the machinists and street railway workers also left the council. Despite this serious split, a successful sympathy strike was organized. The Federated Railway Trades (shop workers) introduced a motion in the ETLC calling for a meeting of all Edmonton trade unionists to plan for a strike. At that meeting the machinists successfully moved for a strike vote of all unions to report to a Central Strike Committee composed of representatives from both sides of the previous split. This vote resulted in a 1,676–506 vote for a strike with 34 of the 38 unions voting casting pro-strike ballots; eleven locals, however, failed to vote. Major strike support came from railway carmen, machinists, railroad shop workers, street railway workers, coal miners, building trades workers, and civic employees. The strike held until the Committee called it off and was marked by a minimum of disorder of any kind. This partially resulted from the tacit support the strike received from pro-labour Edmonton Mayor Joe Clarke, who RCMP security regarded as less than trustworthy.[43]

In Calgary the huge CPR shops were central both to the city's economy and to its trade union movement. Carmen, machinists, and all the other Railroad Shops Federated Trades exercised a considerable thrust for and experience of amalgamation. During the war years, the machinists came to dominate the CTLC and, as Taraska has argued, forged "a new working-class solidarity which led to class conscious action."[44] Militance and political lobbying on the part of munitions workers led to a Provincial Munitions Commission ruling that war contracts should go only to union shops. Thus by the end of 1915 the war shops were fully unionized. Skilled machinists' leaders such as Socialist and Labour Alderman A. Broach, R.J. Tallon, and H.H. Sharples came to dominate the local council and to push it successfully into local politics. Tallon became president of

Division 4 of the Railway Employees Department of the American Federation of Labor in 1917 which represented over 50,000 shopcraft workers on the Canadian railways. The Division, created to negotiate directly with the Railway War Board, entered negotiations with the CPR in April 1918. After heated negotiations the Board offered parity with the United States McAdoo Award which was rejected by an overwhelming Division 4 vote. Armed with this rejection, Division 4 leaders threatened a nation-wide rail strike. A series of walkouts led to dire threats from the government and the active intervention of the AFL which ordered Division 4 to accept the Board's offer. In September reluctant railway shop workers did so but in Calgary trouble flared up quickly when the CPR victimized some freight handlers who had not been formally allowed to enter Division 4. The freight handlers struck demanding the McAdoo Award. Calgary Labour Council unions voted in favour of a general strike in support of the freight handlers and a shopcraft workers' strike began on 11 October 1918. Street railway workers and civic employees also struck in sympathy. The threat to prosecute under Privy Council Order 2525 banning all strikes proved futile when Alberta courts refused to uphold it. A compromise, arranged by Senator Gideon Robertson, ended the affair in late October but general strike tactics had definitely been sustained. This set the scene for the following year's city-wide metal trades strike in April and the subsequent sympathy strike in May and June. Predictably the major support during the general strike came from the CPR Ogden shops and the Metal Trades Council. One outstanding feature of this strike was the creation of an extremely active Women's Labor Council.[45]

In British Columbia, the SPC-controlled Vancouver Trades and Labour Council (VTLC) responded more slowly and deliberately to events in Winnipeg. In mid-May VTLC President Harold Winch of the longshoremen and Secretary Victor Midgley wired Winnipeg congratulating the workers for their "cohesion" which "augured well for the future."[46] The following week they warned the Borden government that any military interference in Winnipeg would force them to call a general strike and simultaneously requested that all Vancouver trade unions take a vote on the question.[47] One week later they issued the following demands:

> Realizing that while there are many problems that face the workers that cannot be solved under capitalism, and that the end of the system is not yet: also realizing that the present situation is a political one, due to the action of the Dominion Government in the Winnipeg strike, and that as taking care of the soldiers ... are working class problems, the majority of the soldiers being members of the working class, therefore be it resolved that the following be the policy of the workers in Canada now on strike, or about to come on strike in support of the Winnipeg workers:
>
> 1. The reinstatement of the postal workers....
> 2. The immediate settlement of the postal workers' grievances.
> 3. The right of collective bargaining through any organization that the workers deem most suited to their needs.

4. Pensions for soldiers and their dependents.
5. A $2,000 gratuity for all those who served overseas.
6. Nationalization of all cold storage plants, abattoirs, elevators....
7. A six-hour day.

They closed by calling for the strike to continue until either the demands were granted or the government resigned and called new elections.[48] The strike, which commenced on 3 June, initially saw 37 unions out but this actually increased in the first few days of the strike. As elsewhere, it found its major support among the metal trades, in the shipyards, and on the street railway. Unique to Vancouver as a major port, however, was the militant support of longshoremen, sailors, and other marine workers. As in Calgary, a series of women's meetings met with enthusiastic support.[49]

While the SPC provided leadership and intellectual sustenance, their reluctance and fears were manifest. Even at the final preparation meeting on 2 June, William Pritchard posed the question less than enthusiastically:

> Their comrades were in the fight, and it was now a question of standing by them, and, if necessary, going down with them—or, later, going down by themselves. His advice was: "If you are going to drown—drown splashing!"[50]

Two weeks later at an SPC educational, W.W. Lefeaux explained that party policy did not include promoting strikes, only analyzing and explaining them.[51] The strike ended in confusion a week after Winnipeg's return to work. A recommendation from the strike committee to go back earlier had been voted down by rank-and-file militants.[52] The strike committee's final report to the VTLC indicated that 45 unions had struck over the course of the strike, but admitted the initial vote had been a narrow 3,305–2,499 victory. Although 57 per cent of those voting favoured the strike, the under 6,000 votes represented only 40 per cent of VTLC members.[53]

In Prince Rupert a sympathy strike had commenced earlier on 29 May when railroad workers left their jobs, while in Victoria the sympathy strike developed very slowly with considerable reluctance being shown by Victoria TLC leaders. Nevertheless almost 5,000 workers left their jobs on 23 June, following the lead of the Metal Trades Council, and remained out until early July.[54] A smaller sympathy strike also took place in New Westminster.

These Canadian events captured the attention of European militants. On 14 June 1919, in Turin, Italy, Antonio Gramsci described "The Revolutionary Tide" which had brought "the struggle on a world scale." "The revolution can no longer be exorcized by democratic swindlers, nor crushed by mercenaries without a conscience," the Italian revolutionary argued. Gramsci's youthful optimism stemmed partially from his view of current world struggles and specifically of those in Canada where, he argued, "industrial strikes have taken on the overt character of a bid to install a soviet regime." Meanwhile, in Glasgow, John MacLean enthused about "the great Canadian strike," which, he argued, had stimulated American labour's "general rank-and-file strike which terrorized the union leaders."[55] While these claims appear exaggerated in retrospect, the important point here is that 1919 was an international event, or as MacLean termed it: "class war on an international scale." It was no more limited to Canada than it was to Winnipeg within Canada. In the years from 1917 to 1920, a working-class movement whose internationalism had been destroyed in 1914, ironically responded with an international surge of class militancy which knew no national limits and few, if any, historical precedents.

One little-known example of the international nature of the uprising can be drawn from Newfoundland, then a self-governing British colony in the North Atlantic. The story of Newfoundland's working class largely remains to be written but in the years 1917 to 1920 at least it resembled closely the Canadian and international pattern of revolt. In the immediate pre-war years Newfoundland fishermen and loggers had commenced to organize. The meteoric rise of the Fishermen's Protective Union, representing both groups of workers, led not only to industrial gains but to great political success and legislative reforms. In the later war years, an economic crisis which revolved around profiteering and rampant inflation led to an investigation which found that the St. John's merchants had indeed engaged in rapacious price gouging. In 1917, St. John's workers created the Newfoundland Industrial Workers' Association (NIWA), an avowedly industrial unionist organization which immediately proceeded to organize workers across the island. Thus, Newfoundland workers conformed to the international wave of industrial unionist unrest. Equally the NIWA found its leadership in the railway shops of the Reid Newfoundland Company and among local socialists and drew its membership from St. John's metal shops and the foundry. Its major industrial battle against Reid Newfoundland involved a three-week strike of 500 railway workers in spring 1918 which involved threats of an island-wide walkout and extensive sympathetic activities in St. John's.[56]

The international literature on the post-war upsurge has blossomed of late and important articles by Larry Peterson and James Cronin have chronicled these red years in rich international comparison.[57] As has often been the case, the comparative insights offered by international labour and working-class history open some interesting avenues for investigation. First, however, let us eliminate a few dead ends of previous Canadian investigation. In the aftermath of the strike, the *B.C. Federationist* concluded: "The first lesson that workers must learn is that only by organization and cohesion, not only in each centre, but throughout the country, can they resist the encroachments of capital."[58] Similar statements have often been used to buttress a "western revolt" notion of 1919, arguing that only workers west of the Lakehead behaved "radically." The lesson, however, surely lay not in a regional understanding of the revolt but rather in the reverse—namely, the necessity of perfecting nation-wide organization. The defection of the AFL, the TLC, and much of the international union leadership had left the working-class movement fragmented and, although the SPC leadership tried valiantly to fill the gap, the consequent breakdown in communications and lack of a national focus proved costly. While the established weekly labour press and the emergent daily strike bulletins were remarkably vibrant and blanketed the country with an extraordinary and rich range of labour opinion, they carried little national coverage. Thus workers in Vancouver knew little of Amherst, and District 18 miners lacked direct contact with their Nova Scotia District 26 comrades. The revolt was not western, however, it was national; but the size and regional fragmentation of the country proved a major impediment to systematic national organization and co-ordination.

Second, there is no doubt that the AFL and TLC leadership, not to speak of the railroad running trades leadership, played reprehensible roles. They undoubtedly exploited their image as respectable labour leaders who believed in the sanctity of contracts. We must add, however, that this ideological and political battleground existed within the North American labour movement everywhere, not only on both sides of the border but also at both ends of each country. The struggle within the TLC so often depicted as east/west was not so simple. At the 1917 TLC convention in Ottawa the debate on the executive's collapse on the issue of conscription and their decision not to resist the law once enacted revealed no simple regional vote. In a lengthy debate 28 delegates spoke with only nine fully supporting the executive of which only two actually supported conscription. The nineteen speakers who opposed the executive included eleven eastern delegates and eight westerners.[59] Eastern opponents included moderate Toronto socialists John Bruce and Jimmy Simpson and Montreal radical machinists Tom Cassidy and Dick Kerrigan. Cassidy engaged in the debate's major rhetorical flight, albeit prescient in light of events in 1919:

> When the machine guns are placed on the streets of Winnipeg to shoot down strikers, also in Montreal, Vancouver Island, and other places, it shows that these organized soldiers are willing to shoot their fellow workingmen. I am not afraid to die.... The masters of the world must be whipped.... We have only one enemy and that is the international capitalist class.

When the vote finally came the major amendment, introduced by Alberta leaders Farmilo and Ross, failed narrowly 101 to 111. Since there were only 44 western delegates present, it should be clear that there was considerable eastern opposition to conscription as well. Indeed when a conciliatory division on conscription itself was taken only ten delegates voted in favour of the calling-up of manpower.

At the 1918 TLC convention in Quebec where seething western discontent eventually led to plans for the Calgary Conference of March 1919 similar non-regional divisions were evident. Westerners represented only 45 of 440 delegates. While radical motions were consistently lost and elections to executive positions saw moderates emerge victorious, nevertheless there were far more votes for radical positions than simply those of the west. For example, the one roll call vote on a Winnipeg motion to release all conscientious objectors from prison was narrowly defeated 99 to 90. The minority radical vote was composed of 58 eastern delegates and 32 western, while the conservative vote included two westerners and 97 easterners. The clear lesson to be learned was that the west should send more delegates.[60]

When the TLC met in Hamilton in fall 1919 the battle between craft unionism and the OBU for control of the labour movement was raging. In that context and with OBU members and sympathizers either departed or expelled, it should not surprise us that the Convention witnessed much red-bashing. Yet there was also an undercurrent of support for industrial unionism and disgust for the TLC's failure to support Winnipeg workers. There was vociferous eastern criticism of the TLC leadership. Toronto delegate Birks denounced "organized officialdom within the trade union movement as something opposed to the spirit and mind of the rank and file."[61] District 26 leader J.B. McLachlan introduced a motion for a general strike demanding the restoration of freedom of speech and of the press and the repeal of the Criminal Code amendments passed during the Winnipeg General Strike.[62] Toronto carpenter McCallum, speaking "as a member of the working-class movement," argued that craft unions were outmoded and asked "Why ban men who demand change?"[63] St. Catharines' delegate Grant "advocated the adoption of the shop steward as the most effective form of organization."[64] Later Ottawa stonecutters introduced a motion for broad joint strikes and denounced their international for ordering them back to work during a general building trades strike in May 1919. As one delegate argued, "the boss beat us because we were divided into small locals." Winnipeg's George Armstrong availed himself of this opportunity to condemn "the machinery of the AFL which made massed action impossible."[65]

Similar battles went on within the international unions as well. For example, the 1920 convention of the IAM saw bitter debate about the expulsion of OBU supporters. Montreal and Toronto machinists led a losing but fiery effort to defend their comrades.[66]

The fight in the Canadian labour movement thus rested on different views of labour's future organization. The western SPC leaders looked to the OBU as the way forward. Despite much historical debate about the intellectual orientation of the OBU, which I will not detail here, the OBU was certainly not syndicalist. An organization led by the SPC could never have been anti-political and thus the supposed "turn" to politics after Winnipeg is nonsense. The political aims of the SPC never varied.[67]

The strike wave, of course, gained SPC leadership only begrudgingly for that very reason. The SPC doubted the wisdom of the industrial actions but had no choice but to lend its leadership skills to the working-class militancy which engulfed the nation. They never, however, viewed 1919 as a nascent revolution.

They were politically too experienced for that. While Joe Knight and Carl Berg in Edmonton allowed their rhetoric to exceed the SPC line in the heady days of June 1919, the leading Vancouver comrades never lost sight of the limitations of the situation. Thus, *The Soviet* could argue, displaying the syndicalist tendencies of Knight and Berg:

> In Winnipeg and Toronto today the same condition is observable. The General Strike by paralyzing industry, paralyzes government. The Strike Committees are forced to rule the cities, to "exempt" certain industries and services in order to provide for elementary human needs; they must police the cities themselves. Willy-nilly "this production for use and not for profit" is undertaken for the benefit of the workers. It displaces the capitalist government which operated for the benefit of the bourgeoisie....[68]

Vancouver's *Red Flag,* on the other hand, was consistent and cautious. The OBU, it noted, simply represented:

> ... a decided urge towards industrial unionism which has lately become very insistent. We have referred to this movement several times and have criticized it and analyzed it. That is our function. We don't initiate movements, we seek to understand them. We realize that beyond a very transitory influence, great movements are not caused by individuals, they are the result of conditions.[69]

Later, after the Winnipeg General Strike has commenced, they warned:

> It may be that some half-baked socialist is voicing Revolutionary phrases in Winnipeg. We doubt it. We know that a bunch of workers who are able to keep their heads in spite of the extreme provocation to which they are being subjected will not allow any muddle head from their own ranks to precipitate trouble.[70]

Simultaneously, the *B.C. Federationist* editorialized:

> Neither the Seattle nor the Winnipeg strikes were revolutionary upheavals. They were strikes in the one instance for higher wages, and in the later case, for the recognition of the right to collective bargaining. Is that a revolutionary strike?

In that same editorial they cautioned against violence and promoted discipline "because the ruling class have the guns, and if blood is shed, it will be the blood of the working class." In a revolution, they continued, it was necessary to "control the means of coercion," and there was no such opportunity in Canada.[71] A week later they again emphasized. "The strike is not a revolutionary strike," and argued instead: "The issue is political. The workers must take the matter up on those lines, and wring political concessions from the master class, and beat them at their own game."[72] All of this fits well with William Pritchard's now famous aphorism: "Only fools try to make revolutions, wise men conform to them."[73]

Ironically, Aaron Mosher, the president of the Canadian Brotherhood of Railroad Employees, shared the SPC perspective to the degree that he recognized that radical leaders could not be held responsible for the labour revolt. In a letter volunteering his services to Prime Minister Borden, he noted:

> Numerous telegrams we are receiving from our local branches throughout the entire west asking authority to strike and the fact that some of our members have gone on strike after authorization was denied them, leads me to believe that it is not just a few labour agitators at Winnipeg who are causing the unrest. In most cases, I am sure the rank and file in the labour movement are forcing the leaders to take the stand they have taken, and it would be well to look into this phase of the situation.[74]

Commissioner Perry of the Royal North West Mounted Police argued similarly in his "Memorandum on Revolutionary Tendencies in Western Canada:"

> At the foundation of all this agitation is the general restlessness and dissatisfaction. The greater number of labour men, and probably of the community as a whole, are in an uncertain, apprehensive, nervous and irritable temper. Perhaps these agitators are but the foam on the wave.[75]

Let us take Mosher's advice and Perry's metaphor and close this paper with a consideration of the causes of the "wave" of unrest.

Eric Hobsbawm, some 20 years ago, suggested that:

> The habit of industrial solidarity must be learned ... so must the common sense of demanding concessions when conditions are favourable, not when hunger suggests it. There is thus a natural time lag, before workers become an "effective labour movement."[76]

Writing ten years later, Michelle Perrot argued: "The strike is a weapon of conquest, the major instrument of a working class more and more desirous and capable of improving its lot, more and more fascinated by the possibilities of the strike."[77] By 1919, Canadian workers had certainly become an "effective labour movement" and they also had developed in wartime conditions a considerable fascination with "the possibilities of the strike." Indeed, as this paper argued earlier, the 1919 revolt represents a return, albeit at a higher level of intensity, to the pre-war pattern of conflict. This intensification was fueled by the addition of new groups of workers to the struggle. These new groups included public service workers, west coast loggers, and previously unorganized or at best partially organized groups of industrial workers such as those in Toronto's and Montreal's packing houses and garment shops. Among these last groups of workers, as also in Winnipeg and certainly as in the coal mines of District 18, another crucial new ingredient was present—ethnic solidarity. In 1919, momentarily at least, the divisiveness of ethnicity was surpassed in the struggle. A Canadian working-class movement which had been swamped with new immigrants from eastern and southern Europe in the pre-war years had matured, coalesced, and to some degree at least, commenced the process of incorporating the new workers into the movement. These "new" Canadian workers, as we are only now coming to realize, often were not "new" to the working class. Indeed Finns, Jews, and Ukrainians often arrived with a more extensive socialist background than their much celebrated English and Scot immigrant comrades. A brief Winnipeg example demonstrates this point poignantly. In the aftermath of the strike a number of "aliens" were transported to Kapuskasing, Ontario to await deportation. All had been arrested in the riot on Bloody Saturday. The *Strikers' Defense Bulletin* provided short biographies of thirteen ethnic workers. One German sheet metal worker joined twelve east Europeans hailing from Galicia (seven), Bukovina (two), "Austrian Poland," the Ukraine, and Russia. Occupationally, they included two boilermakers' helpers, a carpenter, a teamster, and eight labourers. Of the labourers, three were unemployed and the others worked for the city, on the railroad, in a restaurant, in the railway shops, and for Swift's. This state-selected group of foreign-born Winnipeg workers demonstrates graphically the ethnic presence in the Winnipeg strike. This presence was not unique to Winnipeg.[78]

In addition to the new ethnic component of the labour movement there was also a more pronounced presence of women workers. The new involvement of public sector workers brought groups of telephone operators and civic employees, while organization also spread to department store clerks and waitresses, and, of course, into the heavily female garment trades. In Winnipeg, Toronto, Calgary, Vancouver, and elsewhere women workers played important roles in the 1919 strikes, both as strikers and as members of Women's Labour Leagues and Councils which, in some cases, emerged during the general strikes.[79]

Thus the structural transformation of the working class generated by the Second Industrial Revolution and by the ongoing process of the concentration and centralization of capital, which on some levels weakened the working-class movement, simultaneously stimulated an enhanced capacity for collective resistance at the workplace. Thus, scientific management and other managerial innovations, which attacked what Robert Morris has usefully termed the "moral economy of the skilled man," began the process of generating an industrial union response.[80]

The rapid urban expansion generated by monopoly capitalist growth also played its role in the revolt. The working-class neighbourhoods of Toronto's and Montreal's garment districts or those associated with the huge metal plants and railroad shops in those cities and in the west became centres of workers' lives and slowly began to generate working-class community institutions. Northend Winnipeg is perhaps the most celebrated example, but all Canadian cities developed equivalent districts. While sometimes ethnically segregated, these areas often took on instead occupational associations as in Toronto's stockyard area or even Toronto's Junction district. In this period before the automobile's dispersal of the working class, a relationship continued to exist between domicile and workplace. We need to know much more about these communities and their role in sustaining working-class opposition. Neighbourhood may have played another role as well. Witness after witness before the Mathers

Commission complained of poor and expensive housing in Canadian towns and cities. This near-universal complaint also undoubtedly contributed to the working-class revolt of 1919 and helped to widen it beyond simple workplace issues. Thus the general and sympathetic strikes extended beyond organized workers to embrace many workers outside the unions.

Also helping to widen the conflict in a similar fashion were the inter-related issues of inflation, the cost of living, and war profiteering. Recent econometric work on real wages in the first three decades of the twentieth century confirms that "real wage rates declined significantly during the First World War."[81] The new national index compiled by Bertram and Percy shows a low of 85.5 in 1917 (1913 equals 100), while Eleanor Bartlett's work on Vancouver shows the low point as either 1917 or 1918, depending on the choice of indices. What is clear in these studies and in earlier studies of Montreal, Toronto, and Winnipeg is that workers suffered a real decline on a national basis during the second half of the war. These econometric data provide the hard confirmation, for those who still need it, of the testimony of hundreds of workers before the Mathers Commission. They complained continuously of high food prices, of blatant profiteering, and of bureaucratic ineptitude, as well as of inflationary rents and inadequate housing. These complaints united all workers in ways that the more limited workplace battles sometimes failed to. Moreover the political dynamite in this situation was the clear dichotomy between a government which refused "fair wages" and conscripted manpower, and a government which allowed blatant profiteering and refused to conscript wealth. The transparency of the relationship between capital and the state in the war years allowed socialist propaganda to reach a growing and increasingly sympathetic audience. Demands for nationalization of abbatoirs, cold storage plants, and elevators, which might at first seem surprising, must be viewed in this context. As Cronin has argued in the European context, the coincidence of these consumer demands with intense struggles at the point of production helped to deepen class conflict into something approaching conscious class struggle.[82]

The violent repression in Winnipeg, the strike trials and the martyrdom of the leaders, the creation of the Royal Canadian Mounted Police, the conscious victimization of thousands of strikers, the TLC's retreat into craft exclusivism, all suggest a bleak aftermath and a story of defeat.[83] Yet as late as September 1919, Commissioner A.B. Perry of the new RCMP, an acute observer of labour radicalism, warned of the continuing "general state of unrest" which he found "far from satisfactory." Further, he cautioned:

> The leaders of the recent movement are determined, resourceful men; that their aims and objects are revolutionary in character has been clearly established. They have sustained a temporary setback, but to think we have heard the last of them is only resting in a false sense of security.[84]

The war on the labour left did continue and proved successful in the short term.

Yet the seeds of industrial unionism would survive to sprout later. Moreover, if the 1920s and early 1930s appear as a period of relative national labour quiescence, the phenomenon is far from unique. The working-class movement in other advanced industrial countries also slipped into what Yves Lequin has recently termed "the great silence," a period which stretched from the end of the great revolt until the resurgence of industrial unionism in the mid to late Depression years.[85] The fascination with industrial councils and various other welfare capitalist schemes which was so evident in the Mathers Commission and in the National Industrial Conference also had ambiguous results. The seemingly tame industrial councils often provided the basis for the new thrust to real industrial unions when the time was again propitious for working-class struggle.[86]

Defeats should not be confused with failure and perhaps the SPC leaders should be allowed to write their own epitaph. In Winnipeg, F.W. derived the following "Lessons of the Strike:"

> This is only a local momentary defeat on a world-wide battle front. Remember that permanently we cannot lose. Every struggle ... a lesson in class solidarity. Every brutal act of suppression brings capitalism nearer to its inevitable doom.... Courage, fellow workers. Study your class position and you cannot lose.[87]

Meanwhile in Vancouver, Comrade C.K. addressed "The Burning Question of Trade Unionism," echoing a Daniel DeLeon pamphlet title. Developing a "dialectical" position against the old "philosophy of misery" school, he argued that trade unions must be viewed not simply as they are but rather as they might develop. The events of 1919, he wrote, led inexorably to the workers' recognition of the need for political action. He closed on an optimistic note which, although too reminiscent of Second International evolutionism, nevertheless might be a message for all of us in this period of renewed attacks on labour:

> There is a benevolent appearing old gentleman wearing long white whiskers clad in a nightshirt and carrying a scythe. He is known as "father time." The fact is not generally known but he is a socialist of the most pronounced revolutionary type. He is very busy among the trade unions these days. He is working for us.[88]

Notes

1. Royal Commission on Industrial Relations, Evidence, Victoria, B.C., 26 April 1919, 242–3. (Henceforth cited as Mathers Commission.) One SPC view of the Commission is *Causes of Industrial Unrest* (Winnipeg 1919), a pamphlet published by SPC Local No. 3.

2. Mathers Commission, Evidence, Edmonton, Alta., 6 May 1919, 987–90.

3. *Ibid.,* Moose Jaw, Sask., 9 May 1919, 1330–42.

4. *Ibid.,* Sudbury, Ont., 17 May 1919, 1968–72.

5. *Ibid.,* Toronto, Ont., 28 May 1919, 2940–4.

6. *Ibid.,* Hamilton, Ont., 21 May 1919, 2261–81.

7. *Ibid.*, Montreal, Que., 29 May 1919, 3255–60.

8. For a partial reconstruction of this evidence from newspaper sources, see Nolan Reilly, "The General Strike in Amherst, Nova Scotia, 1919," *Acadiensis,* 9 (1980), 56–77; see also *Eastern Federationist,* 14 June 1919.

9. Mathers Commission, Evidence, New Glasgow, N.S., 5 June 1919, 3533–55.

10. *Ibid.*, Halifax, 4 June 1919, 4355–9. On Dane, see Clifford Rose, *Four Years with the Demon Rum* (Fredericton 1980), 5–9, 83.

11. *Ibid.*, Calgary, Alta., 3 May 1919, 786.

12. *Ibid.*, Saskatoon, Sask., 7 May 1919, 1036.

13. *Ibid.*, Regina, Sask., 8 May 1919, 1191.

14. *Ibid.*, Montreal, Que., 29 May 1919, 3163.

15. See Russell Hann's excellent introduction to Daphne Read, comp., *The Great War and Canadian Society* (Toronto 1978), 9–38.

16. David Montgomery, "Strikes in Nineteenth-Century America," *Social Science History,* 4 (1980), 100.

17. All strike data in this paper are drawn from recalculations for the Historical Atlas of Canada, volume III. These recalculations are based on the addition of Maritime provinces material compiled from local sources by Ian McKay of Dalhousie University and on a careful re-examination of all the "incomplete" files available in the PAC, Department of Labour, Strikes and Lockouts files. This work commenced by Peter DeLottinville has been carried through to completion by Douglas Cruikshank. These data currently being compiled for publication in the Atlas provides an entirely new data series for Canadian strike activity. For a report on McKay's work, see his "Strikes in the Maritimes, 1900–1914," *Acadiensis,* 13 (1983), 3–46.

18. David Bercuson, *Confrontation at Winnipeg: Labour Industrial Relations, and the General Strike* (Montreal 1974) and Reilly, "The General Strike."

19. Craig Heron and Bryan D. Palmer, "Through the Prism of the Strike: Industrial Conflict in Southern Ontario, 1901–14," *Canadian Historical Review,* 58 (1977), 423–58.

20. Unless other sources are cited this account draws on PAC, Department of Labour, Strikes and Lockouts files as well as on the original published version, *Labour Gazette,* 20 (1920), 267–94.

21. For a brief account, see Terry Copp, *Anatomy of Poverty* (Toronto 1974), 134–5.

22. *Gazette* (Montreal), 28 May 1919.

23. *Ibid.*, 6 June 1919.

24. *Ibid.*, 20 June 1919. For a brief reminiscence of the emerging Montreal red world, see Catherine Vance, *Not by Gods, But by People: The Story of Bella Hall Gauld* (Toronto 1968), 19–44. On the Vickers strike see *Ontario Labor News.* (Toronto), 1 July 1919.

25. On Cobalt, see Brian F. Hogan, *Cobalt: Year of the Strike, 1919* (Cobalt 1978); on Kirkland Lake, see Laurel Sefton MacDowell, *'Remember Kirkland Lake': The Gold Miners' Strike of 1941–42* (Toronto 1983). 58–60, and Wayne Roberts, ed., *Miner's Life: Bob Miner and Union Organizing in Timmins, Kirkland Lake and Sudbury* (Hamilton 1979), 1–2.

26. J.T. Montague, "Trade Unionism in the Canadian Meat Packing Industry," unpublished Ph.D. thesis, University of Toronto, 1950, 31–8 and George Sayers Bain, "The United Packinghouse, Food and Allied Workers," M.A. thesis, University of Manitoba, 1964, 35–67.

27. *Machinists Monthly Journal,* 31 (April 1919), 330, cited in Donald Wright, "Belshazzar, the Medes, and the Persians: The Rise and Fall of the Metal Trades Strike in Toronto, 1919," unpublished paper, Dalhousie University, 1979. Planning for 1919 took place at the second Provincial Convention of the IAM in late November 1918. See *Labour Gazette,* 19 (1919), 51–2. See also *Ontario Labor News,* 1 May-1 July 1919.

28. For details see David Jay Bercuson, ed., *Alberta's Coal Industry 1919* (Calgary 1978); Bercuson, *Fools and Wise Men: The Rise and Fall of the One Big Union* (Toronto 1978), 196–214; Allen Seager, "Socialists and Workingmen: The Western Canadian Coal Miners' Movement, 1900–1920," paper presented at American Historical Association Meetings, December 1982.

29. Nolan Reilly, "The General Strike," his "Notes on the Amherst General Strike and the One Big Union," *Bulletin of the Committee on Canadian Labour History,* 3 (Spring 1977), 5–8, and his "The Emergence of Class Consciousness in Industrial Nova Scotia: A Study of Amherst, 1891–1925," Ph.D. thesis, Dalhousie University, 1982. See also *Eastern Federationist,* 24 May-21 June 1919.

30. Borden Papers, PAC, MG 26 H vol. 113 pt. 1 and pt. 2, file OC 564 (henceforth Borden Papers.) See, for example, N.W. Rowell to White, Toronto. 26 May 1919; White to Rowell, Ottawa, 26 May 1919; T.L. Church to Borden. Toronto, 27 May 1919; Church to Borden, 31 May 1919; Church to Borden, 2 June 1919.

31. The literature on the munitions industry, the IMB, and labour unrest is growing, but for contrasting views, see: D.J. Bercuson, "Organized Labour and the Imperial Munitions Board." *Relations Industrielles,* 28 (1974), 602–16; Peter Rider. "The Imperial Munitions Board and its Relationship to Government, Business, and Labour, 1914–1920," Ph.D. thesis, University of Toronto, 1974, esp. ch. 9: Michael Bliss, *A Canadian Millionaire: The Life and Business Times of Sir Joseph Flavelle, Bart., 1858–1939* (Toronto 1978), esp. 270–2, 280–4, 320–5, 378–81; Myer Siemiatycki, "Munitions and Labour Militancy: The 1916 Hamilton Machinists' Strike," *Labour / Le Travailleur,* 3 (1978), 131–51; Craig Heron, "The Crisis of the Craftsman: Hamilton's Metal Workers in the Early Twentieth Century," *Labour / Le Travailleur,* 6 (1980), 7–48; and, for Toronto metal trades background, Wayne Roberts, "Toronto Metal Workers and the Second Industrial Revolution, 1889–1914," *Labour / Le Travailleur,* 6 (1980), 49–72.

32. TTLC, *Minutes,* 2. 16 March, 6, 20 April 1916, including correspondence from Draper and Watters of the TLC.

33. Siemiatycki, "Munitions and Labour Militancy," 141.

34. TTLC, *Minutes,* 1. 13, 15 May 1919; *Ontario Labor News,* 15 May 1919.

35. Borden Papers, Rowell to White, 26 May 1919 and White to Rowell, 26 May 1919. Statistics from *Ontario Labor News,* 1 June 1919.

36. *Ibid.,* Church to Borden, 27 May 1919 and "Minutes of Toronto Meeting."

37. *Ibid.,* Borden to R.O. Hawtrey, 2 June 1919.

38. Low estimate is Department of Labour; high estimate is given by Mayor Church in letter to Borden, 2 June 1919. The *Globe* decided on 8000. See *Globe,* 30 May-7 June 1919.

39. TTLC, *Minutes,* 7, 21 August, 3 October, 6 November, 4, 18 December 1919, 22 January, 19 February 1920; Michael J. Piva, "The Toronto District Labour Council and Independent Political Action, 1900–21," *Labour/Le Travailleur,* 4 (1979), 126–8. See also *The New Democracy* (Hamilton), 31 July, 7 August 1919.

40. Data on additional Saskatchewan locations from W.J.C. Cherwinski, "Organized Labour in Saskatchewan: The TLC Years, 1905–45," unpublished Ph.D. thesis, University of Alberta, 1972, chapter 2, and his "Saskatchewan Organized Labour and the Winnipeg General Strike, 1919," unpublished paper, Memorial University of Newfoundland, 1976; for Prince Rupert, see *B.C. Federationist,* 30 May 1919; for Radville through Souris, see Walter Scott Ryder, "Canada's Industrial Crisis of 1919," unpublished M.A. thesis, University of British Columbia, 1920, 36. How reliable this last list of whistle stops (literally) is, isn't clear. Ryder, however, was writing in the immediate aftermath of the event and most of these are railway junction towns where there were probably significant groups of shopcraft workers.

41. On Brandon, see A.E. Smith, *All My Life* (Toronto 1949), ch. 3–6: Kathleen O'Gorman Wormsbecker, "The Rise and Fall of the Labour Political Movement in Manitoba, 1919–1927," M.A. thesis, Queen's University, 1977, esp. ch. 2: Brandon Trades and Labor Council, *Strike Bulletin,* 21-31 May 1919; *Western Labor News* (Winnipeg), 7, 9 June 1919. On the earlier Brandon strike, see *Confederate* (Brandon). 4 April 1919 and *Western Labor News,* 25 April, 7 May 1919.

42. On Saskatchewan see Cherwinski, "Organized Labour," ch. 2 and his "Organized Labour and the Winnipeg General Strike."

43. For the Edmonton strike, see William R. Askin, "Labour Unrest in Edmonton and District and its Coverage by the Edmonton Press, 1918–19," unpublished M.A. thesis, University of Alberta, 1973 and Carl Betke, "Influence and Community: The Ambiguity of Labour Organization in Edmonton, 1906–1921," unpublished paper presented at the Canadian-American Urban Development Conference. University of Guelph, August 1982. See also *The One Big Union Bulletin* (Edmonton), 25 March 1919; *Edmonton Strike Bulletin,* 5, 11 June 1919; and *Edmonton Free Press.* 12 April-12 July 1919.

44. For Calgary, see Elizabeth Ann Taraska, "The Calgary Craft Union Movement, 1900–20," unpublished M.A. thesis, University of Calgary, 1975, quotation at 46 and *Calgary Strike Bulletin,* 30 May-24 June 1919.

45. *Ibid.,* ch. 5 and *Labour Gazette,* 18 (1918), 615, 759, 857, 1005 and 820, 974–5.

46. *B.C. Federationist,* 16 May 1919 and Vancouver Trades and Labor Council, Executive Minutes, 15 May 1919. See also Paul Phillips, *No Power Greater* (Vancouver 1967), 80–1; *Strike Bulletin* (Vancouver), 9-26 June 1919; *The Camp Worker* (Vancouver), 2 June 1919; *The Vancouver Citizen,* 16 June-3 July 1919; and *The Critic,* 26 April-12 July 1919.

47. *Ibid.,* 23 May 1919; Borden Papers, G.H. Deane to Borden, Vancouver, 27 May 1919, J. Kavanagh, Secretary VTLC, to Borden, 27 May 1919; and VTLC, Executive Minutes, 22, 27, 28 May 1919.

48. *B.C. Federationist,* 30 May 1919.

49. For list of unions supporting the strike, see *Ibid.,* 6 June 1919. On women, see *Strike Bulletin,* 16 June 1919. It is worth noting the *Citizen,* the viciously anti-union publication of the Citizens' Committee, propagandized actively for women's support. See, for only two examples, "To the Women," 20 June 1919 and "Women! With Whom?" 21 June 1919.

50. *B.C. Federationist,* 6 June 1919.

51. *Ibid.,* 20 June 1919.

52. *Ibid.,* 27 June, 4 July 1919.

53. *Ibid.,* 4 July 1919. For another brief account of the Vancouver Strike, see Elaine Bernard, "Vancouver 1919," *Democrat* 20 (June-July 1980).

54. Phillips, *No Power Greater,* 80–1. See also the short memoir by machinist Arthur J. Turner, *Somewhere—A Perfect Place* (Vancouver 1981), 22–6, for a brief memory of the Victoria Sympathy Strike. See also *Semi-Weekly Tribune* (Victoria), 14 April-30 June 1919 and Victoria Trades and Labor Council, Minutes, esp. 9 June 1919.

55. Antonio Gramsci, *Selections from Political Writings (1910–1920)* (New York 1977). 61; Nan Milton, ed., *John MacLean: In the Rapids of Revolution* (London 1978), 190, 137.

56. On Newfoundland, see Melvin Baker, Robert Cuff, Bill Gillespie, *Workingmen's St. John's: Aspects of Social History in the Early 1900s* (St. John's 1982). Also Robert Cuff, "The Quill and the Hammer: Labour Activism in Newfoundland and Nova Scotia. 1917–1925," Honours B.A. thesis, Department of History, Memorial University of Newfoundland, 1980; Bill Gillespie, "A History of the Newfoundland Federation of Labour, 1936–63," unpublished M.A. thesis, Memorial University of Newfoundland. 1980; John Joy, "The Growth and Development of Trades and Manufacturing in St. John's, 1870–1914," unpublished M.A. thesis, Memorial University of Newfoundland, 1977; and Ian McDonald, "W.F. Coaker and the Fishermen's Protective Union in Newfoundland Politics, 1909–1925," unpublished Ph.D. thesis, University of London, 1971.

57. Larry Peterson, "The One Big Union in International Perspective: Revolutionary Industrial Unionism 1900–1925," *Labour/Le Travailleur,* 7 (1981), 41–66; James E. Cronin, "Labor Insurgency and Class Formation: Comparative Perspectives on the Crisis of 1917–1920 in Europe," *Social Science History,* 4 (1980), 125–152.

58. *B.C. Federationist,* 4 July 1919.

59. Trades and Labour Congress of Canada, *Proceedings,* 1917, 141–55. For a good example of similar fights in the U.S., see Cecelia F. Bucki, "Dilution and Craft Tradition: Bridgeport, Connecticut, Munition Workers, 1915–1919," *Social Science History,* 4 (1980), 105–124. Also see John Laslett. *Labor and the Left* (New York 1970), *passim.*

60. *Ibid.,* 1918, 138–9. Note that my count is slightly at variance with Gerald Friesen, 'Yours in Revolt': Regionalism, Socialism, and the Western Canadian Labour Movement," *Labour/Le Travailleur,* 1 (1976), 141. The point, of course, remains the same. His count, however, is 29 west and 51 east vs. 3 west and 81 east.

61. *Ibid.,* 1919, 165.

62. TLC, *Proceedings,* 1919, 156–7. See David Frank, "The Cape Breton Coal Miners, 1917–1926," unpublished Ph.D. thesis, Dalhousie University, 1979, 315–19.

63. *Ibid.,* 166.

64. *Ibid.*

65. *Ibid.,* 190–2.

66. On the IAM, see *Proceedings,* 1920, especially 129–40, 559–62, 248–56, 187–98, 380. See also *Bulletin* (Winnipeg), April-August 1919.

67. The syndicalist "accusation" has come ironically from both ends of the ideological spectrum over time. Gideon Robertson, for example, simply, and I believe sincerely, equated the OBU with the IWW. Later communist historians, refusing to forgive Bob Russell's refusal to join the CPC, have made the same charge. More recently some historians have repeated the error, while not necessarily sharing either Robertson's or the CPC's political position. See, for example, *Canada's Party of Socialism* (Toronto: Progress, 1982), 32–3; James Foy, "Gideon Robertson: Conservative Minister of Labour, 1917–1921," unpublished M.A. thesis, University of Ottawa, 1972; Bercuson, *Confrontation at Winnipeg,* 89; Bercuson, *Fools and Wise Men, passim;* A. Ross McCormack, *Reformers, Rebels, and Revolutionaries: The Western Canadian Radical Movement 1899–1919* (Toronto 1977), 98, 112–3, 143 ff: Martin Robin, *Radical Politics and Canadian Labour 1880–1930* (Kingston 1968), 150–1, 171–7, 275. This argument is not unique to this paper, of course. See Peterson, "One Big Union," 53–8 and Friesen, 'Yours in Revolt,'," 139–40 for similar interpretations.

68. *The Soviet* (Edmonton), 1, 13 (20 June 1919).

69. *Red Flag* (Vancouver), 1, 9 (22 March 1919).

70. *Ibid.,* 1, 18 (24 May 1919).

71. *B.C. Federationist,* 23 May 1919.

72. *Ibid.,* 30 May 1919.

73. Gloria Montero, *We Stood Together: First Hand Accounts of Dramatic Events in Canada's Labour Past* (Toronto 1979), 14. Also, of course, the source of Bercuson's title.

74. Borden Papers, A.R. Mosher to Borden, 29 May 1919.

75. Department of National Defence, RG 24, vol. 3985, N-S-C 1055-2-21, *Secret.* "Memorandum on Revolutionary Tendencies in Western Canada," prepared by Assistant Comptroller, RNWMP.

76. E.J. Hobsbawm, *Labouring Men* (London 1964), 144.

77. Michelle Perrot, *Les Ouvriers en grève, France 1871–90,* Tome I (Paris 1974), 64.

78. The new literature on ethnic workers is already too voluminous to list, but note especially Varpu Lindstrom-Best's work on the Finns and Orest T. Martynowych's essays on Ukrainian socialism. See, also, the special issue of *Canadian Ethnic Studies,* 10 (1978) on ethnic radicalism. For the Winnipeg data, see *Strikers' Defense Bulletin,* 1, 4 (27 August 1919). For additional Winnipeg evidence see Donald Avery, "The Radical Alien and the Winnipeg General Strike of 1919," in Carl Berger and Ramsay Cook, eds., *The West and the Nation* (Toronto 1976), 209–31 and his "Ethnic Loyalties and the Proletarian Revolution," in Jorgen Dahlie and Tissa Fernando, eds., *Ethnicity, Power, and Politics in Canada* (Toronto 1981), 68–93.

79. On Vancouver telephone operators and the General Strike see Elaine Bernard. *The Long Distance Feeling: A History of the Telecommunications Workers Union* (Vancouver 1982), 50–65.

80. Robert Morris, "Skilled Workers and the Politics of the 'Red' Clyde," unpublished paper, University of Edinburgh, 1981. As Morris notes, his echo of Edward Thompson's "moral economy" is intentional.

81. On the war economy in general see R.T. Naylor, "The Canadian State, the Accumulation of Capital, and the Great War," *Revue d'études canadiennes,* 16, 3 and 4 (1981), 26–55. On inflation specifically see: Terry Copp, *Anatomy of Poverty,* for Montreal, Michael J. Piva, *The Condition of the Working Class in Toronto;* Harry Sutcliffe and Paul Phillips, "Real Wages and the Winnipeg General Strike: An Empirical Investigation," unpublished paper, University of Manitoba, 1973; Gordon Bertram and Michael Percy, "Real Wage Trends in Canada 1900–26," *Canadian Journal of Economics,* 12 (1979), 299–312; and Eleanor Bartlett, "Real Wages and the Standard of Living in Vancouver, 1901–1929," *B.C. Studies,* 51 (1981), 3–62. For a slightly later period, see Michael J. Piva, "Urban Working-Class Incomes and Real Incomes in 1921: A Comparative Analysis," *Histoire sociale / Social History,* 31 (1983), 143–65. See also for a U.S. comparison, Frank Stricker, "The Wages of Inflation: Workers' Earnings in the World War One Era," *Mid-America,* 63 (1981), 93–105. For the general U.S. economic context, see David M. Gordon, Richard Edwards, Michael Reich, *Segmented Work, Divided Workers: The Historical Transformation of Labor in the United States* (New York 1982), 127–64.

82. Cronin, "Labour Insurgency and Class Conflict," *passim.* See also his *Industrial Conflict in Modern Britain* (London 1979), 109–20.

83. Much of this has been chronicled elsewhere. For an apologetic but detailed description of the creation of the RCMP see S.W. Horrall, "The Royal North-West Mounted Police and Labour Unrest in Western Canada, 1919," *Canadian Historical Review,* 61 (1980), 169–90. On victimization, especially of postal workers, see Borden Papers, various letters June to September 1919, pp. 62179–257. On one particularly unseemly aspect of TLC behaviour, see Tom Traves, 'The Story that Couldn't be Told': Big Business Buys the TLC," *Ontario Report,* 1, 6 (September 1976), 27–9.

84. A.B. Perry, "Draft Memorandum," 1 September 1919. Royal Canadian Mounted Police Papers, volume 1003, PAC.

85. Yves Lequin, "Social Structures and Shared Beliefs: Four Worker Communities in the Second Industrialization," *International Labor and Working Class History,* 22 (1982), 1–17.

86. On Councils in Canada, see Bruce Scott, 'A Place in the Sun': The Industrial Council at Massey-Harris, 1919–1929," *Labour / Le Travailleur,* 1 (1976), 158–92; Tom Traves. *The State and Enterprise: Canadian Manufacturers and the Federal Government 1917–1931* (Toronto 1979), 86–94; and Foy, "Gideon Robertson." For U.S. comparisons see Stuart D. Brandes, *American Welfare Capitalism, 1880–1940* (Chicago 1976), *passim,* but esp. 119–48.

87. *Socialist Bulletin* (Winnipeg), 1, 7 (July 1919).

88. *Red Flag,* 1, 22 (21 June 1919). For an academic echo of labour's educational gains from the strike, see D.G. Cook, "Western Radicalism and the Winnipeg Strike," M.A. thesis, McMaster University, 1921, which argues, on the basis of interviews with Winnipeg strikers, that: "The gains of the strike were many for the labour group. The six-week's strike was like a college course in Economics. Papers were read, issues discussed, and many addresses were given by the leaders. Many of the labour men became enlightened as to the real struggle. There grew a strong spirit of solidarity in the rank and file of labour." (62).

CHAPTER
7 THE GREAT WAR

Although Canada entered the Great War enthusiastically at Great Britain's side in August 1914, from a national perspective the experience ultimately proved traumatic, both because of the brutally wasteful nature of the conflict itself, and because of the divisions within Canadian society that it exposed. Myopic popular fervour masked the fact that at the outset Canadians had no common understanding of the role their country was to play. Was Canada simply a colony giving loyal support to the Mother Country, or was she a nation in her own right fighting in the defence of the same noble principles as the other Allies? This question was vitally important because upon its answer depended the character and extent of Canadian involvement.

A touchstone of the debate was the question of recruitment for the Canadian Expeditionary Force. In 1914 virtually all Canadians agreed that the Canadian military contribution must be strictly voluntary in nature. 'Canada wants no unwilling defenders,' *The Globe* of Toronto pontificated on 10 November 1914, 'coercion is wrong—in Toronto as in Berlin.' As the conflict stretched into months and then years, placing enormous strains on Canada's manpower resources, Canadians became increasingly divided by ethnicity, region, class and occupation, both about the extent of their country's military contribution and about the appropriateness of the voluntary recruiting system. Inevitably, therefore, Prime Minister Robert Borden's announcement on 18 May 1917 of his government's determination to adopt compulsion for overseas military service resulted in a national crisis of unprecedented dimensions, the echoes of which, it could be argued, have resonated from that day to this.

Understandably, discussion of Canada and World War I has revolved around the conscription crisis of 1917, with historical interpretations of the event ranging from the accusation of Laurier biographer, O.D. Skelton, that in opting for compulsion Prime Minister Borden's main objective was not so much to win a war as to win an election, to A.M. Willms's spirited brief in Borden's defence argued principally on the grounds of military necessity. More recently, studies such as those of Granatstein and Hitsman, Barbara Wilson and R.M. Bray have attempted to explain the divisiveness of conscription by reference to the evolution within Canada of the divergent English- and French-Canadian nationalistic responses to the Great War, while New Left historians such as Greg Kealey emphasize the class dimensions of the issue.

The articles reprinted here offer two contrasting perspectives on the question of recruitment itself. In 'Unrequited Faith: Recruiting the CEF 1914–1918,' R. Craig Brown and Donald Loveridge conclude that the Borden administration's ultimately misplaced faith in the principle of voluntarism reflected a certain naïveté on the part of Canada's leaders, military and political. Quite a different picture emerges from James W. St. G. Walker's, 'Race and Recruitment in World War I: Enlistment of Visible Minorities in the Canadian Expeditionary Force.' For Canada's visible minorities, it is argued, the war and recruitment exposed a darker, unattractive side of both Canadian governmental policy and Canadian society.

Suggestions for Further Reading

Armstrong, Elizabeth, *The Crisis of Quebec, 1914–1918.* New York: Columbia University Press, 1937. Reprinted Toronto: McClelland and Stewart, 1974.

Bélanger, Réal, "Albert Sévigny et la participation des canadiens français à la grande guerre," *Revue internationale d'histoire militaire*, 54 (1982) 80–108.

Berger, Carl, ed., *Conscription, 1917.* Toronto: University of Toronto Press, 1969.

Bray, R.M., "'Fighting As An Ally': The English-Canadian Patriotic Response to the Great War," *Canadian Historical Review,* LXI, 2 (June 1980) 141–168.

Gagnon, J.P., "Les soldats francophones du premier contingent expeditionnaire due Canada en Europe," *Guerres Mondiales et Conflits Contemporains*, 1990, 40 (157), 83–101.

Granatstein, J.L. and J.M. Hitsman, *Broken Promises: A History of Conscription in Canada.* Toronto: Oxford University Press, 1977.

Kealey, G., "State Repression of Labour and the Left in Canada, 1914–20: The Impact of the First World War." *CHR*, LXXIII, 3 (1992), 281–314.

Keshen, J., "All the News That Was Fit to Print: Ernest J. Chambers and Information Control in Canada, 1914–1919," *CHR*, LXXIII, 3 (1992), 315–343.

Morton, D., "Junior But Sovereign Allies: The Transformation of the Canadian Expeditionary Force, 1914–1918," *Journal of Imperial and Commonwealth History*, 8, 1 (1979) 56–67.

Nicholson, G.W.L., *Canadian Expeditionary Force, 1914–1919.* Ottawa: Queen's Printer, 1962.

Socknat, T., "Canada's Liberal Pacifists and the Great War," *Journal of Canadian Studies*, VIII, no.4 (Winter 1983–4), 30–44.

Wilson, Barbara M., *Ontario and the First World War, 1914–1918: A Collection of Documents.* Toronto: The Champlain Society, 1977.

UNREQUITED FAITH: RECRUITING THE CEF, 1914–1918

R. Craig Brown and Donald Loveridge

On the morning of October 2, 1914 some thirty thousand Canadian soldiers found themselves crowded into thirty ships lying at anchor in Gaspé Basin, impatiently waiting the assembly of warships which would escort them to war. Those on deck soon spotted the imposing figure of Colonel Sam Hughes, Minister of Militia and Defence, in full uniform, proceeding in a launch from ship to ship. Colonel Sam, never one to miss an occasion for attention-grabbing, was passing out thick bundles of his farewell message to his boys. "Soldiers" the valedictory proudly proclaimed, "The world regards you as a marvel."

By now the men of the First Contingent were all too familiar with Colonel Hughes penchant for exaggeration. Among them were hundreds of recent immigrants who had served in the British army. They, at least, knew that a few weeks of drill and rifle practice had not made the Canadians into the efficient fighting force they would one day be. The Minister's message, the official historian of the Canadian Expeditionary Force records, was received "with mixed feelings."[1]

That did not matter to Hughes. His 900 word statement was intended for another, more important, audience. Carefully worked into the patriotic prose and inspirational verse was his account of the miracle of Valcartier; how he, not quite single handedly, had created a training camp on the sandy banks of Jacques Cartier River a few miles from Quebec City and assembled there the eager volunteers from the cities, towns and farms of Canada.

> Within six weeks you were at your homes peaceful Canadian citizens. Since then your training camp has been secured; three and a half miles of rifle ranges—twice as long as any other in the world—were constructed; fences were removed; water of the purist quality was laid in miles of pipes; drainage was perfected; electric light was installed; crops were harvested; roads and bridges were built; Ordnance and Army Service Corps buildings were erected; railway sidings were laid down, woods were cleared; sanitation was perfected so that illness was practically unknown, and thirty-three thousand men were assembled from points some of them upwards of four thousand miles apart. You have been perfected in rifle shooting and today are as fine a body—Officers and Men— as ever faced a foe.[2]

Four years later, at 6:30 on the morning of November 11, Canadian Corps Headquarters was advised that all hostilities would cease at 11 a.m. At the appointed hour an unaccustomed, almost eerie quiet settled over the lines. The first moment of victory was a time for reflection. In England, a Canadian soldier, recuperating from his wounds, wrote that "the people are taking the good news

From the *Révue internationale d'histoire militaire*, 54, 1982, 53–79. Reprinted by permission of the *Révue internationale d'histoire militaire* and the authors.

very quietly . . . Nearly every family has lost someone, and a great many two or three sons."[3] And, despite the joyous celebrations that erupted from Halifax to Victoria a few hours later, so it must have been in the hundreds of thousands of Canadian families which had sent one or more of their boys to war.

So much had changed since Colonel Hughes had directed his launch to and fro in Gaspé Basin. His original contingent had grown into a Corps of four divisions and supporting arms, commanded, after June 1917, by a civilian soldier from Canada, Lt. General Sir Arthur W. Currie.[4] Hughes himself was no longer Minister of Militia and Defence, having been fired by the Prime Minister, Sir Robert Borden, in November 1916. His Department was now run by Major General S.C. Mewburn, a Liberal member of Borden's Union Government, and its staff had grown from 919 employees in 1914 to more than 5,700 administrators, clerks and typists. Since Hughes' departure, many of them worked in a separate Ministry of Overseas Forces with headquarters in London.[5] The voluntary recruiting that supported the CEF through the first years of the war had been replaced by conscription in 1917. On Armistice Day 105,016 conscripts were available for service of whom 96,379 were on strength and 47,509 had already proceeded overseas.[6] One of Hughes' inspirations, a "Shell Committee" to act as an agency for British munitions contracts in Canada, had been undermined by scandal and replaced, late in 1915, by the Imperial Munitions Board, directed by businessman Sir Joseph Flavelle and employing thousands of men and women in munitions production.[7]

When Hughes issued his first chaotic call for troops the nation was in the midst of a sharpening depression. Manufacturers reported that their plants were operating at less than fifty percent of capacity. Local correspondents of the *Labour Gazette* detailed the news of young men on the move everywhere, going from town to town, looking for a job. By 1918 the munition workers in Flavelle's factories were only a tiny fraction of an industrial army, working overtime in plants and mines, in a booming war economy. And Canada's farmers were producing and selling more agricultural products, at higher prices, than they ever had before. By 1917 there were serious shortages of manpower in the factories and on the farms of Canada, shortages as threatening to the war effort as the reinforcement crisis in the CEF which forced the passage of the Military Service Act.[8]

The manpower crisis had its roots in the hasty, unlimited commitments made by the Borden Government in August, 1914. The first was a decision to send whatever number of men were needed overseas to fight. Characteristically, Hughes announced in New York City on October 7, 1914, that "we could send enough men to add the finishing touches to Germany without assistance either from England or France."[9] In Halifax in December Borden was more moderate but equally sanguine about his military manpower policy. Would, he was asked, the expeditionary force eventually reach 100,000 men? "I prefer to name no figure," he replied. "If the preservation of our Empire demands twice or thrice that number, we shall ask for them."[10]

That was easy to do in the winter of 1914–15. Borden, like his counterparts in London and Paris still anticipated a quick, decisive victory. And, up to that time, the countless hours he had spent trying to boost production in Canada with orders from the Allies for war material had yielded only disappointing results. The second commitment made in August, 1914, to seize the opportunities of war to revive the Canadian economy, remained an empty dream.

There was one more pledge that was easy to give in December, 1914. As Borden talked about raising men for the CEF, he observed that "Canada will answer the call as readily and as fully as its men [have] volunteered since August. There has not been, there will not be, compulsion or conscription."[11]

The commitments to raise as many men and produce as many goods as necessary never changed during the Great War. But, as the war dragged on, with such an appalling wastage of manpower, and as war production steadily increased, it became ever more difficult to recruit men for military service. An examination of the administration of military manpower policy during the war and its relationship to the demand for labour in factories and on farms provides an interesting insight into the history of the CEF. It is not possible, in this short essay, to survey recruiting for all units of the CEF. Instead, we will analyse the recruiting of infantry battalions, the largest single portion of the Expeditionary Force. Unlike earlier discussions of this subject, our study will be based on the effective military force, i.e., the men shipped overseas, rather than on the men who enlisted for service, of whom tens of thousands were discharged in Canada for a variety of reasons.[12]

* * *

The raising of the First Contingent under the personal direction of Colonel Hughes was marked by confusion and chaos. Discarding a prepared plan of mobilization in the Military Districts across Canada, the Minister initially ordered each Local Militia unit commander to enroll men for a divisional contingent and send nominal rolls to Ottawa. There followed a flurry of amendments, additions and contrary instructions which confused and exasperated the local and District Officers as they tried to process the eager applicants for overseas service. Eventually 30,621 men, including 19,299 in 17 CEF infantry battalions and another 1,071 in a separately organized battalion, Princess Patricia's Canadian Light Infantry, found their way to the ships awaiting escort in Gaspé Basin.[13]

The men came from 130 Militia units from every region of Canada. Significantly, more than sixty percent were raised in urban areas and almost half of the men, 48.4%, came from western Canada where the effects of the depression were most severe. Another 31.3% came from heavily industrialized Ontario.[14] Many of these soldiers were among the tens of thousands of unemployed men who had been looking for work in the summer of 1914. For them the army at least would provide shelter, clothing, food and $1.10 a day. Even measured against the hazards of military life, that was better than the prospect of spending another bitter winter on the streets of Canada's cities.

The other remarkable fact about the First Contingent was that sixty percent of its men had been born in the British Isles. Undoubtedly many of them had a more profound sense of the threat the war posed to the Empire than did young Canadians of military age. But unemployment also affected their decisions to enlist. Canada was a nation of immigrants and more than ten percent of the population came from the British Isles. A very large proportion of these British immigrants were single males of military age and this was especially true in the western provinces where the number and proportion of single British-born males far exceeded that in any of the eastern provinces.[15] Unemployment, therefore, and a comparatively large number of single British-born males in the population, in large measure account for the extraordinary large contribution that the western provinces made to the manpower of the First Contingent and to the next phase of voluntary recruiting.

The second phase of voluntary recruiting, for First Contingent reinforcements and a second contingent, began before the first men had reached England. It was far more orderly than the first. Perhaps the chaos at Valcartier convinced Hughes that a more systematic approach was necessary; perhaps his absence in England, leaving the administration of his Department in the more capable hands of Major-General W.G. Gwatkin, Chief of the General Staff, and Major-General Eugene Fiset, the Deputy Minister, explained the change. In any case, preliminary mobilization and training of recruits was delegated to the local militia units in the Military Districts.

Over the next eleven months, through September, 1915, seventy-one infantry battalions were authorized. Thirty-four of them not only recruited a full battalion but also sent one or more drafts of some 250 men overseas. Only two, the 70th from Essex, Kent, Lambton and Middlesex Counties in Ontario and the 57th from Quebec City, failed to send a full strength battalion overseas. Again the largest number of men came from western Canada, 41.4% of the total, closely followed by Ontario's contribution of 38.3%. Twelve percent of the men raised in the second phase of recruiting came from Quebec in four French and six English-speaking battalions. Eight percent of the men were recruited in the Maritime Provinces in six full strength battalions, two of which also sent extra drafts overseas.[16]

In the Quebec and western military districts a clear distinction between recruiting in urban and non-urban areas developed at the beginning of this period and it was beginning to emerge in Districts One and Two in Ontario by the end of the period. Seventy percent of the men raised in Quebec and sixty percent in the western provinces were enrolled in battalions which recruited exclusively in urban areas. In Ontario this type of recruiting did not begin until June 1915 and twenty percent of the 34,352 infantrymen sent overseas from the Province in this phase were raised in Toronto, Hamilton and London battalions.

This phase of recruiting also had its problems. Initial training was hindered by lack of equipment for several battalions. "The training of a unit cannot be pushed far when it has no equipment," an Inspector-General reported of the

58th Battalion at Niagara-on-the-Lake. "1/3 of men have no clothing, 1/2 or more have no shirts. They are short of boots and have no ammunition." Severe weather, winter quartering and the departure of local militia officers for overseas service further set back training schedules as did a serious outbreak of spinal meningitis in units at Toronto's Canadian National Exhibition grounds and in Belleville in the winter of 1914–15. Beyond that, the militia officers training the raw recruits had to cope with major disciplinary problems. Three hundred men had to be discharged from the 25th and 130 from the 26th battalions in the Maritimes. In several Ontario units a ten percent wastage of manpower because of misconduct discharges was reported. The 41st, a singularly ill-fated Quebec battalion, had 88 NCO's and other ranks absent without leave on the day the Inspector-General appeared.[17]

The other responsibility of the militia units, mobilization of recruits, was equally troublesome. Raising a battalion for overseas service was an expensive business and, apart from the equipment supplied—in due course!—by the Government of Canada, the costs had to be borne by the local units. One estimate came to more than $13,000:

Advertising	$ 2,554
Dodgers, Letters, etc.	1,690
Street cars	464
Postage	220
Signs for depots, etc.	850
Office supplies, telephone, rent, etc.	930
Autos, repairs, etc.	656
Sundries	520
Brass & Bugle Bands	2,000
2 Field Kitchens	2,500
Misc.	1,000
	$13,384 [18]

Regimental funds were quickly dissipated and fund raising appeals had to be launched in the community to cover the costs of recruiting.

Moreover, after the Spring of 1915, when casualty lists became a daily feature in the press, the realization dawned that there was not going to be a decisive battle: the war was going to be long and difficult, and characterized by a shocking wastage of manpower at the Front. Now some members of the Militia and self-appointed spokesmen for the "better elements" in society banded together in Speakers Patriotic Leagues and Recruiting Leagues to assist the Militia's recruiting efforts. But these organizations became increasingly outspoken in their criticism of Militia recruiting. The job of mobilization and training was too big and too expensive for the Militia to handle. Far more men were going to be needed to fight the Kaiser and a much greater and more efficient recruiting effort was necessary. The logic of the argument, some spokesmen added, was a more centralized recruiting effort, more direct support from the Department of Militia and Defence, and a scheme of national registration to rationalize recruiting and, perhaps, as a prelude to conscription.[19]

The response from Ottawa was in exactly the opposite direction. Why not, the Government's new recruiting policy seemed to ask, capitalize upon popular clamour for men by handing the responsibility for raising battalions over to these zealous patriots? In the fall of 1915 the Department announced that henceforth the local regiments of Militia would be bypassed in the recruiting effort and that individual citizens and communities would be authorized to raise battalions on their own if they would assume the costs of recruiting.

Given a direct role to play, the patriots, especially in the West and in Ontario, responded with unprecedented energy. 123,966 men, in 170 battalions, were sent overseas in the final phase of voluntary recruiting from October 1915 to October 1917. Sixty battalions, 33.9% of the total, were raised in the western provinces and another 75 battalions, 42.4% of the total, in Ontario. Far fewer men were recruited in the Maritimes and Quebec, but even in these regions the battalions organized, fifteen in the Maritimes and thirteen in Quebec, exceeded the number recruited by the Local Militia units in the preceding phase.[20] At first glance this patriotic phase of recruiting, with the initiative in the hands of neither local nor central military authorities, appears to have been a triumphant vindication of voluntarism and local enthusiasm.

A closer look changes the perspective. 72,296 men, almost sixty percent of the total, were raised in the first three months of this two year period. Another thirty-eight percent were recruited in the next six months, following Sir Robert Borden's announcement on New Year's Day, 1916, that the authorized force level for the CEF had been raised to a half-million men. Then, from July 1916 to October 1917, a mere 2,810 men were raised and sent overseas in infantry battalions. The last infantry battalion for CEF service, the 258th, was organized in Quebec in April 1917 by Colonel Pierre-Édouard Blondin, Postmaster General in Borden's Government. It embarked in October with 231 men. Blondin's experience was not unique. The last Maritime battalion, organized in August, 1916, sent 247 men overseas and the last western battalion, the 251st, raised in Winnipeg, embarked with four officers and 168 other ranks.[21] In short, in the final phase of voluntary recruiting, enthusiasm peaked in the last three months of 1915 and then quickly evaporated. Save for Blondin's effort, not a single infantry battalion was organized in the 13 months from November 1916 to the first call up of conscripts in January, 1918.

What had happened? A large part of the problem can be attributed directly to the mode of recruiting authorized in the final phase. Lacking central organization and control, the citizens raising battalions engaged in ruinous competition for men. Three battalions were organized in Toronto in December, 1915, another in January 1916 and six more in February, 1916. In that same month at least six battalions were recruiting in Winnipeg and three in Edmonton. In the Militia phase of recruiting only two battalions, 2.8% of the total, failed to recruit to full strength. In the patriotic phase, 120 battalions, 73.6% of the total, were sent overseas at less than full strength and ten battalions, 6.1% of the total, were disbanded. Even appeals to men to enlist in special identity battalions seldom worked. Thirty-eight such units, Highlanders, Sportsmen, Bantams, Chums, Pals, Frontiersmen and others, were organized in this phase. Ten of them, including five Highland battalions and one "Dry" battalion from Winnipeg, were raised to full strength. But six others had to be disbanded and the remainder were all under strength.

Unbridled competition had other devastating effects. As soon as men were raised by a battalion's organizers they were sent back to the streets to recruit their friends. Even the most elemental training suffered. The 240th was raised in Lanark and Renfrew Counties in June, 1916. In May, 1917 the Officer commanding Military District 3 wrote:

> At the time this unit was formed, recruiting was not very brisk and consequently the efforts of all of the officers were devoted to securing men. As recruits were obtained they themselves were used as recruiting agents especially among their own acquaintants. Training, therefore, was not performed on any extensive scale . . . The Commanding Officer appeared to consider training of very secondary importance and he devoted much of his time to recruiting both for his own and Forestry Battalions.[22]

The battalion was sent overseas two weeks later with 389 men.

Discipline suffered even more. The Inspectors General's reports tell a dismal tale. The 145th and 146th, both in training at Valcartier in the late summer of 1916, each lost a hundred or more men in five weeks between inspections. The 180th, an Ontario battalion, had 336 men away without leave when it was inspected and 300 men missed parade when the 199th, a Quebec battalion, was inspected. A western battalion, the 210th, recruited 1,020 men, 782 were left when it was inspected; 152 had been discharged and 59 had deserted. Two months later, almost 300 more had disappeared. Only 500 officers and men embarked for overseas.[23] Understrength, poorly trained, lacking discipline, the Inspectors General repeatedly recommended that battalions raised in this phase of recruiting be sent overseas as drafts to be amalgamated into previously organized battalions.

But an unorganized recruiting system and competition between battalions for men were not the only problems encountered by recruiters in the patriotic phase. By the winter of 1915–1916 the Government's plans for domestic war production were falling into place and there was a steadily rising demand for manpower in the agricultural and industrial sectors of the economy. An Inspector General noted that recruiting for the 232nd, a Saskatchewan battalion, had been "very poor." "The reason assigned, [was] not so much the scarcity of men in the country but to the demand for labour at an excessively high rate of wages."[24]

This was true across rural Canada and especially in the west where wages for farm labour skyrocketed in the latter war years and elaborate schemes were developed to import agricultural workers from the United States.[25]

It was no less true in Canada's cities where, as in the earlier phases of recruiting, the recruitment of men for the CEF was concentrated. By late 1915 war contracts were accumulating in ever increasing number; the Shell Committee had been replaced by an agency of the British Ministry of Munitions, the Imperial Munitions Board, and hundreds of contracts for military supplies for the Canadian Government were being distributed by the War Purchasing Commission.[26] The result was a remarkable explosion of industrial activity in every region of Canada, accompanied by corresponding growth in other sectors of the economy from mining to transportation to finance.

Because government statisticians used different bases to measure the number of industrial workers employed before 1917, no reliable figures on the size of the industrial workforce are available for the early war years. But Department of Labour estimates of unemployment among unionized workers indicate unemployment of union workers was below the national average in Halifax, St. John, Toronto, Winnipeg, Regina, and Edmonton in at least 7 of the 11 quarters from June 1916 to December 1918. Other indicators point to a similar trend. Between 1915 and 1917 the average rate of return on capital invested in manufacturing increased in every province; it doubled in Quebec, more than doubled in Nova Scotia and Ontario and almost tripled in Manitoba and Alberta. Using 1917 as a base year, value added to manufacturing increased more than 10% nationwide in 1918 and by 12% in Ontario and Saskatchewan, 16% in New Brunswick and 35% in British Columbia.[27] Crude as these indicators are, they strongly suggest that industrial production, and its consequent draw on manpower in the urban areas of Canada, rose sharply from 1916 on and cut deeply into the potential manpower supply for military service.

The organizers of infantry battalions, therefore, not only had to compete for men among themselves, but also with the factories and shops of Canada. Beyond that, as the Canadian Corps grew in size and responsibility, opportunities for enlistment in other branches of the service, many of them considerably less risky than the infantry, expanded greatly, as did recruiting activity for the British flying services, the Royal Naval Air Service and the Royal Flying Corps.[28] The result was a precipitate decline in enrollment in infantry battalions in urban areas, ending with the meagre contribution, after June, 1916, of 172 men from Winnipeg and 297 from Toronto.

Rural areas, where farmers were constantly badgered by the Government to increase their acreage and production did no better. The five non-urban battalions raised in Ontario after June 1916 contributed a total of 1,124 men, the strength of a single battalion, to overseas service. In western Canada only one battalion, the 249th in Saskatchewan, was recruited after June 1916. In the following year it sent 550 men to Quebec for further training.[29]

But, if the Government's military manpower and wartime production policies were working against each other, and if infantry recruiting had collapsed by the late spring of 1916, why did the Government wait for another year to introduce the Military Service Act? Many factors delayed the decision. The Government, for example, seems to have based its military manpower policy upon monthly enlistment figures which grossly understated the forthcoming infantry manpower crisis by taking no account of wastage through discharge or desertion during the training of men in Canada.[30] But even the use of embarkation rather than enlistment statistics could have been misleading. Because of the long period of time between the date when a battalion was recruited and it embarked, thousands of men recruited in late 1915 and early 1916 were only being sent overseas in late 1916 and early 1917. Thus, Borden and his colleagues could easily have concluded in the spring of 1917 that the infantry manpower crisis was less serious than, in fact, it was. Finally, as depressing as earlier casualty rates were, it was only in 1917 that the fully developed Corps, fighting as a complete unit, suffered casualties at a truly alarming rate.

Borden made the fateful decision to impose conscription during his trip home from the Imperial War Cabinet meetings in the late spring of 1917. At those meetings, and in private talks with Lloyd George and other members of the British Government, he had become privy, for the first time during the war, to the secret information and projections of the British on the duration of the war. Undoubtedly the sombre news influenced his decision. Even more was he influenced by the tragic spectacle of row upon upon row of bedridden wounded Canadian boys in the hospitals he visited in France and Britain. His commitment to their cause and their sacrifice was total and unquestioning. He was answering the "call from the wounded," "the men in the trenches and those who have fallen" he explained on May 18, 1917 when he announced that there would be conscription.[31]

The announcement touched off a furious debate in the House of Commons. The passage of the Military Service Act and the subsequent formation by Borden of a Union Government to implement it have been the subject of equally intense argument among politicians and historians ever since, as they have calculated the effects of conscription upon French-English relations, farmers, trade unions and the Liberal and Conservative Parties.

Some facts are beyond dispute. Among the men of military age in Canada the response was overwhelmingly negative. Of the 401,882 Class I registrants, males aged 20 to 32 who were single or widowers with no children, no less than 93.7% immediately applied for exemption. And tens of thousands more failed to register and became defaulters. The number of registrants who volunteered for service or reported by order in the initial phase of implementation of the Act was tiny, 4.5% of registrants nationally, varying from 10.5% in British Columbia to 1.6% in Quebec. In every province and region of Canada, not just in Quebec, it was evident that popular enthusiasm for military service had been bled dry.[32]

Many advocates of conscription argued that a nationally directed compulsory military manpower policy was the only way to achieve a balanced allotment of military responsibilities between sectors of the economy and among regions of the country. Some, playing upon long-standing animosities between French and English Canada, and obsessed by Quebec's low rate of contribution to the voluntary recruiting effort,[33] went further to claim that the Military Service Act would, at last, force French Canadians to assume their share of the military burden. Driven by the passions of war, few were prepared to concede that demographic and historical factors went far to explain why Quebec (and, to a lesser extent the Maritime Provinces) had contributed comparatively fewer soldiers to the war effort than Ontario and the western provinces. As noted above, the voluntary recruiting system, at least in its first and second phases, was dependent upon the local militia units and was heavily biased in favour of recruiting single men. The significantly higher proportion of single males of military age, both native Canadians and British immigrants, in the West and in Ontario, and the deep roots of the militia in Ontario society help to account for the high rates of recruitment in both regions. By contrast, the proportion of males of military age who were married was well above the national average in Quebec and the Maritime Provinces and the militia exercised much less influence in the societies of the Maritime Provinces and had frittered away by neglect whatever modest attractions it had once had in French Canadian society.[34] The bias towards recruiting in urban areas also helps to explain why French Canadians failed to respond to the voluntary recruiting effort. Not only did the vast majority of French Canadians live outside the two largest cities of Quebec,[35] but only one quarter of the battalions recruited in the Montreal and Quebec districts sought to attract French Canadian recruits.[36] In short, in the Maritime provinces, and even more so in Quebec, the smaller proportion of single males of military age in the population, a concentration on urban recruiting and a legacy of neglect of French Canadians in the Militia go far to account for the failure of men in those regions to respond to the voluntary recruiting effort.

Conscription did tend to balance out the military manpower contribution of the regions. Though still below the national average of 5.6% of the military age group made available for service under the Military Service Act, Quebec's contribution of 5% matched Ontario's 5.1% and approximated the 5.5% contribution from the Western Provinces.[37] But it was grudgingly given. The number of defaulters was exceedingly high, even when account is taken of confusion in the counting and classification of defaulters in the Hull office of Military District 3 and in Districts 4 and 5.[38] Only 1.6% of Quebec's Class 1 registrants reported for service; 98% applied for exemptions. And Appeal Tribunals rejected only 9.3% of exemption claims as compared with 13% in the Maritime and Western regions and 15% in Ontario.[39]

Too much, however, can be made of Quebec's, or French Canada's opposition to conscription, implying, as it does, that there was substantially more support for the Military Service Act in other regions of the country. That doubtless was true among the politicians supporting the Union Government and the voters in Ontario and Western Canada in the 1917 election. It certainly was not true among the Class I registrants in any region of the country. Among them, one broadly based group, the farmers of Canada, illustrates the point. In comparative terms they had been left alone during the voluntary phases of recruiting and they were no more willing to be coerced than they had been to be coaxed into military service. Promised exemptions by the Unionist Government candidates in the 1917 election campaign, 97.4% of the farmers who were Class I registrants applied for exemptions. Only 12.6% of those claims were refused by the Tribunals established under the Military Service Act.[40]

The Government's solicitous regard for agrarians apparently came to an abrupt end, however, when Sir Robert Borden announced the cancellation of all exemptions and the call up of all 20–22 year old Class I registrants in April, 1918. Farmers in every region of the country were outraged and charged that the exemption promise had been a cheap political trick. It mattered not that the call up was Borden's response to the roll back of Allied armies before the German spring offensive on the Western Front. A Nova Scotia farmer complained to his Member of Parliament that "this conscripting farmers is the worst slur on the conservative government yet."[41] District registrars for the Military Service Act reported that the cancellation of exemptions was "generally unpalatable," "created a measure of consternation" and a "feeling of resentment" among farmers.[42]

But the effect of the cancellation upon the farming community was, in fact, not as severe as it appeared. Registrars were instructed to take care to avoid conscripting hardship cases, to grant and renew harvest leaves, and to grant leaves of absence on compassionate grounds. More significant still, registrars were ordered "to call the men with urban addresses in priority to those living in country districts." Reflecting upon the effect of the cancellation in his final report, the registrar in Halifax "did not observe that the farming industry was seriously handicapped by this call, and the fishing industry was very slightly affected. Large industrial concerns in the mining and steel centres were more seriously affected."[43]

The otherwise comprehensive report of the Director of the Military Service Act does not indicate how many young farmers were called for service as a result of Borden's announcement. But if we assume a constant proportion of 20–22 year old farmers to all 20–22 year olds with exemptions, 31.9%, through the process of cancellation and calling up, then only 17,146 young farmers were called up.[44] If we add farmers who reported for service and who had exemption claims denied to those whose exemptions were cancelled, 42,098 farmers, 25.3% of farmers who registered, were called for service under the M.S.A. 71,363 non-farmers reported for service or had their exemptions denied or cancelled, 29.1% of non-farmer registrants. In western Canada the bias towards farmers was much sharper. 23.3% of western farmer registrants and 39.3% of non-farmers were called for service.[45]

Thus, if the administration of the Military Service Act tended to bring more balance into the manpower contributions of the regions of Canada, it was less effective in balancing the contribution of farmers and non-farmers to the military manpower effort. In fact, the more liberal policy toward farmers that existed during the voluntary recruiting period was codified in the regulations made under the Military Service Act both before and after the call up of the 20–22 age group. In part the favouritism of agrarians was accidental; voluntary recruiting tended to centre upon urban areas of high population density. In part it was a matter of design; ever increasing agricultural production for export was an essential component of the Government's war policy.

But so too was industrial production for the war effort and our examination of the recruiting of infantry reveals that the conflict between military manpower policy and industrial policy surfaced during the winter and early spring of 1915–1916, long before the agrarians raised their powerful protest against the Military Service Act. Indeed, given the patterns of voluntary recruiting, that conflict undermined the voluntary recruiting system and precipitated the conscription crisis.

* * *

The history of Canadian manpower policy in the Great War, climaxing in the conscription crisis, has been characterized by a distinguished military historian as a story of "broken promises."[46] That it was; from Borden's 1914 pledge that there would be no conscription to the 1917 election promise to exempt farmers. Yet, from another perspective, it could just as convincingly be called a story of unrequited faith: faith, initially, that the war would quickly end; faith that the patriotic response of the people of Canada would enable the country to send as many men as necessary to the Front and, at the same time, be a major supplier of war material; faith that even with an inadequate bureaucracy and little planning somehow, someway, everything would come out right. Most especially, faith in the principle of voluntarism.

In the end, faith was not enough. Applied to the military manpower policy in an ever more decentralized system of voluntary recruiting, it was dashed by the duration of the war, the appalling wastage of men at the Front, and the Canadian Government's own wartime economic policies. But even when coercion became necessary, the legacy of faith in voluntarism tempered the coercive nature of the Military Service Act. Under the liberal exemptions policy in the Act, 86.8% of all claims for exemption were allowed: only 28% of all Class I registrants were called for military service.

Reflecting upon Borden's decision in 1916 to raise the authorized force level of the CEF to 500,000 men, Sir Thomas White, the Minister of Finance, wrote that "We simply went on faith, feeling instinctively that means could be found to enable us to carry it out."[47] That simple confession spoke volumes about Canada's military manpower policy, from the guns of August to Armistice Day.

Notes

The authors would like to thank Miss Barbara Wilson of the Public Archives of Canada for her advice and assistance in the preparation of this essay.

1. Colonel A. Fortescue Duguid, *Official History of the Canadian Forces in the Great War, 1914–1919,* vol. 1, 104. See also Colonel G.W.L. Nicholson, *Canadian Expeditionary Force, 1914–1919,* 31.

2. Cited, Duguid, *Official History,* Appendices, no. 149, 122–23. For other accounts of the chaos and the accomplishment of the training at Valcartier see Duguid, *Official History,* chs. 1–2, Nicholson, *CEF,* ch. II, and Robert Craig Brown, *Robert Laird Borden, A Biography, Vol. 2, 1914–1937,* 12–15.

3. Nicholson, *CEF,* 482–84; Metro Toronto Library, Baldwin Room, Neil Family Papers, "Harry" to "Dear Bros and Sisters," November 10, 1918.

4. On Currie see H.M. Urquhart, *Arthur Currie: Biography of a Great Canadian* (Toronto, 1950); J.A. Swettenham, *To Seize the Victory: The Canadian Corps in World War I,* (Toronto, 1965); A.J.M. Hyatt, "Sir Arthur Currie and Conscription: A Soldier's View," *Canadian Historical Review,* L, 3, September, 1969, 285–96; and R. Craig Brown and Desmond Morton, "The Embarrassing Apotheosis of a 'Great Canadian': Sir Arthur Currie's Personal Crisis in 1917," *CHR,* LX, 1, March, 1979, 41–63.

5. On the Overseas Ministry see the fine history by Desmond Morton, of the Overseas Ministry and the CEF 1914–1920, *A Peculiar Kind of Politics: Canada's Overseas Ministry in the First World War.* Toronto: University of Toronto Press, 1982.

6. Nicholson, *CEF,* Appendix "E," SS1. Colonel Nicholson's figure of 96,379 on strength includes 16,296 draftees on unexpired harvest or compassionate leave. On conscription and the implementation of the Military Service Act see, *inter alia,* J.L. Granatstein and J.M. Hitsman, *Broken Promises. A History of Conscription in Canada* (Toronto, 1977). Chs. 1–3; Robert Craig Brown and Ramsay Cook, *Canada, 1896–1921. A Nation Transformed* (Toronto, 1974) ch. 13 and Brown, *Borden,* 2 chs. 8–10.

7. The history of the Imperial Minister's Board is described in David Carnegie, *The History of Munitions Supply in Canada 1914–1918* (New York, 1925) and in Michael Bliss's excellent biography, *A Canadian Millionaire: The Life and Business Times of Sir Joseph Flavelle, Bart., 1888–1939* (Toronto, 1978) chs. 10–13 and 15.

8. For a brief sketch of the Canadian economy during the Great War see Brown and Cook, *Canada, 1896–1921,* ch. 12.

9. Cited, J.C. Hopkins, ed., *Canadian Annual Review,* 1914, (Toronto, 1915), 217.

10. Cited, Brown, *Borden, 2,* 22.

11. *Ibid.*

12. Colonel Duguid's figures indicate that 616,557 enlisted in the CEF, either voluntarily or by compulsion. Of these, 421,510 or 68.4% served overseas. Some explanation of the difference may be found in remarks to the House of Commons by Sir Edward Kemp on July 6, 1917. He then explained that 76,000 of the 425,000 who had volunteered for service had been discharged in Canada. The largest groups discharged were medically unfit (33,887), absentees struck off (13,081) and men "not likely to become efficient" (5,345). Duguid, *Official History,* 51; *Canadian Annual Review, 1917,* 307, 311.

13. See Appendix "A" and Duguid, *Appendices,* no. 84, 51–53.

14. In this paper we are not using the contemporary Canada Census distinction between urban and non-urban populations. Instead, we use a much more limited definition of urban recruiting that developed from recruiting patterns from 1914 to 1917, distinguishing between battalions recruited exclusively in defined urban areas and those recruited over larger areas. So defined, our definition of urban includes Quebec City and Montreal in Quebec; Toronto, Hamilton and London in Ontario; Winnipeg and St. Boniface in Manitoba; Regina, Moose Jaw and Saskatoon in Saskatchewan; Calgary and Edmonton in Alberta; and Vancouver, New Westminster and Victoria in British Columbia. The pattern of recruiting is defined in the reports of the Inspectors General on the battalions raised and because no battalions were raised exclusively in urban areas in the Maritime region, all battalions from that region have been classified as non-urban. Obviously, however, this classification, which is necessary for consistent analysis, greatly undervalues the recruitment of men in urban areas across Canada.

15. See Charts A, B and C and 6th *Census of Canada, 1921,* Vol. 2, Table 24 and Table 25.

16. See Chart D.

17. RG 9, II, B5, vol. 5–7 (Inspectors-General Reports on CEF Battalions), Reports on Battalions 19–86. On the 41st Battalion see Desmond Morton, "The Short Unhappy Life of the 41st Battalion, CEF," *Queen's Quarterly,* LXXXI, Spring, 1974.

18. *Canadian Annual Review, 1916,* 308.

19. On the Speakers Patriotic League and related organizations see Barbara M. Wilson, editor, *Ontario and the First World War, 1914–18, A Collection of Documents,* (Toronto, 1977), xxix–xxxvii and 8–21 and R. Matthew Bray, 'Fighting as an Ally': The English-Canadian Patriotic Response to the Great War," *CHR,* LXI, 2, June, 1980, 141–68.

20. In addition, seven special function Forestry and Railway battalions were raised nationally or in more than one region.

21. Public Archives of Canada, RG 24, vols. 1344–54, File HQ 593-3-25. (Embarkation Officer's Report for the CEF).

22. PAC, RG 9, II BS, vol. 7. (Inspector General's Reports).

23. PAC, RG 9, II BS, vols. 5–7.

24. PAC, RG 9, II BS, vol. 7.

25. See *The Agricultural Gazette of Canada,* III, 1916, 245–48, 351; IV, 1917, 387–93, 493; and V, 1918, 864–67, 940–44 and *Eleventh Annual Report of the Department of Agriculture of the Province of Saskatchewan,* Regina, 1916. After the entry of the United States into the war in 1917 the supply of American farm labour was greatly restricted. As partial compensation for that, and for the movement of agrarian labourers into the industrial work force in Canada, a "Soldiers of the Soil" movement was organized in most provinces in 1917–18.

26. See, for example, RG 14, D2, vol. 37, Sessional Paper 149, "Second Report of the War Purchasing Commission, Jan 1, 1917 to March 31, 1918" which lists the bidders for and the 2,467 contracts awarded during that period.

27. Calculated from quarterly reports in the *Labour Gazette, 1916–1919* and from statistics on manufacturing in *Canada Year Book, 1922–23,* 415–16.

28. See Gilbert N. Tucker, *The Naval Service of Canada* Vol. 1, Ottawa, 1952 and S.F. Wise, *Canadian Airmen and the First World War; The Official History of the Royal Canadian Air Force* Vol. 1, Toronto, 1980.

29. PAC, RG 9, II BS, vol. 7.

30. See footnote 12.

31. Brown, *Borden, II,* chs. 7–10.

32. See Canada, House of Commons, Sessional Papers, 1919, no. 246, 86 and Chart E.

33. Across Canada 12.33% of the military age group (males 15 to 44 years of age in 1911) had enlisted in infantry battalions and embarked for overseas service before the implementation of the Military Service Act. By region the rates were: Maritimes, 9.96%; Quebec, 4.69%; Ontario, 14.42% and Western Canada, 15.52%. See chart A.

34. See Morton, *Ministers and Generals, passim* and *Canada and War. A Military and Political History,* Toronto, 1981, chs. 1–2.

35. See 5th *Census of Canada, 1911,* vol. 2, 357–65.

36. In contrast, in New Brunswick, where recruiting was not concentrated in identifiable urban areas, five of the seven infantry battalions contained large numbers of Acadian recruits.

37. See Chart F.

38. See Sessional Paper 246, 1919, 138–40; 145–48.

39. See Chart E. It should not be assumed that reference to Quebec in this paragraph refers only to French-speaking Canadians living in the Province. The statistics available for administration of the MSA in Quebec do not differentiate between French and English speaking registrants. Moreover, the 98% rate of claims for exemptions indicates the unpopularity of conscription among all Class I registrants.

40. See Chart G.

41. Provincial Archives of Nova Scotia, M.G. 2, E.N. Rhodes Papers, vol. 580, no. 8951, letter to Rhodes, May 9, 1918.

42. Sessional Paper no. 246, 1919, 139, 149, 136.

43. *Ibid.,* 132, 17, 136.

44. Total 20–22 with exemptions = 104,149

    Total 20–22 farmers with exemptions = 33,284 or 31.96%

    Total 20–22 exemptions cancelled = 65,610

    $\qquad\qquad$ 31.96% total = 20,969

    Total 20–22 gp. called for service = 53,649

    $\qquad\qquad$ 31.96% total = 17,146

45. Calculated from Charts F and G.

46. Granatstein and Hitsman, *Broken Promises,* chs. 1–3.

47. Cited, Brown, *Borden, II,* 34.

CHART A   Military Age Groups: Male Population 15–44 Years Old in 1911

Province or Region	15–44 Male Population	% Total
PEI	19,715	1.0
Nova Scotia	111,184	5.9
New Brunswick	77,904	4.1
Maritime Provinces	208,803	11.1
Quebec	442,703	23.4
Ontario	638,079	33.9
Manitoba	132,571	7.0
Saskatchewan	167,608	8.9
Alberta	129,444	6.9
British Columbia	162,229	8.6
Western Canada	591,852	31.3
CANADA	1,888,825	100.0

Source: *Canada Year Book, 1913*, 82–84.

CHART B   Males 15 and Over—Canadian, British and Foreign Born in 1911

Province or Region	Number	% Canadian Born	% British Born	% Foreign Born
PEI	31,370	96.68	2.61	.70
Nova Scotia	166,870	89.27	7.58	3.17
New Brunswick	116,626	92.80	4.35	2.84
Maritime Provinces	314,866	91.32	5.88	2.81
Quebec	627,002	89.00	5.46	5.54
Ontario	925,948	71.42	19.42	9.16
Manitoba	172,989	43.21	30.50	26.29
Saskatchewan	206,889	38.61	23.90	37.49
Alberta	162,346	31.30	25.22	43.48
British Columbia	205,657	28.78	34.59	36.62
Western Canada	747,881	35.38	28.65	35.96
CANADA	2,623,820	67.68	17.08	15.24

Source: *6th Census of Canada, 1921*, Vol. 2, Table 24, 118–19.

CHART C Single Males 15 and Over—Canadian, British and Foreign Born in 1911

Province or Region	Number	% Canadian Born	% British Born	% Foreign Born
PEI	12,952	97.79	.67	1.54
Nova Scotia	72,600	90.93	5.59	3.49
New Brunswick	50,840	93.92	2.90	3.17
Maritime Provinces	136,392	92.69	4.12	3.18
Quebec	287,115	90.59	3.96	5.44
Ontario	380,689	75.10	16.29	8.61
Manitoba	82,660	55.76	23.76	20.47
Saskatchewan	110,505	44.92	18.93	36.14
Alberta	91,174	37.51	21.34	41.16
British Columbia	84,492	39.17	32.77	28.09
Western Canada	368,831	44.19	23.78	32.03
CANADA	1,175,285	71.18	14.24	14.59

CHART D Strength of Infantry Battalions Raised in Canada Before Military Service Act

Time Period of Organization / Total No. Battalions	Full Plus One or More Drafts	Full	Full to Half Strength	Less Than Half Strength	Disbanded	
Aug-Sep 1914 First Contingent 17		16	1[x]			17th Battalion had sailing strength of 665. Duguid *Appendices*, #84, pp. 50–51.
Oct 14-Sept 15 71	37	32	2			
Oct 15-Dec 15 85		25	52	7	1	
Jan 16-Jun 16 72	2[*]	13[**]	29[***]	21	7	[+]Includes 5 special function battalions raised across Canada.
Jul 16- 13			3[****]	8	2	[x]Excludes 2 battalions raised for Siberia in 1918. [+]Includes 2 special function battalions raised across Canada.
258	39	86	87	36	10	

[*]Both special functions.
[**]2 special functions.
[***]1 special function.
[****]2 special functions.

Calculated from RG 24, vols. 1344–54, File HQS 93-3-25 (Embarkation Reports).

CHART E   Administration of the Military Service Act by Regions

	Requisitions & Exemptions Claims			Reports for Service Volunteer / By Order				Exemptions Refused				20–22 Class			
	Total Class 1	Exemptions Claimed Number	% of Class 1	Rpts for Service Initially Signed	Minus Low Category	Rpts for Service	Rpts for Service as % Class 1	Exemptions Refused by Appeal Tribunals	As % of Claims	As % of Class 1	20–22 Exempted (Cancelled)	20–22 Called for Service	20–22 Called as % Class 1	20–22 Called as % of 20–22 Exempted
Maritimes	47019	43340	92.1	3679	1462	2217	4.72	6083	14.04	12.94	12139 (7819)	6534	13.90	52.83
Quebec	115602	113291	98.0	2311	423	1888	1.63	10691	9.44	9.25	43290 (26340)	20884	18.06	48.24
Ontario	124965	116092	92.9	8873	1157	7716	6.17	18649	16.06	14.92	29408 (18188)	15355	12.29	52.21
Western Canada	114296	103906	90.9	10390	3891	6499	5.69	14507	13.96	12.69	19321 (13263)	10876	9.52	56.32
CANADA	401882	376629	93.7	25253	6933	18320	4.5	49930	13.26	12.42	104149 (65610)	53649	13.3	51.51
PAGE	94	94	94	44	44	44		100			101 (116)	54		

Calculated from Sessional Paper 246, 1919.

CHART F Infantry Manpower Made Available to CEF as % of 15–44 Age Group in 1911

	15–44 Age Gp in 1911	1st Contingent		Militia Recruiting 10/14—1915		Patriotic Recruiting 10/15—1917		MSA Made Available for Service		MSA Served in CEF		Total Made Available for CEF		Total Served in CEF	
		Number	% Age Gp	Number	% Age Gp	Number	% Age Gp	Number	% Age Gp	Number	% Age Gp	Number	% Age Gp	Number	% Age Gp
Maritime Provinces	208803	836	.4	7472	3.6	12476	6.0	14778	7.1	10599	5.1	35582	17.0	31403	18.0
Quebec	442703	3064	.7	10750	2.4	6968	1.6	22288	5.0	19050	4.3	43040	9.7	39832	9.0
Ontario	638709	6044	.9	34376	5.4	51668	8.1	32676	5.1	27087	4.2	124764	19.5	119175	18.7
Western Provinces[x]	591852	9335	1.6	37105	6.3	45386	7.7	52446	5.5	26619	4.5	124272	20.9	118445	20.0
CANADA[+]	1888825	19299	1.0	89703	4.7	123966	6.6	105016[++]	5.6	96379[++]	5.1	337984	17.9	329347	17.4

[x]Includes bns raised interprovincially 10/14—1917.

[+]Canada figures include 7 nationally raised Forestry and Railway bns 1916 and 1917.

[++]Nicholson figures, CEF, 551 which include those on harvest leave at armistice.

CHART G Farmers Under Military Service Act by Region

	Farmers Reg'd	As % Reg'd	Exemptions Claimed	As % Farmers Reg'd	Allowed Medical	As % Farmers Claimed	Other Claims Allowed	As % Farmers Claimed	Claims Disallowed	As % Farmers Claimed	20–22 Class						
											With Farm Exempt	As % Total Claim	As % Farmer Reg'd	As % Total Reg'd	Reports for Service	As % Farmers Reg'd	As % Total Reg'd
Maritimes	17012	36.2	16438	96.6	3837	23.3	10422	63.4	2179	13.3	2138	13.0	13.0	4.5	574	3.4	1.2
Quebec	36947	32.0	36916	99.9	2834	7.7	26715	72.4	7267	19.7	13713	37.1	37.1	11.9	131	0.4	0.1
Ontario	45706	36.6	45058	98.6	11960	26.5	29657	65.8	3441	7.6	8786	19.5	19.2	7.0	648	1.4	0.5
Prairie Provinces	64537	67.1	61689	95.6	7396	12.0	46836	75.9	7457	12.1	8562	13.9	13.3	8.9	2848	4.4	3.0
Western Provinces	66819	58.5	63669	95.3	8224	12.9	47883	75.2	7562	11.8	8647	13.6	12.9	7.6	3150	4.7	2.8
CANADA	166484	41.4	162081	97.4	26855	16.6	114677	70.8	20449	12.6	33284	20.5	19.9	8.3	4503	2.7	1.1
AGE	102		102		103		103		103		101				102		

Source: Sessional Paper 246, 1919.

RACE AND RECRUITMENT IN WORLD WAR I: ENLISTMENT OF VISIBLE MINORITIES IN THE CANADIAN EXPEDITIONARY FORCE

James W. St.G. Walker

Contemporaries called it 'the war to end all wars' and 'the war to make the world safe for democracy.' During it, women throughout the North Atlantic world stepped forcefully into public affairs; subject populations in central Europe emerged into national self-determination; the proletariat triumphed beyond the Eastern front. But if World War I has thus been deemed 'progressive,' whatever its horrible cost, it was not intended as a liberal social instrument. For example, the relations between categories of people termed 'races' were regarded as immutable, and therefore expected to emerge from the war intact. Science and public opinion accepted that certain identifiable groups lacked the valour, discipline, and intelligence to fight a modern war. Since those same groups were also the subjects of the European overseas empires, prudence warned that a taste of killing white men might serve as appetizer should they be enlisted against a European enemy. The obvious conclusion was that this must be 'a white man's war.'

This decision was reached by virtually all the protagonists, but it was modified by an admission that since the subject races would clearly benefit from the victory of their own masters, they might be allowed to do their bit for the cause as appropriate to their own perceived abilities. Early in the war, when they constituted the empire's largest reserve of trained men, British Indian troops from the 'martial races' of the subcontinent were committed to France. But when the nature of the conflict became evident, and British forces available, it was discovered that Indian combat troops were unsuitable for Europe. Most were diverted to the Middle Eastern campaigns, where their targets were non-Europeans, though thousands of Indian labourers remained in Europe. Similarly New Zealand sent a Maori infantry unit to Gallipoli, and a Maori labour unit to Belgium and France. Even sensitive South Africa agreed, when labour shortages were most pressing in 1916, to enlist blacks for non-combat duties in Europe. China's contribution as an ally was to provide 50,000 'coolies' to labour behind the lines in France. Typically contrary, France itself began the war

From the *Canadian Historical Review*, LXX, 1, 1989, 1–26. Reprinted by permission of University of Toronto Press Incorporated.

This article was presented at the Canadian Ethnic Studies Conference, Halifax, in October 1987. I am grateful to the Social Sciences and Humanities Research Council for financial assistance, and to the following for their critical comments: John Armstrong, Norman Buchignani, Michael Craton, Thamis Gale, Roy Ito, Desmond Morton, Palmer Patterson, John Stubbs, Stephanie Walker, and Glenn Wright.

using its 'force noire' only at Gallipoli and as garrison troops in the French colonies, but the huge losses of men on the Western Front overcame the doubts of the high command and in 1916 African troops appeared in the European trenches. When the Americans entered the war in 1917, black volunteers were at first rejected. Though later recruited and conscripted in large numbers, fewer than 10 per cent ever fired a rifle in the direction of a German; the overwhelming majority were consigned to non-combat service battalions.[1]

Canada shared the Western ideology of 'race,' and Canadian wartime practice generally was in step with the allies: until manpower needs at the front surmounted the obvious objections, killing Germans was the privilege of white troops. Even when called upon, members of Canada's 'visible' minorities were accompanied overseas by a set of presumptions about their abilities which dictated the role they were to play and which limited the rewards they were to derive.[2] An examination of policy towards them and of their participation in the war offers a temporary opening in the curtain which typically covers Canadian racism, revealing some details from the set of stereotypes applied to certain minorities. The curtain also lifts upon the determination and self-confidence of Canadian minorities, and their struggle to be accorded equal responsibilities as well as equal opportunities. The struggle is further revealed, in many instances, as a community effort: communities encouraged, organized, and financed the enlistment of their young men, and those men volunteered in order to gain group recognition and to further the rights of whole communities.

In August 1914 a surge of patriotism, assisted by severe unemployment, prompted the enlistment of more than the 25,000 volunteers initially required for the first CEF contingent. For over a year, in fact, the supply of men exceeded demand: recruiting officers could afford to be selective, and one of the selection criteria was the 'race' of the applicant. Under the terms of the minister of militia's 'call to arms,' existing militia units enrolled volunteers directly, and the local militia officers had complete discretion over whom to accept.[3] There was one exception, however: within days of the first shots in Europe, the Militia Council forbade the enlistment of native Indians on the reasoning that 'Germans might refuse to extend to them the privileges of civilized warfare.' This directive was not, however, made public, and some recruiting officers remained ignorant of it. Indian youth, like their white counterparts, were anxious to participate and presented themselves to their local units. Many were enlisted only to be turned away when their Indian status was discovered. Some were able to slip through undetected, with or without the collusion of their commanders, so that the early contingents did contain some native soldiers despite the official policy.[4]

Members of other 'visible' groups were less successful. Individual unit discretion appears to have kept East Indians entirely outside the Canadian forces, and in British Columbia, where most of them lived, Japanese were rejected completely. The fate of Chinese Canadians is less clear, but if any were accepted in the early years of the war their numbers must have been extremely small.[5] In a memo of November 1914 responding to a query on 'coloured enlistment,' the militia would only refer to the established policy that personnel selection was a matter for each commanding officer, though the chief of general staff offered the prevailing opinion: 'Would Canadian Negroes make good fighting men? I do not think so.'[6] One Cape Breton black volunteer, who decided that 'It's a job that I'll like killing Germans,' was told he was ineligible to join any white unit; a group of about fifty blacks from Sydney, who went to enlist together, were advised: 'This is not for you fellows, this is a white man's war.'[7]

The Canadian volunteers rejected by this policy were not content to accept either their exclusion or the reasoning that went with it. They sought enlistment in large numbers, and insisted on knowing why their offer was not accepted. As early as November 1914 the black community of North Buxton was complaining to Ottawa and seeking corrective action; from Hamilton blacks came the charge that it was 'beneath the dignity of the Government to make racial or color distinction in an issue of this kind'; blacks in Saint John condemned recruitment discrimination and added for the record an account of the discrimination they met daily in their home city.[8] Saint John MP William Pugsley, at the request of Ontario and New Brunswick black representatives, raised the issue in the House of Commons. The government insisted that 'there is no Dominion legislation authorizing discrimination against coloured people,' and the militia was able to state that 'no regulations or restrictions' prevented 'enrollment of coloured men who possess the necessary qualifications,' but no remedies were offered or comment made upon clear evidence of exclusion for 'racial' reasons.[9] And yet the urge to enlist persisted. A group of Cape Croker Indians applied to four different recruitment centres and were rejected from each one; Japanese in British Columbia made repeated attempts to enlist; blacks in Nova Scotia travelled from one unit to another hoping to find acceptance.[10] To some extent this persistence must have been prompted by young men's sense of adventure and patriotism, but they were moved as well by a consciousness that a contribution to the war effort could help to overcome the disadvantages faced by their communities. The Japanese believed that war participation would earn them the franchise, a hope that was shared by some Indian groups. Blacks maintained that a war for justice must have an impact on 'the progress of our race' in Canada.[11]

White intransigence was not overcome by these efforts, but a compromise seemed possible: if whites and non-whites could not stand shoulder to shoulder in defence of the empire, perhaps they could stand separately. 'Coloured candidates are becoming insistent,' a Vancouver recruiter complained, and his superior advised that 'as white men will not serve in the same ranks with negros or coloured persons,' the only solution was to create a separate unit.[12] Because of the numerous black applications in Nova Scotia, several similar suggestions were made, and one commanding officer, though rejecting individual blacks, agreed to accept an entire platoon if one were formed.[13] On the 'reliable information' that 10,000 blacks inhabited Edmonton region from whom 1,000 could easily be recruited, Alberta district commander Cruikshank, with the support of the lieutenant governor, offered to create a black battalion since a racially integrated Alberta regiment 'would not be advisable.' On the same principle General Cruikshank proposed that a 'Half-Breed Battalion' be recruited in Alberta.[14] More insistent and widespread were suggestions to raise distinct regiments of native Indians. Every province from Ontario west produced proposals to enlist natives in segregated units where, under careful supervision of white officers, their 'natural' talents as fighters and marksmen could best be utilized.[15] Some of these suggestions were enthusiastically endorsed by the affected groups, believing that as a recognizable unit they could gain more attention for their communal cause,[16] but none were more energetic than the Japanese. In August 1915 the Canadian Japanese Association of Vancouver offered to raise an exclusively Japanese unit. Receiving a polite reply, the association began to enlist volunteers, eventually 227 of them, who were supported at Japanese community expense and practised their drill under British veteran and militia captain R.S. Colquhoun. With one company thus trained, the association made a formal offer to the government in March 1916 of a full battalion.[17]

The Japanese offer, like every other proposal to create a racially defined battalion, was rejected by Militia Headquarters. Officials doubted that enough volunteers from any group could be found to create and maintain a unit as large as a battalion, and furthermore its members could not be used as reinforcements in other battalions, as was frequently required in trench warfare, if integration should prove difficult. Privately, the combat abilities of blacks and Indians were considered questionable, and although Japanese were regarded as 'desirable soldiers,' their enlistment was feared as a step towards enfranchisement. Individual 'half-breeds,' blacks, and Japanese were theoretically admissible into all militia units. 'There is no colour line,' insisted the adjutant general, but commanding officers were free to accept or reject any volunteer for any reason.[18] One incident more than any other provoked this statement. In November 1915 twenty black volunteers from Saint John were sent to Camp Sussex, where they were told to go instead to Ontario where a 'Coloured Corps' was being formed. Protesting that this action was 'shameful and insulting to the Race,' the Saint John blacks pressed their case with the governor general and militia minister Sir Sam Hughes. Apparently outraged, Hughes ordered a full investigation into the incident and promised that there would be no racial barriers and no segregated units in his army. When the Sussex commanding officer complained that it was not 'fair' to expect white troops 'to mingle with negroes,' a sentiment supported by all the commanding officers in the Maritime district, militia officials quickly explained that local commanders retained their discretionary powers: 'it is not thought desirable, either in the interests of such men themselves or of the Canadian Forces, that Commanding Officers should be forced to take them.'[19] Whatever Hughes's intentions, the statement reinforced the status quo. It remained a white man's war.

At the outbreak of the war a surplus of volunteers had afforded considerable latitude in selecting recruits. By the spring of 1915, when the second Canadian Contingent sailed, trench warfare had eroded all hopes for a short and glorious war, and casualty rates were horrifying. Domestic production competed with the armed services for manpower, just as more and more men were required for the trenches. Selectivity became less rigid, as height, medical, and marital requirements were relaxed, and the recruitment method itself came under scrutiny. In the fall of 1915 a new policy was substituted, enabling any patriotic person or group to form a battalion. This 'patriotic phase,' distinguished from the earlier 'militia phase,' led to the proliferation of new units and to rivalries among them for the available manpower. Since the fighting regiments were not being reinforced directly by new recruitment, the 'patriotic' policy also meant that the units thus raised almost inevitably had to be broken up on arrival in Europe to be used to fill the gaps caused by casualties in the existing regiments. The entire situation was compounded by Prime Minister Borden's announcement that, as of 1 January 1916, Canada would pledge 500,000 troops to Europe. With prevailing casualty rates, it would require 300,000 new recruits per year to maintain this figure in the field.[20]

All these developments—the scramble for men, the raising of special regiments, and their use as reinforcements for fighting units overseas—had implications for recruiting 'visible' minorities. First to fall was the restriction against Indian enlistment. Certain regiments had been discreetly recruiting Indians since 1914, but when Ontario's new 114th Battalion was being formed in November 1915 its commander hoped to enlist four companies of Brantford and region Indians. His superior, the Toronto district commander, lent support to the plan on the understanding that all Indians recruited in his division would be transferred to the 114th. It was apparently this limited plan, consistent with the 'special units' policy, that was at first approved by the militia minister; Indians already in other regiments were invited to transfer to the 114th, and the new battalion was permitted to recruit Indians outside its own geographical territory.[21] The memo that went out to commanding officers, however, stated that Indian enlistment was henceforth authorized 'in the various Units for Overseas Service,' and this impression was reinforced in individual letters to commanders permitting Indian enlistment. The confusion amongst recruiting officers was shared by the chief of general staff, Willoughby Gwatkin, who confessed that he did not know whether open enlistment was now the rule or whether Indian battalions were to be formed.[22] Meanwhile, the 114th was advertising itself, even in the public press, as *the* Indian unit, and at least a dozen regiments transferred their Indian recruits to the 114th.[23] In the event, pressure from other battalion commanders convinced divisional headquarters to cease transferring Indians to the 114th, which was therefore unable to fill more than two Indian companies. The result was a concentration of Indians in the 114th, but others were scattered individually throughout the battalions willing to accept them.[24]

It was perhaps this reigning confusion over special units, coupled with the pressure to find a half million men, that led to one of the war's most discouraging episodes for black Canadians. In November 1915 J.R.B. Whitney, editor of a Toronto black newspaper, the *Canadian Observer,* wrote to Hughes asking if the minister would accept a platoon of 150 black men provided it would be maintained at that strength throughout the war. Hughes warmly replied that 'these people can form a platoon in any Battalion, now. There is nothing in the world to stop them.'[25] On this basis Whitney began to advertise through the *Observer,* and enlisted volunteers in the projected platoon. Early in January 1916 he was able to report to Hughes that he had enlisted a number of Toronto recruits, adding a request to second a black enlisted man for a recruitment tour of southwestern Ontario. Hughes passed this on to the adjutant general, W.E. Hodgins, for action, and this latter official was forced to return to Whitney for an explanation of what was meant by all this. In the process Hodgins discovered that no arrangement had been made with any battalion commander to receive a black platoon. In fact, advised Toronto's General Logie, it was doubtful if any commander would accept 'a coloured platoon' into 'a white man's Battalion.' Hodgins therefore decided that permission to recruit a black unit could not be granted, and he asked Toronto division so to inform Mr. Whitney. On 15 March Whitney received a blunt letter from the Toronto recruiting officer stating that as no commanding officer was willing to enlist them, the plan must be abandoned.[26]

A very hurt Whitney asked for a reconsideration; he had already gathered forty volunteers and could not now tell them to disband. An embarrassed Hodgins begged Logie to find some unit prepared to admit Whitney's platoon, and Logie diligently conducted a canvas of his district. The responses from battalion commanders dramatically revealed the prevailing feelings among the military leadership in 1916. Most rejected the idea without explanation, stating simply their unwillingness to accept blacks. Several acknowledged that white recruitment would be discouraged, and dissatisfaction aroused amongst men already enlisted. Some confirmed that they had already rejected numbers of black volunteers. The most ambiguous answer came from the 48th Highlanders, whose adjutant stated that 'we have, being a kilted regiment, always drawn the line at taking coloured men.' No one apologized or offered any positive suggestions. No one seemed to think his prejudices would not be understood, and shared, in headquarters. Logie replied to Hodgins that the situation was obviously hopeless. Whitney's personal appeal to Hughes provoked sympathy and some furious cables, but the result could not be changed. Even with a half million soldiers to find, Ontario's military establishment could not 'stoop' to the recruitment of blacks.[27]

But Ottawa desks had been shaken, and General Gwatkin was ordered to write a report on 'the enlistment of negroes in the Canadian Expeditionary Force.' Besides Whitney's experience, overtures from black Nova Scotians had become more difficult to ignore, since they were supported by several influential Conservative politicians.[28] Gwatkin's memorandum was scarcely complimentary, but it did offer an opportunity for blacks to join the war. 'Nothing is to be gained by blinking facts,' Gwatkin began:

> The civilized negro is vain and imitative; in Canada he is not being impelled to enlist by a high sense of duty; in the trenches he is not likely to make a good fighter; and the average white man will not associate with him on terms of equality. Not a single commanding officer in Military District No. 2 is willing to accept a coloured platoon as part of his battalion; and it would be humiliating to the coloured men themselves to serve in a battalion where they were not wanted.
>
> In France, in the firing line, there would be no place for a black battalion, CEF. It would be eyed askance; it would crowd out a white battalion; it would be difficult to reinforce.
>
> Nor could it be left in England and used as a draft-giving depot; for there would be trouble if negroes were sent to the front for the purpose of reinforcing white battalions; and, if they are good men at all, they would resent being kept in Canada for the purpose of finding guards &c.

Gwatkin concluded with the recommendation that blacks could be enlisted, as at present, in any battalion willing to accept them, and that a labour battalion could additionally be formed exclusively for them.[29] On 19 April 1916, with Prime Minister Borden presiding, the Militia Council decided to form a black labour battalion headquartered in Nova Scotia, provided the British command would agree. This approval was received three weeks later.[30]

'It is a somewhat peculiar command,' admitted Adjutant General Hodgins, after some difficulty was experienced in finding a qualified officer willing to head a black battalion. But Prime Minister Borden, himself a Halifax politician, took a personal interest in the new project and suggested the name of a potential commander, Daniel H. Sutherland. On 5 July, the day after Sutherland's acceptance, the Nova Scotia No 2 Construction Battalion (Coloured) was formally announced. Officered by whites, the unit was authorized to recruit blacks from all across Canada.[31] The black community in Nova Scotia heartily welcomed the formation of the No 2. 'Considerable joy and happiness' erupted, particularly among the young men, for the No 2 seemed to recognize that 'they were men the same as everybody else.' The African Baptist Association, at its 1916 annual meeting, expressed the view that through the No 2 'the African race was making history,' and pledged to do all in its power to encourage enlistment.[32] Although the all-white No 1 Construction Battalion complained bitterly about its name, fearing association with 'work which might be done by the negro race,'[33] no doubts seem to have been uttered by black representatives at the nature of the work or the fact of segregation.

By the summer of 1916 Canadian blacks, Indians, and Japanese were all being actively recruited into the services. Following the rejection of the Canadian Japanese Association's offer to form a full battalion, militia authorities encouraged other battalions to accept the volunteers who had already received basic training through their private efforts. The association itself promoted this policy, appealing to Alberta's General Cruikshank to permit Japanese to enlist in his district, since BC commanders remained adamantly opposed. On his return trip to Vancouver from Ottawa, where he had gone to present the case for a Japanese battalion, association president Yasuchi Yamazaki met with Cruikshank in Calgary, and the general immediately wrote to battalion commanders with the offer of up to 200 Japanese recruits.[34] The response was overwhelmingly positive. The 192nd Battalion offered to receive all 200, and the 191st asked for 250, but this was vetoed from headquarters as 'there is no objection to the enlistment of odd men, but large numbers are not to be enlisted.' Advertisements from Alberta recruiters appeared in Vancouver's Japanese language press, and temporary recruiting offices were established in British Columbia, though this latter practice was contrary to regulations. Battalions from other provinces, too, sought Japanese recruits. Eventually 185 served overseas in eleven different battalions, mainly in the 10th, 50th, and 52nd infantry battalions. It was undoubtedly at this time that individual Chinese were being enlisted by under-strength battalions.[35]

The rivalry to recruit Japanese was being reflected in the much larger campaign to enlist native Indians. The 114th began with the advantage of being identified as an Indian battalion, and confusion continued for several months over whether all Indians, recruited before or since December 1915, were to be transferred to it. Some Indians who had enlisted in other regiments applied to transfer to the 114th; others asked not to be transferred because they preferred not to serve with 'Mohawks.'[36] The Department of Indian Affairs lent its official support to the 114th recruitment drive, and seconded Charles Cooke to the regiment with the honorary rank of lieutenant. Described as 'the only male Indian employed in the Service at Ottawa,' Cooke toured the Ontario reserves on behalf of the 114th, sometimes in the company of an Indian commissioned officer, stressing the pride and the opportunity derived from serving in an identifiably Indian unit. Although by this time it had been determined that only two companies, that is half the battalion, would in fact consist of Indians, the 114th stressed its Indian connection. The regimental badge contained two crossed tomahawks, and its band, composed mostly of Brantford reserve Iroquois, gave concerts which included Indian war dances.[37]

Other battalions were not slow to enter the recruitment race. Hodgins's attempt to settle the 114th's jurisdiction, by giving it authority to recruit Indians beyond its regimental territory but not *exclusive* authority, seems merely to have stimulated rivalries. Other commanding officers sought to entice Charles Cooke into their service; one battalion allegedly was offering a $5 recruitment bonus to Indians plus a free trip to Europe in case the war ended before they went overseas; others were reportedly recruiting young boys from the residential schools. In July 1916, when Colonel Mewburn called for a report on Indians enlisted in Military District 2, headquartered in Toronto, the 114th had 348, including five officers, and 211 others were arrayed across fifteen different units. This did not include the 107th battalion, raised in Winnipeg and commanded by G.L. Campbell, a senior Indian Affairs official. At first intended as an all-Indian battalion, the 107th shared the experience of Ontario's 114th and eventually enlisted approximately one-half its membership among Indians.[38]

Although these numbers were all recruited, at least ostensibly, into infantry battalions, there were parallel efforts to enlist Indians in non-combatant labour and construction units, particularly for forestry. Duncan Campbell Scott, the senior Indian Affairs official, urged this movement through Indian agents across Canada. When white officers and recruits in forestry units, primarily on the west coast, objected to working amongst 'Indians and Half-breeds,' authority was granted to establish separate native companies and platoons.[39] One of the construction units to recruit amongst Indians was none other than the No 2, from Nova Scotia. Five Indians joined the No 2 at Windsor, Ontario, allegedly on the promise of becoming non-commissioned officers. Once enlisted they claimed to be disgusted by the fighting, gambling, and drinking going on in the No 2 camp, and they called for a transfer. When Colonel Sutherland's response was slow, Chief Thunderwater of the Great Council of the Tribes took up the Indians' case, claiming 'a natural dislike of association with negroes on the part of Indians.' The adjutant general in Ottawa and General Logie in Toronto had to become involved before this entanglement could be settled and the Indians moved to the 256th Railway Construction Battalion, which had a large Indian component. Chief Thunderwater admonished the adjutant general 'that you so arrange that Indians and negroes are kept from the same Battalions.'[40]

The reason the No 2 was in Windsor, Ontario, was that Sutherland had been given authority to recruit nationally, though this clearly meant that he could recruit blacks, for whom there was no inter-regimental competition. Information was sent to every commanding officer in the country authorizing 'any of the coloured men in Canada, now serving in units of the C.E.F., to transfer to the No. 2 Construction Battalion, should they so wish.' Several black volunteers did transfer from other units, at least some with the overt encouragement of their officers.[41] Within Nova Scotia a regimental band was organized, holding recruiting concerts in churches and halls wherever a black audience might be attracted. In the larger black communities, Citizens Recruiting Committees were formed to encourage enlistment, the Rev. W.A. White of the African Baptist Church in Truro gave 'stirring' speeches, and black church elders lent moral support.[42] Early recruiting reports were satisfying, but by November 1916 Sutherland felt it necessary to undertake a more active campaign outside Nova Scotia. His request to recruit in the West Indies was turned down, but funds were authorized in January 1917 to take the band on a tour to Montreal and Toronto, and black centres in southwestern Ontario. After a decline between October and December, recruitment picked up again in January, most of it in Windsor, Ontario, where many American blacks joined the Canadian unit.[43] In western Canada Captain Gayfer established a recruiting office in Edmonton, from which he too conducted tours and spoke in black churches. He later moved his headquarters to Winnipeg, leaving a black enlisted man in charge of the Edmonton office while a white lieutenant visited British Columbia. All across Canada young black men were being advised that 'the need of the day' was for pioneers and construction workers whose contribution to the movement forward to victory was vital.[44]

Two years into the war, recruitment policy towards 'visible' minorities had been reversed completely. But during those two years, the ardour to join their white brethren in the defence of Canadian democracy had been somewhat dampened among the minority youth. Japanese recruitment never remotely approached the thousand men projected by Yamazaki, perhaps because they were not allowed to serve in recognizable units as they believed was essential to win rights for their community. Native Indians did have the opportunity to enlist in concentrated units, but where such units existed they never recruited up to their authorized strength. The fact was that the invitation to serve was coming too late, and after a discouraging demonstration of majority attitudes towards their potential contribution. The Six Nations, who had offered their assistance as allies to the King in 1914, now opposed recruiters on the ground that they were an independent people and would enlist only upon the personal appeal of the governor general and recognition of their special status.[45] Other Indian groups complained that 'We are not citizens and have no votes, as free men'; anti-recruiters followed recruiters around the reserves, speaking out against Indian enlistment during 'Patriotic' meetings, reminding Indians of their grievances and the many government promises made to them which had been broken throughout history.[46] Other factors interfered as well. There was resentment against recruitment methods, including reports of intimidating tactics and the enrolment of underage boys. Indignation followed a rumour that overseas the Indians would be disguised as Italians, thus preventing any recognition for their accomplishments. Complaints from Indians already enlisted, alleging racial discrimination and inferior treatment in the forces, filtered back to the reserves. Other letters from Indians at the front described 'the awfulness of war' and 'openly advised the Indians not to think of enlisting.'[47]

Nor did black Canadians fail to register scepticism at the recruitment campaign. In Nova Scotia, where black community leadership was won over, many individuals 'were feeling keenly that their Loyal offers of service were refused in so many instances,' and were reluctant now to join the No 2. Blacks in the west told recruiters the same thing.[48] Resentment at previous insult was reinforced by continued insult: in Winnipeg black recruits were derided and called 'nigger' by medical staff assigned to examine them. When Colonel Sutherland decided to move his headquarters from Pictou to Truro, he rented a suitable building and had begun furnishing it when the owner suddenly cancelled the contract. The same thing happened to Captain Gayfer when the owner of his recruiting office cancelled the contract 'on account of color of recruits.' Eventually established in Truro, black recruits met segregation in the local theatre. Rumours percolated through the black communities as well, for example that they were to be used only as trench diggers in France.[49] Although several prominent whites, notably Nova Scotian MPs Fleming McCurdy and John Stanfield and businessman H. Falconer McLean, assisted in the formation and recruitment of the No 2, the military hierarchy itself was less than enthusiastic, perhaps feeling that the black battalion had been imposed on them for political reasons. The chief of general staff regarded the unit as 'troublesome.' It took Sutherland two months to gain approval for his tour beyond Nova Scotia, and then only with the strictest admonitions to economize. Western recruiter Gayfer was denied office supplies, had his transport warrants delayed, and received no rations or barrack accommodation for his recruits.[50] And yet Sutherland received constant memos and cables asking him when his unit would be ready for overseas service. The first target was three months; after seven months, Sutherland was told to prepare the men already recruited for sailing, and new recruits could follow later; eventually it was in March 1917, nine months after recruitment began, that the No 2 embarked for England, and with only 603 men enlisted of an authorized strength of 1033 other ranks.[51] Because it arrived in Britain below battalion strength, the No 2 was converted to a labour company of 500 men, and Sutherland was reduced in rank to major.[52]

It was not only 'visible' minority youth who had developed a reluctance to volunteer. In July 1916 recruitment in general plumetted, from monthly peaks near 30,000 earlier in the year to fewer than 8,000, and continued to fall to around 3,000 a month. Not a single battalion raised after July 1916 reached its full strength, from any part of Canada. Employment in domestic war production, and increasing awareness of the carnage at the front, caused the virtual collapse of the voluntary system just at the time when the push was being made to enlist 'visible' minorities. In May 1917, when casualty rates in Europe were more than double new recruitment, Prime Minister Borden announced his intention to introduce conscription with the cry that 'the battle for Canadian liberty and autonomy is being fought today on the plains of France and Belgium.' The Military Service Act, when effected later that year, was less than a popular success among those liable to its call. Over 90 per cent of them applied for exemption.[53]

Canada's Indians were immediate and outspoken in denying the legality of their conscription. 'Indians refuse to report,' cabled one anxious Indian agent. More sophisticated responses referred to the fact that Indians were 'wards of the government,' legally 'minors' and treated as children: surely children were not being called to defend the empire? Since they had no vote, and no voice in the conduct of the war or of the councils of state, it was unfair to expect them to participate now in the war. 'We cannot say that we are fighting for our liberty, freedom and other privileges dear to all nations, for we have none,' stated an Ontario Indian declaration. BC Indians considered 'that the government attitude towards us in respect to our land troubles and in refusing to extend to us the position of citizens of Canada are unreasonable, and until we receive just treatment ... we should not be subject to conscription.' Still others quoted the treaties made in the 1870s, and the negotiations surrounding those treaties, during which Indians were assured that they would never be called to war. Petitions flowed to Ottawa, and even to the King: if they were not to have the rights of citizens, they must not be forced to perform a citizen's duty.[54] Similar petitions came from BC Japanese, pointing out that although they were naturalized Canadians they lacked the franchise and other citizenship privileges, and they claimed exemption from obligatory military service.[55] In these objections to conscription there was a scarcely submerged articulation of the 'war aims' of Canadian minorities: if it was to be their war, it must result in the extension of equality to their people.

The government hesitated. Indians were first granted an extension of the time required to register; then they were advised officially to seek exemption under some existing regulation, such as agricultural employment.[56] Finally, on 17 January 1918, an order in council exempted Indians and Japanese, on the grounds of their limited citizenship rights and, for the former, the treaty promises. The order also referred to the War Time Elections Act which had deprived certain naturalized Canadians of the franchise and at the same time relieved them of military service. In March the regulations were amended so that any British subject disqualified from voting at a federal election was exempted from conscription. Despite the fact that they would already have been covered by this regulation, East Indians were granted a special exemption order three months later.[57]

This did not of course apply to black Canadians, who already enjoyed the franchise and therefore remained liable to conscription. The No 2, still smarting from its demotion to a labour company, immediately requested that all blacks conscripted across Canada be sent to it, so that it could be restored to battalion status. The No 2 proposal was promoted by Nova Scotian MP Fleming McCurdy, among others, and was received sympathetically by the new militia minister, General Mewburn, who confessed that 'The whole problem of knowing how to handle coloured troops has been a big one for some years back.' A collection depot was established in London, Ontario, where No 2 reinforcements could be made ready for overseas, and orders were sent to commanding officers to transfer all 'coloured men' to the London depot. The wording of the order did not appear to leave the commanders with any choice in keeping black conscripts in their own units.[58] In March, when it began to seem that black numbers were lower than anticipated, No 2 recruiters travelled to Detroit to attract black Canadians living there, but this was squelched by Ottawa on the grounds that 'we are not hunting for coloured recruits but merely making a place for them as they come in under the Military Service Act.' Again, when the British-Canadian Recruiting Mission in New York announced that 'about two thousand colored British subjects have registered,' some or all of whom could be sent to reinforce the No 2, Ottawa's answer was a terse 'none required.'[59] Deciding that the number of black conscripts coming in, directly or by transfer, was not worth the effort, Ottawa ordered the abandonment of the London reception centre in May. Sutherland was informed that his company would not be restored to battalion strength after all.[60]

There was one more try. The Rev. William White, chaplain to the No 2 and as an honorary captain 'the only colored officer in our forces,' wrote an impassioned letter to the prime minister. 'The coloured people are proud that they have at least one definite Unit representing them in France,' he stated, requesting that the conscripted blacks be sent to strengthen the No 2.[61] As a consequence Major Bristol, secretary to the Canadian overseas militia minister in London, was asked to make a report. In a response labelled 'personal,' Bristol admitted that 'these Niggers do well in a Forestry Corps and other Labour units,' but since numbers were so limited 'the prospects of maintaining a battalion are not very bright.' Following a survey of district commanders, it appeared that scarcely more than too identified black conscripts were already enlisted, and 'on this showing it would hardly be possible to carry out the suggestion made' to use them to enhance the No 2. The plan was dropped once and for all.[62] Fifty-five black conscripts already gathered in Halifax were trained in Canada as infantrymen, together with white conscripts, but on arrival in England they were placed in a segregated labour unit. Eventually assigned to the 85th Battalion, the Armistice intervened before they could leave Britain.[63]

The ambivalence and the frankly racist confusion surrounding their recruitment was reflected in the overseas experiences of the enlisted minorities. The Japanese, it appears, were consistently used as combat troops, which was their purpose in volunteering.[64] The Indians had a mixed reception. The 114th, recruited with such pride as an Indian unit, was broken up on arrival in England and the men assigned to different battalions, many for labour duties. The 107th, also recruited with an Indian identity and as a fighting unit, was converted to a pioneer battalion in France, where the men dug trenches and built roads and muletracks under direct enemy fire, with heavy casualties. Some Indians did go to the front as combatants, but a sizeable contingent served in forestry work, chiefly within Britain itself.[65] Those blacks who served individually in combat regiments, since their admission had been entirely voluntary on the part of their officers, apparently met few problems. When the 106th Battalion was broken up, for example, its black members went to the Royal Canadian Regiment as reinforcements on the front lines, where they were welcomed. Undoubtedly there were many more where blacks served without incident.[66] But the No 2 itself, as a separate unit with its own administration and records, leaves a different trail. To avoid 'offending the susceptibility of other troops,' it was suggested that the black battalion be sent overseas in a separate transport ship, without escort. Since their sailing occurred during the war's worst period for German submarine attacks, it is fortunate that this suggestion was rejected by the Royal Navy.[67] The battalion arrived in England under strength, and the decision was made not to absorb the men into different units, where whites might object, but to keep them together as a labour company attached to the Forestry Corps in French territory. Working as loggers and in lumber mills, and performing related construction and shipping work, the men of the No 2 were established near La Joux, in the Jura region of France, with smaller detachments at Cartigny and Alençon. Although they laboured side by side with white units, the black soldiers were segregated in their non-working activities. Remote from any means of amusement, they had to await the creation of a separate 'coloured' YMCA for their evenings' entertainment. When ill, they were treated in a separate 'Coloured Wing' of the La Joux hospital. Those who strayed from military discipline were similarly confined in a segregated punishment compound. An extra Protestant chaplain had to be sent into Jura district 'as the Negro Chaplain is not acceptable to the White Units.' Always regarded as a problem and never seriously appreciated, the No 2 was disbanded with almost unseemly haste soon after the Armistice was announced, though the demand for forestry products remained high, and they were among the earliest Canadian units to leave France.[68]

The treatment received by 'visible' Canadians did not originate with the military; recruitment policy and overseas employment were entirely consistent with domestic stereotypes of 'race' characteristics and with general social practice in Canada. And Canadian attitudes themselves were merely a reflection of accepted and respected Western thought in the early twentieth century. Racial perceptions were derived, not from personal experience, but from the example of Canada's great mentors, Britain and the United States, supported by scientific explanations.[69] In these circumstances it is notable that the Canadian military, while by no means avoiding the influence of prevailing ideology, at least had the independence to be less restricting than most of the allies. For example, General Headquarters advised the Forestry Corps to reorganize the No 2 to conform to imperial standards, as were applied to South African, Chinese, and Egyptian 'coloured labour' units. This would have affected their pay and privileges, and for black non-commissioned officers it would mean a reduction to private. Colonel J.B. White, Forestry's La Joux commander, rejected this directive because 'the men of this Unit are engaged in exactly the same work as the white labour with whom they are employed . . . and it is recommended that no change be made.' Headquarters withdrew the order and the men of the No 2 continued to be treated as other Canadian forestry units.[70] One reason for assigning the No 2 to French territory was to avoid contact and comparison with other British 'coloured labour' units 'who are kept in compounds, and not permitted the customary liberties of white troops.'[71] Black American troops in France were completely segregated, forbidden to leave their bases without supervision, and barred from cafés and other public places. Friendly relations with French civilians led to the strictest measures, including the arrest of blacks who conversed with white women, and to an official American request to the French military beseeching their co-operation in keeping the races separate. British East Indian troops were restricted in their off-base activities and were liable to a dozen lashes for 'seeking romance' from white women. Senior army officials objected to East Indian sick and wounded being treated by white nurses. South African black labourers were kept in guarded compounds. Throughout the ranks of the Allies, with the partial exception of the French, non-white soldiers and workers were humiliated, restricted, and exploited. It was simply not their war.[72]

Generally speaking, the efforts of 'visible' enlisted men did not gain recognition for themselves or for their communities at home. Postwar race riots in the United States generated the worst violence experienced by black Americans since slavery. Attempts by Punjabi veterans to gain moderate political reforms led to the infamous Amritsar Massacre in April 1919, where 379 peaceful demonstrators were killed and 1,208 wounded while trapped in a box-like park. French use of African troops to occupy defeated Germany led to condemnation by the Allies and to international censure for subjecting white Germans to the horrors of black authority.[73] Respect, evidently, had not been won by four years in defence of Western ideals. There was even a Canadian incident to illustrate this situation: on 7 January 1919 at Kinmel Park Camp in Britain, white Canadian soldiers rioted and attacked the No 2 ranks on parade after a black sergeant arrested a white man and placed him in the charge of a 'coloured' escort.[74] Far from expressing gratitude for their services, the militia minister in 1919 seemed unaware that the No 2 had even existed.[75] It is true that individual Japanese veterans were granted the franchise, belatedly and grudgingly in 1931 by a one-vote margin in the BC legislature, and native Indians actually serving in the forces were enfranchised by the War Time Elections Act and its successors, but their families and other members of their communities remained as only partial Canadian citizens.[76] Especially indicative of their failure to attain genuine acceptance was the fact that at the outset of World War II, 'visible' volunteers would again be rejected altogether or directed towards support and service functions consistent with their peacetime stereotypes.[77]

During World War I about 3,500 Indians, over 1,000 blacks, and several hundred Chinese and Japanese enlisted in the Canadian forces. To their number must be added the many who tried to enlist and were rejected. Though there was an understandable resistance to later attempts to recruit and conscript them, still the numbers in uniform were impressive, a demonstration of loyalty and a confidence that accepting equal responsibilities would win the advantages of Canadian citizenship. Individual exceptions occurred, but as a group they were denied that equal opportunity to defend their country and empire.

Stereotypes which at first excluded them continued to restrict their military role, and even survived the war. In 1919 respect and equality remained beyond reach. Lessons which could and should have been learned in the first war had to be taught all over again in a second global conflict.

The experience of 'visible' minorities in World War I illustrates the nature of Canadian race sentiment early in this century. Most abruptly, it demonstrates that white Canadians participated in the Western ideology of racism. This was true not only in the general sense of accepting white superiority, but in the particular image assigned to certain peoples which labelled them as militarily incompetent. Canadian history itself should have suggested the contrary—blacks and Indians, for example, had a proud record of military service prior to Confederation—but the stereotypes derived from Britain and the United States were more powerful than domestic experience. Some degree of cynicism is discernible in the rejection of 'visible' volunteers, for example, the fear that military duty would enable them to demand political equality, yet it is not possible to read the entire record without concluding that most white Canadians, including the military hierarchy, were convinced by the international stereotypes and their supporting scientific explanations. This was carried to the point where Canada's war effort was impeded by prejudices for which there were no Canadian foundations.

Equally interesting is what the World War I experience reveals about the minorities themselves. Their persistence in volunteering, their insistence upon the 'right' to serve, their urgent demand to know the reasons for their rejection, all suggest that 'visible' Canadians had not been defeated by the racism of white society, had not accepted its rationalizations, and were not prepared quietly to accept inferior status. They retained a confidence in themselves, most obviously that they could achieve a glorious war record if given the opportunity. While recognizing the restrictions imposed on themselves and their communities, they were convinced that by their own efforts and the goodwill of white Canada they could remove those restrictions. Their appeals to parliament and the crown reveal as well that they had not lost faith in British/Canadian justice. The minority campaigns during World War I, for recruitment and later against conscription, were only possible for persons convinced that they were equal and could achieve recognition of their equality. Their loyalty to Canada and the empire included loyalty to an ideal which the dominant majority had forgotten.

Notes

1. For example, see Jeffrey Greenhut, 'The Imperial Reserve: The Indian Corps on the Western Front, 1914–15,' *Journal of Imperial and Commonwealth History* II (1983): 54–73, and 'Sahib and Sepoy: An Inquiry into the Relationship between the British Officers and Native Soldiers of the British Indian Army,' *Military Affairs* 48 (1984):15–18; Keith L. Nelson, 'The Black Horror on the Rhine: Race as a Factor in Post-World War I Diplomacy,' *Journal of Modern History* 62 (1970): 606–8; Fred Gaffen, *Forgotten Soldiers* (Penticton, BC 1985), 24, 74–5; B.P. Willan, 'The South African Native Labour Contingent, 1916–1918,' *Journal of African*

History 19 (1978): 61–86; C.J. Balesi, *From Adversaries to Comrades in Arms: West Africa and the French Military, 1885–1918* (Waltham, Mass. 1979), 112–13, 120–1; C.M. Andrew and A.S. Kanya-Forstner, 'France, Africa, and the First World War,' *Journal of African History* 19 (1978): 11–23; A.E. Barbeau and F. Henri, *The Unknown Soldiers: Black American Troops in World War* II (Philadelphia 1974); J.D. Foner, *Blacks and the Military in American History: A New Perspective* (New York 1974), 109–32. Black combat troops remained an American embarrassment. The all-black 93rd Division, for example, was first offered to the British army, and upon refusal was eventually attached to the French army for its combat service. The Chinese 'coolies' were shipped across Canada, en route to and from France, in sealed railway carriages. There are voluminous files on this episode in the Directorate of History, Department of National Defence (DND), Ottawa, and in RG 24 at the National Archives of Canada (NA).

2. A small but growing literature is available on the subject of minority Canadian participation in the world wars. Pioneering chapters on black Nova Scotians in M. Stuart Hunt, *Nova Scotia's Part in the Great War* (Halifax 1920), 148 53, and Ontario blacks and Indians in Barbara M. Wilson, *Ontario and the First World War, 1914–1918: A Collection of Documents* (Toronto 1977), cviii–cxiv, 166 75, are being supplemented with more detailed studies. Gaffen's *Forgotten Soldiers* is a colourful description of native Indian soldiers in both world wars, a welcome addition to James Dempsey's brief account, 'The Indians and World War I,' *Alberta History* 31 (1983): 1–8, and a useful corrective to Duncan Campbell Scott, 'The Canadian Indian and the Great World War,' in *Canada and the Great World War* (Toronto 1919), III, 285–328. Calvin W. Ruck, *Canada's Black Battalion: No. 2 Construction 1916–1920* (Halifax 1986), is anecdotal and illustrative, with portraits and quotations from several of the black veterans themselves. The first scholarly treatment of the No 2 is Major John G. Armstrong's 'The Unwelcome Sacrifice: A Black Unit in the Canadian Expeditionary Force, 1917–1919,' unpublished paper presented at RMC Military History Symposium, March 1986. Roy Ito, *We Went to War: The Story of the Japanese Canadians who Served During the First and Second World Wars* (Stittsville, Ont. 1984), is a valuable combination of scholarship and reminiscence, though most of the attention is paid to the second war. Further detail on World War II can be found in Patricia Roy, 'The Soldiers Canada Didn't Want: Her Chinese and Japanese Citizens,' *Canadian Historical Review* (CHR) 59 (1978): 341–58.

3. Robert Craig Brown and Donald Loveridge, 'Unrequited Faith: Recruiting the CEF 1914–1918,' *Revue internationale d'histoire militaire* 51 (1982): 56; Desmond Morton, *A Military History of Canada* (Edmonton 1985), 130; G.W.I., Nicholson, *Canadian Expeditionary Force, 1914–1919* (Ottawa 1962), 18, 19, 212, 213.

4. NA, RG 24, vol. 1221, file 593-1-7, vol. I, telegram, 8 Aug. 1914, Scott to Hughes, 16 June 1915, and reply, 23 June, Nethercott to Hughes, 11 Oct. 1915, Armstrong to Hughes, 10 Oct. 1915, and replies, 18 Oct., Brown to Hodgins, 9 Oct. 1915, and reply, 22 Oct. Gaffen, *Forgotten Soldiers,* 20, points out correctly that since 'race' was not recorded on recruitment documents, it is not possible to give precise numbers on Indian volunteers. The same caveat should apply to the other minority groups discussed here as well.

5. After the war, the minister of militia and defence, Hugh Guthrie, told the House of Commons that the CEF had enlisted 'something like twelve' Chinese and no East Indians; *Debates,* 29 April 1920, 1812. Several sources refer to larger numbers of Chinese veterans in postwar Canada, for example, Jin Tan and Patricia Roy, *The Chinese in Canada* (Ottawa 1985), 15, Edgar Wickberg et al., *From China to Canada: A History of the Chinese Community in Canada* (Toronto 1982), 200, and Carol F. Lee, 'The Road to Enfranchisement: Chinese and Japanese in British Columbia,' IBC *Studies* 30 (1976): 57–8. A search of the records in the National Archives of Canada and the Directorate of History, Department of National Defence, failed to identify these men. Some could have served as British 'coolies' rather than as Canadian soldiers. Guthrie's comment does suggest that a small number were enlisted as regular soldiers, an impression confirmed by Professors Graham Johnson and Edgar Wickberg who report in a personal communication, 31 Oct. 1987, having seen photographs of Chinese in the uniform of the CEF. A separate Sikh regiment had been suggested as early as 1911, apparently with favourable comment from Sam Hughes, but no action was ever taken; Norman Buchignani, personal communication, 14 Oct. 1987. On British Columbia's rejection of all Japanese volunteers see NA, RG 24, vol. 4740, file 448-14-262, vol. 1, Cruikshank, circular letter, 26 April 1916.

6. NA, RG 24, vol. 1206, file 297-1-21, memo, 13 Nov. 1914, Gwatkin to Christie, 30 Sept. 1915.

7. NA, RG 24, vol. 4562, file 133-17-1, Bramah to Rutherford, 4 Oct. 1915, and reply, 6 Oct.; Ruck, *Black Battalion,* 58, quoting interview with Robert Shepard. Despite these obstacles, some Nova Scotia blacks are reported to have been in the first contingent which left Canada in October 1914. Ibid., II.

8. NA, RG 24, vol. 1206, file 297-1-21, Alexander to Hughes, 13 Nov. 1914, Morton to Hughes, 7 Sept. 1915, Richards to Duke of Connaught, 4 Oct. 1915, Hamilton to Duke of Connaught, 29 Dec. 1915.

9. House of Commons, *Debates,* 24 March 1916, 2114–15; NA, RG 24, vol. 1206, file 297-1-21, Edwards to Stanton, 31 Jan. 1916, Hodgins to Stewart, 16 Oct. 1915.

10. NA, RG 24, vol. 1221, file 593-1-7, Duncan to Scott, 19 Nov. 1915; RG 24, vol. 1860, file 54; RG 24, vol. 4740, file 448-14-262, vol. I; RG 24, vol. 4562, file 133-17-1. Bramah to Rutherford, 4 Oct. 1915.

11. Ito, *We Went to War* 8ff; NA, RG 10, vol. 2640, file 129690-3, Jacobs, circular letter, 17 Aug. 1917; RG 24, vol. 1206, file 297-1-21, *Canadian Observer,* 8 Jan. 1916.

12. NA, RG 24, vol. 1206, file 297-1-21, Henshaw to Ogilvie, 7 Dec. 1915, Ogilvie to Hodgins, 9 Dec. 1915.

13. Ibid., Tupper to Hughes, 11 Nov. 1915, Allen to Rutherford, 14 Dec.; NA, RG 24, vol. 4562, file 133-17-1, Langford to Rutherford, 23 Sept. 1915, Borden to Rutherford, 23 March 1916.

14. NA, RG 24, vol. 4739, file 448-14-259, McLeod to Cruikshank, 25 Nov. 1915 and 20 Jan. 1916, Munton to Cruikshank, received 11 March 1916, Cruikshank to Hodgins, 11 March 1916, Brett to Cruikshank, 13 March 1916, Martin to Cruikshank, 17 March 1916; RG 24, vol. 4739, file 448-14-256, 'Half Breed Battalion,' 1915.

15. NA, RG 24, vol. 1221, file 593-1-7, vol. I, inspector of Indian agencies, Vancouver, to Fiset, 23 Dec. 1915, Jackson to Ruttan, 20 Dec. 1915, McKay to Hodgins, 3 Jan. 1916, Donaldson to Hughes, 26 Nov. 1915, Read to Militia Council, 3 Feb. 1916, Rendle to Department of Indian Affairs, 17 Feb. 1916, Henderson to Hughes, 18 March 1916.

16. For example, see *Canadian Observer,* 8 and 15 Jan. 1916; NA, RG 24, vol. 1221, file 593-1-7, vol. 1, Chief Thunderwater, on behalf of the Council of the Tribes, to Hodgins, 29 May 1916; RG 24, vol. 1469, file 600-10–35, White to McCurdy, nd; RG 24, vol. 4662, file 99-256, resolution BC Indian Peoples, 1 Feb. 1916.

17. NA, RG 24, vol. 1860, file 54, 'Recruiting—Special Units and Aliens,' numerous letters and telegrams, Jan.-April 1916; Roy Ito, personal communication, 18 Nov. 1987. An overseas battalion in the CEF consisted of approximately 1,000 men grouped in four companies each with two platoons.

18. NA, RG 24, vol. 1860, file 54, Gwatkin to Yamazaki, 21 April 1916; RG 24, vol. 1206, file 297-1-21, Gwatkin to Christie, 30 Sept. 1915, Hodgins to Tupper, 11 Nov. 1915, Hodgins to Armstrong, 19 Nov. 1915, Gwatkin to Hodgins, 22 Dec. 1915, Hodgins to Ogilvie, 23 Dec. 1915, Hodgins to Gwatkin, 21 March 1916, MacInnes to Hodgins, 25 March 1916; RG 24, vol. 1221, file 593-1-7, vol. 1, Fiset to inspector of Indian agencies, Vancouver, 29 Dec. 1915, Hodgins to McKay, 3 Jan. 1916, Gwatkin, memo, 12 Feb. 1916, Ogilvie to Hodgins, 23 March 1916; RG 24, vol. 4599, file 133-17-1, Hodgins to Rutherford, 29 Oct. 1915; RG 24, vol. 4739, file 448-14-256, Hodgins to Campbell, 15 July 1915, Hodgins to Cruikshank, 20 Nov. 1915; file 448-14-259, Hodgins to Cruikshank, 9 Dec. 1915 and 23 March 1916, Cruikshank to Martin, 27 March 1916; Ito, *We Went to War,* 25.

19. RG 24, vol. 1206, file 297-1-21, Richards to governor general, 20 Nov. 1915, *Saint John Standard,* 20 Nov. 1915, Hughes to Richards, 25 Nov. 1915, Fowler to GOC Halifax, 25 Nov. 1915, Hodgins to GOC Halifax, 29 Nov. 1915, reply, to Dec., Hodgins to GOC Halifax, 22 Dec. 1915, Gwatkin to Hodgins, 22 Dec. 1915, MacInnes to Hodgins, 25 March 1916. Interestingly, at least one commanding officer interpreted the minister's statement as a direct instruction. Lt Col W.H. Allen of the 106th Battalion, Halifax, accepted sixteen black Nova Scotians into his unit, though he reported that it discouraged white volunteers, since 'word has come from Ottawa that there is to be no distinction of colour for enlistments.' Allen to GOC Halifax, 14 Dec. 1915.

20. Brown and Loveridge, 'Unrequited Faith,' 59, 60; Morton, *History,* 135–41, 147; Nicholson, *Canadian Expeditionary Force,* 212–15, 223; J.L. Granatstein and J.M. Hitsman, *Broken Promises: A History of Conscription in Canada* (Toronto 1977), 22–59.

21. NA, RG 14, vol. 1221, file 593-1-7, Logie to Hodgins, 23 Nov. 1915, and reply, 26 Nov., Logie to Hodgins, 27 Nov. 1915, and replies, 6 Dec. and 10 Dec.; RG 24, vol. 4383, file 34-7-109, transfer order, 11 Dec. 1915.

22. NA, RG 24, vol. 1221, file 593-1-7, Hughes to Donaldson, 4 Dec. 1915, Hodgins to McLean, 9 Dec. 1915, Hodgins, circular letter, 10 Dec. 1915, Gwatkin to Hodgins, 6 Jan. and 4 May 1916.

23. NA, RG 24, vol. 4383, file 34-7-109, 'Enlistment of Indians in CEF,' numerous reports, OC 44th Regiment to Logie, 17 Jan. 1916, Scott to Logie, 19 Jan. 1916, and reply, 21 Jan., OC 114th Battalion to Logie, 27 Jan. 1916.

24. Ibid., Logie to OC 114th Battalion, 22 Jan. and 28 Jan. 1916, Hodgins to Logie, 31 Jan. 1916, Hodgins to Baxter, 8 Feb. 1916.

25. NA, RG 24, vol. 1206, file 297-1-21, Whitney to Hughes, 24 Nov. 1915, and reply, 3 Dec. A platoon would contain about 125 men in a standard CEF overseas battalion.

26. Ibid., *Canadian Observer,* 8 and 15 Jan. 1916, Whitney to Hughes, 19 Jan. 1916, and reply, 26 Jan., Hodgins to Logie, 3 Feb., 8 and 13 March 1916, Logie to Hodgins, 4 and 10 March 1916, Trump to Whitney, 15 March 1916.

27. Ibid., Whitney to Logie, 24 March 1916, to Kemp, 29 March 1916, Hodgins to Logie, 31 March 1916, Logie to commanding officers, 3 April 1916, Logie to Hodgins, to April 1916, Whitney to Hughes, 18 April 1916, Hughes to Logie, 3 May 1916, and reply, 4 May. Battalion replies to Logie's appeal of 3 April 1916 are found in NA, RG 24, vol. 4387, file 34-7-141, as are copies of much of the correspondence cited from file 297-1-21.

28. NA, RG 24, vol. 1206, file 297-1-21, Christie to Gwatkin, 29 Sept. 1915, Allen to GOC Halifax, 14 Dec. 1915; RG 24, vol. 4562, file 133-17-1, Langford to Rutherford, 23 Sept. 1915; RG 9, 111, vol. 81, file 10-99-40, McCurdy to Harrington, 16 July 1919.

29. NA, RG 24, vol. 1206, file 297-1-21, 'Memorandum on the enlistment of negroes in Canadian Expeditionary Force,' 13 April 1916.

30. Ibid., Militia Council minutes, 19 April 1916, cable to War Office, 19 April 1916, and reply, 11 May.

31. Ibid., Militia Council, memo, 2 June 1916; RG 24, vol. 1469, file 600-10-35, Hodgins to Gwatkin, 5 June 1916, and reply, 11 June, Hodgins to Sutherland, 13 June 1916, and reply, 4 July.

32. Ruck, *Canada's Black Battalion,* 27, quoting interview with Mrs Mabel Saunders; African Baptist Association, annual meeting, minutes, 1916.

33. NA, RG 24, vol. 1469, file 600-10-35, Ripley to Hodgins, 7 and 15 July 1916, Hodgins to Ripley, 10, 19, and 21 July 1916.

34. NA, RG 24, vol. 1860, file 54, 'Recruiting—Special Units and Aliens'; RG 24, vol. 4740, file 448-14-262, Ityama to Cruikshank, 24 April 1916, Cruikshank, circular letter, 26 April 1916.

35. Ibid., OC 192nd Battalion to Cruikshank, 28 April, 19 May, 4 Aug. 1916, Cruikshank to OC 192nd Battalion, 16 and 20 May and 1 Aug. 1916, Cruikshank to Hodgins, cable, 4 May 1916, and reply, same date, Cruikshank to Yamazaki, 5 May 1916; Ito, *We Went to War,* 34, 70 and App. 111, and personal communication, 18 Nov. 1987. RG 24, vol. 1860, file 54, gives the number of Japanese Canadians enlisted as 166, while the militia minister reported 194 Japanese enlistments; House of Commons, *Debates,* 29 April 1920, 1812. On Chinese recruits see note 5, above.

36. NA, RG 14, vol. 1221, file 593-1-7, vol. 1, Chief Thunderwater to Hodgins, 29 May and 20 June 1916; RG 24, vol. 4383, file 34-7-109, Mewburn to OC 119th Battalion,

26 April 1916, OC 227th Battalion to Mewburn, 4 May 1916. Although the adjutant general directed in February that Indian transfers should thereafter be carried out only when 'special circumstances exist, as in the case of brothers,' Colonel Mewburn was still writing in April demanding the transfer of Indians to the 114th. See Hodgins to Baxter, 8 Feb. 1916.

37. NA, RG 24, vol. 1221, file 597-1-7, vol. 1, Cooke to minister of militia, 15 Dec. 1916; RG 24, vol. 4383, file 34-7-109, Hodgins to Logie, 31 Jan. 1916, Baxter to Hodgins, 2 Feb. 1916, Scott to Logie, 22 Jan. 1916, Logie to Hodgins, 22 Feb. 1916, Thompson to Mewburn, 13 April 1916; Gaffen, *Forgotten Soldiers,* 23.

38. NA, RG 24, vol. 4383, file 34-7-109, Hodgins to Logie, 22 Feb. 1916, Thompson to OIC Divisional Recruiting, 1 March 1916, Thompson to Mewburn, 20 April 1916, Mewburn to OC 227th Battalion, 10 April 1916, and reply, 26 April, various regimental reports to Mewburn, July 1016; Gaffen, *Forgotten Soldiers*, 23.

39. NA, RG 10, vol. 6766, file 452-13, Scott to Renison, 15 Jan. 1917, cables to Indian agents, 15 Jan. 1917, Militia Department to Tyson, 5 April 1917; RG 24, vol. 1221, file 597-1-7, vol. 1, Scott to Fiset, 15 Jan. 1917, vol. 2, Ogilvie to Hodgins, cable, 22 March 1917; RG 24, vol. 4662, file 99-256, Ogilvie to Hodgins, 23 March 1916, Reynolds to Ogilvie, 20 March 1917, Tyson to Scott, 21 March 1917, Ogilvie to Hodgins, 22 March 1917.

40. NA, RG 24, vol. 1221, file 593-1-7, vol. 1, Chief Thunderwater to Hodgins, 30 Dec. 1916, 2 Jan. 1917, Hodgins to Logie, 8 Jan. 1917, vol. 2, John to Thunderwater, 19 Feb. 1917, Mrs Maracle to Thunderwater, 17 Feb. 1917, Thunderwater to Hodgins, 23 Feb. 1917, Hodgins to Logie, 9 and 22 March 1917, Logie to Hodgins, 15 and 24 March 1917. Colonel Thompson of the 114th Battalion had rejected the offer of Whitney's Toronto black volunteers by explaining 'The introduction of a coloured platoon into our Battalion would undoubtedly cause serious friction and discontent.' RG 24, vol. 4387, file 34-7-141, Thompson to Logie, 4 April 1916.

41. Ibid., Wright to Logie, 4 April 1916; RG 24, vol. 4680, file 18-25-2, Adjutant General's Office to district commanding officers, circular letter, 16 August 1916; RG 24, vol. 4486, file 47-8-1, transfer order, 28 Aug. 1916.

42. NA, RG 24, vol. 1469, file 600-10-35, Sutherland to McCurdy, 7 Aug. 1916, Hodgins to Sutherland, 8 Aug. 1916; RG 24, vol. 1550, file 683-124-2, Sutherland to Hodgins, 27 Nov. 1916, to McCurdy, same date.

43. NA, RG 24, vol. 1469, file 600-10-35, Sutherland to Hodgins, 25 Aug. 1916, Elliott to Hodgins, 19 Oct. 1916, Hodgins to Sutherland, 1 Dec. 1916; RG 24, vol. 1550, file 683-124-2, Sutherland to Hodgins, 27 Nov. 1916 and 4 Jan. 1917, memorandum, Minister's Office, 5 Jan. 1917, adjutant general to GOC Halifax, 23 Jan. 1917; RG 24, vol. 4486, file 47-8-1, Morrison, memo, 31 Aug. 1916. The Sailing List of the No 2 Construction Battalion, 28 March 1917, contains information on the birth place, recruitment place and date for each man, so that monthly and regional totals can be compiled.

44. NA, RG 24, vol. 4739, file 448-14-259, Duclos to Cruikshank, 8 Sept. 1916, Gayfer to Cruikshank, 6 and 18 Sept. 1916, 9 and 15 Oct. 1916; No 2 Recruitment Poster, Ruck, *Canada's Black Battalion,* Appendix, 126.

45. NA, RG 10, vol. 6765, file 452-7, Cooke to Scott, 12 Feb. and 4 March 1916; minutes of the Six Nations Council, 15 Sept. 1914, in Wilson, *Ontario and the First World War,* 174.

46. NA, RG 24, vol. 1221, file 593-1-7, vol. 1, Chief George Fisher to Gray, 19 Feb. 1916; RG 24, vol. 4383, file 34-7-109, Baxter to Williams, 18 Dec. 1915, Whitelaw to Baxter, 31 Dec. 1915; RG 10, vol. 6765, file 452-7, Cooke to Scott, 4 April 1916.

47. NA, RG 24, vol. 1221, file 593-1-7, vol. 1, Chief Thunderwater to Hodgins, 20 June and 29 Nov. 1916, Indian Mothers from Saugeen Reserve to Sir Robert Borden, 12 Oct. 1916, Smith to Scott, 1 Oct. 1916; RG 10, vol. 6765, file 452-7, Cooke to Scott, 28 Feb. 1916.

48. NA, RG 24, vol. 1469, file 600-10-35, Sutherland to Hodgins, 18 Dec. 1916; RG 24, vol. 4599, file 20-10-52, Gayfer to Gray, 22 Nov. 1916; RG 9 111, vol. 81, file 10-9-40, Sutherland to Perley, 27 April 1917.

49. NA, RG 24, vol. 4599, file 20-10-52, Gayfer to GOC Winnipeg, 23 Oct. 1916, to Gray, 22 Nov. 1916; RG 24, vol. 1469, file 600-10-35, Stackford to McCurdy, 7 Sept. 1916, Sutherland to Hodgins, 17 Jan. 1917, to Kemp, 18 Jan. 1917; RG 24, vol. 4558, file 132-11-1, GOC Halifax to Sutherland, 5, 8, and to Sept. 1916; Ruck, *Canada's Black Battalion,* 24, and Appendix interviews.

50. NA, RG 24, vol. 1469, file 600-10-35, Gwatkin to Hodgins, 18 Sept. 1916; RG 24, vol. 1550, file 683-124-2, Militia Ottawa to GOC Halifax, 23 Jan. 1917; RG 24, vol. 4739, file 448-14-259, Gayfer to Cruikshank, 6 Sept., 18 Sept., 4 Oct., and 7 Nov. 1916, and replies, 9 Sept., 19 Sept., 10 Oct., Cruikshank to Grant, 6 Nov. 1916, Aitken to Cruikshank, 9 Nov. 1916.

51. NA, RG 24, vol. 4558, file 132-11-1, Hodgins to GOC Halifax, 31 July 1916, to Sutherland, 22 Dec. 1916. Sailing List, No 2 Construction Battalion, 28 March 1917. Of the 603 enlisted men and non-commissioned officers (not including white officers), 342 were Canadian-born, 72 were West Indian, 169 American, and 20 of various other nationalities. Nova Scotia supplied 296, Ontario 207, and the west 33.

52. NA, RG 9 111, vol. 81, file 10-9-40, Sutherland to Perley, 27 April 1917, McCurdy to Perley, 1 Oct. 1917, and reply, 1 Nov., White to Stanfield, 18 Oct. 1917.

53. Brown and Loveridge, 'Unrequited Faith,' 55–6, 60–4, 67, App. D, 76; Nicholson, *Canadian Expeditionary Force,* 344, 347, 350, App. C, 546; Morton, *History,* 153, 156–8; Granatstein and Hitsman, *Broken Promises,* 60–104; A.M. Williams, 'Conscription 1917: A Brief for the Defence,' CHR 37 (1956): 338–51.

54. NA, RG 10, vol. 6768, file 452-20, Mississauga of New Credit to Scott, 22 Oct. 1917, Nishga to prime minister, Nov. 1917, Chief Peter Angus to the King, 13 Nov. 1917, Committee of Allied Tribes to prime minister, 17 Nov. 1917, BC Indian agent to department, 26 Nov. 1917, Chief John Prince to Scott, 27 Nov. 1917, Garden River Reserve to governor general, 4 Dec. 1917, Katzelash band to Department of Indian Affairs, 4 Dec. 1917, Kitzumkalwee band to department, 4 Dec. 1917, Michipicoten band to department, 5 Dec. 1917, Edmundston, NB, Reserve to department, 15 Dec. 1917, Manitoba Rapids Reserve to department, 24 Dec. 1917, Hurons of Lorette to governor general, 10 Jan. 1918; RG 24, vol. 1221, file 593-1-7, vol. 2, Military Sub-committee to Chisholm, 28 Nov. 1917, and reply, 29 Nov.

55. DND, DHist, minister of justice to Governor General in Council, 31 Dec. 1917.

56. NA, RG 10, vol. 6768, file 452-20, Scott to Ditchburn, 1 Dec. 1917, to Anaham Reserve, 14 Dec. 1917.

57. PC 111, 17 Jan. 1918; Military Service Regulations, Sections 12 and 16 as amended, 2 March 1918; PC 1459, 12 June 1918.

58. NA, RG 24, vol. 1469, file 600-10-35, McLean to McCurdy, to Oct. 1917, McCurdy to Perley, 14 Nov. 1917, White to McCurdy, nd, Gwatkin to adjutant general, 21 Oct. 1917, Shannon to adjutant general, 16 Jan. 1918, McCurdy to Mewburn, 17 Jan. 1918, and reply, 21 Jan., adjutant general to Shannon, 5 Feb. 1918, Shannon to adjutant general, 13 and 21 Feb. 1918, adjutant general, circular letter to commanding officers, Feb. 1918, White to Sir Robert Borden, 11 Aug. 1918.

59. Ibid., Young to Milligan, 13 March 1918, Shannon to adjutant general, 19 April 1918, adjutant general to Shannon, 24 and 30 April 1918, British-Canadian Recruiting Mission, New York, to adjutant general, 1 May 1918, and reply, 2 May.

60. Ibid., adjutant general to Brown, 8 May 1918, to Sutherland, 22 May 1918.

61. Ibid., White to Sir Robert Borden, 11 Aug. 1918.

62. Ibid., Bristol to Creighton, personal, 26 Aug. 1918, Creighton to AG Mobilization, 14 Sept. 1918, cable to commanding officers, 17 Sept. 1918, and replies, Creighton to Bristol, personal, 28 Sept. 1918. The record of black conscripts provided by commanding officers showed London, Ont. 23, Toronto 10, Kingston 4, Halifax 55, Saint John 13. The Military Service Council asserted, however, that it had 'no record of coloured men who are liable to draft, as all men are shown according to Nationality regardless of colour.' Ibid., Captain Newcombe, memo, 25 Sept. 1918.

63. Ruck, *Canada's Black Battalion,* 37–9, and interview with Isaac Phills, 57.

64. Ito, *We Went to War,* 70 and App. 111. Of 185 volunteers, 54 were killed and 119 wounded.

65. NA, RG 9 III, vol. 5010, War Diaries, 107th Pioneer Battalion. In 1918 the 107th was disbanded and the men absorbed into an engineering brigade. See also Gaffen, *Forgotten Soldiers,* passim.

66. Ruck, *Canada's Black Battalion,* 65, interview with Sydney Jones of the 106th. At a black veterans' reunion in 1982, reference was made to eight different units, besides the No 2, in which the survivors had enlisted; ibid., chap. 6, Reunion and Recognition Banquet. Mr Thamis Gale of Montreal, himself a World War II veteran and whose father was in the No 2, has been assiduously tracking down every black to serve in the CEF. From his as-yet unpublished results it appears that there may have been more than 1,200 blacks in the CEF, which would mean over 600 distributed in various units outside the No 2; personal communications, 16 and 24 June 1986 and 14 Feb. 1988.

67. NA, RG 24, vol. 1469, file 600-10-35, Mobilization to Gwatkin, 19 Feb. 1917, and reply, nd, memo to naval secretary, 21 Feb. 1917 and reply, 23 Feb.; Hunt, *Nova Scotia's Part,* 149–50.

68. NA, RG 24, vol. 1469, file 600-10-35, Morrison to Bristol, 20 Dec. 1917; RG 9 III, vol. 1608, file E-186-9, director of forestry to YMCA, 9 June 1917, OC No 12 District to

Timber Operations, 17 Jan. 1918, OC No 9 District to Timber Operations, 19 Aug. 1918, director of timber operations to General Headquarters, 28 Nov. 1918, and signal, 30 Nov. 1918; RG 9 III, vol. 4616, file C-B-8, assistant director to director, Chaplain Services, 20 Feb. 1918; RG 9 III, vol. 4645, folder 747, War Diaries, 2nd Canadian Construction Coy (Colored), vol. 11–10, 13, and 22 March 1918, vol. 12–14 and 17 April 1918, vol. 13–8 and 12 May 1918.

69. There is of course a huge literature on the nature and extent of Western racist thought, and it is not considered necessary to recount its features here. Studies which explicitly set Canadian developments within a broader context, usually imperial or continental, include Carol Bacchi, 'Race Regeneration and Social Purity: A Study of the Social Attitudes of Canada's English-Speaking Suffragists,' *Histoire Sociale / Social History* 11 (1978): 460–74; Carl Berger, *The Sense of Power: Studies in the Ideas of Canadian Imperialism, 1867–1914* (Toronto 1970), and *Science, God, and Nature in Victorian Canada* (Toronto 1983); Douglas Cole, 'The Origins of Canadian Anthropology, 1850–1910,' *Journal of Canadian Studies* 8 (1973): 33–45; Terry Cook, 'George R. Parkin and the Concept of Britannic Idealism,' *Journal of Canadian Studies* 10 (1975): 15–31; Robert A. Huttenback, *Racism and Empire: White Settlers and Colored Immigrants in the British Self-Governing Colonies, 1830–1910* (Ithaca and London 1976); and Howard Palmer, 'Mosaic Versus Melting Pot? Immigration and Ethnicity in Canada and the United States,' *International Journal* 31 (1976): 488–528.

70. NA, RG 9 III, vol. 1608, file E-186-9, Provisional Mobilization Store Table for a Labour Company, White to GHQ, 10 Jan. 1918, and reply, 14 Jan.

71. NA, RG 9 III, vol. 81, file 10-9-40, Morrison to Bristol, 20 Dec. 1917.

72. DND, DHist, 'Secret Information Concerning Black American Troops'; Foner, *Blacks and the Military,* 121–2; Balesi, 'From Adversaries to Comrades,' 112–13; Jeffrey Greenhut, 'Race, Sex and War: The Impact of Race and Sex on Morale and Health Services for the Indian Corps on the Western Front, 1914,' *Military Affairs* 45 (1981): 72–3; Willan, 'South African,' 71–3.

73. Nelson, 'Black Horror,' passim; Robert C. Reinders, 'Radicalism on the Left, E.D. Morel and the Black Horror on the Rhine,' *International Review of Social History* 13 (1968): 1–28; John C. Cairns, 'A Nation of Shopkeepers in Search of a Suitable France,' *American Historical Review* 79 (1974): 718; Bernard Shaw, *What I Really Wrote About the War* (New York 1932), 322–3; Robert A. Huttenback, *The British Imperial Experience* (New York 1966), 175–89.

74. NA, RG 9, III, vol. 1709, file D-3-13, Collier to OC Canadian Troops, 10 Jan. 1919; Ruck, *Canada's Black Battalion,* 58–60, interviews with Robert Shepard and A. Benjamin Elms. See also Desmond Morton, 'Kicking and Complaining: Demobilization Riots in the Canadian Expeditionary Force, 1918–19,' CHR 61 (1980): 341, 343, 356.

75. House of Commons, *Debates,* 20 June 1919, 3741.

76. Ito, *We Went to War,* 73; Roy, 'Soldiers,' 343; Provincial Elections Act Amendment Act, *Statutes of British Columbia,* 1931, C 21; War Time Elections Act, *Statutes of Canada,* 1917, C 39.

77. See, for example, NA, RG 24, vol. 2765, file 6615-4-A, vol. 6, secret memorandum no. 1, to all chairmen and divisional registrars, 20 Nov. 1941, and order from adjutant general to all district commanders, 12 July 1943; RG 27, vol. 130, file 601-3-4, 'Conscription of East Indians for Canadian Army'; DND DHist, 'Sorting out Coloured Soldiers' and 'Organization and Administration: Enlistment of Chinese'; *The King's Regulations and Orders for the Royal Canadian Air Force,* 1924, amended 1943; *Regulations and Instructions for the Royal Canadian Navy,* amended by PC 4950, 30 June 1944. Ito and Roy give considerable detail on Chinese- and Japanese-Canadian efforts to enlist during World War II.

CHAPTER

8 THE IMMIGRANT ADJUSTMENT IN WESTERN CANADA

Dissatisfaction with a Canadian past dominated by political and economic factors led to the renovation of Canadian history in the decades following World War II, though it was the 1970s before new methodologies, different approaches and alternate subject matter became prominent. Nowhere was the impact greater than in the study of Canadian society. In 1958 few argued with A.R.M. Lower's *Canadians in the Making: A Social History of Canada* which romanticized the "sturdy yeomanry" of his youth in the "horse and buggy" age. Lower spun yarns about "the tinkle of the bells on the 'cutter' as it rolled along in the moonlight over the snow, with plenty of 'buffalo robes,' a good horse, and, if you were lucky, your best girl beside you." The book was certainly a good read with some excellent insights, but it was an elitist, impressionistic, long personal essay. This anecdotal approach invited critics who asked other questions of different sources from different perspectives. While Lower might tell tales about the quaint "New Canadians," such an approach to the immigrants and their adjustment was no longer adequate.

While the traditional images of the immigrant were not always incorrect, they were frequently superficial and often misleading. Ethnocentric panegyrics would continue to be written, but in the 1970s and 1980s academics turned to studies of demography, literacy, standards of living, housing, kinship, social mobility and class structure, with quantification a favoured methodology. The overall result was a very different appreciation of the "New Canadians."

The readings included in this chapter represent two of the more recent approaches. The first selection by Robert Harney, published in *Urban History Review* in 1978, illustrates the dramatic changes that were taking place in ethnic studies. "Boarding and Belonging: Thoughts on Sojourning Institutions" is an analysis of Italian migrant workers in Canada. Harney's innovative analysis centred on the household and the extended family in the urban setting. Using oral interviews as well as other techniques, Harney demonstrates not only the uniqueness of the experience but indicates that the sojourners knew it was an "important social and cultural formative period" in their lives. The second article is by a geographer and represents yet another approach to the study of immigrant groups. In "Kinship and Society in the Ukrainian Pioneer Settlements of the Canadian West" John C. Lehr combines both a spacial and sociological analysis to explain the block settlements and their expansion in the west. While the nature of the "blocks" has long been recognized, Lehr's analysis of kinship adds a new dimension. The "social ties" within the group, he concludes, explain "many of the paradoxes of Ukrainian settlement."

Suggestions for Further Reading

Avery, Donald, *Dangerous Foreigners: European Immigrant Workers and Labour Radicalism in Canada* (Toronto: McClelland and Strewart, 1979).

Burnet, Jean (ed.) *Looking Into My Sister's Eyes: An Exploration into Women's History* (Toronto: Multicultural History Society of Ontario, 1986).

Burnet, Jean R. with Howard Palmer, *"Coming Canadians": An Introduction to a History of Canada's Peoples* (Toronto:McClelland and Stewart, 1988).

Epp, Frank H., *Mennonites in Canada, 1920–1940: A People's Struggle for Survival* (Toronto: Macmillan, 1982).

Palmer, H. (ed.) , *Immigration and the Rise of Multiculturalism* (Toronto: Copp Clark, 1975).

Parr, Joy, *Labouring Children: British Immigrant Apprentices to Canada, 1869–1924* (Montreal: McGill-Queen's University Press, 1980).

Potrebenko, Helen, *No Streets of Gold: A Social History of Ukrainians in Alberta* (Vancouver: New Star, 1977).

Ramirez, Bruno, *On the Move: French-Canadian and Italian Migrants in the North Atlantic Economy, 1860–1914* (Toronto: McClelland and Stewart, 1991).

BOARDING AND BELONGING: THOUGHTS ON SOJOURNER INSTITUTIONS

Robert F. Harney

The gap between the subject matter of migration studies and that of North American urban and ethnic history has narrowed in recent years. Historians of migration now study in detail the precise local causes of the movement from old world locations and the pattern of the consequent diaspora. At the same time, those who study major American cities and small industrial towns have begun to show some appreciation of the relationship between migration causes and settlement. In most studies, however, there remains a lacuna between accounts and explanations of the crossing and the history of ethnic institutional and neighborhood life on the North American side. Although we have moved from Oscar Handlin's compelling, if often incorrect, metaphors of "uprootedness" and "in fellow-feeling" to explain the processes of migrating, ghettoizing, and acculturating, we continue to depend too much on mono causal agents of settlement such as family chain migration or the padrone system.[1] Using these ideas to carry them over the rough spots in narration, historians lose sight of the important mental transition from sojourner to settler among newcomers, and of the formative period in ethnic settlement when male sojourners predominated. Even if it is a proper reflection of the sojourner's ambivalence as a man neither in his home place nor reconciled to his new place, this lack of study destroys our chance to discover the stages of cultural and institutional transition from migration to sojourning and settlement.

Abrupt transition from the locus of emigration to full-fledged ethnic settlement and the use of padronism or extended family as *deus ex machina* to turn migrants into urban North Americans can be found in even the best recent studies of immigrants in cities, as, for example, in H. Nelli's *Italians in Chicago* and J. Barton's *Peasants and Strangers: Italians, Rumanians and Slovaks in an American City.*[2] Nelli, building a model of padronism and an indistinguishable

Urban History Review, No. 2–78 (October, 1978), pp. 8–37. Reprinted by permission of the author and the editors of the *Urban History Review.*

mass of the exploited for whom the generic "southerner" provides both a class and ethnic identity, must wait until the newcomers have broken the sojourning thrall enough to be on Chicago's registered voter rolls or in commercial directories before he is able to study geographical and occupational mobility. For the sojourning period, he offers nothing but the stock characters, padrone and southerner, and a few biographies of exceptional immigrants. There is, in his account, neither a history and analysis of sojourner institutions nor a guide to the changing sentiments, intentions, and ethnic identity of the newcomers.

Barton makes more effort to explain the pattern of settlement in North America in terms of old world causes such as family and *paese* (home town) loyalties and the larger push factors that existed in specific European areas. There is, however, no "interior" history of the migrants. We do not know their frame of mind, their levels of expectation, nor how long they intended to stay. Nor is any thought given to whether knowing these things would enable us to understand better the pace of acculturation or the intensity of ethnic persistence in Cleveland. So, although Barton implements the best ideas of Handlin about the migrant as a villager and of Vecoli about family and *paese* reconstitution in the city, his chapters on the Old World remain strangely disjoined from those which deal with the new ethnic institutions of the city such as benevolent societies, visible ethnic business enterprises, and parishes. By failing to appreciate and study the informal, often amoebic, institutions of the sojourning period and by maintaining stock characters like the padrone and the "southerner," the historian fails the immigrant in his continuous, if tortuous, journey from migrant to "ethnic" and retrospectively confirms the stereotyping of male sojourners as Wops, Bohunks, birds of passage, *cafoni*—the faceless guestworkers of North America at the turn of the century.[3]

It is my belief that a chrysalis of the ethnic settlement of the North American ethnic group itself, its boundaries and its content, can be found in those first years of urban migrant life, now shrouded in creation myths and filio-pieties. Careful study of the sojourner, his frame of mind, his needs, his amoebic institutions, and the impact of the sojourn on his identity will demonstrate this. Such study will require the use of oral testimony as well as a change in approach. In fact, North American historians have ceased to view immigration, the ethnic colony, and acculturation as an obvious continuum, and, in the face of startling ethnic persistence, more time has been spent rethinking the relationship between the last two pictures in the triptych than between the first two. The distinctions between migrants and immigrants, sojourners and settlers[4] is not always made and the result is that family settlement is very often seen as the first stage of ethnic neighbourhood life.

Now, when so many excellent local studies of specific ethnic groups and their settlement are appearing, it seems the right time to reassert the need for thorough comparative studies of the migration, sojourning, and settlement patterns of each ethnic group. Stock characters such as steamship agents, immigrant bankers, foraging foremen sent to Europe to recruit, and labour brokers need to be studied as part of an economic structure rather than simply appearing on the stage in the immigrant drama. Households with boarders, extended families, boarding-houses, padrone-run bunkhouses and commissaries, informal *paese* clubs, mutual aid and burial societies—all elements in the sojourner's world—require analysis as institutions,[5] if we are to understand the transition from sojourning to settling to ethnicity in terms worthy of historians rather than those of latter day restrictionists or settlement house workers.[6]

I will look at the institution of boarding from the perspective of the sojourner and the settler. We must first remove some of the confusion that surrounds the practice of boarding among newcomers, and then we can see it as a form of entrepreneurship for some settlers, as a social institution fulfilling most needs for sojourners, and finally, as a frame within which aspects of North American ethnicity were defined. Two points need to be made at the outset. In attempting to show the entrepreneurial and institutional nature of boarding, I am not denying the important contribution made to the subject from the perspective of household and family studies. For example, Modell and Hareven's excellent study, "Urbanization and the Malleable Household: An Examination of Boarding and Lodging in American Families," although it does not pay attention to sojourning as a concept, informs most of my thinking on the places of households in the study of boarding.[7] Also, I am aware that much damage is done to separate ethnic traditions and patterns of boarding by my cross-cultural approach. I wish only to show in this paper that the condition of being a sojourner, which was shared by most male migrants of the so-called "new migration" of the twentieth century, encouraged similar institutions among all groups.[8]

Questions of morality and definition linger from then, and, before we can discuss the role of boarding in the sojourner economy and society, some confusions need to be sorted out. The Dillingham Commission, despite its misuse of the statistics on boarding, offered in 1911 a sensible classification of varieties of the boarding phenomenon among newcomers. The three general categories listed were: households consisting of two or more families living together; households consisting of one or more families with boarders and lodgers; and "scattering households" in which no family is present and called for this reason "group households." This last category divides into "either ... a group of men who share all expenses or ... a 'boarding house' usually [run by] a man without a family, and boarders and lodgers."[9]

Two subspecies of the first and last classifications have received most attention from historians. The household of an extended family has been the focus of chain migration studies, and the boarding house/inn as an adjunct of padronism has interested those who view migration a strict relationship of labour, flowing through brokers, to capitalist demand. The phenomenon of several families, related or from the same old country locale, living as a single household was not uncommon, especially for short periods of time while people inserted themselves into the North American economy. However, one or more families living with relatives or fellow countrymen as boarders was far more than a "malleable household": it was also a complex network of informal trust, written contract, and cash exchange. Oral testimony shows that there was almost always exchange of money, precision about services rendered and terms of *modus vivendi,* as well as careful accounting of food and other costs. Analysis of boarding among sojourners then as simply family or household history does fall short of the cash nexus that existed and animated the institution at least as much as "in fellow-feeling" did. The other subspecies, which skews our understanding of boarding much more than a too simple view of family and paesanism, is the extreme form of exploitation found in padroni inns and isolated work camps.

Confusing the traits of remote work camps with boarding itself is the same as identifying private enterprise with monopoly capitalism. Indeed, it was monopoly—through cultural or geographical isolation—of lodging, transport, job opportunity, and food supply which produced the extreme forms of exploitation. In both Canada and the United States, work camps on the railways, shanties near coal patches, isolated barge canal campsites, and lumber camps led to virtual enslavement ... a condition which was luridly detailed by social reformers and immigration, industrial, and royal commissions. This spectre of the padrone-run commissary and bunkhouse or of the overcrowded inn near train stations and harbours created the aura of depravity and criminality which surrounds all of the Dillingham Commission's third category, "group households."[10]

In the case of Sicilians in the southern United States and the Chinese along the entire west coast of the Americas, insertion into the North American economy, often to replace black slave labour, was so reminiscent of negro servitude that the housing of the newcomers was naturally compared to slave quarters.[11] In 1930, an exposé of padrone and company-run camps in West Virginia showed that Italian migrant labour was often shanghaied, threatened with physical violence, and that camp security was maintained by armed guards and, in one case, a gatling gun.[12] Thus, the housing of foreign sojourners and the image of slavery ran together in the public mind. In the cities, immigrant entrepreneurs sometimes kept their employees in crowded lodgings near their shops. Especially in cases when those employees were immigrant minors, such as Greek or Basilicatan bootblacks or Syrian and Lebanese confectioners and pedlars, boarding became associated with white slavery and child abuse.[13]

Boarding in the city was rarely seen as the product of rapid population growth and poor urban planning or, conversely, as the sojourner's choice. For Nelli's Chicago, it was the padrone control of lodging itself which served as the mechanism by which target migrants were trapped and sojourners transformed into settlers.

> Unemployed workers who remained in Chicago had no problems in obtaining food or lodgings, for padroni and Italian bankers saved and operated tenement houses where they encouraged guests to indulge in extravagance in order to place them more completely in debt.[14]

Turn-of-the-century eyewitnesses noted the geographical proximity of "employment agencies, saloons, cheap lodging houses, lunchrooms, and cheap or second-hand clothing stores."[15] Amy Bernardy saw the same link between boarding and labour exploitation in Boston's North End:

> The problem of capital and labour shines through between the lines in the notice outside the banchista's office: "need 300 men for work on the railroad." The horror of the unsanitary and degrading accommodations shows itself beneath the laconic sign: "bordo" or "'we take in boarders."[16]

In Toronto, a cluster of bankers, travel agencies, and hotels existed in the heart of the first 'Little Italy' in the St. John's Ward; the Venzia Hotel, a steamship agency, an "immigrant bank," and a working class hotel dominated the main intersection of the second neighbourhood around St. Francis (St. Agnes) Parish. The Royal Commission which dealt with fraudulent labour practices surrounding the importation of Italian labour to Montreal demonstrated the close ties between the Canadian Pacific's recruiters, the padrone, Antonio Cordasco, and a number of boarding houses.[17] Inevitably the boarding of alien migrant males became almost synonymous in Canadian cities, as it already was in the rural work camps, with exploitation and monopoly of services. In fact, any sense that sojourners might prefer such a boarding system was lost in a haze of moral outrage. The very place of boarding as an aspect of the commerce of migration rather than an exploitative end in itself became lost. The United States Industrial Commission of 1901 heard this testimony: "However, I have called the attention of the commission to many cases of Italian hotel keepers who have tried to get hold of the Italian immigrants in order to speculate upon them." And boarding was identified with outright violent crime as well. "Others have told me," wrote the director of Ellis Island, "how they were led to boarding houses where they were beaten and robbed or shanghaied to some far off mine, quarry, or construction site."[18]

If boarding came into the cities from the remote work camps with a criminal record, in the city, the sojourners and their lodging system were immediately caught in yet another vortex of moral and sociological confusion. Boarding was associated with overcrowding, tenement conditions, and the dangers of the "lodger evil." All of those masks of social disintegration intensified when the "pipeline to the cesspools of Europe" was attached. The lodger evil itself, of course, had emerged as a moral issue only when the majority of boarders in the city ceased to be middle class and were replaced by rural, lower class migrants and foreigners.[19] In that sense, ethnic and cultural disparities were merely a convenient rallying cry for the city reformers and social gospellers, but reform, inspired by the social gospel or not, and prejudice fed on each other. J.S. Woodsworth, describing immigrants in Winnipeg and Toronto, could not comprehend why Galicians would live "twenty-four in one room where only seven should have been. Fancy such conditions," he added, "with illimitable prairies stretching to the north and west."[20] Thus, someone like Woodsworth could see boarding as an aspect of clannishness, a failure to acculturate, and a judgmental category which served to portray the sojourners (not incorrectly, only maliciously) as being like Emily Dickinson's rats, "the concisest tenants of the Earth," providing unfair competition for native stock. By living and surviving in the bestial nests of the boarding house, sojourners not only lowered standards, but also threatened to succeed. In Toronto, the muckraking newspaper *Jack Canuck* clearly expressed the danger that the sojourner might prove to be the fittest breed in the industrial city: "Not so the Italian. He is content to 'pig-in' with a crowd of others and live under conditions which an Anglo-Saxon would be ashamed of."[21]

The Report of the Toronto Medical Health Officer Dealing with the Recent Investigation of Slum Conditions in Toronto, Embodying Recommendations for the Amelioration of the Same, prepared for the city by Dr. Hastings in 1911, contained a typical interplay of hostility toward boarding, foreigners, and the burgeoning industrial city itself. Charts of overcrowded rooms, dark rooms, rear houses, tenement houses, common lodging houses, cellar dwellings, and one-roomed dwellings—all obviously employed as indices of squalor and social disintegration—were juxtaposed page on page with lists of ethnic households in the neighbourhoods studied in the report.[22] Boarding then, rather than being approached as a possible variation on the "malleable household," a sign of the resilience and initiative of migrant networks, was treated as urban pathology.[23]

If we can pass from the moralizing and emotion that surrounds turn-of-the-century boarding to its social reality, a different set of questions can be asked about the institution itself: questions about the uses of family and household to cope with a new North American situation, about boarding as a form of ethnic entrepreneurship and proprietorship—one of the earliest such forms—and as a community institution and a force shaping the boundaries of ethnicity itself. Further questions about the role of boarding in establishing the *ambiente* and density necessary for an ethnic settlement, and indeed, in moving the sojourner into the position and attitudes of a settler need answering as well. A new perspective, informed by much oral testimony and by the concept of sojourning, when combined with an understanding of different ethnic household traditions, should enable us to see boarding as one of those key institutions now lost in the mists between migration and permanent settlement.

Whether we are dealing with a family with boarders or a "group household," no amount of rhetoric about paesanism and kinship ties should draw us away from the economic matrix of the institution as it was understood and used by both the boarder and the keeper of boarders. For the boarders, the nature of the arrangement satisfied the needs of their sojourning frame of mind. That frame of mind (*mentalitá*) called for maximizing savings, minimizing potentially costly encounters with the host society, and, as much as circumstances permitted, recreating or remaining in the *ambiente* of the home country.[24] Considered in these terms, one can see that the family-run boarding system was not so much a different institution from the "group household" as it was a felicitous and highly efficient form of it. Enterprise, a labour intensive and administrative organization around a working wife and serving children, was not only a traditional aspect of the European rural family but was also an efficient adaptation of that tradition to the city. The study of boarding benefits enormously from recent interpretations of the role of women in the work force and reassertions of older ones about the family as a single economic unit.[25]

Boarding then was a practical use of family and village ties as well as of certain qualities within the pre-industrial family itself. Historians have rarely felt that they could penetrate the complex nucleus of fellow-feeling and entrepreneurship in the relationship of relatives and fellow villagers, who lodged together in North America.[26] In 1941, Oscar Handlin's eloquence could not hide the fact that he had thrown in the towel with the remark that, among the Boston Irish, "no matter how cramped the quarters of those already settled, there was always room *for the sake of rent, charity or kinship.*"[27] Even in Vecoli's articulate critique of Handlin's *Uprooted,* the sojourner's family and "belongingness with his fellow townsmen" are contrasted with padronism, as if the former had no cash nexus.[28] Since then, perhaps because of the heritage of padronism or the image of sex roles, the study of boarding among Italian migrants remains too dichotomized. Certainly Slavic and Hungarian studies have no trouble in dealing with the family with boarders and the "missus" of the establishment as both a household and a well organized business enterprise.[29]

Thomas Kessner's recent study of Jewish and Italian social mobility in New York City concludes that "lodgers represented the closest of neighbours and immigrants were careful to choose those of similar ethnic origin and religious background. These boarders became part of the immigrant household." Kessner notes in passing that in 1880 most Italian *bordanti* in the city were unrelated to the family with whom they formed a household, and that even by 1905, by which time chain migration could presumably have done its work, over 62% of *bordanti* were unrelated to the household in which they lived.[30] All this suggests more family enterprise than chain migration and kinship.

Among Italian lodgers, words like *bossa* for the keeper of the house, *bordo* for their arrangement, and *bordante* to describe themselves were borrowed and the Italian expression *covivenza* was rarely used. Perhaps an ethno-linguist could explain what qualities in the Italian North American household were sufficiently alien to require such borrowing. That boarding confused the newcomers themselves can also be seen in the attempt to force an ascriptive setting.

Older boarders were called uncle by the young women who, after marriage to a boarding-boss, found themselves wives and keepers of boarders. Younger lodgers called the lady of the house auntie or *nonna* (grandmother), and *la padrona* when they referred to her with third parties. Hungarians usually referred to the boarding-boss's wife as the "miszisz."[31] Many of these terms were obviously used to impose vigorous sexual controls on the boarding house, but they also reflect the attempt to make the institution fit either household or family situations which could be understood from the old world experience.

The use of terms of respect or of familial designations between boarder and the boarding-boss's wife cannot obscure either the menial labour status of the woman who ran the boarding establishment or the precise business arrangements which existed between boarder and keeper. Although oral testimony invariably emphasizes the atmosphere of trust, family values, and sense of shared fate in early Italian Canadian boarding, further questioning always brings out descriptions of highly structured arrangements about services rendered, payment for services, controls on boarder behaviour, and on the organization of boarding itself. These latter aspects are clearer in the "group household" than in the family with boarders or the boarding-boss variations, but they are present in all forms of immigrant boarding.

A Methodist colporteur in Toronto complained that Sicilian women in the 1900s were so busy tending to boarders that they could not come to church gatherings; he did not understand that caring for a group of *bordanti,* or a boardinghouse, was an occupation for the whole family and a profession for the wife of the household: "Thus the rooming house is lucrative because it utilizes almost completely the family spare time labour. Similar is the case with lunch bars, grocery stores, etc."[32] Whether we can find sufficient material in traditional sources, such as assessment rolls, income statistics, and city directories, to measure how lucrative keeping boarders was as an ethnic enterprise, the psychic saving involved in keeping the mother and wife at home to work and in maintaining the family as a single economic unit was clearly supplemented by much real profit from taking in sojourners.[33]

Fortunate the settler who could turn his household and his dependents into a source of income while still working outside the home himself. He was like the rich *contadino* of the old country who owned a draft animal which could be rented out for extra income. A wife as a beast of burden in the boarding business was certainly the equivalent of a mule in southern Italy or Macedonia, and small children were as valuable an asset as healthy sons had been on the land.[34] The profit margin for the family with boarders was potentially great, limited only by the energy of the family, the size of the house, the satisfaction of the clientele, and, very occasionally, public inspection and intervention. For example, in Toronto in 1911, at a time when an Italian unskilled sojourner could earn about $2 a day as a labourer, a Toronto Italian family collected $3 a month from each of thirty boarders. The house they used rented for $28 a month. Depending on food arrangements, clear profit as well as free shelter accrued to the entrepreneurial family, and the husband was able to work full time outside of the home. In other instances, men paid $1.25 a week or the equivalent of a day's wages on board. The Hastings Report remarked darkly that there was "some evidence that certain small hotels and old rooming houses are about to undergo the dangerous transformation into foreign lodging houses."[35] If the Report saw such changes as heralding the spread of slum conditions, we should see it as proof of a successful entrepreneurial form and evidence of the existence of a satisfied clientele. Egisto Rossi, a special commissioner for the Italian government, calculated the sojourner's reasons for supporting a boarding system:

> Accepting my conclusions about the second and third points, it should be noted that the cost of food and lodging in Canada does not differ much from that of the United States. With 3 or 4 dollars a week, a manual labourer can live well enough in both countries. Certainly, our labourers do not spend on average more than 15 dollars a month, and that, when you consider that they earn usually about $1.25 to $1.75 a day, enables them to save and to return to Italy at the end of a season with some *gruzzolo di denato* (nest egg).

Thus, there is every reason to believe that groups of sojourners would have created boarding institutions if entrepreneurial families and boarding bosses had not done so.[36] That is, after all, what the existence of so many "group" or "scattering households," as described by the Dillingham Commission and many other contemporaries, signifies.

Despite the camaraderie and intra-ethnic warmth that emerges from much of the oral testimony, boarding was a business. In an oral history of Pennsylvania immigrants, the authors describe a boarder in a South Slav establishment who found his "plate [turned] upside down at the boarding house when he did not have work." Moreover, the definitions of services to be rendered between keeper and boarder, regardless of kinship or paesanism, were so precise and so quickly surrounded by local custom that it very soon did not depend on the ritual of affecting kinship described earlier. Whether the mistress of such a "malleable household" was called la padrona, auntie, or the missus, if she took money for bed and board, she accepted a more rigorous set of commitments for service than any boardinghouse boss.[37] The woman was responsible for serving the boarders in a way that closely resembled the duties of a peasant wife to her husband. (Perhaps that is why, in the Hungarian case, the missus was assumed by many boarders also to share sexual favours with them, and why Italian feminists like Amy Bernardy railed against boarding as a source of adultery.)[38]

Giovanni Verga, in one of his short stories about Sicilian life, describes the obligations of a good peasant wife thus: "She made sure that he found a fresh sheet on the bed, the macaroni made, and the bread for the following week already leavening."[39] The female boardinghouse keeper, and this varied considerably from ethic group to ethnic group, washed the workers soiled work clothes, bedding and dirty underclothes, and sometimes even the back and legs of the boarders themselves when they came in from mines and factories. The services rendered require much more study, for the status of women and the sexual mores of each country of emigration must have affected services offered in North American boarding arrangements.

Contractual arrangements revolved around the food supply, clothing, and bedding, but it was the first of these that seems almost to have been a preoccupation. A Roumanian account indicates that groups of boarders sometimes moved in search of better food.[40] For historians and social scientists who fear that contemporary emphasis on varieties of ethnic cuisine may trivialize ethnicity, the study of the place of food in boarding is instructive. The food supply was the most flexible of the sojourner's costs, and its preparation, along with language and daily contact with boarders of the same origin, was the most salient aspect of the sojourner's struggle to insulate himself from cultural change. The boarder balanced his concern to maximize savings with his need for ample and hearty food in labour intensive job situations. He refused usually to sacrifice fully his *ambiente* and culture by eating food prepared in an "English" or North American style every day of the week.

The boarding-boss or the housewife with boarders wished to maximize profits while not alienating clientele. Again, it is obvious that excesses occurred where isolation and company indifference gave the commissary or those in charge of the food supply a virtual monopoly. For example, since most foremen and section bosses of Italian work gangs on the Canadian Pacific Railroad depended on Montreal padroni for their supply of Italian food, the railroad navvies in isolated camps paid as much as five times the going city rate for mouldy bread and tainted sardines (anchovies). In the city, competition between forms of lodging and perhaps greater "fellow-feeling" caused more balance between the profit motive and the workers' tastes and requirements. On the other hand, taste in food did maintain ethnic boundaries. Certainly sojourners saw it as an important difference between themselves and other groups, and it was used as a reason for maintaining ethnically homogeneous bunkhouses at many work sties. "All Japanese stay in same bunkhouse. The Canadians live in a separate bunkhouse and of course didn't like to eat Japanese food from our Japanese cook." What was true of isolated camp sites was equally true of the city, and *Jack Canuck,* lamenting the clannishness of Italians and the fact that they received work from the city through subcontracts, remarked: "It is said that the Italian employed by the city of Toronto refuse to buy any other than Italian macaroni. That they live in gangs of from 6 to 9 in one room ... ."[41] The newspaper's bitter comment tells us something about the place of boarding in the creation of ethnic density, of making other ethnic enterprises such as food importation possible, and the importance of food in defining ethnic boundaries and choice of housing.

Although carefully arrived at agreements between a boarding-boss and his boarders or in a "group household" might be expected, the degree of organization in the arrangement of meals in the household with boarders is a bit startling. Even in warm, family-based, and *paesani* (fellow townsmen) boarding circumstances, the question of food supply was matter for careful accounting and individual, if usually unwritten, contracts. In one household, a hurdy gurdy man and his wife kept three or four younger boarders, often men from their *paese*. In the kitchen was a great black stove with separate pots of food prepared by each lodger for himself. An affluent or prodigal man might be preparing veal while a boarder more concerned about the cost of prepaid steamship tickets limited himself to the same meatless minestra or pasta every day. Yet another had made a full board arrangement with the family and ate their prepared meal with them. Everyone took his food from the stove and sat down to eat at the kitchen table together.[42]

A Slovak migrant in the Niagara peninsula described his boarding arrangement thus:

> The rooming house ... see we paid the lady a dollar a month for cooking. You paid a dollar and we paid the room extra. And every week she bought what she need in the grocery store. She was purchaser. She chose—sometimes she says well tomorrow we're going to have real meat or something like that—or breaded veal or pork chops. Okay everybody agree. And then, end of the week—Sunday usually—they calculate everything—how much she spent—and then she spread the expenses amongst all of us. We pay a dollar and she had a free board. And her husband had to pay same as we do.[43]

The ethos of this arrangement hovers between family, trust, and good business, and the possible mutations of the boarding arrangement seem endless. Without a much larger sample, and some attempt at controlling that sample by time, place, and ethnic group, it is difficult to tell how much old world traditions affected the nature of the arrangement, but it should be clear that the simple line between family and enterprise is quite useless. For example, a Donau-Schwaben (German from Hungary) boarding house in Welland, Ontario had only lodgers who were related to one another and the owner. The lady of the household cooked for all the men, but:

> We paid so much a week and she cooked. She cooked for us and we could buy our own food and take it to her and she cooks it or sometimes the butcher came to the house. Butcher send young fellow and he notes down what you want and the next day they delivered it.[44]

The boarding system was further complicated by whether the household was responsible for preparing the lunch pail for each worker/boarder as well. In that instance, the matter could range from a commitment to so many sandwiches or cold sausage per day to no agreement. (In Toronto, for example, many Polish and Lithuanian boarders in the Niagara-Queen Street factory district found it easier to save by buying monthly lunch tickets from local Chinese and Macedonian restaurants who had packed lunches waiting for them each morning as they passed by.)

The sojourners' preoccupation with their meal arrangements grew from two different sources. First, as the most variable of their expenses, it bore constant and close scrutiny by men committed to saving. However, we must not deny the centrality of familiar cuisine to their maintenance of popular culture while away from the homeland. Moreover, it seems likely that boarding as an important and pioneering form of enterprise in immigrant neighbourhoods would not have existed if those who maintained boarders could not meet their dietary and culinary demands. Those Roumanian boarders in Cleveland expected a Sunday noon meal of noodle soup, pork meat, and dumplings. They demanded sauerkraut, sausage, and pureed white beans a certain number of times a week.[45] Like the Italian labourers who would only eat imported pasta, the Roumanians were practising a primitive but determined consumer power. Their existence made possible small entrepreneurial successes for those who imported pasta and tomatoes or made sauerkraut to some old country formula. Storefronts, *ambiente,* and ethnic settlement followed.

Concern over the cost, quality, and ethnicity of food existed in the "group households" as much as in the family with boarders where instead of agreements with *la padrona,* the boarders had to evolve a regime as a group. The organization of a cooking roster, rent payments, a budget of shared costs for food and drink, and even the laying out of rules for behaviour between boarders took time and consensus. Sometimes one would be hard put to tell the difference between a commercial boarding-boss and the sort of authoritarian leader who emerged to dominate such households. Usually the latter was an older member of an extended family of males involved in the boarding establishment, or a village man whose reputation had been great in the old country as well. He might differ from a boarding-boss only in so far that his power lay in his influence rather than in proprietorship over the location.[46] In other cases, remarkable democracy prevailed. More oral testimony, especially about weekly budget meetings and arrangement of a roster, will certainly show that "group boarding" nurtured the more formal institutions of the later community, such as burial societies, mutual aid organizations, and *paese* clubs. Some boarding establishments sounded more like settlement houses or fraternal organizations than households anyway. Peter Roberts described what he, as a social gospeller, had found to be an ideal "group household" of Japanese in Omaha:

> One of the best samples of housekeeping I have ever seen was done by the 140 Japanese who lived in the House of the Good Shepherd in South Omaha. A board of managers had charge of the affairs of the group. The secretary of the board kept all records, accounts, and transacted all business with outsiders; the commissary had charge of the feeding of the group; the cooking, washing, and scrubbing were systematized, and each member was bound by a set of rules that secured peace and order.[47]

As we turn to the role of boarding the dynamic of changing ethnic identities in North America, we should observe that for the true sojourner, the boarding place, whether under a padrone system, with a family, or in a "group household," provided a means of living with one's own on a scale larger than the family, and yet, smaller than the host society or even of that North American invention, the ethnic group. The lodging place served as the focus of "fellow-feeling," of gossip about townsmen and countrymen who were mavericks, philanderers, or drunks, of the news' network coming from the home village, of intelligence about job opportunities, of the arranging of marriages and the travel of other family members, and finally, of who were reliable merchants, money-lenders, and go-betweens. It was the place to play old world card games and spend leisure time. In that sense, the boarding house, especially if one includes the saloons and ancillary enterprises often in its immediate environs, had for the sojourner a variety of the ethnic "completeness of institutions"[48] that Raymond Breton had described as necessary to a later stage of ethnic development.

In its informal and amoebic way, boarding provided for all the needs of the sojourners. If we could keep that in mind, the early period of ethnic settlement, dominated by male migrants and boarding arrangements, could be understood not in terms of the failure of acculturation or the pathology of marginality, but as a period when the sojourners' needs were met and when those entrepreneurs who drew their income from serving and exploiting the sojourners began the formation of permanent settlement and, indeed, of an ethnic bourgeoisie. One need only think of the sojourner's agenda to predict those institutions which would grow up in his presence and those which would be retarded.[49] Institutions of acculturation or culture mattered little. There were no children to educate in the new ways or to make steadfast in the old. For most of the groups involved, the presence of women was required to make ethnic parishes necessary. On the other hand, the sojourners did require ethnic food, rough leisure in the form of saloons, coffee-houses, and billiard rooms, steamship agencies, banks, employment bureaus, and some form of mutual aid or burial insurance. Just as oral testimony can show the presence of successful immigrant enterprise before city directory or tax roll evidence existed,[50] interviews also confirm that early community business notables and leaders of *paese* clubs or benevolent societies began as heads of group households or as boarding house bosses. Dr. Juliana Puskas of the Hungarian Academy of Sciences has pointed out that in those groups, such as the South Slav and the Hungarian, where the "miszusz" had a special role in running the boarding establishment, many such women were the moving spirits and first officers of parish and benevolent society committees.[51]

One suspects that the study of boarding and especially of the "group household" could bring us to the very heart of the relationship between ethnic identity and socio-economic reality, as well as providing a means of understanding the shifting boundaries of that identity. At a simple level, boarding often provided a neighbourhood with the density and concentration of people necessary to attract or create institutions which more overtly nurtured a separate ethnic existence. At a more important level, boarding as a form of clustering people from the same homeland began the process of breaking down extreme localism, even when each household seemed to represent only one local origin, and thus, led to what Helen Lopata has described as the "gradually emerging fabric" of North American ethnicity.[52]

If we look closely at the place and scale of "fellow-feeling" in boarding, we can begin to grasp the way in which localism and ethnicity among the sojourners existed as both a continuum of identities and as conflicting loyalties or, at least, loyalties of different intensities. For example, when in Upton Sinclair's *The Jungle,* Jurgis Rudkus and his Lithuanian group reach the Chicago stockyard area, they find housing that seems to reflect both their Lithuanian ethnicity and the melting pot:

> There were four such flats in each building, and each of the four was a "boarding house" for the occupancy of foreigners—the Lithuanians, Poles, Slovaks, or Bohemians. Some of these places were kept by private persons, some were co-operatives.[53]

Rudkus, however, did not end up in that boarding-house because he was a Lithuanian, he was led to it by a man from his own village: "The two families literally fell upon each others' necks—*for it had been years since Jokubas Szedvilas had met a man from his part of Lithuania.*" In almost every account of boarding, what appears to be camaraderie based on large ethnic definitions recedes upon closer examination, and one finds people from one village, town, or district clustering together. Optimum size for "group households" and families with boarders tended to stay within such parochial definitions of their group. In such instances, at least within the boarding establishment, ethnicity did not extend beyond the *paese* or local area of emigration. Yet boarding was an expedient and a functional institution for sojourners, allowing them to adapt their sense of "fellow-feeling" to the scale of ethnicity imposed upon them by the nature of their migration, their jobs, or their lodgings.

A look at a single sojourner's experience can demonstrate this point. Paul Bertoia, an immigrant from near Udine in Friuli, the northeast of Italy, arrived alone in Toronto after World War I. In search of work and relatives, he went on to Edmonton. There he stayed in a boardinghouse/inn known to its residents as the Roma Hotel. One floor was occupied completely by Friulan sojourners, and the next floor by Trevisans from a neighbouring region of Italy. Each floor had its own cooking, dialect, card games, and camaraderie, even though the inn was named for Italy's capital and the native Edmontonians considered everyone in the building an Italian migrant. When Mr. Bertoia boarded with kinfolk in Drumheller, he associated chiefly with people from his home town near Udine, and later, when he came to Toronto, became involved in benevolent organizations like the Fratellanza which took in members from all over the Italian peninsula.[54] His ethnic reference group changed according to his setting.

Men who found themselves in more remote work situations with few *paesani* with them seem to have developed a sense of belonging to a larger Italian or Italian Canadian ethnic group more quickly than those who were able to lodge with *paesani:*

> Question: Were there a lot of people working on that job from your home town in Calabria?
>
> Answer: No. They were mostly from other provinces. Was mixed you know. Mostly from southern Italy. In this gang we passed the winter in this converted horse stable—we were all Italian.[55]

Mr. Carnovale, the man who answered the above query, had three possible reference groups other than acculturation to Canadian ways: his *paese,* his region defined either as Calabria or the Italian south (Mezzo giorno), or the nation state of Italy. It is impossible to doubt that the background of the men with whom he sojourned and boarded did not affect his commitment to one identity or another, or at least his pace along a continuum from *campanilismo* to an Italian Canadian ethnic sense. In that way, detailed study of the social setting of the migrants might begin to yield answers about the historical process of ethnicity.

In an account of a Macedonian "group household" in Toronto in 1920, we can see how the smallest details of the boarding organization could cement village ties or break them down either in favour of a larger Macedonian identity or of acculturation. A father defends his son who has burnt the daily stew prepared for other boarders. There is an angry exchange of words, and, despite the fact that they are all fellow villagers, no turning back. Some moved and found new households; they passed either into the so-called "English" boarding houses or found another Macedonian "group household." In either case, the real conditions of their sojourn caused them to move away from their village loyalties and identity.[56]

If a burnt stew could threaten "fellow-feeling," it should also show that boarding in a "group household," even of fellow townsmen, was no idyll.[57] All the tensions of inter-family jealousies and of life without womenfolk existed. For those families who left after such a contretemps, the "group household" and the village or *paese* that is served in the diaspora lost meaning in that sense which Harold Isaacs, quoting Robert Forst, felt was at the core of ethnicity: as "the place where, when you've got to go there, they've got to take you in."[58] For the many ethnic identities in flux at the turn of the century, boundaries moved, not just because of the broad categories of prejudice used by the North American host society, but also because of the vicissitudes of the sojourning community. Boarding situations, length of sojourn, and neighbourhood density meant that local identities brought from the Old World gave way, although never for various ascriptive purposes disappearing, in favour of North American ethnicity. Toronto's Italians appeared out of a skein of earlier relationships in which Calabrese generally boarded with Calabrese, and

Abruzzese with Abruzzese. (Sicilians and Friulians did not mix at all with the mainland Southern Italians.) Even people from regions living together represented a change from localism. At the turn of the century people from the original towns of settlement like Laurenzana and Pisticci had formed their own boarding households and institutions. The Dillingham Commission had counted Brava (Cape Verdean coloured Portuguese) as a separate ethnic group and had listed their boarding houses separately. Ruthenes, Galicians, and Bukovinians found their larger identity as Ukrainian only slowly.

In a sense, not only were ethnic institutions born in the sojourning years, so was North American ethnicity itself. Historians who wish to understand the relationship between the social and geographical processes of migration and the growth of ethnic identity would do well to look more closely at those first years of sojourning and at the institutions adapted to cope with North America. The sojourners themselves knew that it was an important social and cultural formative period. The Appalachian saying of our time sums it up nicely: "We ain't what we want to be and we ain't what we're going to be, but we ain't what we were."[59]

Notes

1. O. Handlin, *The Uprooted* (Boston, 1951), R. Vecoli, "Contadini in Chicago: A Critique of the Uprooted," *Journal of American History,* Vol. L.1 (December 1964), pp. 404–417.

2. H. Nelli, *Italians in Chicago, 1880–1930: A Study in Ethnic Mobility* (Oxford, 1970), offers a detailed chapter on geographical settlement with no analysis of institutions before 1920. A later chapter uses the padrone system to explain occupational patterns. See also, J. Barton, *Peasants and Strangers: Italians, Rumanians and Slovaks in an American City, 1890–1950* (Harvard, 1975). Chapter II uses chain migration to make the leap from a statistical analysis of old world emigration to a skimpy and anecdotal knowledge of sojourning communities. Moreover, there is some disjuncture between emigration locations and origins of Cleveland migrants.

3. R. Juliani, "American Voices, Italian Accents: The Perception of Social Conditions and Personal Motives by Immigrants," *Italian Americana,* Vol. 1, No. 1 (Autumn 1974), pp. 1–25; and "The Origin and Development of the Italian Community in Philadelphia," in J Bodnar, ed. *The Ethnic Experience in Pennsylvania* (Lewisburg, 1973), pp. 233–261. Juliani's use of oral testimony and background in sociology allows him to say more about the mind set of first arrivals, their institutions and "paesani services."

4. P. Siu, "The Sojourner," *American Journal of Sociology,* Vol. 58 (July 1952), pp. 34–44. Siu describes the sojourner as, not a "marginal man," but one committed to maintaining himself in a manner which will enable him to re-insert himself easily in his country of origin.

5. Of the institutions mentioned, probably the padrone system has received most systematic attention from historians. See L. Iorizzo, "The Padrone and Immigrant

Distribution," in S.M. Tomasi and M.H. Engel, eds., *The Italian Experience in the United States* (Staten Island, 1970), pp. 43–75; R.F. Harney, "The Padrone and the Immigrant," *The Canadian Review of American Studies,* Vol. 2 (Fall, 1974), pp. 101–118; H.B. Nelli, "The Italian Padrone System in the United States," *Labor History,* Vol. 5, No. 2 (Spring, 1964), pp. 153–167.

6. There were of course many excellent studies of specific institutions by contemporary social scientists. Two which deal with the sojourners well are G. Abbott, "The Chicago Employment Agency and the Immigrant Worker," *American Journal of Sociology,* Vol. XIV, No. 3 (November 1908); and E. Bradwin, *The Bunkhouse Man* (New York 1928). I am using institution in the simplest sense—a relationship or behavioural pattern of importance in the life of a community or society.

7. John Modell and Tamara Hareven, "Urbanization and the Malleable Household: An Examination of Boarding and Lodging in American Families," *Journal of Marriage and Family,* Vol. 35 (August 1973), pp. 467–78.

8. The only detailed study of an ethnic boarding house that I am aware of is A. Vazsonyi, "The Star Boarder: Traces of Cicisbeism in an Immigrant Community," in Tractata Altaica (Wiesbaden, 1976), pp. 695–713. This is an ethnological romp through the mores and arrangements of mid-American Hungarian boarders.

9. *U.S. Immigration Commission, 1907–1910 Reports* (henceforth cited as *Dillingham Commission*), Vol. 1, *Abstracts,* pp. 422–438. For agreement with Modell and Hareven that the semantic distinction between boarding and lodging was irrelevant, see *Dillingham Commission,* Vol. 26, pp. 79–80. Although padronism and so-called immigrant hotels fall under the last classification, group household, it is clear that many inns and hotels that ran in traditional commercial terms also were essentially ethnic institutions. See D. Esslinger, *Immigrants and the City, Ethnicity and Mobility in a 19th Century Midwestern Community* (Port Washington, 1975), p. 45, has an interesting account of German hotels in downtown South Bend but does not seem to see the phenomenon as an aspect of ethnic enterprise or of the changing Polish and German ethnic boundaries of the roomers.

10. See *Reports of the Industrial Commission* (Washington, 1910) Vol. XV, pp. x–xii; and *Royal Commission appointed to inquire into the Immigration of Italian Labourers to Montreal and the Alleged Fraudulent Practices of Employment Agencies* (Ottawa, 1905). *Dillingham Commission,* II, p. 427.

11. J. Scarpaci, "Immigrants in the New South: Italians in Louisiana's Sugar Parishes, 1880–1910," in F. Assante, *II Movimento migratorio Italiano dall'unita nazionale ai giorni nostri* (Naples, 1976), pp. 206–209. In the Chinese case, the steamship agents' "holding pens" for migrants at Macau bound for America were called barracoons, the word for slave quarters in most of the Iberian world. See John Foster, *American Diplomacy in the Orient* (Boston, 1903), p. 280.

12. "Forced Labor in West Virginia," *The Outlook,* June 13, 1903.

13. T. Saloutos, *The Greeks in the United States* (Cambridge, 1964), pp. 52–53; *Dillingham Commission,* Vol. 2, pp. 401 & 405.

14. H. Nelli, *Italians in Chicago,* p. 60; for the concept of the target migrant, see J.M. Nelson, *Temporary versus Permanent Cityward Migration: Causes and Consequences* (MIT, 1976).

15. G. Abbott, "The Chicago Employment Agency," p. 294.

16. A Bernardy, *America Vissuta* (Torino, 1911), p. 316.

17. See *Royal Commission (Italians); and R.F. Harney, "Chiaroscuro: Italians in Toronto, 1885–1915," Italian Americans,* Vol. 1, No. 2 (Spring 1975), pp. 143–167.

18. *Industrial Commission,* Vol. XV, p. 157; B. Brandenburg, *Imported Americans* (New York, 1903) described all the frauds and violence visited on migrants in process; E. Corsi, *In the Shadow of Liberty* (New York, 1937), p. 38.

19. Modell and Hareven, "Urbanization and the Malleable Household," p. 470. The 'lodger evil' among immigrants also was subject to confusion about extended families and about how kinship might make household proximity more respectable no matter how remote. For example, the Dillingham Commission remarked that "many persons in few rooms is not so serious a matter when all are members of the family as when strangers are included in the household." *Dillingham Commission,* Vol. 1, p. 748. So it was not the quality of life, the health hazard, but really the "moral climate" that mattered to the authorities.

20. J.S. Woodsworth, *Strangers Within Our Gates* (Toronto, 1909), pp. 217–220.

21. *Jack Canuck,* January 1, 1912, p. 14. *Saturday Night* at least sensed the relationship of this condition to sojourning (January 20, 1912), p. 2, "He is probably counting the hours to that longed for day when he too shall appear at Salerno and jingle money in his pockets."

22. *Hastings Report,* pp. 16–17. The list of families by nationalities included all groups but Anglo-Celts. The three districts chosen for analysis were St. John's Ward, the Eastern Avenue area, and the Niagara Street district. All were heavily immigrant, commercial, and the last two were industrial as well. They were not however the most squalid in the city. The juxtaposition of ethnicity with social problems was quite misleading since British lower class and Canadian pathological slum neighbourhoods were not included in the study.

23. V. Greene, "The Polish American Worker to 1930: The Hunky Image in Transition," *The Polish Review,* Vol. XXI (1976), pp. 63–78. On page 65 it is pointed out that even sympathetic observers of Slavic group households left the impression that "the workers still required non-group leadership to effect the necessary reforms" in immigrant life including housing. This same view persists among students of European guestworker systems who feel that boarding or hotel accommodations "lead to a ghetto-like life and prevent any contact with the local community … (and thus) retard a positive process of learning." W.R. Bohning, "The Social and Occupational Apprenticeship of Mediterranean Migrant Workers in West Germany" in M. Livi-Bacci, ed., *The Demographic and Social Pattern of Emigration from the Southern European Countries* (Florence, 1972), p. 226. This view like that of the turn-of-the-century Toronto assumes that integration is the only proper course for sojourners.

24. See P. Siu, "The Sojourner"; V.G. Nee and B. de B. Nee, *Longtime Californ': A Documentary Study of an American Chinatown* (New York, 1973) Chap. II "The Bachelor Society"; R.F. Harney, "Men Without Women Italian Migrants in Canada, 1885–1930," a paper presented to the AIHA-CIHA Joint Sessions (Toronto, Oct. 28, 1977).

25. Traditions among South Slavs like the *zadruga* and *drustvo* and the role of wives in running *czarda* in Hungary obviously made adaptation to being a boarding house mistress easier for female immigrants from those groups. For the Italians, M.H. Ets, *Rosa: The Life of an Italian Immigrant* (Minnesota, 1970), and the story of Rosa Mondavi in A. Pellegrini's *Americans by Choice* (New York, 1956), pp. 138–147, demonstrate the almost involuntary economic performance of immigrant wives. See J. Scott and I.L. Tilly, "Women's Work and the Family in 19th Century Europe," *Comparative Studies in Society and History* (Jan. 17, 1975); C. Golab, "The Impact of the Industrial Experience on the Immigrant Family: The Huddled Masses Reconsidered," *Immigrants in Industrial America 1850–1920,* Richard Erlich, ed., (University Press of Virginia: September 1977); and V.Y. McLaughlin, *Family and Community: Italian Immigrants in Buffalo 1880–1930* (Cornell University Press, 1977).

26. The study of ethnicity would profit from more awareness of issues in the study of the formation of nationality and growth of national feeling. For example, see A. Smith, *Theories of Nationalism* (London, 1971); and K. Deutsch, *Nationalism and Social Communication* (MIT, 1953). Both suggest that the scale of fellow-feeling is a function of the economic and social network which proves most useful.

27. Oscar Handlin, *Boston's Immigrants* (Harvard, 1941), p. 101.

28. Rudolph Vecoli, "Contadini in Chicago," pp. 408–411.

29. See for example, G. Prpic, *The Croatian Immigrants in America* (New York, 1971); M. Byington, *Homestead: The Households of a Mill Town* (Pittsburgh, 1910); T. Bell, *Out of This Furnace* (Pittsburgh, 1976); I. L. Adamic, *From Many Lands* (New York, 1919), and Vazsonyi, "The Star Boarders."

30. T. Kessner, *The Golden Door. Italian and Jewish Immigrant Mobility in New York City, 1880–1915* (New York, 1976), p. 100.

31. For the uses of "miszisz," see Vazsonyi "The Star Boarder"; C. Panunzio, *The Soul of the Immigrant,* shows the typical Italian use of "padrone" to describe the head of the establishment; "Bordo" and "bordante" ("bordisti") are terms discussed by Amy Bernardy in *Italia randagia attraverso gli Stati Uniti* (Turin, 1914), pp. 88–122. Louise Tilly's thesis on the formation of the Milan working class, 1881–1911, shows the use of the proper Italian *covivenza* to describe urban boarding of newcomers there (Toronto: History Department, 1972), R.F. Harney, Director, p. 291. The uses of family terms like auntie, nonna, uncle, and daughter to reduce tension and define roles is mentioned in most oral testimony.

32. John Kosa, *Land of Choice: The Hungarian in Canada* (Toronto, 1957), p. 31.

33. J. MacDonald and L. MacDonald, "Chian Migration, Ethnic Neighbourhood Formation and Social Networks," in C. Tilly, ed., *An Urban World* (Boston, 1974), p. 231. This, like most sources, concentrates on the importance of sheltered work for Latin immigrant women rather than on the entrepreneurial role of family.

34. J. Marlyn, *Under the Riles of Death* (Toronto, 1971), pp. 19–22, presents a convincing picture of the ambivalence of the children of boardinghouse keepers toward their role in the intended household. Lithuanian and Polish landlords in Chicago often rented out the better units to tenants but lived in the worst rooms themselves to minimize costs: see Victor Greene, *For God and Country: The Rise of the Polish and Lithuanian Ethnic Consciousness in America, 1860–1910* (Madison, 1975), p. 53.

35. *Hastings Report,* pp. 8 and 14.

36. E. Rossi, "Delle Condizioni del Canada respetto all 'immigrazione italiana," *Bollettino dell' Emigrazione #4,* Anno 1903. Although the economics of boarding usually is described in terms of the boarding-boss or family with boarders profit, it must be remembered that the sojourner clientele made the system work. It was they, maximizing their savings to meet old world needs, who accepted crowded conditions and minimal service. A convincing local example can be found in R. Wilson, *A Retrospective: A Short Review of the Steps Taken in Sanitation to Transform the Town of Muddy York into the Queen City of the West* (Toronto, 1934), p. 32, which describes a three-room cottage with twenty Italian boarders thus: "They were all jolly good natured fellows and were highly amused at the visit of the health inspector and his inquiries as translated by the boss ... "—hardly the atmosphere of white slavery and padronism. In the Canadian case, a special service offered by the ethnic boarding system was credit for room and board over the long winter months of unemployment. Nick Lombardi speaks from the perspective of the boardinghouse keeper: "We had a couple, not because we needed them, but because they were good friends and they wanted to stay with us. We all used to eat together. And if they didn't have the money, daddy and mom never used to worry. They knew they'd pay off the debt in the summer." (Taped Interview, The Multicultural History Society of Ontario, June 1, 1976). His friend, Paul Lorenzo, remembers the situation from the sojourner's view: "We used to live over where they put the new Mount Sinai Hospital, near Mt. Carmel church on McCaul Street, in an Italian boarding house—$2.50 a month. There were about 8 or 10 boarders in the house. In the winter time, we can't pay the rent—we have no money. You must wait for summer to return so you can go out and work again and pay your debts ... And when you'd go to the store you had to sign a book since you had no money. And my father kept his own book too, so that he would never be cheated." (Taped Interview, The Multicultural History Society of Ontario.)

37. This story was gathered by John Bodnar and Carl Oblinger of the Pennsylvania Museum of Man and will appear in a forthcoming oral history volume. P. Roberts, *The New Immigration* (New York, 1914), p. 131. The sick, wounded, and unemployed threw off the three shift bed rotation and were often evicted. Gina Petroff (Taped Interview, Oct. 12, 1976) tells the story of a man known as Nick Coca Cola. "Anyway he been sleeping on the third floor. Not working. He never get up two days, just sleep and stay there day and night, and the name is Nick ... There's Depression and nobody give work to you. So anyway they kept him for a little while over ... and then they kicked him out." (Unless otherwise cited, all oral testimony is from the collection of the Multicultural History Society of Ontario. A computerized guide to that collection is in process.)

38. See Vazsonyi, "Traces of Cicisbeism"; and A. Bernardy "Da un relazione de Amy Bernardy su I' emigrazione delle donne e fanciullo italiane nelle Stati Uniti," *Bollettino del' Emigrazione* (1909).

39. "Nanni Volpe," in G. Verga, *The She Wolf and Other Stories* (Berkeley, 1958), p. 160.

40. "The Boarding House," from *The New Pioneer* in V. Wertsman, *The Romanians in America, 1748–1974* (Dobbs Ferry, 1975), p. 62.

41. *Jack Canuck,* Vol. 1, No. 14 (January, 1912); T. Hiramatso (Taped interview).

42. Mary Caruso (Taped Interview, Dec. 7, 1976). Her grandfather, a hurdy gurdy man, left the boarding enterprise completely to his wife.

43. Michael Guzei (Taped Interview (Slovak Barr)).

44. John Krar (Taped Interview Donau-Schwaben #260 Frei) *Dillingham Commission,* Abstracts, Vol. 1, pp. 422–552. "Many variations upon this arrangement are met with but some form of it constitutes the method of living usually followed by *recent immigrant households*" (read, sojourners.)

45. V. Wertsman, *The Romanians,* p. 63.

46. Stoyan Christowe, *This Is My Country* (New York, 1938). The leader of a "group household" although he depended on a coterie of elders or kin, exercised control.

47. P. Roberts, *The New Immigration,* p. 124.

48. R. Breton, "Institutional Completeness of Ethnic Communities and the Personal Relations of Immigrants," *American Journal of Sociology,* Vol. 70 (September 1964), pp. 193–205. Anna Kaprielian (Jan. 24, 1978, Armenian)—same sense of the completeness of a sojourning institution comes out of this conversation. "He had a house. The first floor was a coffee shop and library. People would go there and play backgammon, cards, read books (whoever could read). Armenians would congregate there. Everyone would tell his story, talk about his family. They'd write letters ...."

49. For those who believe that the sojourning attitude shapes a migrant's relations with North America, studies about occupational mobility and acculturation should reflect the intensity of the migrant's desire to insert himself as much as it does North American conditions. The contrasting of Jewish settlers and Italian sojourners as to rates of occupational mobility without tolerance to their frame of mind and attitude about staying in the United States becomes silly. See Betty B. Caroli, "Italian Settlement in American Cities," in H.S. Nelli, ed., *The U.S. and Italy: Proceedings of the 9th Annual Conference of the AIHA* (Washington, 1976), pp. 156–158.

50. For example where would a man who sold balloons at Toronto parades who also was chief money lender in the Italian community, a man who lost his arm in an abattoir accident but made a comfortable living escorting brides back and forth from Macedonia, and all the informal keepers of boarding establishments fit in the gross measures of mobility and status such as S. Thernstrom's *The Other Bostonians* (Cambridge, 1973). Some synthesis of oral testimony and quantitative methods would greatly enhance the value of urban studies.

51. Conversation with Dr. Juliana Puskas, Toronto, January 25, 1978. Dr. Puskas has spent the last year visiting Hungarian committees in the U.S. and Canada.

52. H. Lopata, *Polish American Status Competition in an Ethnic Community* (New York, 1976), pp. 608 and 19–20 gives a clear sociological view of ethnicity as a historical process, in which the *okolica,* the physical and psychic unit of group identity, changes in North America.

53. Upton Sinclair *The Jungle* (New York, 1965), first edition 1906, p. 32.

54. P. Bertoia (Taped Interview Friulian, March 1, 1978). Ethnic identities among sojourners were nowhere near as hard-edged as prejudice and the ethnic groups own retospective falsification now make them appear. Finns, Swedes, and Finn Swedes

who lived near quarries on Cape Ann in Massachusetts changed ethnic loyalty with boarding houses. See P. Parsons & P. Anastas, *When Gloucester Was Gloucester: Toward an Oral History of the City* (Gloucester, 1973), p. 21.

55. John Carnovale (Taped Interview, Italian, The Multicultural History Society of Ontario.)

56. F. Tomev (Taped Interview, Macedonian, December, 1977). In a given boarding house, there would be all "pro Bulgarian" or all patriarchist Macedonians and men from the same village would not board together if their politics differed. The sources of this rising ethnic consciousness lay in local, neighbourhood developments which affect all immigrants, even the most articulate. See Victor Greene, *For God and Country: The Rise of Polish and Lithuanian Ethnic Consciousness in America, 1860–1910*, p. 5.

57. H.N. Brailsford, *Macedonia—Its Races and Their Future* (London, 1906), p. 102, "Is your village Greek, I asked him, or Bulgarian. Well, he replied, it is Bulgarian now but four years ago it was Greek ... .The Bulgarians heard of this and they came and made us an offer. They said they would give us a priest who would live in the village, and a teacher to whom we need pay nothing. Well sir, ours is a poor village, and so of course we became Bulgaria." For all peasant migrant groups, ethnicity was far more local and malleable than we have assumed.

58. H. Isaacs, *Idols of the Tribe* (New York, 1975), p. 43.

59. M. Pei, *What's In a Word* (New York, 1968), p. 52.

KINSHIP AND SOCIETY IN THE UKRAINIAN PIONEER SETTLEMENT OF THE CANADIAN WEST

John C. Lehr

In the European colonization of the frontierlands of the New World, various nationalities have tended to seek the company of their fellows in settlement. At the time of the agricultural settlement of the Canadian prairies, this was acknowledged as a natural inclination by the Dominion Government when it set aside special areas for the settlement of such groups as Doukhobors and Mennonites.[1] By locating with their fellows, new settlers could in some measure secure a familiar social, religious, and linguistic environment which, in the opinion of the Department of the Interior, did much to promote successful agricultural settlement.

The drive to seek out familiar milieux is common to all peoples. In-group preference is so nearly universal that it competes with physiological drives for food or sex for recognition as a basic human trait.[2] Yet while group settlement

From *The Canadian Geographer*, 29, 3, 1985, 207–219. Reprinted by permission of The Canadian Association of Geographers.

has been noted as a feature of the agricultural settlement of western Canada, the contributions of kinship and society to that area's distinctive social geography have been largely neglected. As an initial step toward correcting this situation, this essay presents an examination of the spatial form and internal structure of the block settlements of one of the most significant groups to settle independently in western Canada, the Ukrainians. It identifies the nature and role of social ties and divisions within this immigrant community. It argues that intra-group relationships were strongly expressed in both the micro- and macro-geography of Ukrainian settlement, and that they were in large measure responsible for the occupation of sub-marginal homestead land by Ukrainians in parts of the Canadian west.

GROUP SETTLEMENT

English-speaking settlers of the western Canadian agricultural frontier were fortunate to be settling a territory that, in many important respects, maintained the basic societal framework of their points of origin. They encountered familiar elements of law and administration; the creed of the ruling majority was Protestant; and English was the de jure, if not the de facto, language of all in the newly settled west. Nonetheless, ties of blood and custom were still sufficient to cause many English-speaking immigrants to cluster together in settlement.[3] Even independently minded American settlers, when surrounded by "foreigners," lost little time in seeking new homesteads within an area of English-speaking settlement.[4]

For the "foreign" settlers the social experience of settlement was far different. British laws, Anglo-Saxon customs, the Protestant creed, the English language, often the Latin script, were unfamiliar, even incomprehensible. Only settlement among their fellows offered some amelioration of the alien British ambiance. Among their country- and kin-folk, foreign settlers could hope to retain some elements of their homeland society and culture. Group settlement allowed them to practise their own religion, gave spiritual comfort, and ministered to their psychological well-being.

Several ethnic or religious groups settling in the west sought the social security of group settlement, but few extended their quest as far as the Ukrainians. Many were seemingly content to achieve a general sense of "at homeness," and were comforted by a few transposed common elements of their national culture. There was little perpetuation of "old-country" regional groupings within the larger ethnic group settlement, and little, if any, homogeneity was displayed at the micro-scale. This was the situation, for example, with the three areas of Irish settlement in eastern Canada examined by Mannion.[5] It was no less true of the Mormon settlement in southern Alberta.[6] In both instances the circumstances of emigration caused unifying factors to predominate, and divisive forces within the group were submerged by common religious and cultural elements.

Group settlement was by no means universal in the international migration of Europeans, but it has been remarked that most group settlements "have a decided 'locality flavour' about them," in that "the majority of the group derive from one particular area of Europe."[7] Contributing to a study of cultural integration among immigrants some thirty years ago, C.A. Price defined four levels of group settlement: village, district, regional, and national. He cautioned, however, that what "at first sight appear to be concentrations of this or that nationality very often turn out to be simply numbers of migrants from one particular village or district."

For the most part, geographers have concentrated on explaining the creation of the macro-geography of group settlement in the New World. Bohland, Brunger, and Ostergren are among the few to have extended the level of geographical inquiry to the consideration of familial and old-country village ties in settlement.[8] In his pioneering study of the social role of the pioneering process, Dawson dealt with social ties in a general fashion, and a number of Canadian geographers have since commented on the tendency of territorially defined sub-groups to concentrate in different parts of a common settlement area.[9] Apart from Richtik's examination of kinship linkages among Ontario British settlers in Manitoba, however, analyses of the macro-geography of ethnic settlement in the Canadian west have stopped short of examining the role of kin linkages in settlement.[10]

UKRAINIAN SETTLEMENT

Ukrainian immigrants from the Austrian-administered provinces of Halychyna (Galicia) and Bukovyna (Bukowina) began to settle in western Canada in 1892. Until 1896, they all located near Star, in east-central Alberta, but with the trickle of Ukrainian immigrants turning into a flood in that year, a number of other Ukrainian settlements were established throughout the parkland belt, in an arc from Edmonton in the west to Winnipeg in the east.

When the outbreak of the First World War terminated their emigration, there were an estimated 170,000 Ukrainians in Canada.[11] The majority had sought homestead land in western Canada, and almost all of them had come from western Ukraine, an area governed until 1919 by Hapsburg monarchs of the Austro-Hungarian Empire. Halychyna and Bukovyna were economically depressed and politically oppressed agricultural backwaters of Austrian dominion.[12] The Ukrainian population of these provinces was almost entirely peasant, identified little with Austria, and was ruled by an alien, or alienated, aristocracy. The peasantry possessed little affection for the multinational Austria of which it was a part, and it did not possess a strong sense of ethnicity in the national sense. Most loyalties were bounded by the restricted horizons drawn by the limited mobility of peasant life in eastern Europe in the nineteenth century. The family, the village, the church, and, to a lesser extent, the province were the foci of peasant emotion and loyalty.

As Ukrainians arrived in western Canada they established a well-defined pattern of behaviour, sufficiently different from the norm to elicit comment from the colonization officers of the Department of the Interior who settled thousands of immigrants of all nationalities on the homestead lands. The Ukrainians were marked as "peculiar people" by Immigration Commissioner William F. McCreary, who wondered at their refusal of prime wheat-growing prairie land in favour of the less fertile woodlands on the northern fringes of the parkland belt. Their determination to settle together was soon found to be a major problem in the administration of western settlement.[13] It also became a major factor in the development of the basic geographical pattern of Ukrainian settlement in western Canada (figure 1). In the early years, group or block settlement was favoured by the Department of the Interior, since it simplified the tasks of the colonization officers and reduced the chances of failure in settlement.[14] Once begun, however, the process acquired an almost uncontrollable momentum of its own, as Commissioner McCreary reported to the deputy minister in 1898: "They are apparently an obstreperous, obstinate, rebellious lot. I am just about sick of these people. They are worse than cattle to handle. You cannot get them, by persuasion or argument, to go to a new colony except by force. They all want to go where the others have gone."[15] This single-minded determination created a distinctive geography of block settlements across the west. The macro-geography of these blocks reflects the Ukrainians' desire for woodlands, but their internal structure—their micro-geography—reflects the intensity with which the benefits of a familiar milieu were pursued.

SETTLEMENT STRUCTURE

There are many incidental references to the internal morphology of Ukrainian block settlements in western Canada, and many authors have commented on the tendency of Ukrainian pioneers to settle on an old-country village basis.[16] More substantial comment has been provided by Goresky, Lazarenko, and Royick, who have identified specific village groupings in the Star-Vegreville block settlement of Alberta.[17] Pohorecky and Royick have identified linguistic differences among the Ukrainians in Alberta, which they hold to reflect the perpetuation of old-country dialects in the New World.[18] Since dialect survival is dependent on the grouping of dialect speakers in settlement, the implication is that such groupings were perpetuated in Ukrainian settlements in Alberta, a contention that is supported by evidence from Goresky and Byrne.[19]

Old-country villages were commemorated in the landscape of the prairie provinces in toponyms transferred by the settlers from Ukraine. The villages of Ispas, Stry, Luzan, and Shepenge (or Szpenitz, but properly Shypyntsi) in

Alberta, and Jaroslav, Senkiw, Melnice, Zbarazh, and Komarno in Manitoba, are but a few examples.[20] However, since the Ukrainians were seldom in a position to name places—that was the preserve of the railway companies and the English-speaking surveyors and administrators—the strongest record of Ukrainian occupance and of old-country village ties survives in the names of their rural schools and school districts, where examples abound.

That the Ukrainians perpetuated their old-country village groups in western Canada is not as significant as the frequency with which they did so. This trait was sufficient to impart to the Ukrainian block settlement an internal structure that varied little. Since it is impractical to examine all Ukrainian block settlements in western Canada, data from three areas will be drawn upon in a discussion of the various hierarchical linkages found within such settlements. Those selected are the Star-Vegreville block of central Alberta, the first established and ultimately the largest Ukrainian settlement; the Manitoba Interlake (Pleasant Home) block; and the Stuartburn block in southeastern Manitoba (figure 1).

FIGURE 1   Ukrainian Settlements in Western Canada, 1914

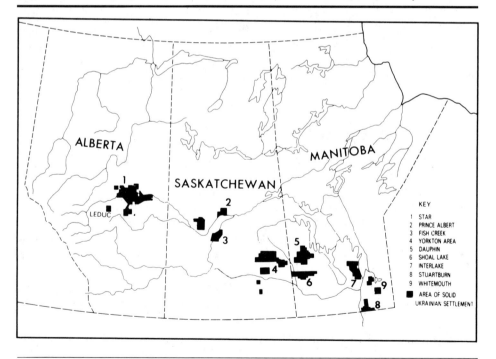

Sources: Public Archives of Canada, RG76; and Records of Homestead Entry, Alberta, Saskatchewan and Manitoba.

KINSHIP AND VILLAGE TIES

In most peasant societies, families are generally large and non-nuclear. Indeed, it is not unusual for peasants to be related to the majority of their fellow villagers by ties of blood or marriage. Nor is it unusual to find that the concepts of village and kin are virtually synonymous. Ties to kinfolk are strong, and they are kept strong by economic and social interdependence, heightened by the restricted horizons of village life. To the peasant in nineteenth-century Ukraine, loyalties were to family, village, locality, district, and province rather than to the more abstract concepts of nation, state, or even ethnicity. Just as villagers grouped together in settlement when they emigrated, so groups of villagers from the same region tended to group together, thereby perpetuating old-country district groupings. Although village groups are here considered in isolation, in both social and spatial terms the village was a *holon;* it functioned as a unit in its own right, but it was also part of a higher group within a hierarchy (figure 2).[21] To conceive of the village as a discrete social or spatial unit is misleading. It was only one unit in a closely integrated hierarchy and cannot be separated from its place within the district or region, although analysis necessitates that it first be considered in that way here.

FIGURE 2   Social Structure and Interrelationships in Western Ukraine

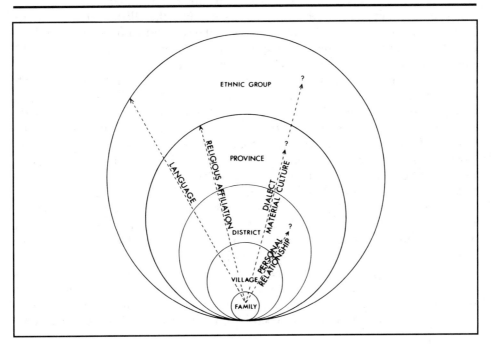

Contemporary observers of Ukrainian settlement made frequent comment on its cohesiveness, as evidenced by the immigrants seeking out their fellows and kin.[22] Records of homestead cancellation are equally revealing. In those areas of Alberta settled by Ukrainians, homestead entries were frequently cancelled, even after improvements had been made, when settlers sought to relocate near more recently arrived relatives.[23] Social reasons were cited on the declarations of abandonment almost as frequently as environmental ones. A terse scrawl, "My brother has moved and I wish to homestead beside him" or "I wish to locate near friends," barely conveys the strength of the magnetism that family and friends exerted on the socially isolated settler.[24] Interviews with surviving settlers and their families in Alberta and Manitoba confirmed that the vast majority of immigrants chose their locations because they "wanted to be with friends—to help out in hard times and stick together."[25] Todor Kutzak, a pioneer of Sirko, Manitoba, was more blunt: "When I arrived in Canada in 1905 I headed for Gardenton where I had an uncle who would feed us when we [Kutzak and friend] arrived."[26] The great majority of over 250 Ukrainian settlers who were interviewed in a research project in 1971, and who gave reasons for settlement in a specific area, mentioned the presence of friends, relatives, or fellow villagers as a major factor in their decisions.[27] Several also commented that they subsequently changed their location so as to secure an even tighter family settlement.

The spatial impact of the close agglomeration of settlers on the basis of family groups can be illustrated by the Stuartburn area of Manitoba (figure 3). This area was first settled in 1896, and already by 1900 the Ukrainian settlement had extended over five townships, and a number of distinct old-country village and district agglomerations were apparent. In Township 1, Range 6 East, 12 families from the village of Bridok, Zastavna District, Bukovyna, had settled in a well-defined cluster, although there was a certain amount of mixing with 13 families from the village of Onuth, also of Zastavna District (figure 4). Villagers from Lukivci, Chernivci District, Bukovyna, had settled alongside them, but they remained almost totally separate, even after five years of settlement. In the northern area of the Stuartburn block, 45 families from Senkiw (Synkiw), Zalishchyky District, Halychyna, were less tightly grouped. They formed two closely linked clusters centred on Township 2, Range 6 East, which together contained 33 of the Senkiw families. A similar pattern was evident with the settlement of families from the village of Postolivka of Huisatyn District, Halychyna. The first Postolivka settlers took land in 1897, on Section 36, Township 1, Range 5 East, and subsequent arrivals settled on adjoining sections. In 1898, a second nucleus of Postolivka settlers was established some twelve miles east, in the centre of Township 2, Range 7 East. The reason is difficult to determine, for at the time of the establishment of the second group there was no shortage of vacant homestead lands surrounding the initial settlers from Postolivka. Since the second group also clustered in its settlement,

FIGURE 3 District of Origin of Ukrainian Settlers at Stuartburn, Manitoba, 1901

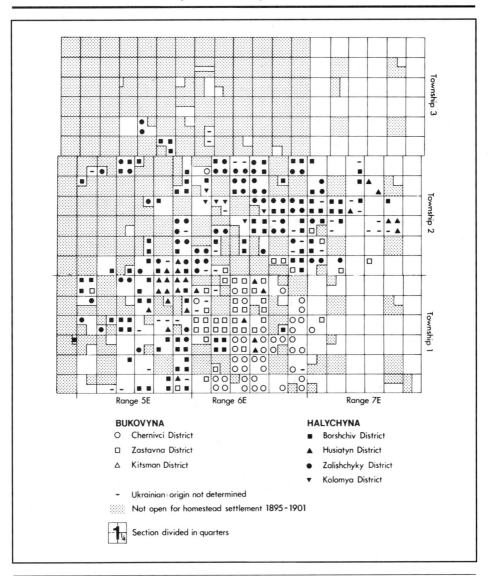

Sources: V.J. Kaye, *Dictionary of Ukrainian Pioneer Biography* (Toronto: Ukrainian Canadian Research Foundation, 1975); Township General Registers, Department of Lands, Government of Manitoba; and field research in southeastern Manitoba. Reprinted from J.C. Lehr, "The Peculiar People: Ukrainian Settlement of the Stuartburn District of S.E. Manitoba," in *Building Beyond the Homestead,* ed. David C. Jones and Ian MacPherson (Calgary: University of Calgary Press, 1985).

FIGURE 4 Villages of Origin of Bukovynan Settlers at Stuartburn, Manitoba, 1901

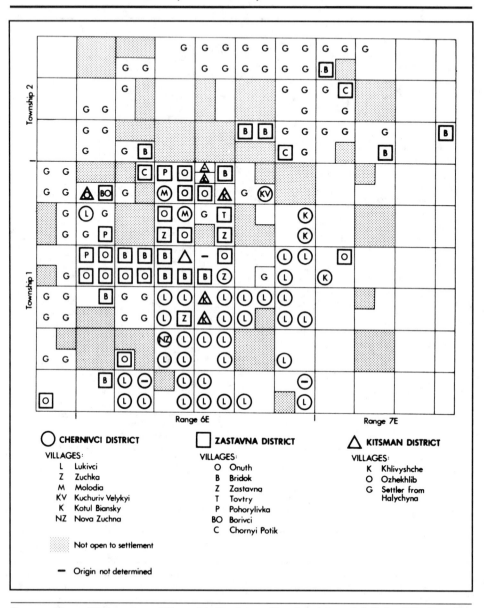

Sources: Kaye, *Dictionary;* and Township Registers. Reprinted from J.C. Lehr, "The Peculiar People: Ukrainian Settlement of the Stuartburn District of S.E. Manitoba," in *Building Beyond the Homestead,* ed. David C. Jones and Ian MacPherson (Calgary: University of Calgary Press, 1985).

kinship was probably a factor, for all but one of the second group held the surname Podolsky, and travelled to Canada on the SS *Christiana,* arriving at Halifax on 12 July 1898.[28] As far as can be ascertained, no members of this family settled outside this group of settlers.

Kinship was undoubtedly a major factor in the perpetuation of old-country village ties. Thirteen of the 32 families comprising the Lukivci group had the surname Kossowan, four Zyha, and three Shypot (figure 5). While this in itself is not conclusive evidence of kinship, it certainly points in that direction. It is usually impossible to determine kin linkages created through marriage, yet marital ties may have been as effective as blood relationships in maintaining closely clustered patterns of settlement.[29] At all events, what appear to be three large family groups account for over half of the immigrants from the village of Lukivci who settled in the Stuartburn district.

FIGURE 5 Family Groups of Settlers from the Village of Lukivci, Bukovyna, at Stuartburn, Manitoba

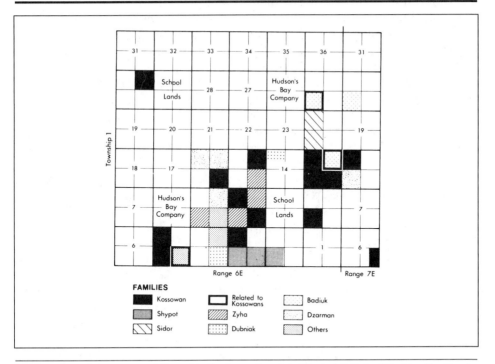

Sources: Kaye, *Dictionary;* and Township Registers. Reprinted from J.C. Lehr, "The Peculiar People: Ukrainian Settlement of the Stuartburn District of S.E. Manitoba," in *Building Beyond the Homestead,* ed. David C. Jones and Ian MacPherson (Calgary: University of Calgary Press, 1985).

The general pattern of old-country village agglomeration was replicated in the Ukrainian settlement of the Manitoba Interlake region. Settlers from the village of Bereziv Vyzhnyi, Kolomya District, Halychyna, settled together in Township 17, Range 2 East (figure 6). Members of another small group from the village of Luka, Buchach District, Halychyna, were apparently all related and formed a close settlement occupying seven quarters on two adjoining sections. Villagers from Melnycia, Borshchiv District, Halychyna, also formed a small, loosely clustered settlement in Township 17, Range 3 East.

In summary, agglomeration of settlers on a basis of old-country village origins was common within Ukrainian block settlements throughout the Canadian west. Furthermore, kinship was a factor of considerable significance in perpetuating what were, in effect, European social organisms on the Canadian settlement frontier.

DISTRICT AND PROVINCIAL SEGREGATION

Agglomeration in settlement by district and province of origin was another marked feature of the Ukrainian block settlements, perhaps even more marked than agglomeration by village. Most notably of all, at the highest level in the hierarchy, there was an almost total separation between settlers from Halychyna and Bukovyna.

Contiguity of settlement by district of origin is clearly evident in the Stuartburn block (figure 3). This settlement contained immigrants from seven districts in the western Ukraine: Borshchiv, Husiatyn, Zalishchyky, and Kolomya in Halychyna, and Chernivci, Kitsman, and Zastavna in Bukovyna.

In the case of Zalischyky District, the majority of settlers came from Senkiw, yet others from villages within Zalischyky District settled beside them. Notably, immigrants from Kolodribka village, although settling on adjacent quarter-sections, also chose sites within an area of Zalishchyky District settlement. Similarly, immigrants from four villages in Husiatyn District—Postolivka, Zelena, Khorostkiv, and Tovstenko—all settled together. Those from Postolivka, who formed the majority, also constituted the geographical hub of the Husiatyn settlement.

Settlers from Bukovyna came from three districts: Chernivci, Kitsman, and Zastavna. The few settlers from Kitsman District did not locate together, but those from Chernivci and Zastavna settled as two distinct groups within the same area (figure 4). Eighty-two percent of the settlers from Chernivci were from the village of Lukivci, so in that case district settlement was virtually synonymous with village settlement. Among those from Zastavna District, however, there were villagers from Bridok (13 families), Chornyi Potik (3 families), Tovtry (1 family), Pohorylivka (3 families), and Zastavna town (2 families). All settled together (see figure 4).

A similar pattern was manifested in the Interlake area of Manitoba, where a number of groups tended to cluster according to district of origin (figure 6).

FIGURE 6 Ukrainian Settlers in the Manitoba Interlake District

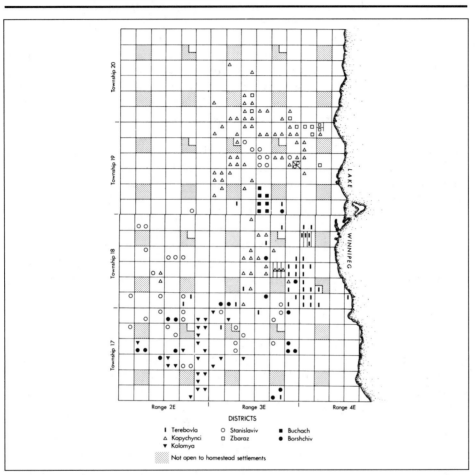

Sources: Kaye, *Dictionary;* and M. Ewanchuk, *Spruce, Swamp and Stone* (Winnipeg: Published by the author, 1977).

Considering the unorganized and loosely administered process of land selection and settlement, the social cohesion shown by these settlers was remarkable.

Social cohesion was also manifested in the separation of settlers by their province of origin, although this pattern was obscured by the fact that some block settlements contained immigrants from only one province. The Interlake block, for example, was settled initially by immigrants from Halychyna, and those from Bukovyna entered only in small numbers and toward the end of the settlement period. In contrast, the Stuartburn district in Manitoba and the Star-Vegreville district of Alberta were settled almost from the beginning by immigrants from both provinces. A clear separation developed between the two groups, replicating old-country social and spatial groupings on the settlement frontier of western Canada.

In the Alberta case, Bukovynian settlers expanded north and east from the initial point of Ukrainian settlement near Star, while those from Halychyna confined themselves to areas west and south of the Bukovynan territory (figure 7).[30] Mixing was unusual and was generally confined to those areas that were last to be settled: the sub-marginal lands of the boreal forest north of Smoky Lake and the eastern-most district of Ukrainian settlement beyond Myrnam. These areas were mainly settled after 1905 by re-migration from the area around Wostok, Andrew, and St. Michael. Most settlers were the sons of pioneers seeking homestead land of their own. Otherwise, there was little mixing between the two groups; the contact zone remained shallow and easily defined.[31]

A similar pattern was evident in the Stuartburn district, where Bukovynan immigrants formed a solid contiguous block of settlement in the townships along the American border (figure 3). As in the Star-Vegreville case, their separation from the Halychyni began to break down only in the areas last to be settled. Similar circumstances prevailed in the final phase of settlement in both areas: a scramble for a rapidly diminishing area of homestead land in the general area of Ukrainian settlement, and a good deal of re-migration by the sons of the earlier Ukrainian settlers.

The separation of the two groups was voluntary. It was not due to any deliberate action by government agents, although there is considerable evidence of connivance by the Department of the Interior: "I found I had to put the Bukowinians and Galicians in two separate groups as they were not friendly with each other ... There was some religious difference between them which appeared to cause friction. Probably there was some obscure racial trouble as well, tracing back to the past history of these people."[32] In fact, the division of the Ukrainian block settlement on the basis of old-country provincial origin is explainable in terms of Catholic-Orthodox rivalries and conflicts that were heightened by the provincialism of the Ukrainian peasant.

It is difficult for outsiders to appreciate the intensity of feeling that was associated with the religious differences between the Orthodox Bukovynans and the Uniate (Greek Catholic) of Halychyna.[33] To many of the Ukrainian peasants, religion was the cornerstone of life. Religious affiliation meant more than adherence to a style of worship; it carried strong national and political overtones. The Greek Catholics feared Russophile sympathies by the Orthodox who, for their part, were equally suspicious of Roman Catholic and Polish dominance of the Uniate Church. This rift was exacerbated by differences in folk culture between Halychyna and Bukovyna, and by the mental images each group had of the other.[34]

FIGURE 7 Ukrainian Settlement in the Star-Vegreville Block of East-Central Alberta to 1914

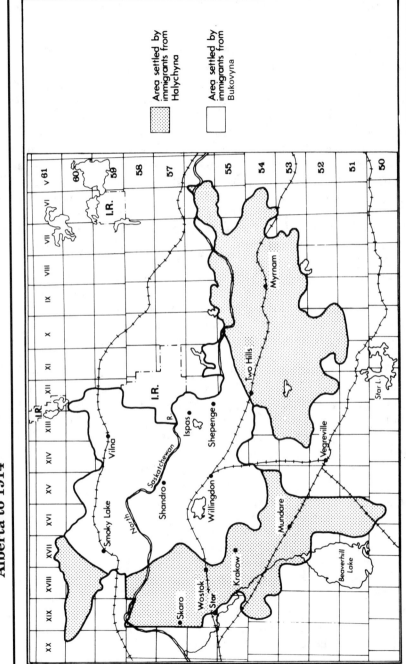

Source: Data from Records of Homestead Entry, Alberta.

To many Bukovynans, people from Halychyna were stereotyped as miserly and without compassion; to the latter, Bukovynans were unsophisticated, bucolic "hayseeds."[35]

The intensity of their mutual antipathy was early remarked upon by many officials of the Department of the Interior who worked with the two groups. In 1897, Commissioner William McCreary noted that the Bukovynans "do not affiliate, and, in fact are detested by the Galicians."[36] Considerable trouble was experienced when officials disregarded such animosities and treated the Ukrainians as a homogeneous group. Colonization Agent C.W. Speers reported one such instance: "After a little trouble which arose, the Galicians, not wishing to go with the Bukowinians—verily the Jews not wishing to deal with the Samaritans—I assured them they were all Canadians now under free institutions and they were well satisfied as we agreed to colonize them in different parts of the Township."[37] The Department of the Interior rapidly learned to accommodate itself to these prejudices. Indeed, it soon became the practice to segregate the Bukovynans from the Halychnyi even while in transit and during their stay in the Winnipeg immigration sheds.[38]

It is more difficult to account for the perpetuation of a clear pattern of settlement by district of origin. Religious allegiance along old-country provincial lines played an important role in maintaining segregation at the macro-level; family ties clearly account for segregation at the micro-level, at the scale of the old-country village. Yet strong district loyalties operated between these extremes, as well.

Two explanations can be advanced: regional consciousness and chain migration. There is little doubt that the limited horizons of the peasant world heightened local loyalties. In some cases, peasants' horizons scarcely extend beyond their own villages, but in the densely settled environments of western Ukraine, social contacts and kinship linkages often extended over a number of villages, all of which fell within a relatively restricted geographic area. This seems to have been the case in the Stanislaviv District settlement of the Manitoba Interlake, where many families came from the village of Mariampol and its immediate environs. Unfortunately, paucity of data makes it impossible to determine the extent to which district settlement was actually "locality settlement." It is also unwise to ascribe too little physical mobility to the Ukrainian peasant at the turn of the century. Marital ties, for example, spanned the Prut River between Halychyna and Bukovyna and were directly responsible for the initial close settlement of immigrants from Halychyna and Bukovyna in the Stuartburn area. The relationship between the Storeschuk and Zahara families, from Halychyna and Bukovyna respectively, was a major factor in securing the presence of both groups in Stuartburn, although subsequent settlement saw them segregate.[39]

The second possible explanation for segregation at the district level is chain migration. According to Price, this mechanism, whereby knowledge of immigration opportunity is diffused through personal contacts between the old and new lands, accounts for most old-country groupings in New World settlement.[40] He suggests that chain migration was largely responsible for the growth of the Ukrainian population in Canada, and there can be little doubt that it was a factor of primary importance. The effect of immigration propaganda should not be overlooked, however. Dr. Josef Oleskow, an influential advocate of Ukrainian emigration to western Canada, advised Ukrainian emigrants to try to settle near to, or alongside, other Ukrainians or other minority groups from the ethnically Ukrainian areas of eastern Europe. The consensus of those Ukrainians who wrote on the subject was that in settlement abroad the peasant should follow the advice of the Ukrainian aphorism: "svyi do Svoho—Let each keep to his own."[41]

CULTURE AND MOBILITY

The internal morphology of the Ukrainian block settlement may be interpreted as the spatial manifestation of the strong cohesive social forces found within a traditional peasant society. These were sufficiently strong to have a considerable effect on the decision-making process in homestead selection. Ukrainian immigrants were apparently prepared to rank social factors above environmental factors in their decision-making in settlement, and traded off economic prosperity against the opportunity for social and cultural satisfaction.

When Ukrainian settlers first entered into sub-marginal sandy and stony lands in the Stuartburn and Interlake districts, they were probably unaware that the lands were "left overs" and "totally unfit for grain growing or other types of farming."[42] Marunchak, a historian of the Ukrainians in Canada, attributes this to poor judgement of new conditions, compounded by lack of time for experimentation,[43] and these were certainly factors. Yet they do not explain why Ukrainians continued to homestead in notoriously poor areas, even after they were warned against doing so.[44] They may not have fully understood the limitations of the sites they chose, but to assume that most peasant farmers were totally naive in such matters strains the bounds of credulity.[45] Rather, the Ukrainians evaluated land according to criteria quite different from those employed by non-Slavic, market-oriented pioneers.[46] Above all, they were apparently prepared to overlook deficiencies in aspects of land quality if, by so doing, they could remain within, or in contact with, a chosen cultural and social environment. Indeed, they sometimes took as homesteads land abandoned as unfit for settlement by earlier Ukrainian settlers, as in the Sniatyn area of Alberta. The reasons given for abandonment, such as "mostly covered by water," "all sand and bush and not fit for farming," "too much water and too many stones," or "land flooded for past two years," reflected conditions usually evident to the most casual observer![47] It is difficult to believe that settlers who were obliged to wade waist-deep to their homesteads, as some did in the Interlake and Stuartburn districts, did not have doubts about the quality of the land in the area.[48] Yet Ukrainian immigrants persisted in going into such areas, despite the efforts of Crown Agents to persuade them otherwise. By 1900, government interpreter Cyril Genik was advising Ukrainian immigrants to go to Alberta where good land was still available, and to avoid Stuartburn and the Interlake.[49] His advice went unheeded by those with connections in these areas, and sub-marginal land continued to be homesteaded.

CONCLUSION

The *initial* decision of the first Ukrainian pioneers to locate within a specific area was influenced by such factors as a desire for timber, the quest for a wide resource base, a fear of the prairie, poor evaluation of land quality, lack of mobility, and ignorance of alternative areas open to homesteading. The *perpetuation* and *expansion* of settlement, in contrast, was largely dependent upon the willingness of subsequent Ukrainian settlers to rank social-cultural factors above economic or environmental ones. Such decisions were essentially individual, but uniformity of choice created a pattern of group behaviour in which the tide of settlement thrust many into sub-marginal areas. This argument does not imply that the Ukrainians were immobile either as individuals or as a group. Nor is it meant to suggest that this behavioural pattern in settlement was confined to the Ukrainians. An incident at Fish Creek, Saskatchewan, where Ukrainian immigrants defied the efforts of the Crown to dictate their point of settlement in the west, was a dramatic refutation of the former, and Richtik has argued that settlers from Ontario displayed a similar pattern of behaviour in their settlement of southwestern Manitoba.[50] Faced with the choice of locating on a less desirable site or settling away from their friends, Ontario settlers, like the Ukrainians, often chose the former. Less desirable *sites* were chosen because of their more desirable *locations*.

The crucial difference between the Ontario and Ukrainian settlers lay in the extent to which each group was prepared to pursue social advantages. Ontario settlers soon reached the point at which they were not prepared to accept a further decline in land quality. In moving away from their fellows to secure better land they demonstrated that their kinship ties were neither as strong nor as meaningful as those of the Ukrainians. A few Ukrainian settlers also moved away from the block settlements in attempts to secure better land, but usually after they had been in the country for some time. Often they were the children of early immigrants, and when relocating to new areas they frequently did so in groups. One such group moved from the Manitoba Interlake to Prelate, Saskatchewan;[51] another from Stuartburn moved to Rycroft in the Peace River district.[52]

There is scattered evidence to suggest that although the initial decisions in settlement were those of the man, much of the subsequent inertia was due to the reluctance of the woman to break her social ties. Confined to the farm and less exposed to assimilative pressures, the woman most needed the social ties transferred from the homeland. In the absence of the daily intercourse of village life the pioneer woman became more reliant on the presence of neighbours and friends. To move away, even for economic benefit, was intolerable.[53]

Social ties, it is clear, explain many of the paradoxes of Ukrainian settlement.[54] The initial occupation of much of the poorer sub-marginal land by Ukrainian settlers is explainable only in such terms, and their continued occupation is easily understood in the light of those ties of which Edmund Burke spoke in 1775: "Close affection . . . grows from common names, from similar privileges, and equal protection. These are ties which, though light as air, are as strong as links of iron."[55]

Notes

1. H. Schlichtmann, "Ethnic Themes in Geographical Research on Western Canada," *Canadian Ethnic Studies* 9, 2 (1977): 9–41.

2. D.R. Taft and R. Robbins, *International Migrations: The Immigrant in the Modern World* (New York: Ronald Press, 1955), 111.

3. J.M. Richtik, "Manitoba Settlement, 1870–1886" (Ph.D. diss., University of Minnesota, 1971), 558–62.

4. *Winnipeg Telegram,* 26 June 1889.

5. J.J. Mannion, *Irish Settlements in Eastern Canada: A Study of Transfer and Adaptation* (Toronto: University of Toronto Press, Department of Geography Research Publications, 1974), 13.

6. J.C. Lehr, "Mormon Settlement Morphology in Southern Alberta," *Albertan Geographer* 8 (1972): 11–12.

7. C.A. Price, "Immigration and Group Settlement," in *The Cultural Integration of Immigrants,* ed. W. D. Borrie (Paris: UNESCO, 1959), 273–74.

8. J. Bohland, "The Influence of Kinship Ties on the Settlement Pattern of Northeast Georgia," *Professional Geographer* 22 (1970): 267–69; A. Brunger, "A Spatial Analysis of Individual Settlement in Southern London District, Upper Canada, 1800–1836" (Ph.D. diss., University of Western Ontario, 1973), 104–7; and R.C. Ostergren, "Prairie Bound: Migration Patterns to a Swedish Settlement on the Dakota Frontier," *Ethnicity on the Great Plains,* ed. F.C. Luebke (Lincoln, NB: University of Nebraska Press, 1980), 54–72.

9. C.A. Dawson, *Group Settlement, Ethnic Communities in Western Canada,* Canadian Frontiers of Settlement Series 7 (Toronto: Macmillan, 1936), 278–79.

10. Richtik, "Manitoba Settlement," 558–62.

11. W. Darcovich, ed., *A Statistical Compendium of the Ukrainians in Canada 1891–1976* (Ottawa: University of Ottawa Press, 1980), 500–2.

12. See P.F. Sugar, "The Nature of the Non-Germanic Societies under Habsburg Rule," *Slavic Review* 22 (1963): 17; I.L. Rudnytsky, "The Ukrainians in Galicia under Austrian Rule," *Austrian History Yearbook* 3 (1967): 394–429; E.G. Balch, "Slav Emigration at its Source," *Charities and the Commons* 16 (1906); 171–83; J.P. Himka, "The Background to Emigration: Ukrainians of Galicia and Bukovyna, 1848–1914," in *A Heritage in Transition,* ed. M.R. Lupel (Toronto: McClelland and Stewart, 1982), 11–31; and A.M. Shepakov, *Ukrains' ka Trudova Emigratsiya v S.Sh.A. i Kanadi [Ukrainian Workers' Emigration to the U.S.A. and Canada]* (Kiev: Akademiya Nauk Ukrains'kaya, R.S.R., 1960), 13–45.

13. W.F. McCreary, Commissioner of Immigration, Winnipeg, to J.A. Smart, Deputy Minister of the Interior, Ottawa, 14 May 1897, RG76, vol. 144, file 34214, pt. 1, Public Archives of Canada (hereinafter PAC). This file contains an extensive correspondence between McCreary and Smart covering the period 1897–1900, in which may be found numerous references by McCreary to the Ukrainians' determination to stay together.

14. Ibid., 13 May 1897.

15. Ibid., 20 May 1898.

16. P. Yuzyk, *The Ukrainians in Manitoba: A Social History* (Toronto: University of Toronto Press, 1953), 42; V.J. Kaye, *Early Ukrainian Settlements in Canada 1895–1900* (Toronto: University of Toronto Press for the Ukrainian Canadian Research Foundation, 1964), 142; V.J. Kaye, *Canadians of Recent European Origin: Survey* (Ottawa: Department of National War Services, Citizenship Division, 1945), 46; J.G. MacGregor, *Vilni Zemli: Free Lands* (Toronto: McClelland and Stewart, 1969), 157; C.H. Young, *The Ukrainian Canadians* (Toronto: Thomas Nelson and Sons, 1931), 75; J. Stechishin, *Istoriya Poselen'nya Ukraintsiv u Kanadi [History of Ukrainian Settlement in Canada]* (Edmonton: Ukrainian Self-Reliance League, 1975) 242–47; M. Ewanchuk, *Istoriya Ukrains'koho Poselen'nya v Okolytsi Gimli [A History of the Ukrainian Settlements in the Gimli Area]* (Winnipeg: Trident Press, 1975), 24–28; and P. Zvarych [Svarych], "Do Pytan'nya Rozvytku y Postupu v Materiyal'niy Kul'turi Ukrains'kykh Poselentsiv u Kanadi" ["On the Problem of Development and Progress in the Material Culture of Ukrainian Settlers in Canada"], in *Zbirnyk na Poshanu Zenona Kuzeli* (Paris: Shevshenko Scientific Society, 1962), 151.

17. I. Goresky, "Early Ukrainian Settlement in Alberta" in *Ukrainians in Alberta,* Ukrainian Pioneers' Association (Edmonton: Ukrainian Pioneers' Association of Alberta, 1975), 17–38; J.M. Lazarenko "Rusiw Pioneers in Alberta," in *Ukrainians in Alberta,* 38–41; and A. Royick, "Ukrainian Settlements in Alberta," *Canadian Slavonic Papers* 10 (1968): 278–97.

18. Z.S. Pohorecky and A. Royick, "Anglicization of Ukrainian in Canada between 1895 and 1970; A Case Study in Crystallization," *Canadian Ethnic Studies* 1 (1970): 150.

19. Goresky, "Early Ukrainian" and "Minutes of the Founding of One of the First Ukrainian Greek Catholic Churches in Alberta, March 1900," *Canadian Ethnic Studies* 6 (1974): 67–69; also T.C. Byrne, "The Ukrainian Community in North Central Alberta" (M.A. thesis, University of Alberta, 1931), 31.

20. See E.G. Mardon, *Community Names of Alberta* (Lethbridge: University of Lethbridge, 1973); J.B. Rudnyc'kyj, *Manitoba Mosaic of Place Names* (Winnipeg: Canadian Institute of Onomastic Sciences, 1970); and J.B. Rudnyc'kyj, *Canadian Place Names of Ukrainian Origin* (Winnipeg: n.p., 1951). Rudnyc'kyj disputes Komarno as a transferred toponym; he claims that it is derived from the Ukrainian "komar," or mosquito, and means "full of mosquitoes."

21. A. Koestler, *The Ghost in the Machine* (London: Pan Books, 1970), 65.

22. For example, *The Russell Banner,* 22 Oct. 1903.

23. See, for example, the pioneer biographies in *Ukrainians in Alberta,* 263–556.

24. Declarations of Abandonment, N.W. 20, Township 55, Range 16 West, 4, and N.W. 20, Township 55, Range 15 West, 4, Homestead Files, Provincial Museum and Archives of Alberta.

25. Interview with John Gregorchuk, Arbakka, Manitoba, 8 Oct. 1975. See also interviews with George Alexiuk, Sundown, Manitoba, 15 July 1975; Mrs. M. Sportak, Vita, Manitoba, 3 July 1975; Mrs. Wasylyna Koshelanyk, Caliento, Manitoba, 3 July 1975; N. Chornopysky, Vita, Manitoba, 8 Oct. 1975; George Penteliuk, Arbakka, Manitoba, 10 Oct. 1975; Andrew Lamash, St. Michael, Alberta, 15 June 1972; Andrew Basisty, Andrew, Alberta, 6 June 1972; and Mrs. W. Melynyk, Delph, Alberta, 30 May 1972. Immigrants from the same village gravitated together even in the emerging ethnic enclaves in western Canadian cities: see M. Vinohradova, "Recollections of a Pioneer Woman," *The Ukrainian-Canadian* (March 1972): 22–24.

26. Interview with Todor Kutzak, Sirko, Manitoba, 10 Oct. 1975.

27. Project SUCH (Save Ukrainian Canadians' Heritage), under the Opportunities for Youth Programme, was undertaken during the summer of 1971. It aimed at interviewing Ukrainian settlers, or their immediate families, to compile a collection of oral history and folklore. The data collected, comprising 251 General Information Questionnaires, 58 Detailed Informant Sheets, and some 200 hours of tape-recorded interviews, are now held in the Ukrainian Arts and Crafts Museum, 1240 Temperance St., Saskatoon.

28. V.J. Kaye, *Dictionary of Ukrainian Canadian Pioneer Biography: Pioneer Settlement in Manitoba* (Toronto: Ukrainian Canadian Research Foundation, 1975), 165–66.

29. In the case of the settlers from Lukivci, the Badiuk family was linked by marriage to the Kossowan family, and at least one of the four families that appeared to be unrelated to any others in the area was, in fact, related to the Kossowans by marriage. In one account of Ukrainian settlement in the Interlake district, it is indicated that

a good many village groups were bound together by marital ties (M. Ewanchuk, *Spruce, Swamp and Stone: A History of the Pioneer Ukrainian Settlements in the Gimli Area* (Winnipeg: Published by the author, 1977), 19–23.

30. The Ukrainian settlement at Star was established by immigrants from the Kalush district of Halychyna. The first Bukovynan settlers did not arrive in Canada until 1896.

31. Data abstracted from the Homestead General Registers and Records of Homestead Entry, Provincial Museum and Archives of Alberta. Supplementary data were derived from *Ukrainians in Alberta*, 263–556, and from field research in east-central Alberta.

32. T. McNutt, "Galicians and Bukowinians" in *The Story of Saskatchewan and Its People*, ed. J. Hawkes (Chicago-Regina: S.J. Clarke, 1924), 731–32.

33. A good indication of the intensity of feeling that accompanied religious affiliation in the pioneer environment is given by MacGregor, *Vilni Zemli*, 164–82, in his discussion of the religious conflicts between Orthodox and Uniate pioneers in Alberta.

34. On differences in the material culture of the two groups, see J.C. Lehr, "Ukrainian Houses in Alberta," *Alberta Historical Review* 21, 4 (1973): 9–15.

35. Interviews within the Ukrainian community of east–central Alberta, 1971–75. See J.C. Lehr, "The Process and Pattern of Ukrainian Rural Settlement in Western Canada, 1891–1914" (Ph.D. diss., University of Manitoba, 1978) 318–19.

36. McCreary to Smart, 15 May 1897, RG76, vol. 144, file 34214, PAC.

37. C.W. Speers to McCreary, 9 July 1897, RG76, vol. 144, file 34214, PAC.

38. Handwritten diary of Anton Keyz.

39. Interview with Stephan Storeschuk, Gardenton, Manitoba, 21 July 1975.

40. Price, "Immigration," 270.

41. J. Oleskow, *O Emigratsii* [*On Emigration*] (L'viv: Michael Kachkowskyi Society, 1895), 39. The first Ukrainians to settle in western Canada chose to locate in east-central Alberta, to be close to a small group of *Völksdeutsche* (ethnic Germans) from the western Ukraine. The *Völksdeutsche* were conversant with Ukrainian, and the newcomers had close relations with them in their early years. The proximity of *Völksdeutsche* was also a major determinant in the selection of lands by the first Ukrainians to settle in the Stuartburn district, at Grenfell, and at other points in the west. In addition, Poles, Romanians, and, on occasion, on an individual basis, Jews were closely associated with Ukrainian settlement. Poles, usually from western Halychyna, settled alongside Ukrainians from that province in the Skaro area of Alberta and at Cook's Creek in Manitoba. Romanians from Bukovyna settled at Marea Boian, Alberta, replicating a previously close geographical relationship between Romanian and Ukrainian villages in Bukovyna. Similarities of religion, a common understanding of languages, and a shared peasant *Weltanschaaung* explain these associations. Ukrainians from Halychyna probably had comprehension, even fluency, in Polish, and were of the Greek Catholic (Uniate) church; some were

even of the Roman Catholic church. The Romanians shared with the Bukovynans a common adherence to Orthodoxy, mutual comprehension of language, and certain folkways and attitudes.

42. M.H. Marunchak, *The Ukrainian Canadians: A History* (Winnipeg: Ukrainian Free Academy of Sciences, 1970), 86.

43. Ibid., 43.

44. A.B. Woywitka, "Homesteader's Woman," *Alberta History* 24 (1976): 20; and M. Ewanchuk, *Pioneer Profiles: Ukrainian Settlers in Manitoba* (Winnipeg: Published by the author, 1981), 128–29.

45. Most Ukrainian immigrants were from an agricultural background. Few of the emerging Ukrainian industrial proletariat were involved in agricultural settlement in Canada. Although some of the better educated, non-farm elements of Ukrainian society migrated to Canada before 1914, few did so before 1905, and they seldom went on to the land. In 1901, it was estimated that only 2 percent of Ukrainian settlers in the Dauphin region were literate. This may be an unduly low estimate, but an examination of signatures on applications for homestead entry in Alberta between 1892 and 1914 suggested that less than 20 percent of all Ukrainian applicants were literate. On literacy rates, see *Winnipeg Telegram,* 2 Jan. 1901; and Canada, *Sessional Papers,* 1897, "Department of the Interior," 120.

46. J.C. Lehr, "The Rural Settlement Behaviour of Ukrainian Pioneers in Western Canada, 1891–1914" in *Western Canadian Research in Geography: The Lethbridge Papers,* ed. B. M. Barr, B.C. Geographical Series 21 (Vancouver: Tantalus Research Ltd., 1975), 51–66; and interview with Stefan Yendik, Frazerwood, Manitoba, 12 Nov. 1974.

47. Declarations of Abandonment, Records of Homestead Entry, S.E. 18, Township 57, Range 18 West, 4; N.E. 10, Township 59, Range 17 West, 4; S.E. 22, Township 59, Range 17 West, 4; and N.W. 30, Township 57, Range 16 West, 4, Homestead Files, Provincial Museum and Archives of Alberta.

48. Ewanchuk, *Pioneer Profiles,* 128.

49. Ibid., 66; Woywitka, "Homesteader's Woman," 20; and Wasyl Mihaychuk, "Mihaychuk Family Tree" (unpublished typescript, n.d.), 2 pp.

50. Richtik, "Manitoba Settlement," 558–62. For details of the confrontation between officials of the Department of the Interior and Ukrainian immigrants at Fish Creek, Saskatchewan, see Kaye, *Early Ukrainian Settlements,* 300–8; and John C. Lehr, "Government Coercion in the Settlement of Ukrainian Immigrants in Western Canada," *Prairie Forum* 8 (1983): 179–94.

51. *Ukrainians in Alberta,* 357.

52. Woywitka, "Homesteader's Woman," 21–22; and *Ukrainians in Alberta,* 286–87.

53. E. Shlanka, "Krydor Community No 13, Interviews of Pioneers" (April 1944, typewritten ms), 5; J.S. Woodsworth "Ukrainians in Rural Communities: Report of

Investigation by the Bureau of Social Research, Governments of Manitoba, Saskatchewan and Alberta" (Winnipeg, 25 Jan. 1917, typewritten ms), 130; and Ewanchuk, *Spruce, Swamp and Stone,* 22–23.

54. Merrill explains the density of Ukrainian settlement in the Riding Mountain area of Manitoba as a reflection of the immigrants' desire to maintain close family ties; see L. Merrill, "Population Distribution in the Riding Mountains and Adjacent Plains of Manitoba and Saskatchewan, 1870–1946" (M.A. thesis, McGill University, 1953), 64–91; also MacGregor, *Vilni Zemli,* 184–85.

55. Edmund Burke, Second Speech on Conciliation with America, 22 Mar. 1775, House of Commons.

CHAPTER

9 THE GREAT DEPRESSION AND UNEMPLOYMENT POLICIES

The "Great Depression" of the 1930s almost haunts Canada. Fear of a similar catastrophe and comparisons with current difficulties pervaded both academic and non-academic literature as well as political programmes for fifty years afterwards. The economists dominated the early studies on the 1930s, followed closely by political apologists for one or the other of the Bennett Conservatives or the King Liberals. Some of the best studies concentrated on the third parties, especially the Cooperative Commonwealth Federation, the *Union Nationale* and Social Credit, and their impact on political culture. There was also a significant body of Marxist literature, which stressed the failures of the system, but which also emphasized the conditions of the destitute, primarily the single males. While all of these works made token reference to the pain and suffering during the 1930s, especially in the West, most were concerned with political, ideological or developmental agendas of one sort or another. To the economists, for example, the depression provided the justification for their Keynesian and post-Keynesian models.

By the 1970s a more dispassionate examination of the 1930s began to take place, although the political aspects continued to dominate. In the first selection, "Canadian Unemployment Policy in the 1930s," James Struthers offers a revisionist view of the convoluted positions taken by federal leaders, though his content remains traditional and his essential concern is with politics. His final comment demonstrates his cynicism about the leadership: "By 1945, then, Canadians were finally ready to fight the Great Depression of the 1930s."

The depression they planned to avoid was the one with long lines of destitute men at soup kitchens, with crowds of men in relief camps or riding the rails, and with threatening masses of men on picket lines. Rarely did images of women enter the picture, yet women were perhaps even greater victims in the 1930s than men. It was women who were left behind to make do when the men hit the rails. It was women who had to raise the children, often without any assistance. It was women who had to serve potatoes three times a day, if they had them, and it was women who had to lay the dead when the men were away. While the plight of women has been graphically recorded in books like *The Wretched of Canada* (1972), edited by L.M. Grayson and Michael Bliss, and Barry Broadfoot's *Ten Lost Years, 1929–1939: Memories of Canadians Who Survived the Depression* (1973), some suspect a conspiracy of silence over their condition in that decade. After all, there were hundreds of thousands of unemployed women, and where are their pictures? They are the subject of Ruth Roach Pierson's "Gender and the Unemployment Insurance Debates in Canada, 1934–1940." If Pierson is correct it was not an oversight that women were excluded both from images of the Depression and the beneficence of the government. "Masculine independence and feminine dependence" were consciously legislated by a patriarchal system that discriminated on the basis of gender.

Suggestions for Further Reading

Bird Patricia, "Hamilton Working Women in the Period of the Great Depression," *Atlantis*, VIII, no. 2 (Spring 1983), 125–136.

Broadfoot, Barry, *Ten Lost Years, 1929–1939: Memories of Canadians Who Survived the Depression*. Toronto: Doubleday, 1973.

Coulter, Rebecca, "Young Women and Unemployment in the 1930s: The Home Service Solution," *Canadian Women Studies*, VII, no. 4 (Winter 1986), 77–80.

Dumas, Evelyn, *The Bitter Thirties in Quebec*, trans. Arnold Bennett. Montreal: Black Rose Books, 1975.

Grayson, L.M., and Michael Bliss, eds., *The Wretched of Canada: Letters to R.B. Bennett, 1930–1935*. Toronto: University of Toronto Press, 1972.

Horn, Michiel, ed., *The Dirty Thirties: Canadians in the Great Depression*. Toronto: Copp Clark, 1972.

Struthers, James, *No Fault of Their Own: Unemployment and the Canadian Welfare State, 1914–1941*. Toronto: University of Toronto Press, 1983.

CANADIAN UNEMPLOYMENT POLICY IN THE 1930s

James Struthers

I

One of the problems of discussing unemployment during the Great Depression is the danger of becoming overcome by a sense of déja vu. Today unemployment officially stands at over 12% of the workforce; perhaps as many as 2,000,000 Canadians are without work and according to the Economic Council of Canada the jobless total is unlikely to drop below 10% until 1987. Yet despite these appalling figures, our government, as in the 1930s, tells us it cannot act to create jobs because its first priority must be to reduce the deficit in order to restore business confidence.

Although the arguments behind today's economic policies are certainly different from those of the 1930s, many of the essential moral homilies remain unchanged. Canadians in the 1980s, like their parents and grandparents of the 1930s, are being told they can't expect to hope for recovery without practising severe restraint, self-discipline, hard work, and much tightening of belts. Despite these frightening parallels, however, we haven't yet been surrounded by soup kitchens, relief camps, food vouchers, bankrupt provincial governments, and trainloads of hungry single men 'riding the rods' in search of work or relief. Yet all these sights and problems were characteristic of the failure of governments to respond to unemployment during the 1930s. Why this was so I'll attempt to explain in this paper.

To a large extent the unemployment policies pursued by R.B. Bennett and Mackenzie King in the 1930s were continuations of approaches and attitudes towards joblessness that had been widespread in Canada before 1930. Canadians had become well acquainted with cyclical unemployment—or trade depressions as they were then called—well before the 'dirty thirties.' The 1870s, the early 1890s, and the years 1907–08, 1913–15, and 1920–25, were all periods of heavy unemployment in this country. From this perspective it's best to think of the Great Depression as simply the most intense and long-lasting of a series of "waves" of unemployment which battered all western industrial economies during the last half of the 19th and first third of the 20th centuries.

Because of our climate we were also quite familiar with seasonal unemployment. Canada is infamous for being an 'eight months country.' Each winter tens of thousands of Canadians working in the country's great outdoors industries—construction, agriculture, forestry, fishing, and transportation—

From *Windy Pine Occasional Paper No. 2* (Peterborough: Canadian Studies Programme, Trent University, 1984). Reprinted by permission of Trent University.

routinely lost their jobs, often for up to six months of the year due to bad weather. Even in the boom years of the so-called 'roaring twenties' (1926–29), winter unemployment rates averaged well over 10% of the workforce. So the sight of hungry, jobless men walking the streets in search of work or relief was quite familiar to most urban-dwellers in Canada.

Why, then, did the Great Depression take us so much by surprise? Why, for example, didn't Canada follow Great Britain's lead in 1911 by devising new institutions and policies, such as a national system of unemployment insurance and a state employment service, to cope with the problem of joblessness? There were a number of reasons for our unpreparedness but three were particularly important. In the first place, seasonal unemployment was predictable. Winter was a fact of Canadian life; therefore, newspapers, politicians, businessmen, and others argued that workingmen should save up enough money during the summer to tide themselves and their families over the winter. Moreover, it was simply assumed (without any evidence) that wages for seasonal labour were high enough to allow them to do so. To provide the seasonally unemployed with relief, it was argued, would discourage habits of thrift, frugality, and self-reliance.

As for cyclical unemployment, attitudes towards this problem were shaped by two factors. First, recovery in the past had always occurred eventually. The market did correct itself. Therefore, all a country could do was to 'tough it out' by practising restraint and doing nothing to discourage business confidence, especially on the part of foreign investors. Secondly, Canada was a New World society with a developing farm frontier. It was also a country which, in the three decades before 1930, had become increasingly preoccupied with rural depopulation. And it was a country in which farmers were still politically powerful and were continually complaining about the shortage of farm help at affordable wages. For these reasons, legislation such as unemployment insurance, which might be appropriate in more crowded, congested, and highly urbanized societies such as Great Britain, was deemed by business and farm leaders to be inappropriate for Canada. There was always work for the unemployed, even if only for room and board and little more, they argued, on the nation's farms during the winter. If life in the city was made too easy through doles and unemployment insurance for the idle, might not even more men and women be encouraged to leave the land altogether?

Finally, working-class political pressure, in the form of strong trade unions and labour parties, was extremely weak in Canada before World War II. Farmers and businessmen, on the other hand, were politically powerful. Hence governments responded to their views on the unemployment question and not to the views of those who were most likely to become unemployed.

As a result of these attitudes, Canadian governments, although well acquainted with unemployment before 1930, were hopelessly ill-equipped for dealing with it. No one kept unemployment statistics; there was no efficient state employment service; no public welfare departments existed at the federal or provincial level and there were only four at the municipal level. In all of Canada before 1930 there were less than 400 trained social workers. Relief, where available, was granted by private religious charities or by 19th century poor law "Houses of Industry," both of which operated at the local level. In Toronto as late as 1932, jobless men still had to line up at the local House of Industry, first built in the 1830s, to get a bag of groceries or a basket of coal and were expected to saw wood or break rocks in exchange for this miserly relief. Moreover, with the brief exception of the years 1920–21, when the threat of unemployed World War I veterans loomed large throughout Canada, provincial governments along with Ottawa denied any responsibility for coming to the aid of the jobless. Public relief where given was an exclusively local matter financed solely out of local taxes, chiefly on property. One of the sad ironies of the "dirty thirties" was that although no other country, except perhaps the United States, was more economically devastated by the Great Depression than Canada, no other country was as ill-prepared for dealing with its consequences. On the eve of 1930 we lacked even the bare bones of a permanent welfare structure for relieving those in need.

II

The origins of Canadian unemployment policy in the Depression lie within the 1930 federal election. On the one hand Mackenzie King went into the election—at a time when unemployment was about 12%—denying that there was a jobless problem and bragging that he would not give a 'five cent piece' to any Tory provincial government for unemployment relief. King also claimed that the whole idea of an unemployment crisis was simply a Conservative pre-election plot.

Bennett, on the other hand, made what from our perspective today seem like recklessly extravagant promises. He claimed he would 'end unemployment,' 'abolish the dole,' and provide 'work and wages for all who wanted it.' Not surprisingly, Bennett won the election, largely on the strength of his promises to do something about the unemployment crisis.

Despite the boldness of his rhetoric, however, (which reflected his egotism, arrogance, and over-confidence in his own abilities) Bennett really had very traditional ideas about how to deal with unemployment. Like King, he believed the problem in 1930 was largely a seasonal and temporary phenomenon which would quickly right itself. Unlike King, Bennett as a good Tory, also believed that sharply boosting the protective tariff would stimulate investor confidence, create jobs by reducing reliance upon imports, and ultimately force other nations to lower their trading barriers against Canadian exports. It was through these tariff hikes that Bennett hoped to 'end unemployment.'

But these hikes would take time to produce results. Since Bennett had promised to provide jobs immediately, he also introduced a $20,000,000 emergency relief act in the summer of 1930 to tide people over with what was expected to be a difficult winter. $16,000,000 was to be spent on public works and, most significantly, the projects were to be administered by local and provincial governments who together were expected to contribute 75% of their cost. Unemployment relief, Bennett insisted like King before him, was primarily a local responsibility. Ottawa's help was on a temporary, emergency basis only, and would last only until the effects of his tariff hike were felt.

Through providing money for relief projects such as provincial road-building Bennett also hoped to deal with another pressing problem. Transient, unemployed single men, largely immigrants, were trapped in Canadian cities because the lumber, construction, and agricultural industries which normally drew them out of cities were closed down. Such men, cut off from family ties, coming from different cultural backgrounds, and with nothing to lose, were considered to be a serious menace to law and order. Bennett's relief projects would draw them out of the cities and put money into their pockets for the winter months ahead.

Between the fall of 1930, when he first took office, and the spring of 1932, Bennett adhered to this policy of using public works or relief works as they were called, to fight unemployment. Indeed, throughout the fiscal year 1931–32 his government spent almost $50,000,000 or more than twice as much as it had the previous year on this approach. Nevertheless, by the spring of 1932 unemployment stood above 20% of the workforce and the federal deficit was over $151,000,000, almost half of total government revenue for that year. As a result, Bennett quickly became disillusioned with public works as a means of relieving unemployment.

In the first place, he had used this approach only as a temporary stop-gap expedient. Neither he nor anyone in his government were believers in Keynesian deficit-spending as a way out of depression; therefore there was no expectation that public employment could be used in itself as a recovery strategy. Moreover, by 1932 it had become obvious that the Depression was more than a 'temporary' problem. Secondly, by 1932, local and provincial governments, especially in the west, could no longer afford to pay their 75% share of the cost of these increasingly expensive relief works and Bennett had no intention of assuming a larger share of the cost. Finally, Bennett and Canadian businessmen were increasingly alarmed at the size of the federal deficit and the level of taxation which in themselves appeared to be a threat to investor confidence, and hence a barrier to recovery.

For all these reasons, then, Bennett reversed his unemployment policy in the spring of 1932 virtually abandoning reliance on public works and instead depended almost solely upon direct relief or the provision of a 'dole' to tide the unemployed over the worst of the Depression until recovery began. His chief unemployment policy, now that tariffs and public works had failed, was to attempt to eliminate the deficit and to balance the federal budget. This meant keeping expenditure on the jobless down to the lowest level consistent with their physical survival. At the same time, Bennett also refused to modify his policy that unemployment relief was primarily a provincial and local responsibility. His government would pay only one-third the cost of direct relief in any town or city and would contribute nothing to the costs of its administration.

III

Once Bennett opted for a policy of direct relief as his sole remaining means of dealing with unemployment, he entered into a nightmare of contradictions, ironies, and paradoxes which he had never anticipated and which would ultimately destroy his administration. Five such anomalies were of particular importance. The first was the paradox of residency requirements for relief. Since local governments, under Bennett's policy, had to assume anywhere from one-third to one-half the cost of relief on a rapidly diminishing and highly regressive property tax base, they attempted to limit their own relief costs in the only way possible, namely by restricting eligibility for relief to their own municipal residents. Only those who could prove anywhere from six months to, in some cases, three years continuous residence in a city before applying for the dole were deemed eligible to receive it. In a country like Canada with a geographically diverse and highly mobile labour market, many of the unemployed who had been on the road looking for work could not qualify for relief when they needed it. To get the dole they had to return to their home town which they had left in the first place because there was no work. Bennett's policy, then, discouraged the unemployed from looking for work outside their town or city for fear of becoming ineligible for relief.

Transients also posed a contradiction. Tens of thousands of Canada's unemployed were immigrant, seasonal workers—bunkhouse men—who by the very nature of their work on the frontier could not qualify for relief in any city. Bennett's earlier public works policy had, in part, been intended once again to get them out of urban areas. Now, without public works, they had no choice but to drift back into Canadian cites where they could find neither relief nor work. As a result, transient single men 'riding the rods' from town to town were quickly recognized as a serious menace to law and order. Since the cities refused to assume responsibility for them, and since Bennett refused to assume responsibility for relief, he decided upon another alternative suggested to him by General Andrew McNaughton of the Canadian army—relief camps, run by the Defense Department. Here the men could be kept out of the cities, provided with room, board, and clothing and put to work on useful projects to preserve their morale. There was only one hitch. Since Bennett had already abandoned public works as a relief policy, the men couldn't be paid a wage, not without arousing serious unrest from married unemployed men on direct relief. Instead they were paid a 20¢ daily 'allowance' in return for their labour in the camps.

Why would single men go into such camps for 20¢ a day? Cut off from direct relief in the cities, they had no choice except starvation, which is why the 20,000 men in the camps after 1933 quickly referred to them as 'slave camps' and ultimately organized the relief camp strike and 'On to Ottawa Trek' of 1935, which ended in a bloody two-hour riot with the RCMP in Regina. As one camp inhabitant cynically put it in 1933, 'You come in broke, work all winter and still you are broke. It looks like they want to keep us bums all our lives.'

Relief standards posed a third source of contention. By insisting on primary local and provincial responsibility for the financing of relief, and by assuming no share in the cost of administering relief, Bennett's government ensured that relief scales—that is, how much money or its equivalent in food vouchers a family would receive—varied dramatically from city to city, depending upon the health of local economies and the political complexion of local city councils. A survey by the Canadian Welfare Council of relief standards in 50 Canadian cities during September 1936 showed just how far such scales of aid could differ. In London, Ontario, a family of five could receive no more than $40.39 a month for food, fuel, and shelter costs. That same family in Toronto could get $58.87; in Hamilton $34.40; in Ottawa $45.32; in Quebec City $26.66; in Calgary $60.00; and in Halifax a mere $18.86. Such gross variations in support within cities of comparable living costs was, of course, morally indefensible. Within Ontario, the Canadian Association of Social Workers discovered, in a survey of 107 municipalities, that not one provided the food allowance recommended by the Ontario Medical Association as the minimum necessary to maintain nutritional health. Food allowances in Toronto alone were 40% below the minimum standard which the League of Nations defined as necessary to maintain health. Since Bennett had promised, when elected in 1930, to 'abolish the dole,' such gross variations and substandard levels of support in a policy of direct relief which his administration had initiated, was political catastrophe.

The bankruptcy of first local and then provincial governments was the fourth disastrous consequence of Bennett's relief policy. By insisting that local and provincial governments were to be held primarily responsible for the cost of relief, Bennett's unemployment policy concentrated the fiscal cost of the Depression where its impact was greatest—that is, in western Canada. By 1932, all four western provinces were technically bankrupt because of the cost of paying their two-thirds share of direct relief and were only kept solvent by continual federal loans and grants. By 1937 Ottawa would be paying 85% of all relief costs in Saskatchewan; 71% in Alberta; 69% in British Columbia; and 68% in Manitoba; while still insisting that relief was a local responsibility. In Ontario and Quebec, in contrast, Ottawa paid only 29% and 32% respectively of relief costs.

To give an equally paradoxical example of the contradictions of this policy, in Forest Hill, a very wealthy area of Toronto with few unemployed, per capita relief costs to taxpayers averaged only $4.00 a month in 1934. In East York, a working-class borough only a few miles away, with almost 50% of its population on relief, the cost of the dole averaged $25.00 a month per taxpayer. Yet the people of Forest Hill, in many cases, were the employers of those living in East York. By drawing municipal boundary lines around themselves, they could enjoy the lowest relief taxes in Canada and shove the burden of the Depression onto their unfortunate employees.

The final irony of direct relief was the fact that you had to be totally destitute to receive it. Insurance policies, bank savings, home equity, automobiles, everything of value had to be liquidated in many municipalities before a family could become eligible for the dole. Hence, what was the point of saving for a rainy day if you knew beforehand that all your assets would be confiscated before you could become eligible for aid? Far better to spend your money while you had it, since if you lost your job you would soon be just as badly off as the man down the road who had saved nothing.

IV

Because of contradictions such as these, by 1933–34 Bennett was desperately looking for alternatives to his relief policy. There were two directions he could go. The first, urged increasingly by the provinces, the municipalities, organized labour, some social workers, and the unemployed, was to take over total responsibility for unemployment relief instead of continuing to contribute on a one-third basis. Had Bennett followed this option, residency requirements for relief could have been abolished; the provinces, particularly in the west, and the municipalities would once again have been fiscally solvent; and most importantly the levels of assistance for families on the dole across Canada could have been raised to a national minimum standard sufficient to ensure that everyone received at least enough food, shelter, and clothing to remain healthy and to enjoy reasonably decent living standards.

Bennett had absolutely no interest in taking this route, however. In the first place, it would have cost far more to the federal government, already concerned primarily in reducing, not increasing, its deficit. Secondly, it would have necessitated the creation of a permanent federal welfare bureaucracy at a time when Bennett was still convinced that the unemployment crisis was temporary. Finally, and most importantly, Bennett and his advisors believed that a national minimum standard of relief would increase the numbers of those unemployed. Why? Because wage rates for those already working in Canada, particularly unskilled labourers, had been so lowered by the Depression (clothing workers in Montreal and Toronto, for example, often made only $10.00 for a 60 hour work week) that for a large segment of Canada's working-class a dole which provided healthy and decent living standards would be preferable to work.

This was certainly the conclusion of Charlotte Whitton, Canada's most well-known social worker, an arch social conservative, and Bennett's key advisor on relief policy in the 1930s. In a 1932 report to the government on relief in western Canada, Whitton told Bennett that 40% of those living off the dole on the prairies didn't really need it; that the very existence of direct relief in the west was drawing tens of thousands of farm families into the western cities during the winter, thus artificially boosting the unemployment rate; and that by contributing to local and provincial relief efforts, Bennett's government had only succeeded in making thousands of immigrant and poor rural families "permanently dependent at a scale of living which they never had and never will be able to provide for themselves."

With this kind of advice coming from the chief executive of the Canadian Welfare Council it was small wonder that Bennett himself concluded in 1934 that the people had become "more or less relief-conscious and were determined to get out of the Government, whether it be municipal, provincial, or federal, all they could." Instead of opting to take over total responsibility for unemployment relief, Bennett decided over the winter of 1934 to move in exactly the opposite direction: to sever all of Ottawa's ties with the dole and turn the whole ugly, embarrassing business completely back to the provinces and municipalities.

From this perspective, unemployment insurance, which the British had pioneered in 1911, began to appear more and more attractive as a policy alternative for the Bennett government. In the first place, at a time when unemployment still hovered at 20% of the workforce, Bennett simply could not withdraw from direct relief and abdicate all responsibility for the jobless. He had to have some political alternative to put in its place. Unemployment insurance fit the bill nicely for a number of reasons. Businessmen, particularly bankers and insurance company and real estate executives, favoured such a measure by 1934. These financial organizations now held many worthless municipal and provincial bonds and had become convinced that direct municipal relief was a highly inefficient way to finance the costs of unemployment. Far better, such businessmen argued, to build up an unemployment fund in good times through insurance premiums which could be used to aid the jobless during depressions. Better yet, unemployment insurance seemed to reinforce thrift. Since the premiums were compulsory, it forced workers to defer part of their incomes for a rainy day. Thus, unlike the dole, it didn't reduce everyone to complete and utter destitution before they could become eligible for aid. Moreover, because 80% of the cost of unemployment insurance could be financed by compulsory premiums paid by workers and employers, it would cost the federal government only a fraction of what was presently being spent on relief. As a result, unlike the dole, unemployment insurance would not interfere as directly with the widely shared desire among businessmen to see a balanced federal budget.

Finally, precisely because it was called unemployment "insurance," actuarial science, not nutritional standards of human need, could provide an arbitrary ceiling on benefits which in any case would always be kept to a fixed percentage of existing wage rates. In this way unemployment insurance seemed to pose no threat to the market-determined distribution of income. Under the legislation Bennett eventually introduced in the early months of 1935, Canadians had to work a minimum of forty weeks over two years to be eligible for any benefits whatsoever, which in any case were set at a maximum of $11.40 a week for a family of five, almost 40% below the $17.30 a week which the Montreal Council of Social Agencies recommended as the minimum amount necessary to maintain health.

Under Bennett's unemployment insurance act, then, only those workers who were most regularly employed could qualify for benefits and the levels were set low enough to ensure that in no case would life on unemployment insurance be preferable to any form of work offered by Canadian employers anywhere in the country. In other words, unemployment insurance, as drafted by Bennett's advisors, was designed to reinforce the work ethic and to provide a perfect political cover for a federal withdrawal from relief. It was not designed to reduce poverty or to provide unemployed Canadians with a level of support adequate to maintain health and decency.

Most importantly, unemployment insurance offered nothing to the 1.2 million Canadians who were already on relief in 1935. Since their family breadwinners were obviously not working, they could not pay any premiums or qualify for benefits. It was a good idea for future depressions, but unemployment insurance really provided no solution to the problems of the 1930s.

Nevertheless, Bennett proceeded with his strategy. In June 1934, he told the premiers that all federal support for relief would be cut off on August 1st. After tremendous political pressure, he subsequently modified this policy to a 22% federal cut-back in relief spending. Then, in September, Bennett asked the provinces whether they would be willing to surrender their exclusive jurisdiction over unemployment insurance to Ottawa. Outraged by his high-handed pressure tactics and unilateral cut-backs, the premiers understandably refused. As a result, faced with an election and almost certain defeat in 1935, Bennett simply introduced his unemployment insurance bill in Parliament as part of his package of New Deal reforms, knowing full well that without provincial agreement the bill was probably unconstitutional and hence useless, as indeed it turned out to be.

After five years in office, Bennett went down to spectacular defeat in the 1935 election, his party losing all but 39 seats. He also left a very meagre legacy for his successor, the Liberal leader Mackenzie King. The attempt to provide work for the jobless had been abandoned after 1932; relief standards across Canada were grossly inadequate everywhere; four provincial governments were technically bankrupt; single unemployed men in the relief camps had walked out and rioted in their attempt to reach Ottawa; and unemployment insurance, the only creative piece of legislation on the jobless crisis to emerge from Bennett's administration, was clearly unconstitutional.

V

In what ways, if any, did Mackenzie King pursue different policies for the remainder of the Depression? Unlike Bennett in 1930, King made no promises in the 1935 election beyond pledging to provide sober, orderly government. As a result, he had no political I.O.U.'s to redeem. In fact, the most striking aspect of King's unemployment policy is that from December 1935 until the spring of 1938 it was virtually a carbon copy of Bennett's. In the first place, he continued to insist that the jobless were primarily a local and provincial responsibility. Secondly, after a quick hike in federal relief contributions immediately after the election, King began systematically to cut back on Ottawa's support of the dole to such an extent that by 1937, in cities such as Winnipeg, Ottawa was paying only 20% of relief costs and on a national basis, only 30%, compared to the one-third share Bennett had paid throughout most years of his administration. Like the Tory prime minister, King's first priority was to balance the budget.

King's administration also refused to define any national minimum standard of relief, based on medical or nutritional standards. Instead, his government defined a national *maximum*. In October 1937 King's minister of labour, Norman Rogers, announced that Ottawa would in no province pay more than 30% of the dole's cost, and in every city the standard of living on relief had to be kept below the average going rate for unskilled labour in the surrounding area, in order that "work incentives" could be enforced. This policy was adopted at a time when most provinces had no minimum wage for men.

Although King did abolish Bennett's hated relief camps for single men in 1936, the alternative he put in their place was, in many ways, much worse. This was a farm placement scheme which paid about 45,000 of Canada's single unemployed $5.00 a month to work on farms across the country. This was less than the infamous 20¢ daily "allowance" the men had received in the camps, and there was no guarantee that food, clothing, shelter, and medical care provided by individual impoverished farmers across Canada would be comparable to what the army had offered in the relief camps. As one army commander pointed out when the camps were shut down in 1936 and many men refused to leave, "the men prefer to stay where they have 'regular hours' and good food, rather than leave for farms, where they have to work harder, longer hours, and for lower wages, with a possibility that they may not collect their wages in the fall." Although cynical in its conception, King's farm placement scheme nonetheless did solve the problem of chronic unrest among transients. Spread out individually across Canada rather than concentrated in the camps, single men proved almost impossible to organize politically after 1936.

King's overall unemployment strategy duplicated Bennett's in two other ways. As Bennett had done after 1932, until the severe recession of 1938, King rejected public works as an antidote to unemployment, in marked contrast to the massive works schemes pioneered by Franklin Roosevelt's New Deal south of the border. Instead, King relied totally on direct relief as a means of caring for the jobless. King also refused to enact an unemployment insurance plan, claiming that the political opposition to the measure by New Brunswick, Quebec, and Alberta made impossible the unanimous consent which he claimed was necessary for a constitutional amendment.

In only two areas did King take actions significantly different from Bennett's. In April 1936 he appointed a National Employment Commission, chaired by Montreal industrialist Arthur Purvis, to investigate the unemployment and relief situation and to come up with recommendations for reform. Secondly, in August 1937, he appointed a Royal Commission on Dominion-Provincial Relations, chaired by Supreme Court justice Newton Rowell, to investigate and attempt to straighten out the tangled web of federal-provincial financial relations, particularly the continuing inability of the western provinces to stay fiscally solvent without federal loans and grants.

The most significant result of both these commissions is that they ended up saying the same thing. The NEC, which reported in January 1938, and the Rowell-Sirois Commission, as it came to be called, which reported in May 1940, both argued that the first step in combatting unemployment and restoring fiscal solvency to the provinces and local governments was for Ottawa to put in place immediately a national employment service and system of unemployment insurance, and to assume total financial and administrative responsibility for unemployment relief. In short, both commissions argued that Ottawa should take the route both Bennett and King had rejected throughout the entire depression, namely to accept primary responsibility for unemployment. The jobless crisis, both commissions argued, was a *national* problem, reflecting Canada's national economy; consequently, relief to those without work should be first and foremost a national responsibility. Only Ottawa through its unlimited taxing power, they argued further, possessed the fiscal strength to pay for these relief costs. Finally, reflecting the new Keynesian sophistication being developed within the department of finance, both commissions concluded that only Ottawa could inject enough purchasing power into the economy through insurance and relief payments and public works to push levels of demand up high enough to stimulate economic growth and thus ultimately to eliminate unemployment.

It would be pleasant to report that after receiving this sensible advice, King realized the error of his ways and reversed his economic policies. In fact, he did no such thing. When he discovered that the NEC was about to recommend federal control of relief, King pulled out every stop he could to kill the Commission's final report. When that proved impossible, thanks to Arthur Purvis' integrity, King simply ignored it. Why? The reason was best expressed by Mary Sutherland, King's closest confidant on the NEC and the author of a dissenting minority report. In it, Sutherland articulated the basis for Ottawa's continued resistance throughout the 1930s to accepting primary responsibility for the jobless. "No matter which government is responsible for and administers relief ...," Sutherland wrote, "there will be constant pressure to increase the benefits and to enlarge the base of admittance to benefits. If responsibility is centralized in the Dominion government, the counter-pressure from local taxpayers will be eased. The irksome, unwelcome, and hard check provided by necessity, by municipal officials, harassed by mounting demands on diminishing revenues, will be removed."

In short, Sutherland, like King and R.B. Bennett, believed that national responsibility for relief would cost too much and would erode the work ethic. If Ottawa controlled relief, it would have to define a national minimum standard of support, or in effect a national poverty line, across the country. In a country like Canada with widely diverse regional wage rates and living standards, such a national minimum would inevitably be higher than existing wage rates for many of the working poor. The result would be to attract this class out of work and onto relief, thus increasing unemployment. Sutherland's argument was, in this sense, almost identical to the one first put forward by Charlotte Whitton in her 1932 report on relief in western Canada. Only by keeping relief a local responsibility and local governments on the edge of bankruptcy could relief costs and benefit levels be kept to the barest minimum.

Ironically, putting more purchasing power directly into the hands of the jobless and their families in the form of higher relief benefits was exactly what *was* needed in order to push up consumption and effective demand to levels that would in turn encourage investment and employment. But as long as the Bennett and King administrations continued to approach the relief question from the angle of its effects upon the work ethic of individuals rather than upon the purchasing power of all the unemployed, they simply could not see this. As a result, in their relief policy, as in their wider economic policies of balanced budgets, a sound dollar, and regressive taxation, Bennett and King inhibited the chances of recovery.

VI

In 1940, after World War II had begun, Canadians finally did see enacted a constitutionally valid scheme of unemployment insurance. The pressures of war and the need for national unity had dissolved the political objections of the three dissenting provinces. More importantly, King's own fear of post-war unemployment, and of how jobless veterans would respond to relief of the 1930s variety, now galvanized him into making unemployment insurance a first priority of the government, particularly with an election looming on the horizon in 1940. Wartime mobilization and the potential labour shortage also gave the federal government a vital need for creating a national employment service, motive which had not been present during the heavy labour surplus of the 1930s. Finally, the necessity for massive war expenditures gave Ottawa an overpowering political argument for trying out new Keynesian ideas such as deliberately incurring large deficits, a policy which would have left most Canadian businessmen aghast in the Depression.

The tragedy of unemployment policy in the 1930s is that strategies for dealing with joblessness which *were* politically possible, indeed essential in the context of the war, were not deemed possible, given Canada's political landscape in the Depression. The essential continuity and the essential failure of the policies pursued by both R.B. Bennett and Mackenzie King lay in their refusal to accept that the unemployed were a national responsibility. This refusal, in turn, was rooted in what might be termed the dilemma of 'less eligibility' in a market economy. In a private enterprise system, business and the market set wage levels and living standards. During the 1930s, for many *working* Canadians, these standards and wages were below what was necessary to ensure a decent and healthy standard of living. As a result, both the Bennett and King governments believed they could not provide higher relief benefits for the jobless without attracting many of the working population onto the dole. Without direct state intervention or trade union pressure to improve working conditions and living standards for low income Canadians, or in other words, without massive intervention into the marketplace, the government felt limited in the benefits it could provide for the unemployed. And in the political context of the 1930s, given the absence of a serious political threat from the left or a strong labour movement, the pressure simply was not there for either Bennett or King to move in a direction that would have been regarded by Canadian businessmen as serious meddling in their affairs.

Only war, with the full employment it would bring and the strong labour union organization it would permit, could create a political climate in which it would be possible to effect these kinds of permanent structural reforms to underpin working-class incomes. By 1945, then, Canadians were finally ready to fight the Great Depression of the 1930s.

GENDER AND THE UNEMPLOYMENT INSURANCE DEBATES IN CANADA, 1934–1940

Ruth Roach Pierson

On 22 January 1935, in a House of Commons debate on the extent of unemployment in Canada, J.S. Woodsworth cited an account of murder and suicide from the *Winnipeg Free Press* of 18 December 1934. A Valour Road man had returned to his home to find his baby boy aged 18 months drowned in the bathtub, his five year-old daughter strangled, and his wife poisoned. The wife had come to Canada

From *Labour/Le Travail*, XXV (Spring 1990), 77–103. Reprinted by permission of the Canadian Committee on Labour History.

from England four years previously. The husband had not been able to find steady work for some time. The family had been trying to survive on relief, but, according to the *Free Press,* "there had not even been enough money in the house to buy the poison," a germicide, that the wife had ingested. In the note she had left on the kitchen table, she wrote " 'I owe the drug store 44 cents: farewell.' "[1]

In the narrative of the Great Depression, both as told at the time, and in the main by historians after the fact,[2] it is men who fill the ranks of the unemployed—men who ride the rails, men who stand in the bread-lines, men who sell apples on street corners. Single unemployed women have a shadowy presence at best.[3] The married woman appears not as a person in her own right. If she was employed, she was seen as a symbol of the cause of unemployment among men and, if dependent, as a symbol of the high cost of male unemployment to society.[4] The Great Depression was construed as a period of gender crisis. The focus of concern at the time, however, was masculinity in crisis, for the perception of crisis was framed by the belief that the position of head of household and family provider was an essential property of masculinity, a position that male unemployment undermined. While female unemployment was trivialized, male unemployment was seen not as undermining but rather as intensifying what was believed to be woman's complementary and natural role as nurturant wife and mother.[5]

Given the near invisibility of the army of unemployed women in the perceptions of politicians then,[6] and of mainstream historians more recently, it is not surprising that the subject of the female worker rarely surfaced in the unemployment insurance debates of the 1930s; nor is it surprising that gender issues, and the implications of legislation and policies for women, are not central to James Struthers' classic account of the emergence of Unemployment Insurance in Canada.[7] But if we understand gender to be a fundamental social category, we are justified in asking where and how concern for women fits into the Depression-era discussion of unemployment insurance. And if we further understand gender to be relational, to be a category comprising all that which shapes social relations between the sexes,[8] then we are justified in examining the gender implications for women of the silences regarding them: that is, of the measures that made no mention of them, of the concepts into which they were invisibly enfolded, and of the assumptions through which masculine priority was inscribed.

Unemployment insurance (UI) legislation was introduced and passed in the Commons only once during the Great Depression, in 1935, although a further bill was drafted in 1938. The initial UI legislation appeared as the only developed part of the omnibus Employment and Social Insurance bill which passed third reading in March 1935. But after the election in October resoundingly defeated R.B. Bennett's Conservative government and returned the Mackenzie King Liberals, the bill was never implemented. Although the bill's easy passage had testified to broad public support,[9] Bennett had not sought the consent of the provincial premiers to the idea of federal jurisdiction over unemployment insurance and other essential social services. When, in 1937–8, King considered introducing an Unemployment Insurance bill similar in basic outline to the UI provisions of the 1935 Act, his fear of effecting Ottawa's jurisdiction over unemployment relief far outweighed his commitment to a federal UI scheme. Because he was also wary of triggering a dominion-provincial jurisdictional row, and knew that the Judicial Committee of the Privy Council of Great Britain had, in December 1936, declared the Employment and Social Insurance Act of 1935 *ultra vires,* King sought the provincial premiers' support for amending the British North America Act to grant constitutionality to federal unemployment insurance legislation. But once it was clear that only six of the nine premiers were prepared to offer unreserved support, King used this lack of unanimity to justify postponing introduction of the UI bill, pending the report of the Royal Commission on Dominion-Provincial Relations. The Rowell-Sirois Commission Report eventually concluded, in February 1940, "that the care of employables who are unemployed should be a Dominion function."[10] But it was the outbreak of war in September 1939 that, as Struthers notes, "created the compelling new reason for unemployment insurance,"[11] namely, the perceived need to safeguard veterans and the enlarged war-time civilian labour force against the widespread unemployment expected in the wake of demobilization and the return to peace-time production. On 18 June 1940, King could tell the Commons that all provinces now agreed to an enabling amendment to allow for the introduction of the UI bill. And on 11 July 1940, he announced British Parliamentary approval of a constitutional amendment giving the federal government power over unemployment insurance.[12] In the first days of August, the legislation quickly passed both houses of the Canadian Parliament and became law.

The debate on unemployment insurance in Canada revolved around these three pieces of legislation: the UI provisions of the Employment and Social Insurance Act of 1935, the Unemployment Insurance Bill of 1938, and the UI Act of 1940. Participants in the debate were many and included Members of Parliament, the ministers of labour, finance, and insurance and their top civil servants, trade union leaders, spokesmen for associations of manufacturers and financial institutions, members of governmental commissions, members of women's organizations, and academic social investigators. Of great influence behind the scenes were A.D. Watson,[13] Chief Actuary, Department of Insurance, and Hugh Wolfenden, his actuarial associate and consultant on contract until their falling out over the 1940 legislation. Also influential was the British expert D. Christie Tait of the International Labour Organization, who was brought in to review the 1938 draft bill and whose views helped shape the 1940 Act. It is in the vision of unemployment insurance articulated in the proposals for, the drafts of, and the responses to UI legislation that we shall search not only for the positioning of women in the scheme but also for the gender assumptions implicitly embedded in the entire discourse. In particular, we want to examine how a sex/gender system was inscribed in the overall conceptualization of unemployment insurance as well as in the paragraphs of draft and enacted legislation and in the administrative structure created for its implementation.[14]

Sex Distinctions in Contribution and Benefit Rates

We can isolate seven components of the legislation that were crucial in determining coverage: the method of calculating amount of contribution and amount of benefit; the provision of dependants' allowances; the setting of an income ceiling; the naming of categories of uninsurable employment (that is, the exception of certain occupations); the imposition of statutory conditions of eligibility for benefit; the qualification period; and the method of calculating the benefit period. In only one of these components was the female sex mentioned explicitly. This was in the 1935 Act's provisions for calculating contributions and benefits. (Married women received explicit mention in the 1935 schedule governing "special cases," and wives in the discussion of and clauses covering dependants' allowances, as we shall see.) The 1935 Act divided all insured persons into four major groups by age, and then further subdivided each group by sex. A flat rate of contribution was set for each sex (always higher for males) within each major age group. Accordingly, in all age categories, girls paid a lower contribution than boys, and women a lower one than men. As benefits were related in part to contributions, it followed that girls would receive lower benefits than boys, and women lower benefits than men of the same age.[15] The flat-rate system and the graduation of the rate according to distinctions of age and sex derived from British unemployment insurance legislation, the general model for the Canadian UI legislation until 1940.[16]

The 1938 draft bill, however, while retaining the four major groups based on age distinctions, eliminated sex distinctions entirely.[17] As Chief Actuary Watson noted in March 1938, the new UI bill was marked by an "absence of any distinction in benefits or contributions as between men and women, or as between boys and girls."[18] Given, as already mentioned, that unemployment in Canada in the 1930s was largely regarded in political and academic circles as a male problem and unemployed women as a consequence received little official concern, and given that the discourse at every level of the society from radio drama to university lecture castigated married women in paid employment for taking jobs from men,[19] how can we account for the 1938 draft bill's elimination of the distinction based on sex?

Insofar as policy analysts, legislators, and political and labour activists thought about women during the Great Depression, they tended to divide them into two categories, that of female worker and that of wife/mother.[20] It was, by and large, ideologically anathema for a woman to combine these two categories in herself.[21] Those who did risked putting themselves outside the solicitous embrace of public policy. Let us consider, for instance, the unwed mother who, by necessity, combined motherhood with work for pay because she was ineligible for a mother's allowance (only one of the provinces with such legislation—British Columbia—provided allowances for unmarried mothers, and then only under exceptional circumstances).[22] Bearing the stigma of having transgressed patriarchal morality and largely bereft of child care facilities,[23] the single mother had to scrounge in the dregs of the job market for employment. A second type of woman who violated the female worker/wife and mother dichotomy was the employed married woman. Even before the Depression, women with paying jobs who married were forced to resign from federal and provincial civil service posts, and from teaching positions and other white-collar jobs.[24] During the Depression, as already has been noted, social censure directed at married women for causing male unemployment intensified.[25] As the Depression worsened, married women's right to employment became an increasingly divisive issue among members of the National Council of Women of Canada as local Councils of Women, and even some Business and Professional Women's Clubs, went on record as opposed to married women working for pay.[26]

Of the two categories, the single woman worker tended to take a back seat in social policy to the wife/mother whom the hegemonic ideology constructed as the dependant of a bread-winning husband/father. The dominant frame in operation at the time, no matter how divergent from social reality,[27] was the conception of the male worker as the head of household and therefore deserving of a "family wage,"[28] that is, a wage sufficient to support both the man's unwaged children and the children's unwaged, housekeeping mother.[29] This conception would frame the theory informing Leonard Marsh's *Report on Social Security for Canada 1943,* the document regarded as the founding text of 'the welfare state' in Canada.[30]

Hegemonic as this master frame was, it did not completely obscure the existence of women workers nor, provided they were single, totally preclude concern for their welfare. The Left, in particular, admitted the single woman worker into the fold of workers whose interests it sought to protect and advance. But given that the Left was little different from society as a whole in subscribing to the woman as worker/woman as mother dichotomy,[31] it was principally as non-mothers that women and their labour-market interests qualified for the attention of trade union spokesmen and male socialists, communists, and eventually liberals. Usually when trade unionists and left-to-liberal politicians took up the banner of sexual equality, it was for female non-mothers.[32] On the whole, only when thus "desexed"[33] did women workers acquire eligibility for equal treatment. In other words, equality of situation was usually required for women to be considered eligible for equality of treatment. And it was with this understanding of equality between the sexes in mind that J.S. Woodsworth rose in the House, as he did on a number of occasions, to criticize the discrimination according to sex in UI contributions and benefits that was inscribed in the 1935 Act.[34]

In the politically radicalized atmosphere of the Depression, opposition to discrimination on the basis of sex was *de rigeur* among members of the CCF and the CPC. And the "equal treatment of both sexes"[35] as regards contributions and benefits that was incorporated into the 1938 bill reflected the liberal opinion of British expert D. Christie Tait that it was necessary to acknowledge the "increasing reluctance among many people to making such a discrimination in unemployment insurance."[36] The Fifth Convention of the Canadian Federation of Business and Professional Women's Clubs had protested as "unequal pay for equal work" the lower UI contributions and benefits established for girls and women in the 1935 legislation.[37] And the Ottawa Women's Liberal Club had passed a resolution disapproving of "the discrimination between the sexes with regard to the scale of insurance payments and benefits."[38] But the discrimination so signified was less that against dependent wives and mothers than that against single women workers who, in their independent state, were more similar to men. It was possible, in other words, to entertain at one and the same time disapproval of discrimination on the basis of sex and the notion that married women should be supported by their husbands.

Gender in the Flat versus Graded Rates Debate

At the same time, however, the single woman admissible to equality with men on the grounds of independence was crucially different from the large proportion of men in the labour force who were married with dependants.[39] By 1940, those consulted in the revising of the 1938 bill for submission to Parliament were concerned to address the 'social injustice' that they saw entailed in the abandonment of sex categories for setting the rate of contributions and benefits while a flat rate within age categories was retained. Perceived as a 'social injustice' was the flat rate system's non-accommodation of the fact that "men usually have more dependants than women and therefore need a higher benefit."[40] Although both the 1935 Act and the 1938 Bill had provided for dependants' allowances, the amount of allowance was not regarded as sufficient to compensate for the 1938 elimination of the sex-based differential in basic benefit. Clearly, the concept of sexual equality resided uneasily within the master frame of male breadwinner entitled to a 'family wage' to support a dependent wife and children. While the single working woman's independence qualified her for equality with the working man, the married woman's presumed dependence threatened to disqualify her from such equality, and the married male worker claimed a position of more equal than others.[41]

This male claim was based on the concept of the 'family wage.' From its frequent invocations in Commons debates, and from its service as the implicit rationale underpinning dependants' allowances for spouses, one can see that the concept of the 'family wage' was widely accepted as common sense. MPs across party lines invoked the 'family wage' as an ideal or as a principle of social justice. For example, on 12 February 1935, G.D. Stanley of the Conservative Party identified as "the ideal to which [the male worker] strives" the possibility of becoming "self-supporting," which Stanley defined as the condition of a male worker's being able, "during his working years, ... to earn enough to provide for the maintenance of his family during his whole life."[42] On 18 February 1935, Woodsworth of the CCF criticized the capitalist wage system in Canada for the social injustice of "fixing the price of labour" while having "no regard ... to the conditions necessary to maintain the labourer and his wife and family in a state of well-being."[43] And on 9 April 1935, H.B. McKinnon of the Liberal Party made a case for including dependants' allowances in minimum wage legislation on the grounds that "a man with a family of six or seven or eight should be given some consideration over and above what is given to the man who is single."[44]

Civil servant Eric Stangroom of the federal Department of Labour recognized as one of the positive "social effects" of incorporating dependants' allowances within an unemployment scheme the fact that fewer children would be forced into employment, and wives would not be obliged to take on "unsuitable work."[45] Both the 1935 Act and the 1938 draft bill provided for dependants' allowances and allowed that both adults and children could be dependants. The dependant adult was defined in Section 15 (2) of the 1938 draft legislation as "the wife or dependent husband of the insured person, or a female having the care of the dependent children of the insured person."[46] Used without the qualifier "dependent," the term "wife," it should be noted, here bore the social meaning of "dependence" as the very essence of its signification in a way that not even the term "children" did. Moreover, while it was acknowledged that women could have dependent husbands as well as dependent children, it was also assumed by Chief Actuary Watson, among others, that "the dependants of women claimants will be relatively unimportant."[47] Indeed, provision for dependants' allowances was made on the assumption that "the dependants of female wage-earners are relatively few." To support this claim, British data was cited to show that in 1924 only about 2 per cent of working women had adult dependants and only about 2.7 per cent had dependent children.[48] Canadian civil servants assumed, in the complete absence of hard data, that the proportion of female workers with dependent children "would *probably* be lower in Canada as *probably* relatively few women with children are wage earners."[49]

In the discussions surrounding the drafting of the 1940 UI legislation, the question of how to deal in a 'socially just' way with the need of the male head of household for a higher benefit than the single male or female worker turned on the relative merit of a "graded rating" versus the "flat rating schemes" embodied in the 1935 Act and the 1938 Draft Bill.[50] Pivotal to the proposed "graded rating" system was the use of a fixed ratio to allow contributions and benefits to vary in direct relation to income. In other words, the varying amount of contribution to be paid and amount of benefit to be collected were both to be computed in terms of a set proportion of the individual worker's usual earnings.

As early as 1935, Tom Moore of the Trades and Labour Congress of Canada had asked the Senate Committee on Unemployment Insurance to consider "graded benefits 'proportionate to the man's earnings.'" William Beveridge had recommended earnings-related contributions and benefits to the British Royal Commission on Unemployment Insurance of 1930–32 (sometimes referred to as the Gregory Commission). The United States had shown a preference for graded rates from the start.[51] By 1938 social policy experts writing in Canada, such as L. Richter in the *Dalhousie Review*[52] and D. Christie Tait in his Report to the Dominion Government,[53] had been criticizing the flat-rate system of contributions and benefits for its unfairness to higher-paid workers. With their deeply entrenched suspicion that the social-insurance recipients would sooner collect benefits than put in a good day's work, many Canadian social-policy drafters and analysts were as wedded to the principle of 'less eligibility' as their British counterparts.[54] In the context of unemployment insurance, honouring this principle meant that the benefit collected had to be set at a level lower than the recipient's usual earnings, otherwise "overinsurance" would occur.[55] Applied within a flat rate system, it meant that contributions and benefits had to be fixed low enough that the insurable worker "earning the lowest rate of wages"[56] would not receive more in UI benefits than his/her normal earnings. According to the 1935 Act and the 1938 Draft Bill, the total benefit possible for a claimant could not exceed 80 per cent of the person's average weekly pay while employed.[57] For so long as they were employed, the more highly-paid insurable workers enjoyed the advantage of contributing a lower proportion of their wages to the UI fund than the less well paid. Once unemployed, however, those who had enjoyed a higher income level would receive in UI benefit a much smaller proportion of their former wages and, as a consequence, would suffer a sharp drop in their standard of living. Following this line of reasoning with respect to Canada's vast regional differences, Labour Minister N.A. McLarty concluded in the Commons debates of 1940 that because "the unemployment benefit can never rise as high as wages, ... the yardstick used to measure UI benefits would necessarily have to be the lowest wages paid in the lowest wage-paid area in the country."[58] It was the graded system's elimination of the leveling effect of the flat-rate system of benefit computation that helped fuel the "strong intellectual argument," noted by Watson in 1940, that the graded system would be more "socially just."[59] Here, clearly, the concept of social justice needs to be read as encompassing the maintenance of wage and salary hierarchies. According to a memo Gerald H. Brown, assistant deputy minister of labour, sent Watson in May 1940, the introduction of graded contributions and benefits would protect the higher standard of living of higher wage earners.[60]

If the existence of wage and salary hierarchies was not perceived as 'socially unjust,' there was some sense that sex-based hierarchies of contribution and benefit might be. The ideology of sexual equality in wages and social benefits was prevalent on the Left, as we have seen, at least insofar as the single female worker could be assimilated to the norm established by the male worker. In 1935, the All Canadian Congress of Labour had raised objections to the system of flat rates graduated "according to age and sex," and recommended its replacement "by a scale of contributions [graded] according to earnings."[61] The 1938 bill had dispensed with sex-based differentiations, but, despite the retention of dependants' allowances, the very removal of sex distinctions in a flat-rate system was seen by some, as mentioned earlier, to violate the principle of the 'family wage,' and penalize the male head of household.[62] The adoption of a system of variable rates, graded according to income, appeared to be the solution to the problem. The differentiation on the basis of sex, by which girls and women in each age group were to pay and receive less in contributions and benefits than boys and men, was "the result," Stangroom reflected in 1939,

> of [a] tradition which has had a bad psychological effect on the efficiency of the woman, who feels she is held cheaply; on the employer, who feels a woman should be paid less; and on the male worker, who feels, from the age of 16 when he enters the scheme, that he is superior by reason of his sex alone.[63]

Stangroom concluded that "an employee contribution equal as to both sexes" should be a feature of any future UI plan contemplated by the Canadian Parliament. Earnings-related contributions and benefits achieved that end and therefore established "a principle more easily defended," for they would not "give to the women wage earners a status of inferiority," as, according to the Ottawa Women's Liberal Club, the 1935 sex-discriminatory provisions had done.[64] Graded contributions and benefits, moreover, "would appeal as more logical and realistic than a division by age and sex."[65] The 1939 response of Watson, the pragmatist, was that "there may, however, be sound reasons for treating men and women technically alike. It certainly does simplify the scheme."[66]

Albeit by 1940, studies showed that the graded system was, in fact, more complicated to administer, in the end it was its potential for creating the illusion of sexual equality that commended the earnings-related system to those concerned with averting charges of sex discrimination. As the May 1940 report comparing flat versus graded rating systems succinctly stated, the latter "dispenses with the sex distinction question, and achieves the same end."[67] In other words, the 1940 adoption of the graded-rates system gave the appearance of formal equality in Canadian UI legislation by eliminating any explicit differentiation in contribution or benefit based on sex. At the same time, however, in the absence of any concurrent social program to change the sexually unequal wage structure of the Canadian labour market, the graded-rate system, calculated as it was in direct relation to individual earnings, implicitly embedded sexual inequality in contributions and benefits into the Canadian unemployment insurance scheme. In the language of the authors of the report outlining the case for the earnings-related system,

> A direct grouping by wages rather than by sex would establish a sounder relationship [between contributions and earnings and between earnings and benefits] which would not be so unfavourable, psychologically, to female labour....

It would, in other words, achieve the desired smoke-and-mirrors effect. At the same time, the report openly acknowledged that the variable-rate system, relative to earnings, would "give public recognition to the common circumstance of lower wages for women as a fixed principle."[68] Given that the report acknowledged that legislated inequality on the basis of sex had a negative psychological effect on women while it simultaneously called for recognition of "the usual difference in wages between men and women" as a matter of "fixed principle," one might paraphrase the report's position as 'No inequality but inequality anyway.' On the one hand, inequality between the sexes would not be explicit in the UI legislation, while on the other there would still be real inequality because women were lower paid than men and would therefore contribute and benefit less.

Provision for Dependants

The earnings-related system, then, was heralded for removing the 'social injustice' of sexual inequality from UI legislation by sleight of hand. Equally important to drafters and supporters was the conviction that the graded rating "does not involve [the] injustice" of penalizing men, who "usually have more dependants than women," as it was believed the flat-rated scheme with no provision for sex categories would have done.[69] Dichotomized into either single female workers or dependent wives and mothers, women as dependants, not independent single women, were the prime objects of social policy throughout the 1930s–1950s, except during the war emergency years. (Women who did not fit into one or the other of these categories tended to fall through the holes of the emerging social security net.) Because the assumption was that most women were dependants, the concept of dependency is the key to understanding many of the gender issues raised in the UI debates.[70] Within the master frame that assigned economic primacy to the man on the grounds of his heading a household of dependants, the claim to dependants' allowances was the logical extension of the claim to a 'family wage.' On this basis, both the 1935 Act and the 1938 UI bill included provisions for dependants' allowances in which a "wife" was by definition classified as a dependant.

Those who were as concerned with expediency as with social justice, like the author of the memo on "The Problem of Dependency in Unemployment Insurance" circulating within the Departments of Labour and Insurance in spring 1940, believed that the 'family wage' should be honoured through provision of dependants' allowances because "the existence of dependants arouses a sense of responsibility in the workman."[71] But for civil servants and their advisors, and the Conservative and Liberal politicians whom they served, the commitment to the 'family wage' and, by extension, dependants' allowances was limited by their concerns about the costs of a social security system, and by their overriding commitment to preserving wage differentials. Throughout the debates on unemployment insurance in Canada, a distinction was drawn between "predictable" and therefore respectable and "insurable" need, on the one hand, and "absolute" need, on the other.[72] UI legislation was never intended to address the latter, the need of the destitute, of the long-term unemployed and of the unemployable. The Dominion Actuary could compare the unemployment insurance scheme proposed in 1940 with the dole, relief, or unemployment assistance and pronounce UI the "soundest socio-economic institution on the whole."[73] But if the first proposed UI legislation had been implemented in 1934 or 1935, a time of high unemployment, it would not have relieved the existing joblessness, as both its authors[74] and its critics[75] well knew. Nonetheless, there were some provisions in the 1935 UI Act, as L. Richter pointed out, that "satisfie[d] the social principle." However restrictedly, they addressed need by providing training and rehabilitation programs, loans for the fares of unemployed men to move to where work was available, and an employment exchange system. Included in the list of provisions addressing need was the "payment of additional benefit for families without any increase of the premium."[76] Asked for his opinion in 1935, an American consultant criticized the inclusion of dependants' allowances in UI plans precisely because they introduced "an element of payment according to need."[77]

By 1940, the issue of whether the new UI bill should or should not include dependants' allowances was muddied by the debate taking place over family allowances.[78] There was a strong belief on the part of some highly placed civil servants in the Departments of Labour, Insurance and Finance that the retention of dependants' allowances in UI legislation and the introduction of family allowances were mutually exclusive. This belief dovetailed with the assumption that the proposed, earnings-related system of setting UI contribution and benefit levels dispensed with the need for dependants' allowances in a UI scheme. It was assumed that, under a graded system that related contributions and benefits directly to earnings, since men earn more, the higher UI benefits they would receive would be sufficient for them to meet their responsibilities as family providers. Dependants' allowances, therefore, could be eliminated. This assumption was used to argue that the graded-rate system would not be more expensive than the flat-rate system because the latter was "accompanied by dependants' allowances" which increased the cost of UI.

Eric Stangroom, in particular, articulated this line of reasoning in a series of memos to Watson in May and June, 1940, on flat versus graded rates and "the problem of dependency." A supporter of an independent scheme of "Family Endowments or Family Allowances regardless of the employment or unemployment status of the breadwinner or breadwinners," Stangroom felt that the retention of dependants' allowances in a UI benefit scheme "would prejudice the introduction of Family Allowance schemes...."[79] Stangroom recognized that having to provide for family dependants had the positive effect of stabilizing a male work force. But in the context of the debate over Family Allowances, Strangroom's desire to detach dependants' allowances from UI led him to argue that dependants' allowances were a matter of need, and need was not a matter to be addressed by Unemployment Insurance.[80] To corroborate his argument, he cited the statistics that

> In Canada between 1934 and 1936, as much as 15.6% of male wage-earners and 49.5% of female wage-earners would not even receive the allowance for an adult dependent [and one dependent child], because their average wage while in employment was less that $12 weekly.[81]

"The truth," he contended, was that "the great need of [Canadian] families" was the result of "a wage situation"; that is, due to pervasive low wages, "need exists in many of the families of the nation *even when the breadwinner is at work.*" In other words, social reality fell far short of the ideal of the 'family wage,' and it was not UI's job to bridge this enormous shortfall. The most "needy" kinds of employment were excluded from the proposed UI scheme anyway, Stangroom pointed out.[82] He feared, moreover, that if dependants' benefits were introduced, they would be difficult to abolish.[83]

Watson, in contrast, held that not providing dependants' allowances in a UI scheme would be difficult, as they were provided under other social insurance measures, such as Workman's Compensation, the Old Age Annuity Scheme in the U.S. Social Security Act, and Canada's Civil Service Superannuation Scheme. Alert to questions of cost, Watson suggested that "there might be advantages in limiting the dependants to children alone rather than including wife and children," but, he conceded, "it might also be difficult to get acceptance for that view."[84] To those who opposed the inclusion of dependants' allowances in the belief that they "would militate against the adoption of family allowances," Watson years later recalled arguing that their inclusion "would hasten rather than retard family allowances."[85] On balance, Watson, ever the pragmatist, recommended "a thorough-going recognition of dependants" in the 1940 UI bill "as in the Act of 1935"[86] to obviate the necessity for additional assistance or relief measures.[87]

Given the prevailing assumption that most women were dependants and were, therefore, to be provided for by men, whether daughters by fathers or wives by husbands, the major channel through which UI coverage was to be extended to women was the provision of dependants' allowances. That the drafters of the UI legislation seriously considered either dispensing with dependants' benefits altogether or not including wives (dependants by definition, as we have seen) says something about the lesser importance, in the eyes of the policy makers, of women relative to men, of wives relative to husbands and of daughters relative to fathers, as well as of the expendability of the 'family wage' principle. Indeed, the debate over UI dependants' allowances versus 'family allowances' was, in large part, a debate over the function of the wage. Although lip service was paid regularly to the principle of the 'family wage,' it was well known that wages did not vary according to need, that is, that dependants' allowances were not built into wages. In a sense, the advocates of 'family allowances' regarded this measure as *the* solution to the non-reality of the 'family wage'. Moreover, dependants' allowances as an integral part of the unemployment insurance benefit package threatened to contravene the 'less eligibility' principle as applied to UI, and cause what bureaucrats and policy analysts of the day called "overinsurance."[88] As Stangroom wrote in his analysis of the problem of dependency in UI, "whatever our decision, it seems that benefits should not exceed wages ... or overinsurance will result, with the danger of malingering."[89] To grant more, in an unemployment insurance benefit package that included dependants' allowances, than a person could earn while in waged or salaried employment would, it was feared, destroy the work incentive.

Initially, dependants' allowances were not a feature of the early drafts of the 1940 UI bill. In the end, partly as a result of representations from labour, particularly Quebec labour, the 1940 UI Act did contain provision for dependants' allowances. They were included in the legislation, however, just as the sex distinctions in contributions and benefits had been excluded from the 1938 bill, by sleight of hand. Watson told the story in 1951. The base benefit rate had been originally set at 40 times the average daily/weekly contribution. A person earning between $5.40 and $7.50 a week and paying a 12 cent weekly contribution would have received a weekly benefit of $4.80. Asked to evaluate the relationship of benefits to contributions in the original 1940 Bill with an eye to increasing the latter to cover dependants' allowances, Watson remembered having found the benefits "to be very considerably in excess of" the contributions. In disagreement with him, however, were those who thought that the rates of benefit were already "so moderate" that they could not possibly be further decreased, but who were "equally reluctant" to propose higher contributions for the sake of dependants' allowances. "Some practical decision had to be reached quickly," Watson recalled in 1951, because "the bill had to go forward into the Senate the next day or perhaps the day after that." The compromise solution was to bring in dependants' allowances through the back door by reducing the base benefit rate from 40 times the average daily/weekly rate of contribution to 34 times for those claimants without dependants, and by allowing only claimants with dependants to receive benefits of 40 times their average contribution.[90] Now, with respect to those covered by UI who had been earning between $5.40 and $7.50 a week, the unemployed person with dependants would receive $4.80 in weekly benefits while the person without, only $4.08.[91]

The "differential on the basis of dependency"[92] thus amounted not to a "15 per cent supplement to [the] base rate" for claimants with dependants, as Struthers describes it,[93] but rather to a reduction to 85 per cent of the base rate for claimants without dependants. In other words, claimants without dependants both were penalized for not having them, and expected to subsidize the 'allowances' for those who did. As it was widely assumed that few women in the labour force had dependants, this measure can hardly be regarded as designed to be of advantage to female workers. At the same time, since the major provision of unemployment insurance for women was to be by way of their dependence on men, to disguise "the differential on the basis of dependency" as a supplement for dependants was not only to mask the cut in the base benefit rate for the single worker but to disregard the real material needs of wives and children living in households organized on the basis of the 'family wage.' Nonetheless, being by definition connected to the labour market only indirectly through their husbands, married women were to have access to unemployment insurance through the dependants' benefits (however meagre) extended to their male providers. As already noted, married women in paid employment did not fit comfortably into the master frame. Upon marriage, women were presumed to enter a state of dependency in which husbands would provide for them. Therefore, for a married woman to claim unemployment insurance was a contradiction in terms or, what was greatly feared, a way to defraud the system. Hovering on the edges of the UI debate in the 1930s was the suspicion that women workers who married would make fraudulent claims. This was the subject of a series of memos exchanged between Watson and Wolfenden in late 1934. Wolfenden clearly delineated two feared scenarios as follows: the woman who had worked long enough to qualify for UI benefits before marriage would, on marriage, leave employment and make claims; or the married woman would continue in paid employment only long enough to qualify for benefits.[94] That both of these cases would have already been covered by the exclusion from benefit of all those who voluntarily severed their employment contract "without just cause" attests to the strength of the fear. The perceived anomalousness (and feared duplicity) of gainfully employed, married women was written into the 1935 Act. Section 25 gave the Unemployment Insurance Commission power to make regulations in respect of "special classes," that is, to impose additional conditions and terms as the commissioners saw fit. This section identified five classes of "anomalies": a) casual workers; b) seasonal workers; c) intermittent workers; d) "married women who, since marriage or in any prescribed period subsequent to marriage, have had less than the prescribed number of contributions paid in respect of them;" and e) piece workers.[95] This section of the 1935 legislation closely followed the British UI Anomalies Act and Regulations of 1931. The framers of Canada's 1938 Bill and 1940 Act, however, felt that the schedule for anomalous cases could be simplified by eliminating both married women and intermittent workers once the "ratio rule," to be discussed below, was built into the UI scheme.

Indirect Methods of Controlling Women's Access to Benefit

In addition to direct, there were also indirect methods of controlling women's access to UI benefit. The remaining five of the seven sets of regulations governing eligibility and coverage all affected women without explicitly mentioning either the female sex or married women. Most importantly, there was, throughout all the drafts from 1935 to 1940, the scheme's inherent bias toward 'the good worker,' the 'good risk.' The framers of the Canadian UI legislation were well aware of the fact that Great Britain's UI scheme had collapsed in the 1920s under the sheer weight of the numbers of unemployed. As the initial drafting in Canada was undertaken at a time of mass unemployment, it is no wonder, then, that the framers exercised great caution, and sought to make eligibility regulations strict and coverage strictly limited. Watson's (and Wolfenden's) preoccupation with actuarial soundness so unmistakably informed the 1935 legislation as to draw fire from CCF critics who attacked the principle as contrary to the interests of workers.[96]

By its thoroughgoing application of a ratio formula that related benefit period to employment and contributory history,[97] the 1938 bill was decidedly framed to reward the steady worker. Moreover, as a summary of the 1938 bill disclosed, the reduction in the number of future benefit days by past claims would penalize the worker who might make what were labelled "trifling claims." In general, the scheme was to function in such a way that "the more he works the greater his benefits."[98] The 1940 legislation retained the "ratio rule," establishing, within a qualifying period of 30 weeks worked over any two-year period, a fixed ratio of five to one between the number of days of paid contributions and the number of days of benefit. Thirty weeks (or 180 days) of employment and contributions within twenty-four months got one six weeks (or 36 days) of benefit. Five years of insurable employment and contributions got one an entire year on UI. As Watson wrote to Arthur MacNamara, Chairman of the Committee on Unemployment Insurance, Dependants' Allowance Board, Department of National Defence, "one important purpose of an unemployment insurance Act ought to be, although not always observed, to give benefit for a good long period to a person who has had a good employment record and then falls on evil days."[99]

Certainly, as Labour Minister McLarty told the House in July 1940, the ratio rule for computing of benefit days was an incentive for "insured persons to try to improve their benefit status by keeping employed."[100] Equally true, as Tait pointed out in discussing the disadvantages of the ratio rule in 1938, was the fact that "the insured worker may be entitled to only a short period of benefit for the simple reason that he has suffered a great deal of unemployment through no fault of his own."[101] Overlooked by (or invisible to) all was the fact that, through no fault of *her* own, the average woman worker was handicapped in the race for 'good worker' status, since circumstances dictated that she had less access than the average male worker either to steady or to long-term insurable employment. Indeed, rather than expressing concern about any possible harmful effects on the woman worker, architects of the 1938 and 1940 legislation heralded as a positive outcome of the ratio rule that it would *disadvantage* married women. Tait, for example, cited as support for the adopting ratio rule an Australian's opinion that it

> would prevent serious anomalies arising from an undue drain on the fund on the part of casual, intermittent and seasonal workers and married women and thus it may avoid the necessity for complicated regulations like the Anomalies regulations in Great Britain.[102]

As we have seen, the schedule for anomalous cases in both the 1938 Draft Bill and the 1940 Act was simplified by the elimination of married women and intermittent workers.

As explicated by Watson in 1934, the proposed UI scheme was designed to alleviate short-term, but not structural, seasonal, or cyclical joblessness.[103] Nor, he could have added, as Tait did in 1938, was it to alleviate the intermittent unemployment of the irregularly employed.[104] In their attempt to negotiate the contradiction between the assumed dependency of wives and the non-realization of the 'family wage,' women, particularly married women, turned to just the sorts of catch-as-catch-can, temporary, and improvised jobs in the 'informal' economy that were deemed uninsurable. And insofar as they did (and had to do) this, women were excluded from unemployment insurance coverage.

According to the 1935 Act, part-time workers were not by definition ineligible, but they were required to contribute for the equivalent of 40 weeks before acquiring eligibility, a condition that a woman working two or three days a week or less would have taken a long time to fulfill.[105] Two changes in the 1940 Act brought some increase in access to benefit for the less regularly employed. One was the reduction of the qualifying period from 40 to 30 weeks worked over two years, and the second was the option of making daily, rather than weekly, contributions towards establishing qualification period. The latter opened the door somewhat to those who would have found it impossible to meet the "continuous employment" requirement of the 1935 legislation.[106] Despite these two changes, the 1940 Act still put UI coverage well beyond the reach of most 'intermittently' or 'irregularly' or 'casually' working women.

In a Canadian economy still heavily reliant on male labour in the primary (and seasonal) industries of agriculture, logging, and fishing, the relegation of seasonal unemployment to the status of an anomaly was bound to affect adversely a large proportion of working men. Furthermore, agricultural labour, logging and fishing were explicitly excluded from insurance coverage, on various grounds, in all the drafted and enacted UI legislation from 1934 to 1940. As part of its mandate to examine the possibility of extending coverage, the

Unemployment Insurance Commission began recommending inclusion of such areas of heavy male employment as lumbering, and certain occupations within agriculture, as early as 1945.[107] With the exception of nursing, the excluded categories of employment in which women predominated had to wait almost three decades for inclusion.

The most general principle of exclusion incorporated in the 1930s and 40s UI legislation was the income ceiling. Excluded in the 1940 Act was any employment (in the 1935 Act and 1938 Bill, any non-manual employment) which paid more than $2,000 a year.[108] The ruling belief was that, first, the well paid and, second, the securely employed did not have to be insured against the contingency of unemployment, since, in the first case, the person could afford to save enough for a rainy day, and, in the second, unemployment was unlikely. As civil servants were regarded as falling into the second category (the permanently employed), those in the federal and provincial public service as well as municipal employees were all excluded from coverage.[109] The secure employment argument was used also as a rationale for excepting school teachers.[110] Whether in the case of female school teachers or female civil servants, the argument was wholly inappropriate, given that neither teaching nor the civil service meant job security for women. Except during the war, when qualified teachers and civil servants were scarce, the policy of most school boards and provincial and municipal civil services as well as of the federal government itself (until 1955), was to require women to relinquish their positions at marriage or, alternatively, at first pregnancy. Certainly a far tinier proportion of the female than of the male labour force would have been excluded on the basis of earnings exceeding $2,000, a condition coincident with the assumption of male independence and female dependence.

In addition to teaching, the two other most salient female-dominated occupations, marked for exclusion from UI coverage in all the bills and enactments from 1934 to 1940 were hospital and private nursing, and domestic service performed in private homes.[111] By one fell swoop, between 30 and 40 per cent of women in the paid labour force were thus denied access to UI coverage. The rationales for exclusion were various, some identical to those regarding male-dominated occupations. The argument advanced for excluding professional nurses, for instance, was that "they collect their own fees," making their relationship to their employer "analogous to that of physician and patient or solicitor and client."[112] While this assimilated nurses to the model of the highly paid male professional, it conveniently overlooked the discrepancy in fee between nurse and doctor or nurse and lawyer. Nursing probationers, on the other hand, were excluded "because they hardly get enough money to clothe themselves."[113] Registered nurses and nurses in training were thus caught between being falsely identified with doctors and lawyers on the one hand, and, on the other, the decision by the original framers of the Canadian unemployment insurance scheme not to include the economically most vulnerable within the scheme's catchment.[114]

While cleaners of clubs and business premises were to be eligible, domestic servants employed in private homes were not.[115] The rationale advanced for their exclusion was administrative difficulty. As McLarty explained to the House in July 1940, their inclusion

> would make the administrative machinery in the matter of inspection so top heavy and complicated that the cost would be out of proportion to the good which would be accomplished.[116]

Agriculture and fishing were also excluded on the grounds that these were occupations carried out far from centres of inspection.[117] Despite the difficulty of supervision, which he conceded, Tait, in his 1938 Report, had argued for reconsidering the exclusion of agriculture, horticulture and forestry, but not of domestic service.[118] The argument of administrative difficulty would prove much more tenacious in the case of domestics than, for instance, in that of loggers or fishermen. One good reason was the perpetual shortage of domestic help. Despite widespread joblessness in the Depression, demand for domestic servants outran supply; and the war only exacerbated the shortage. The administrative argument with respect to paid household labour conveniently disguised the policy of using domestic service as an alternative unemployment insurance scheme for unemployed women.[119] It was an occupation for which, in any case, women were believed to be eminently well-suited.

Another statutory general condition of eligibility for benefit that limited access for women, particularly married women, was the requirement that the claimant be "capable and available for work."[120] For married women, availability was sharply curtailed by the subordination of the wife to the husband in location of residence[121] and, for mothers of young children, by the scarcity of child care facilities. The married woman's lack of mobility, in other words, put geographical limits on her job searching capacity which were as severe as the time limits that child rearing responsibilities imposed on job seeking mothers. Moreover, married women would not have been eligible for the loans provided by the 1935 Act's Section 14 to pay the fares of unemployed workers moving to where work was available.[122] Clearly, the discrimination against women embodied in the regulations regarding availability for work was structural.

Gender and the UI Administrative Structure

Gender was also inscribed in the administrative structure which UI legislation mandated for implementing the scheme. A three-person agency, called the Unemployment Insurance Commission, was created to oversee the entire operation of UI. A dispersed federal bureaucracy of employment service and unemployment insurance offices was to be set up in regional divisions and in cities and towns across Canada. Each region's central office was to act as a clearing house for vacancies and applications for employment and to make this information available to the local offices. Regional insurance officers would be hired to handle unemployment insurance claims. To handle disagreement over claims, the Commission was empowered to set up regional courts of referees and to appoint regional deputy umpires and a national umpire. Provision was also made for the appointment of inspectors authorized to investigate workplaces concerning compliance with UI regulations. To advise and assist the Commission, an Unemployment Insurance Advisory Committee, consisting of a chairman and four to six members, was to be appointed by the Governor in Council.[123]

Not surprisingly, male administrative control of the operation of UI was ensured from the start. It is true that, at the regional and local level, women (if unmarried, of course) could be hired as employment placement or unemployment insurance officers. And during the war, with the male labour shortage, the lifting of the marriage bar, and the creation of the Women's Division of National Selective Service, the labour of both married and unmarried women was drawn upon to fill some of these jobs in many parts of Canada. But, in keeping with the rest of Canadian state structures, within the higher echelons of the UI administration (that is, within the Commission itself, the inspectorate, and the hierarchy of appointees to implement the appeal procedure), no provision was made to ensure that a proportionate number of women would take up positions. The one exception was the Unemployment Insurance Advisory Committee. Although the 1935 Act was silent on the issue of the sex of those appointed to serve, Prime Minister Bennett conceded in the House on February 21, 1935, that, "if it is thought desirable, ... I contemplate that one of the members ... shall be a woman."[124]

And indeed Section 36(1) of the 1938 Draft Bill stipulated that the Unemployment Insurance Advisory Committee (UIAC) should be composed of a chairman and not fewer than four nor more than six other members, "one of whom shall be a woman." For some reason, this stipulation, present in Section 83(1) of the 1940 Act at first reading, was dropped before final passage.[125] Nonetheless, a woman was appointed to the first UIAC formed in December 1940.[126] The aim of having one woman on the UIAC, however, was not to ensure that women workers were represented in proportion to their labour force participation. Instead, this gesture toward sexual equity reproduced a gender asymmetry widespread in western discourses of representation since the 18th century, wherein diversity and plurality have come to characterize the category 'men,' while women have been collapsed into the unified and homogeneous category of 'woman.'[127] Far removed from unemployment insurance as this practice might seem, its relevance can be discerned in the discussion about the composition of the UIAC. Memos exchanged among Commissioners and labour department officials spoke of the need to select representatives of employers, of labour,[128] of government, and one woman. Underlying this search was a conception of men being diverse, and of women being 'all the same.' Quite beyond consideration was the idea that women might also be divided into workers, employers, and government officials, and hence that there might be need to find representatives of women workers, women employers, women government officials. Otherwise dichotomized into women workers in the public sphere and dependent wives in the private domain,[129] women were reduced to a single category when it came to the representation of their public capacities.

Conclusion

On close examination, then, gender pervaded the 1934–40 debate on unemployment insurance, and was inscribed in every clause of the resulting legislation. The indirect limits on women's access to UI benefit derived in large measure (as Diana M. Pearce has argued with respect to unemployment compensation in the U.S.) from the mismatch between the normative worker targeted by the programme, the male breadwinner, and female labour market participation patterns. Less mobile than men, women were less likely to meet the available, able and willing to work requirements of UI regulations. Disproportionately concentrated in low-paying and irregular or intermittent jobs, women would have more difficulty fulfilling the statutory conditions for eligibility: the minimum earnings and minimum work-time qualifications. And as quitting a job voluntarily did not entitle one to unemployment insurance, also disqualified would be any woman who voted with her feet, and left a position because of intolerable work conditions or sexual harassment.[130]

Moreover, women were more or less closed out of the supervisory, adjudicative, inspectorate and decision-making levels of the UI administrative structure. The only possibility for women's needs and interests to receive a hearing was created by the requirement (later dropped) that one of the four to six members of the Unemployment Insurance Advisory Committee be a woman. While Canadian UI legislation contributed to the gendered complementarity of masculine independence and feminine dependence, and to the dichotomization of women into either single workers assimilated to the male norm or dependent wives/mothers, the gendered asymmetry or representation in UI's administrative structure contributed at the same time, paradoxically, to the conceptualization of men as multiple and diverse and to that of women as singular and uniform.

In most depictions of unemployment during the Depression, the plight was viewed as visited directly on men, indirectly on women. The gender crisis thus triggered was a crisis in masculinity, an undermining of what was believed to be the male identity's intrinsic tie to the role of head of household and provider. The parallel discourse on unemployment insurance similarly gave precedence to the wage earning of men, as their income-earning capacity was construed as central to the male's identity both as worker and husband/father. While the Left made liberal gestures toward an ideology of sexual equality, these were

constrained by the hegemonic assumptions framing the debate for all participants. Chief among these was the construction of breadwinning as a masculine
responsibility, a construction whose normative dimension was intensified in
the Depression despite its increased divergence from actuality. A complementary intensification occurred in the renewed enforcement of married women's
dependency. In contrast to men's, women's economic and familial identities
tended to be viewed as being divided if not contradictory. Separated into single,
independent working women on one side, and dependent wives/mothers on the
other, women's incorporation into UI provisions was twofold, and their access
to unemployment insurance benefit limited in both direct and indirect ways.
As workers assumed not to have dependants, women's lower contributions and
benefits were only a concern for those disturbed by explicit, formalized sex distinctions. That women's wages were lower than men's was accepted, by
government officials, as a fixed characteristic of the labour market. The framers
of the UI legislation sought to preserve, not eliminate, wage differentials of
both class and gender. That the unemployment insurance scheme would be
structured by the inequities women faced in the labour market was largely a
matter of indifference to them. As it was assumed that most women would be
provided for by a male relative, women's principal access to benefit was to be
through the indirect channel of dependants' allowances. The sleight-of-hand
provision for dependants in the 1940 Act, however, revealed the hollowness of
the government's commitment to the 'family wage.' Ideologically dominant as the
concept of the 'family wage' was, its rhetorical deployment by the makers of
social policy appears to have functioned more to disenfranchise married women
and enforce their dependence than to entitle dependent wives and children to
adequate provision.

Notes

The author wishes to thank Paula Bourne for her assistance with the research for this
paper, Dr. Jane Lewis for her assistance with its conceptualization, and Philinda Masters
for her assistance with its editing. Research for the paper was funded by a grant from the
SSHRCC "Women and Work" Strategic Grants Programme.

1. Canada, House of Commons, *Debates,* 22 January 1935, 85. Woodsworth was quoting from the *Winnipeg Free Press,* 18 December 1934.

2. See, for example, Michiel Horn, ed., *The Dirty Thirties: Canadians in the Great
   Depression* (Toronto 1972); A.E. Safarian, *The Canadian Economy in the Great
   Depression* (Toronto 1970); H. Blair Neatby, *The Politics of Chaos: Canada in the
   Thirties* (Toronto 1972).

3. Abraham Albert Heaps, a Labour spokesman, made one of the rare inclusions of
   women along with men among the unemployed when, in the parliamentary debate on unemployment insurance of January 1935, he referred to the "vast numbers
   of men and women at present out of work." Canada, House of Commons, *Debates,*

29 January 1935, 288. Beyond Agnes Macphail, one of the only other MPs to express concern for the plight of unemployed women was Charles Grant MacNeil, whose concern for "single, unemployed women transients" focused less on their material deprivation than on their lack of protection from sexual exploitation, which he believed would result in moral ruin and the attendant problems of unmarried motherhood and venereal disease. ("The problem of unmarried mothers is becoming more acute, the problem of illicit alliances is more acute.... the problem of venereal disease is becoming more acute.") Canada, House of Commons, *Debates,* 8 February 1937, 670–1; 2 March 1937, 1434.

4. See Wendy Kozol's analysis of the use by the U.S. New Deal Resettlement Administration (later Farm Security Administration) of photographs of mothers in rags holding children in their arms in the doorways of shacks and other makeshift shelters to symbolize the poor's adherence to patriarchal ideals of family and motherhood, and thereby establish that the poor were deserving of relief. Wendy Kozol, "Madonnas of the Fields: Photography, Gender, and 1930s Farm Relief," *Genders,* 2 (Summer 1988), 1–23.

5. For example, in her study of family violence through examination of the records of child protection agencies in Boston, Linda Gordon has disclosed that social workers "considered the stresses of the Depression as mitigating circumstances of (his) violence as they did not in the case of (her) neglect." Linda Gordon, *Heroes of Their own Lives—The Politics and History of Family Violence: Boston 1880–1960* (New York 1988).

6. In parliamentary debate on the National Employment Commission's provision for a committee on women's employment, Agnes Macphail rose to comment on how little attention the House had paid to the plight of unemployed women. To make her case, she cited the fact that there were no camps for single destitute women as there were for men. "The problem of the young and old unemployed women should be given careful consideration," she argued, "because it has been given very little consideration in the past in connection with any projects to employ unemployed persons on public works and so on. One would almost think," she concluded, "that there was no problem in connection with unemployed women; that it did not exist, when in fact it is a serious problem." Canada, House of Commons, *Debates,* 7 April 1936, 1907–8.

7. James Struthers, *'No Fault of Their Own': Unemployment and the Canadian Welfare State 1914–1941* (Toronto 1983).

8. When I speak of gender as a fundamental category of social historical analysis, I understand gender to encompass all discourses, practices and structures shaping (and shaped by) the prescribed and prevailingly actualized social relations between the sexes. See, among others, Joan Kelly, "The Social Relation of the Sexes: Methodological Implications of Women's History," in *Women, History, and Theory: The Essays of Joan Kelly* (Chicago 1984), 1–18; Joan W. Scott, "Gender: A Useful Category of Historical Analysis," *American Historical Review,* 915 (December 1986), 1053–75; Joan Wallach Scott, *Gender and the Politics of History* (New York 1988).

9. There were only three dissenting votes. See Struthers, *'No Fault',* 129.

10. National Archives of Canada [NAC], RG40, Records of the Department of Insurance, Vol. 24, file 7, Extract from Book II of the Recommendations of the Royal Commission on Dominion-Provincial Relations. Not submitted until February 1940.

11. Struthers, *'No Fault',* 197.

12. Canada, House of Commons, *Debates,* 18 June 1940, 864–5; 11 July 1940, 1532.

13. Not to be confused with Sir Alfred Watson, the British Government Actuary in the 1920s and early 1930s.

14. In a recent article, Alice Kessler-Harris takes a very different approach to the discussion among working people during the Depression as to "who was and was not entitled to work." Conflating gender perception with a notion of separate spheres, Kessler-Harris argues that it was neither of those but rather working people's concern for the integrity of "the family" and a working-class conception of justice that shaped working people's responses to the Depression. "In the code of honour of working people, jobs belonged to the providers." And the concept of the provider could include "widows, single women and married women with unemployed or disabled husbands as well." How does this qualification relate to the popular perception that "a male who worked would ... 'spend his income to the support of his family while the [married?] woman spends for permanent waves, lip sticks'?" Did "males who had other means of support" really face "the same criticism as married women?" Kessler-Harris calls "not gender specific" the perception that men should be "'men and provide for their mothers, sisters, wives and daughters, and womanhood ... restored to its pedestal motherhood'." What she means is that such a view could be and was held by both men and women. But who would claim that a gender ideology is held by members of only one sex? In her rush to downplay or "decenter" the category of gender, Kessler-Harris sometimes goes too far, as in her claim that "one of the nation's first and most immediate responses [to the Depression-triggered "discussion of who was and was not entitled to work"] was to exclude the spouses of wage earners from the labour force." Male spouses? On the basis of her own evidence, one could conclude that the conception of who deserved employment was as deeply gendered as the notion of "the family" was patriarchal. Alice Kessler-Harris, "Gender Ideology in Historical Reconstruction: A Case Study from the 1930s," *Gender & History,* 1 (Spring 1989), 31–49.

15. NAC, RG 40, Series 3, Vol. 24, file 4, The Employment and Social Insurance Act, Bill 8, Passed by the House of Commons, 12 March 1935.

16. L. Richter, "Limitations of Unemployment Insurance," *Dalhousie Review,* 18 (July 1938), 229–44.

17. NAC, RG 40, Series 3, Vol. 24, file 5, The National Employment Insurance Bill, 1938.

18. NAC, RG 40, Vol. 24, file Unemployment Insurance (6): Drafting 1938 Bill, Watson's Actuarial Report of 15 March 1938.

19. Ruth Roach Pierson, Introduction to Chapter Six, "Paid Work," in Beth Light and Ruth Roach Pierson, eds. and comps., *No Easy Road: Women in Canada 1920s–1960s* (forthcoming).

20. The National Employment Commission's "Summarized Report on Co-ordination of Aid" stated: "Of 3,375,000 women and girls fifteen years of age and over, who might by reason of age be eligible for gainful occupation a large proportion are married and are, therefore, not seeking employment or gainful occupation." NAC, RG 27, Records of the Department of Labour, Vol. 3358, file 12, "Summarized Report on Co-ordination of Aid," 20 March 1937, 39.

21. With reference to postwar Britain, Denise Riley has written that "the dominant rhetoric described the figure of woman as mother and woman as worker as diametrically opposed and refused to consider the possibility of their combination." Denise Riley, "Some Peculiarities of Social Policy concerning Women in Wartime and Postwar Britain," in Margaret Randolph Higonnet, Jane Jenson, Sonya Michel, and Margaret Collins Weitz, eds., *Behind the Lines: Gender and the Two World Wars* (New Haven 1987), 260.

22. NAC, MG 28, I 10 Canadian Council on Social Development, Vol. 63, file 497, Aid to Dependent Mothers and Children in Canada: Social Policy Behind our Legislation, 1942.

23. Those religious orders providing sanctuary for single mothers and their offspring tended to accept the death of the 'illegitimate' infant, the incarnation of the sin of its parents, as a 'blessing.' See Andrée Lévesque, "Deviants Anonymous: Single Mothers at the Hôpital de la Miséricorde in Montreal, 1929–1939," in Katherine Arnup, Andrée Lévesque and Ruth Roach Pierson, eds., *Delivering Motherhood: Maternal Ideologies and Practices in the 19th and 20th Centuries* (London 1990), 108–25.

24. Veronica Strong-Boag, *The New Day Recalled: Lives of Girls and Women in English Canada, 1919–1939* (Toronto 1988), 62–3.

25. Pierson, Introduction to Chapter Six "Paid Work," in *No Easy Road.*

26. According to Margaret Hobbs' research for her PhD thesis on women and work in the Depression, University of Toronto, forthcoming.

27. See, for an example from the USA, Lois Rita Helmbold, "Beyond the Family Economy: Black and White Working-Class Women During the Great Depression," *Feminist Studies,* 13 (Fall 1987), 629–55. Thanks to Margaret Hobbs for this reference.

28. Ruth Roach Pierson, Introduction to Chapter Five "Unpaid Work," in *No Easy Road;* Hilary Land, "The Family Wage," *Feminist Review,* 6 (1980), 55–77; and Michèle Barrett and Mary McIntosh, "The 'Family Wage': Some Problems for Socialists and Feminists," *Capital & Class,* 11 (1980), 51–72; Martha May, "The Historical Problem of the Family Wage: The Ford Motor Company and the Five Dollar Day," *Feminist Studies,* 8 (Summer 1982), 399–424.

29. Or her substitute. As Sonya Michel has noted with respect to the United States, "public policy during the Depression upheld the ideal of the conventional family with a wage-earning father and housekeeping mother." Sonya Michel, "American Women and the Discourse of the Democratic Family in World War II," in Higonnet *et al., Behind the Lines,* 156.

30. See particularly Leonard Marsh, Part IV: "Family Needs," *Report on Social Security for Canada 1943,* with a new Introduction by the Author and a Preface by Michael Bliss (Toronto 1975), 195–232.

31. A minority within the political Left were sympathetic to the concerns of married women workers. Nonetheless, the view that came to predominate was one that favoured the 'family wage.' See Joan Sangster, *Dreams of Equality: Women on the Canadian Left, 1920–1950* (Toronto 1989).

32. Sangster, *Dreams of Equality.*

33. Riley, "Some Peculiarities of Social Policy concerning Women," 261.

34. Canada, House of Commons, *Debates,* 18 February 1935, 914; 8 March 1935, 1537–8.

35. NAC, RG 40, Series 3, Vol. 24, file 6 (1935–39), A Summary of the 1938 Draft Unemployment Insurance Bill.

36. NAC, RG 40, Vol. 24, file Unemployment Insurance (7), D. Christie Tait, "Report on a Proposed Unemployment Insurance Bill in Canada," n.d. (probably early 1938).

37. NAC, MG 28, I55, Papers of the Canadian Federation of Business and Professional Women's Clubs, Vol. 43, Minute Book 1, Minutes of the 5th Convention, CFBPWC, Calgary, 3-6 July 1935, 9–10.

38. At its 31 January 1935, meeting. NAC, MG 26, K, R.B. Bennett Papers, Vol. 793, Reel M-1461, 503874.

39. According to data used by the Department of Insurance in 1940, 39.8 per cent of male wage-earners were married in 1921 (58.4 per cent were single) and 40.4 per cent were married in 1931 (57.6 per cent were single). NAC, RG 40, Vol. 24, file 6, A Summary of the Draft Unemployment Insurance Bill (1938), January 1940.

40. NAC, RG 40, Series 3, Vol. 24, file 7, "The Principles of Flat and Graded Employee Contributions and Benefit, as Applied to a Projected Canadian Unemployment Insurance Scheme," memo attached to a letter to A.D. Watson from Gerald H. Brown, Assistant Deputy Minister, Department of Labour, 8 May 1940.

41. Catharine MacKinnon has identified the tendency to establish men as the norm against which women are measured as a salient feature of law and other social discourses and institutions. Women, she has written, "have to meet either the male standard for males or the male standard for females." Catharine MacKinnon, *Feminism Unmodified: Discourses on Life and Law* (Cambridge 1987), 71–2. I am grateful to Sherene Razack for bringing this point to my attention in "Feminism and the Law: The Women's Legal Education and Action Fund," PhD thesis, University of Toronto, 1989.

42. Canada, House of Commons, *Debates,* 12 February 1935, 768.

43. Canada, House of Commons, *Debates,* 18 February 1935, 914–15. Apparently Woodsworth was unaware of any contradiction in his espousal in the same speech of a principle of "social justice" that contravened the principle of the 'family wage,' namely that "men and women should receive equal remuneration for work of equal value."

44. Canada, House of Commons, *Debates,* 9 April 1935, 2565–66.

45. NAC, RG 40, Vol. 24, file Unemployment Insurance (6), Eric Stangroom, "Some Aspects and Anomalies of the British Unemployment Scheme as They Might Relate to Possible Canadian Legislation," December 1939.

46. NAC, RG 40, Vol. 24, file Unemployment Insurance (6), "Notes on the Unemployment Insurance Draft Bill (1938)," n.a.

47. NAC, RG 40, Vol. 24, file Unemployment Insurance (6), Watson's Actuarial Report, 15 March 1938.

48. NAC, RG 40, Series 3, Vol. 24, file (6), A Summary of the Draft Unemployment Insurance Bill (1938), January 1940. In 1915 the Fabian Women's Group in Britain had estimated that 50 per cent of working women were partially or wholly maintaining others. The validity of their sample was questioned by B. Seebohm Rowntree and Frank D. Stuart, who put the figure at 12 per cent. Ellen Smith, *Wage Earning Women and their Dependants* (London 1915), and B. Seebohm Rowntree and Frank D. Stuart, *The Responsibility of Women Workers for Dependants* (Oxford 1921). Thanks to Jane E. Lewis for these references.

49. NAC, RG 40, Series 3, Vol. 24, file 6, A Summary of the Draft Unemployment Insurance Bill (1938), January 1940, author's emphasis.

50. NAC, RG 40, Series 3, Vol. 24, file 7, "The Principles of Flat and Graded Employee Contributions and Benefits, as Applied to a Projected Canadian Unemployment Insurance Scheme," memo attached to a letter to A.D. Watson from G.H. Brown, ADM/Labour, 8 May 1940.

51. *Ibid.,* 3.

52. L. Richter, "Limitations of Unemployment Insurance."

53. NAC, RG 40, Vol. 24, file Unemployment Insurance (7), D. Christie Tait, "Report on a Proposed Unemployment Insurance Bill in Canada," probably early 1938.

54. Struthers. *'No Fault',* 6–7, 85, 100, 135, 147, 181, 188, 205, 207, 211–12.

55. NAC, RG 40, Series 3, Vol. 24, file 7, "The Problem of Dependency in Unemployment Insurance," received by Watson from Eric Stangroom, 5 June 1940.

56. NAC, RG 40, Vol. 24, file Unemployment Insurance (7), D. Christie Tait, "Report on a Proposed Unemployment Insurance Bill in Canada," 45.

57. NAC, RG 40, Series 3, Vol. 24, file 7, "The Problem of Dependency in Unemployment Insurance," received by Watson from Eric Stangroom, 5 June 1940.

58. Canada, House of Commons, *Debates,* 16 July 1940, 1786.

59. NAC, RG 40, Series 3, Vol. 24, file 7, Memo. from Watson to Gerald R. Brown, Assistant Deputy Minister, Department of Labour, 6 May 1940.

60. NAC RG 40, Series 3, Vol. 24, file 7, "The Principles of Flat and Graded Employee Contributions and Benefit, as Applied to a Projected Canadian Unemployment Insurance Scheme," memo attached to a letter to Watson from G. H. Brown, ADM/Labour, 8 May 1940. In a comparison of the 1935 and 1940 Acts, the following argument was advanced in support of abandoning the flat rate system of calculating contributions and benefits: "If circumstances compel an insured man to subsist on benefits for several months, the man of high income (within the scope of the Act) will suffer greater hardship than the man of low income because he will have higher obligations in the way of rent and other fixed expenses." NAC, RG 50, Records of the Unemployment Insurance Commission, Vol. 24, file 1-2-2-9, Memorandum of 7 May 1940.

61. Cited by Woodsworth. Canada, House of Commons, Debates, 8 March 1935, 1534.

62. NAC, RG 40, Series 3, Vol. 24, file 7, "The Principles of Flat and Graded Employee Contributions and Benefit, as Applied to a Projected Canadian Unemployment Insurance Scheme," memo attached to a letter to Watson from G. H. Brown, ADM/Labour, 8 May 1940.

63. NAC, RG 40, Vol. 24, file Unemployment Insurance (6), Stangroom's memo re. Some Aspects and Anomalies of the British Unemployment Scheme as They Might Relate to Possible Canadian Legislation, December 1939, 16–17.

64. In resolution passed by the Ottawa Women's Liberal Club on 31 January 1935. NAC, MG 26, K, R.B. Bennett Papers, Vol. 793, Reel M-1461, 503874.

65. *Ibid.*

66. NAC, RG 40, Vol. 24, file Unemployment Insurance (6), Watson's response to Stangroom's Memo. re. British Scheme, 1939, 7.

67. NAC, RG 40, Series 3, Vol. 24, file 7, "The Principles of Flat and Graded Employee Contributions and Benefit, As Applied to a Projected Canadian Insurance Scheme," memo attached to a letter to Watson from G.H. Brown, ADM/Labour, 8 May 1940.

68. *Ibid.*

69. *Ibid.*

70. See Jane Lewis, "Dealing with Dependency: State Practices and Social Realities, 1870–1945," in Jane Lewis, ed., *Women's Welfare, Women's Right* (London 1983), 26–30.

71. NAC, RG 40, Series 3, Vol. 24, file 7, "The Problem of Dependency in Unemployment Insurance," received by Watson from Eric Stangroom, Department of Labour, 5 June 1940.

72. Watson, the Chief Actuary, Department of Insurance, defended the inclusion of dependants' benefits in the 1940 UI plan on the grounds that, although they depended on marital status and dependants, because these variables were taken into account regardless of need in the sense of 'absolute' need, they did not contravene the "insurance principle" of predictable need. NAC, RG 40, Series 3, Vol. 24, file 7, Memo from Watson to G.H. Brown, ADM/Labour, 16 January 1940.

73. *Ibid.*

74. In June 1934, Dominion Actuary Watson more or less advised Bennett that it was an inopportune time to introduce UI. "The plain fact is that until means are found of effecting greater stability than heretofore in social and economic conditions, an unemployment insurance fund is liable to be called upon to bear burdens so uncertain and so incalculable as to set at naught the best considered rates of contributions." NAC, RG 40, Series 3, Vol. 24, file 3, Actuarial Report on Contributions Required under "The Employment and Social Insurance Act," prepared by A.D. Watson, 14 June 1934.

75. In the 1935 debate in the House, Woodsworth criticized the proposed UI legislation for not meeting "the needs of the great mass of the unemployed." Canada, House of Commons, *Debates,* 29 January 1935, 284.

76. L. Richter, "General Principles and European Experience," *The Employment and Social Insurance Bill,* Proceedings of the May 1935 Meeting of the Canadian Economics and Political Science Association, *The Canadian Journal of Economics and Political Science,* 1 (1935), 447. See also A.W. Neill's discussion of Section 14 of the 1935 bill. Canada, House of Commons, *Debates,* 12 February 1935, 771.

77. W.J. Couper, "A Comment From the Point of View of American Opinion," *The Employment and Social Insurance Bill,* Proceedings of the May 1935 Meeting of the Economics and Political Science Association, *Canadian Journal of Economics and Political Science,* 1 (1935), 455.

78. In fact, when Family Allowances were implemented in 1944, even though the cheques were made out to mothers, the amounts were insufficient to counteract the general tendency of Canada's social organization which encouraged women's dependence on men.

79. NAC, RG 40, Vol. 24, file Unemployment Insurance (7), Memo to Watson from Stangroom, 10 May 1940. See also RG 40, Series 3, Vol. 24, file 7, Memo on "The Problem of Dependency in Unemployment Insurance," received by Watson from Stangroom, 5 June 1940.

80. As Eric Stangroom, Department of Labour, responded in a letter dated 17 October 1940, to a query from Angus MacInnis, C.C.F. M.P. from Vancouver, "Personally, I feel that as wages take no account of dependency some system of family allowances might be the proper solution, leaving unemployment insurance to compensate for loss of earnings." NAC, RG 27, Vol. 3454, file 4-1, part 1.

81. NAC, RG 40, Series 3, Vol. 24, file 7, Memo on "The Problem of Dependency in Unemployment Insurance," received by Watson from Stangroom, 5 June 1940. In both the 1935 Act and the 1938 Bill, the total benefit paid to claimants could not exceed 80 per cent of a person's average weekly pay while employed. Thus, for example, under the 1935 Act, a man 21 years of age or older, earning $12 a week, would have been eligible for a maximum benefit package of $9.60 which would have entitled him to draw, beyond the basic benefit of $6.00 for himself, the adult dependant benefit of $2.70 plus benefit for only one dependent child at 90 cents. Because the flat benefit rate for a woman 21 or over was $5.10, while the adult dependant and dependent child benefit rates remained constant, the average weekly pay for an adult working woman would have needed to be approximately $11 in order for her to collect, beyond her own UI benefit, dependants' benefits for one adult and one child.

82. People in low-paid and irregular employment would have faced great difficulty fulfilling the entry requirements for UI under either the 1935 or 1940 Acts or the 1938 draft bill. Introducing a daily rate of contribution option in the 1938 bill and 1940 Act overcame the difficulties with the definition of "continuous employment" encountered when only a weekly contribution was possible, as in the 1935 Act. NAC, RG 50, Vol. 24, file 1-2-2-9, Comparison of 1935 and 1940 Acts, Memorandum from J. MacKenzie, 7 May 1940. The 1940 Act, however, established an earnings floor of 90 cents per day below which a person would not be eligible to collect benefits. NAC, RG 40, Series 3, Vol. 24, file 8, First Reading UI Bill, July 1940, Section 19 (3).

83. NAC, RG 40, Vol. 24, file Unemployment Insurance (7), Memo to Watson from Stangroom, 10 May 1940.

84. NAC, RG 40, Series 3, Vol. 24, file 7, Memo. from Watson to Gerald R. Brown, Assistant Deputy Minister, Department of Labour, 16 January 1940.

85. NAC, RG 40, Series 3, Vol. 26, file 3-25-2, vol. 5, A.D. Watson's Comments on General Review of the UI Act, 1940 by R.G. Barclay, Director of U.I., Parts I & II, as submitted to N. McKellan for comment, 17 February 1951.

86. *Ibid.*

87. NAC, RG 40, Series 3, Vol. 24, file 7, Memo. from Watson to Gerald R. Brown, ADM/Labour, 16 January 1940.

88. NAC, RG 40, Vol. 24, file Unemployment Insurance (6), Eric Stangroom, "Some Aspects and Anomalies of the British Unemployment Scheme As They Might Relate to Possible Canadian Legislation," December 1939, 10, 27.

89. NAC, RG 40, Series 3, Vol. 24, file 7, "The Problem of Dependency in Unemployment Insurance," received by Watson from Eric Stangroom, 5 June 1940.

90. NAC, RG 40, Series 3, Vol. 26, file 3-25-2, vol. 5, A.D. Watson's Comments on General Review of the UI Act, 1940 by R.G. Barclay, Director of UI, Parts I & II, as submitted to N. McKellan for comment, 17 February 1951. The compromise proposal of setting the graded contributions and benefits rate for persons without dependants at 85 per cent of the total for those with dependants was sent to Watson for his appraisal by Gerald H. Brown, ADM/Labour, on 12 July 1940. NAC, RG 40, Series 3, Vol. 24, file 8, letter to Watson from Brown, 12 July 1940.

91. Senator L. Coté was incensed that the differential between those with and those without dependants was so small and threatened to "blow up the whole thing" in the Senate. According to Watson, he was able to reassure the Senator that, "when the opportunity should arise, the differential would be widened." NAC, RG 40, Series 3, Vol. 26, file 3-25-2, vol. 5, Watson's Comments on General Review of the UI Act, 1940 by R.G. Barclay, Director of UI, Parts I & II, as submitted to N. McKellan for comment, 17 February 1951. See also Canada, Senate, *Debates,* 1 August 1940, 412.

92. *Ibid.*

93. Struthers. *'No Fault',* 201.

94. NAC, RG 40, Series 3, Vol. 24, file 2, Wolfenden Memo. re. Married Women, enclosed in a letter to Watson dated 11 December 1934.

95. NAC, RG 40, Series 3, Vol. 24, file 4, The Employment and Social Insurance Act, Bill 8, Passed by the House of Commons, 12 March 1935. The subsequent history of the treatment of married woman workers within UI legislation, complicated, if not to say tortuous, as it is, is the subject of a separate study.

96. Specifically Woodsworth. Canada, House of Commons, *Debates,* 18 February 1935, 915.

97. In a comparison of the 1935 Act and the 1938 bill, Watson singled out, as one of the major differences, the latter's "determination of benefits wholly on the ratio rule principle, instead of partially on that principle as in the 1935 Act and in the British Act." NAC, RG 40, Series 3, Vol. 24, file 8, Memo to MacNamara from Watson, 6 December 1940.

98. NAC, RG 40, Series 3, Vol. 24, file 6, A Summary of the 1938 Draft Unemployment Insurance Bill.

99. NAC, RG 40, Series 3, Vol. 24, file 8, Memo to MacNamara from Watson, 6 December 1940.

100. Canada, House of Commons, *Debates,* 26 July 1940, 1990.

101. NAC, RG 40, Vol. 24, file Unemployment Insurance (7), D. Christie Tait, "Report on a Proposed Unemployment Insurance Bill in Canada," early 1938, 40.

102. *Ibid.,* 42.

103. NAC, RG 40, Series 3, Vol. 24, file 1, Watson's (Revised) Actuarial Report on Contributions, 3 November 1934.

104. NAC, RG 40, Vol. 24, file Unemployment Insurance (7), D. Christie Tait's 1938 Report on UI Bill, 2–6.

105. Frederick George Sanderson, Liberal M.P. for Perth South, Ontario, criticized the Act for its treatment of part-time workers. Canada, House of Commons, *Debates,* 19 February 1935, 990.

106. Canada, House of Commons, *Debates,* 19 July 1940, 1786.

107. NAC, RG 27, Vol. 886, file 8-9-26, part 1, Memo re. Amendments to the Unemployment Insurance Act, 1940, to Chairman and Members of the Unemployment Insurance Advisory Committee from L.J. Trottier, Chief Commissioner, 21 February 1945.

108. First Schedule, Part II (n), 1935 Act: First Schedule, Part II (m), 1938 Draft Bill and 1940 Act.

109. First Schedule, Part II (l), 1935 Act; First Schedule, Part II (k), 1938 Draft Bill and 1940 Act.

110. NAC, RG 40, Vol. 24, file Unemployment Insurance (7), D. Christie Tait's 1938 Report on UI, 32. Another argument developed to justify excepting the teaching profession from UI was that the administration of unemployment insurance was to be organized around an employment service infrastructure, and one could hardly expect a teacher to bypass boards of education and seek placement through an employment office. Canada, House of Commons, *Debates,* 26 July 1940, 1988.

111. First Schedule, Part II, (i), (h), (g), 1935 Act; First Schedule, Part II, (h), (g), (f), 1938 Draft Bill and 1940 Act.

112. Canada, House of Commons, *Debates,* 29 July 1940, 2056.

113. *Ibid.*

114. NAC, RG 40, Series 3, Vol. 24, file 3, Memo. on Excepted Employments, anon., n.d., presumably by Watson in early 1935.

115. Canada, House of Commons, *Debates,* 19 July 1940, 1781.

116. Canada, House of Commons, *Debates,* 26 July 1940, 1988.

117. NAC, RG 40, Vol. 24, file Unemployment Insurance (6), Notes on the Unemployment Insurance Draft Bill (1938), n.a.

118. NAC, RG 40, Vol. 24, file Unemployment Insurance (7), D. Christie Tait, "Report on a Proposed Unemployment Insurance Bill," 27.

119. See Pierson, Introduction to Chapter Six, "Paid Work," in *No Easy Road.*

120. Section 20 (1) (iii) of 1935 Act; Section 16 (1) (iii) of 1938 Draft Bill; and Section 28 (iii) of 1940 Act.

121. According to English Common Law and the Quebec Civil Code, the principle of "the unity of domicile" required that "a wife's domicile, like that of her minor children, [be] that of the husband." It changed as he changed his domicile and not as she changed hers. Indeed, the husband could change his domicile [her "dependent" domicile] against the wife's will "or even without her knowledge." Canada, Royal Commission on the Status of Women in Canada, *Report* (Ottawa 1970), 236–7.

122. Canada, House of Commons, *Debates,* 12 February 1935, 771.

123. NAC, RG 40, Series 3, Vol. 24, file 8, 1940 Bill.

124. Canada, House of Commons, *Debates,* 21 February 1935.

125. NAC, RG 40, Series 3, Vol. 24, file 8, First Reading UI Bill, July 1940; Canada, "The Unemployment Insurance Act, 1940," *Acts of the Parliament of the Dominion of Canada* (Ottawa 1940), c. 44, s. 83 (1).

126. NAC, RG 27, Vol. 163, file 612-01 (68–4), Memo of 3 December 1940 from Minister of Labour recommending appointments to the Unemployment Insurance Advisory Committee. The woman was Miss Estelle Hewson, Secretary of the Border Branch of the Canadian Red Cross, Windsor, Ontario. NAC, RG 50, Vol. 57, file U05— Miss Estelle Hewson, Letter to Dr. W.A. Mackintosh, Chairman, UIC, from Estelle Hewson, 27 December 1940.

127. The Encyclopaedists and philosophes, like Rousseau, called for the diversification of the category of 'man' to reflect the diversity of 'men,' differentiated, as they were seen to be, "by religions, governments, laws, customs, prejudices, climates." Rousseau, *Lettre à D' Alembert* (Garnier-Flamarion edition), 67, quoted in Michèle Le Doeuff, "Pierre Roussel's Chiasmas: from imaginary knowledge to the learned imagination," *Ideology & Consciousness,* 9 (Winter 1981/82), 53. Then the French Revolution abolished the division of society into orders that had applied to women as well as to men and replaced it with a system that drew distinctions among men according to property and occupation but introduced the political treatment of women *en bloc*. It is in that "historic passage from one system of discrimination (by estate) to another (by sex)" that diversity and plurality came to characterize the category 'men' while unity and homogeneity came to characterize the category 'woman.' Le Doeuff, 52.

128. The Unemployment Insurance Act stipulated that "there shall be appointed at least one [member] after consultation with organizations representative of employed persons and an equal number after consultation with organizations representative of employers." "The Unemployment Insurance Act, 1940," s. 83 (3).

129. By definition not in the labour market because not gainfully employed and hence not eligible for unemployment insurance.

130. Diana M. Pearce, "Toil and Trouble: Women, Workers and Unemployment Compensation," *Signs,* 10 (Spring 1985), 439–59.

CHAPTER

10 WILLIAM LYON MACKENZIE KING

If political success is measured by longevity, then Mackenzie King's twenty-two years as Canadian Prime Minister make him a very successful politician indeed. Despite this, few Canadian political leaders have received such widely varying treatment at the hands of historians. To some, King represents the epitome of political craftsmanship, the skilled leader with his mind always on the elusive goal of national unity. For those who subscribe to this point of view, King's handling of the conscription issue during the Second World War was his crowning achievement.

King's detractors, among historians, cannot challenge his political success, but they insist that King's goal was less national unity than the success of his own political career, and they argue that the means he used to achieve his ends were petty, unscrupulous, and sometimes immoral. Far from providing the country with strong leadership, he was a model of ambiguity and indecision: "conscription if necessary, but not necessarily conscription."

A further complication for historians, in attempting to assess Mackenzie King, is his somewhat bizarre personality. Shortly after his death, stories about his experiments with spiritualism began to circulate. His extraordinarily extensive diaries, which he had directed should be destroyed after his death (an instruction which his executors decided to ignore), provide a unique insight into the private personality of a political leader.

The first reading in this chapter is by Blair Neatby, author of all but the first volume of the authorized biography of Mackenzie King. In it Neatby argues, in the context of the Great Depression, that King provided real leadership. Although not a radical in any sense, King was "the conciliator in politics" who could hold his government and his party and his country together in a time of crisis.

The second reading, by Colonel C.P. Stacey, is a chapter from a book in which Stacey attempted to analyse what he termed "the private world of Mackenzie King."

436

Some of Stacey's conclusions, particularly those relating to King's sexual proclivities, are controversial and have been challenged. In the reading reprinted here, Stacey examines the question of the extent to which King's public policies were influenced by spiritualism during the Second World War.

The author of the third reading, Joy Esberey, disagrees with Stacey that King led "a double life." Rather, she claims, "the separation of the private and public King is invalid." Drawing on psychological concepts, she argues that King's political career can only be understood by viewing his public and private lives as integrated rather than contradictory. The private life becomes an explanatory tool rather than something to be explained away.

Suggestions for Further Reading

Dawson, R. MacGregor, *William Lyon Mackenzie King: A Political Biography*. Volume I. Toronto: University of Toronto Press, 1958.

Granatstein, J.L., *Canada's War: The Politics of the Mackenzie King Government*. Toronto: Oxford, 1975.

Neatby, H. Blair, "Mackenzie King and French Canada," *Journal of Canadian Studies*, XI, no. 1 (February 1976), 3–13.

_____, *William Lyon Mackenzie King*, 2 volumes. Toronto: University of Toronto Press, 1963, 1966.

Whitaker, Reginald, "The Liberal Corporatist Ideas of Mackenzie King," *Labour/Le Travailleur*, II (1977), 137–169.

_____, "Political Thought and Political Action in Mackenzie King," *Journal of Canadian Studies*, XIII, no. 4 (Winter 1978–79), 40–60.

WILLIAM LYON MACKENZIE KING: THE CONCILIATOR IN POLITICS

H. Blair Neatby

Mackenzie King is one of the best known and least liked of all our prime ministers. Even today he is a controversial figure; a man who had none of the obvious qualities of a leader and yet a man who survived for an incredibly long time in a very hazardous occupation—he was leader of the Liberal party for almost thirty years and prime minister for over twenty. And not only that, he left an indelible stamp on the country. Whether for good or ill, today's Canada is partly King's making.

Our concern is with the Mackenzie King of the 1930s. Even in those years his contemporaries were puzzled by the man. R.J. Manion, a Conservative opponent,

From *The Politics of Chaos: Canada in the Thirties* (Toronto: Copp Clark Pitman, 1986), 73-87. Reprinted by permission of Copp Clark Pitman.

commented that King was unpopular in the House of Commons and among most Canadians. How could such a man win elections? Manion could only suggest that he was an "opportunist, *par excellence*" and also very lucky.[1]

Prominent Liberals were just as ambivalent. J.W. Dafoe of the *Free Press*, for example, was a very partisan critic of R.B. Bennett but he also had reservations about King. Dafoe never sided with the Liberals who wanted to get rid of King— and there were many such Liberals in the early 1930s—but on the other hand he was never prepared to go farther than to say that King, for all his weaknesses, was the best man available. Most party leaders rouse more enthusiasm.

What is the explanation for this ambivalence? The simple answer is that Mackenzie King himself *was* an ambivalent figure. His career is strewn with apparent contradictions and inconsistencies. He seemed to be flabby and indecisive; never yes, never no, always maybe or partly, always the smoke screen of qualifications which concealed any decision, or hid the fact that no decision had been made. And yet this apparently indecisive man picked forceful and powerful colleagues; Gardiner, Dunning, Ralston, C.D. Howe—these men were not nonentities. What is more, King controlled and dominated these men. Ralston he dismissed abruptly, without warning. And C.D. Howe once said that the key to King's career was that King was a leader—a telling remark coming from C.D. Howe! The ambivalence shows up in King's policies too. He posed as a social reformer: the first Minister of Labour, the industrial consultant, the workingman's friend. And yet his record of social legislation is a meagre one, and is as easily explained by political opportunism as by political conviction.

King's political longevity becomes more credible if we begin with his concept of political leadership. King did not believe in imposing his will or his policies on his party; he was not an authoritarian leader like Bennett. King believed that his party, and his cabinet, had to be consulted and had to be convinced before a policy could be adopted. He believed in participatory democracy, at least within the party. This didn't mean that he suppressed his own opinions—quite often it meant that he converted others to the policy he preferred. On other occasions, however, it could mean agreement on a policy or a compromise for which he had little enthusiasm. Political leadership for him was like being a conciliator in labour disputes; the successful conciliator is one who comes to understand the point of view of both sides, and who can thus suggest a compromise or a settlement which both sides can accept. The conciliator is not a passive bystander. He tries to create a satisfactory agreement, a consensus. He contributes his own ideas as well as his techniques for arriving at agreement. Although the final outcome cannot be dictated it is often the result of persuasion.

Mackenzie King's reaction to the depression illustrates his activities as a conciliator. Initially King, like many of his contemporaries, saw the depression as a temporary recession. It could not be ignored but at the same time it did not seem to demand drastic or radical measures. King, in the Liberal tradition, believed at first that the economy would recover with little help from governments.

The important thing, from his point of view, was not to obstruct the process but to allow economic laws to operate. Canadian Liberals saw the protective tariff as the worst form of obstruction. By creating artificial barriers to trade, the tariff distorted national economies, and at the same time taxed the poor for the benefit of the rich. It was natural therefore for King in the early 1930s to blame the depression on the tariff which Bennett had just raised to unprecedented levels. Even as late as 1932 King was still focusing on the tariff as the real villain. In the session of that year the Liberal amendment to the budget declared that lower tariffs were "essential to a revival of trade, and improvement of business, and the return of prosperity."

By 1932, however, the traditional emphasis on the tariff no longer satisfied all Liberals. Western Liberals, for example, once so obsessed with the tariff issue, no longer cared. Lower tariffs might reduce the cost of farm machinery but what did this matter when wheat prices were too low to cover the costs of production, much less meet mortgage payments and provide a living? Most westerners by this time had decided that the depression posed new and urgent problems and could only be resolved by new and radical measures. Many of them had come to the radical and almost revolutionary conclusion that the answer lay, not in lower tariffs, but in inflation. Inflation would raise the prices of farm products. It would also raise the prices of the goods which farmers purchased but there would still be a net gain. Most farmers had mortgages on their land and machinery, mortgages based on the inflated prices of the 1920s but which now had to be repaid when dollars were scarce. Inflation, by lowering the value of money, would redress the balance, and make it possible to pay debts in devalued currency. Even in 1932 King had been under strong pressure from western Liberals to go beyond the tariff and opt for some form of inflation. Eastern Liberals were not sympathetic to the idea. They did not represent a debtor community; deliberate inflation was to them shockingly dangerous and even immoral. How could business survive if money had no stable value? There could be no Liberal consensus on inflation under these conditions and so King pacified the westerners by leaving inflation an open question. In the 1932 session at least, the party stayed united on its tariff resolution.

King, however, was sensitive to shifting political currents. Personally he would have been happy to continue to concentrate on the tariff issue; inflation seemed to him morally wrong and unlikely to foster economic recovery. But as party leader he could not ignore the feelings of his western followers. The party must be kept united. If Liberals could not agree to concentrate on the tariff, some new basis of agreement was needed. Inflation did not look like a promising avenue. In addition to King's personal misgivings, it was clear that eastern Liberals would not support that policy.

It was here that King illustrated his capacity for leadership—for his type of leadership. In the fall of 1932 he met with some prominent Liberals, a select group which included Vincent Massey and J.W. Dafoe as well as active politicians like Lapointe and Ralston. They argued about tariff policy, railway policy and, inevitably, about monetary policy. All of these men were Liberals with concern for the underprivileged but also with a healthy respect for free enterprise and existing social institutions. They were not likely to opt for simple panaceas such as printing money. All of them could remember the postwar inflation in Germany a dozen years earlier, when people had gone to the bakery with a wheel-barrow of paper marks for a loaf of bread. But on the other hand, what of the argument that the value of money had already changed during the depression? The depression could be seen as a period of deflation; to say that the prices had declined was only another way of saying that the value of money had increased. Would it be possible to manipulate the money supply to increase prices without having a runaway inflation? How could the money supply be safely adjusted? What about a central bank?

Mackenzie King was intrigued by the possibility. He had once been trained as an economist but he knew little about the complexities of velocity of circulation and rediscount rates, so he consulted Professor Curtis, an economist at Queen's University. From him King learned that a central bank would be necessary if a policy of controlled inflation was ever adopted, but that a central bank did not necessarily mean inflation. Here was the compromise King was looking for. He knew his party could not be united on a policy of inflation but both western and eastern Liberals might be persuaded to agree on the establishment of a central bank. The compromise might be summed up as "inflation if necessary but not necessarily inflation."

It was not enough for King to decide on a policy. Bennett was the kind of leader who announced his decisions in radio broadcasts but for King political leadership involved consultation and discussion. When Parliament reassembled in January of 1933 King therefore announced to caucus that a Liberal platform needed to be hammered out and proposed a number of caucus committees to discuss the various planks. All of the committees—tariffs, railways, social welfare—encountered some difficulty in reaching agreement, but the committee on monetary policy was almost a free-for-all, as he knew it would be. King, however, used all his considerable talent as a conciliator. He attended all the meetings, began by suggesting the central bank as a possible basis of agreement, listened carefully to the contradictory views, drafted what he hoped would be an acceptable policy statement after three weeks, allowed the debate to continue for another two weeks, revised his draft slightly to meet the criticisms and finally got all members of the committee to agree that the draft was at least acceptable—as far as it went. The final consensus was that the Liberal party advocated a central bank. It went farther, however, and also stated that the supply of currency and credit should be determined by the needs of the community.

This was still vague. Liberals might still disagree on what the needs of the community were; but the platform was nonetheless a radical advance in party policy. The Liberal party had affirmed that government should control monetary policy, that it should manipulate currency and credit. Money was no longer sacrosanct; governments on this basis would be as responsible for the supply of money as they were for the level of tariffs or taxes. From King's point of view, what was even more important was that all members of the party had agreed. This policy represented a consensus on which the party was united. It was no mean achievement to have negotiated such a radical shift in policy without alienating any of his followers.

The Liberal platform of 1933 remained the official platform of the party through the election campaign of 1935. It had been difficult enough to arrive at a consensus and King had no urge to open up the Pandora's box and start all over again. In any case, he did not think it was necessary. He was sure that the Liberals would win the next election. It seemed the part of wisdom to be as flexible as possible; to adopt general principles without being committed to specific measures. The party favoured freer trade, closer cooperation with provincial governments, more efficient administration—but few details were spelled out.

It required a good deal of self-confidence to avoid specific promises. Other parties were less reserved. R.B. Bennett had his New Deal. The C.C.F. had its Regina Manifesto of 1933. H.H. Stevens' Reconstruction party was promising a wide range of measures which would restore prosperity. Social Credit had its inflationary panacea. Many Liberals feared that they would suffer defeat if they did not participate in this auction. King, however, was convinced that the Canadian voters had had enough of reckless and unfulfilled promises. He was sure that they would have more respect for a party which offered a stable and responsible administration. In the welter and confusion of three new parties and a Conservative party which had changed its spots, the Liberal party would offer cautious reform. The Liberal slogan in 1935 was "King or chaos." As a slogan it reflected accurately enough the political situation. The Liberal party was the only party with significant support across the country. If it did not win, there would be no majority government. The slogan also reflected King's view that the Liberal party would win without offering anything more specific. The voters confirmed his analysis: they returned 171 Liberals in a House of 245, the largest majority in Canadian history up to that time.

Any slogan, however, is an oversimplification. Chaos was still possible, even with King in office. The multiplicity of parties in 1935 was a reflection of fundamental divisions within the country. One out of every five voters had voted for new parties, radical parties, parties which had not even existed in 1930. And even within the older parties, Conservative and Liberal, there were differences and divisions which had not been resolved. These political divisions were based on deeply rooted divisions within Canada itself. The grievances of western Canada, for example, explain why both the C.C.F. and Social Credit parties drew their strength from that region. The Liberal party itself was a coalition of regional and cultural blocs, and there was no guarantee that it would hold together in the face of the continuing economic crisis.

Mackenzie King, when he returned to office in 1935, had no new or novel policies. In many ways he was still the King of an earlier era. In 1921 he had come into office during an economic recession. His government had economized, it had balanced its budget and even reduced the national debt, it had lowered tariffs and taxes. Within a few years prosperity had returned, and King believed that there was a cause and effect relationship. He was convinced that these policies had brought prosperity once and that similar policies in the 1930s would produce similar results. He did not close the door on new ideas, but he hoped that the tested remedies of the past would still be effective.

He began with the traditional Liberal policy of freer trade. Within three weeks of taking office he had signed a trade agreement with the United States. Negotiations had begun when Bennett was still Prime Minister but Bennett had not been enthusiastic. King had no reservations, although the implications were far-reaching. It was the first formal trade agreement with the United States since the Reciprocity Agreement of 1854 and it marked the turning away from the ever-increasing tariff barriers between the two countries which had reached their peak with the Hawley-Smoot tariff and the Bennett tariff, both in 1930. A further trade agreement was signed three years later, this time involving Great Britain as well as the United States. The trend was clearly towards increased trade with the United States. It is a trend which has continued ever since until today the relationship is almost symbiotic.

Freer trade, especially with the United States, was expected to benefit Canadian producers of natural products by increasing their markets. It was a traditional Liberal policy and the effects would be gradual at best. The same traditional and cautious approach could be seen in the first budget of the new government. No new expenditures were proposed but corporation taxes and the sales tax were increased. The aim was to balance the budget, to have the federal government live within its means.

Even monetary policy scarcely reflected the long-drawn-out discussion over inflation. R.B. Bennett had established a central bank in 1934. The Bank of Canada which he set up was a banker's bank, independent of the federal government and primarily concerned with financial stability. The Liberal government amended the constitution of the Bank of Canada to establish federal control and eventually federal ownership. It was thus in a position to determine the supply of currency and credit on the basis of the needs of the community. Under Graham Towers, however, the Bank of Canada had already established a policy of easy money. Chartered banks had plenty of money to lend at low rates of interest. The policy of easy money was continued but neither Towers nor the government under King was prepared to print more money.

Special measures were introduced for the drought areas on the prairies, where crop disaster continued to be almost the normal way of life. Some marginal crop land was turned back to grazing land and an insurance scheme was introduced to provide some income for farmers in a year of crop failure. The Wheat

Board, established under Bennett, was continued under the Liberal government. What improvement there was, however—and there was some—had little to do with federal policies. Crop failures and acreage reductions in Canada and elsewhere in the world gradually eliminated the world wheat surplus and wheat prices increased, although they were still below a dollar a bushel. The price trend was at least encouraging, and if rains would come and if grasshoppers and rust and frost would stay away, the farmers could hope to get off relief.

At this stage there was nothing radical, nothing really novel, nothing that was not consistent with traditional and orthodox Liberalism. The orthodoxy of the new government is most clearly shown in its efforts to economize, to balance the federal budget. The greatest drain on the budget was still the heavy relief expenditures: unemployment relief and farm relief. Soon after taking office King appointed a National Employment Commission, which was asked to do two things. It was to reorganize the administration of all relief expenditures, in the hope that a more centralized and more efficient administration would eliminate duplication and reduce costs. It was also asked to recommend measures which might be taken to create employment opportunities and so remove men from the relief rolls.

The National Employment Commission was not able to introduce many economies. Most of the relief was administered by provincial and municipal governments and, even though the federal government was providing much of the money, there was little the federal government could do to change the system. It was a different story when it came to recommending positive measures to foster employment. The Commission argued that employment was not a local but a national problem. A factory might close down in Hamilton but the cause was elsewhere—in the declining purchasing power in the Maritimes or the prairies perhaps, where men could no longer afford to buy the products of the factory. Two major conclusions were drawn from this analysis. Because the Canadian economy was national and not local or provincial in scope, unemployment must be seen as a national problem. The Commission therefore recommended that the federal government should take over the full cost of unemployment relief. The Commission went much farther, however; it argued that some positive action could be taken to reduce unemployment. Instead of economizing and trying to balance the budget, it recommended increased federal expenditures and reduced taxation in times of depression. The motor of the economy was seen as investment. When private enterprise was not prepared to invest money—when there was a depression—governments should deliberately incur deficits in order to counterbalance the deficiency. John Maynard Keynes had arrived in Canada.

Mackenzie King's initial response to these suggestions was more than negative: it was hostile. He paid little attention to the positive proposals; he was shocked even at the suggestion that the federal government should pay the full cost of unemployment relief. The federal government was having enough trouble meeting its financial obligations as it was; it seemed absurd to aggravate its problems by taking over more responsibilities. King was reacting like a traditional federalist, insisting that both levels of government, federal and provincial, should look after their own affairs. It was at this time, in the fall of 1937, that King decided to set up yet another royal commission—the Rowell-Sirois Commission on Dominion-Provincial Relations. If the federal system was going to be changed it would not be changed unilaterally, by having the federal government volunteer to take on new burdens.

But the positive proposals of the Employment Commission were not forgotten. The 1938 session might be the last session before the next election. King suggested to the Minister of Finance, Charles Dunning, that he plan a pre-election budget. For King this meant a balanced budget, for he was sure that responsible Canadians wanted a government which lived within its means. Charles Dunning agreed; he too believed that government deficits were undesirable, if not immoral. Dunning's first draft of his budget proposed a small surplus.

King and Dunning, however, were surprised to find that some cabinet ministers no longer believed in balanced budgets. Norman Rogers, Minister of Labour, had been converted by the Employment Commission. He argued that Dunning should budget for a deficit and talked of an additional $40 million for public works to inject money into the economy. Dunning threatened to resign if this policy was adopted; Rogers threatened to resign if it wasn't. Other cabinet ministers took sides. It was the kind of situation in which King the conciliator took over. He was not convinced by the arguments but he was, as always, convinced that the party must be kept united. Eventually he proposed $25 million of additional expenditure as a compromise and set up a cabinet committee to decide how the money would be spent.

The budget of 1938 was a turning point in fiscal policy in Canada. For the first time a government had consciously decided to spend money to counteract a low in the business cycle. In addition to the expenditures in the budget the government also offered loans to municipalities for local improvements and passed a National Housing Act to encourage the building of homes. Consistent with this Keynesian approach, the government also reduced some taxes and offered some tax exemptions for private investors. The idea of a static and balanced budget was gone. In its place was a fiscal policy of stimulating economic recovery by government deficits and by direct economic incentives.

The new fiscal policy did not work any miracles. Recovery would not come until the war, when deficit financing and government investment in the economy became a patriotic duty. But the budget of 1938 marks the beginning of a new concept of the role of government in Canada. Until then the federal government had concentrated on providing public services such as railways and canals, police forces and national defence, post offices, and more recently old age pensions and unemployment relief. The taxes it had collected were designed to pay for these services. It had now undertaken a new and significantly different responsibility: that of balancing the total economic investment, private and public, in order to balance the national economy. The implications would be far-reaching. The government budgets of our day are dominated by this new role. Looking back to the 1930s we can now see that it was the most radical and most constructive innovation of that depression decade.

And yet it is still difficult to visualize Mackenzie King as a radical. He was not an innovator; he was not a man with original ideas. Indeed, he still continued to believe that eventually governments should balance their budgets and let free enterprise flourish. Certainly he did not appreciate the significance of the Keynesian revolution. King's strength was in his commitment to a policy of party unity, and in his capacity to accept and adopt new ideas when the alternative was a division within the party. This concept of political leadership had brought King a long way since 1930. On monetary issues he had begun with the certainty that inflation was sin but had come to accept the idea of a central bank which might manipulate currency and credit on the basis of social need. On fiscal policy he had begun with the traditional ideas of a limited role for government with balanced budgets and had come to accept the idea of government responsibility for controlling the level of economic activity.

Under King the Liberal party did respond, gradually and tentatively, to the pressures of a revolutionary decade, and under his leadership it responded without disintegrating into warring factions. To be leader of a still united party four years later was in itself no small achievement. The risk of party schisms had been real. More significant, the party still seemed to have popular support. Mackenzie King's policies had not been dramatic but his concept of political leadership had averted possible chaos.

Notes

1. R.J. Manion, *Life Is an Adventure* (Toronto, 1937), p. 290.

WAR: THE PRIME MINISTER SWEARS OFF

C.P. Stacey

The autumn of 1939 brought the war which Canadian politicians, remembering the desperate domestic crisis of 1917, had had particular reason to hope might be averted. The outbreak had a special consequence for Mackenzie King. In effect, he swore off spiritualism for the duration.

On 1 September Hitler, no longer "careful", invaded Poland. On the evening of the 2nd, King and Joan Patteson held at Kingsmere what turned out to be the craziest of all their sessions with the little table.[1] It began with King's

From *A Very Double Life: The Private World of Mackenzie King* (Toronto: Macmillan, 1976), 190–204, 244. Reprinted with the permission of the Master and Fellows of Massey College.

father announcing that Hitler was dead: "He was shot by a Pole." King's mother, Laurier, Gladstone, and Max King followed; and William Lyon Mackenzie drew a parallel between himself in 1837 and the German dictator:

> *I did not want to shed a drop of blood*
> *I was driven to desperation*
> *Hitler did not want to have war*
> *He has become desperate.*

At this point there was an interruption. It was 11 p.m. O. D. Skelton telephoned to say that at midnight (London time) the British Cabinet had decided to have Sir Nevile Henderson, the British Ambassador in Berlin, deliver an ultimatum to Germany demanding the withdrawal of German troops from Poland, failing which there would be immediate war. King and Skelton agreed that the British should have allowed more time. King then returned to the table. His father's spirit still asserted that Hitler was dead, and said, "The French and British will agree to a conference when they hear of Hitler's death." King asked, "Are you sure this is not all subconscious thought and desire asserting itself?", but the spirits insisted, and the sitting ended with his mother declaring, "War will be averted."

This very peculiar personal problem added to King's anxieties at this desperate moment. He wrote in his diary:[2]

> ... The real issue:—Christ vs. anti-Christ. I felt strongly tonight, after conversation J. and I had, that there are some things that [as?] Asquith said which we were not meant to know in the sense of attempting to know them by the senses, but which could be known only to Faith. In other words, that the spiritual things must be spiritually discerned; that we must not hope to get the profound spiritual experiences and truths through material agencies. Least of all, must we seek to convince ourselves as to courses of conduct in great decisions by occult means. The Roman Catholic church, I believe, is right in recognizing the existence of phenomena of the kind, but in recognizing its [sic] dangers. Evil and Good exists [sic] in the Hereafter as well as the here and now. Men may be guided by evil spirits or by good spirits....

On 4 September the Prime Minister added a rather formal note to his memorandum of the *séance* of the 2nd:

> This all makes perfectly clear either that a lying spirit has come in somewhere, or that sub-conscious wishes dictate the words expressed.—I felt terribly exercised at this for I felt at the time it was not truth, however, that it would serve as a guide to future action & belief as to worth of "automatic writing"—I felt I should perhaps not have sought to use the table to discover the course of events. I had a feeling at the time that it was a sort of betrayal of faith so to do.—Like in Lohengrin.[a] Elsa determined to know what it was not intended she should know— It is faith one must be guided by and intuition—our guide [WLMK Sept. 4]

---

[a] King had been seeking for explanations of Hitler in the Wagner operas.

Here King seems to be repudiating the little table, while reserving judgement as to automatic writing. From this moment the familiar pencilled memoranda of sittings at the little table vanish from King's diary, and references to the table disappear from the text.

The Prime Minister's motives in abandoning the table at this particular point are interesting to speculate upon. The doubts he records about the genuineness of the information it gave him could have arisen at any time, and in fact they had arisen at the time of the knighthoods affair in 1934, "lying spirit" and all. But war is a more serious business than peace, and the leader of a country at war has reason to be especially cautious about the sources of his information and the influences that bear upon him. What is more, he has particular reason to be cautious about his public image. It would have been highly dangerous to King politically at any time if the Canadian public had been informed of his spiritualistic proclivities; with the country at war, it would have been instantly fatal, and King undoubtedly was well aware of it.

It is interesting that King suggested that the table's messages were a product of "subconscious thought"—his own, of course—(though it was surely very simple-minded to ask the spirits about it). Joan had suggested this in 1934. I am left wondering whether, for King, the table had finally become a sort of game, which he enjoyed enormously but did not absolutely believe in, and which he could give up without serious injury to his life.

It should be added that with the outbreak of war King's tolerance for Hitler was at an end. On 23 January 1940, *à propos* of the refusal of General Hertzog of South Africa to believe in Hitler's desire for world domination, he wrote, "I shared that view myself at the time but I have changed it in the light of what has developed since this war began. Germany could not have developed the military machine she has nor proceeded in any way she did unless she were bent on world domination by terror and violence."

The little table was a highly personal and private operation, and very few people apart from King and the Pattesons knew about it. It is questionable whether his secretaries knew, for his records of the *séances* held across it were written by himself in longhand. The danger of the wrong people coming to know about the table was therefore comparatively slight. *Séances* held with mediums were a different matter. When King consulted a medium he was putting his career in her hands and in those of her associates.[b] Moreover, in wartime the steps of a Prime Minister were apt to be dogged by the press even more than in peace. In these circumstances it is not surprising that he severed almost all

---

[b] I have been assured that many people in Kingston knew of King's consulting a fortune-teller there. But this never reached the newspapers, or if it did it was not published. In spiritualism, as in other matters, King was lucky. The mediums he dealt with were sincere and dedicated people who kept his confidence and were not interested in making money out of him. He would have been an ideal blackmail target, but so far as I know no such attempt was ever made on him.

connection with the spiritualistic fraternity in Britain during the war. He made two wartime visits to London, in 1941 and 1944. In striking contrast with his actions earlier and later, during these visits there were no *séances*. Of his spiritualist friends, the only ones he had contact with were the Duchess of Hamilton and some members of her circle; and none of these contacts seems to have been closer than a telephone conversation. In 1941 he did not even manage to speak to the Duchess (she was trying to get him as he left his hotel to return to Canada), but he sent her a farewell telegram. In 1944 he recorded what appears to have been a telephone talk with her: "She is most understanding. She had hoped to have me meet a number of friends. But realized what the situation was."[3]

In the course of these visits King did not darken the doors of the London Spiritualist Alliance, where before and after he was wont to make arrangements for meetings with mediums. In October 1945, when he had revoked his self-denying ordinance against spiritualism, he went back there again to see Miss Mercy Phillimore, the Secretary of the Alliance. "I was amazed," he wrote, "to learn it was nine years since I had last been there or seen her."[4] He had apparently not been there during his 1937 visit.

The general absence of *séances* from King's diary for the years 1939–45 does not mean that it is a dull or conventional document. It is true that it is basically an enormously valuable dictated record of public business, a detailed day-to-day account of the direction of the Canadian war effort, having as its highlights King's memoranda of his conversations with Churchill, Roosevelt, and other great figures of the crisis. But—well representing the double life that King continued to lead—it continues also to be highly eccentric. It describes—often in King's difficult longhand—his psychic experiences, and in particular his dreams, which he normally terms "visions".[c] Almost every day's diary entry commences with an account of the overnight vision. Frequently, but not always, it stars the deceased members of his family. And frequently King's attempts at interpretation are as curious as the dream. Here, from the early days of the war, is an example taken at random. King records how he felt cold in the night and put an extra quilt on his bed. Then came the vision. He was following a well-known Ottawa lady through the streets of the capital, with an umbrella in his hand. They turned into "a sort of Club or room where a lot of men seemed to be lying in pyjamas.... Suddenly the word 'Mac' and 'Max' came very strongly before me, and I felt at once it was my brother the Doctor who was advising me that it was the covering on me which was causing the damage. The men lying in pyjamas stood for lighter form of bed clothing.... Once I threw off the brown quilt which I had added for the cold, I began to feel relief of body and mind...."

---

[c]"Was surprised to find I had been keeping records of visions from 1934, etc., re future—quite clearly recognising later in the day & often in year the vision coming true—(I recall how mother emphasized these are not dreams, they are visions)...." (Diary, 9 Jan. 1938).

King's final conclusion was, "I am quite certain that those who are nearest to me are watching over me hour by hour, and that this was another evidence of it...."[5]

Also increasingly prominent in these wartime diaries is the old obsession with the position of the hands of the clock. Perhaps this and the dreams are compensating King for the loss of the little table. One could give innumerable examples. One is enough. On 25 August 1943 President Roosevelt visited Ottawa; and King wrote a "Memo re hands of clock" as they were at various times that day, beginning with "Exactly 10 past 8 when I looked at clock on waking—straight line", and including "12 noon when noon day gun fired & I read my welcome to President—together", not to mention "25 to 8 when I was handed in my room a letter from Churchill re supply of whiskey to troops ...—both together". Occasionally King is still found consulting the tea-leaves, though not, I think, to discover the future course of the war.[6]

It must further be said—and it will probably surprise nobody—that King's rejection of spiritualism for the duration was not total. Like a drinker who has taken the pledge, but secretly resorts at intervals to the bottle, he occasionally returns to the old ways. The death of Pat I in July 1941, an episode of enormous importance to King, resulted in a *séance* over the little table in which King's parents reported Pat's arrival in the Beyond. They did not mention receiving the "messages of love" that King had entrusted to him. But they described his happy reunion with the Pattesons' dog Derry: "They know all about hunting for rabbits and squirrels." (At this point, Joan remarks, "I hope there are no cats in heaven—it would be hell if there were.") Joan, it is to be feared, did not always take the little table quite as seriously as King.

This sitting was closely followed by two more, arising out of King's plan to visit Britain shortly—another very important matter (flying the Atlantic was novel and serious business for an elderly politician in 1941). In one, Sir Wilfrid Laurier tells him to go by bomber plane and adds that the weather will be bad for flying in September; his mother tells him that Churchill will be delighted to see him ("He likes you very much"); and W. E. Gladstone tells him that the war will be over before Christmas, and that the President loves him, and wants to see him before he goes to England. (That did not happen, but King did have a telephone talk with Roosevelt before he took off.) The other sitting consisted mainly of advice about the will that King was making. All three were recorded in the old way, in pencilled memoranda written by King and placed in the diary.[7] This revival of the table seems to have been a brief and isolated incident.

As with the table, so with *séances* and with mediums. They were rare, but it cannot be said that there were none. Notably, there was one in Toronto in August 1942. King was visiting the office of his publishers, the Macmillan Company of Canada. Conversation with an official of the company revealed that she was a spiritualist and resulted in a spur-of-the-moment *séance* with a "little medium" that evening before the Prime Minister caught the Ottawa train. A galaxy of talent attended: not only King's relations and Laurier, but

Queen Victoria, Florence Nightingale, Anne Boleyn, Sir Frederick Banting, Norman Rogers, and others. King had never seen the medium before.[8] One is amazed by his imprudence in putting his career at the mercy of this unknown young woman. It seems likely that he would not have done so had he had more time to think. As always, he was lucky; the story did not get out. But every such episode must have widened the circle of people who knew about the Prime Minister's peculiarities.

In addition to these recorded incidents, we have to reckon with the possibility that others went unrecorded. Did the secret tippler perhaps hold some sessions at the little table without telling the diary? It may be worthwhile to note something about the record of the epoch-making sitting of 2 September 1939. Except for the pencilled memorandum of it, there is no direct reference to it in the diary. It may be recalled that the text states that King's doubts arose "after conversation J. and I had". This is certainly the table sitting. Elsewhere the text says, "had J. come over for a little *talk, reading and conversation* together" (the italics are mine). The word *conversation* was sometimes used as a synonym for *séance* or *sitting*. Here it was doubtless used to conceal the real meaning from the secretary to whom King was dictating.[d] But when we find King writing, for instance, in 1941, "I spent an hour or so with J. in conversation. Had an exceptionally interesting talk,"[9] is this a concealed reference to a session with the table? It is quite conceivable, but it seems impossible to be certain.

The war's interference with King's spiritualistic activities does not seem to have depressed him. There is no return of the morbid desire for contact with his mother that is found in the diary before the first *séances* with Mrs. Wriedt in 1932. He now thought he knew what he had wished to know. On 18 December 1943, the anniversary of his mother's death, he recalls in some detail the events of 1917, and how he failed to reach Ottawa in time. He proceeds in terms that can only be called triumphant:

> My mother is nearer to me today than she was in her last day upon earth and I am nearer to her.... she has come back to me and I have now the assurance that she is at my side and that we will be together for ever.

At the end of this account of Mackenzie King's involvement with the spirit world, one faces the question, so often asked, Did he conduct the affairs of Canada in accordance with what he believed to be advice from the Beyond? And the answer is quite clearly No.

After King's death, reports of his spiritualistic activities at once began to be published, and his friend the Duchess of Hamilton was quoted in print as saying that he "fully appreciated the spiritual direction of the universe and was always seeking guidance for himself in his work".[10] Joan Patteson, who knew him better than anyone else, was much disturbed. She said nothing publicly, but

---

[d] King dictated his account of the *séances* in Toronto in August 1942 to J. E. Handy, who thus became aware of the Prime Minister's spiritualistic activities, if he had not been before.

she wrote to Violet Markham at this time, "*never* did he allow his belief to enter into his public life—or [himself to] be guided by anything he found in his search for Reality, as he put it. He looked forward to re-union & he longed to feel that those who loved him, still loved & watched over him & that death did not end but rather began the real life."[11] Mrs. Patteson knew more about King's private than about his public life, but all the evidence fully supports her. Blair Fraser, assiduously interviewing in 1951 the mediums whom King had consulted in the United Kingdom, came to the same conclusion.[12] Blair Neatby, after years of research in the diary and King's other private papers, saw no reason to differ. The spiritual communications King received, he writes, "did no more than confirm his confidence in his own judgment and strengthen his conviction that he was on the right path". He comments on King's "infinite capacity to rationalize, to accept what he wished to believe and to reject the rest".[13]

My own reading leaves me in no doubt of the soundness of these conclusions. A good deal of the evidence has been presented in the foregoing pages. As throughout his life, Mackenzie King in his spiritualistic period was a worried and insecure individual seeking for support. It was support, strength, not advice, that he asked for and received from the spirits. Mainly, he wanted approval, and by a strange coincidence that was what he usually got. The spirits did not, in general, tell him what to do; they told him that what he had done, or what he had decided to do, was right. Thus they sent him on his way with confidence renewed.

Though requests for help are fairly commonly recorded in the diary or in King's notes of *séances,* there are remarkably few requests for advice. At one point however, in January 1935, he did show a tendency to make such requests. He asked Lord Oxford for advice "as to demanding an election", and Oxford told him to try to force one. A week later he asked Laurier to advise him on how long to speak on the Address in reply to the Speech from the Throne; and Sir Wilfrid said, "Speak for an hour and a half.... Speak on trade and labour ... try to touch the high spots only, give up reading figures, or quotations. Try to be humorous, light touches help to relieve the monotony...."[14] I have no doubt whatever that both these replies actually represented plans already formed in King's mind, and now returned to him by his subconscious self with the stamp of approval of two great, dead Liberals. (Humour was an aspiration only; King had always known that he was not capable of it.)[e]

What King would have liked to have, apart from general encouragement, was information about future events. (What politician, what human being, would not?) We have seen him seeking it, in the comic case of the knighthoods in 1934 and in the episode of the election in 1935. In both, the information he received was wrong. The things King got over the little table, I have suggested, came out of his own head; and there were no revelations about the future to be had from there.

---

[e]"I cannot be other than earnest. I often wish I could be humourous [*sic*] but I cannot, it is a decided limitation" (Diary, 20 Jan. 1904).

King constantly refers to receiving "guidance"; but these references are normally after the fact. After a successful day in Parliament, he is likely to feel that he has been "guided". The examples early in 1935 just given are isolated. Apart from them it would be difficult to find many instances in which he asked one of his correspondents in the 'Beyond' to tell him what to do in a specific situation.

It would be strange, nevertheless, if the irrationalities of King's private world never boiled over into his other world—the rational world of public business. And I believe that this did in fact happen during the greatest political emergency of his career, the Cabinet crisis over conscription in the autumn of 1944.

King told the Governor-General's secretary, after the crisis was over, that it was "wholly the power from beyond" that had saved the day: "I was a mere instrument in working out a higher will."[15] It was a characteristic phrase, though commoner in the privacy of the diary than in conversation. The detailed record in the diary contains no indication, during that long agony, that King felt he was receiving actual guidance. The "little table", we have seen, was not much in use during the war. But to me, at least, the diary does indicate that at one very important point King acted on a basis of intuition rather than reason.

Sir Wilfrid Laurier, it has been made amply clear, was never far from King's mind. And he went into this supreme crisis in 1944 full of memories of the earlier battle over conscription in 1917 and what it had meant for Sir Wilfrid and the Party. When, on 13 October, he received Colonel Ralston's cable telling him that he was returning from England at once in order to raise grave questions, King wrote: "It is a repetition of the kind of thing that led to the creation of the Union government after Borden's return from England [in May 1917]. That will not take place under me."

When trying to write the history of this episode some years ago, I thought I was faced with an interesting conundrum. Ralston told King that the time had come to adopt overseas conscription, and said that if this was not done he would have to resign. For nearly a fortnight King devoted himself to trying to argue Ralston out of resigning. On 26 October he told the Minister of National Defence that it was his duty as a soldier, and his duty under the oath he had sworn as a Minister of the Crown, to remain at his post. And then, on 1 November, when Ralston was still prepared to go on discussing the problem and to seek a compromise, King suddenly and without warning dismissed him from the Cabinet.[16] This seemed to me a little strange; and I examined the diary with care in an attempt to discover just when and why King changed his mind. I thought, and still think, that I found the turning-point on the evening of 30 October.

By this stage of the controversy nerves were certainly fraying. After a long and trying Cabinet meeting, King found awaiting him at Laurier House a telegram from George Fulford, Liberal Member for Leeds. It demanded universal overseas conscription. King remembered Fulford as a strong opponent of his family allowance ("baby bonus") project in the Liberal caucus. Fulford, moreover, though evidently no spiritualist himself, was a son of one of King's close friends in spiritualism, the lady who had introduced him to Mrs. Wriedt; the name Fulford on any document was perhaps likely to have a rather special impact upon him. At any rate the telegram triggered an extraordinary reaction in King's mind. He suddenly became convinced that there was in the Cabinet a conspiracy against him personally. This is what he wrote in the diary:

> This, at once, caused me to feel exactly what the conspiracy is, because I believe it has come to be that. It is not merely a question of conscription. The same men who are for conscription are the same identically as those who opposed most strongly the family allowances and other social reforms in the budget: Ilsley, Ralston, Howe, Macdonald, Crerar and Gibson? [*sic*] It is perfectly plain to me that in pretty much all particulars my position is becoming identical to that of Sir Wilfrid Laurier's [*sic*] where his supposedly strongest colleagues left him, one by one, and joined their political enemies and became a party for conscription. They will find that at this time they have not the Wartimes Election Act to assist them in a campaign....[17]

From this moment, I think, King was determined to dismiss Ralston, presumably because he thought of him as the kingpin of the conspiracy. The difficulty is that the diary never says so; it continues to talk in terms of Ralston's impending *resignation*. But what King *did*, as distinct from what he *wrote*, gives a different impression. The day after the revelation from the Fulford telegram, he sent for General McNaughton and obtained his promise to take the National Defence portfolio if Ralston "resigned". That afternoon he again recorded his conviction that he was the intended victim of a conspiracy: "As I sat in Council, I thought of [*sic*] what was happening to me, was exactly the same as had happened to Sir Wilfrid. I can see this whole thing has been worked out as a plot. Some of the men who were incensed at the proposal at the start are now coming round, being fearful."[18] Yet still he says no word indicating that he has a purely personal counterplot, a plan to strike the conspirators before they can strike him. Why? One explanation occurs to me. Edouard Handy, to whom King dictated the diary, was very, very reliable. But there are some risks that no wise politician takes; and this was the deadliest secret of King's career. Unfortunately, there is no private handwritten diary at this point.

Before the Cabinet met on 1 November, King took steps obviously designed to provide against other conscriptionists leaving with Ralston. He telephoned W. P. Mulock and T. A. Crerar asking them not to commit themselves to anything hasty at the meeting. He did not dare approach J. L. Ilsley and Angus L. Macdonald, Ralston's closest associates, but he did make a curious proposal to the Governor-General. He suggested that if Ralston, Ilsley, and Macdonald all resigned, His Excellency should accept Ralston's resignation, but not Ilsley's or Macdonald's, at least for the moment. This would surely have been an interesting constitutional innovation. As the Cabinet was actually assembling for the meeting, King told Louis St. Laurent that McNaughton was willing to take National Defence. This politic hint to his Quebec lieutenant was the only word he had spoken on the subject. As he entered the meeting, having told nobody else—nobody at all—what he intended to do, he had on his side one of the most potent of the principles of war—surprise. Late in the afternoon he exploded his mine; and Layton Ralston gathered up his papers and left the Cabinet room—alone.[19]

If it seems strange that King recorded nothing in advance about his intention to dismiss Ralston, it is at least equally strange that later he denied that he had dismissed him at all. He appears to have denied it in the Cabinet on 7 November, before a tableful of men who had seen it happen; and he denied it in the diary that day and again six days later, although this contradicted the detailed account of the dismissal that he had written in the diary at the time. He had apparently convinced himself that Ralston had carried out his threat of resignation, and that was all.[20] It is all very peculiar, and one wonders what King's colleagues thought about it.

The fact is that there was no Cabinet conspiracy against King. The evidence is now pretty complete—there seems little likelihood that much more will come to light—and none of it supports the conspiracy theory. King himself seems to have recorded no evidence for it. The plot existed only in his mind. It was a product of irrational intuition, in the same class with the information King's dead father gave him about the knighthoods in 1934.[f] And yet I think it is evident that King made it the basis of a great act of policy. The most remarkable thing about the whole affair is that it turned out so well for King. Not only did he survive the crisis, but it left him stronger than ever. I have suggested elsewhere[21] that, though his strategy was non-existent, his tactics in the Ralston case were flawless and typically deadly. I might have added that he was probably the luckiest tactician who has operated in Canada since General Wolfe.

Notes

1. Notes of sitting, Kingsmere, 2 Sept. 1939 (original Diary, 1939, Vol. 133).

2. 2 Sept. 1939.

3. August-September 1941. April-May 1944. See especially 5 and 6 Sept., 1941, and 17 May 1944.

4. 17 Oct. 1945.

5. 18 Sept. 1939.

6. Memo (original Diary, Vol. 145, p. 719). Tea-leaves, e.g., 2 July 1943.

7. Notes of sittings, Kingsmere, The Farm, Wednesday, 16 July 1941; Moorside, 3 Aug. 1941; and (no place), 11 Aug. 1941 (original Diary, Vol. 139). Pickersgill and Forster, *Mackenzie King Record*, Vol. 1, 235.

---

[f] King would not have admitted this. See page 192 of *A Very Double Life: The Private World of Mackenzie King*, which quotes a passage where he makes a firm distinction between information received over the table and "intuition—our guide". (For full particulars of C.P. Stacey's biography, see p. 378.)

8. 5 Aug. 1942.

9. 2 Feb. 1941. For more probable case, see Diary, 11 Oct. 1942 (transcribed from "Book F").

10. Article by Fred Archer in *Psychic News* (London), reprinted in *Evening Citizen,* Ottawa, 11 Oct. 1950.

11. 17 Dec. 1950 (Markham Carruthers Papers, M.G. 32, F. 6, P.A.C.).

12. "The Secret Life of Mackenzie King, Spiritualist", *Maclean's,* 15 Dec. 1951.

13. Neatby, 407–8.

14. Notes of sittings, 202 Elgin Street, 6 Jan. 1934 [1935], and 13 Jan. 1935 (Diary, 1935).

15. 8 Dec. 1944.

16. Stacey, *Arms, Men and Governments,* 441–59.

17. 30 Oct. 1944.

18. 31 Oct. 1944.

19. *Arms, Men and Governments,* 456–9.

20. *Ibid.,* 466.

21. *Ibid.,* 459–60.

FRIEND OR FIEND: KING AND HITLER

Joy Esberey

William Lyon Mackenzie King is one of the best known and least understood of all Canadian prime ministers. He was 'to his own great satisfaction ... prime minister longer than any man in British history.'[1] But it is not longevity alone that matters. It has recently been suggested that Mackenzie King's approach to politics 'took such deep roots that people mistook it for politics itself.'[2] This lonely bachelor, apparently devoted to the memory of his mother and obsessed by life beyond the veil, has been described as an enigma, yet has been explained in simple one-dimensional terms. A direct consequence has been the tendency to separate Mackenzie King's private life from his public career, an approach which makes much of his behaviour inexplicable except in the crude terms of hypocrisy or political expediency. This misleading and dysfunctional 'double vision' of King is challenged in this study, which provides a comprehensive analysis of King's personal development and a consideration of selected examples of his political behaviour to demonstrate that the separation of the private and public King is invalid.

From *Knight of the Holy Spirit: A Study of William Lyon Mackenzie King* (Toronto: University of Toronto Press, 1980), 3-8, 208-15, 223-224, 231-232. Reprinted by permission of the University of Toronto Press.

Because the impact of his personality is considered to be an essential dimension of King's political actions, it is not enough to rely on selected incidents in King's life or on the obvious Freudian explanations of some of his reactions. Instead I have attempted to trace the development of the main lines of the personality from its roots in the family to its flowering in the adult political leader. To do so the accepted picture of the King family has had to be redrawn to show a more balanced view of King's relationship with his parents, especially his mother, and of his interaction with his siblings. His patterns of behaviour are traced from this source through the search for appropriate sexual and occupational roles to the crisis of identity and its eventual partial resolution in political self. At the same time I give some attention to the development of his attitudes, especially the importance of religion and the cult of money, and to the general perceptual framework, dominated by the idea of the enemy, through which King viewed the world.

The analysis of King's personality is to a considerable extent a study of neurotic tendencies. Most of his apparently bizarre behaviour is explicable in these terms, as are many of the apparent paradoxes in his career. To suggest that King's behaviour reflected neurotic trends is neither to judge nor to condemn. The clinical label is useful only in so far as it is a key to identifying a complex and interrelated set of interactions and defences, which had political as well as personal repercussions. It should be noted that these tendencies, while pronounced, were debilitating rather than incapacitating. To the extent that the defences could be related to the constructive facets of his personality, King was able to maintain contact with reality and to function relatively effectively in the uncertain world of politics. To the extent that King failed to achieve his objectives, these time- and energy-consuming defences cannot be dismissed as marginal to understanding his political career.

Selecting an approach for the analysis of personality involved choosing a framework for the study, a level of analysis, and a method of presenting conclusions. For the basic study of King's personality the concept of the life cycle developed by Erik Erikson seemed the most useful.[3] It covers the whole life span of the subject without neglecting the formative years. It gives due attention to the impact of socialization and to environmental factors without losing sight of the epigenetic dimension of the personality. Erikson views the life cycle as a sequence of developmental stages within which conflicts between opposing forces must be resolved. It is a dynamic concept which gives due regard to the place of set-backs and regressions in the total growth pattern termed personality. Perhaps the most important virtue is that the life cycle offers a systematic way of organizing ideas about the growth of personality and it presents specific things to look for, giving a description of the external and internal factors that will indicate a successful or unsuccessful solution to the crisis of each stage. Thus this approach enables one to examine the idiosyncrasies of the personality with some objectivity.

Having selected the framework I then considered the level at which the analysis should be developed. Greenstein suggests 'three overlapping but analytically separable operations: the characterization of phenomenology, the dynamics, and the genesis of personality.'[4] Of these the emphasis was placed on the first two. The phenomenology constituted the basis on which the deeper layers of the analysis are identified and consists of the identification of recurring patterns of behaviour. The dynamics then relate to the circumstances under which these patterns of behaviour become dominant and how the various patterns interact with each other. Although it may be interesting to speculate on the causes of various patterns of response, evidence is lacking on the early years of most political leaders, and as causal answers are not essential to an understanding of personality in action they need be developed no further.

The problem of presenting the personality and relating it to political behaviour was less easily resolved. King's political activity could not be fully covered without having the analysis of the life cycle swamped by a vast sea of detail.[5] I therefore decided to concentrate on presenting those aspects of personality which had important political consequences and to incorporate where necessary additional explanatory material drawn from both Freudian and neo-Freudian sources.[6] As Erikson's work constitutes a bridge between these two schools this compromise did not involve any theoretical incongruity. Although the analysis of King's life and career is arranged in a generally chronological pattern, this study is in no sense a biography. The story of King's life and times has already been told by the historians. This work retreads old ground only when it presents a challenge to existing views.

The application of the insight gained from an understanding of King's personality to his political career also raised methodological problems. Any study of a career as long as King's must be selective. Each incident in his political life is in itself the product of a multi-faceted and complex process and is interrelated to every other incident. Some of these incidents are important enough to the overall pattern of personality development to require detailed analysis; others are not. The criteria for importance are the contribution each incident makes to the general patterns of behaviour which constitute the adult personality and the amount of time and energy the subject expended on each response.

Some of the examples were obvious. The importance of party and party leadership in a parliamentary system of government is such that it can be neglected only by the foolhardy. The fusion of personal and political identity in King's case, however, made it evident that this was one area which could not be ignored. The focus of King's relations with governors-general and with his support staff, on the other hand, is important because it was idiosyncratic of King to devote so much personal concern to these matters. The relationship with Buchan is also important as a link in the search for supportive others so characteristic of King's interpersonal relations.

The selection of illustrative material from the field of policy making was more difficult. It was tempting to consider the dramatic developments of the 1940s when the war, the conscription crisis, and the social-welfare policy proposals of the post-war period dominate the field. But these events climaxed rather than characterized his career, and since they are already well documented in existing literature an interested reader would have little difficulty applying the insight of the psycho-analytical study to these examples. I therefore restricted my choice to those areas where the type of explanation that personality studies offer would be most helpful. One of the subjects that conventional explanations have not explained satisfactorily is why King persisted in emphasizing the tariff issue long after it had ceased to be of popular concern. This study offers an explanation along with a consideration of the apparent ambiguities in King's relation with the British government. The visit to Hitler and King's attitude to personal diplomacy were selected to illustrate the consistency of behavioural patterns in King's career and the way in which such well-entrenched actions were not always politically efficacious.

The discussion of these events must of necessity be limited, and the structural and environmental components of the interaction are given less attention than the psychological necessities. This emphasis is not reductionist but a logical progression from the original objective. In attempting to demonstrate the connection between personality and political behaviour emphasis must be given to psychological elements. Nowhere in this study do I suggest that only psychological explanations are needed to understand King's political behaviour. I do maintain, however, that the personality variable is crucial to this understanding. I suggest that the inner psychology of the leader ensured that particular sets of circumstances produced specific results and that another leader given the same set of circumstances might have chosen another course. The settlement of the dispute over the relative importance of personal and environmental factors must await detailed studies of specific incidents in which both variables are adequately examined. This study aims only to provide the basis for the personality dimension of such works. Similarly, within the limits of this study, it was not possible to offer any conclusions about the contribution King's personality made to his success. Discussion of this problem would involve an examination of the whole Canadian political process, the electoral system, and the historical climate of the times. My aim is to illuminate the psyche in action in the political field, not to rewrite the history of the 1920s and 1930s, although to the extent that King and the Liberal party dominated these decades the two cannot be completely separated. The study makes heavy demands on the reader because it assumes some knowledge of the incidents and individuals mentioned. The focus at all times is on King and the complexities of his personality.

Obviously, King's diary constitutes an essential source for any study of his personality, but it should not be the only source. An equal amount of attention must be given to the family and personal letters in the King papers. King was an enthusiastic and diligent correspondent throughout his life and often devoted dozens of pages in his letters to incidents that only merited a few lines in the diary. Much that is obscure in the diary can be explained in the light of letters written at the time and subsequently returned to King.[7]

It is equally clear that neither source can be taken at face value. They constitute a complex integration of King as he was and King as he wished to be. It is the analyst's task to sift the 'real' self from the 'idealized' self, and the defence mechanisms from the factual descriptions. This is a complex process and one can do little more now than identify the signals of inner conflict—fatigue, inconsistent reactions, repetition—hidden under the surface narration of feelings and events.

It is possible that King's diary represented a substitute 'wife-confidante' but it is not clear that it was intended to be a secret.[8] The first entry in the first volume (6 September 1893) expressed the hope that 'the reader may be able to trace how the author has sought to improve his time.' And the sentiment is repeated the following January and at various places throughout the volumes. Even when King went so far as to declare, 'this journal is strictly private,' as he did on the fly leaf in 1902, he continued to write 'and none should look upon its pages save with reverent eyes.' Obviously, 'strictly private' in King's view did not mean for his eyes only.

Nevertheless, a diary is a personal rather than a public work, and the author is less concerned with communicating with others than with a personal record and self-evaluation; consequently, large sections of the entries are ambiguous or even obscure. In reading a diary, it is essential to seek the author's meanings rather than impose standard or preconceived ideas on the material. Thus a certain circularity is inevitable: without the diary, it is impossible to present an accurate picture of King's personality, but without a clear view of King's personality it is impossible to understand the diary. A simple phrase—'tonight was practically wasted'—means little in itself without some understanding of what the individual considers a waste of time, an understanding that might be obtained, for example, by comparing his intentions with his actions.

In interpreting the diary it is helpful to keep in mind that King was essentially Victorian in his outlook and responses. Anyone familiar with the writings of nineteenth-century evangelical Christians will have little difficulty with the style of the King diaries. They show the same emotionalism, the same extensive use of Christian symbolism, the same 'conscious record of sins,' the compulsive self-examination, and concern for mental and spiritual well-being that dominated the private papers of such people.[9] This piety is as much a part of King's personality as his pragmatism in later years. These were not two different faces of the same man; they were an integrated whole. But the integration was often imperfect and it required a great deal of psychic energy to maintain. The diary was one of the avenues wherein this endeavour could be sustained: 'I am taking up this diary again as a means of keeping me true to my true purpose ... it has helped to clear me in my thoughts and convictions ... I shall seek to be true in what I record in its pages ... revealing a desire to work ... to make the will of God prevail among men, to achieve personal righteousness, truth in thought & word, purity in heart, constancy and courage in action.'[10] It was the earnest Christian rather than the scholar or the politician who set the tone of the diary.

Friend or Fiend: King and Hitler

King's visit to Hitler in 1937 was probably the most controversial of all his actions in external relations, yet it was also the action most characteristic of his personal style. He had shown great faith in the efficacy of face-to-face contact in industrial conflict, and his association of industrial and international disputes would ensure that his thoughts would turn in this direction as the European situation became more threatening. His impulsive interview with Mussolini in 1928 had set a precedent which could be followed. King had taken the opportunity while in England in 1936 to propose such private negotiations to Prime Minister Baldwin, and the following year he discussed the desirability of such meetings of heads of states with Franklin Roosevelt.[11]

King's early enthusiasm for summit diplomacy, later to become an important facet of international relations, was in part derived from his perception of the European situation. On 15 June 1936 he had observed in his diary that: 'The European situation as it is today has nothing to compare with it at any time. No man can have to do with public affairs without feeling the necessity of coming to grips with it first hand.' In one sense the European situation offered a perfect example of a problem which he felt uniquely qualified to resolve—the building of confidence through the 'personal individual effort ... [of] men of different countries.'[12] He hoped that his talents as an intermediary could lead others to seek his aid. At the beginning of the year he had noted: 'I would be happy beyond words were I called on to intervene in the European situation. It would be the greatest joy of my life—but it seems too great a mission to expect.'[13]

His belief that through intervention he could avert war had a national as well as a personal component. He sought to make Canada's voice heard in 'a situation which threatens to engulf her in a world war and which, by being heard, might prevent such an appalling possibility.'[14] His confidence was derived from a simplistic view of both the European crisis and Hitler: a situation viewed in terms of juvenile personal associations and a projection onto the German leader of his own hopes and desires. His decision is best considered in his own words:

> I had been born in Berlin in Canada, in a county which had several communities of German names, and had represented that county in Parliament. Had also lived one winter in Berlin and felt I knew the best sides of the German people ... if I were talking to Hitler I could reassure him what was costing him friends was the fear which he was creating against other countries. That there was not so far as Canada, for example, and other parts of the Empire were concerned, any thought of continued enmity toward Germany but a desire to have friendly relations all around.

On talking the matter over with Skelton, he still feels very strongly that it would be resented in Canada; that it would only be flattering Hitler by having him feel that some more persons were coming to him; that he was so much of an anglo-maniac, that nothing could influence him. That his speech three months ago that he was following his star of destiny just as a somnambulist walks in his sleep, showed how completely mystical he was, and unwilling to view anything to influence him in any way from different sides.

My own feeling is that I made Canada's position vis-à-vis Europe and Great Britain, very plain, that to go to Germany might undo a little of the solid position in which I had already placed matters by creating doubts and suspicions as to what underlay the visit of Germany. It might also seem to obligate us to side with the British, should war come later. The Jingo press of Canada might misconstrue it all. My feeling, therefore, is that while I feel I could do some good and might do a great deal at this juncture, unless something should come up before I go away which would give a real reason for going, it might be better not to take the risk involved ...[15]

The following year he reconsidered this verdict when in the course of discussions with the German ambassador the possibility of an interview with Hitler arose. King accepted the invitation and with the approval of Chamberlain made the trip to Berlin.

The outcome of the visit was predetermined by two personal factors. King had throughout his life demonstrated a tendency to be very impressed by and enthusiastic about new situations. His enthusiasm often later gave way to misgivings and disappointment, but King made only one visit to Berlin. In the light of his determination to avoid overseas entanglements and his belief that peace was still a viable alternative, King was already strongly predisposed to see Hitler in a favourable light. It has already been observed that an individual's commitment to a particular course of action creates unconscious barriers to information that threatens this belief. Hitler did not fit into the category of enemy as long as he was willing to listen to King and to appear to accept King's interpretation of the issues.

The structure of the interview only reinforced this predisposition. A great deal of the diary record of the encounter focuses on the physical surroundings and appearance of Goering and Hitler, and the whole entry reflects King's personal satisfaction in the formal courtesy and laudatory tones of such diplomatic occasions. He did not hesitate to read personal approval into the slightest gestures, observing that 'Hitler nodded his head as much as to say that he understood,' and 'he would turn and look at me sideways and would smile in a knowing way as much as to say you understand what I mean.'[16] There was none of the lack of courtesy, the personal invective, the criticism of the opponent that King associated with the enemy.

To a man obsessed with signs and divine guidance there were many auguries of God's purpose. His Bible reading the day of the meeting was by chance just that chapter that he had read to his mother prior to her death. His day was filled with meetings and symbols associated with 'witnesses' and parallels.

He could believe that 'it would seem to be the day for which I was born—Berlin 1874.' Nor did King have any difficulty with the German leader, and noted: 'while he was talking ... I confess I felt he was using exactly the same argument as I had used in the Canadian Parliament last session.'[17]

In his summary King stressed Hitler's mysticism, his deeply religious nature, his humble origins, and the fact that he was 'a teetotaller, and also a vegetarian, unmarried, abstemious in all his habits and ways.' These were the characteristics of the virtuous not of the enemy, as was the need for 'quiet and nature to help him think out the problems of his country.' A man who had so much in common with Mackenzie King, who could look 'most direct at me in our talks together,' who 'never once became the least bit restless during the talk,' could not be other than 'eminently wise.'[18]

King saw and heard only those things that he needed to see: 'a genuine patriot,' a 'simple peasant,' a man 'with whom it should be possible to work with a good deal of trust and confidence,' and was completely duped.[19] Once he returned to Canada he did not find it difficult to find further evidence to reinforce his original misperception:

> I felt I wanted to read to Joan something re Hitler, to talk of his life. I had cut out recently articles concerning him. I am convinced he is a spiritualist—that he has a vision to which he is being true—His going to his parents' grave at the time of his great victory—or rather achievement—the annexation of Austria was most significant—I read aloud from Gunther's Inside Europe, concerning his early life—his devotion to his mother—that Mother's spirit is I am certain his guide and no one who does not understand this relationship—the worship of the highest purity in a mother can understand the power to be derived there from—or the guidance. I believe the world will yet come to see a very great man—mystic in Hitler. His simple origin & being true to it in his life—not caring for pomp—or titles, etc., clothes—but reality—His dictatorship is a means to an end—needed perhaps to make the Germans conscious of themselves—much I cannot abide in Nazism—the regimentation—cruelty—oppression of Jews—attitude towards religion etc., but Hitler ... the peasant—will rank some day with Joan of Arc among the deliverers of his people, & if he is only careful may yet be the deliverer of Europe. It is no mere chance that I have met him, & von Ribbentrop & Goering & the others I did—it is part of a mission I believe ... 'Divine Commission Fulfilled' says Hitler etc. The world scoffs at these. They are given in ridicule—but they are I believe true—He is a pilgrim—his love of music—of Wagner Opera—his habits abstinence, purity, vegetarian, etc., all evidence of the mystic who is conscious of his mission & lives to it. Strange this bringing together of Hitler & Bunyan, both I believe are meant to guide me at this time to the purpose of my life—which I believe to be to help men to know the secret of the path to peace, in industrial & international relationships—If I can only live to that they will know I have been with Him that end will be achieved. I pray God I may so live that men see that I have been with him.[20]

It is important not to downgrade the influence of King's meeting with Hitler merely because subsequent events proved King's perceptions of the man to be so wrong. Despite his attempts to transcend the limits of his finite existence King was no more omniscient than any other mortal; rather his personal defence made him even more liable to misinterpretation than others. Nevertheless, it is possible to agree with Nicholas Mansergh that this misperception of Hitler's intent made little difference to King's actions: 'essentially it was the situation in Canada, not the situation in Europe that determined his approach.'[21] And he was able to confront Hitler with Canada's intentions. This does not detract from the emphasis which King placed on this personal impression and which could have affected his sense of the imminence of danger. He steadfastly held to the belief that his view of Hitler was the correct one. He told Tweedsmuir the following year: 'I shall be interested in knowing whether it is not agreed [by Chamberlain and Halifax] that my little visit to Berlin, a year ago, was not helping to inspire a little more in the way of confidence ... I think you will agree that what I told you of different attitudes and probable developments was not wide of the mark.'[22] A few months later King observed: 'I believe, however, that it will be found in the end that Hitler is for peace, unless unduly provoked.'[23]

King could respond enthusiastically to Munich because he believed he had been instrumental in it. In many ways it seemed that Chamberlain was a substitute for King himself. Throughout 1937 King had dwelt in his private record on his capacity as a conciliator in a world where such a need was clearly visible. In October, in the course of interpreting one of his visions he had written:

> I am sure all this struggle is to help me in the field of international relations. It is to enable me to speak with conviction on the application of the Principles that make for Peace being a condition of mind and heart, in the nation as the individual, resulting from application of right principles bringing into being right policies in the former & right conduct in the latter—till we all 'become of one mind,' from 'being like minded'—This seems to me to be the process of spiritual evolution, from *being like minded to Christ thro' him, becoming one with God.* In this way the soul preserves its individuality and identity, and finds both preserved as they lose themselves in God, unless we lose our lives, we cannot find them. Instead of a multitude of souls, we become one soul with the One soul.[24]

He wondered about the possibility of leading a mission to Japan and told Tweedsmuir: 'How grateful I am that Chamberlain went to see Hitler! You may recall how strongly I urged these personal contacts. While it is not yet clear that war will be avoided, it is altogether certain that but for Chamberlain's meeting with Hitler we all should have been in the throes of a world war today.'[25] As Violet Markham sadly observed to Tweedsmuir, 'Hitler I fear pulled a good bit of wool over our friend Rex's eyes.'[26]

King's responses, however distasteful to some Canadians today, were perfectly consistent with his general beliefs. King was an appeaser by conviction rather than as an expedient, and his actions need to be judged in the context of Martin Gilbert's position: 'Appeasement, both as an attitude of mind and as a policy, was not a silly or treacherous idea in the minds of stubborn, gullible men, but a noble idea, rooted in Christianity, courage and commonsense.'[27] It was a policy in which, through patient and conciliatory reactions, men would be given an opportunity to declare themselves with the forces of good or those of evil. King had repeated in a public broadcast in 1936 the views he had expressed in *Industry and Humanity:*

> Fundamentally, the world struggle of today is one between the contending forces of good and evil. It is a part of the never-ending conflict between the forces activating those who, by their thoughts of others, and their unselfish acts, are seeking to further 'the law of Peace, Work and Health,' and the forces actuating those who, by their greed and selfish ambitions, are furthering 'the law of Blood and Death.'[28]

In times of stress King was inclined to consider some of his British allies among the latter rather than the former. King's tendency to see old threats and dangers would be accentuated by suggestions such as the proposal for an imperial war conference or cabinet. In 1936 he had been preparing himself for possible conflict by 'going pretty carefully through Lloyd George's "War Memories" ... I owe it to the country and to my work to anticipate ... the matters to be given consideration "prior to or in the event of war".'[29] Inevitably in times of stress King was dominated by the tensions of the past as much as by the problems of the present, but because he had surrounded himself with able men this perceptual difficulty did not seriously affect his capacity to lead.

The war with all its serious complications was at the same time a great triumph for King. His success in bringing a united Canada into the war has been described as 'one of the outstanding achievements of Commonwealth statesmanship.'[30]

Notes

1. Nicholas Mansergh, *The Commonwealth experience* (London, 1969), 17.

2. William Christian and Colin Campbell, *Political Parties and Ideologies in Canada* (Toronto, 1974), 2.

3. Erik H. Erikson, *Childhood and Society* (Middlesex, Eng., 1965); *Insight and Responsibility* (New York, 1964); *Identity, Youth, and Crisis* (New York, 1968); *Identity and the Life Cycle* (New York, 1959); *Young Man Luther* (New York, 1968); *Gandhi's Truth* (New York, 1969).

4. F.I. Greenstein, *Personality and Politics* (Chicago, 1969), 65.

5. J.E. Esberey, 'Personality and Politics: A Study of William Lyon Mackenzie King' (unpublished PhD thesis, University of Toronto, 1974).

6. Karen Horney, *The Neurotic Personality of Our Times* (New York, 1937); *Neurosis and Human Growth* (New York, 1950); *Our Inner Conflict* (New York, 1945). Helen

Deutsch, *Neurosis and Character Types* (New York, 1965). O. Fenichel, *The Psychoanalytical Theory of Neurosis* (New York, 1945). G. Mahl, *Psychological Conflict and Defense* (New York, 1971). D. Shapiro, *Neurotic Styles* (New York, 1965).

7. The main source of primary material on King is the W.L. Mackenzie King collection in the Public Archives of Canada (PAC). There are extensive references to King in other collections in this repository. Among published sources one would note: R. MacGregor Dawson, *William Lyon Mackenzie King, A Political Biography, 1874–1923* (Toronto, 1958); H. Blair Neatby, *William Lyon Mackenzie King, 1924–1932* (Toronto, 1963); *William Lyon Mackenzie King, 1932–1939* (Toronto, 1976). F.A. McGregor, *The Fall & Rise of Mackenzie King* (Toronto, 1962). J.W. Pickersgill and D.F. Forster, eds, *The Mackenzie King Record,* 4 volumes (Toronto, 1968–70). Earlier volumes of interest include: H.S. Ferns and B. Ostry, *The Age of Mackenzie King* (Toronto, 1955); H.R. Hardy, *Mackenzie King of Canada* (Toronto, 1949); Andrew Haydon, *Mackenzie King and the Liberal Party* (Toronto, 1930); Bruce Hutchinson, *The Incredible Canadian* (Toronto, 1952); O.E. McGillicuddy, *The Making of a Premier* (Toronto, 1922); Norman Rogers, *Mackenzie King* (Toronto, 1935). University of Toronto published a microfiche edition of King's diaries in two parts, 1893–1931 in 1974 and 1932–47 in 1980.

8. J.L. Granatstein, *Canada's War: the Politics of the Mackenzie King Government 1939–1945* (Toronto, 1975), v.

9. C.P. Stacey, *A Very Double Life: The Private World of Mackenzie King* (Toronto, 1976), 11.

10. Diary, 1 Jan. 1902.

11. Diary, 5 Mar. 1937.

12. WLMK to Buchan, 8 Sept. 1936 (BP).

13. Diary, 5 Jan. 1936.

14. Diary, 15 Jan. 1936.

15. Diary, 1 Oct. 1936.

16. Diary, 29 June 1937.

17. Ibid.

18. Ibid.

19. WLMK to Anthony Eden, 6 July 1937.

20. Diary, 17 Mar. 1938.

21. Mansergh, *Commonwealth Experience,* 382.

22. WLMK to Buchan, 23 July 1938 (BP).

23. WLMK to Buchan, 6 Sept. 1938 (BP).

24. Diary, 18 Oct. 1937.

25. WLMK to Buchan, 20 Sept. 1938 (BP).

26. Violet Markham to Buchan, 20 Aug. 1939 (BP).

27. Martin Gilbert, *The Roots of Appeasement* (London, 1966), 3.

28. J. Eayrs, *In Defence of Canada: Appeasement and Rearmament* (Toronto, 1965), xi.

29. WLMK to Buchan, 24 Aug. 1936 (BP).

30. Mansergh, *Commonwealth Experience,* 284.

CHAPTER
11 WORLD WAR II: THE DIEPPE DEBACLE

In marked contrast to the country-wide outbursts of patriotic enthusiasm in August, 1914, Canada's declaration of war on 10 September, 1939 was greeted sombrely and hesitantly by Canadians of all class and regional stripes. Setting the tone was Prime Minister William Lyon Mackenzie King, whose government's initial efforts were directed toward ensuring that Canada's part in the conflict was restricted to a level commensurate with its relatively junior international status. Haunted by the bitterly divisive national consequences of the conscription crisis of World War I, King sought to limit Canada's manpower commitment by channelling the country's resources and energies into such non-combatant contributions as the British Commonwealth Air Training Plan. This was an eminently reasonable policy during the winter of 1939–1940, given the state of suspended military animation popularly dubbed 'The Phony War' which then prevailed.

In the spring of 1940 the very foundations of King's carefully-crafted war strategy collapsed, a casualty of the German *blitzkrieg* which swept first northward into Denmark and Norway, and then westward through the Netherlands, Belgium and into France. With the evacuation of the British Expeditionary Force from Dunkirk on 4 June and France's capitulation little more than a week later, Great Britain alone of the major powers faced Nazi Germany, its largest remaining ally the Dominion of Canada. In these new circumstances, a very different Canadian contribution, both in scale and in scope, became necessary. At home, Canada's dramatically changed role was reflected in the National Resources Mobilization Act of June, 1940, the federal government's master plan to mobilize the country's entire military and industrial resources. Abroad, by the fall of 1942 the Canadian army establishment in Great Britain had swelled to five divisions, quintuple the number originally envisaged, to say nothing of the vastly expanded air, naval and merchant marine forces in place.

In contrast to the horrendous trench warfare experiences of the Canadian Expeditionary Force in World War I, for two years after the fall of France the only Canadian soldiers to see battle were the two ill-fated battalions dispatched to Hong Kong in December, 1941, another controversial chapter in Canada's military history. Instead the Canadian army marked time, training at various locations across Great Britain while the Allied Command marshalled the forces necessary to launch a final grand assault on German-controlled continental Europe. That inactivity was itself a factor in the decision to commit two Canadian infantry brigades to an exploratory raid on the heavily fortified French resort town of Dieppe on 19 August 1942. Unfortunately, Dieppe has gone down in the annals of Canadian military history as a tragic debacle, a perfect example of Murphy's Law at work, when everything that could go wrong, did.

The three articles reprinted here present a range of perspectives on the major questions associated with the Dieppe raid. Why was it launched in the first place? Why did it go so terribly wrong? Who was to blame? What, if any, lessons of value for the planning of future operations, specifically the Normandy invasion, were learned from the whole sad affair? Was it ultimately justifiable militarily?

Introducing the subject is Brian Loring Villa's 'The Bare Facts of a Historical Tragedy.' In presenting the 'bare facts,' Villa also signals his interpretation of Dieppe and its implications. To comprehend the full weight of his argument about the culpability of Lord Mountbatten, largely immune from criticism for more than a generation, students are advised to consult *Unauthorized Action: Mountbatten and the Dieppe Raid*, Villa's 1989 monograph from which this article was excerpted. The second reading, 'The Significance of Dieppe,' taken from Col. C.P. Stacey's *The Canadian Army 1939–1945, An Official Historical Summary*, reflects the immediate post-war Canadian military point of view, which was to stress the raid's vital importance for later planning operations. Like Villa, fifty years after the event Peter J. Henshaw has serious reservations about several aspects of the official account of the Dieppe affair, the most critical of which is captured by the title of his recent (1994) article in *Queen's Quarterly*, 'The Dieppe Raid: the Quest for Action for All the Wrong Reasons,' reprinted here.

Suggestions for Further Reading

Campbell, J.P., *Dieppe Revisited: A Documentary Investigation.* London: Frank Cass, 1993.

Drolet, G., "Dieppe: 1942–1992," *Canadian Defence Quarterly*, 22, 1, Special #2 (1992), 36–42.

Fanshawe, R.J., "Dieppe: Unforgettable Lessons," *Marine Corps Gazette*, 77, 2 (1993), 57–59.

Greenhous, B., *Dieppe, Dieppe*. Outrémont, Qué: Éditions Art global, 1993.

Robertson, T., *Dieppe: The Shame and the Glory*. Toronto: McClelland and Stewart, 1963.

Stacey, C.P., *The Canadian Army 1939–1945: An Official Historical Summary*. Ottawa: King's Printer, 1948.

———, *Six Years of War: The Army in Canada, Britain and the Pacific.* Vol. I. Ottawa: Queen's Printer, 1955.

Villa, B.L., *Unauthorized Action: Mountbatten and the Dieppe Raid.* Toronto: Oxford University Press, 1989.

THE BARE FACTS OF A HISTORICAL TRAGEDY

Brian Loring Villa

Just before dawn on 19 August 1942 a swarm of landing-craft approached the coast around the sleepy port town of Dieppe on the English Channel. The largest raid in history was on. A flotilla of 250 small naval craft were engaged, and overhead the largest single air battle of the war was about to get underway. Over 50 squadrons, some 800 fighters—Spitfires, Hawker Typhoons, and Hurricanes (more than had been engaged in the Battle of Britain)—would see action that day, many flying repeat missions, together with approximately 100 light and medium bombers—Blenheims and Bostons. Six thousand men would soon be trying to storm ashore from the landing-craft.

The coastline is generally straight, but at Dieppe it forms a small horseshoe with high cliffs on either side. At the centre lies the town, through which the river Arques makes its way to the sea, forming in succession narrow inner and outer harbours. It was from this small town, huddled about the inner harbour, that in peacetime the ferry unloaded British tourists—most of them heading for Paris. Because the harbour and river were shunted to the east, it had been possible to develop the rest of the gap between the cliffs most attractively with a broad promenade. A strip of pebbled beach stretched almost from cliff to cliff between the esplanade and the sea. Fronting on this promenade at the western end was a large casino. In peacetime this ocean front was the scene of all the small pleasures of a minor resort. Now the two-storey casino was heavily fortified, the beach was covered by machine-gun points along the housefronts, and, at the ends, by pill-boxes and a tank that had been set in concrete. These strong-points, together with guns sited in caves on both headlands, permitted enfilade (raking fire) right across the beach—a most effective form of fire, since any advancing force must at some point intersect it. A defending force would not even have to calculate range. Meanwhile, at a distance of two to three miles inland, Dieppe was circled by a perimeter of field batteries, just beyond a cordon of barbed wire, that gave protection from airborne attack in the rear, while heavy coastal batteries set back on the cliffs, well off to each flank, defended against attack from the sea. Just inland was a small airfield near Arques-la-Bataille.

Dieppe's defences constituted a very considerable German investment. Though the town itself was of slight importance, the Germans saw in Dieppe an obvious point for a British attack: it was within the range of RAF support and it was familiar as the terminal of the Dieppe-Newhaven ferry. Furthermore, Hitler had reason to suspect action at the coastal towns. In February 1942, after German divisions had overrun much of European Russia, Stalin stunned the West by signalling, in an astonishingly public way, his willingness to negotiate with Germany and his unhappiness with his Western allies. He declared publicly that Hitlers may come and go but Germany as a great nation would always remain, and that the Soviet Union was fighting simply in self-defence. The Foreign Office analysis noted with alarm:

> The whole speech, in fact, ignores the [Anglo-Soviet] Alliance or the whole war other than the 'liberation of Soviet Territory.' It would be hard to devise anything more deliberately unfriendly. And at the same time it holds out an unmistakeable hand to the Germans to the extent of hinting that the ousting of Hitler, though it would be 'welcome,' is not in Stalin's view an absolutely essential 'result' of the war for the 'liberation of our Soviet land.'[1]

There were three possible explanations, depending on how desperate the Soviet leader was and how convoluted were his calculations. Stalin might be genuinely seeking to arrange an immediate truce of sorts; or, by suggesting the possibility of a separate peace, he might be trying to force his Western allies to help him resist Germany; he might believe that galvanizing the West would force Germany to grant better terms. Indeed, he might be trying to keep all three irons in the fire. In any case, the Western powers were under intense pressure to reassure Stalin with some measure of military assistance.

For his part, Hitler drew a prescient conclusion from Stalin's speech. In a directive of 23 March he stated that the Western powers would be impelled by 'obligations to allies, and political considerations' to employ what capability they had to mount raids, possibly even committing airborne forces. Accordingly, he ordered that German troops along coastal regions susceptible to British attack were to be kept permanently in a high state of readiness.[2]

Hitler's erratic intuition was working at top form. Planners in Britain were indeed coming under the sort of pressures he predicted. At Combined Operations Headquarters (COHQ)—headed since October 1941 by the young Lord Louis Mountbatten, who was just beginning his meteoric rise in the British military establishment—staff planners were thinking out the implications of renewed pressures from the War Cabinet to help the Soviet Union. Anticipating that they would lead to further demands for raids, one of the principal Naval planners, Captain John Hughes-Hallett, was drawing up a list of possible targets for the raiding season that would begin late in May.[3]

Hughes-Hallett recognized that a lot of small raids would be necessary, but that they would scarcely satisfy the Soviet Union or Cabinet. Something big and impressive would therefore be needed. Thus the plan for a huge raid on

Dieppe came into being. As Field Marshal Montgomery's biographer, Nigel Hamilton, noted in 1981: 'Every military consideration argued against this expensive form of exercise, and it is noticeable that the Germans declined utterly to indulge in such operations on the British coast.' But Hitler did not have to worry about public opinion and the press. Hughes-Hallett, knowing that from its inception the raiding program had been envisaged as a dimension of psychological warfare, also knew that Britain would be forced into doing something drastic. And indeed, before he and the staff could work up the full plans, pressures for action in Cabinet built up so quickly that Mountbatten was forced to lay the project prematurely before the approving authority, the Chiefs of Staff Committee. This body was composed of Mountbatten himself, initially sitting in only for commando operations, and each of the highest-ranking officers of the three services: the First Sea Lord, Admiral Sir Dudley Pound, for the Navy; General Sir Alan Brooke, who had just taken over the chair from Pound, for the Army; and Chief Air Marshal Sir Charles Portal, for the Air Force. They gave hasty, tentative approval to Mountbatten's project, and assigned it the code-name *Rutter* (it would later be changed to *Jubilee*), on the understanding that the plan would be refined by Combined Operations, as the co-ordinating and supplying agency, and by the three Force Commanders, who would be charged with carrying it out.[4]

The commanders nominated were, initially: the Canadian Major-General J.H. Roberts for the Army, who would command all Allied ground forces; Air Vice-Marshal Trafford Leigh Mallory for the Air Force; and Rear-Admiral H.T. Baillie-Grohman (also later replaced by Captain John Hughes-Hallett) for the Navy. One of the most curious aspects of the raid was the employment of the 2nd Canadian Division to form the bulk of the attacking force, from which followed necessarily the appointment of its commander, Roberts, as the Army force leader for the Dieppe raid. Roberts was new to divisional command; even as a regimental commander sent to France after Dunkirk, he had not seen combat. Nor had the men under him. How, Montgomery's biographer has asked, 'could anyone believe that a Combined Operation, using untried soldiers, could successfully smash its way into the heart of Dieppe and beyond—to the airfield of Arques—in a matter of hours and then be successfully re-embarked on the following tide?' Those chosen to lead the operation presumably thought they would find a way to do the impossible.[5]

In the succeeding months the plan was fleshed out by an exceptionally cumbersome process. The fundamental principle of the British military forces was that the commanding officer, charged with executing a plan, must give final approval. He could, in theory, refuse to accept it when first proposed, or subsequently could refuse to commit his troops to the engagement if he thought the plan was fundamentally unsound, or if he felt the necessary conditions on which it was predicated no longer existed—a reason that led to the cancellation of several raids. Given this right of negative veto, it was vital that force commanders be engaged from the beginning in the planning process, but since there were three commanders for *Rutter,* planning was a very difficult process. Added to this was the great imponderable of having assigned the lion's share of ground operations to Canadians. The overall Canadian Commander, General A.G.L. McNaughton, delegated responsibility to the Commander of the Canadian Corps, Lieutenant-General H.D.G. Crerar, who in turn delegated it to General Roberts, whose 2nd Canadian Division would be committed. This was consonant with the above-cited British military doctrine. But it was felt that the Canadians ought to be given a little more help than usual, perhaps because few had much confidence in either General Roberts (who had no experience of divisional combat command or amphibious operations) or his principal adviser for planning, Lieutenant-Colonel Churchill Mann. Therefore a significant modification was made in the procedures. Since Canadian troops were under Home Forces Command, their commanding officer, General Sir Bernard Paget, was asked to keep a watchful eye over the whole plan as it developed. He delegated this unusual advisory role to General Montgomery, who was then commanding the southeast sector.[6]

Principal responsibility for advising General Roberts and Colonel Mann went, of course, to the Combined Operations organization, which may be said to have existed for the purpose of giving advice. In recognition of this, Mountbatten's original title had been Adviser on Combined Operations. (COHQ, it should be noted, did not have the forces or the commanders for large operations, and had to request appropriate commands to participate on a temporary basis.) As soon as COHQ had blocked out the concept of the operation and received approval from the Chiefs of Staff, its role in the planning process was purely advisory, although it was weighty, because the staff at COHQ were still regarded as the experts in this sort of warfare and because they had first conceived the plan.

There were many hands in formulating the plan for Dieppe: COHQ, the Air Force Commander, the Ground Force Commander, and whatever advice was given him from Canadian Army and Corps staffs, the Naval Force Commander, the Home Forces staff, and particularly the South-East Command. The reader will readily recognize in this multitude of planners a prescription for disaster. The Canadian commander naturally tended to rely on the British advisers at COHQ and Home Forces, whereas they, thoroughly imbued with the principle of a commander's veto, assumed that if Roberts was not complaining, he must be approving the plan. Though everyone paid lip-service to the principle that command, authority, and responsibility were undivided, these elements were in fact thinly spread all over the military establishment. This point was first made by the official Canadian historian, C.P. Stacey, and it is still a very telling one indeed.[7]

Those acquainted with organizational and bureaucratic models of decision-making, as first formulated by Professor Graham Allison, will recognize a further complicating factor. The advisers had to think of what was good for Roberts and his men, but they also had to think about what was good for their own institutional interests. Not surprisingly, they tended to compromise on differences, and as long as Roberts did not protest, they cheerfully assumed that everything was proceeding well. Roberts, knowing that this was his first opportunity to prove himself and that another might not be coming for a long time, made a point of never being difficult.

As different agencies made their suggestions, the plan underwent a number of significant changes. COHQ had itself originally favoured one that called for flanking attacks, which would converge on Dieppe from the rear. But it was feared, particularly by Montgomery, that the flanking attacks might never develop the steam to take the town, and without that achievement the raid would be seen by the public as a failure. Recognizing that much of the project's importance derived from the public perception of it, Montgomery supported the much riskier notion of making a frontal attack simultaneous with the flanking attacks, because this alone might give promise of capturing the town. Since it was becoming so clear that the raid's primary purpose was to grab headlines, one might have expected Combined Operations to make a powerful argument for the maximum amount of fire support from air and sea forces to ensure success. Strangely, when Mountbatten presented the rough outline to the Chiefs of Staff for their approval, he limited himself to remarking that there were many problematical aspects to the raid that would have to be worked out, but he did not then try to extract any substantial commitment of forces.[8]

A fundamental flaw in the whole conception was revealed when the planners sat down to figure out just when and where every landing vessel would be in the final approach. It was soon felt that there were too many simultaneous assaults in the Dieppe area, and that a traffic jam of sorts would occur if they all went in at the same time. Hence, to ensure clarity of command and control, it was decided that the flanking attacks would precede the frontal assault by half an hour (a frontal attack could not precede because, without taking the batteries on the flanks, any force approaching the centre would be destroyed by raking fire).[9]

This decision to let a half-hour elapse between the two major components of the assault constituted a major and, in the end, fatal change in plans. Everyone had recognized that while the flanking attacks always had some chance for limited success, the frontal assault in the centre, against the well-defended port itself, was a very doubtful proposition. Only with complete surprise could its capture be envisioned. This need for tactical surprise had been written into the outline plan, and the landing of tanks was to be employed for shock effect. But now the port was to be given a half-hour's warning by the start of the flanking attacks. Without surprise there might still have been some hope of succeeding if much heavier preliminary bombardment, and more extensive naval fire support, had been assigned. But the more preparatory fire support there was, the less would be the element of surprise. It was a vicious circle. This called for hard choices and crisp decision-making.

A clear decision should now have been taken, either to increase the air and naval support massively or to abandon the project. These options were never squarely confronted. No one could entertain any reasonable hope that without achieving tactical surprise in the centre, and with only minimal fire support, the frontal attack had any chance of succeeding. On 5 July, just six weeks before the raid, the German propaganda minister Goebbels, an amateur strategist at best, said that the enemy might be tempted to land on the French coast 'in a fit of military madness.' The day after the raid, with the beaches strewn with bodies amidst the wreckage of tanks and landing craft, that judgement did not seem far off the mark. One can easily understand why a German officer, interrogating the prisoners of war, wanted to hear their explanation for an operation that seemed to him to be clearly too big for a raid and just as clearly too small for a lodgement. For many, this has become the classic question about, if not the judgement on, the operation.[10]

Quite astonishingly, the planned amount of fire-power in support was actually reduced on 5 June, when—while Mountbatten was away in America—the preliminary heavy bombardment was cancelled. Montgomery and the Force Commanders obviously felt that restoring the prospects of surprise and facilitating the movement of the tanks they hoped to land were preferable to heavy preliminary bombardment, which their advisers apparently did not think could be made heavy enough.[11]

A number of other important events occurred between these crucial changes in June and the final modifications. A series of training exercises were carried out, as well as two full-scale dry runs, *Yukon I* and *II,* in the Bridgport/West Bay area of the Dorset coast. In the course of *Yukon I* on June 11, it became apparent that the exact synchronization of so many simultaneous landings was difficult to achieve with the precision required as to both timing and location. This first trial was deemed a dismal failure; hence the raid on Dieppe was postponed to early July. An attempt to execute the plan—called *Rutter*—was made between 2 and 8 July, but after the men had boarded the craft that were to take them across the Channel, and been told what the objective was, the weather worsened. They were still confined to the vessels, awaiting better conditions, when five days later the Luftwaffe made an attack on the assembled craft. Because the weather forecast for the last possible day of favourable moon and tides was still poor, the force was disbanded. German intelligence was certainly good enough to draw the obvious conclusions. The following day a Führer order went out over Hitler's signature. Noting German victories on the Russian front, Hitler expressed his conviction that the Allies had the choice of 'immediately mounting a major landing in order to create a second front or of losing Soviet Russia as a political and military factor.' He concluded that it was 'highly probable that enemy landings will shortly take place in the area of C-in-C West.' 'The most probable area,' he believed, would be 'the Channel coast, the area between Dieppe and Le Havre, and Normandy.'

Additional defensive measures were ordered, and the key commanders were to report to Hitler on a daily basis on the measures taken. It is not clear whether this circular order was available to British intelligence.[12]

As some 6,000 men, with varying degrees of knowledge of the plan, returned to the barracks and pubs of Britain on 8 July, General Montgomery recommended to his superiors that the raid be cancelled for good. There is no record that this recommendation was discussed by the Chiefs of Staff Committee. It is recorded however that Mountbatten argued that the option of reviving plans for the raid should be considered, because so much time and effort had been invested. The Chiefs agreed, which meant that the forces assigned to *Rutter* would continue to be held in reserve under Mountbatten's control until a decision was taken one way or another. Since Montgomery was not the least bit interested in any attempt to revive the project, it was undoubtedly by mutual accord that he was cut out of the chain of responsibility, even though the Canadian troops continued to be assigned to his command. The Naval Force Commander, Rear-Admiral H.T. Baillie-Grohman, was also reluctant to have anything more to do with the operation and was similarly cut out.[13]

Despite the negative opinion of such experienced commanders, COHQ was convinced that a revival of the operation was feasible and proceeded to try to make it so. A major problem would be attempting to maintain security. The troops must not be allowed to suspect that the raid might be mounted again. In a patent exercise in wishful thinking, it was assumed that both the troops and their morale were in such perfect condition that no further training—which might indicate another attempt—should be undertaken. This was a tragic mistake, for as Lord Lovat, the only commander who achieved his assigned objective, later observed, the plan required a 'split-second standard of excellence.' Hughes-Hallett decided to reduce dependence on large infantry landing ships; much of the attacking force would make the whole crossing in smaller landing-craft. They would leave from various points in southern England to avoid presenting a target or tipping off German intelligence. While these last two decisions improved the chances of concealing intent by dispersion, they added to the difficulty of navigating through the very narrow channel that would be cleared of German mines and also through the congestion of craft off Dieppe. This use of a multitude of smaller craft also made it more likely that the necessary synchronization of the landings, always the critical problem, would prove difficult, particularly as the smaller unarmoured landing-craft were designed for short runs of five to ten miles, not the 70 miles to Dieppe—none of the training exercises had been based on so long a run by these craft. Finally, the employment of this unwieldy formation made it much more difficult to turn around should some last-minute danger, like the appearance of a German coastal convoy, appear. Somewhat more sound was the decision to substitute commandos for the airborne troops that were originally designated to take out the major flanking batteries. But the commandos had to be carried in by more naval craft, adding further to the congestion.[14]

The preliminary order for the operation, now called *Jubilee,* was issued by Combined Operations on 31 July. On the evening of 17 August the troops began their movement, leaving on the night of the 18th.[15]

Scores of books in prose, and even some in poetry, have been written solely about the military side of the engagement. The main events of that sad morning, beginning at 0450, can be told briefly. From east to west along the Channel front it was mostly a tale of disaster, punctuated by a few minor successes. At the extreme eastern end, where No. 3 Commando was supposed to take out a major coastal battery, 23 landing-craft approached the beach and came under intense fire; only six actually reached shore. All the commandos aboard five of the remaining six vessels became casualties in the final run-in, or shortly after landing. Only men from the one remaining landing-craft came through the fire and managed to keep the heavy coastal battery out of action for most of two hours. A little to the west, the assault at Puys by the Royal Regiment and the Black Watch achieved nothing. They landed 15 minutes late—8 minutes after the Germans had sounded the alert. Of the 500 who landed, only six soldiers returned unwounded. The rest were dispatched by a defending force numbering little more than 60 effectives.

The frontal attack on the centre by the Royal Hamilton Light Infantry and the Essex Scottish was a disaster, though it had started out promisingly. For the first minute or two after the fighter-bombers had shot up the harbourfront, the German defenders seemed dazed. But moments later German machine guns and mortars blazed into action as the first craft unloaded their men. 'High explosive bursting on shingle, the rattle of small-arms fire, the dull roar of distant naval guns and sharp report of high-velocity field pieces, the howling of aircraft engines, the screams of wounded men—these sounds in deafening combination numbed the minds of soldiers who had never before been under fire.' Though the first landings were perfectly timed, and two battalions were landed abreast, support from the destroyers offshore and the fighters overhead was insufficient. The tanks that were to provide some of the fire-support arrived fifteen minutes late, and by then momentum had been lost. Raked by withering fire, many of the infantrymen simply huddled beside the low sea-wall separating the beach from the promenade to await the end. A few units pushed ahead and managed to enter the town, but they could do little. Of the 27 tanks unloaded, about half managed to cross the sea-wall; but none penetrated the tank barriers protecting the town itself. Eventually all 27 had to be abandoned. A desperate attempt by General Roberts to reinforce the eastern half of the main assault by the Essex Scottish, by throwing in the Fusiliers de Mont-Royal, was of no avail because the former were largely still pinned against the sea-wall and the latter were unloaded at the wrong beach. Much more worthy of reinforcement was the action being carried out to the west by the South Saskatchewans and Cameron Highlanders, who were landed in reasonably good shape, the latter managing to penetrate some 2,000 yards inland in their attempt to enter the town from the flank; but before they could reach their objective, general evacuation had already been decided on (at 0900, nearly four hours after landing).[16]

The only real major success of the whole morning was at the extreme western end of the front. There Lord Lovat led No. 4 Commando in a successful assault on a German coastal battery, putting it entirely out of action. By 0830 he and his men had done their job and been successfully evacuated. Elsewhere, pulling the men off the beaches under vicious fire proved almost impossible. As Hughes-Hallett later recalled: 'I doubt whether a withdrawal has ever been attempted under such terrible conditions.' Heavy casualties attended the evacuation and the rear guard was forced to surrender. By 1250, when a destroyer made a last cautious approach to the beaches to see who might be left to evacuate, there was little to be seen save the bodies of the dead and the burned-out hulks of abandoned tanks and landing-craft. There was nothing to do but limp back home.[17]

Perhaps the single most important factor in these tactical reverses was the delay in the landings—all scheduled to occur in the half-hour between 0450 and 0520—even though none were off by more than 20 minutes. Mistimings, of course, affected vital elements of the plan. There had never been any chance of surprise at the centre because the flanking attacks were to commence half an hour earlier. Surprise for the enveloping attacks was nevertheless thought possible—though it would depend on the precisely timed arrival of units on the beaches. But any one of the many seemingly minor delays dashed this hope. It has been argued that some of the fateful delays were due to bad luck; particularly the unexpected collision with a small enemy convoy of the craft carrying the commandos for the easternmost attack. The resulting fire-fight certainly warned the Germans at two points east of the town, Puys and Berneval. Not surprisingly, after this collision some jittery landing-craft crews, aware both of the delay and of a possible alert, made for good reason their final approaches to the beach at a speed much greater than had been planned. The noise-level of the landing-craft engines was correspondingly loud, and many of the German defenders who had not heard the fire-fight were thus alerted.[18]

The collision, however, cannot be ascribed merely to bad luck for two reasons. First of all, the presence of enemy convoys was not the exception but the rule. They were constantly working the coasts because Dieppe was a frequently used terminus for the Germans. Moreover, two warnings of the convoy's likely route had been sent by the Commander-in-Chief Portsmouth to the *Jubilee* force shortly after their departure from England. Had this been a small commando operation, it would have been possible to make necessary adjustments by timing the final approach somewhat differently, or by making an end-run; but since it was a large operation in which exact synchronization of multiple parties was essential, these options were not available. The only feasible course was to cancel the operation. This was not done. It has been argued that there was a failure in signal transmission, which prevented the timely receipt of the warnings, but this has never been established. It seems more likely that the new Naval Force Commander, Hughes-Hallett, decided not to throw away the last chance to carry out this mission. He was nothing if not determined. He and Mountbatten later claimed that because bad-weather forecasts had been given, it had taken great courage to leave Portsmouth and commit the men to action. In fact the weather predictions were particularly good (as the weather in fact turned out to be). Such vaunted courage, or stubbornness, could more accurately be applied to the decision to proceed after two warnings about the German coastal convoy had been sent to Hughes-Hallett at 0127 and 0244. The collision with the convoy occurred one hour after the second warning.[19]

The cumulative effect of all these events—the clash with the convoy, the mistimings, the failure to neutralize all the key batteries, the loss of surprise for the frontal attack—translated into massive casualties. In some cases landing-craft returned without having attempted to disembark soldiers. Of the nearly 5,000 Canadians who embarked, nearly 1,000 were spared in this way. Of the remaining 4,000 who did attempt to land, only thirty per cent returned alive. In other words nearly 2,700 were killed or captured. Photographs of the gutted-out landing-craft, from which no survivors could possibly have emerged, and pictures of the carnage on the beaches, are still shocking today.[20]

About 1,300 of some 1,900 prisoners-of-war had managed to avoid being wounded, and a high proportion of these men, after enduring the misery of prisoner-of-war status for three long years, eventually returned home at war's end. By any standards this was a terrible balance-sheet. Dieppe may have been the biggest raid in history, and the largest air battle of the Second World War, but it also won the dubious distinction of being, as Nigel Hamilton has observed, 'the most tragic and, in ratio to participating forces, the most costly Allied offensive of the war.'.[21]

The dreadful news was not reported immediately. British newspapers and radio stations were allowed to carry some word of the operation even as the raid was ending, but naturally the accent was on the positive. 'Morale of returning troops reported to be excellent,' was the message Mountbatten sent to Prime Minister Churchill in Cairo the next day. 'All I have seen are in great form.' To the War Cabinet he reported that the lessons learned would be 'invaluable' in planning the future cross-Channel invasion, and Churchill wired on the 21st: 'My general impression of "Jubilee" is that the results fully justified the heavy cost. The large scale air battle alone justified the raid.' When it had become evident that a disaster was in progress, the government moved to restrict coverage. In the meantime, however, inaccurate reporting had done some damage. The American press—seemingly unaware that the number of U.S. rangers who participated in the raid was approximately fifty—headlined that the Yanks were storming Europe, an affront that left a lasting wound in Canadian-American relations. Canadian headlines were similarly sensational, though they at least managed to identify the main force correctly.[22]

Initial enthusiasm wore off in a matter of hours. On the evening of 19 August, CBC correspondent Rooney Pelletier, broadcasting to Canada, spoke of a 'noble occasion' and a 'day of of high honour,' but he warned that the 'electric enthusiasm' was all a bit premature. 'It seems wise to exercise a bit of caution,' Pelletier advised, 'before shouting full-throated hosannahs.' The next day the first detailed report by Ross Monroe was published in Canadian newspapers. Headlines announced a 'Blazing, Bloody Battle.' Underneath Monroe explained that 'Canadian shock troops had a rough time of it at several points and losses probably will not be small.' As the full dimensions began to sink in, a new phase commenced (not ended yet) in which commentators and analysts, and later historians, tried to see some good emerging from the operation. In a letter to Mountbatten at the time of the Normandy landing in July 1944, Eisenhower credited Dieppe with having provided many useful lessons. Since Eisenhower had long been a friend and booster of Mountbatten's, this confirmation of what had become a received opinion might well have been challenged when it was later invoked by Mountbatten to defend the operation.[23]

Within two weeks of the raid a report was released from the Canadian headquarters that tried to justify it as a vital learning experience. Its principal author, the Canadian military historian C.P. Stacey, admits now that this was something of a rationalization. Subsequent historians, offering points and counterpoints, have had no better success in presenting a convincing justification, though they have written so many studies that the literature on Dieppe is nearly as extensive as that on the Normandy invasion—completely out of proportion to Dieppe's military importance. Much bitterness has simmered under the surface of the long debate. Just a few months after the raid, Lord Beaverbrook confronted Mountbatten at a dinner party: 'You have murdered thousands of my countrymen. You took those unfortunate Canadian soldiers .... They have been mown down in their thousands and their blood is on your hands.' Beaverbrook was not alone in thinking this. For many Canadians, Dieppe has assumed the same importance Gallipoli has for Australians.[24]

How did such a disastrous undertaking come about when the odds against its success were well known? Why has there never been any clear designation of responsibility? Who, in the end, was finally responsible? These questions are answered in the pages that follow—in the course of which a large window is opened on the desperate first two years of the Second World War.

Notes

1. Baggallay to Eden, 12 and 13 February 1942 and Foreign Office staff minutes on same, FO 371/32875; Ewer to Ridsdale, 27 February 1942, F0371/32876 and Staff Minutes on same.

2. The 23 March 1942 directive is in U.S. Government, *Führer Directives and Other Top-Level Directives of the German Armed Forces, 1942–1945* (GPO, Washington, 1948), pp. 21–2.

3. Hughes-Hallett often tried to explain how the list of targets was chosen. The two most important accounts are in his unpublished memoirs, tentatively titled *Before I*

Forget, and his interview with John Secondari in 1967. The former—hereafter referred to as Unpublished Memoirs—exists in two copies with slight variations and unfortunately different paginations; one is in the Mountbatten Papers MB1 B47 and the other in the National Archives of Canada, Ottawa (with traces of four different paginations!), MG 30 E 463. I have used the most legible NAC pagination. (I have relied principally on the chapters titled 'Combined Operations' and 'Dieppe.') The interview with Secondari is preserved in the Mountbatten Papers MB1 B67/2. Bernard Fergusson, in *The Watery Maze: The Story of Combined Operations* (London, 1961), a book much approved of by Mountbatten, claims that the 'final reason for choosing Dieppe was the fact that the planners had already ruled it out as a desirable place to capture in the early stages of a real invasion, and we should therefore be giving nothing away by raiding it now' (p. 169). What Fergusson presumably had in mind was the fact that it was recognized very early that all the Channel ports were too easy to destroy, as usable ports, by the enemy before their capture, and any attempt to seize them was unlikely to prove worthwhile. But if this was what Fergusson had in mind, why then did he justify a raid in which the raiders risked all in an attempt to capture Dieppe when they could much more easily have raided the hinterland or devastated some less well-fortified place?

4. Nigel Hamilton, *Monty: The Making of a General, 1887–1942* (London and New York, 1981), p. 549.

5. Ibid., p. 552.

6. Many explanations have been advanced for the involvement of Montgomery and South-Eastern Command. But as Hughes-Hallett credits the decision to Churchill, one must conclude the motive was principally political, i.e. he wanted to avoid criticism that Dominion troops were used casually as cannon fodder. Hughes-Hallett, Unpublished Memoirs, MG 30 E 463, NAC, pp. 128, 152. (These memoirs, which at first glance seem tame, are in fact rich in important detail. They are the best statement of the Mountbatten/Hughes-Hallett position and merit publication.)

7. C.P. Stacey, *Six Years of War,* Volume 1 of the Official History of the Canadian Army in the Second World War (Ottawa, 1966, corrected 4th printing), p. 399.

8. J. Hughes-Hallett, 'The Mounting of Raids,' in *Royal United Services Institute Journal, XCV* (November 1950), 585, and Unpublished Memoirs, pp. 152–4, MG 30 E 463, NAC; COS (42) 42nd (O) 13 May 1942, also COS (42) 139th (same date).

9. 'There was no margin of time, or indeed of sea room.' Hughes-Hallett's Unpublished Memoirs, pp. 168–9, 153, MG 30 E 463, NAC. His amazingly complex navigation 'Track Chart' for this operation is preserved in DEFE 2/336.

10. Goebbels is quoted in Michael Balfour, *Propaganda in War 1939–45* (London, 1979), p. 279; interview with Major Brian McCool in Ronald Atkin, *Dieppe 1942: The Jubilee Disaster* (London, 1980), p. 249.

11. The abandonment of the bombing has always been blamed by Mountbatten and his defenders on Montgomery, who was in the chair at the meeting of 5 June when this was first accepted. Blame he certainly deserves but it must be noted that the suggestion was first made at a meeting of 1 June, for part of which Mountbatten was present. Nor could it be said that he was ignorant of the real reasons for the reluctance of Bomber Command to lend its craft for raids; see Chapter 7 of this book.

For the meeting of 1 June see DEFE 2/546. There is also a copy of the minutes in the Baillie-Grohman Papers at the National Maritime Museum, Greenwich (Dieppe folder).

12. The most accurate and complete translation of the German Army West warning orders is to be found in the late Stephen S.W. Roskill, 'The Dieppe Raid and the Question of German Foreknowledge' in *Royal United Services Institute Journal,* CIX, No. 633 (February, 1964), pp. 27–31.

13. On Montgomery's recommendation to cancel, see Field Marshal Bernard Montgomery, *Memoirs* (London, 1958), p. 76, also Brigadier Maurice Chilton, of Montgomery's South-Eastern Command, to Crerar 7 July, File 220C1.009(D3) DND; COS (42) 64th (O) 6 July 1942; Hamilton, *Monty,* p. 505. Judging by the memoirs of Goronwy Rees (see below), his representative for *Rutter* planning, Montgomery was never much interested in the project and probably did not like having responsibility without authority. One can well believe, therefore, his 1962 statement for the CBC program 'Close-Up' that he was 'delighted, absolutely delighted' at the cancellation, which was the impression Rees had at the time. Transcript of 'Close-Up: Dieppe' in Directorate of History, National Defence Headquarters, Canada (hereafter DND), 594/009(D13), and Goronwy Rees, *A Bundle of Sensations* (London, 1960), p. 157. For many years Mountbatten and his supporters explained the replacement of Baillie-Grohman as something involuntary—due to his sudden posting elsewhere— but on two occasions at least Mountbatten claimed that it was his decision, in 1950 telling Churchill that it was because Baillie-Grohman was a 'sick man' and in 1971 telling Hughes-Hallett that he had pushed Baillie-Grohman aside because he (Hughes-Hallett) could do a much better job. The truth is more probably that Baillie-Grohman refused to have anything to do with the revival of *Rutter,* being dismayed by the lack of professionalism in Mountbatten's organization. Mountbatten's draft replies to Churchill's questions are attached to Mountbatten to Ismay, 29 August 1950, Ismay Papers, Liddell Hart Centre, King's College, London (hereafter KC); Mountbatten to Hughes-Hallett, 3 September 1971, in MG 30 E463 NAC. On Baillie-Grohman's criticism of COHQ, see pp. 193–5 of this book.

14. Lord Lovat, *March Past* (London, 1978), pp. 242, 245, 272–3, 275.

15. Combined Plan, 31 July 1942, 75/10 DND.

16. W.A.B. Douglas and Brereton Greenhous, *Out of the Shadows: Canada in the Second World War* (Toronto, 1977), p. 113.

17. Hughes-Hallett, Unpublished Memoirs, p. 188, NAC.

18. Hughes-Hallett, untitled comments on Robertson manuscript in the Hughes-Hallett Papers, IWM.

19. Hughes-Hallett had boxed himself in badly, having loudly complained about too many Force Commanders who cancelled operations for the slightest reason. He would have looked very foolish had he returned to England without having landed the men. The warning is to be found in DEFE 3/187. Professor F.H. Hinsley's silence on this in his official history, *British Intelligence During the Second World War,* is hard to understand, particularly as intercepts and their use were a major concern of his study. There is no mention of the failure to get this intelligence to the Naval Force Commander in his long appendix on the role of intelligence in the

Dieppe raid. John Campbell of McMaster University, to whom I am indebted for drawing this to my attention, is writing a study that will deal with the problem of these intercepts.

20. T. Murray Hunter, *Canada at Dieppe* (Ottawa, Canadian War Museum, 1982), pp. 39–41.

21. Hamilton, *Monty,* p. 549. Mountbatten to Churchill, 20 August 1942, CAB 120/69.

22. New York *Journal-American, Daily News, New York Post, Toronto Star, Windsor Daily Star,* all 20 August 1942.

23. Sound recordings, from Canadian Broadcasting Corporation archives accompanying Doug Stuebing, *Dieppe 1942* (Toronto, 1967). Mountbatten had in fact written to Eisenhower to claim some of the credit for Normandy. Eisenhower's response, saying in effect that he had managed to avoid the mistakes of Dieppe, may be read more than one way. Mountbatten to Eisenhower, 25 June 1944, and Eisenhower to Mountbatten, 11 July 1944, both in Mountbatten file, Eisenhower Papers, Abilene, Kansas.

24. C.P. Stacey, *A Date with History* (Ottawa, n.d. but *c.* 1982); 'The Curious Case of Lord Beaverbrook,' Mountbatten Papers, p.10, MB1 C20; cf. Tom Driberg, *Beaverbrook, A Study in Power and Frustration* (London, 1956), p. 291.

THE SIGNIFICANCE OF DIEPPE

C.P. Stacey

The raid on Dieppe was perhaps the most hotly discussed operation of the war. Tactically, it was an almost complete failure, for we suffered extremely heavy losses and attained few of our objectives. After the Normandy landings of 6 June 1944, however, the raid appeared in a new perspective; and historically it is in the light of the events of that later day that it must be judged.

It is in order to glance first, however, at its immediate consequences within the Canadian Army Overseas, and in Canada. There is no doubt whatever that in the Army it produced a new sense of pride. After nearly three years of disappointment and frustration, it had been demonstrated that this Canadian Army could fight in the manner of that of 1914–18; and the bad luck and the losses did not diminish the confidence thus engendered.[1] At the same time, the experience of Dieppe undoubtedly led Canadian soldiers to view the question of their own employment more soberly. There was less demand now for immediate assault upon the Germans in the west; the magnitude of such an enterprise was more clearly apparent than before, as was the need for the most detailed preparation, the most careful training, the most exacting discipline.

From *The Canadian Army, 1930-1945* (Ottawa: King's Printer, 1948), 83-86. Courtesy of the Department of National Defence, Canada.

At home in Canada the effects were different. Soldiers and civilians look at such things from widely separate points of view. Canadian civilians, particularly those who had lost relatives, saw only the casualty lists and the failure. It was quite impossible, without helping the enemy, to make any announcement of the actual lessons learned; and as the raid was followed by another long period of inactivity by the Canadian forces, public opinion continued to dwell upon it for months, and comment, frequently very ill-informed, continued in the press and elsewhere. Although, as has been made apparent, the responsibility for the tactical plan was widely distributed, and the Canadian share was limited, it was declared with the utmost assurance, in at least one respectable publication, that the project for a raid on Dieppe and the plan for it were almost exclusively the work of Canadian officers and proved the bankruptcy of Canadian generalship; and there can be little doubt that such criticism did something to undermine the hitherto unassailable prestige of General McNaughton with the public.

So much for the Canadian results of the operation. More important was its influence on future planning.

Needless to say, it was closely analysed at Combined Operations Headquarters, and a detailed report was prepared incorporating the official "lessons learned." It is unnecessary here to state these lessons in full, but the most important should be summarized. One of them was that in future, "assaults should be planned to develop round the flanks of a strongly defended locality rather than frontally against it" unless overwhelming close support was available. Another was the necessity for the formation of "permanent naval assault forces with a coherence comparable to that of any other first line fighting formations," and the desirability of training Army formations intended for amphibious assaults in close co-operation with such Naval forces. (This was subsequently done, we shall see, before the Normandy landing, and with the happiest results.) Still another was the importance of maintaining flexibility in the army plan, by providing the commander with a strong reserve to be available to "exploit success" at the points where it may be achieved. (It might have been added that unless means can be found for ensuring that the commander receives early and accurate information of events ashore, his reserves will be no use to him.) But the paramount lesson was "the need for overwhelming fire support, including close support, during the initial stages of the attack." This, it was recommended, should be provided "by heavy and medium Naval bombardment, by air action, by special vessels or craft working close inshore, and by using the fire power of the assaulting troops while still sea-borne." The Naval Force Commander, incidentally, had reported that in his opinion a battleship could have operated off Dieppe during the first hours of daylight without undue risk and would probably have turned the tide ashore in our favour.

Two other lessons, not so specifically stated in the official document, decidedly affected our later planning. First, it had been made pretty clear that the

classical plan of securing a beach by landing infantry at dawn was not prac-
ticable in the face of well-organized defences. A new technique of landing and
support was required, and largely on the basis of the Dieppe experience it was
developed before the Normandy assault of 1944. Secondly, it had been shown
that the military plan in such operations must not depend upon precise timing
of the landings. Although in general a very high standard of precision was attained at Dieppe, we have seen that in at least two cases relatively slight
inaccuracies in timing had most serious results. This possibility was avoided
in planning the 1944 assault.

Some of these lessons were obviously not new. Others there might have
been considerable difficulty in deducing from earlier history. However this may
be—and as explained above Combined Operations Headquarters had been
keenly conscious of the pressing need for a large-scale modern experiment—
these tactical conclusions do not perhaps wholly exhaust the effects of the
Dieppe operation.

On 7 June 1944, the day following the momentous landings in Normandy,
General Crerar "briefed" a large group of Canadian officers on the operations
which had just begun. He spoke in part as follows:

> ... To commence with, I think it most important that, at this time, all of you
> should realize what a vital part the gallant and hazardous operation of the
> raid in force on Dieppe, by 2 Cdn Inf Div, has played in the conception, planning
> and execution of the vast "Overlord" operation. I shall, therefore, give you in
> briefest outline this important background.
>
> Until the evidence of Dieppe proved otherwise, it had been the opinion in
> highest command and staff circles in this country that an assault against a
> heavily defended coast could be carried out on the basis of securing tactical
> surprise, and without dependence on overwhelming fire support, in the critical
> phases of closing the beaches and over-running the beach defences.
>
> If tactical surprise was to be the basis of the plan, then bombardment, prior
> to imminent "touchdown" obviously required to be ruled out. Dependence on
> tactical surprise also implied an approach under cover of darkness and landing
> at first light. Adequate air superiority, after surprise had been achieved and
> throughout the operation, was, of course, considered essential, and required to
> be assured.
>
> Very briefly, such were the conceptions held by those on the highest levels con-
> cerned with planning the operation against Dieppe, and however hazardous
> the operation, it was natural, and proper, that after nearly three years of war,
> without any fighting by Canadian troops, the responsibility for carrying out
> this essential preliminary to future large scale invasion should come to a
> Canadian Division.
>
> I am not going to take up your time by analysing the results and lessons of
> Dieppe ... I will, however, make it clear that from the study of those experi-
> ences emerged the technique and tactics first demonstrated by the 3 Cdn Inf Div
> in "Pirate" exercise last October, and that this technique and these tactics,
> were those adopted for the vast combined operation which took place yesterday.

One more point in the nature of a personal opinion. Although at the time the heavy cost to Canada, and the non-success of the Dieppe operation seemed hard to bear, I believe that when this war is examined in proper perspective, it will be seen that the sobering influence of that operation on existing Allied strategical conceptions, with the enforced realization by the Allied Governments of the lengthy and tremendous preparations necessary before invasion could be attempted, was a Canadian contribution of the greatest significance to final victory.

The contrast between the plan of the Dieppe assault and that followed on 6 June 1944 is, indeed, most striking. For the puny bombardment by four destroyers which covered the Dieppe frontal attack, the "Overlord" plan substituted the fire of a tremendous naval force including six battleships; in place of the brief attack by cannon-firing Hurricanes, we have the combined efforts of the British and American Bomber Commands, dropping more than 11,000 tons of bombs in twenty-four hours; we have engineer assault vehicles, amphibious tanks, new support craft of many types (including rocket bombardment ships); and we have the army helping to clear the way for its own assault with self-propelled artillery firing from tank landing-craft. These devices and techniques, in many cases, stemmed directly from the experience of Dieppe, although the lessons of many later amphibious operations also helped to shape them. The casualties sustained in the raid were part of the price paid for the knowledge that enabled the great operation of 1944 to be carried out at a cost in blood smaller than even the most optimistic had ventured to hope for. The assault on the famous Atlantic Wall was regarded as a most perilous and uncertain enterprise. When in the course of a week or so after D Day it became fully clear that the thing which men had hoped for, but scarcely expected, had really come to pass—that General Eisenhower's armies had smashed the barrier at a single blow and established themselves solidly in France—the name of Dieppe was suddenly on many lips. That much-criticized undertaking had made an essential contribution to the success of the most momentous operation of war ever attempted.

The Allies were not the only people to extract lessons from the Dieppe raid. The Germans likewise studied it with care; and it clearly had considerable influence upon their subsequent system of defence in France. The evidence indicates that it convinced them that any attempt at invasion could be destroyed on the beaches. Their efforts, they decided, should be concentrated upon preventing landings and particularly the landing of armour. This was reflected in the arrangement of their coastal defences, which in Lower Normandy were simply a thin line along the beaches, almost entirely without "depth."

NOTE: Laymen may not appreciate fully the difficulties of the Dieppe raid on the naval side. All experience shows that no operation of war is harder than landing troops in darkness with precision as to time and place. In this, the first large combined operation of 1939-45, thirteen groups of craft sailed from three ports at varying speeds. The assault craft, we have seen, had a 10-mile run-in. As noted above, a high general standard of precision was attained in spite of these difficulties; but the plan was such that relatively minor inaccuracies had serious consequences. In other respects the plan for handling the naval assault force was an almost complete success, and served as a model for later and larger operations.

Dieppe served also to confirm the Germans in the belief that a basic consideration in the Allies' minds at the very outset of an invasion would be the capture of a major port, and thus encouraged them to devote their best efforts to developing heavy defences about such places. Thus the Germans were, as a result of the raid, centring their defence upon the ports when simultaneously the Allies, also in part as a result of the raid, were increasingly turning their attention to the possibility of invading over open beaches without immediately gaining a major port. The great conception of the prefabricated harbour owes something to the lessons learned at Dieppe concerning the difficulty of capturing a German-held port.

An uncovenanted result of the Dieppe raid was thus to warp the Germans' system of defence in North-West Europe to our advantage.

Notes

1. It was the present writer's observation, however, that the operation's favourable effects upon morale were at least partly undone, as time passed, by the influence of the reports of continued criticism in Canada.

THE DIEPPE RAID: THE QUEST FOR ACTION FOR ALL THE WRONG REASONS

Peter J. Henshaw

> *"The extent to which the raid went according to plan and still ended in utter disaster illustrates how fatally flawed was the conception of the operation from the first; how easily military leaders desperate for action could delude themselves into thinking that audacity and surprise were a substitute for sound strategy and adequate fire power."*

Though uncertainties continue to plague accounts of the decision to launch the Dieppe raid on 19 August 1942, the tragic details of events that day are clear enough. The intention was to capture a minor port on the French channel coast using two brigades of Canadian infantry, which would land at dawn supported by tanks, British Commandos, Royal Marines, a few American Rangers, a handful of destroyers, and most of the fighter aircraft in Britain. In their brief time ashore, the attackers were supposed to cause maximum havoc before beating a hasty retreat. Planners compiled a small catalogue of tasks to be performed: inspect a radar station, demolish a railway tunnel, attack an airfield, overrun a German headquarters, destroy coastal batteries, tow away barges, etc. None of these had any intrinsic significance. The raid was really no more than an

From *Queen's Quarterly*, 101/1, 1994, 103-115. Reprinted by permission of *Queen's Quarterly*.

attempt to exercise the Allies' supposed dominance in the air and at sea, provoking the Luftwaffe into a battle it was sure to lose, proving that whatever number of German troops were deployed in the west, the Allies could, with their amphibious capabilities, overwhelm specific targets at will.

Events in the skies above the Normandy coast and on Dieppe's unforgiving shingle proved quite the opposite. The Luftwaffe, with all of the advantages possessed by the RAF in the Battle of Britain, could inflict greater casualties than it suffered; the German army, with relatively few troops in prepared positions, could bring an assault by a numerically superior force to a standstill on the beaches and keep it pinned there, making the withdrawal just as suicidal as the attack.[1]

The raid was to have been the first of a series of such operations, favoured by the RAF as an opportunity to employ its fighter aircraft to advantage, and favoured by Winston Churchill as an extension of the irregular warfare and audacious strategies of which he was so enamoured. It was conceived in Lord Louis Mountbatten's Combined Operations Organization, which in 1942 was rising in size and importance, given the status almost of a fourth armed service, as Churchill sought to bypass what he saw as the inertia and timidity of regular Army and Royal Navy staff.

The rise of Combined Operations was also linked to some of the largest problems of coalition warfare faced by the British government, not least that of trying to persuade both the Soviet Union and the United States of Britain's devotion to opening a second front in northwest Europe at the earliest practical moment. The Soviet Union needed evidence that its allies were not holding back whilst the two titans of the continent ground each other down on the eastern front; the United States needed reassurance that its decision to make the defeat of Germany a priority over the war against Japan was the right one, and that delays in returning to the continent stemmed not from the British government's preoccupation with defending the Empire but from the real problems of building up a force that might defeat the German army on the north European plain.[2]

To the urge for large scale raids as a means of offsetting pressure for an immediate second front (not only from the Soviets and Americans but also from some of Churchill's domestic political foes, including Lord Beaverbrook) must be added the determination of the Canadian Army to find useful employment for itself in Europe before a third year of inaction elapsed. Canadian troops had been arriving in Britain since 1939. Some were sent to France in 1940, not long enough to engage in any serious fighting, but long enough for a lieutenant-colonel in the Royal Canadian Horse Artillery to win a reputation for tenacity by returning to Britain with all of his regiment's guns. This was "Ham" Roberts, who by 1942 had been promoted to the command of the 2nd Canadian Division, which would undertake the Dieppe raid. At the end of 1941, three Canadian infantry divisions and an armoured division were already in Britain, another armoured division was on its way, and plans were set in motion for these units to form part of the 1st Canadian Army, with its own field headquarters under the command of Andrew McNaughton.

McNaughton wanted Canadian divisions to remain together in Britain, poised to join the decisive land campaign against Germany itself. Regardless of this policy's intrinsic merits, the refusal to allow Canadian formations to serve in North Africa (McNaughton thought that there was too much dispersal of Allied forces in order to uphold British prestige around the world) and the impossibility of staging a successful return to northwest Europe before 1943 at the earliest (the shortage of landing-craft was enough to ensure that) meant that the Canadian Army in Britain was bound to remain inactive for at least the first three and a half years of the war. Raids launched from Britain seemed to provide an ideal escape from the dilemma of either keeping the Canadian Army united but unoccupied in Britain or detaching units for service elsewhere, with the possibility that unity, once lost, might never be regained. For this reason, McNaughton and Harry Crerar (the latter taking command of Canadian troops in Britain while McNaughton recovered from illness) insisted that Canadian troops must play a leading role in raids launched from Britain and should be chosen to undertake the attack on Dieppe.[3]

The British Army may have been less concerned than Combined Operations, the Canadian Army, and RAF Fighter Command to justify either its claim to resources or even its organizational integrity through participation in large-scale raids, but it could not afford to show any lack of enthusiasm for such operations. To do so was to invite Combined Operations to take complete control of amphibious operations (including the final return to the Continent) and to invite the Canadian Army in Britain to operate outside the authority of the British Army in Britain (known as Home Forces).[4]

Crerar seems to have pushed for the employment of Canadian troops in a raid on Dieppe almost as soon as the idea of such an operation emerged in Combined Operations Headquarters. Home Forces stepped in as quickly as it could to assert its authority over the operation. No operation involving troops drawn from Home Forces—which, in the British Army's eyes, included the Canadian Army in Britain—could be launched without the approval of Home Forces' commander Sir Bernard Paget. Paget delegated his responsibility for supervising the military planning to the commander of the available Canadian divisions, a lieutenant-general already well known for his puritanical eccentricities, blunt opinions, and ruthless efficiency—Bernard Montgomery.

Montgomery insisted that the detailed military planning should be done by Roberts and his staff from the 2nd Canadian Division, free from the interference of Combined Operations "amateurs" or senior Canadian officers such as McNaughton and Crerar, who argued that they should be involved by virtue of their status as commanders of a national army. Montgomery wanted Roberts, who as military force commander would fight the battle, to make the plan.

Yet by the time Roberts became involved, his room for manoeuvre in planning was so tightly constrained by the framework of the outline plan (concocted by Combined Operations and Home Forces staff) and the requirements of the other services that the final plan could hardly be called his own.[5]

The outline plan for operation *Rutter* (as the operation would be known until its cancellation in early July) set out the objective of capturing Dieppe by a frontal assault launched 30 minutes after landings had been made east and west of the headlands that rose sharply at either end of the main beach. The flank landings were to touch down as near as possible to first light. Airborne forces were to deal with the covering coastal batteries. A heavy air bombardment was to be the prelude to the attack.

The main changes made after the outline plan had been handed over to the force commanders—Ham Roberts (Army), Tom Baillie-Grohman (Navy), and Trafford Leigh-Mallory (Air Force)—were first that the frontal assault would be launched 60 minutes after the landings on the flanks (enough time, it was hoped, for the headlands to be captured), and secondly that the preliminary air attack by heavy bombers would be replaced by an attack at dawn by fighter-bombers. The reasoning seems to have been that night attack on Dieppe (Bomber Command refused to expose its forces in daylight) might be so wildly inaccurate that it would merely alert the defenders and block the streets against the advance of Canadian tanks (which were thought to be the key to success) without seriously disrupting the defences. Reliance was placed on surprise and on the accuracy of a fighter-bomber attack launched minutes before the landings. Baillie-Grohman (the officer with the greatest experience of combined operations—much more indeed than Mountbatten) thought that the lack of heavy air support made support from naval guns all the more vital. He called in vain for the employment of an old battleship or cruiser to lend supporting fire. The British Admiralty could not be persuaded to expose a capital ship in the channel in daylight—knowing that these large ships would have to remain just off the French coast for the duration of the operation, or else forgo air cover. And in any case, the Admiralty was sceptical of the value of naval gunfire against coastal targets.

The force commanders clearly remained concerned by the paucity of supporting fire because on 3 July, the day before the raid was scheduled to be launched, a heavy air attack on Dieppe was reintroduced into the plan—only to be removed again later the same day for reasons that remain obscure. By then, the men and equipment of the 4th and 6th Canadian Infantry Brigades and the Calgary Tank Regiment had already been loaded into the assault ships and landing craft that would carry them across the channel. To have cancelled the raid at this stage must have been almost unthinkable.[6]

But why had no one insisted that the operation be abandoned at an earlier stage? Roberts may have been at the point of calling for cancellation on 2 July, when Crerar intervened to shore up the major-general's will, persuading him that the only problem was Roberts' own lack of confidence. Leigh-Mallory, too, had deep misgivings about the plan, warning Sir Sholto Douglas (commander-in-chief of Fighter Command) three days earlier that the raid was certain to produce heavy casualties in the air. (Douglas' reply was blunt: "I certainly do not propose to call the operation off.... Unfortunately one cannot often win a battle without considerable casualties.") Baillie-Grohman seems to have kept his reservations to himself until after the operation was cancelled. Perhaps the hope of a last-minute addition of effective heavy air support was sufficient to overcome the doubts of the force commanders until the preparations for the raid had gained so much momentum that even they were unwilling to stand up and take responsibility for cancellation. Or perhaps they were carried along by Montgomery's preoccupation with promoting and exuding confidence, or by the determination of Mountbatten, McNaughton, Crerar, and Douglas (for their own particular reasons) to get the forces under their command into immediate action.[7]

Though the expedition was ready to sail on the evening of 3 July, unfavourable weather forced repeated postponements until the operation was finally cancelled and the troops dispersed on 7 July.

That same day, Montgomery recommended that the operation be cancelled for all time. He had doubts about the feasibility of maintaining security after all of the troops had been told of the objective. He had also begun to question the wisdom of a plan likely to leave the attacking troops ashore long enough to be threatened by a German armoured division whose presence (eight hours' distance from Dieppe) was confirmed just days before the raid was cancelled. If Montgomery were quietly relieved by the cancellation, Roberts must have been so too. He and Baillie-Grohman circulated a memorandum critical both of the intelligence available to them and of the way the raid had been planned. If the decision had been in the hands of Montgomery, Baillie-Grohman, and Roberts, the July cancellation of the raid might have been final.[8]

Others were not so certain that new life could not be breathed into the operation. Mountbatten and Jock Hughes-Hallett—the Combined Operations naval adviser most closely associated with the project's genesis—strove to keep the raid alive. They feared seeing the summer raiding season draw to a close with nothing for Combined Operations to show for all its claims and efforts—hardly the way to silence the organization's many detractors. The RAF and Fighter Command must have been concerned that there might be no decisive engagements in the air (and hence no significant assistance lent to the Soviet Union) in 1942 unless the operation was revived. McNaughton and Crerar must have been disturbed by the prospect of another year passing with no battle experience gained—a situation sure to increase pressure for the breakup of the nascent 1st Canadian Army. They joined the revival without hesitation. By the time Home Forces was told about *Jubilee* (as the revived operation would be known) participation by the 2nd Canadian Division (under Crerar's supervision, not Montgomery's) was a *fait accompli.*[9]

Eleven days earlier, before *Rutter* had been finally cancelled, Mountbatten had secured the Chiefs of Staff Committee's agreement that he *should* consider remounting the operation at a later date if it could not be launched on 8 July. Mountbatten and McNaughton were convinced that security was not a problem. On 17 July, McNaughton himself persuaded Paget that security had not already been compromised. That same day, Mountbatten proposed that the committee should give him the executive authority to mount and launch *Jubilee* and should appoint Hughes-Hallett as the new naval force commander. While Baillie-Grohman would, in this way, simply be replaced (left conveniently to continue in a new post), Montgomery was excluded at the insistence of McNaughton (who argued that an operation by Canadian troops must be supervised by a Canadian commander).

The Chiefs of Staff Committee, though agreeing to Hughes-Hallett's appointment as force commander, was reluctant to give Mountbatten the additional powers that would enable him to "mount" and "order" the operation. (There was no small measure of uncertainty amongst members of the committee about what the terms "mount" and "order" meant in practice.) Mountbatten's proposal was considered twice more without result. Mountbatten's response was to revise and clarify his demands, threatening an enquiry into his status as Chief of Combined Operations if they were not met. On 27 July the committee accepted Mountbatten's new procedure for raids. From that moment, Mountbatten had the authority to launch any raid (including, it seems, *Jubilee*) without submitting a final plan to the committee for approval, subject only to the concurrence of the commanders whose forces were involved.[10]

This meant that, for better or for worse, the military side of the operation had become an exclusively Canadian responsibility, with Roberts the force commander, Crerar the "responsible military officer," and McNaughton overseeing the employment of Canadian troops on behalf of the Canadian government. After the raid ended in failure, Crerar would claim that the *Rutter* military plan had been completed under Montgomery's direction and had not been changed in any significant way for *Jubilee,* except for the substitution of seaborne commandos for paratroops. In fact, under Crerar's supervision at least one other significant change was made, and others were considered. Furthermore, tides dictated that troops were likely to be ashore longer in *Jubilee* than they would have been in the 8 July plan.

Roberts seems to have been persuaded to go along with the raid's revival on the understanding that definite improvements could and would be made to the plan. He may have hoped for simultaneous landings on the flanks and on the main beach in front of Dieppe. This would have provided the frontal assault with the maximum cover of darkness and the greatest chance of achieving surprise. What Roberts ended up with was a compromise. The impossibility of finding sufficient room at sea for the landing-craft to make simultaneous landings meant that the frontal assault would commence 30 minutes after the landings on the flanks—enough time for surprise to be lost, though not enough time for the flanks to be secured (as Montgomery hoped would be the case in the 60 minutes allocated for this task in his plan).

Roberts may also have expected the revived operation to include heavier air support. Leigh-Mallory was certainly anxious to find a way of employing heavy bombers without breaking Bomber Command's rule that they should never be exposed to German day-fighter aircraft. Bomber Command's offer of a potentially inaccurate night raid was rejected by the force commanders as being worse than no heavy air support at all.

The only change to *Jubilee's* plan that represented a definite improvement on its predecessor was an element introduced not by the action of the planners but by the shortening of the hours of daylight as the summer solstice receded. The longer nights of August meant that the attacking forces could set sail in darkness, thereby lessening the risk that they would be tracked across the channel by German reconnaissance aircraft.[11]

The senior staff of Combined Operations, the Canadian Army, and Fighter Command (the commands with most to lose in terms of men and equipment, the most to gain in terms of prestige) were sufficiently desperate for action that they were able to persuade themselves that *Jubilee's* plan was, if anything, better than that of *Rutter,* and that security was not a problem (as it turned out not to be). A more objective analysis would have led them to the conclusion that the second plan was no better than its predecessor, and may even have been worse.

But for these men and the organizations they controlled, the drive to revive the raid had become entwined with the need to justify their favoured strategy and tactics for winning the war, their claim to power and resources, their autonomy, or even their corporate existence. Indeed, so jealous was Mountbatten of his new powers that he seems not to have told the Chiefs of Staff Committee even informally that Dieppe would be attacked on 19 August. It is, nevertheless, far from obvious that the committee would have objected to the final plan for *Jubilee* had Mountbatten still been required to present this plan to the committee for approval. The committee's responsibility for approving the military side of the final plan had, in effect, been delegated to McNaughton and Crerar. If these two Canadians had no objections, why should the committee, or for that matter Churchill (in his capacity as minister of defence), have stepped in to cancel the raid?

McNaughton and Crerar, along with Mountbatten, the RAF commanders, and the local naval commander, were nothing if not determined. They pushed ahead with *Jubilee,* confident in their own assessments of its viability, no doubt reassuring themselves that a plan, which in its earlier stages had been scrutinized in almost every quarter, could not go far wrong.

How far it could go wrong can hardly have been imagined. German defenders had no foreknowledge of the raid. Some were alerted by a chance encounter between assault ships and a German coastal convoy. Others were manning defences as a matter of routine. Allied air superiority was sustained, though at great cost. The insurmountable problem was that the advantage of surprise, where achieved, was transitory, and in the absence of Allied heavy fire support the defenders could hold the attackers at bay almost indefinitely. In the inevitable confusion of battle, Roberts sent reinforcements into an already hopeless situation, merely swelling the number of casualties. By 9 a.m. the failure of an attack that had begun some four hours earlier was apparent. Due to the problems of communication, the original schedule proved impossible to alter, and the withdrawal could only begin at 11 a.m. as planned. By 1 p.m. most of those still ashore had surrendered. Of the roughly 4,000 Canadian troops who actually landed, 3,367 were killed, wounded, or taken prisoner. Losses in the air were also heavy: 106 Allied aircraft (Leigh-Mallory had predicted 120) as against 48 German aircraft destroyed. The navy lost one destroyer, five tank landing-craft, and 28 lesser craft.

Almost immediately there began at the highest levels of Allied command an unseemly tussle to apportion blame. This was not simply a matter of taking responsibility for the casualties. At stake too was the issue of which individuals and organizations should plan the return to the Continent. Mountbatten reacted to criticism from another member of the British Chiefs of Staff Committee by emphasizing the failings of every organization but his own. The story rapidly gained currency that "the Canadians" had changed a more intelligent Combined Operations plan. This story was soon changed, with the blame shifting to army planners—including Montgomery, by that time in North Africa. Roberts proved to be an easy target throughout, charged with reinforcing failure. More recently the case has been made that Mountbatten revived the operation without the authorization of the British Chiefs of Staff, the result being the implementation of a plan that would either have been rejected or sent back for improvements. More recently still, it has been argued that the operation was so obviously flawed that Churchill and the British Chiefs of Staff must have known that it would fail. The fragmentary and sometimes misleading nature of official records suggests that there may never be widespread agreement on the reasons why the raid was revived and launched.[12]

What can be said is that the outcome of the raid probably owed less to any conspiracy—either to subvert the authority of the British Chiefs of Staff Committee or to launch an operation that was certain to fail—than to the profound and perplexing problems of coalition warfare faced in 1942 by British and Canadian leaders. These problems led some of them to favour a large-scale raid as a demonstration of their commitment to an early second front; as a justification for the existence of an organization created for the express purpose of launching dramatic amphibious operations; as a way to defend the integrity of a national army; but above all as the most obvious alternative to inaction. The extent to which the raid went according to plan and still ended in utter disaster illustrates a number of points—how fatally flawed was the conception of the operation from the first; how easily military leaders desperate for action could delude themselves into thinking that audacity and surprise were a substitute for sound strategy and adequate fire power; how difficult it was to halt an operation, even of highly dubious utility, after it had gained momentum from the investment of valuable time and resources; and finally how in wartime the urge for action to justify a wider strategic policy or an organization's existence could blind leaders to an operation's disastrous defects.

Notes

The following shows the sources of unpublished information used in this paper. The most important published sources are shown in the works cited.

1. Details of the plan can be found amongst the records of almost all the organizations involved in the raid. See the records of the 1st Canadian Corps in the National Archives of Canada (NA) RG 24, vol. 10,750; Combined Operations records in the Public Record Office, London (PRO), DEFE 2/542 and 544; Admiralty, Portsmouth Station records, PRO, ADM 179/226; and RAF Fighter Command records, AIR 16/746–748.

2. PRO, Cabinet Historical Section records, CAB 106/3, "History of Combined Operations Organization," confidential unpublished history, 1956, chapters 3 and 4.

3. NA, McNaughton papers, MG 30 E133; Crerar papers, MG 30 E157.

4. AIR 16/760.

5. Imperial War Museum, London, (IWM), Haydon papers, Haydon's correspondence with Hughes-Hallett, Henriques, and Skrine, August to October, 1958. Department of National Defence, Ottawa, Directorate of History, Transcript of television program "Close-Up: Dieppe," interview with Lord Montgomery.

6. ADM 179/220, Orders for *Rutter,* 29 June 1942. AIR 16/760, Leigh-Mallory to Bomber Command and the reply, 3 July 1942.

7. AIR 16/760, Leigh-Mallory to Douglas, 29 June 1942 and the reply 30 June 1942. National Maritime Museum, London (NMM), Baillie-Grohman papers, "Flashlights into the Past," unpublished memoirs.

8. RG 24, vol. 10,750, file 220C1.009 (D3), Chilton to Crerar 7 July 1942 and Montgomery to Crerar, 5 July 1942; Baillie-Grohman papers, Notes on Staffs and Planning for *Rutter,* 9 July 1942.

9. NA, Hughes-Hallett papers, MG 30 E463, "Before I Forget," unpublished memoirs. McNaughton papers, vol. 248, July war diary.

10. PRO, Chiefs of Staff Committee minutes, CAB 79/56, COS(42) 64th(O), 2, 6 July 1942. CAB 79/22, COS(42) 211th, 9, 20 July 1942; 213th, 3, 21 July 1942; 214th, 5, 22 July 1942; 218th, 11, 27 July 1942. PRO, War Office, Directorate of Military Operations and Intelligence papers, WO 106/4117, Mountbatten to Hollis, 23 July 1942.

11. IWM, Hughes-Hallett papers; PRO, Chief of the Air Staff's papers, AIR 8/895, note by Slessor, 12 May 1942; AIR 16/764, Combined Plan, 31 July 1942.

12. Admiralty, War History Cases, ADM 199/1079 and 1199. CAB 127/24, Mountbatten to Brooke, 31 Aug. 1942. B.L. Villa, *Unauthorized Action: Mountbatten and the Dieppe Raid* (Toronto: 1989). D. and S. Whitaker, *Dieppe: Tragedy to Triumph* (Toronto: 1992).

WORKS CITED

Campbell, J.P. *Dieppe Revisited: A Documentary Investigation.* London: 1993.

Greenhous, B. *Dieppe, Dieppe.* Montreal: 1993.

Hinsley, F.H. *British Intelligence in the Second World War: Its Influence on Strategy and Operations.* Vol. 2. London: 1981.

Hughes-Hallett, J. "The Mounting of Raids," *Journal of the Royal United Services Institute,* XCV, Nov. 1950.

Rees, G. *A Bundle of Sensations: Sketches in an Autobiography.* London: 1960.

Robertson, T. *Dieppe: The Shame and the Glory.* London: 1963.

Roskill, S.W. *The War at Sea.* Vol. 2. London: 1956.

Stacey, C.P. *History of the Canadian Army in the Second World War: Six Years of War.* Vol. 2. Ottawa: 1955.

Villa, B.L. *Unauthorized Action: Mountbatten and the Dieppe Raid.* Toronto: 1989.

Whitaker, D. and S. *Dieppe: Tragedy to Triumph.* Toronto: 1992.

CHAPTER

12 IN SEARCH
OF QUEBEC

No subject has galvanized Canadian attention in recent decades more than the position of Quebec in the federation. Canadians everywhere have struggled to understand the French-English relationship, and governments at all levels have legislated, administered, implored, cajoled, plotted and otherwise sought answers to the "Quebec question." Parti Québécois governments in Quebec have added a critical dynamic that may or may not alter the debate. Academics have spent entire careers dissecting the issues, and there has never been a shortage of information or opinion; consequently there are almost as many approaches to the subject as people writing about it. "The Mystery of Quebec," to use the phrase of Laval political scientist Leon Dion, alternately fascinates, eludes and confuses not only those who study it but those who write about it.

The three articles offered here, therefore, are a selection from a wide spectrum. They may simply represent the views of the individuals who wrote them. They may also represent a cross-section of opinion. In the first selection, "A Half-Century of Cultural Evolution in Quebec," sociologist Guy Rocher examines the "profound cultural changes" that he believes help to explain the "mystery." Another sociologist, Hubert Guindon, attacks the "political fairy tales" frequently used to explain the Quebec of the 1960s and 1970s. In "Quebec and the Canadian Question" he argues that the modernization and secularization of Quebec society and institutions were the creators of the new Québécois. There is no "mystery" in his interpretation. The final and most recent study by Ralph Peter Güntzel is also on the 1960s and 1970s. A labour historian, Guntzel examines the activities and ideologies of the *Confédération des syndicats nationaux*, the second largest labour union central in the province. Again there is little doubt about what happened. The workers who originally spoke with a "social-democratic and socialist voice" in their pursuit of a new society abandoned the English-Canadian left and turned to the sovereigntists in the 1970s.

Suggestions for Further Reading

Behiels, Michael D., ed., *Quebec Since 1945: Selected Readings*. Toronto: Copp Clark Pitman, 1987.

Blais, Andre, and McRoberts, Kenneth, "Public Expenditure in Ontario and Quebec, 1950–1980: Explaining the Differences," *Journal of Canadian Studies,* XVIII, no. 1 (Spring 1983), 28–53.

Borins, Sanford F., "Capital Accumulation and the Rise of the New Middle Class," *The Review of Radical Political Economics,* XII, no. 1 (Spring 1980), 17–34.

Coleman, William D., *The Independence Movement in Quebec, 1945–1980*. Toronto: University of Toronto Press, 1984.

Guindon, Hubert, *Quebec Society: Tradition, Modernity, and Nationhood,* edited and with an introduction by Roberta Hamilton and John L. McMullan. Toronto: University of Toronto Press, 1988.

Dion, Leon, "The Mystery of Quebec," *Daedalus* 117,4 (Fall 1988), 283–318.

Fournier, Pierre, *The Quebec Establishment*. Montreal: Black Rose Books, 1976.

Jones, Richard, *Community in Crisis*. Toronto: McClelland and Stewart, 1972.

McRoberts, Kenneth D., *Quebec: Social Change and Political Crisis*. Toronto: McClelland and Stewart, 1988, 3rd. ed..

———, "The Sources of Neo-Nationalism in Quebec," *Ethnic and Racial Studies,* VII, no. 1 (January 1984), 55–85.

Pinard, Maurice, and Hamilton, Richard, "The Class Bases of the Independence Movement: Conjectures and Evidence," *Ethnic and Racial Studies,* VII, no. 1 (January 1984), 20–54.

Trofimenkoff, Susan, *The Dream of Nation: A Social and Intellectual History of Quebec*. Toronto: Gage, 1983.

A HALF-CENTURY OF CULTURAL EVOLUTION IN QUEBEC[†]

Guy Rocher

Introduction

When I was a young sociology professor, in the early 1950s, my colleagues and I used to receive invitations from Canadian universities to explain why Quebec had not changed, why it hung on to its past and seemed to be rooted in the eighteenth century. However, since the late 1960s, we have been invited to talk about why Quebec has changed so rapidly, the ways in which it has evolved, and what it is likely to become in the short or long term.

From Michael D. Behiels, ed., *Quebec Since 1945 Selected Readings* (Toronto: Copp Clark Pitman Ltd., 1987), 289–299. Reprinted by permission of University of Toronto Press Incorporated. Translation courtesy of Copp Clark Longman Ltd.

[†] "Un demi-siècle d'évolution culturelle au Québec," *University of Toronto Quarterly 50,* 1 (Fall 1980): 15–28. Translated by Barbara Krever.

This is a small and perhaps too personal an indication of the changes that Quebec has undergone during the past few years, but it is significant nonetheless. Anyone who had left Quebec in the 1930s and had come back today would discover a society profoundly changed, or at least one that gives the impression of having undergone profound changes. Of course, it could be an illusion; we will return to that later. At any rate, relations with other people, institutions, literature, and the general climate in Quebec lead us to believe in a definite evolution. The past fifty years have certainly not been characterized by stability, continuity, or a maintenance of the status quo. As well, if one consults the recent writings of the "professional observers" of society—political scientists, ethnologists, sociologists— the image of a Quebec that is moving, changing, and being transformed becomes even stronger, almost an obsession, or at the very least, commonplace.[1]

It would be wrong, however, to think that no change took place before the 1930s. Many developments had taken place at the end of the nineteenth and the beginning of the twentieth centuries, but these affected mostly the social organization and the structures of Quebec and hardly touched its mentality. The industrial revolution and urbanization took place in Quebec during these years. From the rural and artisanal society that it was until the mid-nineteenth century, Quebec became progressively more industrialized and urbanized, and the population began to cluster around certain large urban centres, first around both Quebec City and Montreal and ultimately mostly around Montreal. The decline of Quebec City's role as the second most important industrial centre is a major and unfortunate event in the structural and cultural development of Quebec.

Franco-Québécois reacted to this period of urbanization and industrialization *with a pre-industrial mentality*. Undoubtedly this is what struck the observers of the 1930s and 1940s: Quebec resembled a place where two large streams of water met without mingling. Elements of traditional and industrial society existed side by side without interpenetrating; in rural Quebec, large regions remained well-protected enclaves of purely traditional society.

Quebec was industrial in its production methods and yield, its division of labour, the development of its territory, and the urban concentration of its population; it was pre-industrial in its mentality, its ideology, its morality, and its ethos, so much so that one hesitated to call Quebec an industrial society. It was rather, according to the title of Everett C. Hughes' book written at this time, a society "in transition."[2]

This can be explained partly by the fact that Franco-Québécois were not responsible for the industrialization of Quebec. It was carried out under the auspices of foreign, or at least English-Canadian, capital and by means of a qualified labour force of which French Canadians constituted only the lower levels. Any profit that French Canadians gained was not as partners or shareholders, but only as subordinates. A harsh light is shed on the situation when one studies the linguistic dividing line in companies, which was at the level of the foreman in most important enterprises until around the 1950s: the foreman was generally bilingual, so as to be able to speak French to his employees and English to the office staff and to superiors in the company. It is only recently that the linguistic dividing line for Francophones has begun to be raised from one echelon to another to the top or head-office level, where it is now.[3]

Within North American industrial society, Francophone Quebec had retained the appearance of a sort of homogeneous cultural reserve characterized by the predominance of the Catholic Church, the alliance between the state and the Church, a government that could be called "clericocratic" (so much so that Quebec was referred to in English as "the priest-ridden province"), an educational system still marked by the influence of the eighteenth century, a moral code directly inspired by the Catholic religion, and a family lifestyle that sociologists called "traditionalist."

As for culture in the stricter, less anthropological, sense, literary and artistic production was very uneven. Apart from certain breakthroughs that were remarkable precisely because they were isolated cases, on the part of a few poets (such as Émile Nelligan, Saint-Denys Garneau) or painters (such as Borduas), the greatest share of literary and artistic production was inspired by a rhetoric and aesthetic that did not belong to this century.

Culture, both in anthropological and in the more restricted sense, has undergone a radical and dramatic evolution in the last few decades. This does not exclude the fact that certain structural changes have also taken place over the same years. There has been a rapid and unexpected decline in the birth rate, resulting in a decrease in population unprecedented in Quebec's history; there is also the process of state-building, which entailed an increase in public bureaucracy, and an ever-increasing intervention in sectors that had previously been controlled by the church or by private enterprise. However, these structural transformations were themselves the product of cultural evolution, of the change in the mentality, mind, and soul of Franco-Québécois.[4]

My task will be to describe a few of the profound cultural changes that have taken place in contemporary Quebec and to look at a few explanatory factors. I will end with a few judgements on the present and the future.

A Culture in the Process of Modernization

One of the most visible traits that characterizes the recent evolution of Québécois culture is the flourishing of that culture. For almost two hundred years, it was polarized between two linguistic and cultural communities, the French and the English. It remained so almost until the Second World War. The Francophone community was particularly homogeneous due to its religion, historic roots, customs, mentality, and lifestyle. The English-speaking community in Quebec, while less unified, still had a distinct style: it had its traditions, its leadership, its own universe that made it different from other English-speaking communities in other parts of Canada.

Two things happened. First of all, the homogeneity of the Francophone community broke down. There was no longer the same religious unanimity, and consequently a diversity of personal rules of moral conduct came to replace the former unity. Tradition and the past lost their position of privilege. Also, in the economic sector, new professions and diverse interest groups sprang up. New elites appeared that were representative of new social groups.[5] "Unanimity is no more," was the way Gérard Pelletier summed it up in a resounding article that appeared in the magazine *Cité libre* in the late 1950s.

Secondly, the Anglophone community became diversified as well, less from the inside than from the addition of new elements. Immigration over the last thirty years has added to its number. The old Anglophone stock was supplemented by Allophones from Greece, Italy, Germany, and from Latin countries or regions such as Spain, Portugal, and South America. The majority of immigrants—especially those who arrived in Quebec after the Second World War—chose to live in the Anglophone community: they adopted English as their language and sent their children to English-speaking schools, whether Protestant or Catholic.[6] This is one of the most powerful causes of Quebec neo-nationalism, of the separatist or sovereign ideology, and of the recent language legislation (Bill 101). But a true "assimilation" of these Allophones into the Anglophone community of British origin never came about: the Allophones adopted the English language and elements of Anglophone culture without being entirely accepted or integrated into the original Anglophone community. As a result, what we usually call the "Anglophone community" in Quebec has become a very complex reality, made up of disparate elements of diverse origins and cultures.

Quebec, then, became a pluralistic society from the cultural point of view. Value and identity conflicts became more and more intense; this is a new reality with which Quebec must learn to live.[7]

A second characteristic, which is not without a link to the first, is the recent secularization that can be observed in the Québécois mentality, especially in the Francophone community. If the Catholic Church has withdrawn from public power and turned inward upon itself, abandoning to the state the many functions that it used to serve in teaching, health, and social assistance, it is because it now has only limited aid and support from the population of Quebec. Québécois no longer turn to the church first; they no longer expect services and instruction from it. Recruitment of clergy has almost run dry, both for men and women, and consequently religious communities and clergy are no longer able to fill the functions they had previously. For a growing number of Québécois, a greater dissociation than before has taken place between religion and morality, with the latter no longer necessarily obeying the commands of the former. Even couples who have remained attached to the Catholic Church, and who have taken the sacraments faithfully, have resorted to the use of contraceptives in family planning without feeling a contradiction to their religious allegiance.

Another important trait of contemporary Quebec: it has been much more open to the world than before. Quebecers, Francophones as well as Anglophones, were always great travellers. Long ago, many of them were *coureurs des bois,* explorers, navigators, etc. As well, many Québécois families had members, male and female, who were missionaries in China, Africa, South America, or in the Canadian North. Many of the accounts related in the missionaries' sermons made up a frequently repeated and lively folklore of exotic stories.

Today, Québécois themselves travel for their own pleasure. Almost all young Québécois have travelled outside of Quebec; many have stayed for quite long periods in various countries in Africa, Asia, South America, as well as in Europe or in the United States. Of course, their experiences abroad are more or less superficial, depending on the individual case, and the resulting influence on the rest of their lives is not always substantial. But, for the majority of young Québécois, Quebec is no longer the centre of the world or the only measure of things; they have experienced culture shock elsewhere and will be marked by it forever....

The last trait that deserves to be emphasized is the diversification and proliferation of art forms on the part of artists, performers, writers, poets, Franco-Québécois *chansonniers.* In spite of the fact that it happened rather late, Quebec is nonetheless in the process of making itself more and more well-known, especially in the Francophone world, for its poetry, novels, theatre, and music. Without exaggerating the quality of the literary and artistic work it has produced, one can at least maintain that it is enjoying a period of rebirth, that it is making its comeback in the contemporary world of literature and the arts.

One word can perhaps sum up this cultural evolution of the past few years: modernization. It is an ambiguous term, one that sociologists tended to overuse for some time and that they now hesitate to use. The evolutionary connotation that it seems to carry is objectionable. It remains nonetheless that, if we exclude any value judgement as to whether modernization is good or bad, fortunate or harmful, we can recognize a society's leap into the twentieth century. This is what happened in Quebec, especially to its Francophone community.

A Few Explanatory Factors

It is very probable that the gap between an industrial society and the pre-industrial mentality was becoming more and more unbearable in Quebec, and, by the 1940s, one could predict that Quebec could not survive much longer under such circumstances. There was a sort of schizophrenia involved in living inside a mental universe that was dissociated from everyday reality.

The Second World War contributed greatly to the evolution toward a more modern mentality. There is a definite reason why historians date historic periods in relation to certain wars. Throughout human history, wars have had considerable influence on people's lives, mentalities, beliefs, ideologies. Quebec did not escape from the immense shakeup of the Second World War. Many women went to work in wartime industries, while a great number of young men in the army and in military campaigns were going through unanticipated experiences. At the end of such a disturbing period, Quebec could never be the same. Perhaps it was due to these events in particular that Quebec became more open to the outside world, as was mentioned earlier.

Another factor is the educational revolution that took place at this time. This is not to say that this revolution is only a recent one. During the 1930s, there was a great debate, which I believe was a sign of things to come, surrounding the introduction of sciences into the traditional classical curriculum, which had been based mainly on arts and philosophy and which had neglected math and the precise sciences. The curriculum had remained true to the intellectual universe of classicism, or at least this was the defence for what it had become. In the 1950s, those who supported the teaching of science triumphed. The classical curriculum was substantially modified.[8]

However, it was in the 1950s and even more in the 1960s that major reform was undertaken. Reform in the 1930s only applied to classical education; the changes in the 1960s would transform the whole system.

While still remaining distinct from each other, the Protestant and Catholic sectors were unified under one authority, with identical standards and rules. But it was especially the Catholic sector that underwent profound changes, with regard to its structures, programs, and mentality. This transformation was characterized in particular by the abandonment of the classical curriculum, such as it was, by the unification of the whole of the system (which had up until then been made up of parts more or less independent of each other), by democratizing access to secondary, college, and higher education, by creating a broader range of programs, and by reasserting the value of public education, which for a long time had been neglected for private education. For those who were educated in the Quebec system thirty or forty years ago, today's system is unrecognizable. That is what very often causes confusion and anguish for parents who no longer feel capable of following their child in an educational system that has almost nothing in common with the one they knew.[9]

Are these changes in education a reflection of cultural evolution or an agent of this transformation? The educational revolution, especially in the 1960s, was probably both. It was both prompted by and an indication of a new mentality and it helped to accentuate the new aspects of this mentality.

Finally, this evolution in Quebec can probably not be explained without reference to the changes in mentality that took place in the whole of contemporary Western civilization. It is possible that, for reasons not yet analysed, Quebec, and especially the Francophone community in Quebec, has been more sensitive than other societies to the great cultural transformations that Western civilization has seen in the last few decades. At any rate, some sectors of Québécois society have enthusiastically welcomed cultural innovation, whether in the area of morals, literary or artistic creation, political ideologies, or counterculture. This can be observed, for example, in young poets, feminist movements, in the formation of certain "communes," and in various religious movements alike.

Progress or Regression?

In the face of this evolution, one can wonder whether the new conditions that are predominant in Quebec are more or less favourable than before for the cultural development of individuals, groups, and for the whole of society. Are the changes that we just mentioned unfortunate disturbances that created havoc in a universe that was until then orderly and relatively functional? Or is it a question of a cultural and spiritual renewal apt to come soon to fruition?

First of all, it is true that for some years now Quebec has experienced a renewal of political conscience. When they left the Catholic Church, Québécois turned to political power, which required them to take on roles and responsibilities that they had up until then refused. At the same time, the question of national identity, an old problem, latent in the French-Canadian conscience for more than 150 years, re-emerged in many different ways—Québécois neo-nationalism, FLQ revolutionary and other secret movements, periods of terrorism and violence, and the emergence of the Parti Québécois. Many English-Canadians tend to interpret these phenomena more negatively than positively. However, all these stirrings of political thought and criticism made up a favourable atmosphere for cultural development in Quebec, an important source of inspiration for many artists in their novels, poems, plays, songs. There are not often great nationalistic moments in the life of a people; such moments are often marked by violence and by a certain romanticism that touches every human being.

Bill 101, the recent legislation on language in Quebec, can be seen in the same light. The legislation also suffers from a bad reputation in English-Canadian circles, where they have tried to paint it as repressive and even tyrannical legislation. The English-language press, especially in Quebec but also in other provinces, lashed out against this bill. People too easily forget to consider the bill as an important gesture of self-affirmation on the part of the Franco-Québécois community. There were not only economic reasons that led the government of Quebec to enact this law, whose obvious aim was to re-establish a certain balance of power between Quebec's two linguistic communities in the areas of employment and the economy; there was also the pressure of a nationalistic ideology that found support in pride in the language, in its purity and quality as well as in the use to which it was put. This bill was an attempt to express the new-found respect for the French language, both as a vehicle for expressing thought and as a symbol of cultural identity. It is understandable that the caricature that Canada's English-speaking community too often made of it was particularly irritating for a good number of Franco-Québécois. Lack of understanding of the current evolution of contemporary Quebec was only too obvious in this situation and was quite shocking.

It is obvious that relations between the Franco-Québécois community and other linguistic communities in Quebec have not improved. One can even say that they are more tense than they have ever been.[10] The "two solitudes" that Hugh MacLennan described symbolically in his novel still exist; one could say that they have been replaced by several solitudes, with the increase of new ethnic communities (Greek, Italian, Portuguese, Spanish, etc.). There are still very few cultural exchanges between Francophone, Anglophones, and Allophones in Quebec. One group is unaware of the activities of another, even when there is not a climate of mistrust and misunderstanding between them. It is probably the Anglophone sector that has made the most progress in the area of cultural exchange. A growing number of Anglo-Québécois have made great efforts to gain a better knowledge of the language and culture of their Francophone compatriots, probably at the time of the latter's political and cultural awakening. For their part, the Francophones are still too obsessed with themselves and too involved with their cultural and political renewal to have the time and inclination to understand other cultural groups in Quebec. The great possibilities for reciprocal enrichment characteristic of such a co-habitational situation as we have in Quebec have not yet been explored. And for now, it is probable that the political climate will remain a negative factor, such that one cannot expect a rapid change in this situation.

Another factor is that both the Francophone and Anglophone communities are deeply marked by the American influence, and this influence is becoming stronger. It is easy to assume that the Francophone community is protected from American influences by its language. There is, of course, a certain barrier, but it is insufficient, considering the powerful pressure represented by American civilization at our doorstep. The influence of that civilization leaves its mark on the entire world, far beyond geographical limits and language barriers.

For both Anglophones and Francophones in Quebec, as well as for the whole of Canada, the proximity of the American colossus surely represents the greatest challenge to the future. Will we be able to develop a culture of our own, with its own originality, without being a simple copy of U.S. culture? Personally, I believe it is purely utopian to think that either Canadian or Québécois culture can be totally and entirely independent of American culture. But I also think that it is possible for a collectivity such as ours not to give in passively to this influence, but rather to assimilate U.S. culture, to integrate it with our past and with what we have already acquired of it, and to turn all this into a new product that would have a certain originality. In order to do this, it will be necessary to know how to communicate with the most lively intellectual circles in the United States (which we do infrequently in Canada and even less in Quebec), those that harbour inner feelings of dissent about U.S. civilization. American influences flood our homes and our lives, especially through the mass media and through the consumer habits we share with our neighbours to the south.[11] But we have not yet been able to seek out that which is intellectually and spiritually exciting in the U.S., that which is non-conformist and goes against the well-established order.

In Quebec, protest movements, whether by youths, the left, or within the Catholic church, have almost no contact, strangely enough, with their American counterparts. They believe it preferable to take their inspiration from European movements, whether French, German, or British. However, they have much more in common with American than European movements. This is a strange paradox. And if we do not solve this ambiguity, we will never be able to assimilate American culture (assimilate in the strong sense of the term, i.e., to make it our own by adapting it to ourselves and transforming it to fit our substance): we will only be under its influence and ultimately be its victims.

There is an encouraging phenomenon that can be observed in Quebec over the last few years: the development of cultural forces in regions other than Montreal and Quebec City. There has been first an economic, and increasingly, a cultural, focus in regional development. For example, people are beginning to object to the fact that, all too often, radio and television carry exclusively Montreal-based programs, and that programming on the whole is too much influenced by Montreal. We are seeing small, more or less militant groups beginning to take charge of regional cultural development. This is happening, for example, to community radio and television, to Radio-Québec, to a certain regional press, to regional and local educational institutions.[12]

There is evidence here more of frustrated aspirations than of gratification. The regions, especially the peripheral ones, still only have limited financial and human resources for taking charge of and supporting cultural institutions of good quality. Moreover, a long-lived habit of passivity makes it difficult and sometimes problematical for the population to participate in new regional enterprises that are sometimes daring and sometimes even suicidal. It is always a minority, and always the same one, that finds itself participating in all the business activities in a region. Often, because of this, the clientele, which is not yet ready to take part in a regional enterprise, is dissatisfied, as are those who support a regionalist ideology of participation.

In spite of these difficulties and limits in regional cultural development, I believe that there is hope for the future. Regions outside Montreal and Quebec City harbour cultural wealth that is rooted in the past and that is kept up in a more authentic way than in the major centres. This is one of the sources of original cultural development from which we could profit in developing a North American, non-U.S., culture.

Let us end by coming back to a remark made at the beginning of this article: was there perhaps a tendency to exaggerate the actual changes that Quebec underwent during the last two decades? There was a time, especially in the 1960s, when we built up the changes into an ideology. Evolution was good, status quo bad; virtue resided in change, and stopping meant stagnation. The effect was that we wanted to see change everywhere, and we probably saw more than there was.

At present, we are witnessing, in Quebec as well as almost everywhere in the world, a return to conservative positions that are more reassuring, more orderly, and apparently wiser. Changes that came about in the 1950s and 1960s have come to a standstill. Important sectors of the population, even of youth, are questioning the changes that came about, for example, in the school system or in the intervention of the state in cultural matters, and are hoping, strangely enough, to revert to the way things were. This new and rather unexpected situation forces us to take a look at the ground covered, to wonder what has really changed and whether we were so afraid of witnessing change that we overestimated the extent of the cultural evolution.

These doubts, applying both to the extent of changes that were brought about and to their appropriateness, create a climate of perplexity that is hardly favourable to an intense cultural life and activity. We are living rather in an atmosphere of inhibition, of discomfort, of timidity, which does not encourage innovation, inventiveness, or imagination. After being marked by the "new wave" of youth in the 1960s, our era has just entered a phase that seems dominated by a feeling of old age. If we believe in demographic findings, and if we attribute a certain importance to them, we will have to wait several years before we emerge into more enlightening times!

Conclusion

Must we end on this pessimistic note or may we add a few words of optimism? It seems to me that a mixture of the two is appropriate. Some conditions that are favourable to the cultural development of Quebec and others that are not rub shoulders, thus making an analysis of the present situation difficult and any prediction of the future uncertain.

But it is perhaps precisely because of this tension of uncertainty, debate, value conflicts, and ebb and flow of past and future ideologies that a new cultural development could flourish. Great periods of cultural creation were not all associated with times of peace, calm, collective euphoria, and confidence in the future—far from it! But we must make certain that the forces that inhibit the free and creative spirit will not be dominant enough to stifle positive motivations and inclinations.

How to succeed? Merely the will of individuals and groups is not enough. Success depends on accidents of history, on games of chance, on the imponderables of great historic tendencies. Individuals are not in complete control of history; the future is revealed only partially, and often falsely, to them. But the will to realize something, in spite of the trials of the times in which we live, leads us all to try to leave our mark.

Notes

1. The list of works mentioned here could be long, as there has been extensive material written on Quebec in the last few years. We limit ourselves to mentioning some of them while keeping in mind that the list if far from exhaustive. The first works quoted are in English, the order being chronological: Hugh Bingham Myer, ed., *The Quebec Revolution* (Montreal: Harvest House, 1964); Ramsay Cook, *Canada and the French-Canadian Question* (Toronto: Macmillan, 1966; reprinted by Copp Clark Pitman, 1986); Edward M. Corbet, *Quebec Confronts Canada* (Baltimore: Johns Hopkins University Press, 1967); Marcel Rioux, *La Question du Québec* (Paris: Segher, 1969); Fernand Dumont, *La Vigile du Québec* (Montreal: Hurtubise HMH, 1971), Marcel Rioux and Yves Martin, eds., *La Société canadienne française* (Montreal: Hurtubise HMH, 1971), first published in English: *French-Canadian Society* (Toronto: McClelland and Stewart, 1964); Jean-Luc Migué, ed., *Le Québec d'aujourd'hui. Regards d'universitaires* (Montreal: Hurtubise HMH, 1971); Claude Ryan, ed., *Le Québec qui se fait* (Montreal: Hurtubise HMH, 1973); Gabriel Gagnon and Luc Martin, ed., *Québec 1960–1980. La crise du développement* (Montreal: Hurtubise HMH, 1973); Marcel Rioux, *Les Québécois* (Paris: Seuil, 1974); Denis Monière, *Le Développement des idéologies au Québec, des origines à nos jours* (Montreal: Québec Amérique, 1977); Edouard Cloutier and Daniel Latouche, eds., *Le Système politique québécois* (Montreal: Hurtubise HMH, 1979).

2. Everett C. Hughes, *French Canada in Transition* (Chicago: University of Chicago Press, 1941). For the history of industrialization in Quebec, see for example, Albert Faucher's article "Le Caractère continental de l'industrialisation au Québec," *Recherches sociographiques* 6, 3 (1965): 219–36.

3. Everett C. Hughes' study reveals a great deal about the situation in the 1930s. The split in the early 1970s is well described by Serge Carlos, *L'Utilisation du français dans le monde du travail au Québec,* Study E3, carried out on behalf of the Commission of Inquiry on the Position of the French Language and on Language Rights in Quebec (Quebec, July 1973).

4. See the two articles by Gary Caldwell and B. Dan Czarnocki, "Un rattrapage raté. Le Changement social dans le Québec d'après-guerre, 1950–1974. Une comparison Québec/Ontario," *Recherches sociographiques* 18, 1 (1977): 9–58, et "Un rattrapage raté II La Variation à court terme," *Recherches sociographiques* 18, 3 (1977): 366–96. The two authors discuss particularly what they call the "disjunctive" model that I suggested for an analysis of the evolution of Quebec since the Second World War. However, they reproach me for having minimized the structural changes that took place during this period and for having concentrated on cultural changes. It is a question of emphasis: without denying certain structural changes, I believe that they were enveloped and even carried along by the great cultural transformations that Quebec has undergone in the last three decades.

5. Guy Rocher, "Multiplication des élites et changement social au Canada français," *Revue de l'Institut de sociologie* 1 (1968): 79–94.

6. See, for example, Richard J. Joy, *Languages in Conflict* (Ottawa, 1967), particularly chapter 9, "Immigration: 95% English-speaking."

7. This evolution and the present situation are thoroughly described and analysed in the government of Quebec's White Paper, *La Politique québécoise du développement culturel* (Quebec: Éditeur officiel, 1978), vol. 1, chap. 3.

8. Nicole Gagnon, "L'Idéologie humaniste dans la revue *L'Enseignement secondaire*," *Recherches sociographiques* 4, 2 (1963): 167–200, reproduced in *École et société au Québec,* edited by Pierre W. Bélanger and Guy Rocher, 2nd ed. (Montreal: Hurtubise HMH, 1975), 1: 59–89.

9. Much has been written on this reform. One could consult, in particular, the *Rapport de la Commission d'Enquête sur l'enseignement au Québec* (Quebec, 1963, 66), 5 volumes. The reform is also put in perspective in *Rapport Parent, dix ans après* (Montreal: Bellarmin, 1975) and in numerous articles in various issues of the magazine *Prospectives*.

10. Rainer Knopff, "Language and Culture in the Canadian Debate: The Battle of the White Papers," *Canadian Review of Studies in Nationalism / Revue canadienne des études sur le nationalisme* 6, 1 (1979): 66–82. The author analyses certain ambiguities in the linguistic policies of the Lévesque and Trudeau governments, but his analysis is ambiguous as well. This in itself shows the difficulty of the subject. It also seems that the Liberal Party of Quebec, under the direction of Claude Ryan, is not ready to clear up these same ambiguities.

11. Gilbert Maistre, "L'Influence de la radio et de la télévision americaines au Canada," *Recherches sociographiques* 12, 1 (1971): 51–75.

12. In this regard, the Radio-Québec Bill, as it was recently amended, constitutes a very important step forward. It establishes regional committees with important responsibilities for programming and production of programs; at the same time, it modifies the board of directors by having half of it made up of presidents of the regional committees. Thus, there is a chance that Radio-Québec could, two or three years from now, become a public television body where part of the programming would be planned and carried out in the regions. This would be the culmination of a long evolution, as much in the regions as in the central offices of Radio-Québec and in the Government of Quebec.

QUEBEC AND THE CANADIAN QUESTION

Hubert Guindon

A century and a half ago, after the Rebellion of 1837, Lord Durham observed in his famous report that when he looked for the cause of the unrest, he found, to his astonishment, 'two nations warring in the bosom of the same state.' He proposed a simple remedy: 'I believe that tranquility can only be restored by subjecting the province [of Quebec] to the vigorous rule of an English majority.'

Were he to return today, Lord Durham would no doubt be astonished to learn that, despite the application of his proposed remedy, his initial observation holds true. Quebec and English Canada still seem to be 'two nations warring in the bosom of the same state.' Today the viability of Canada as a political entity remains in question. And for the Québécois it is *the* question, the distinctively *Canadian* question.

From *Quebec Society: Tradition, Modernity, and Nationhood,* (Toronto: University of Toronto Press, 1988), 125–146. Reprinted by permission of University of Toronto Press Incorporated.

How are we to understand Quebec and its place (or lack thereof) in Canada? For most English Canadians, the rise of the separatists in Quebec has been inexplicable. Quebec, that quiescent paragon of rural provincialism, has suddenly been transformed into a seat of rabid nationalists intent on the dismemberment of Canada.

If this change seems inexplicable, it is because it does not fit the political stereotypes and cultural myths that English Canadians long used to interpret Quebec as an archaic, traditional society. Ruled by an autocratic clergy fiercely possessive of its own powers and opposed to democracy, modernization, or social progress, Quebec, it was said, was a rural backwater of poverty, illiteracy, and political despotism.

This political/cultural vision of the French in Canada did not emanate from bigoted Orangemen. Strangely enough, it was the conceptual framework of the politically liberal anglophone academics of the 1950s, and it was shared and disseminated by the 'progressive' French-Canadian intellectuals in and around *Cité Libre* magazine, who then lived in Montreal and went on in the 1960s and 1970s to work mainly in Ottawa. (That move may seem particularly surprising, but it was theoretically predictable. Minorities are often known to internalize the majority's view of themselves, and when people from a minority want to chart a career in the majority setting, it is a necessary precondition that they adopt the common mindset.)

Political fairy tales are always with us, and only belatedly do we become aware of them. It is, therefore, easier to spot distortions of social reality in the older ones than in the current ones. How are we to understand what has really been going on in Quebec these past few decades? What processes have made the Canadian question so urgent for the Québécois?

I have argued elsewhere ['The Modernization of Quebec and the Legitimacy of the Canadian State'] that the delegitimation of the Canadian state in the eyes of the Québécois is a consequence of the modernization of Quebec, which took off with the provincial government's massive intervention in the areas of health, education, and welfare. In this chapter I explore this issue at somewhat greater length and disentangle some of the separate threads in the modernization process. This necessitates distinguishing between the processes of government involvement, secularization, and political alienation.

The modernization of Quebec was heralded by the beginnings of large-scale government involvement in the structure of Quebec society in the early 1960s—a process now called the Quiet Revolution—and by the overthrow of the Union Nationale party, which had held provincial power. The secularization process became visible six or seven years later, as a massive dropout rate among priests and nuns became noticeable. Finally, political alienation became clear in the late 1960s, as the independence movement took shape: the Mouvement Souveraineté-association, the precursor of the Parti Québécois, was created.

The Quiet Revolution

Antecedents: social unrest in the 1950s

The modernization of Quebec is popularly described as beginning with the Quiet Revolution, as if it had sprung full-blown from the traditional society preceding it. That, of course, is nonsense. The Quiet Revolution was preceded by a decade of unrest, during which more and more Québécois came to question their society and its capacity to meet their needs.

Labour unrest The designation of a single event as the beginning of any social change is always arbitrary. Nevertheless, a logical starting point for this history is the strike of the asbestos miners in 1949, a highly symbolic event. Quebec's asbestos mines, largely American-owned, were virtually closed down by this strike involving some 5,000 workers, who were mainly seeking better job conditions. Their unions were affiliated with the Canadian Catholic Confederation of Labour (the predecessor of the Confédération des syndicats nationaux of CNTU), which until this time had stressed co-operation with management; they received backing from many other Quebec unions, which put aside their history of internecine quarrels and came together to support the asbestos workers. The dispute became particularly bloody, partly because of the goon-squad tactics of the police, who were under orders from the ruling Union Nationale party to aid management and break the strike.

The strike rapidly became much more than a labour dispute. It signalled a questioning of the whole internal political and social order of Quebec society. For many years, the institutional Church had backed the political regime of Maurice Duplessis and the Union Nationale. Now two bishops openly broke with the Church, instituting collections in the parish churches of their dioceses in support of the workers. (One of them, Archbishop Charbonneau of Montreal, was eventually forced to resign his see as a consequence.) Equally significant, the intelligentsia of Quebec, who normally did not choose sides in labour disputes, mainly supported the workers.

The whole event was deeply revealing of the kinds of changes that were beginning to occur in Quebec. Here was an American corporation (at that time we did not have the word 'multinational' to describe it) with English-speaking managers and French-speaking workers who were contracting asbestosis. In retrospect, it seems amazing that under such circumstances it was Maurice Duplessis, not the Johns-Manville Corporation, and the provincial police, not the anglophone management, who became the scapegoats and villains in the political unrest that grew out of this prolonged strike.

The world of the arts This unrest spread during the 1950s, through the social, political, and cultural institutions of Quebec's traditional society. The world of the fine arts was ready for it. In 1948, Paul-Emile Borduas, an influential painter, lost his teaching position for writing a manifesto, *Le Refus Global,* that called for artists to reject the ideological hegemony exercised by the institutional Church, and to demand total freedom of expression. Although Borduas subsequently went into self-imposed exile, his message left its imprint.

Social welfare   Unrest also developed in the area of what is now called social welfare (it was then still called charity). New professionals, such as social workers, were beginning to emerge and become critical of Church control over the welfare institutions and the lack of professional qualifications of many who cared for the socially disadvantaged, the economically deprived, and the mentally disturbed. This growing dissatisfaction with the traditional ways of organizing social activities was an echo from the area of labour, where a growing critique of paternalism foreshadowed a push toward unionization and formalized collective bargaining as the normal way of organizing work.

Education   It was in the area of education that the loudest demands for change were heard. During the mid-1950s, a teaching brother anonymously published a series of letters, collected as *Les Insolences du Frère Untel* (in translation, *The Impertinences of Brother Anonymous*), which satirically decried the education system, at the time almost entirely controlled and run by the Church. The articles, which were very funny, attracted broad attention within the middle class, partly because the author castigated the atrocious distortions of his students' spoken and written French, coining the term *joual* (a colloquial pronunciation of *cheval*) to refer to their language. That lower-class French could be spoofed meant that a middle class had been sufficiently developed to constitute a willing audience for such humour. These educated Québécois were equally ready to read the satirical criticism of the 'yearly pilgrimage' to Quebec City that was undertaken by each school board in order to have its budget approved. Such mockery was a way of demanding new, more professional bureaucratic structures to handle educational needs.

By the end of the 1950s, educational concerns had shifted to the universities. Three law students of the Université de Montréal staged a sit-in in Premier Duplessis's waiting-room, with the well-publicized purpose of achieving a statutory grant system for the universities—in other words, more automatic transfer of public money to institutions of higher learning. Once again, case-by-case administration was being criticized.

In retrospect, another episode can be seen to herald the secularization of Quebec's public institutions. In reaction to a request by the Jesuits to obtain a charter to start a new French university in Montreal, the newly formed Association des Professeurs de l'Université de Montréal published a booklet entitled *L'Université dit Non aux Jésuites.* The Jesuits failed to obtain the charter.

Health care   Health institutions were also an object of social dissatisfaction. The costs of health care, which were rising fast, were borne exclusively by the patients or their kin. A twofold demand was emerging: increased involvement of the state in funding and, as a consequence, secularization of health-care institutions. In the meantime, lay people were increasingly questioning the selflessness of the religious orders that oversaw the administration of these institutions.

The end of the decade   Toward the end of the decade, two events occurred that foreshadowed two political developments: the impending demise of the Duplessis regime, and the eventual rise of the independence movement.

In the first, two priests, Fathers Dion and O'Neill, castigated the political immorality of the Union Nationale party—Duplessis's political vehicle—in a clerical periodical, *Ad Usum Sacerdotum*. The article was leaked and widely publicized and acclaimed. The fact that the charge of immorality was made by clerics who were neither parish priests nor bishops but university professors may have been significant. Certainly, they received no official rebuke. Only the bishop of rural Gaspé made a faint—and inconsequential—rebuttal. Thus, the decade that had begun with the toppling of an archbishop from his see for his expression of sympathies for the workers in a strike declared illegal by the Duplessis regime, ended with a formal, direct attack on the political immorality of that regime—an attack that went unchallenged and its authors unpenalized.

The first ripple of the independence movement, like that of the Quiet Revolution, surfaced in a labour dispute. In 1959, producers at Radio-Canada, the French network of the CBC, tried to start a trade union. The management objected that producers were managers and therefore could not be granted certification as a union. The producers went on a strike that lasted for more than two months and galvanized public attention. Once again, amazingly, the villains of the tale were not the francophone bureaucrats of Radio-Canada but the Canadian Parliament, not the minister responsible for the operation of the CBC, but Confederation itself. The asbestos strike had signalled the questioning of the internal socio-political regime of Quebec society. A decade later, the Radio-Canada strike began the eventual questioning of the external political and economic constraints on the development of Quebec society.

Agents: the emerging middle classes

The evolution of the social unrest of the 1950s in the fields of labour, welfare, education, politics, and communications raises the question of who, sociologically speaking, was politically restive and why. The reception given *Les Insolences du Frère Untel* was one indication among many of the existence of a new middle class; in Quebec's increasingly differentiated society, it was this group that felt, articulated, and progressively disseminated social unrest.

The massive urbanization that had accompanied the Second World War and immediate post-war period in Quebec had put pressure on the traditional institutions that dealt with education, health care, and welfare. The new demographic conditions required a radical and sudden increase in the scale of these institutions, which, in turn, transformed their nature. New, expensive technologies and increasingly specialized expertise required large-scale organizations in order to service a greatly expanded clientele with up-to-date levels of service. These public and para-public institutions became a major and growing labour market for members of the new middle classes: in contrast to the self-employed petite bourgeoisie of tradition, they were salaried professionals and semi-professionals developing their careers in large-scale bureaucratic organizations. In the eyes of this new middle class, Quebec institutions urgently required state money if they were to grow and thus modernize Quebec society. And the Duplessis regime was so slow to respond as to be proclaimed reactionary.

When the priorities of the new middle class became the priorities of the state, the Quiet Revolution was officially under way. This happened after Duplessis's death, when Paul Sauvé became premier in 1950. He had been in office barely three months before sudden death ended his term; it was seen as a terrible and personal loss by the whole of Quebec society. Since he had had no time to implement any changes, the deep sense of bereavement was a consequence of his promise of change (*désormais*—'henceforth'), which had included three solemnly declared intentions:

1. To provide statutory grants to universities.
2. To establish a royal commission to study the feasibility of free hospitalization.
3. To revise the pay scale for the civil service.

All three promises were soon met, if not by Sauvé's Union Nationale, then by the Liberals, who won the following election on the slogan 'It's time for a change.'

Certainly, many of the new Québécois middle class had a sincere commitment to the ideology represented by these goals. But simple sociological analysis shows that the modernization of health and education met the requirements of their career interests, as well as the needs of social progress. Statutory per capita grants to universities and per diem subsidies for hospital beds meant that state money now flowed automatically from the public treasury into educational and health institutions. These institutions were therefore able to plan rapid development. The statutory grants were politically popular because they provided free services to hospital patients as well as subsidized education for university students; they were also, especially in their design, an inducement for institutional growth. At universities, for instance, no limits were set on the number of students—money flowed from the province simply on a head count:

the effect was to induce these institutions to increase their student enrolments rapidly. With such growth, access was secured for more and more people, thereby democratizing the educational system. Simultaneously, moreover, as resources soared, these institutions could attract an increasingly qualified (and increasingly specialized) staff and reward them accordingly. Full-time careers in these institutions, once very scarce for the laity, became plentiful, and soon the introduction of the practice of tenure meant that they also became, in the universities, lifetime careers.

That the Quiet Revolution meant social progress is beyond question. It achieved increased accessibility and democratization of education, as well as improvements in the quality and accessibility of health care. It meant greater financial and bureaucratic participation by the state and rapid growth of public and para-public institutions, as well as the growth of new elites. That it also involved the secularization of Quebec society was neither so clearly foreseen nor, probably, intended. Unanticipated consequences of periods of rapid change are, however, the norm rather than the exception.

The Secularization of Quebec Society

Secularization is frequently associated with modernization in sociological literature. But the links between the two are usually far from clear and far from convincing. At the theoretical level, 'secularization' is generally defined in terms of the shrinking importance of magic and religion, as a result of the expansion of science and the scientific method. The narrowing sphere of the sacred corresponds to the expansion of knowledge, at the expense of faith and myth. Yet to conceive of secularization as a fading of myths rather than an emergence of new ones is to miss the point. Moreover, this idealistic view of secularization fails to take account of how the process takes shape and how it unfolds historically.

If the theoretical perspective on secularization is often rooted in epistemology (theories of knowledge), the popular perspective is usually put more crudely in institutional terms of ignorance and education, as a by-product of increased (mass) education. People erroneously assume that the world of knowledge and the world of meaning are the same thing. In fact, education has or should have something to do with knowledge, while secularization has to do with the world of meaning, quite another matter indeed.

Secularization is a question of politics, not epistemology. Historically, secularization started with the separation of the Church from the State, with constitutional proclamations in France and the United States, not of a churchless society, but of a churchless state. In the case of France, this proclamation was made at the time of the Revolution to formalize the break with a feudal past. In the United States, the American Revolution needed to distance the state from an official religion (and therefore from all religions), in order to proclaim freedom of religion and accommodate the denominational pluralism of the citizens.

No such political imperatives ever existed in Britain or its dominion of Canada, where a break from feudalism never occurred (although the evolution of capitalism did) and where freedom of religion became politically tolerated and practised, not constitutionally proclaimed. Yet one can argue quite correctly that secularization took place in the nineteenth and twentieth centuries in both Britain and English Canada. The process was the institutional consequence of the break from Roman Catholicism.

The term 'institutional secularization' refers to the process by which institutions initiated, staffed, or managed by clerics came under lay control. In the sixteenth and seventeenth centuries, when the Protestant churches broke from Roman Catholicism, whole societies were deprived of the organizational structure of the religious orders whose missions were to aid the poor, to tend the sick, and to provide education (to the extent that it had been developed). Thus new institutions had to be organized on a community basis under the aegis of the Protestant churches, with increased lay participation through voluntary associations. For these structural reasons, the process of institutional secularization took place much earlier in Protestant countries than in Catholic countries. By the nineteenth century, voluntary associations were well established in Protestant countries and gradual secularization of institutions was taking place. Higher education in Ontario, for example, followed this pattern. Although denominational rivalry long ensured considerable religious homogeneity among the clients and the administrators of institutions (and will probably continue to do so for some time in many places), effective and legal control by the laity, through non-profit organizations, has become firmly rooted in the social structure of Protestant countries.

In contrast, the secularization of social institutions in most Catholic countries did not take place until after the middle of the twentieth century.[1] In fact, both the number of religious orders and their membership increased dramatically during the nineteenth and early twentieth centuries in Catholic countries; the Church became progressively more involved in social institutions during that period of transition when the poor, the sick, and the ignorant, as Everett C. Hughes once put it, no longer belonged to their kin and did not yet belong to the state.

This brief historical outline sets the stage for the analysis of the secularization of Quebec, which, it must be remembered, was—and still is—a Catholic society. We will address three issues: the secularization of institutions, the massive dropout from the ranks of the clergy during the mid-1960s, and finally the substantial drop in religious practice.

The social institutions

As the Quiet Revolution swept Quebec, the Church had neither the human nor the financial resources necessary to develop the educational and health-care institutions required to meet social needs as defined by the new middle classes. These needs were broadly defined indeed: nothing short of universal access to free education up to the university level, and heavy subsidies thereafter; free hospitalization for all citizens; and (later in the 1960s) free medical care. When the State accepted such a mandate, it sealed the fate of the Church in the whole area of social institutions. Such massive and rapid investment of public money required the development of a public bureaucracy to act on behalf of the public will (at least theoretically). Neither the Church as an institution nor the traditional community elites could be the agents of this institutional development. New elites—trained in everything from accounting to engineering, from personnel to industrial relations, from purchasing to architectural design—would swell the ranks of the new middle classes in the ever-growing public bureaucracies.

Although massive growth of public institutions took place during the 1960s, the traditional institutions had already felt great demands during the 1950s. Increasing enrolments had put pressure, for instance, on the traditional *collèges,* the institutions that had offered elite youths secondary and undergraduate education from a classical curriculum. (This *cours classique* was generally the only francophone education available beyond the elementary level.) As the number of students rose, these institutions, once staffed almost exclusively by clerics, had to begin hiring lay teachers, who cost much more than clerics. Yet state subsidies amounted to very little—some $15,000 a year per institution. The same pattern was observable in health care. In brief, the demand for education and health care was outstripping the supply. The costs of expanding the existing facilities were essentially borne by their clients and, to a real but undocumented extent, by the Church—most of whose patrimony, one can assume, was spent in this transitional period of growth preceding the financial and administrative take-over by the State and its emerging professional bureaucrats.

Once the state decided to modernize and expand the educational system by the use of incentives, the secularization of the education system was greatly accelerated. This acceleration had nothing to do, as is commonly assumed, with a growing loss of religious belief or decrease in religiosity. Rather, it came from simple economic calculation at the community level. As long as the costs of education were borne locally, through taxes raised from local pockets, it made local economic sense to have clerical teachers, who cost much less than lay teachers because they lived communally and frugally and were low-level consumers. However, once the provincial government bore an overwhelming share of the costs of education, it quickly dawned on local business people (who made up most local school boards) that it made much more sense—if not to the total local community, at least to its merchants—to seek lay people with the highest possible qualifications. Not only were their salaries highly subsidized; they were big spenders with an assured income. In contrast to nuns and priests, lay teachers paid taxes and got married. Everyone—the hairdresser, the car dealer, the real-estate agent, and the insurance salesperson—could expect some share of the action. When principle and self-interest so neatly coincided, no wonder institutional change was both swift and harmonious.

While communities were securing immediate economic advantage, however, their control over local institutions was being sapped. Whether community elites were aware of this erosion or felt it was a fair trade-off, the fact is that bureaucratic centralization soon eclipsed the importance of the community. Norms as well as subsidies started to come from outside. Since loyalty is most often a function of dependence, the loyalty of the teaching staff belonged no longer to the school board but to the professional association, which bargained with government for working conditions and salary. In the process, school boards came to represent the government more than the community.

Similar analyses could be made in the realm of social welfare. The voluntary agencies that had traditionally been organized, staffed, and managed by the Church in local communities were now to be organized by lay professionals employed by state agencies.

This massive modernization initiated by the growing state bureaucracies was far from unique to Quebec society. It was common to all industrially developed countries, in fact. What was unique to Quebec (and to similar Catholic societies elsewhere in North America) is that the sudden, rapid secularization of social institutions was mostly conflict-free.

The exodus of clergy

During the late 1960s and the early 1970s, Quebec, like English Canada, the United States, and some European countries, quite suddenly saw a new phenomenon: priests and nuns left their vocations in droves. Part of the process may be explained by ideological changes within the Catholic church and part by the fact that the Vatican increasingly facilitated the release of individuals from their clerical vows. Equally facilitating these 'defections' in Quebec was the fact that, contrary to the situation before the Quiet Revolution, priests or nuns who left orders could now quite easily find a place for themselves within the social structure. No longer were former clerics—especially priests—viewed as having committed spiritual treason by leaving the sacred calling; no longer could a defector cope only by either leaving the society or concealing his or her previous occupation. Suddenly, with the change in the social order, ex-priests could (and did) enter the growing ranks of the public and semi-public bureaucracies. The change was so thorough and so pervasive that priests who taught religion at the Université de Montréal, which holds a pontifical charter, were able, because of tenure, to keep their positions after quitting the ranks of the clergy and celibacy. Such a situation would have been inconceivable less than a decade earlier.

Paradoxically, the same reasons that had prompted men and women to enter the clergy in remarkable numbers in the none-too-distant past could also explain the sudden, massive exodus. Without doubting the selflessness and sincere motives of those who became priests, brothers, or nuns, one can argue that, in social terms, joining the clergy of Quebec had certainly not involved downward social mobility. For women, it had meant an assurance of comfortable, if austere, living quarters and an escape from the burden of large families and domestic chores, while gaining access to socially esteemed occupations in teaching and nursing. The lifestyle of nuns, although basically other-worldly, certainly matched and often surpassed the conditions under which most married women from the same social backgrounds could expect to live. The social distance that nuns maintained from the civil society was compensated by the deference given them by the laity. The majesty of their convents contrasted with the urban tenements their married sisters occupied. Deprived of the privileges of married life, they were equally spared its burdens; on balance, entering a convent was not—and was not perceived as—an irrational decision.

For men, joining the clergy, regular or secular,[2] meant entering a career that could lead to important institutional positions. In the secular clergy, the career paths mainly involved pastoral duties in the urban and rural parishes of a geographically circumscribed diocese. A young man began as a curate, receiving only a very low stipend beyond room and board, but could fully expect to become a parish pastor some day. Promotions, based primarily on seniority, would lead as parish priest from a small, possibly rural, parish to a large urban parish. As he moved from small to large parish, his income rose substantially because it was a function of both the wealth and the size of his parish. The 'good income' years made a relatively secure retirement possible.

For the regular clergy, the career patterns varied according to the kinds of institutions run by the order—from novitiates for the training of future priests to colleges and sometimes universities, as well as shrines, publications, and social agencies involved with co-operatives or credit and trade unions. A man could aspire to positions of leadership, public recognition, and gratitude as his career reached its apex.

Quebec had long had a relatively high percentage of people who chose to follow these patterns. More or less simultaneously with the Quiet Revolution, decisions to enter the religious life suddenly shrank to a trickle, and defections increased dramatically, especially among younger nuns and priests—those who were beginning, not terminating, their careers. The shrinking role of the Church in the newly emerged social order was certainly a key factor. The Church, which had previously offered both full career patterns and social esteem, could now promise neither. One can also say that the Catholic hierarchy unwittingly helped to curtail the potential of clerical careers. Bureaucratic centralization of resources and decision-making, which became hallmarks of the new social organization, did not spare the Church itself. The career patterns of the secular clergy were drastically altered. Parish priests were suddenly transformed into functionaries on a fixed salary—and a low one at that. Any surplus resources were centralized by the bishop, who was, so the rationale went, in the best position to assess the needs of the various parishes and distribute the resources. Bureaucratically unimpeachable, this doctrine led to measures that sapped the morale of the secular clergy by suddenly eliminating the traditional pattern of rewards. Worse, parish priests and their curates realized that a priest who joined the ranks of the rapidly growing para-public institutions as a salaried professional made more than four times their income, was exempt from pastoral duties, could live in a private apartment, and, as a learned man of science, was more visible, better known, and socially esteemed in both the lay and the clerical worlds.

The decrease in religious practice

'Tradition,' Everett Hughes once pointed out in conversation, 'is sacred only so long as it is useful.' If tradition involves a mix of the sacred and the utilitarian, it follows that the first people to question its sacred character will be those for whom tradition is no longer useful. And indeed in mid-twentieth century Quebec, it was the intelligentsia and the new middle classes—whose careers and interests were no longer served by the traditional culture, institutions, or leadership—who first challenged the legitimacy of all three.

For traditional Quebec society, including the elites, visible religious practices were interwoven with almost every part of life. Many of these folkways all but disappeared over a very short time. For example, people had been accustomed to locate themselves by referring to the parish in which they resided; this custom rapidly disappeared as the majority of people no longer knew the names or the general locations of parish churches.

It would not be misleading to say that most of the population drifted into secularization through inattention. For the majority, estrangement from religious practice developed as a result of the Church's growing irrelevance in meeting their everyday needs. Schools were no longer linked to the Catholic parish; teachers were more apt to be lay than clerical; hospitals and clinics were professionally administered by specialists who lived far from where they worked, and neither knew nor cared to know about their clients in other than a professional capacity. The secularization of charity in the professionally operated agencies of the state left the Church not only with a shrinking role but also with half-empty buildings whose material upkeep became increasingly dependent on the continuing popularity of bingo.

The falloff was evident both in the important decisions of life and in the minutiae of daily living. Stanley Ryerson has observed in conversation how deeply Quebec society has changed: nowadays, people no longer doff their hats or cross themselves when passing in front of a church. When what was commonplace becomes bizarre, when automatic, unreflecting, customary behaviour becomes unusual over a very short time, one suspects that deep changes separate the present from the immediate past. In every respect except calendar time, centuries—not decades—separate the Quebec of the 1980s from the Quebec of the 1950s.

No longer visible, now basically silent, the Church, once a dominant institution in social and collective life, withdrew to service the spiritual and private needs of those still seeking its counsel. As its political clout faded, the voice of its critics became louder. The political liberals and conservatives maintain that the Church was, in large measure, responsible for the economic underdevelopment of Quebec, because it did not impart to its flock the 'right' values, those that inspire entrepreneurial leadership and economic success. Under its leadership, they argue, Quebec's institutions failed to adapt to the requirements of a modern industrial society. The Marxists, on the other hand, take the Church to task for having collaborated with the anglophone bourgeoisie in exploiting its flock, the working class. Both charges are ideologically inspired distortions. The Church, however, no longer answers its critics. Is this a dignified silence, or the sign of its collapse as an institution?

The Canadian Question

By the late 1970s, a modern and secular social order had indeed emerged in Quebec society. Quebec had put its internal house in order, in line with other developed societies. In spite of this—maybe because of this—Quebec remained politically restive. It was readying itself to challenge the legitimacy of another sacred institution: the Canadian state. The internal issue of Church and society having been resolved, the external issue of state and society rose to the top of the political agenda. For Quebec society that was *the* Canadian question.

A *lament for two nations*

Seldom, if ever, do a conquered people give their consent to a conquering state. Conquered subjects' loyalty to the state is always suspect. This is so true that loyalty oaths are routinely administered to and taken by future civil servants. In times of crisis in national unity, these forgotten oaths become instruments of social control for those who fear for the state's security. The point is raised here not to underscore the vulnerability of those fragile freedoms known as civil liberties, but rather to call attention to the historically enduring price of political domination. Both those who created the state and those who are subject to it are forever condemned to wishful thinking: the first, to the dream of national unity, the latter, to the dream of national independence.

Those who dream of national unity are also forced to lament the absence of a commonly agreed-on history. In Canada in the 1960s, the Royal Commission on Bilingualism and Biculturalism went to great lengths and considerable expense to document this great gap. (On second thought, the commission might have realized it owed its very existence to that regrettable fact.)

Commonly agreed-on history presupposes a common celebration of either a glorious past or a common victory over an undesirable past. France can claim both; Britain can claim the first; the United States, the latter; and Canada neither. The cruelty of this observation is mitigated by the fact that political consensus can also be built on shared visions of the future. Such visions, however, must be based on the correction of history, not its denial. 'Unhyphenated Canadianism' is a mirage based on the confusion of individual biography with group history. All immigrants have a biographical break with a past in which the country of origin somehow, to some degree, became undesirable—often because of denied opportunity or political persecution; the country of adoption, by the mere fact of receiving the immigrants, symbolizes a land of opportunity or a refuge from oppression, both of which are good reasons for thanksgiving. In contrast, the French and the English in Canada are burdened with historical continuity. In both cases, the breaking with the biographical past creates not a new citizen but a marginal one. And while marginal people may invent myths and create new visions, a new political order without group consent remains beyond reach.

A political order is a symbolically mediated structure. In other words, the state, to be legitimate, must rely on the substantial—not just formal—consent of the governed. Formal consent can be engineered by manipulation, trickery, propaganda, publicity, and deception, or it can be claimed on the basis of sufficient numbers alone. Shared consent, however, requires shared meanings, shared myths. The French and the English in Canada may have a common fate, but they share no political myths. The closest they have come was the belief that Canada was a partnership between the French and the English, an idea formalized in the compact theory of Confederation, which presents dualism as central to the nature of the state. John Porter spoke of 'charter groups'—while admitting the junior status of one of them. Stanley Ryerson called Confederation an 'unequal union.' Lester Pearson, in striking the Royal Commission on Bilingualism and Biculturalism, spoke of the 'two founding races.' The commission, sensitive to the connotations that might be evoked by the word 'race,' preferred to speak of 'two societies and two cultures.' Pierre Trudeau watered the concept down still further, referring to two language communities (as though language without culture can be the basis of community) and many cultures. One need say no more to illustrate either the inability to define what Canada is or the incapacity of words to cover up an embarrassing social and political reality.

The last person to speak candidly about the social and political reality of Canada in unambiguous, well-established English words was Lord Durham, in his description of 'two nations warring in the bosom of the same state.' As mentioned at the beginning of this chapter, he recommended the subjugation of the French to the vigorous rule of the British, advice that was heeded but that did not succeed. Before Confederation, following this advice required thwarting democratic principles. With Confederation, those principles ensured political domination of the French nation.

Ever after, the word 'nation' to describe the French fact in Canada was banned from the political vocabulary of Canadian academics and politicians. To make credible this semantic confusion, it became customary to refer not to the Canadian *state* but to the Canadian *nation*—creating unity not politically but semantically.

Such obfuscation obviously requires education. Denying reality rather than assuming it is characteristic of Canadian politicians, not of ordinary Canadian citizens. On leaving or entering Quebec, Québécois and non-Québécois alike quickly perceive the reality of cultural and social differences. Some people are dumbstruck by the differences. Others are paranoid about them. Both types of reaction testify to the reality of social and cultural boundaries. The fact that this dual reality cannot find a political expression in the Canadian political system constitutes its basic vulnerability.

The compact (or dualist) theory of Confederation, the myth that so many French Canadians clung to so that they could symbolically legitimate a dignified commitment to the Canadian state, suffered an ignominious death with the patriation of the Constitution in 1982; one partner, they discovered, could force patriation without the consent of the other. That the death blow was struck by a prime minister who was himself partly French-Canadian made it no less lethal; that it involved political trickery transformed the constitutional process from grand ritual into tragic farce, making the final demise of illusion seem unreal and senseless. Rumour has it that Prime Minister Trudeau's ruthlessness in patriating the Constitution was motivated by his frantic determination to secure a niche for himself in Canadian history. Secure a niche he did indeed: whether it will be an enviable one is quite another matter.

The destruction of dualism as a shared myth through the forcible patriation of the Constitution constitutes a proof by political action, rather than national argument, of a doctrine close to Trudeau's heart: that Quebec is a province *comme les autres*. In other words, Quebec is not the homeland of a people, it is merely a region of the country, one region among ten.

In legal fiction, Quebec has become a province *comme les autres;* in social reality it has not. It also is different economically; only in the province of Quebec is the economy controlled by a minority who differ socially, culturally, and ethnically from the inhabitants. This social and historical fact has arisen partly because of the Canadian state. Therein lies its tainted legitimacy. Therein, too, lies the reason it gave birth to the dream of national independence among its subjects in Quebec.

The unreachable dream

The dream of national independence in Quebec society took root when the 'partnership' between French and English in the Canadian state was still a dominant theme in the political rhetoric. In effect, it was the suspicion that English Canadians did not in fact share this political myth that gave rise to the political alienation of the intelligentsia in Quebec society.

While the 1950s were ushered in by the strike in the asbestos mines, the 1960s were opened by the strike at Radio-Canada. Both events heralded basic changes in the socio-political order. The asbestos strike led to the Quiet Revolution a decade later. The Radio-Canada strike led, some fifteen years later, to the election of the Parti Québécois. With the Quiet Revolution sprang up a modernized and secularized society, founded by the state and managed by bureaucratically employed professionals. With the independence movement was born an enduring, credible challenge to the legitimacy of an externally imposed political order.

As already stated, both strikes at first glance seem paradoxical. The asbestos strike involved a multinational corporation with English-Canadian management and French workers, but it led to a questioning of the Duplessis regime and the social power of the Church. The strike at Radio-Canada involved a conflict between producers and management within the exclusively French network of the CBC but ended by being defined in ethnic terms. Neither interpretation is really paradoxical. The contradiction between objective fact and social response would be real enough in normal times, but in times of social unrest and of heightened tension it is not unusual for an event to be invested with meanings that transcend what actually happens. The discrepancy signals the major redefinitions of historical situations that precede a challenge of a political order.

The strike at Radio-Canada, unlike many strikes, directly affected the intelligentsia and initiated their political alienation. Soon they scrutinized the federal government's institutions to ascertain the amount and level of participation of francophones within them. They found this participation appallingly low, giving substance to the emerging conviction that the Canadian state is 'theirs, not ours.' Moreover, as the Royal Commission on Bilingualism and Biculturalism eventually substantiated, the few francophones who did work in these institutions had to check their mother tongue at the door. At the Montreal Harbour Board, for example, bilingual civil servants received a routine memo from their francophone boss: 'Since everybody in the department is bilingual, all reports must be written in English.' It made perfect administrative sense internally. Externally, when leaked to the press, it made no political sense, except as an example of Lord Durham's 'vigorous British rule.'

The memo was quoted in the first of a series of editorials by André Laurendeau, the prestigious editor of *Le Devoir*. Some months later Prime Minister Lester Pearson struck the Royal Commission on Bilingualism and Biculturalism. Noble men filled with good intentions and alarmed by the strains threatening the state, the commissioners came forth with recommendations that perpetuated, rather than eliminated, those strains. By refusing to recommend a language regime based on territory, which would have ensured the francophone majority in Quebec access in their own language to the large corporate sector of Montreal, they proclaimed Quebec the model for the treatment of 'minorities' and urged the rest of Canada to follow suit toward their French minorities. In effect, they recommended leaving Quebec untouched, in terms of language policy, and adopting measures they thought would ensure the viability of French communities outside Quebec.

This viability could not be ensured, however, since postal services and radio and television programming in French were no replacement for a vanishing economic base. Furthermore, they could not convince the politically restive Québécois that Quebec was a model, since within that 'model' they had to choose between a public-sector career in French or a private-sector career in English. If Quebec was to be a province *comme les autres,* as Trudeau insisted, it seemed elementary to correct that strange discrepancy. More skilled in provocation than in integration, Prime Minister Trudeau dismissed the terms of reference of the Royal Commission on Bilingualism and Biculturalism and proclaimed Canada to be bilingual and multicultural. While the proclamation pleased those citizens who were neither French nor English, it certainly did not guarantee any substance to ethnic cultures since they would not be celebrated in their own languages; what it did guarantee was state funds to enable colourful celebrations of official pluralism.

The official bilingualism adopted by the Canadian state was politically irrelevant for the modernizing Québécois majority and politically resented in most of English-speaking Canada. In Western Canada it smacked of privilege, since the few French Canadians living there were fully bilingual but now able to get federally funded French-language radio and television, not to mention bilingual labels on their cornflakes, while the overwhelming majority of new Canadians could not receive such services in their cultural languages. The reasons of state clashed with the logic of community, and the reasons of state prevailed, pitting the ethnic Canadians against the French Canadians. The very same result was achieved in Quebec by the failure of the senior government to act, leading, in 1974, the junior government under Robert Bourassa—no wild-eyed separatist but a tame Liberal—to introduce Bill 22, *la loi sur la langue officielle.* Replacing a 1969 act that had the same intent but was less comprehensive, Bill 22 announced that French was the language of the workplace and of government services. It also restricted anglophone education to children who demonstrated a prior knowledge of the English language. Thus, although the new law was loudly denounced by the anglophone media, one of its most immediate effects was to alienate from the Liberal party many of Quebec's new Canadians, who resented having to learn not one but two languages to qualify for effective citizenship.

The vocal opposition to Bill 22 in English-speaking Quebec was disseminated throughout the rest of Canada, leading the Canadian Air-Traffic Controllers' Association to challenge, in 1976, the federal official language policy. Specifically, the air controllers, fearful of eventual bilingual requirements, struck to protest the use of French by francophone pilots when talking to francophone controllers; safety in the air was threatened, the union's public statements suggested, unless both parties had to use English at all times. Until now, implementation of the federal bilingual policy had been passively resisted, as the successive annual reports of the Commissioner of Official Languages ritually attested to. The CATCA strike was, however, an official challenge by a special-interest group. Trudeau responded by solemnly proclaiming in a television address that this challenge constituted a major threat to national unity, packed his bags, went off to Bermuda, and left the whole matter in the hands of Transport Minister Otto Lang—who promptly surrendered to the demands of CATCA.

Only months later, provincial elections brought to power, to the consternation of English Canadians, the Parti Québécois, whose announced goals included the peaceful attainment of independence for Quebec. One of its first actions was to complete the francization of Quebec that Bourassa had begun. It enacted Bill 101, *la charte de la langue française*, which makes French the normal language of work, education, and public life in Quebec. Basically, its authors considered Ontario the model for the treatment of the other official language. But what is normal in Ontario and elsewhere in Canada is considered by those regions to be outrageous in Quebec.

In response to the election of a 'separatist' government in Quebec, Trudeau struck a Task Force on Canadian Unity, headed by Jean-Luc Pepin and John Robarts. Its report, however, did not take sufficient umbrage at Bill 101 and was not only ignored but swiftly denounced, on the very day of its release, by Don Johnston, MP for Westmount–St Henri, then a Liberal backbencher but soon to be promoted to Trudeau's cabinet. Proud of his interview in the electronic media, Johnston eventually had the transcript translated into French and distributed in both languages to his constituents. In it, he solemnly proclaimed his and his constituents' rejection of the Pepin-Robarts Report. The grounds? First, history teaches us one thing: if you leave a minority at the mercy of a majority, its rights will not be protected. And that is what the Pepin-Robarts Report did. Second, our French-Canadian compatriots would be 'condemned' to live all their lives only in French, a fate presumably worse than death. If Don Johnston was right about the fate of minorities at the hands of majorities, he made it the duty of every self-respecting Québécois to become an *indépendantiste*. By equating living one's life only in French to a sentence, he clearly shows that taking the role of the others is not an automatic consequence of living in their midst.

The Parti Québécois had won its electoral victory preaching sovereignty-association—political independence for Quebec within an economic union with Canada—but had promised to seek a specific mandate before attempting to negotiate the change with Ottawa. A referendum was announced for May 1980, and the federal Liberals combined with the provincial party to throw enormous amounts of money and advertising into the campaign. The referendum failed—a joyless victory of national unity. English Canadians stopped holding their breath, even when the PQ unexpectedly won another victory at the polls the next year. What the referendum had done was to make the dream of national independence unreachable.

Then Trudeau delivered on his promise of 'renewed federalism'; in 1982 the Constitution was repatriated without Quebec's consent. The PQ resisted federal blandishments to sign, but in its eagerness to retain power, it loosened some requirements of Bill 101 (which even in its original form was felt by some Québécois to give insufficient protection to the French culture and language), and it announced a new, quasi-federalist platform that drove several well-known *indépendantistes* to leave its ranks. Those moves proved too much for the Quebec electorate. Although they had voted overwhelmingly against the Liberals in the federal election of 1984, sweeping the Conservatives to victory, a few months later they voted almost as decisively *for* the provincial Liberals—the party that, after all, had come to power in 1960 under the slogan *maîtres chez nous*.

The outcome of the referendum and the purge of the *indépendantistes* from the Parti Québécois spells not the end of Québec's 'national' movement, but the end of its embodiment by a specific political party. It also means that the strategy to achieve independence will not follow the route of party politics. A return to less institutionalized forms of political mobilization is not to be excluded.

Conclusion

This essay ends on a melancholy note of disillusionment with statesmanship and party politics in this country. It does not claim to be non-partisan or dispassionate. It is a plea, a public and desperate one, for the youth of this country to distance themselves from the political culture they are exposed to. It is especially a plea to young English Canadians not to accept either the new demonology on Quebec or the idea that all is returning to 'normal' there, but to resolve to help to bring to birth eventually a state that will truly enjoy the consent of the governed.

Notes

Originally published in M. Michael Rosenberg, William B. Shaffir, Allan Turowetz, and Morton Weinfeld, eds., *An Introduction to Sociology* (Toronto, 1983).

1. The exception was France, where after the Revolution the state took over the direct organization of education, producing bitter internal conflict that lasted more than a century.

2. Catholic priests may be regular or secular clerics. The regular clerics are those who are members of a particular order, such as the Basilians, the Sulpicians, and the Jesuits, and live under its rule (hence 'regular'); they take vows of celibacy, poverty, and obedience (to the hierarchy of the order). Although an order sometimes accepts the responsibility of running a parish, each views itself as having one or more special mandates, which in Quebec before the 1960s was most often education, health, or some form of social service for active orders. (Some orders are strictly contemplative.)

   In contrast, secular clerics take a vow of celibacy, but not of poverty or obedience. They work under the local bishop (whose assignment comes from Rome) and run most parishes, as well as other institutions under direct diocesan control.

   All nuns and religious brothers are regular clerics.

THE CONFÉDÉRATION DES SYNDICATS NATIONAUX (CSN), THE IDEA OF INDEPENDENCE, AND THE SOVEREIGNTIST MOVEMENT, 1960–1980

Ralph Peter Güntzel

In early June 1979, the CSN, Québec's second-largest labour union central, held a special convention on the national question. The one thousand delegates were to discuss a variety of issues related to Québec's constitutional status and the socio-economic condition of francophones in Québec. On the third day of the convention, several high-ranking CSN officers led by the central's vice-president, André L'Heureux, proposed a resolution in support of independence for Québec. A long and intense debate ensued. In the end, only one quarter of the delegates rallied behind the pro-independence proposal.[1] This vote did not

From *Labour / Le Travail*, 31, Spring 1993, 145–173. Reprinted with the permission of the editor of Labour/Le Travail.

mean, however, that the CSN endorsed federalism. Quite the opposite: in early April 1980, the CSN recommended to its members to vote yes in the referendum in order to permit the Parti Québécois government to negotiate sovereignty-association. On the eve of the Québec referendum, the CSN position on the issue of separation was ambiguous. To explain this ambiguity one has to go back in CSN history to the time of the Quiet Revolution.

The evolution of the CSN position on the independence question during the 1960s and 1970s can be divided into three phases. From 1960 to 1966, the CSN opted for federalism and provincial autonomy and rejected separation. From 1966 to 1972, most CSN leaders and many rank-and-file members came to favour independence. As a result, the CSN gradually moved away from its federalist stand and became increasingly sympathetic toward independence. In 1972, though, this process came to a halt. For the remainder of the decade the union central avoided any clear-cut stand. This paper seeks to cast light on the rise of separatism within the CSN after 1966, as well as its hesitation waltz during the 1970s. Both phenomena can only be understood with a prior knowledge of the ideological radicalization which the union central underwent between 1960 and 1980. Hence, I will first give an account of the CSN's socio-economic outlook, and then discuss its stance on constitutional questions. Although this study does not pretend to be a comparative analysis, the experiences of Québec's other union centrals are considered briefly as well.

I

The Confédération des travailleurs catholiques du Canada (CTCC) was founded in 1921 under the influence of the Roman Catholic Church. For a long time it adhered to Catholic social doctrine and defined as its goal the defence of traditional French-Canadian values, particularly against such adversaries as the international, religiously neutral unions. In pursuit of this goal, the CTCC opposed state intervention in the social and educational fields, and advocated collaboration with the business community.[2] It was only in the 1940s and 1950s that the CTCC leadership's socio-economic outlook began to change. Gradually the idea of preserving traditional French-Canadian society was supplanted by the ideology of 'catching-up.' The central now wanted Québec to copy the institutions and standards of other Western societies. CTCC demands aimed at parity with Ontario in terms of salaries, work conditions, labour relations, health services, and the education system.[3]

Many of the proposals aired by the CTCC-CSN were to be taken up during Québec's Quiet Revolution. Between 1960 and 1966, Premier Jean Lesage and his Liberal government implemented the ambitious reform programme that was at the heart of the Quiet Revolution. The team around Lesage advocated planning the economy to avoid such disturbances as those Canada had experienced during the first post-war depression, 1957 to 1961. It wanted to render the workplace more humane, and to make systematic provisions for the aged, the unemployed, and the sick, as well as for an efficient, highly-skilled, and professional labour force. Inspired by institutions and standards in other Western societies, the Quiet Revolution's reforms vastly expanded state intervention in the economy, in social, health, and welfare services, and in the educational system. An economic planning council was created, and various provincial capital pools, such as the Société générale de financement and the Caisse de dépôt et placement, were set up. All private hydroelectric companies were nationalized. New hospital insurance benefits gave Québec residents free access to hospital and diagnostic services. The health-care and educational systems, formerly largely administered by the Church and private organizations, now became subject to state control.

The CSN was important in the coalition supporting the Liberal reform drive.[4] The union central also benefited from many Quiet Revolution measures, most particularly the reform of Québec labour relations. With the new labour code of July 1964, Bill 5 in June 1965, and the Civil Servants' Act in August 1965, the right to strike—except where essential services were in jeopardy—was given to workers employed by hospitals, school commissions, and municipalities, to teachers, and to civil servants. It should be noted, however, that extending the right to strike to the public sector had not been among the Liberal Party's original intentions. Rather, it was the demands and pressure of organized labour which led to the new legislation. According to labour historian Jacques Rouillard, these laws placed Québec in the vanguard of North American labour legislation. "Pour la première fois, l'enthousiasme issu de la Révolution tranquille porte les conquêtes sociales au-delà du modèle proposé par les autres sociétés nord-américaines."[5]

All the aforementioned reforms and others, such as the replacement of the spoils system by the merit system, and Bill 16 including the equalisation of spouses in marriage, were introduced within a short time. While the reforms of the Quiet Revolution rapidly followed each other, they gave the population the impression of witnessing not only radical change but even the dawn of a new era. Since all those reforms had a distinctly progressive character, they helped heighten expectations. Many intellectuals, students, and labour union militants expected the reforms to herald a more just and egalitarian society in which wealth would be distributed more equally.[6] Some of them joined radical political movements such as Parti pris, Révolution québécoise, and the Parti socialiste du Québec (PSQ). They could do so without being marginalized because the Quiet Revolution had created a new openness in intellectual life and thereby laid the basis for the free expression of radical ideas. It was in the last phase of the Quiet Revolution, during 1965–66, that radical political movements became increasingly prolific. At the same time, disappointment with the achievements of the Quiet Revolution started to set in. Unemployment rates remained higher and average incomes lower in Québec than in Ontario. Moreover, the instability and insecurity of the economic situation did not change in the least. During the late 1960s and early 1970s, the economic situation deteriorated and unemployment rates began to rise dramatically.[7] At the same time, government debts accumulated. The expansion of the public sector had led to an increase in costs and taxes. Yet while taxes went up the standard of living did not rise.[8]

The disappointment about the results of the Quiet Revolution was particularly pronounced within the CSN. This was largely due to the evolution of public-sector negotiations from 1965 onwards. The rapid rise of unionization in this sector created a situation in which the state and the CSN found themselves to be opponents at the bargaining table and in industrial conflicts. Unlike other employers, the state disposed of legislative powers which it used to enact special back-to-work legislation. Moreover, numerous court injunctions prevented or ended public sector negotiations on the ground that essential services were in jeopardy. Under those circumstances, striking, the classical weapon of unionism, proved to be no longer effective.[9] The multiplication and aggravation of these conflicts during the second half of the 1960s increasingly frustrated and radicalized the CSN. Disappointed with the results of the Quiet Revolution, and more particularly its newly established system of industrial relations, more and more rank-and-file activists and union leaders—particularly in the public sector—started to reassess the power structures of existing society and redefine the character and the form of union activities. They soon concluded that the Québec state was inherently hostile to working-class interests, no matter which party held power.[10] For them the obvious explanation of this hostility was the state's dependence on the business community.[11] In addition they considered it necessary to create new forms of unionism, since the traditional ones had become insufficient.[12] Towards the end of the decade, they came to analyze the market economy from a Marxist viewpoint without, however, employing Marxist terminology. From there they went on to advocate a socialist society and to politicize union activities accordingly.

In the early 1970s, a variety of events reinforced this ideological radicalization. In April 1970, the Parti libéral du Québec came to power. Led by Robert Bourassa, the new government embarked on a pro-business course of which the most prominent features were a disregard for state interventionism and support for private enterprise.[13] Half a year after the provincial elections, the October Crisis and the invocation of the War Measures Act took place. About one quarter of the people arrested during the crisis were labour union activists. This infringement on citizens' civil liberties evoked the wrath of many CSN leaders and rank-and-file members. In the wake of the October Crisis, the CSN became more hostile towards the state apparatus. According to historian Jean-François Cardin, "[la CSN] ne craint plus d'attaquer directement l'Etat et son rôle d'appui à la bourgeoisie dans l'exploitation des travailleurs."[14] The early 1970s also witnessed several dramatic industrial conflicts, such as the strike at

La Presse in 1971. This dispute crested on 29 October of that year, when police violently broke up a demonstration supporting the strikers, leaving behind one dead and several wounded. Thirty-seven militants were arrested on this occasion. Seven months later, CSN president Marcel Pepin and the presidents of Québec's two other labour union centrals were sentenced to jail for one year on the grounds that they had encouraged the illegal public-sector strike of April 1972.[15]

In the aftermath of the Quiet Revolution, the left within the union central underwent both a considerable radicalization and an increase in numerical strength. As a result, the left was able to exercise an ever-growing influence on the CSN's general orientation. In its quest to dominate the central, the left was pitted against a group of more moderate or conservative activists, most of whom belonged to private-sector unions. It would be simplistic, however, to equate the left with the public sector and the right with the private sector. In fact, most public-sector union members were no more radical than their peers in private-sector unions. Most professionals adhered to elitist attitudes and held the average worker in disregard.[16] A 1970 poll of CSN-organized teachers showed that most of them did not think that unions should get involved in political activities.[17] The poll confirmed the findings of the CSN political action committee report presented at the 1968 confederal convention. The report stated that most CSN members were neither politicized nor willing to join the political activities of the labour movement. Quite similarly, in its report to the 1972 confederal convention, the Committee of the Twelve, an *ad hoc* committee on ideological issues, pointed out that Québec's political parties and their ideas exercised a dominant influence among the CSN membership.[18]

While the CSN general membership was unwilling to fundamentally change the socio-economic system, the central's active membership became increasingly radical between the mid-1960s and early 1970s.[19] The rise of the left was greatly helped by the dynamic personality of Marcel Pepin, president of the CSN from 1965 to 1976. Pepin's determination and leadership qualities were unmatched by those heading the right wing of the central.[20] He was surrounded by a group of intellectuals to which belonged Richard Daigneault, Pierre Vadeboncoeur, André L'Heureux, and Michel Rioux. This 'think tank' was sensitive to the wave of protest sweeping through Québec in the wake of the Quiet Revolution, and favoured the radicalization of the union central. Due to its close relationship with the president, the group wielded enormous informal power within the CSN. Its influence on decision-making processes paralleled that of the elected officers. Thus its opponents on the right referred to the group as 'le pouvoir parallèle.'[21] Pepin and his collaborators were pushed forward not only by the general atmosphere of post-Quiet Revolution Québec, by public-sector militants, and union councillors emerging from the student movement and socialist organizations, but also by a radical faction within the CSN's own left wing. Led by Michel Chartrand, the radical left in 1969 conquered the Conseil central des syndicats nationaux de Montréal (CCSNM), a CSN sub-organization which represents all unions in the Montréal region. Under Chartrand's presidency, the CCSNM made ideological commitments which were pathbreaking for the CSN as a whole. In 1970, the CCSNM proposed the CSN should officially reject capitalism and endorse socialism.[22]

Since Pepin and his followers were afraid to jeopardize the unity of the central, relations between the radical faction and the more moderate faction within the left were often characterized by tension and mutual suspicion.[23] Relations between both factions were rendered even more difficult by the personal animosity between Pepin and Chartrand. In 1971, however, all elements of the left joined forces in order to give the CSN the socialist orientation advocated by the CCSNM. The debate on the official ideology of the union central finally erupted in open conflict between the left and right.[24] Aggravated by dissent over which strategy to adopt in the 1972 public-sector negotiations, this conflict split the movement. Being in a minority situation, the right wing decided to leave the union central. The CSN lost about 70,000 members, which equalled one-third of its membership. Many of those who left the CSN went on to found a new, non-political union central, the Centrale des syndicats démocratiques (CSD).[25]

After the departure of the dissenters, almost all leaders of the CSN were partisans of socialism. They agreed on the need for fundamental socio-economic change. They thought the economic activities of society should be planned and aim at fulfilling the needs of the population. Furthermore, they endorsed the principle of collective ownership of the means of production, and of workers' participation in the economic decision-making process. Yet within the framework of these principles, they had different visions of socialism. Some CSN socialists wanted the collective ownership of the means of production to be comprehensive, while others wanted to limit it to certain key sectors such as natural resources. For the latter group, the expansion of the co-operative sector and workers' co-ownership were preferable to the nationalization of the entire economy.[26] CSN socialists took positions somewhere between those of social democracy and communism. In some instances their positions bordered on those of classical social democracy committed to minimize differences of wealth and to nationalize some sectors of the economy. Unlike social democrats, however, CSN socialists were prepared to go much further to eliminate private ownership of the means of production and principle of profit. What made CSN socialists different from communists was their insistence on democratic planning and decision-making. CSN socialists did not envisage a leading role for the Communist Party, nor a proletarian revolution. CSN socialists agreed that socialism should be attained peacefully, but remained unclear on how it should be brought about.

In October 1972, the confederal council—the CSN's highest decision-making body between its confederal conventions—adopted almost unanimously a declaration rejecting capitalism and endorsing socialism.[27] The resolution, though, failed to define socialism and instead called for "la poursuite d'une étude dans tout le mouvement visant à définir le contenu d'un socialisme québécois et les étapes de sa réalisation."[28] This hesitance to take a definite stand not only reflected the varying interpretations of socialism among CSN radicals, but also the insecurity these radicals felt toward the rank-and-file majority of their organization. The fact that the central's leadership was left-leaning did not mean that the right was now absent from the ranks of the CSN. A large number of militants, and a majority of the rank-and-file membership, were opposed to any fundamental socio-economic change, but they remained faithful to the CSN despite its socialist orientation. They found its services satisfactory and distrusted the risk of joining a small, newborn central. Although the members of the confederal council appeared courageous in October 1972, the CSN leadership was deeply affected by the defections. The socialist CSN leaders were well aware that they had to anticipate the reactions of their largely anti-socialist constituency if future disaffiliations were to be avoided. Therefore they decided not to pursue elaborations on official CSN ideology. All plans to discuss the definition of the CSN version of socialism, and the steps required to attain a socialist society, were postponed. Instead, priority was given to the political education of the membership.[29]

In the end, very little energy was devoted to political education since the CSN underwent yet another crisis from 1973 to 1976. The enormous rise of the cost of living led many unions to try to force employers to reopen collective agreements in order to increase salaries. Walkouts and illegal strikes multiplied. The CSN strike fund rapidly became exhausted. This period was characterized by internal struggles about moves to raise per-capita contributions to the strike fund. In the public sector unions were resentful of fee increases. In this sector, strikes were normally ended by special laws and court injunctions after only a few days. However, strike-fund benefits were disbursed only after two weeks of striking. About 20,000 members, mostly nurses and professionals, refused to pay the increases and consequently were forced to leave the CSN.[30]

While the union central was recuperating from its most recent losses over the fee-increase issue, several factions of Marxist-Leninist militants started to make their presence felt. They belonged to a variety of political organizations, the most important of which were En Lutte! and the Parti communiste ouvrier (PCO). They all agreed on the need for a revolutionary overthrow of capitalist society, but were fiercely opposed to each other on various theoretical issues. Although their organizations were tiny, due to their devotion, training, and discipline, the Marxist-Leninists began to exert considerable influence within the CSN. They were most successful in public-sector unions and regional CSN suborganizations such as the CCSNM.[31] With the rise of the communist far left, ideological division within the union central became even more pronounced. In the latter 1970s, despite having lost a large number of members due to ideological differences, the CSN was ideologically less-homogenous than ever. In these circumstances, the CSN leadership found its margin of manoeuverability extremely limited. It was constantly faced with the threat of internal divisions and renewed disaffiliations. Norbert Rodrigue, who succeeded Marcel Pepin as CSN president in 1976, was highly sensitive to this problem.[32] His leadership aimed at consolidating the movement, while cautiously pursuing the socialist education of its membership. Rodrigue avoided new disaffiliations, but made little or no headway regarding the spread of socialist thinking.[33] When he stepped down in 1982, the internal debate on socialism had not taken place. His successors discontinued the socialist discourse without any hesitation.[34]

As is suggested by the example of the Centrale d'enseignement du Québec (CEQ), Québec's third-largest labour union central, the CSN was not the only union central to experience ideological radicalization and factional strife. Originally called Corporation des Instituteurs et Institutrices catholiques, the CEQ was renamed Corporation des Enseignants du Québec in 1967 before it received its present name in 1974. It was only in the late 1960s and early 1970s that the CEQ transformed itself from a professional association into a labour union central. Teachers continued to dominate the central's membership, although the CEQ began to organize non-teachers in 1971. Like the CSN, the CEQ adopted a radical discourse in the early 1970s. Propagating a Marxist analysis of Québec society, the central continuously attacked the state as the defender of the capitalist class. Yet the CEQ did not propose any alternative to the capitalist system. Unlike that of the CSN, the discourse of the CEQ was void of any reference to socialism. The CEQ leadership intended to elaborate upon a vision of society after an internal debate among the rank-and-file membership. Since a large part of the rank-and-file membership did not share the leadership's radicalism, the debate was continuously postponed and eventually dropped. Many CEQ members were sympathetic to social democracy and to the idea of gradual change within the parameters of the market economy. Toward the end of the 1970s the moderates made their presence more strongly felt, and in the early 1980s CEQ radicalism came to an end. The central dropped its Marxist analysis and the language of class struggle.[35]

Unlike the CSN and the CEQ, the Fédération des Travailleurs du Québec (FTQ), Québec's largest union central, did not experience any significant ideological radicalization. Dominated by such social-democratic leaders as Louis Laberge, Fernand Daoust, and Jean Gérin-Lajoie, the FTQ showed remarkable ideological consistency during the 1960s and 1970s. Apart from a brief period of more radical discourse in the early 1970s, the FTQ was content to criticize the market economy, but not to fundamentally oppose it. Advocating state interventionism, economic planning, and the nationalization of certain sectors of the economy, the FTQ favoured a reformist course of gradual change. The central's leadership had little regard for Marxist analysis. As Jean Gérin-Lajoie put it:

> Ce qu'on défend, c'est une action sociale-démocrate [...] L'analyse de classe n'a rien à voir avec la réalité sociale; c'est un concept livresque qu'on n'a pas adapté des endroits d'ou elle provient. C'est un outil d'analyse qui n'a aucune valeur sur le plan de l'action.[36]

During the 1960s and the 1970s, organized labour in Québec spoke with a social-democratic and a socialist voice. More than anything else it was the following three phenomena that forged its ideological outlook: first, the experience of the Quiet Revolution which had brought with it high expectations and bitter disappointments; second, the constraints of public-sector negotiations where employers could frustrate strikes by back-to-work legislation; and third, the climate of protest and criticism that swept through Québec and other Western societies in the late 1960s. Whether more moderate social democrats or more radical socialists provided the leadership for the various union bodies was to some extent a personality question. More important, however, were the experiences in industrial conflicts and the disposition of rank-and-file activists. A social-democratic leadership prevailed in the FTQ, which represented mostly private-sector workers. The CSN and the CEQ, on the other hand, recruited most of their members from the public sector. Frustrated by the course of the disputes in the public sector, many CSN and CEQ rank-and-file activists had become increasingly radical. By the early 1970s, both centrals had a socialist leadership.

The CSN and the CEQ were most comprehensive in their critique of the market economy. Yet they were hesitant to elaborate upon any alternative vision of society. This reluctance resulted not from any lack of zeal on the part of the leadership, but from the ideological heterogeneity of the rank-and-file membership. While many of the most active rank-and-filers were sympathetic to radical socio-economic change, the majority of them, including in particular the more passive members, opposed any such notion. CSN leaders, such as Pepin and Rodrigue, were aware of this gap between the leadership and a large part of the rank-and-file membership. In the 1970s, the CSN presidents hoped to close this gap by adjusting the outlook of the rank-and-filers to their own. Having witnessed the schism of 1972, they were very cautious, however, in their attempts to bring about this adjustment.

II

From its foundation up to the 1950s, the CTCC adhered to a double nationalism which was both French-Canadian and pan-Canadian. The linking idea which enabled the central to combine two seemingly contradictory national allegiances was that of 'the pact between two races.' Canada was perceived as a country made up of French Canadians and English Canadians, both of whom were separated by language and religion as well as by legal arrangements necessary for the preservation of their respective traditions. In order to preserve French Canada's heritage, the CTCC advocated a high degree of provincial autonomy. Regarding Canada as a shelter for traditional French-Canadian culture, the CTCC continuously demanded full equality between French Canadians and English Canadians, bilingualism and biculturalism, and—since the 1940s—the repatriation of the constitution and the transformation of Canada into a republic.[37]

On the eve of the Quiet Revolution, however, the CTCC's constitutional outlook became more ambiguous. On the one hand, the central continued to defend provincial autonomy, since it exercised more influence on the provincial than on the federal government.[38] Yet on the other hand, the rise of intellectuals such as Jean Marchand, Gérard Pelletier, Marcel Pepin, and Pierre Vadeboncoeur made the CTCC increasingly critical of French-Canadian nationalism. For this group of union leaders and councillors, French-Canadian nationalism was responsible for the backwardness of Québec's socio-economic institutions.[39] They led the CTCC to reject the idea of conserving all traits of traditional French-Canadian culture. Instead, the central came to advocate the modernization of the province of Québec along the lines of other Western societies.

As has been seen, in 1960 the Lesage government set out to modernize Québec institutions. Yet unlike the CSN, which merely wanted to reform the socio-economic system, the Liberal government also pursued a nationalist agenda. Lesage's équipe de tonnerre aimed at ending the economic inferiority of Québec's francophone population. Its goal was economic and social equality between the province's francophone majority and anglophone minority. To do so, the Lesage team sought to transfer economic decision-making processes into francophone hands. The provincial government intervened in the economy in order to help expand the tiny francophone business community. It hoped that the existence of a strong francophone business community would ultimately make French-speaking Québecers maîtres chez eux. Lesage's neo-nationalist programme stimulated French-speaking Québecers' national pride. Unlike traditional French-Canadian nationalism, the neo-nationalism of the Quiet Revolution had nothing static and submissive about it. It challenged existing power structures in a province where social-class divisions coincided almost identically with divisions between ethnic groups.[40]

Quiet Revolution neo-nationalism also constituted a conscious break with French Canada's hapless past. Francophones in Québec no longer perceived their collectivity as 'la nation canadienne française' but as 'la nation québécoise.' French-Canadian identity turned into Québécois identity. At the same time, an increasing number of francophones questioned the status of Québec within Confederation. Among the numerous separatist organizations created in the early 1960s, the Rassemblement pour l'indépendance nationale (RIN) was by far the largest one. Like various other separatist parties and movements, the RIN perceived French-speaking Québecers as a colonized people. As Marcel Chaput, co-founder and second president of the RIN wrote, French Canada "a été conquis par les armes, occupé, dominé, exploité, et [...] encore aujourd'hui son destin repose, dans une très large mesure, entre les mains d'une autre nation qui lui est étrangère."[41] Chaput and the RIN wanted to end Confederation, because for them it meant both the political and economic domination of Québec.[42]

Headed by Jean Marchand, CSN president from 1961 to 1965, the union central rejected the idea of separation. CSN leaders saw no need for such a change. More importantly, like their FTQ peers, they feared the possible economic repercussions of independence, including a decline of living standards and increased unemployment.[43] In addition, Marchand, Pelletier, and many others were unwilling to distinguish between traditional nationalism and neo-nationalism. They regarded separatism as just another facet of reactionary French-Canadian nationalism.[44]

In 1964, the CSN leadership created a special committee to study biculturalism, joint programmes, self-determination, and separatism. In early 1965, the committee asked Pierre Elliot Trudeau to draft a memorandum on Québec's constitutional status. Trudeau accepted and produced a document in which separatism was entirely discarded. According to Pierre Vadeboncoeur, Trudeau's text was nothing less than "un pamphlet virulent contre l'indépendance du Québec."[45] The memorandum was favourably received by the leaders of the CSN, the FTQ, and the Union des cultivateurs catholiques (UCC), who intended to present it to the Constitutional Committee of Québec's National Assembly. Vadeboncoeur and André L'Heureux, who had become separatists in 1963 and 1962 respectively,[46] were shocked. They approached Pepin arguing that it would be premature to take a definitive stand on the issue, since public opinion was still evolving. Only after long and difficult discussions—involving Vadeboncoeur, L'Heureux, constitutional expert Jacques-Yvan Morin, and Marcel Pepin—was Pepin finally convinced that Trudeau's text should be revised.[47]

In September 1966, the CSN, the FTQ, and the UCC jointly submitted the memorandum to the Constitutional Committee of the Québec National Assembly in 1966. The memorandum came out in favour of "[un] fédéralisme adapté à la réalité actuelle." The most important of its numerous suggestions to reform the federalist system were: a charter of rights and liberties to be included in the constitution; a supreme court to interpret the constitution; the equality of the two languages on the federal level; bilingualism in those provinces where there was a linguistic minority exceeding 15 per cent of the population or half a million people. The memorandum also wanted the provinces to acquire full responsibility in the cultural, educational, and welfare sectors. In addition, it called for a mechanism to harmonize provincial welfare policies. The document rejected a greater centralization of powers in Ottawa as detrimental to the interests of Québec. It also opposed the concept of associated states as well as the independence option. Any radical change of the constitution was to be avoided. In addition, the memorandum considered Québec sovereignty to be "une hypothèse et non une thèse; une hypothèse insuffisante pour permettre non seulement l'adhésion mais une discussion objective de quelque importance."[48]

Although the CSN membership had no say in composing the memorandum, the CSN 1966 confederal convention did not hesitate to endorse the document retrospectively. It was not long thereafter, though, that the constitutional vision of the CSN leadership was challenged from within the union central.

III

In the 1966 provincial elections, the Lesage Liberals were defeated and Québec separatists gained about nine per cent of the public vote. In the provincial elections four years later, the separatists would win one quarter of the public vote. The significant increase of support for the sovereignty option was largely due to the general disappointment with the immediate results of the Lesage government's economic nationalism. As has been said, the neo-nationalism of the Quiet Revolution was dynamic and expansionist, establishing the economic reconquest of Québec as its ultimate goal. Creating high expectations among French-speaking Québecers, its immediate results were meagre. Throughout the 1960s, the expansion of the francophone business community made little headway. As anglophone control of the private sector remained largely unchanged, francophone mobility in the private sector continued to be limited. The francophone community did not significantly improve its socio-economic status relative to other ethnic groups.[49] The ensuing disenchantment with the continued socio-economic inferiority of francophones directly benefited the separatist movement. Towards the end of the 1960s, more and more francophone Québecers became convinced that the well-being of the francophone collectivity could only be brought about with the help of an independent Québec state.

The rise of separatism in post-Quiet Revolution Québec also affected the CSN. During the period 1966 to 1972, sympathies for independence within the CSN were most pronounced among the professionals, teachers, provincial and municipal civil servants, and public sector-workers in general.[50] Regardless of which sector they belonged to, separatists within the union central were divided into two factions: first, the moderates who wanted to attain independence to end the minority situation of Québec within the Confederation, and to allow francophones to be economically successful; second, the radicals who saw independence as a precondition for the creation of a socialist society in Québec. It was the latter group of socialist separatists who became dominant in the CSN during the 1970s. Originally, this group was formed by union militants and councillors, who previously had been members of the PSQ that was dissolved in 1966. In 1963 the PSQ had been founded by disenchanted New Democratic Party members from Québec. They opposed the centralism of the NDP which, according to them, disregarded the fact that Québec was a nation of its own.[51] Former PSQ members, such as Michel Chartrand and André L'Heureux, no longer saw any viable prospects for co-operation between the left in Québec and the left in Canada. This attitude was most clearly expressed in the following 1972 statement by the Chartrand-led CCSNM:

> Il n'y a plus à espérer, comme le démontre abondamment l'histoire, qu'un mouvement politique populaire né dans l'ouest du Canada puisse gagner efficacement les provinces de l'Est, et inversement [...] Dans un pays comme le Canada, l'impérialisme et le capitalisme n'ont pas à diviser pour régner, vu que les divisions sont déjà profondément inscrites dans la géographie, les cultures, l'histoire, les traditions, les mentalités et les intérêts particuliers entre le Québec d'une part et les provinces anglophones d'autre part.[52]

Under these circumstances, the installation of a socialist government in Ottawa appeared to be only a remote possibility. The creation of a socialist Québec, therefore, necessitated the separation of Québec from Canada. Chartrand, L'Heureux, and other militants on the left of the CSN knew that independence would not automatically lead to socialism. They thought, though, that only independence could make socialism possible.

While forming only a tiny group at the end of the Quiet Revolution, by 1972 the number of separatists among the CSN membership had increased enormously. The growing popularity of separatism was greatly helped by four phenomena: the failure of all CSN efforts to expand into other provinces and into sectors under the jurisdiction of the Canadian labour code in the mid-1960s; the appeal and credibility of the independence option due to René Lévesque's personality and the progressive image of the Parti Québécois (PQ); the language debate beginning in 1969; and the invocation of the War Measures Act in October 1970.

During the mid-1960s, all CSN efforts to expand into areas under the jurisdiction of the Canadian Labour Code failed. All international and interprovincial companies in areas such as communications, including radio, TV, telephone, and transportation, fell under the jurisdiction of this code. Negotiating units in these sectors were Canada-wide. In 1965–66, the CSN tried to win over railway workers in East Angus and Pointe St-Charles, as well as the francophone employees of Radio Canada. In all cases, the workers in question belonged to unions affiliated with the Canadian Labour Congress (CLC). Although enjoying the support of the workers concerned, the CSN was unable to form new unions. This was due to the veto of the Canadian Labour Relations Board, on which the CLC held three seats and the CSN only one. Having met with such disappointments associated with the federalist system of labour relations, many CSN activists and officers began to see federalism more critically.[53] Not long afterwards, the CSN initiative to expand beyond the province of Québec came to nothing.[54]

With the founding of the Mouvement Souveraineté Association (MSA) in November 1967, public debate about Québec's constitutional status intensified significantly. The new importance of the independence option was reflected in the CSN monthly *Le Travail*. Having ignored the issue in previous years, in early 1968 *Le Travail* started to discuss the national question.[55] The fact that this discussion could now take place in the CSN mouthpiece was partly due to René Lévesque's "tremendous personal popularity among workers and trade unionists."[56] As a minister in the Lesage cabinet, he had won the sympathy of organized labour with social-democratic proposals such as complete unionization, free education, and economic planning.[57] In addition to Lévesque's personal prestige, the PQ's social-democratic programme created sympathy for the new party among CSN members and officers. Moreover, in its early years, the PQ appeared to be open to progressive proposals, and even courted workers to join its ranks. Not surprisingly, the PQ came to be seen as the party of political and social change.[58] Lévesque's take-over of the leadership of the independence movement and the founding of the MSA-PQ made the sovereignty option more attractive and more credible. Unlike other separatist leaders, such as Marcel Chaput and Pierre Bourgault (Chaput's successor as president of the RIN), Lévesque had experience in holding political power. The addition of new, distinguished members to the PQ also increased the party's credibility. In autumn 1969, *Cadres,* the journal of the professionals organized within the CSN, commented on Jacques Parizeau's arrival in the ranks of the PQ:

> Personne ne peut [...] contester la compétence économique de Parizeau [...] Avec l'entrée en scène de Parizeau, la notion d'un Québec séparé prend une dimension nouvelle. L'indépendance devient une option politique valable, qui se discute au mérite. Lévesque lui avait donné son caractère sérieux qu'elle n'avait jamais eu. Avec Parizeau, elle cesse d'être une aventure.[59]

The fierce debates on the language issue late in the decade were another reason for the rise of separatism within the CSN. By the end of the 1960s, Québec nationalists demanded government action to make French the language of work in order to ensure greater social mobility for Québec francophones. In addition, they wanted the government to reform the educational system so that immigrants would be forced to integrate into the French-speaking community. They hoped thereby to ward off the perceived threat of the assimilation of francophones. The CSN quickly became involved in the language debate. In January 1969, the central came out in favour of French as the language of the workplace. At the same time the CSN adopted a declaration of principles regarding instruction and culture, which stipulated that the Québec educational system should be founded on language.[60]

During the October Crisis, the CSN again joined the camp of Québec nationalists. As previously mentioned, many of those arrested were labour union militants, the most prominent being Michel Chartrand. In a Common Front with René Lévesque and the PQ, the CSN denounced the invocation of the War Measures Act for its infringement on citizens' civil liberties. An improved relationship between the CSN and the PQ was not the only result of the October Crisis. Equally important was the fact that a significant number of Québecers, within or outside the labour union movement, came to resent the federal intervention. This resentment in many cases led to a questioning of the federal system as such.[61]

Ever since the end of the Quiet Revolution, CSN militants had become involved in a highly-animated and controversial debate on independence. In 1967 the Syndicate professionnel des enseignants criticized the CSN leadership for the 1966 memorandum, and took a clear stand in favour of independence.[62] The teachers' union was supported by the Syndicate des fonctionnaires municipaux de Montréal which demanded that the CSN hold an internal referendum on the independence question.[63] The CSN leadership, however, tried to avoid any formal discussion of the issue, and especially any internal referendum. CSN president Pepin was a diehard federalist who believed Québec could become socialist without having to leave Confederation and who cherished the ideal of anticapitalist solidarity from coast to coast.[64] In addition, he and other CSN leaders did not want any internal divisions about this issue to become evident. In April 1968, the CSN executive committee proposed to conduct an opinion poll instead of an internal referendum. In January 1969, when called to decide on the issue, the confederal council could not come to an agreement and dropped the proposal despite dissent.[65] Yet, the separatists within the central continued to pressure the leadership to hold an internal referendum and to change the CSN position on the national question. Slowly, the power relations within the CSN changed in favour of the separatists. Even before the departure of the right in 1972, various CSN bodies, particularly in the public sector, had taken a pro-separatist stand.[66] With the departure of the largely federalist right, the CSN separatists finally found themselves in a position of strength among CSN leaders and militants alike. The union central, with the votes of the separatists, decided in October 1972 that a formal debate and referendum on the independence issue was to be launched among the membership in order to establish a new CSN position.[67]

The experiences of both the FTQ and the CEQ during the late 1960s and the early 1970s resembled that of the CSN. In both organizations, an increasing number of members came to support separation. As in the case of the CSN membership, this increase was largely caused by the new credibility that separatism enjoyed after the arrival of René Lévesque and the creation of the PQ, by the debates of the language issue, and by the ramifications of the October Crisis. The official discourse of the FTQ and the CEQ reflected the new popularity of the idea of independence. The 1969 FTQ convention discontinued the practice of denouncing separation which dated back to 1963. The 1972 CEQ convention even took a stand in favour of independence. The convention resolved, however, that this endorsement was not to be regarded as the CEQ's official position and that an internal referendum ought to take place in order to establish such a stance.[68] As will be seen, several years were to pass before either CEQ or CSN followed through on their 1972 decisions.

IV

Until 1976 (for the remainder of Marcel Pepin's presidency), no internal debate of the national question took place. The leadership shelved the national question since it wanted to consolidate the membership, and avoid the risk of internal division over the independence issue. In addition, continued financial problems and the debates on fee increases absorbed all energies. Despite the absence of dramatic events, the number of adherents to the idea of sovereignty continued to increase. Separatism now gained popularity among members of private-sector unions. At the same time, on the far left, a group of determined federalists emerged. The Marxist-Leninist militants opposed separation which they thought would alienate Québec workers from the Canadian working class, and thereby benefit their common class enemy, the Canadian bourgeoisie.[69]

In July 1976 Norbert Rodrigue succeeded Pepin as CSN president. For the first time in CSN history, its six-member executive committee had strong separatist leanings. The new CSN president was known to favour the idea of independence. Furthermore, vice presidents André L'Heureux and Francine Lalonde had been very vocal supporters of separation since the early 1960s. (The latter even became a minister in René Lévesque's second cabinet.) Only five months after the CSN leadership change, the PQ came to power on the promise of holding a referendum within four years. Rodrigue concluded that the union central could no longer avoid an internal debate and referendum concerning the CSN stand on the Québec national question.[70] In September 1977, an orientation committee headed by Rodrigue, and including twenty of the central's most influential leaders, was formed. Its function was to conduct and analyze the internal debate on the national question. Most of the committee members were sympathetic to independence.[71] Yet only a minority of committee members, such as Francine Lalonde, André L'Heureux, Michel Bourdon, and Robert Tremblay, wanted to make the propagation of independence the committee's priority. Led by Norbert Rodrigue, the majority of committee members had two other goals in mind: to avoid internal divisions and renewed disaffiliations over the independence issue, and to instill carefully a socialist spirit into the movement.

The committee's preliminary report to the 1978 confederal convention bore witness to this dual aim. The document stated that the CSN "comprend dans ses rangs des travailleurs de différents niveaux de conscience, de différentes sensibilités et allégeances idéologiques et politiques." Inspired by Rodrigue's goal of consolidating the membership, the report proclaimed the necessity of establishing a lowest common denominator position that could be shared by the entire membership. Since the CSN enjoyed no consensus on the issue of separation, the committee considered it premature "de chercher à répondre par un oui ou un non à l'indépendance du Québec."[72] The report also declared openly the committee's second priority:

> Le débat sur la question nationale [...] doit être pour nous l'occasion de poursuivre [...] le débat plus global que nous menons sur notre projet de société [...] Cette démarche de réflexion sur la question nationale pourra [...] exercer une capacité d'attraction afin que plus de travailleurs se retrouvent dans les positions de la CSN.[73]

The document stated that Québec francophones had far less access to better-paid jobs than anglophones. Unlike the neo-nationalists and the advocates of independence, the CSN orientation committee did not propose to remedy this situation by the expanding francophone businesses under the guidance of the Québec state. Instead, the CSN leaders maintained that there was an economic system in existence which provided a structural base on which exploitation might take the form of national oppression. The committee did not yearn for change merely on the character and composition of the business community. Its aim was to end an economic system based on the antagonism of employer and employees. Hence, the committee report urged Québec workers to combine the struggle against national oppression with the struggle against capitalism.[74]

In winter 1978–79, the CSN finally embarked upon its vast internal debate and referendum on the national question. The tone of the debate and the outcome of the referendum were significantly influenced by the deterioration in CSN-PQ relations which the 1970s had witnessed. These relations had become visibly strained after the PQ had attained power in 1976. The earliest tensions, however, had appeared in the early 1970s. Unlike the CSN, the PQ never had envisaged any fundamental change in the socio-economic system. Thus the PQ leadership had little sympathy for the ideological orientation the CSN had adopted in 1972. René Lévesque had never hidden his disregard for radicals on the left, whom he denounced as "les missionaires de la table rase qui grenouillent dans les chapelles marginales de la révolution miracle et de l'ultra-gauchisme doctrinaire des anarcho-patriotes."[75] At a meeting with CSN militants in 1973, Jacques Parizeau criticized the CSN for having chosen "une option politique qui n'est pas la nôtre." He then went on to reject "une transformation totale de la société et des choses comme la nationalisation des terres qui a un sens à Cuba mais pas ici et dont personne ne voudrait ici."[76] Since 1971–72, the PQ leaders took care to distance their party from the CSN so that the public would not associate the PQ with the labour central's radicalism.[77]

Despite the growing gap between the CSN and the PQ, the PQ continued to claim numerous supporters among the CSN membership. Many union members appreciated the PQ's commitments to bring about sovereignty and to implement various social-democratic reforms.[78] Rank-and-file support for the PQ was so noticeable that the CSN executive committee became concerned about it. On the eve of the 1976 provincial election, the CSN executive declared:

> Il importe de mettre nos membres en garde contre l'illusion que le PQ pourrait changer fondamentalement la condition des travailleurs [...] S'il est important de donner une leçon au Parti libéral, il faut être bien conscient qu'au lendemain de l'élection, même si le PQ prenait le pouvoir, nous serions placés devant une autre gouvernement qui, de gré ou de force, serait asservi à la classe dominante.[79]

Once in power, Lévesque's PQ government chose to ignore many aspects of its social-democratic platform in an attempt to gain support from the business community and more-conservative voters.[80] The Lévesque administration, however, did implement several significant social reforms. It raised the minimum wage to the highest level in North America and, until 1979, indexed this to the cost of living. Moreover, it introduced free dental care for children under age 16 years, and set up a public system of automobile insurance against personal injury.[81] Other noteworthy social legislation included Bill 45 which revised the Québec labour code. The bill permitted a unionization vote if more than 35 per cent of the employees had signed union cards, and obliged an employer to rehire a striker after the end of a strike. In principle, the bill prohibited the employment of scabs, but permitted an employer to hire workers during a strike in order to safeguard essential services and protect his or her property.[82] Although the bill was "more progressive than anything existing in any other North-American jurisdiction,"[83] the CSN executive severely criticized the bill for enabling the employer to hire scabs under the aforementioned conditions. To the CSN leadership, Bill 45 proved that the PQ government was by no means favourably disposed towards the workers.[84]

Bill 45 was not the only piece of PQ governmental policy that met with CSN criticism. Cuts in social services and education budgets cost the PQ government much sympathy within the CSN.[85] At the central's confederal convention in June of 1978, its leadership launched a general attack on the Lévesque government. It criticized the government for having restricted the budget for social affairs; for having failed to introduce legislation regarding maternal leave, abortion, and the application of the principle of equal pay for equal work; for having failed to introduce legislation to promote health and security in the workplace; for not having fought against inflation, unemployment, the closing of enterprises, and poverty in general; and for having displayed anti-labour attitudes in the field of industrial relations.[86] The harsh criticisms were only partly inspired by the PQ government's failure to live up to the expectations of CSN socialists. The CSN leadership also wanted to mobilize the rank-and-file membership for the public-sector negotiations which were to be held in 1979.

The 1978 convention took an emotional turn after violence erupted between convention delegates and the provincial police. The clash occurred when about 200 delegates demonstrated at Sainte-Thérèse to express their solidarity with the strikers at the Commonwealth Plywood factory. Several CSN militants were injured on the occasion, the most well-known of them being vice-president L'Heureux. Some militants were arrested; others fled. Those who evaded arrest returned to the convention floor. Many wore bandages, and all had horrifying stories to tell. Feelings ran high, and CSN delegates were quick to denounce the PQ government which they held responsible for the actions of the police. Several CSN delegates ostentatiously destroyed their PQ membership cards on the floor of the convention room, receiving applause from those who had always mistrusted the PQ government.[87] After the incident at Sainte-Thérèse, PQ supporters within the CSN became even more marginalized.[88]

The CSN referendum held in the winter 1978–79 had several noteworthy results. About 4,380 members—2.8 per cent of all 155,704 CSN members—participated in the internal debate and referendum.[89] Only half the participants wanted the CSN to take a stand on the independence issue.[90] There were four reasons why so many opposed such a stand. First, some did not want the CSN involved in political activities at all. These members advocated a purely economic unionism limiting CSN activities to collective bargaining.[91] Second, many were opposed to separation. Fearing the potential economic repercussions of separation most of these federalists were particularly concerned with the prospect of job losses and a decline in the standard of living.[92] Less numerous, but very vocal, were those federalists who defended the thesis that separation would divide workers in Québec and Canada to the class enemy's benefit. Third, a large group did not want the CSN to endorse independence because they considered this to constitute an automatic endorsement of the PQ. They either regarded the PQ as a party defending the interests of the business community or did not want to diminish the bargaining power of public and para-public sector unions.[93] Fourth, a good number of militants were afraid of internal divisions and renewed disaffiliations which might be the result of a CSN stand in favour of independence.[94]

Faced with the ambiguity of its membership and unwilling to take a stand that could be interpreted as an endorsement of the PQ, the majority of the CSN leadership decided to drop the issue of an official stand on the independence question. Led by André L'Heureux and Michel Bourdon, a minority of CSN leaders maintained that the CSN should endorse independence since it was a precondition for ending the national oppression of French-speaking Québecers and for creating a socialist society. Yet, their recommendations were defeated by the orientation committee, the confederal council, and the special confederal convention on the national question of June 1979.[95] Instead, the special convention resolved in favour of "une démarche d'appropriation par le peuple québécois des pouvoirs et des institutions politiques, économiques et culturels."[96] Failing to specify the number and exact nature of the powers and institutions mentioned, the resolution perfectly reflected the varying opinions of the CSN membership.

The orientation committee report presented at the 1979 convention amounted to a full-fledged attack of the PQ government. The document argued that Québec needed to curb foreign control of the Québec economy and develop its weak secondary sector on the basis of advanced technologies.[97] Having established these parameters, the CSN leaders severely criticized the PQ government for its incoherent development strategy and its unwillingness to challenge the hold of American capital on the Québec economy.[98] Despite its wordy condemnation of the separatist leaders, the orientation committee report did display an inherent separatist logic. Under the federalist system only the federal government possessed the powers to restructure the Québec economy. As the CSN leaders well knew, the federal government always had been tied intimately to the Ontario business community, and therefore could not be depended upon where Québec economic development was at issue.[99] The provincial government, however, would be overburdened with such a task since its powers were too limited. Hence, to develop Québec's secondary sector and to attack the foreign domination of the Québec economy would necessitate a massive transfer of powers from Ottawa to Québec. If anything, the CSN project was even more comprehensive than René Lévesque's sovereignty-association.

Since the 1979 special convention on the national question had neither rejected nor endorsed independence, the issue remained far from settled. With the referendum of 20 May 1980 approaching, internal debate intensified. On 11 April 1980, the confederal convention held a special meeting to discuss the CSN's stand on the referendum. While many militants did not want the organization to adopt an official position, both the executive and the orientation committee were determined to endorse a 'yes' in the referendum. As Norbert Rodrigue pointed out, during the previous years the CSN had managed to establish a critical distance from the PQ and its vision of society. Consequently, nobody could mistake a CSN stand in favour of the 'yes' side as an unqualified endorsement of the PQ. Rodrigue also pointed out that Québec needed to appropriate political institutions and powers since this would create better conditions in the workers' struggle for a socialist society.[100] Following Rodrigue's recommendations, the confederal council, with an overwhelming majority, came out in favour of a 'yes' in the referendum.[101]

Like the CSN, the FTQ did not formally endorse independence but took a stand assenting to the negotiation of sovereignty-association. Unlike the CSN, FTQ support for a 'yes' in the referendum failed to ignite protracted discussion. Since the early 1970s, relations between the FTQ and the PQ had been cordial. Their respective visions of society were not as far apart as those of the CSN and the PQ. In the provincial election of 1976, the FTQ had endorsed the PQ. After the PQ had come to power, relations between the FTQ and the PQ government were harmonious. The FTQ leadership was pleased with the PQ governmental record (including Bill 45). Meanwhile, the CEQ was unable to take a stand either on Québec's constitutional status or on the referendum question. The CEQ's ability to make political commitments had become a casualty in the struggle that deadlocked CEQ moderates and radicals. After the PQ had taken power, the moderates were no longer willing to denounce the Québec government as an agent of capitalist interests. When the central's radicals proposed a resolution that supported independence and rejected the PQ's vision of society, the moderates refused to fall in line. The resolution fell through. Furthermore, since the moderates expected the radicals to use the referendum campaign as an occasion to launch an all-out attack on the PQ government, they opted against CEQ participation in the referendum campaign.[102]

As this brief look at the FTQ and the CEQ shows, on the eve of the referendum, none of Québec's three large labour union centrals took a stand in favour of independence. In the CSN and the FTQ, too many rank-and-file members remained partisans of federalism. Furthermore, many CSN members, and most of the central's leaders, wanted to avoid a gesture that could be interpreted as support for the PQ government. This consideration also played a role in the debates within the CEQ. Since its membership consisted almost entirely of teachers who enjoy a high degree of job security, the CEQ was the only union central that potentially could have mustered overwhelming support for independence. Yet the CEQ radicals were determined to link a resolution in favour of independence to a condemnation of the PQ, while the moderates were equally determined to prevent any such condemnation. The same mechanism also made it impossible for the CEQ to take a stand on the referendum question. For the FTQ and the CSN it was less problematical to take such a stand. Dominated by social democrats, the FTQ simply followed up its earlier policies of support for the PQ government. The CSN, on the other hand, was dominated by radicals who faced no significant opposition from moderate social democrats. Thus they could combine a ringing denunciation of the PQ with a recommendation to vote 'yes' in the referendum.

V

Québec sovereigntism and the radicalism of the CSN shared the same roots. Both phenomena were products of the enthusiasm that accompanied the Quiet Revolution and the disenchantment that followed it. Although both concepts challenged the status quo, their ultimate goals were different. CSN radicalism aimed at fundamental change in the socio-economic system and the replacement of the market economy by a socialist economy. Sovereigntism, by contrast, sought fundamental change in Québec's constitutional status and the transformation of the province into a sovereign nation-state. As abstractions, sovereigntism and socialism are not inherently incompatible. It fell to those propagating the two concepts to decide on the degree of compatibility they would have in real life. In the event, the Lévesque-led sovereigntist movement opted for a market economy, while the majority of CSN radicals favoured independence. The CSN radicals did so for two reasons: first, they felt that co-operation between the left in English Canada and the left in Québec was impossible; second, they perceived Québec society at that time as more progressive. PQ sovereigntists and CSN socialists shared the idea of Québec independence. They disagreed in their visions of society: one group advocated the market economy, the other one socialism. Thus their relationship was bound to be discordant.

Ideological dispositions were not the only determinants of the relationship between sovereigntism and socialism in Québec during the 1970s. To a large extent, this relationship was determined by the relative popularity both options enjoyed. In the wake of the Quiet Revolution, sovereigntism flourished much more rapidly than did socialism. Sovereigntist parties had already been in existence when the PQ was founded in 1968. The CSN embraced socialism only five years later. Both sovereigntism and socialism had a high profile in Québec political culture during the 1970s. Neither of them, though, was a complete success by the end of the decade. Although it may have been less attractive than the status quo in 1980, the sovereigntist option certainly was more popular than the socialist one. The defence of French Canada and Québec's autonomy were issues deeply rooted in Québec. The sovereigntist movement could benefit from those traditions, while the socialist movement did not have any such base in the Québecers' collective mentality.

The popularity of sovereigntism was felt even within the ranks of the CSN. Among many rank-and-file members, René Lévesque was more popular than the CSN leaders, and the PQ enjoyed a degree of credibility that surpassed that of the CSN. Many CSN members subscribed to the PQ's vision of society rather than that of the CSN socialists. Consequently, the socialist option lost potential sympathizers and activists. Many of those who had the idealism to invest their time and energy to challenge existing socio-political structures were drawn to the sovereigntist movement rather than the socialist one. By comparison, the group of socialists was small. Since the sovereigntist movement recruited its followers from the pool of potential socialist activists, the CSN socialists saw Lévesque's PQ as a dangerous competitor. The only way to stand up to this competitor was to denounce it continuously and vociferously.

The coexistence of sovereigntism and socialism was tainted by the continuous attacks from the socialists. This type of coexistence could have improved had the PQ made an effort to reach conciliation. Representing only a small constituency, the CSN socialists were only minor players in Québec politics. The fact that the CSN carried little political weight did not endear its CSN socialism to the PQ. Instead of conciliation, the PQ put demarcation on the agenda. With pride, René Lévesque stated:

> Our hands are not in any way tied as far as the unions are concerned [...] We owe not a cent, not a dollar, to the employers, or to the unions [...] We have no organic ties, which means that we can be the government of all the people without being a puppet to any one sector.[103]

The relationship between the PQ and the CSN was characterized by ideological differences, denunciations, and neglect. It is hardly surprising that sovereigntists and socialists rarely joined forces.

Despite ideological differences and mutual disregard, a sovereigntist triumph was in the best interest of the CSN socialists. Once they had come to the conclusion that co-operation with the left in English Canada either was impossible or undesirable, the CSN socialists automatically narrowed their framework to Québec. In order to implement radical socio-economic change within that framework, they needed to patriate all major decision-making processes to

Québec. This reasoning would have been invalid only if Québec society had been considerably more conservative than English Canadian society. This clearly was not the case. Furthermore, as long as the majority of progressives in the province were preoccupied with the cause of sovereignty, socialism was condemned to take a back seat. Only after independence would those idealistic energies be available to take on other struggles. Of course, sovereigntist triumph would not have guaranteed the subsequent triumph of socialism, but only independence could have made a socialist society possible. The CSN socialists could only arrive in the cock-boat in the wake of the sovereigntist man-of-war.

The thought of endorsing an idea identified with the much-criticized Lévesque government certainly made many CSN socialists ill at ease. This uneasiness, though, did not prevent the socialist CSN leaders grouped around Norbert Rodrigue from realizing that the success of socialism depended on the success of sovereigntism. Yet the CSN socialists could not impose their will on the entire CSN membership. The CSN was not a political party; its members shared economic concerns, not political ideologies. As the internal debate of 1978–79 revealed, a large group—possibly one half—of the rank-and-file membership was opposed to a formal endorsement of independence because they were federalists, or because they did not think it proper for the CSN to concern itself with political issues. The long list of disaffiliations during the 1970s had made the CSN leadership very sensitive to rank-and-file opinions. Thus, more than anything else, it was opposition emanating from the rank-and-file membership that prevented an official CSN endorsement of independence in 1979–80.

Notes

I would like to acknowledge with thanks the financial assistance of the Faculty of Graduate Studies and Research, McGill University. I would also like to thank Andrée Lévesque and Auroshakti Jeyachandran who read earlier versions of this article. Finally I would like to express my gratitude to Normand Ouellet, Mario Robert, and Lucie Courtemanche of the CSN documentation service.

1. CSN, *Procès-verbal, congrès confédéral 1979*, 131–2; Louis-Gilles Francoeur, "Indépendance: La CSN ne s'avance pas." *Le Devoir,* 4 juin 1979, 3; Laval LeBorgne, "Une résolution prônant l'indépendance est défaite: La CSN refuse tout appui au PQ," *La Presse,* 4 juin 1979, A12.

2. Louis-Marie Tremblay, *Le syndicalisme québécois: Idéologies de la CSN et de la FTQ, 1940–1970* (Montréal, 1972), 30; Bernard Solasse, "Les idéologies de la FTQ et de la CSN, 1960–1978." *Idéologies au Canada français,* éd. par F. Dumont *et al.,* (Québec, 1981), tome 1, 223; Leo Roback et Louis-Marie Tremblay, "Le nationalisme au sein des syndicats québécois," *Canadian Review of Studies in Nationalism,* 5 (1978), 239. Older accounts often associate the CTCC with timid unionism avoiding confrontation. See for instance Harold A. Logan, *Trade Unions in Canada: Their Development and Functioning* (Toronto, 1948), 579–603; Charles Lipton, *The Trade*

Union Movement of Canada, 1827–1959, 4th ed. (Toronto, 1978), 224–5. Jacques, Rouillard, however, has shown that the practice of the CTCC was more militant than its ideology and that the relatively low strike-rate of the CTCC in the 1920s was not so much the result of its ideology as of its incohesiveness and the large proportion of non-specialized workers affiliated with the CTCC. See Jacques Rouillard, *Histoire de la CSN 1921–1981* (Montréal, 1981), 83–6, 94–5.

3. Roback et Tremblay, "Le nationalisme au sein des syndicats québécois," 239–42, 245. The ideological evolution of the CTCC found its symbolic expression in a change of name: in 1960 the CTCC became the Confédération des syndicats nationaux (CSN).

4. Carla Lipsig-Mummé, "The Web of Dependence: Quebec Labour Unions in Politics Before 1976," in Alain Gagnon, ed., *Quebec: State and Society* (Toronto, 1984), 297, 300; Henry Milner, *Politics in the New Quebec* (Toronto, 1978), 178; Raymond Hudon, *Syndicalisme d'opposition en société libérale: la culture politique de la CSN* (Québec, 1974), 81.

5. Jacques Rouillard, *Histoire du syndicalisme au Québec: des origines à nos jours* (Montréal, 1989), 301. ["For the first time, the enthusiasm generated by the Quiet Revolution takes social gains beyond the model proposed by other North American societies."]

6. *Ibid.,* 409–10.

7. Gérald Bernier et Robert Boily, *Le Québec en chiffres de 1850 à nos jours* (Montréal, 1986), 238.

8. Michael Smith, "The Transformation of Labour relations in Québec: An Analysis." *In Work in the Canadian Context: Continuity Despite Change,* Katherina Lundy and Barbara Warme, eds., (Toronto, 1981), 369.

9. This became apparent in the hospital strike of 1966, the teachers' strike and the strike at Hydro-Québec in 1967, and the conflict at the *Régie des alcools* in 1968–1969. See also Claude Lemelin, "Les deux prochaines années seront loin d'être facile pour la CSN," *Le Devoir,* 17 octobre 1968, 18; Rouillard, *Histoire du syndicalisme québécois,* 408.

10. Solasse, "Les idéologies de la FTQ et de la CSN," 227.

11. For example, see Marcel Pepin, "Une société bâtie pour l'homme," CSN, Procès-verbal, congrès confédéral 1966, 15, 20–1.

12. For example, see also Marcel Pepin, "Le deuxième front," CSN, Procès-verbal, congrès confédéral 1968, 12–42.

13. Rouillard, *Histoire du syndicalisme au Québec,* 410–1.

14. Jean-François Cardin, *La crise d'octobre 1970 et le mouvement syndical* (Montréal, 1988), 261. ["[The CSN] is no longer afraid of directly attacking the state and the part it plays in supporting the bourgeoisie's exploitation of workers."]

15. On the strike at *La Presse* see Marc Raboy, *Movements and Messages: Media and Radical Politics in Quebec* (Toronto, 1984), 81–4. On the public sector negotiations and strike in 1972, see Diane Ethier, Jean-Marc Piotte et Jean Reynolds, *Les travailleurs contre l'Etat bourgeois, avril et mai 1972* (Montréal, 1975).

16. Claude Lemelin, "Les deux prochaines années seront loin d'être faciles pour les dirigeants de la CSN," *Le Devoir,* 17 octobre 1968, 18; Michel Sabourin, "Congrès de la Fédération des ingénieurs et cadres: 'Nous sommes bien payés, petits-bourgeois, mais des travailleurs quand même'—Jean-Guy Rodrigue," *Québec-Presse,* 3 juin 1973, 8.

17. Bernard Chaput, "Faudra-t-il s'en mêler un jour?" *Nouveau Pouvoir,* 1 mai 1970, 2.

18. CSN, Procès-verbal, congrès confédéral 1968, 272–3; CSN, Procès-verbal, congrès confédéral 1972, 93.

19. 'Active members' are those who participate in the activities of their union body on a regular basis. In the case of the CSN, this group was only a minority. On the problem of rank-and-file passivity in the CSN, see Jean-Luc Duguay, "La CSN instituerait une enquête sur la désaffection des conseils centraux," *Le Devoir,* 9 décembre 1970; CSN, Procès-verbal, conseil confédéral, 17–20 novembre 1976, 27; André Lauzon, Serge Demers, Pierre Martin, "Nos pratiques syndicales," *Unité ouvrière,* avril 1979, 9–12; Hudon, *Syndicalisme d'opposition en société libérale,* 354–7.

20. Pierre Vadeboncoeur, "Marcel Pepin: Un nouveau départ," *Nouvelles CSN,* (30 mars 1990), 11–2; Evelyn Dumas-Gagnon, "Que se passe-t-il à la CSN? 2: Au delà d'un conflict de personnalité," *Le Devoir,* 28 décembre 1967, 1, 24.

21. Evelyn Dumas-Gagnon, "Le départ de Sauvé provoque un débat d'une rare violence," *Le Devoir,* 2 décembre 1967, 5; "'Une clique d'intellectuels anarchiques'," *Québec-Presse,* 4 juin 1972, 9. ["the parallel power"]

22. "Le conseil central de Montréal (CSN) propose une déclaration de principe," *Québec-Presse,* 1 février 1970, 9A.

23. For example, see Jacques Lafrenière, "Chartrand: une 'philosophie politique': La CSN veut canaliser la contestation de ses membres," *La Presse,* 25 janvier 1969, 10; "L'affrontement Pepin-Chartrand a eu lieu dans un climat de liberté d'expression," *Québec-Presse,* 18 janvier 1970, 5; Jean-Luc Duguay, "Marcel Pepin à l'ouverture du congrès: La CSN éclatera si elle se lance dans l'action politique partisane," *Le Devoir,* 7 décembre 1970, 1.

24. Jacques Kaeble, "'Ne comptons que sur nos propres moyens': Marcel Pepin: 'L'état d'insécurité des travailleurs est très grand'," *Québec-Presse,* 24 octobre 1971, 15; "Yvon Valcin critique la direction de la CSN," *Le Devoir,* 4 décembre 1971, 2; "L'exécutif du Conseil central de Québec est contre le manifeste de la CSN," *Québec-Presse,* 16 janvier 1972, 18; CSN, Procès-verbal, conseil confédéral, 23–25 février 1972, 12–5.

25. Gabriel Gaudette, "La culture politique de la CSD," *Recherches sociographiques,* 17, 1 (1976), 35–72. See also Pierre Richard, "La CSN perdra 27 000 membres: les fonctionnaires: La désaffiliation acquise de justesse," *Le Devoir,* 26 septembre 1972, 1, 6.

26. The different visions of socialism are discussed in Comité des Douze, CSN, Procès-verbal, congrès confédéral 1972, 81–7. See also the internal working paper *Ne comptons que sur nos propres moyens* (Montréal 1971) and Marcel Pepin's reaction to the working paper in Jacques Kaeble, "'Ne comptons que sur nos propres moyens': Marcel Pepin: 'L'état d'insécurité des travailleurs est très grand'," *Québec-Presse,* 24 octobre 1971, 15.

27. CSN, Procès-verbal, congrès confédéral 1972, 101, 176.

28. *Ibid.*, 176. ["a movement-wide study aimed at defining the components of a Quebec socialism and the steps involved in its realization."]

29. CSN, Procès-verbal, congrès confédéral 1974, 101–3.

30. Louis Favreau et Pierre L'Heureux avec la collaboration de Paul Michel, *Le projet de société de la CSN de 1966 à aujourd'hui: Crise et avenir du syndicalisme au Québec* (Montréal, 1984), 112–3; Rouillard, *Histoire du syndicalisme québécois,* 331, 415.

31. Interview with union councillor Peter Bakvis, Montréal, 29 May 1990; Interview with ex-CSN vice-president Francine Lalonde, Montréal, 19 June 1990; Interview with union councillor Marc Lesage, Montréal, 5 July 1990; Jacques Benoît, *L'extrême gauche* (Montréal, 1977); Irène Ellenberger, "L'action politique syndicale dans les années 1970: Témoinage de Irène Ellenberger, ex-présidente du Conseil sentral de Montréal (CSN)," RCHTQ, *Bulletin,* 40 (Hiver, 1988), 23–43.

32. Pierre Dupont et Gisèle Tremblay, *Les syndicats en crise* (Montréal, 1976), 101–2.

33. In many unions the CSN's socialist discourse met with disinterest or opposition. See for instance: [Paul Cliche, Ginette Galarneau, Fiore Fionda,] "Rapport préliminaire concernant la campagne de consultation sur la question nationale en vue de congrès des 1er, 2 et 3 juin 1979." 17 mai 1979, 4. Archives de la CSN, Dossier "Question nationale 1976–1980," 370 (2–2–2–3); "Les travailleurs face à la question nationale: Quelles questions devons nous nous poser?," *Le Travail,* avril-mai 1979, 9.

34. This rupture with ten years of CSN radicalism has not yet been the topic of systematic analysis. The best account to date has been provided by a group of CSN socialists: Favreau et l'Heureux, *Le projet de société de la CSN,* 167–81.

35. Rouillard, *Histoire du syndicalisme au Québec,* 362–70.

36. Jean Gérin-Lajoie in an interview with Gisèle Tremblay. Dupont et Tremblay, *Les syndicats en crise,* 120. See also Rouillard, *Histoire du syndicalisme au Québec,* 318–22; Solasse, "Les idéolgies de la FTQ et de la CSN," 228–48. [What we are defending is social-democratic action [...] Class analysis has nothing to do with social reality; it's the stuff of books, a concept that has not been adapted from its place of origin. It is an analytical tool that has no value in terms of action."]

37. Louis-Marie Tremblay, *Le syndicalisme québécois: Les idéologies de la CSN et de la FTQ, 1940–1970,* 30–2, 41.

38. *Ibid.*

39. "La CSN et le séparatisme," *Le Travail,* décembre 1961, 5.

40. Kenneth McRoberts, *Quebec: Social Change and Political Crisis,* 3rd ed. (Toronto, 1988), 132; William Coleman, *The Independence Movement in Quebec, 1945–1980* (Toronto, 1984), 92, 99; P.-A. Linteau *et al., Histoire du Québec contemporain: tome 2: Le Québec depuis 1930* (Montréal, 1986), 394; Rouillard, *Histoire du syndicalisme au Québec,* 294; Alain Gagnon and Mary B. Montcalm, *Quebec Beyond the Quiet Revolution* (Scarborough, Ontario, 1990), 9, 18, 25, 45. [(would ultimately make French-speaking Quebecers) masters in their own house.]

41. Marcel Chaput, *Pourquoi je suis séparatiste* (Montréal, 1969), 19. [(French Canada) "was conquered by the force of arms, occupied, dominated, exploited, and [...] even today, its fate rests, to a very great extent, in the hands of an alien nation."]

42. *Ibid.,* 27, 33.

43. "La CSN et le séparatisme," *Le Travail,* décembre 1961, 5; Gabriel Gagnon, "Pour un socialisme décolonisateur," *Parti pris,* septembre/octobre 1966, 49. For the FTQ see, Rouillard, *Histoire du syndicalisme au Québec,* 323; François Cyr et Remi Roy, *Elements d'histoire de la FTQ: La FTQ et la question nationale* (Montréal, 1981), 67–9.

44. In June 1964, the CSN monthly *Le Travail* published a manifesto by Pierre-Elliot Trudeau, Marc Lalonde and others which clearly stated: "Nous croyons au fédéralisme comme régime politique au Canada [...] le séparatisme québécois nous apparaît non seulement comme une perte de temps, mais comme un recul." "Pour une politique fonctionnelle," *Le Travail,* juin 1964, Appendix, 5–6. ["We believe in federalism as the political system for Canada [...] We see Quebec separation not only as a waste of time but as a step backward."]

45. Pierre Vadeboncoeur, "Geoffrey: Une conscience," *Nouvelles CSN,* 2 mars 1990, 11. [(nothing less than) "a virulent pamphlet against Quebec independence."]

46. *Ibid.;* André L'Heureux, Sécrétariat d'action politique, Montréal, janvier 1976, 45. Archives de la CSN, Dossier "Question nationale" 430 (1–9–1–3).

47. "Une grosse vulgarité," *Parti Pris,* février 1965, 18; Vadeboncoeur, "Geoffrey: Une conscience," 9–11.

48. "Mémoire sur les problèmes constitutionels présenté conjointement par la CSN, le FTQ et l'UCC," CSN, Procès-verbal, congrès confédéral 1966, 459–64. [(in favour of) "[a] federalism adapted to current reality."]; ["a hypothesis and not a thesis; an inadequate hypothesis that does not admit of support or even much objective discussion."]

49. This situation was highlighted by the *Report of Royal Commission on Bilingualism and Biculturalism,* published in 1969, which stated francophone Québecers ranked twelfth among fourteen ethnic groups with respect to average income. *Report of the Royal Commission on Bilingualism and Biculturalism,* Volume 3A (Ottawa, 1969), 23.

50. Ralph Güntzel, "La FPPSCQ, la CSN et la question nationale depuis 1964," *Travail, Profession et Société,* 1:1 (printemps, 1990), 4; "La CSN refuse d'enquêter sur l'opinion constitutionelle de ses 225 000 membres," *La Presse,* 27 janvier 1969, 10; "Les dirigeants montréalais de la CSN appuient le PQ," *Québec-Presse,* 22 mars 1970, 3; FNEQ, Procès-verbal, congrès fédéral, 27–29 novembre 1970, 39–40.

51. André L'Heureux, Secrétariat d'action politique, Montréal, janvier 1976, 45. Archives de la CSN, Dossier "Question nationale" 430 (1–9–1–3).

52. "Construire par la base une démocratie socialiste au Québec," *Le Travail,* mai 1972, 3; CCSNM, "Résolution pour l'indépendance du Québec, 14e congrès du CCSNM, avril 1972"; Louis LeBorgne, *La CSN et la question nationale depuis 1960* (Montréal, 1975), 196–8. ["As history amply demonstrates, there is no more hoping that a popular political movement born in western Canada can effectively win the eastern provinces, or vice versa [...] In a country like Canada, imperialism and capitalism do not have to divide in order to rule, given that divisions are already deeply engraved in the geography, cultures, history, traditions, ways of thinking, and special interests between Quebec on the one hand and the English-speaking provinces on the other."]

53. Claude Larivière, "Les libertés syndicales et le pancanadianisme," *L'Action nationale,* LV, 9–10 (1966), 1125–8.

54. CSN, Procès-verbal, congrès confédéral 1966, 368–9; CSN, Procès-verbal, congrès confédéral 1968, 64–5.

55. See, "L'avenir du Québec, c'est surtout l'affaire des salariés," *Le Travail,* janvier 1968, 18–9; "Un statut particulier dans un fédéralisme nouveau," *Le Travail,* mai 1968, 18–9.

56. Leo Roback, "Quebec Workers in the Twentieth Century," in W.J.C. Cherwinski and Gregory S. Kealey, eds., *Lectures in Canadian Labour and Working Class History* (St. John's, 1985), 179–80.

57. Vera Murray, *Le Parti québécois: de la fondation à la prise du pouvoir* (Montréal, 1976), 217.

58. Favreau et L'Heureux, *Le Projet de société de la CSN,* 102.

59. Mario Cardinal, "Enfin un débat des adultes," *Cadres,* septembre/octobre 1969, 12. ["No one can deny Parizeau's abilities as an economist [...] Parizeau's arrival on the scene adds a new dimension to the notion of a separate Quebec. Independence becomes a valid political option to be discussed on its merits. Levesque had given it a credibility it never had before. With Parizeau, it stops being an adventure."]

60. CSN, Procès-verbal, congrès confédéral 1968, 517; "La CSN adopte un programme d'action axée sur la nécessité d'un 2e front," *Le Devoir,* 27 janvier 1969, 3.

61. Jean-François Cardin, *La Crise d'octobre 1970 et le mouvement syndical* (Montréal, 1988).

62. CSN, Procès-verbal, congrès confédéral 1968, 535.

63. *Ibid.,* 521.

64. Jacques Keable, "'Ne comptons que sur nos propres moyens': Marcel Pepin: 'L'état d'insécurité des travailleurs est très grand'," *Québec-Presse,* 24 octobre 1971, 15; Marcel Pepin, "Un camp de la liberté." CSN, Procès-verbal, congrès confédéral 1970, 26.

65. CSN, Procès-verbal, conseil confédéral, 16 et 17 avril 1968, 4–5; CSN, Procès-verbal, congrès confédéral 1968, 335, 513, 515, 521.

66. See for instance, FPSCQ, Procès-verbal, congrès fédéral 1971, 13; FNEQ, Procès-verbal, congrès fédéral, 27–29 novembre 1970, 39–40; CSN, Procès-verbal, congrès confédéral 1968, 535; "Construire par la base une démocratie socialiste au Québec," *Le Travail,* mai 1972, 3.

67. CSN, Procès-verbal, congrès confédéral 1972, 173–7; Pierre Richard, "Optant pour le socialisme: La CSN organisera un référendum sur l'indépendance," *Le Devoir,* 5 octobre 1972, 1.

68. On the FTQ, Rouillard, *Histoire du syndicalisme au Québec,* 324–5; Cyr et Roy, *Eléments d'histoire de la FTQ,* 95–140. On the CEQ, Rouillard, *Histoire du syndicalisme au Québec,* 369; Louise Clermont-Laliberté, *Dix ans de pratiques syndicales: La CEQ 1970–1980* (Québec [1980]), 85.

69. Yves Taschereau, "Ils sont fous," *L'Actualité,* novembre 1976, 50; Benoît, *L'extrême gauche,* 102, 114.

70. CSN, Procès-verbal, conseil confédéral 17–20 novembre 1976, 26.

71. Interview with Peter Bakvis, Montréal, 29 May 1990; Interview with Francine Lalonde, Montréal, 19 June 1990; Interview with Marc Lesage, Montréal, 5 July 1990.

72. CSN, Procès-verbal, congrès confédéral 1978, 185. [(the CSN) "includes in its ranks workers with different levels of awareness, different ideological and political sensibilities."] [(considered it premature) "to try to answer yes or no to the question of independence for Quebec."]

73. *Ibid.,* 150–1; see also, "Eléments pour une discussion de masse: Document de travail," présenté au Comité d'orientation CSN, le 21 décembre 1978, 6–7. Archives de la CSN, Dossier "Question nationale 1976–1980," 370 (2–2–2–3). ["We should consider the debate on the national question an opportunity to pursue […] our own broader, ongoing social debate […] The process of reflecting on the national question may […] have a magnetizing effect that will see more workers drawn to CSN positions."]

74. CSN, Procès-verbal, congrès confédéral 1978, 181.

75. "La peur de faire peur," *Le Devoir,* 20 mai 1980, 9. [(whom he denounced as) "missionaries of the clean slate who grovel in the marginal chapels of the miracle revolution and the doctrinaire ultra-leftism of anarcho-patriots."]

76. "Les travailleurs sont toujours seuls: Marion et Forget vs. Parizeau," *Le Travail,* octobre/novembre 1974, 19. [(the CSN for having chosen) "a political option that is not ours." (He then went on to reject) "a total transformation of society and things like the nationalization of land, which makes some sense in Cuba but not here, and which no one would want here."]

77. Claude Masson, "Pepin joue le tout pour le tout: Face aux dissensions internes à la CSN, il engage une lutte à finir avec Bourassa," *La Presse,* 14 juin 1972, A5; Lipsig-Mummé, "The Web of Dependence," 305.

78. *Québec-Presse,* 29 avril 1973, Supplement 1er mai, 28; "Un million de québécois," *Le Travail,* janvier 1974, 26–31; "C'est comme ça qu'on est," *Le Travail,* 27 juin 1974, 6; CSN, Procès-verbal, congrès confédéral 1978, 163.

79. Comité exécutif de la CSN, "Votons pour renforcer notre capacité de lutter." Document soumis au bureau confédéral de la CSN le 31 octobre 1976. CSN, Procès-verbal, bureau confédéral, terme 1976–1978, 34. ["It is important to warn our members against the illusion that the PQ could make fundamental changes in the condition of workers […] It may be important to teach the Liberal party a lesson, but we must realize that on the day after the election, even if the PQ came to power, we would be faced with another government that was, willingly or unwillingly, a slave to the dominant class."]

80. Don and Vera Murray, "The Parti québécois: From Opposition to Power," in Hugh G. Thoburn, ed., *Party Politics in Canada,* 4th ed. (Scarborough, Ontario, 1979), 245, 251; John Fitzmaurice, *Québec and Canada: Past, Present, and Future* (London, 1985), 198–9; Favreau et L'Heureux, *Le projet de société de la CSN,* 132; François Demers, *Chroniques impertinentes du troisième Front commun syndical, 1979–1980* (Montréal, 1982), 97.

81. McRoberts, *Quebec: Social Change and Political Crisis,* 267–8; Linteau *et al., Histoire du Québec contemporain: tome 2: Le Québec depuis 1930,* 658.

82. Rouillard, *Histoire du syndicalisme au Québec,* 424.

83. Reginald A. Whitaker, "The Quebec Chauldron: A Recent Account," in Gagnon, ed., *Quebec: State and Society,* 83.

84. CSN, Procès-verbal, congrès confédéral 1978, 6, 47–60.

85. Interview with Peter Bakvis, Montréal, 29 May 1990.

86. CSN, Procès-verbal, congrès confédéral 1978, 156–66.

87. Pierre Vennat, "La CSN de retour devant la Commonwealth avec 'son' système d'ordre: 'Cette attaque sauvage est un coup monté'," *La Presse,* 8 juin 1978, A3; Interview with Peter Bakvis, Montréal, 29 May 1990.

88. Interview with Francine Lalonde, Montréal, 19 June 1990.

89. CSN, *Rapport sur la consultation sur la question nationale* (Montréal, 1979), 4; Bernier et Boily, *Le Québec en chiffres,* 316.

90. *Rapport sur la consultation sur la question nationale,* 4.

91. For example, see Response of the *Syndicat des travailleurs de Roberval.* Archives de la CSN, Dossier "Question nationale," 1696 (23–3–4–3) and response of the *Syndicat des employés des Aciers Atlas.* Archives de la CSN, Dossier "Question nationale," 370 (2–2–2–3). The orientation committee did not ask the participants to explain their stand. Yet some of the ballots returned to the committee did give reasons under the heading "other remarks."

92. Interview with Peter Bakvis, Montréal, 29 May 1990; Marcel Pepin, "Pourquoi les travailleurs hésitent devant la thèse péquiste," *Le Devoir,* 19 juillet 1980, 2.

93. *Rapport sur la consultation sur la question nationale,* 5; FNEQ, Procès-verbal, conseil fédéral, 24–27 mai 1979, 10.

94. For example, see Response of the Syndicat national des employés de soutien de la commission scolaire du Cap-de-la-Madelaine, Archives de la CSN, Dossier "Question nationale," 370 (2–2–2–3) and Response of the Syndicat national des employés de Garage de Rimouski. Archives de la CSN, Dossier "Question nationale," 370 (2–2–2–3).

95. CSN, Procès-verbal, conseil confédéral, 3–5 mai 1979, 398–9; CSN, Procès-verbal, congrès confédéral 1979, 131–2.

96. CSN. Procès-verbal, conseil confédéral, 1979, 147. ["a process by which the people of Quebec take over the political, economic and cultural powers and institutions."]

97. *Ibid.,* 74–5.

98. *Ibid.,* 61–7.

99. *Ibid.,* 37–51.

100. CSN, Procès-verbal, conseil confédéral, 11 avril 1980, 927–8.

101. "La CSN décide de rallier le camp du OUI," *Le Devoir,* 12 avril 1980, 7; Laval LeBorgne, "Le conseil confédéral de la CSN vote Oui," *La Presse,* 12 avril 1980, A2.

102. On the FTQ see, Rouillard, *Histoire du syndicalisme au Québec,* 325–7; Cyr et Roy, *Eléments d'histoire de la FTQ,* 155–98. On the CEQ see, Rouillard, *Histoire du syndicalisme Québec,* 369–70; Clermont-Laliberté, *Dix ans de pratiques syndicales,* 86.

103. René Lévesque, *My Quebec* (Toronto, 1979), 45.

CHAPTER
13 E. HERBERT NORMAN, CANADA AND THE COLD WAR

On April 4, 1957, the Canadian ambassador to Egypt, E. Herbert Norman, climbed to the roof of a nine-storey Cairo apartment building, carefully removed his glasses, watch, and jacket, and jumped to his death on the street below. Norman's suicide sent shock waves throughout Canada and sparked a multi-layered controversy that continues to this day. At one level the controversy bears on Norman himself, on his guilt or innocence with respect to the charges of being a Communist spy in the service of a foreign power, presumably the Soviet Union. More generally, the incident raises questions about the impact of the "red scare" on Canada in the late 1940s and early 1950s, about the Cold War mentality that it spawned, and about the Canadian-American relationship during that era.

The immediate circumstances surrounding the Norman suicide are relatively well known. Less than a month before, in March 1957, Norman's name had surfaced in the investigations of the U.S. Senate Subcommittee on Internal Security, dedicated to ferreting out "Red" subversives in high governmental places in the United States and elsewhere. The charges that Norman was a Communist and a threat to Western security were not new ones. Indeed, he had previously undergone two internal security checks by the RCMP, first in October 1950, and again in January 1952. The latter, in fact, had been prompted by accusations made by another witness before that same U.S. Subcommittee on Internal Security. According to notes which Norman left at the time of his death, he was not prepared to go through yet another round of interrogations which were sure to follow the latest allegations. Suicide seemed the only way out.

While what immediately precipitated the Norman suicide may be reasonably clear, less certain (and heatedly debated) are his ultimate motives in choosing this drastic course of action. Was Norman really a Communist spy who feared what another, more intense investigation would reveal? Was he even perhaps the "Fifth Man" so long sought by British Intelligence? Or, was he an innocent Canadian victim of the McCarthyite witchhunts of the 1950s, hounded to death by American innuendo and false accusations? The readings presented here take very different positions on these questions, and rely upon very different kinds of evidence. Indeed, an important aspect of the modern phase of the Norman controversy revolves around the quality of scholarship on the subject. In particular, the two major protagonists, Roger Bowen and James Barros, have been accused of faulty, even misleading, craftsmanship. With respect to all readings on this topic, students should examine carefully the general interpretations and the detailed evidence upon which they are based.

Following in an older tradition of writers such as Charles Taylor, Roger Bowen defends Norman, arguing that his was in reality "murder by slander." In *No Sense of Evil Espionage: The Case Of Herbert Norman*, Chapter 9 of which is reproduced here, James Barros takes the opposite tack, maintaining that there is sound evidence to conclude that Norman's admitted affiliation with the Communist Party had extended well beyond his days as a student at Cambridge University in the mid-1930s, and that that affiliation was much more than simply benign intellectual curiosity. The most recent pronouncement on the subject is that of J.L.Granatstein and David Stafford in their book, *Spy Wars*. Granatstein and Stafford are neither so convinced of Norman's guilt as Barros, nor of his innocence as Bowen, characterizing him as a "casualty of the cold war."

Suggestions for Further Reading

Barros, James, *No Sense of Evil Espionage: The Case of Herbert Norman*. Toronto: Deneau, 1986.

Bothwell, Robert, and J.L. Granatstein, "Introduction," *The Gouzenko Transcripts*. Ottawa: Deneau, 1982.

Bowen, Roger W., *Innocence Is Not Enough: The Life and Death of Herbert Norman*. Armonk, New York: M.E. Sharpe Inc., 1986.

Bowen, Roger W. (ed.), *E.H.Norman: His Life and Scholarship*. Toronto: University of Toronto Press, 1984.

Cuff, R.D., and J.L.Granatstein, "Looking Back At The Cold War," in *Ties That Bind* (2nd ed.). Toronto: Samuel Stevens Hakkert and Co., 1977.

English, John, *Shadow of Heaven: The Life of Lester Pearson, Vol.I: 1897–1948*. Toronto: Lester & Orpen, Dennys, 1989.

Granatstein, J.L. and David Stafford, *Spy Wars*. Toronto: Key Porter Books Ltd., 1990.

Smith, Denis, *Diplomacy of Fear: Canada and the Cold War 1941–1948*. Toronto, University of Toronto Press, 1988.

Taylor, Charles, "Herbert Norman," in *Six Journeys: A Canadian Pattern*. Toronto: Anansi, 1977.

COLD WAR, MCCARTHYISM, AND MURDER BY SLANDER: E.H. NORMAN'S DEATH IN PERSPECTIVE

Roger W. Bowen

Probably no event in recent years involving Canadian-United States relations aroused such a wave of indignation and resentment in Canada as the suicide on April 4 in Cairo of Canadian Ambassador E. Herbert Norman. The general belief was that charges of communism against Mr. Norman, which were revived by the Subcommittee of the United States Internal Security Committee, were directly or indirectly responsible for his death. Canadians were indignant because the charges were regarded as false, as well as because the tactics employed by the Subcommittee were considered reprehensible and unwarranted interference in Canadian affairs.[1] So reads a 'confidential' dispatch sent to the State Department by the American ambassador to Canada two weeks after Norman's fatal leap from a nine-story Cairo apartment building in April 1957. Concerned exclusively with the 'Canadian Reactions to the Suicide of Ambassador E. Herbert Norman,' this dispatch catalogued the plethora of charges which Canadian newspapers levelled against the American government, ranging from 'guilt by association' and 'character assassination' to 'trial by smear.' Extensively quoted was a Toronto *Globe and Mail* article which claimed that 'the smear of Norman was just one more example of a long series of insults and injuries [inflicted] by the Americans on Canada.[2] The highly emotive cries of 'witch-hunt' and 'murder by slander' that issued forth even from the halls of Parliament were similarly recorded in the dispatch to State. Yet the Americans fully understood that while the moral outrage expressed by press and public was no doubt genuine, it could not be sustained, particularly as the moral issue involved was being transmogrified into a political one.[3]

During the first week after Norman's death, Secretary of State for External Affairs Lester 'Mike' Pearson said nothing to indicate that the charges of communism levelled against Norman by the American Senate subcommittee might be grounded in historical fact, but instead remained silent as press reports recalled Pearson's 1951 defence of Norman when the same subcommittee had first alleged Norman's previous association with the Communist party. Pearson had then, on 9 August 1951, reported that the 'security authorities of the Government' had given Norman 'a clean bill of health' and personally praised Norman for being 'a trusted and valuable official of the department.'[4] Seen in this light in 1957 after Norman's death, the expressions of moral outrage by the press seem altogether reasonable. Equally reasonable, and much applauded by the Canadian press, was Pearson's 10 April official note of protest to the

From Roger W. Bowen (ed.), *E.H. Norman: His Life and Scholarship* (Toronto: University of Toronto Press, 1984), 46–71. Reprinted by permission of the University of Toronto Press.

American government that threatened to cease providing security information on Canadians unless the American executive branch could guarantee that future congressional investigatory bodies would be denied unrestricted access. But two days later, and following repeated reaffirmations by the Senate that its information on Norman was correct, the man who could hardly wait to be prime minister, John Diefenbaker, turned the 'Norman affair' into a political football in this election year.[5]

Diefenbaker asked Pearson in Parliament whether the American allegations were 'untrue, unjustified, and had no basis in fact.' Pearson finally came clean on 12 April, replying: 'To say there was no truth in statements about Mr. Norman's past associations would have deceived the country.' Pearson was then pummelled by the press. A typical response to his admission was a 15 April editorial in the Montreal *Gazette* which accused him of having exercised bad judgment in 1951 by giving the public a 'misleading impression' about Norman's involvement in the Communist party. Pearson tried defending himself in an article in the same newspaper two days later. Referring to the 1950–51 RCMP investigation of Norman, Pearson said, 'I concluded that he had had, as a student, ideological beliefs which were close to some brand of Communism. 'I also concluded,' Pearson went on, 'that he regretted these earlier associations and beliefs and had voluntarily abandoned them by the time he entered the Canadian Foreign Service.'[6]

Yet despite his attempts to offer a defence of his position, Pearson's credibility had been damaged. Mr Low, leader of the Social Credit party, summed up Opposition sentiment, and perhaps public sentiment as well, when he said to Mr. Pearson, 'The Minister is letting us know something that he has withheld ever since 1951.'[7] A 'confidential' American dispatch from Ottawa to Washington at this time further explains the effect of Pearson's truth-telling: 'The opposition position on the Norman case has undergone a fundamental change in the last few days. From a position of supporting the Government in its defense of Mr. Norman and in its protests to the United States, it has now accused the government of using the protests for political purposes and of withholding information on the case.'[8] In the more personal terms of how these disclosures affected the way Norman would be remembered by the Canadian public afterwards, the image of Norman as martyr for Canadian nationalism was replaced by Norman the communist.

A secondary but by no means less important consequence of the politicization of Norman's death was the impact it had on Canada's foreign policy. As James Eayrs suggests, some of Canada's more prominent Anglophiles began to call into question the Liberal government's policy under Pearson of volunteering Canadian military forces for peacekeeping purposes in the Middle East.[9] Norman after all had been Canada's ambassador to Egypt until his death. Now critics could point to a one-time communist negotiating with a suspected pro-Russian Egyptian President (Nasser) towards the undoing of Mother England's noble attempt to prevent the Suez Canal from being nationalized. Moreover, now that Pearson's credibility had been damaged by the Norman affair, evidence suggesting that Pearson had also seemed to be all too sympathetic towards Egyptian nationalism (and, conversely, prejudiced against Israel) took on a new light, especially as Pearson himself was being attacked by McCarthyite innuendo. Arthur Blakney reported in the *Gazette* that 'there have been veiled suggestions that the Subcommittee [on Internal Security] could—if it were bent on causing trouble—release secret testimony by ex-communist Elizabeth Bentley tagging Mr. Pearson as a man who was far too close to the inside of wartime communist espionage rings.' The same report also asserted that Pearson could have been 'a source of information to communist espionage rings during the war.'[10] State Department records from this period show that the Americans took these allegations seriously. That the allegations against Pearson, as well as against Robert Bryce for that matter, were not made public by the Senate subcommittee can likely be attributed to pressure placed on the Senate by the State Department, which wished to avoid another Norman affair.[11]

In this sense, the reputations of Pearson and Bryce were not assaulted by the Americans *because of* Norman's death, or rather because of the politicization of Norman's death by both the Americans and the Canadians. But because Norman's death was so politicized, his life was in the process stripped of all meaning. For with Pearson's admission that Norman had once been 'some brand' of communist, the McCarthyites, who had tried him for his past associations, seemed vindicated and the public's memory of Norman formed unidimensionally around the ideological imprint of 'communist.' Only recently have North Americans started to rethink Norman's death in terms of his life and scholarship. Initiated first by a scholarly study of Norman's Japan-related writings by the American 'New Left' scholar John Dower and then a sensitive but excessively psychological treatment by Canadian journalist Charles Taylor,[12] Canadians seem more prepared today to consider Norman's life in the complex terms it deserves. Yet just as political events in 1957 seemed to conspire to obfuscate the meaning of his life and death, so too does the rise of a new 'red scare' threaten once again to distort the real meaning of the Norman tragedy.

Over the past several years, it seems, every reported espionage case in North America or Britain invariably refers to Norman. Most recently, Norman's name reemerged in the context of the Hambleton case which 'proved,' says the popular weekly magazine *Maclean's*, 'that Canada is enmeshed in the international espionage game.'[13] Similarly, when in March 1980 Sir Roger Hollis, chief of British counter-espionage from 1956 to 1965, was accused of having been a 'mole' for the Soviets, Norman was again mentioned by the Canadian press. So too in 1979 was he mentioned in the context of the discovery that Anthony Blunt might have been the 'fourth man' in a Soviet spy ring consisting of Guy Burgess, Donald Maclean, and Kim Philby, all of whom were Norman's contemporaries in Cambridge in the 1930s. And for those swept away by what *Maclean's* calls Canada's 'mood of paranoia,'[14] the publication of Chapman Pinscher's *Their Trade Is Treachery* in 1981 put to rest any lingering doubts about Norman. Therein Pinscher states unequivocally that Norman, along with John Watkins, Canada's ambassador to the Soviet Union between 1954 and 1956, served as a spy for the Soviets.

Old questions have therefore been asked with renewed interest in recent years: Was Norman the long-sought 'fifth man' in a Soviet spy ring? Was he simply a vanquished traitor rather than a victimized martyr? Was he accurately labelled by the Senate subcommittee and just poorly protected by Pearson? Or rather, from an entirely different perspective—one that is supportive of Pearson's 1951 judgment—are not these accusatory questions, offered as they are during a period of heightened political conservatism and fear of communism, simply old grist for neo-McCarthyite mills?

The latter is a rhetorical question and the abbreviated account of Norman's adult life which follows is an attempt to substantiate the claim of Norman's 'innocence.' I emphasize 'innocence' now so there will be no misunderstanding. For some people, belief in Marxism will always remain a 'crime,' albeit of a lesser order than membership in the Communist party. Norman was 'guilty' of both prior to joining External Affairs in 1939, and probably for a good while after that time he still subscribed to a Marxist-humanist vision of historical change. Let it also be mentioned now that after surveying over eight hundred pages of FBI documents, over a hundred pages of State Department material, hundreds of pages of External Affairs files, and all the material held by U.S. Army Intelligence and U.S. Navy Intelligence, I can quite confidently assert that there is not one shred of evidence to suggest that Norman ever served the Soviets or any other foreign country as a spy. Instead, as I shall try to show, this heretofore classified material reveals only that a great many Americans suspected disloyalty on Norman's part because of the people with whom he associated and the ideas he professed. Of course, to believe that any American had the right to attribute 'disloyalty' to any individual Canadian suggests a presumptuousness and arrogance that some Canadians, especially Lester Pearson, saw at that time and decried as a violation of Canada's sovereign rights. As much as anything, the terrible lesson of Norman's death is that he was prosecuted in America by Americans who were ideologically trapped by Cold War, McCarthyite fears. But the deeper meaning of his death can only be captured by looking at his life. To this account, in dangerously abbreviated form, I now turn.

Student Years

By the time Norman was sixteen years old he was already a serious student of Karl Marx. His early correspondence shows that while he, the son of a missionary, could in no way accept Marx's 'unchristian spirit,' he none the less found Marx's condemnation of 'ironfisted capital' appealing. In justifying to his older brother his attraction to Marx's ideas, he quoted an epigram attributed to the King of Sweden: 'If a man under 30 had never been a socialist, he had no heart, and if a man over 30 was a socialist, he had no head!'[15] Still under thirty in 1933, six years later Norman was quoting Marx and Reinhold Niebuhr with equal facility in order to justify revolution in capitalist society. 'Capitalism,' he wrote, 'is now pure stupidity; its historic role has long been finished and is acting contrary to civilization.' 'Reason and Humanity,' he told his brother, 'cannot come about without revolution, so tightly and firmly will the acquisitive society in power fight to preserve its privileges.'[16]

Such was Norman's state of mind when he left Canada with a Victoria College B.A. in the autumn of 1933 for Trinity College in Cambridge, England. Within a month of enrolling, Norman attached himself to the liveliest young socialist group then active in England. He noted in one letter that once he mentioned to other students he had read John Strachey's *The Coming Struggle for Power*, 'you are granted a sesame into their company.'[17] The company to which Norman was admitted was the Cambridge University Socialist Society, then dominated by the young and brilliant radical John Cornford. A class list shows that Guy Burgess, Donald Maclean, Anthony Blunt, and James Klugmann were among Norman's classmates. Kim Philby had already graduated that spring. But it was under Cornford's political guidance that Norman wrote of experiencing an 'intellectual rebirth' upon renouncing 'infantile Canadian Marxism.' 'Under his [Cornford's] tutelage,' Norman proudly wrote four years later, 'I entered the party. I not only respected him and his gifts, both intellectual and political, but loved him.'[18]

He returned to North America in 1935 and the following year entered graduate school at Harvard. Besides working for a doctorate in Asian studies, he involved himself in collecting money and goods to be sent to the anti-Franco Spanish rebels; he helped organize a Canadian affiliate of the American Friends of the Chinese People, an organization supporting Mao's forces; he joined a Marxist study group that included Robert Bryce, later to become an Ottawa mandarin, and Tsuru Shigeto, today a well-known economist in Japan; and he aided Phillip Jaffe, who in the mid-forties was indicted for communist spy activities during the time he headed *Amerasia,* a magazine openly sympathetic to what are now known as 'national liberation movements.' According to Jaffe, Norman was at this time a member of the Canadian Communist party.[19]

By late 1939 Norman was in the process of completing his doctoral dissertation, entitled *Japan's Emergence as a Modern State* and published under the same title in 1940 by the Institute of Pacific Relations. Regarded by most Japanologists today as a pathfinding effort,[20] his book was singular for its heavy reliance upon secondary histories by Japanese Marxist writers; and remarkable for its unabashed use of Marxist terminology in explaining Japan's transition from the feudal epoch to an exploitative capitalist era. This work was followed by another IPR publication, *Soldier and Peasant in Japan* (1943), an unpublished monograph called 'Feudal Origins of Modern Japan' (1944), and in 1949 a biography of Tokugawa period utopian rebel Ando Shoeki, whom Norman likened to seventeenth-century English egalitarians John Lilburne and Gerrard Winstanley. All these later works shared with

Japan's Emergence a striking left-leaning, anti-authoritarian message that was embellished by an iconoclastic radical tone and analysis.

Norman's first writings had a political relevance and impact too important to overlook. His first two books particularly brought him a tremendous amount of acclaim and notoriety in the field of Asian studies. Owen Lattimore, for instance, wrote in 1945 about Norman: 'Widely read in Japanese sources, this young Canadian is already the most authoritative contemporary analyst of Japan's economy, society, and government. He is to some extent a disciple, and in a sense the successor, of Sir George Sansom.'[21] In October, 1945, this very quotation was incorporated into a memorandum to General Thorpe, counter-intelligence chief of the occupation forces of Japan, recommending Norman to the general's attention. A handwritten postscript was added, interestingly, noting that 'Dr. Norman would be too modest to bring this evaluation of his own work to anyone else's attention. Owen Lattimore is, of course, one of the outstanding American writers on China, now a professor at Johns Hopkins University.'[22]

Norman's writings, in other words, earned him the attention and respect of scholars and military people alike. But this prominence was a mixed blessing. Once Thorpe was replaced by General Willoughby, who turned his office into a 'loyalty board' (as we shall see), and people like Owen Lattimore became a target of McCarthyism—or in other words as political power shifted to right-wing forces—Norman's writings and the fame they earned him were turned into evidence of infamy and disloyalty. Should this be difficult to believe, one has only to look at the 17 April 1957 'Summary of Bureau [FBI] Files Re Egerton Herbert Norman' which cites 'Norman's Published Writings for IPR and *Amerasia*' and 'Owen Lattimore "Impressed" with Norman's Work' as two major pieces of evidence against Norman. Ironically, except for one section on 'Norman's Participation in Marxist Discussion Group at Harvard, 1937,' there is nothing in this 'top secret' document about Norman's involvement in Marxist groups during his student years.[23]

Foreign Service Years

Shortly after joining External Affairs in late 1939, Norman was sent to Japan to serve as a language officer in the Canadian embassy. After the outbreak of war, he and the other embassy officials were interned until June 1942, when through a prisoner exchange with the Japanese government they were repatriated to Canada. It was right after the trip home that the FBI first intruded into Norman's life. Upon disembarking from the SS *Gripsholm* he was interviewed by an FBI agent regarding information he might have to offer about 'other passengers.' As he had none to offer, says the 5 September 1942 report, the interview was brief, and the report concluded with the words: 'failure to develop any derogatory information through a personal interview with the subject.'[24] Norman's FBI file was started.

It was added to in 1946, though the event which prompted the newest report occurred in November 1942 in Cambridge, Massachusetts. On 9 November, Norman had contacted the FBI in Boston for the purpose of 'securing from them the property of Tsuru [Shigeto],' Norman's graduate school friend of several years earlier. According to the FBI report, Norman produced a calling card of Tsuru as evidence of his authority to take possession of the property. The report read, 'Norman first claimed to be on an official mission for the Canadian government to obtain the books of Tsuru for the use of the Canadian government in a special investigation. He indicated that he held diplomatic immunity. Norman stated that he was on a highly confidential mission and could not divulge the details of the mission.' Norman likely had only a vague idea about what Tsuru's property comprised, and probably did not know that the FBI had already completed a thorough inventory of Tsuru's possessions. In fact, they consisted of Senate reports on munition hearings, communist propaganda materials, correspondence on the Young Communist League, and so on. Norman most likely gained some appreciation of the sorts of materials involved during his conversation with the FBI agents from whom he was trying to secure Tsuru's possessions. The agent's report reads: 'Later on, during the conversation, Norman changed his story and indicated that he did have a personal interest in the possessions of the subject [Tsuru] and that he was not actually on a special mission for the Canadian Government to obtain this material.'[25]

Norman had been caught in a lie—one, moreover, that made him look all the worse because of the sort of communist materials involved. Without going into details, suffice it to say that this incident followed Norman for the rest of his life. Several hundred pages of FBI reports on this episode appear periodically in Norman's file over the next fifteen years. As late as 1957, interest on the part of the U.S. Senate subcommittee in Tsuru and the Tsuru-Norman connection remained strong. In fact, on 27 March 1957, a week before Norman's death, Japanese citizen Tsuru *voluntarily* testified before the Senate subcommittee regarding his relationship with Norman (and Robert Bryce) in the Harvard Marxist study group.[26] For Norman, this must have been the ultimate betrayal. A generous interpretation might have it that in 1942, the thirty-one-year-old Norman, who was after his repatriation involved in a very sensitive intelligence work aimed against imperialist Japan,[27] risked a great deal to help his Japanese friend by retrieving materials the content of which, if reported to the Japanese wartime government, would most certainly have put Tsuru in prison.

It is easy to imagine that Norman felt compelled to dissemble before the FBI agents precisely because his job in Ottawa from late 1942 until the end of the war involved security and intelligence matters concerned with the war against Japan. Assisting a Japanese national, even a leftist, at this time could have seriously compromised his position with External. Regardless, it must be concluded that this run-in with the FBI was not reported to Ottawa because Norman kept his security job until the end of the war.

Norman's duties at External changed within a month of Japan's surrender when Norman Robertson, under-secretary of state, gave Norman a new assignment to assist in the work of assembling and repatriating liberated Canadians in the Far East. He was sent first to the Philippines, and then to Japan, and was expected back in Ottawa by late September or early October. 'There could not be a better man for the assignment,' wrote Owen Lattimore upon learning of Norman's Far Eastern duty.[28] Apparently the American occupiers thought the same, for in late September or early October the supreme commander for the Allied powers in Tokyo sent a request to Ottawa, asking that Norman be permitted to remain in Japan and serve as a civilian head of an American army counter-intelligence unit. 'We were particularly asked to leave him there awhile, and I agreed rather reluctantly,' wrote H.H. Wrong, acting under-secretary, in late October 1945.[29]

The young thirty-four-year-old Norman was clearly enthusiastic and thrilled with his new assignment; he wrote his wife at this time: 'You have no idea how terribly busy I have been the last two weeks, yet never so excitingly busy in my life. My present position is head of the Research and Analysis Branch of the Counter-Intelligence Section of GHQ—and it is every bit as interesting as it sounds. My boss, the head of CIS, is General Thorpe—a frank, blunt, rough-tongued soldier but so accepts suggestions with so much ease and affability that sometimes it quite astounds me.'[30]

His assignment, as it later became clear, was a precarious one. A major part of his task, defined by the Americans, was first to help arrange for the release of long-imprisoned Japanese radicals who had opposed Japan's war effort—some were communists and Norman was later slandered for assisting in their release—and secondly, to interrogate them. Among those working with him was John K. Emmerson, who himself was later a victim of McCarthyism. A few years later their duty came to be regarded as a 'crime' when Eugene Dooman, who during the war had served as chairman of the Far Eastern subcommittee of the State-War-Navy Coordinating Committee, testified in 1951 that the official attention given by Norman and Emmerson to these Japanese communists served to enhance the public regard for the communists to such an extent that they were able to recruit '100,000' new members. But for Norman, in that job of releasing the imprisoned Japanese communists he was simply following the orders of General MacArthur. Innocently, he wrote of the experience: 'I have never enjoyed anything so much as being able to tell them [the prisoners] that according to General MacArthur's orders they were to be released within a week ... Later we had the opportunity to interview them at greater length and after a few days at liberty they were able to give us political information on current affairs of the utmost interest.'[31]

The work was exhausting, he wrote, often necessitating ten-hour days. What pleasures he enjoyed during this period, he told his wife, came from the occasional tennis game, conversations with Japanese intellectuals, and the close personal associations he had with noted Asian specialists then in Japan, such as T.A. Bisson, Bill Holland, Owen Lattimore, John K. Emmerson, and Shigeto Tsuru, all figures who later figure prominently in the McCarthyite witch-hunt directed at the Institute of Pacific Relations. In another letter (25 November 1945) Norman mentions seeing Jack Service as well, one more Far Eastern expert whose career was badly damaged by the infamous 'China Lobby.'

During this very early phase of the occupation, when the essential policy was to demilitarize and democratize the Japanese state, Norman was enamoured of the MacArthurian radical messianic zeal that prosecuted militarists and protected democrats. Norman easily accepted MacArthur's judgment that the occupation was a 'spiritual revolution' wherein 'freedom is on the offensive, democracy is on the march.'[32] In his own words, Norman believed that MacArthur was 'following a course designed to give the Japanese the maximum opportunity to develop their own democratic institutions.'[33] At the same time, Norman retained a healthy scepticism about the possibility of imposing democracy from above, a view reinforced by his superiors in Ottawa. Dr. Hugh Keenleyside, Norman's superior at the Far Eastern desk during the war, believed in late 1945 that 'there is nothing in MacArthur's record to lead one to think that he has any serious interest in democracy and all that should mean.' Keenleyside worried that the 'enlightened policy' towards both China and Japan of men like John Carter Vincent—later victimized by McCarthyism—in the State Department would be undercut by MacArthur who could not 'know just where the convenience of supporting the old order should be sacrificed to the *necessity* of encouraging a growth of economic as well as political democracy.'[34] Although early on in the occupation Norman tried to dispel such doubts held by Ottawa ('No one is more fully aware of the need for the Japanese to take hold and to perform the task [of democratization] than General MacArthur'),[35] he later echoed doubts similar to those of his superiors once MacArthur 'reversed course' and partially 'de-democratized' Japan. Nevertheless, by the end of his first tour of duty, his pro-occupation views and actions had earned the genuine respect of his commander, General Thorpe, MacArthur's first chief of counter-intelligence. Upon Norman's departure from Japan, General Thorpe wrote the prime minister of Canada, MacKenzie King, on 31 January 1946: 'I should like to express to you my personal appreciation of Dr. Norman's services. His profound knowledge of Japan, his brilliant intellectual attainments and his willingness to give his utmost to our work has made his contributions to the success of the occupation one of great value. During his tour of duty with us, Dr. Norman has won the respect and admiration of all who have been associated with him. It will be difficult, indeed, to fill the vacancy left by his departure.'[36]

In January 1946, given a respite from the occupation, Norman was assigned to the office of Canada's ambassador to the United States, Mike Pearson, who also was serving as Canada's chief representative to the Far Eastern

Commission (FEC), the Allied powers' organization that was *nominally* in charge of overseeing the occupation of Japan. Norman was Pearson's first secretary and the alternate Delegate to the FEC. But when by mid-1946 it had become clear that Norman's talents were being wasted by serving on the powerless FEC, on Pearson's initiative he was reassigned to head Canada's mission to occupied Japan. Pearson wrote to the secretary of state: 'As Mr. Norman is a distinguished Japanologist and served for a time on General MacArthur's staff in Tokyo and later as Canadian delegate on the FEC during its tour of Japan, it was felt that it would be easier to get SCAP's co-operation if Mr. Norman was named head of the mission, and that he was the best man we could send.'[37] MacArthur personally accepted this argument. On 2 August 1946, Norman departed aboard the SS *General Meigs* from Vancouver and arrived in Yokohama on 14 August as Canada's head of the liaison mission. There Norman remained until October 1950 when, in the words of Arthur Menzies, until recently Canada's ambassador to China, he was recalled 'following certain inquiries undertaken as a result of allegations concerning Norman's communist connections.'[38] Thereafter began the nightmare that ended only with his death.

The political atmosphere of the occupied Japan to which Norman returned in August 1946 had changed from the early period which was so evangelically democratic in tone. Occupied Japan of late 1946 can best be characterized by quoting General MacArthur's 'Statement on the First Anniversary of Surrender.' MacArthur made it clear that occupied Japan had become enmeshed in the emerging Cold War, which he depicted as 'dread uncertainty arising from impinging ideologies which now stir mankind.' MacArthur asked, 'Which concept will prevail?' The choice for the Japanese was clear: 'principles of right and justice and decency' or the evil of 'the philosophy of an extreme radical left' that could prove seductive to a nation afflicted by 'generations of feudalistic life.'[39] As far as Norman was personally concerned, once MacArthur began yielding to Cold War rhetoric, his chief witch-hunter, General Willoughby, was permitted to conveniently forget that the Japanese communists whom Norman and Emmerson released in 1945, in order to serve as a countervailing force to rightist tendencies in Japan, had been freed and encouraged to organize political parties and labour unions by MacArthur himself. Unknown to Norman, General Willoughby began investigating Norman as a 'security matter' in October 1946, two months after Norman's return to Japan.[40]

None the less, from all accounts Norman and MacArthur enjoyed a healthy, mutually respectful relationship during much of Norman's last four years in Japan. Though critical of some of MacArthur's policies, Norman admired the general for the missionary zeal he still brought to this crusade for democratization, and MacArthur for his part seemed to have genuinely respected Norman's expertise as a Japanologist. Charles Kades, then a high-ranking functionary in Government Section (G-1) and one of the architects of Japan's constitution, wrote:

> So far as General MacArthur is concerned, I know of my own knowledge that they [EHN and MacArthur] were on excellent terms ... It is my recollection that the first person in GHQ General MacArthur spoke to after the Emperor visited him in the Embassy was Herb Norman, which perhaps is some measure of his closeness to the Commander-in-Chief, and in my opinion Mr. Norman's memoranda and oral advice were very favourably received and influential ... There is no doubt Herb Norman influenced me ... and I frequently turned to him for advice ... When I needed additional personnel for the Government Section who were experts on Japan, he recommended that I try to secure the assignment of then Captain (U.S.N.) Sebald.[41]

Sebald later became America's ambassador to Japan.

For his part, Norman no less admired MacArthur, and seemed to enjoy an intimacy with the General that few might expect. Some of Norman's letters to the general began with 'My Dear General MacArthur,' even as late as July 1950, after the Korean War broke out. One of Norman's then junior advisors in the Canadian mission recently told me the story about MacArthur's personal appearance at Canada's Dominion Day celebration in 1947. MacArthur, who on record was a teetotaller and non-smoker, accepted both a drink and a cigarette from Norman before the two men retired onto the veranda of the legation for a private chat.

Norman's private communiqués to Ottawa, a few of his public speeches, and his private correspondence with the general, however, clearly show that Norman was not uncritical of the man and many of his policies. In a confidential memo to External, dated 28 January 1948, and in response to MacArthur's second anniversary message, Norman wrote: 'The ideas which he stressed in the message were not new and could be criticized for not admitting the slightest possibility that any grounds of criticism of the occupation existed.'[42] He further observed, in referring to emerging Cold War realignments, that MacArthur's policies were designed 'to tie [Japan's] economy to that of the United States.'[43] In a different communiqué of the same year to Ottawa he warned that democratic reform was being undone because of MacArthur's policies aimed at 'de-purging' war criminals: 'Some of the most powerful political forces in Japan today are those commanded by former leaders who have been purged but still exert an indefinable but nonetheless potent influence behind the scenes.'[44]

Publicly, Norman was saying to Japanese audiences that 'there would seem to be dangers inherent in the tendency of the occupation to think of democracy as something institutional.' Institutional reforms, he said, 'were imposed on Japan from the top. These reforms, admirable in themselves, were not initiated by the Japanese, hence they could scarcely command the deepest loyalty ... It is safe to say that not all the changes of the occupation will remain.' In the same speech Norman questioned MacArthur's pronouncement that Japan had by 1948 undergone a 'spiritual revolution' in the name of democracy. He queried, 'If democracy can be measured by written laws, he

[MacArthur] was right, but can it be?' The mistakes of the occupation authorities, he said, grew out of the Cold War which prompted policy that would 'favour the interests of the conservatives in Japan who could be counted upon to be anti-communist.' The result was a 'watering down' of most progressive reforms undertaken earlier on.[45]

Privately, in his letters to MacArthur, Norman also raised questions about the wisdom of certain occupation policies. One of the best examples was his questioning, on humanitarian grounds, of the sentences imposed on two Japanese 'war criminals,' Shigemitsu Mamoru and Togo Shigenori. In pleading for commutation of their sentences, which MacArthur had personally endorsed the day before (22 November 1948), Norman defended his recommendation by saying, 'This may not be legal reasoning but I think at least it has in it a quality of common sense and humanity.' Reduction of their sentences, he further argued, 'will reveal to the Japanese public in a practical manner that the victorious powers are not motivated by a general and indiscriminate sense of revenge.' Norman ended his letter saying, 'I feel that I am carrying out my obligations to my government and also following the dictates of my conscience.'[46] Though MacArthur did not heed Norman's advice on this issue, neither does it appear that he bore Norman a grudge for questioning his wisdom, for three months later MacArthur personally recommended to Ottawa that Norman's rank be upgraded to minister. Lester Pearson, by then secretary of state, immediately endorsed MacArthur's recommendation, adding in a note to the general, '[Norman's] cordial relations with you have resulted in benefits to your Headquarters, as well as to the Government of Canada.'[47] In thanking the general for this vote of confidence, Norman sent MacArthur an autographed copy of his new book, *Ando Shoeki,* and MacArthur responded to this gesture of goodwill by urging Norman to write a general article on Japan, past and present.[48]

But outside the relationship of mutual respect, goodwill, and cooperation between MacArthur and Norman, suspicions regarding Norman's 'loyalty' to the occupation were being voiced. As mentioned earlier, General Willoughby, head of counter-intelligence (G-2) and a notorious right-winger who reputedly said of Franco of Spain that he was 'the second best general in the world,' began investigating Norman for his past communist sympathies. Why Willoughby chose Norman as a target can easily be guessed. One reason stems from Norman's strong criticism of many in MacArthur's staff whom he accused of incompetence or indifference. Norman bemoaned what he termed the loss 'of the old crusading zeal that characterized the earlier phase of the occupation,' and the emerging, 'rather blind and unquestioning faith in all the policies that have emanated from SCAP and a somewhat intolerant impatience with any doubts as to whether there is a discrepancy between the theory and implementation of occupation policy.'[49] He especially regretted the reversal in land reform policy—these democratic advances had been reversed by American 'disinterested officials' and the 'very mediocre and in some cases painfully inept performance of an increasingly conservative Japanese bureaucracy.'[50] In large part the cause of these problems could be found, Norman wrote in a report of February 1950, in the contradiction inherent in the occupation: 'A brief review of the fate of the post-war government of Japan will show that a parliamentary democracy is scarcely compatible with a military occupation.'[51] Shortly thereafter, Norman's assessment was, if anything, even more negative: 'As the year wore on it became more and more evident that GHQ, SCAP, believed it could secure the economic and political stability of Japan by placing its confidence in, and giving support to, the more conservative social forces at work here. This development cast before it a shadow over the future of liberal democracy; it gave hope to the "old guard." '[52]

If Norman's official expression of such sentiments was not responsible for Willoughby's investigation of him, then some of Norman's activities and associations were, once Willoughby began organizing his 'loyalty boards' in order to search for 'leftists and fellow-travellers' working for the occupation. And, of course, once America 'lost' China to Maoist communism, the 'loyalty boards' began operating at a feverish rate. Suddenly, all Far Eastern experts, especially those who advised the State Department, came under suspicion. FBI reports, among which there was one on Norman, were sent to Willoughby from Washington. It was then remembered that Norman had earlier in the occupation worked with Japanese communists; that he was a friend to such Japanese socialist scholars as Hani Goro, and to American Far Eastern experts Owen Lattimore, Bill Holland, T.A. Bisson, Emmerson, and others. Subsequently, it was also learned that Norman had involved himself in organizing a Japan branch of the Institute of Pacific Relations, which for Willoughby was 'a spy ring for Russian Communists,' and 'heavily weighted with known leftists in control positions.'[53] And in 1947, Norman brazenly travelled to an IPR conference in England. The 'evidence' began mounting: he wrote four articles for *Amerasia* in 1937 and 1938, six for *Far Eastern Survey* (1939–45), and six for *Pacific Affairs* (1943–49). These were allegedly 'communist-inspired' journals. Then, after the outbreak of the Korean War, according to speculation in the press, Norman criticized Willoughby's faulty intelligence reports which rejected the possibility of Chinese intervention in Korea. But the *coup de grace,* according to one U.S. security report, was the discovery by the Government of Canada of 'certain communist connections, especially with Israel Halperin,'[54] a Russian-Jewish *émigré* who had been implicated by Igor Gouzenko, the Russian embassy cipher clerk who defected in Ottawa in 1945. Halperin had once shared a dormitory room with his friend Norman in the early thirties when both were undergraduates at the University of Toronto, and later kept in touch it would seem; Norman's phone number was found by the RCMP in Halperin's personal notebook.

The Gouzenko-Halperin-Norman connection had not been made until August 1950, when the FBI asked Counter-Intelligence (G-2) to initiate an investigation of persons listed in the address book of Israel Halperin. The investigation showed, or rather the connection was made for the first time, that in addition to Norman's name appearing in the address book, so too was Tsuru Shigeto's.

Suddenly, the 1942 interrogation of Norman by the FBI over his attempt to secure Tsuru's possessions took on renewed relevance. This information was communicated to the FBI, which in turn sent it on to Ottawa. With little advance warning, Norman was abruptly recalled from Japan on 19 October 1950 on the basis of a 17 October report compiled by the RCMP and most certainly based largely on the G-2 and FBI information.[55] On the basis of these reports, Norman was subjected to intermittent interrogation by the RCMP over a six-week period, ending in late November.

'A pile of bricks does not make a house,' to cite one of Norman's favourite quotations: the evidence against Norman, though considerable, was insufficient and inconclusive. And so the RCMP 'cleared' Norman, noting in a 1 December 1950 report that the original 17 October RCMP report that prompted his recall and which had been sent to the FBI, was no longer valid. The newest report said: 'Of the numerous points supplied at the time, the majority have been absolutely determined to be in error. The remaining few have not been confirmed nor does there appear to be any answer to them.'[56] The most damning comment to appear in the second RCMP report read: 'The worst possible conclusion we can arrive at is the very apparent naivete in his relationships with his fellow man.'[57] The December report also concluded that the October report's findings should be discounted; this too was communicated to the FBI.

But for Norman's sense of well-being, the judged validity or invalidity of the early report mattered little. By all accounts, from both friends and family members, the experience had been terrifying and emotionally exhausting. Though one of his interrogators told me not long ago that Norman had 'stood up' well to the questioning, Norman's close associates say he was still recounting the nightmare years later, especially after the second Senate attack came in 1957.

Shortly after the interrogation ended, he was made head of the American and Far Eastern division, a position he held until July 1952. It was unfortunate that External Affairs retained this archaic combination of American *and* Far Eastern affairs in one division, for in August 1951, when Asianist and ex-communist Karl Wittfogel testified before a Senate subcommittee that Norman was a communist, American State Department figures expressed alarm that a communist was in charge of American affairs in the Department of External Affairs, entitled as he was to inspect 'top secret' material. Ottawa was outraged by this public disclosure and immediately issued a protest, claiming Norman had been 'given a clean bill of health' and remained 'a trusted and valuable official of the Department.'[58] Unofficial Canadian reaction to the McCarran committee disclosures was no less swift and angry. Harold Greer, writing for the *Toronto Daily Star*, suggested that the 'smearing' of Dr. Norman was the result of a 'vendetta' on the part of Major General Willoughby who had been angered by Norman's objections to the increasingly undemocratic policies of the MacArthur occupation of Japan. The Toronto *Globe and Mail* demanded that 'the Federal Government protest strongly to Washington against the manner in which the

Canadian diplomat was smeared with the allegations of Communist sympathies.' The *Globe and Mail* further asserted that in this instance 'the Washington witch-hunt' had insulted Canadian national integrity by not working quietly through regular diplomatic channels; Washington, the newspaper claimed, was treating Canada like a 'poor relation living in the porter's lodge on Uncle Sam's estate.' The *Ottawa Citizen* echoed these remarks, saying that 'the U.S. Congressmen show as much contempt for Canada's sovereignty as the Soviet Union does for Bulgaria's.' The *Citizen* attack ended: 'U.S. Senators would do the cause of world freedom a great service if they confined their star chamber procedures to their own citizens.'[59]

Pearson sought to erase the smear by discrediting the 'unimpressive and unsubstantiated statements by a former Communist [Wittfogel],' before announcing at the conclusion of a press conference on 16 August that Norman would serve as his chief advisor to the 4 September San Francisco Conference on the Japan Peace Treaty.

Politically, however, a 'clean bill of health' only serves to remind the 'once-afflicted' of the disease. Norman confided to a friend in the aftermath of the 1951 publicity, 'You can't wash off the poison of a smear from your emotions.' 'How can you,' he asked in desperation, 'fight back against this sort of thing?'[60] Deeply depressed at losing the sine qua non attributes of a successful diplomat, his private anonymity and his public reputation, Norman passively resigned himself to unattractive and out-of-the-way foreign service positions during the next few years. After a closet post in Ottawa, Norman went off to New Zealand in 1953 as high commissioner for, in the words of one high-ranking Canadian diplomat still in service today, 'a rest and cure.' 'For someone of Herb's calibre,' this same diplomat remarked, 'New Zealand was exile.' Norman, of course, knew this, and suffered diplomatic convalescence passively. Hence, his hopes were renewed when in 1956 Lester Pearson told him of his political resurrection, namely that he was being sent to a diplomatic hot spot, Egypt, as ambassador. According to many who were closest to him at that time, this new and promising assignment served to lift the cloud of depression still troubling Norman, sending him into Egypt filled with enthusiasm and high hopes of being able to make an important contribution to the cause of world peace.

And contribute he did by establishing a relationship of trust with President Nasser following the invasion of Egypt by Israel, England, and France in October 1956. From Norman's dispatches to Ottawa during this period of the Suez crisis, it is clear that his intervention with Nasser was crucial in securing Egyptian acceptance of a United Nations–Canadian peacekeeping force to be stationed in the Sinai. As late (in his life) as 14 March 1957, Norman's personal intercession with Nasser, in this case a late night visit to Nasser's holiday retreat, had the effect of clearing the way for additional Canadian troops to occupy the battle zones.[61] It is something more than mere historical irony that at the same time as Norman was meeting late at night with Nasser to work for peace in the

Middle East, in Washington Norman's old American friend from the early days of the occupation, John K. Emmerson, was undergoing congressional hearings before being appointed to serve as political counsellor in Paris. It was in the course of those hearings that Emmerson mentioned something that members of Congress had not known, that E. Herbert Norman was then serving as Canada's ambassador to Egypt and minister to Lebanon. Emmerson also remarked that he had had the opportunity of meeting with Norman during his stay in Beirut in the fall of 1956. In Emmerson's words, 'the statement was like a shock wave: the sharp investigators [Senators Jenner and Watkins, and Counsel Robert Morris] had not known where Norman was and what he was doing. Both senators asked me to repeat it. Morris asked the senators if they would like to see the evidence in the security files that Norman was a communist. He proceeded to read into the record reports about Norman's communism, laying stress on statements by a former communist, Karl August Wittfogel, that Norman had been a member of a summer Communist study group in 1938 and that he had been identified as a member of the Communist party in 1940.'[62]

Clearly, the record from which Counsel Morris read was the October 1950 RCMP report, the one discredited and superseded by the December 1950 RCMP report which also had been sent to Washington. But no matter; the full text of this meeting between Emmerson and his Senate interrogators was released to the press at 4:30 PM on 14 March. 'Senators Probe Canadian Envoy,' newspaper headlines read, the same 'Canadian Envoy' who was at the very same time meeting with President Nasser in order to ensure peace in the Middle East. Old charges, old evidence, but inserted into a new situation: Would internal saboteurs, 'stab-in-the-back' leftists cause the 'loss' of Egypt from the 'free world' as they had with China? The McCarthyite defenders of freedom, the architects of a new kind of organized stupidity, answered a resounding 'No!' Norman had to go. And thus began the public persecution of Norman that led to his jump from a downtown Cairo apartment building.

Conclusion

But was it 'murder by slander' as some have alleged? Was Norman guiltless of the charges of 'communism'? Had he been slandered?

The answer to these questions, according to official Canadian records, is a yes qualified only by the admission of youthful left-wing sympathies. According to official American records, the answer is an unqualified no. There is, as we have seen, support for both positions. Norman was undoubtedly a communist during his early years, but there is no evidence to suggest he remained a communist during his time as a foreign service officer. Yet there is evidence to suggest he was something of a radical-liberal who believed in, among other things, non-intervention, self-determination for all peoples, popular democracy, and the value of 'national liberation movements.' He supported, for example, what he called 'emergent Arab nationalism,' as a popular struggle for independence, even as he criticized Nasser for demagoguery. Before that he supported the rise of the Japanese Communist party and the labour movement because he saw them as positive countervailing forces to lingering fascist tendencies in the Japanese body politic and as the bearers of a historical, verifiable democratic undercurrent in Japan's past. For similar reasons, earlier in his life he was drawn to support democratic forces in Spain's civil war and communist forces in China's struggle. History, he believed, was on the side of the forces of liberation, and as a historian of transnational background he felt compelled to back those whom he believed were struggling for principles that transcended petty nationalism. That his conception of freedom conflicted with the ahistorical and ultranationalistic McCarthyite conception can be of no surprise to anyone.

Finally, as a Canadian diplomat in a world dominated by American power and U.S.-USSR ideologically based schisms, Norman was especially vulnerable to McCarthyism. Nor was he alone. A secret U.S. Foreign Service dispatch and other sources recently released under the Freedom of Information Act show, as we have seen, that other Canadians were similarly being targeted by McCarthyism at this time, the three most prominent names being Robert Bryce, clerk of the Privy Council; Arthur Menzies, until recently Canada's ambassador to China; and Lester Pearson himself. Bryce had once shared with Norman involvement in a Marxist study group at Harvard and had introduced Tsuru to Norman; Menzies had, along with Norman, joined the Canadian Friends of the Chinese People in the late thirties; and Pearson had helped prevent the Americans from getting Igor Gouzenko to testify in Washington. It may very well be that the international furor raised by Norman's death actually served to protect these other distinguished Canadians from McCarthyism.

But perhaps the more important point to be made about Norman's death was made by Lester Pearson: 'The issue before us, is not only the tragedy of one man, victimized by slanderous procedures in another country and unable to defend himself against them. There is the broader question of principle involved—the right, to say nothing of the propriety, of a foreign government to intervene in our affairs ... Such intervention is intolerable.'[63]

Norman's tragic death can be understood in similar terms, perhaps no less appropriate, as defined by George Grant in his influential *Lament for a Nation*.[64] Grant's book is a lament for the loss of his nation's identity to the all-consuming American leviathan to the south. Norman's story is in a very real sense a story of Canada's loss of one of its own to this same giant, the story of how one Canadian fell victim to the American behemoth run amok.

The imagery is apt, for it reminds us that giants may be both gentle and savage. Canadians no doubt benefit when the giant is gentle and protective, but they will suffer when it feels threatened and strikes out, blindly, even at its friends. Norman was the giant's victim, not really its target as some advocates of a conspiracy theory might suggest. Norman was a victim of its blind fear, albeit a fear expressed in a slow, methodical, organized, though sensibly stupid manner, much in the fashion of a blind person searching for his cane. That the blind giant struck out in fear, hurting friends in the process, might be forgiveable except for the fact that the blindness was self-inflicted.

Notes

1. Department of State, dispatch no. 875, 18 April 1957, file no. 601/42274/4-1857. All American records cited in this paper were obtained through the Freedom of Information Act.

2. Appearing in the *Globe and Mail* on 11 April 1957.

3. Hence, we read in a 17 April 1957 telegram from the American ambassador to Canada to the secretary of state: 'Believe strong Canadian line re exchange security information motivated by domestic political considerations as well as by widespread bitter feelings resulting from Norman suicide. Pearson's detailed statement in Parliament and publicity given to exchange of notes [between U.S. and Canadian governments] would appear aimed at meeting political exigencies rather than at solving basic problem. April 16 speech by conservative leader Diefenbaker indicated intention conservative opposition use Norman affair as political ammunition in election campaign already underway' ('Confidential' telegram, file no. 601.4274/4-1057).

4. Quoted in a U.S. 'Confidential' memorandum, 14 August 1951, State Department document file no. 742.001/8-1451.

5. See note no. 3; and Department of State dispatch 892, 25 April 1957, file no. 601.4274/4-2557.

6. The *Gazette* editorial and Pearson's reply appear in their entirety in 'The Strange Case of Mr. Norman,' *U.S. News and World Report,* 26 April 1957, 153–54. See also 'The Pearson Case,' *Globe and Mail,* 19 April 1957.

7. Reported in 'Confidential' dispatch, 18 April 1957, American embassy in Ottawa, file no. 601.4274/4-1857.

8. The American ambassador's assessment in ibid.

9. See James Eayrs, ed., *The Commonwealth and Suez* (New York, Toronto: Oxford University Press, 1964), 382–8, 416–21.

10. Blakney's article was quoted extensively in U.S. embassy dispatch (Ottawa) of 18 April 1957, file no. 601.4274/4-1857.

11. Department of State, file nos. 601.4274/4-1557; 601.4274/6-958; 601.4274/5-2658. See also 'Intolerable Incident,' *Newsweek,* 22 April 1957, 64. FBI Chief Hoover stated in a secret memorandum of 10 April 1957, 'I want complete summaries of all we have on Norman and Pearson.' FBI file no. 100-346993-73.

12. John W. Dower, *Origins of the Modern Japanese State: Selected Workings of E.H. Norman* (New York: Pantheon, 1975); Charles Taylor, *Six Journeys: A Canadian Pattern* (Toronto: Anansi, 1977): 107–51

13. *Maclean's,* 13 December 1982, 29

14. Ibid.

15. Personal correspondence to brother Howard Norman, 11 July 1927

16. Ibid., 15 May 1933

17. Ibid., 21 October 1933

18. 3 March 1937; Cornford had recently been killed in action in the Spanish Civil War.

19. Personal correspondence, from Jaffe to the author, 25 February 1978

20. See the articles by John W. Hall and George Akita in *Journal of Japanese Studies* 3, no. 2 (Summer 1977), and Herbert Bix's rejoinder in the same *Journal,* vol. 4, no. 2 (Summer 1978).

21. Owen Lattimore, *Solution in Asia* (Boston: Little, Brown and Company, 1945), 38, n. 4

22. No. 201 miscellaneous file, Department of External Affairs, no. 53038440; memorandum dated 22 October 1945

23. FBI file no. 100-346993-73

24. FBI file no. 100-346993-x; the interrogation actually took place on 25 August 1942.

25. FBI file no. 100-346993-2, dated 16 October 1946

26. Tsuru's testimony is quoted at length in the FBI's 'Summary of Information,' file no. 100-346993-73.

27. It appears that Norman's work between 1942 and the end of the war involved the translation and interpretation of captured and/or intercepted Japanese war documents. In the summer of 1943 or 1944 he arranged for security clearance for such work for his older brother who also read Japanese language material with facility.

28. Owen Lattimore to Hugh Keenleyside, 5 September 1945; External Affairs file no. 50061-40 (hereafter External Affairs will be rendered EA)

29. H.H. Wrong to Hugh Keenleyside, 20 October 1945, EA no. 104-C-34

30. Correspondence, 26 October 1945

31. Ibid.

32. Supreme Commander for the Allied Powers (SCAP) *Political Reorientation of Japan II* (Washington, DC: U.S. Government Printing Office), 737, 756

33. Correspondence to his wife, 26 October 1945

34. Correspondence, Hugh Keenleyside to Norman Robertson, under-secretary of state, 4 September 1945; EA 104-CD-34

35. From his speech on 'Japan in Evolution,' given in New York on 16 March 1946 to the Foreign Policy Association

36. EA 50061-40, vol. 3/4-1

37. Ibid., 30 May 1946

38. Personal communication to the author, 20 February 1978

39. SCAP, *Political Reorientation of Japan II,* 756

40. The case remained open until 11 March 1947 and was reopened in May 1950; FBI file no. 100-346993.

41. Personal communication to author, 18 January 1979

42. EA 4606-F-2-40

43. Ibid.

44. EA 4606-E-8-40, vol. 1, 19 January 1948

45. 'Japan since Surrender' (unpublished typescript, 13 pp, 1951?)

46. 23 November 1948 (This letter can be found in the MacArthur Archives, Norfolk, Virginia.)

47. 9 February 1949

48. Norman letter to General MacArthur, 28 February 1949 (MacArthur Archives)

49. EA 10848-10, 26 October 1949

50. EA 10463-B40, 11 August 1949, 4

51. EA 10463-B40

52. Annual Review of Events in Japan for 1950, EA 4606-F-40, part I

53. See note 2 in the 'Conclusion' to this volume.

54. Department of State, 20 March 1957, file no. 601.4274/3-2057

55. Correspondence between G-2 and the FBI between August and October 1950, and references to communication with Ottawa by both, lend credence to this conclusion. Memo from GHQ, Far East Command, to G-2, Washington, 30 November 1950; reference to CIA involvement noted in 30 November 1950 memo from Lt Col Roundtree to Willoughby, G-2, GHQ, inter-office memorandum; and FBI file memorandum, 1 November 1950, file no. 100-346993-6.

56. This finding is one of several incorporated into a review of the Norman case by the American embassy in Ottawa, dated 25 April 1957, file no. 601.4274/4-2557.

57. Quoted in memorandum from U.S. Department of Justice, Ottawa, Liaison office, 7 December 1950, from Glenn H. Bethel to director, FBI, file no. 100-346993-24.

58. See no. 4.

59. All of the above newspapers' remarks are found in a 'restricted' dispatch from Ottawa to Washington, dated 20 August 1951; file no. 310.342/8-2051 XR 742.001.

60. Quoted by Sidney Katz, in *Maclean's,* 28 September 1957.

61. EA, 15 March 1957, file no. 50366-40 (A thirty-year rule restricting quotation prohibits specific citations.)

62. John K. Emmerson, *The Japanese Thread: A Life in the U.S. Foreign Service* (New York: Holt, Rinehart, Winston 1978), 334–5

63. House of Commons, 10 April 1957

64. George Grant, *Lament for a Nation: The Defeat of Canadian Nationalism* (Toronto: McClelland and Stewart, 1965)

SUICIDE

James Barros

The suggestion that Norman's tragic death on April 4, 1957 was due to the actions of the Senate Subcommittee on Internal Security now raises some doubts that this was what drove him to take his own life. A close examination of events before and after he committed suicide shows that the reasons for it are far more complex than would appear at first glance.

The Senate Subcommittee's release on March 14, 1957 of Emmerson's testimony of March 12 included the excerpts from the Summary of Information prepared for General Willoughby in mid-April 1951. This Summary of Information was an amalgam of FBI and RCMP information.[1] The release of the testimony led to a defense of Norman by Pearson which was as forceful as it had been six years earlier. Indeed, in March-April 1957, Pearson was fully supported, at least initially, by the parliamentary opposition leader and future prime minister John Diefenbaker. The opinions of an aroused Canadian public and a press sympathetic to Norman were echoed across the border, although some of the American reaction may have been politically motivated. Ottawa quickly lodged an official protest. Washington was seemingly embarrassed, and though Norman, at first, was "upset," as his deputy Arthur Kilgour subsequently told Ottawa, he was also "somewhat detached."

Morally and politically, Norman's position appeared to be virtually unassailable as the confident tone of his March 19 messages of thanks to both Pearson and Diefenbaker seemed to indicate. Pearson then wrote a personal letter of support in return, which appears to show that he had not only won the government's endorsement but also that of his colleagues and friends. In fact, Pearson's initial comments in the House of Commons had led the embassy staff in Cairo, as well as others, to consider the Norman matter closed. What more could anyone have asked for?

Norman's work habits appeared normal. He never mentioned the Senate Subcommittee to Kilgour, and later inquiries by the embassy staff led to the reasonable conviction that there had been "no sudden and drastic change" in his behaviour. Then about March 21, a week after Emmerson's testimony was released, he showed "signs that he was preoccupied." His secretary "found him somewhat tense," he appeared to lose interest in important matters, yet still adhered to the usual daily schedule. The first recorded occasion when his conduct attracted attention was a reception on March 22, for the Director General of the Food and Agriculture Organization. Norman "appeared to several people to be quite upset."

From *No Sense of Evil Espionage: The Case of Herbert Norman* (Toronto: Deneau, 1986), 143–57, 235–37. Reprinted by permission of Deneau Publishers & Company Ltd.

It was not until several days later, on March 25, that he broached the subject of the subcommittee's activities to Kilgour who, much later, informed External Affairs that he thought that day had "marked perhaps a turning point" in Norman's demeanor. Complaining that the people in Washington were still after him, he produced a newspaper clipping dealing with a statement by the subcommittee's counsel Judge Morris. Referring to Pearson's protest to Washington, the judge had declared that he would press ahead and present, through reputable witnesses and reliable evidence and documentation, those underlying facts that impinged on the United States' security. Kilgour tried to assure Norman the statement was in character with the judge's attitude, and that he saw no reason to believe that his name would resurface. Norman then noted that when Emmerson had previously been investigated in Washington, he had written an affidavit attesting to Emmerson's character. This was not so, as the particular affidavit dealt only with the events that took place at Fuchu prison in October 1945.[2] He reasoned that when the subcommittee had reopened the case, it must have been angered by the affidavit it had found in Emmerson's file. He also maintained that although his acquaintanceship with various individuals—Owen Lattimore especially—had been raised during his own "investigation" in Ottawa, it had not come up in the subcommittee's previous hearings. There is no documentary evidence to support the fact that Norman was ever questioned about Owen Lattimore in Ottawa. While it is true that the subcommittee was not aware of most of his acquaintances, it did know about his relationship with Lattimore during the postwar period when they were both in Tokyo.[3] Norman then observed that the thought that the subcommittee "might be able to reveal apparently *new information disturbed him very much.*"[4] He added that he found it discouraging to work so hard and then to have something like this develop.

For the next several days he continued to work in his office. Then on March 28, during an informal luncheon at the Young Women's Christian Association, "a decisive change" was noted. Though all the Canadians were seated at a single small table, it did not go unnoticed that Norman "scarcely took part in the conversation and in fact did not appear to be mentally with us," as Kilgour subsequently wrote. He also had begun closing his office door which had not been his usual practice, and was sometimes seen scribbling on foolscap sheets of paper or resting on his office couch; in fact, some of the embassy staff thought he looked ill.

On the morning of March 29 he arrived at his office and then asked one of the embassy's Egyptian employees to open the door that led to the roof of the chancery building. Though the ambassador told the employee that he was not needed, he, nevertheless, decided to accompany him. Norman walked around the roof, looking over the sides, and particularly at the highest point which was directly over the garage.

On the same day it was announced in the Egyptian press that Tsuru had been interviewed by the subcommittee. The embassy staff agreed that the news should not be brought to Norman's attention, although he subsequently asked

Kilgour if anything further had developed. He answered in the negative to save his chief additional anguish. Although Kilgour never found out whether Norman had ever learned that the subcommittee had again commenced inquiries about him, it would be safe to assume that in a cosmopolitan city such as Cairo, especially in the circle in which Norman moved, it was only a matter of time before the subcommittee's activities would have become known to him. Mrs. Norman later admitted to Kilgour that Herbert had told her that the subcommittee "probably would eventually interview" Tsuru, since he was temporarily teaching at Harvard University. The fact that he was aware of Tsuru's presence at Harvard prompted an RCMP officer to scribble in the margin of Kilgour's report that Norman "must have still been in touch with him."

For the next three days Kilgour saw virtually nothing of his chief. It appears that he had driven out of Cairo to get away from it all. On at least one occasion he was accompanied by a friend who said Norman had slept in the car a great deal of the time and that he had declared he could sleep for an entire year.

On April 1 and 2 Norman was up and about holding talks with senior Egyptian officials. He still appeared "preoccupied though no more than previously."[5] By this point, Tsuru's public testimony to the subcommittee had been released. Norman admitted to the Canadian journalist King Gordon that he had never been as depressed as he had been during the last weeks. He was convinced that the old communist charge would be revived, and that Judge Morris' boast that nothing would obstruct the subcommittee's investigatory work was a sure sign that a new inquiry was about to be initiated. He dwelt on what he euphemistically called his 1950 investigation, admitting that it had not been inquisitorial, only terribly thorough. Convinced that the RCMP had passed on his file to the FBI, he now feared that the FBI, in cahoots with the subcommittee, might extract information out of context and distort whatever was in his file. These comments to Gordon were, of course, deceptive in the extreme, for Norman well knew from his January 1952 interrogation by Messrs. Guernsey, McClellan, and Glazebrook that the most damaging information about him had been supplied to the RCMP by M15, and not by the FBI. Denigrating the English cousin, however, was less productive than denigrating the American neighbor.

According to Gordon, Norman had no fear that new information might emerge in any renewed investigation. He was very satisfied with the "thoroughness" of the previous one, although he claimed that it had been an ordeal both physically and psychically. He thought that others might become unjustly enmeshed because of the distortions. He also observed that these congressional investigations had no limits when they were intent on destroying someone's name. As an example, he cited the Senate Subcommittee's use of a letter written in September 1940 by William Holland of the Institute of Pacific Relations, stating that any "secret message" to Institute member Philip Lilienthal in Tokyo might be sent in care of Herbert Norman at the Canadian Legation. What Holland seemingly had wanted to say was that any communications not meant for the attention of the Japanese branch of the Institute of Pacific Relations—Lilienthal's mailing address in Tokyo—were to be sent to Norman, in view of growing Japanese criticism of the Institute's excessively pro-Chinese attitude. Norman claimed that he had not known about Holland's letter until it was mentioned in the subcommittee's hearings, and that he naturally would never have agreed to its proposal.

He also thought that External Affairs might be embarrassed if he were once more involved in the subcommittee's questionable activities, despite Pearson's and the Department's complete support. Yet, he felt that neither Ottawa nor Washington could deflect its intentions, if it decided to press for a renewed investigation; as an afterthought, he mentioned that he had awakened the previous night thinking that to be innocent was not sufficient, adding that he had been both conscientious and very discreet in executing his ambassadorial mission. If the question again were to surface he would chuck it all and retire to the country. He characterized the congressional investigations and those who conducted them as "evil." His use of the word evil, according to Gordon, was interesting for he spoke it as if it were an "incarnate" object, something able to destroy life and the world.[6]

At 8:30 the following morning, April 2, Norman visited his Egyptian physician, Dr. Halim Doss. He stayed with him until 10:30, and again visited him that same afternoon between 3:00 and 5:30 p.m. He told the doctor the whole story of his relationship with the subcommittee, and "how he was *worried* about its further investigations."[7] Mentioning that he had discussed the matter with Arthur Kilgour, who had minimized the subcommittee's current activities, he felt that the FBI "contained some vicious elements who might not hesitate to frame him if they were able to do so." He spoke of Alger Hiss who had probably been "framed," and that his only mistake had been to deny that he knew Whittaker Chambers—a statement he could not retract.

It is true that the FBI, like any other security organization, should be kept on a tight leash, yet the thought that it would attempt to "frame" Norman is preposterous, just as his comments about Alger Hiss border on the absurd, even if they were, no doubt, shared at the time by many from the "Liberal Left." Hiss had been found guilty by twenty of the twenty-four jurors who had sat at both his trials. Despite the fact that he had been defended by America's best legal talent, and had invoked every appeal process the American federal system of law had to offer, all his appeals were rejected. Predictably, if Alger Hiss had been charged in Canada he would have been convicted under the draconian strictures of the Official Secrets Act, after facing a judiciary which was and still is, generally, far more conservative than its American counterpart.

Although Dr. Doss insisted that Norman was exaggerating the subcommittee's actions, noting that it had made no further comments, Norman pointed out that it was working behind closed doors. He then showed him about twelve pages of notes he had written. Some were on the embassy's blue air mail stationery and, according to Dr. Doss' disclosure, they resembled the text of a note found after Norman's suicide. The doctor understood, he later told Kilgour, that Norman had subsequently burned them.

Dr. Doss felt that his patient suffered from a "tremendous sense of guilt." He had, in fact, brought this to his attention. He correctly concluded that "he must have had a very strong religious upbringing." Norman had also maintained that "he had *never* been a communist but during his student days he had become very interested in communism because of its international aspects,"[8] casually observing, in this connection, that Soviet Russia had stood up to Nazi Germany. Kilgour later admitted to Ottawa that he had had a similar conversation with Norman, and that both he and Dr. Doss had assured him that there was no reason to take these prewar experiences so seriously, because many intelligent people had walked the same road. According to the doctor, Norman felt that he had "let the Canadian Government down because it previously had said that he had never been a communist but now he was afraid that a [sub]committee in Washington might show that he had *almost* been a communist."[9] The fear that obviously stalked him was that of public exposure.

The following day, April 3, Norman did not appear at the office, but he telephoned Kilgour to invite him to lunch and a chat, since they had not had an opportunity to talk to each other for several days. Since Kilgour had a prior engagement, he visited with him before lunch for approximately an hour. Kilgour thought he looked "quite weary," and Norman observed that the Washington investigation "had got him down." It was Kilgour's impression that he was unaware that Tsuru had testified, as he talked of the previous RCMP investigation and how tiring it had been. He repeated the assertion that the RCMP had been fed information by the FBI—no mention of MI5—recalling that during the Ottawa investigations he had been asked if he knew a certain Cambridge University economist. When he had said he did, it had taken several hours of questioning to satisfy the RCMP. Available documentary evidence shows that no questioning took place on the subject. Norman also claimed that John Foster Dulles had told him in Tokyo that the only thing Alger Hiss had done was not to cooperate with the FBI. Kilgour surmised that he might have "actually expected another prolonged inquiry." Indeed, "he mentioned the possibility of being recalled to Ottawa for investigation—the result of which might be that he was not properly cleared." Ultimately, the discussion led to the mutual decision that Norman should take an immediate holiday in Spain.

Since the Normans and Arthur Kilgour were planning to attend a Japanese movie that evening, Kilgour was invited for dinner. The proposed holiday was discussed before dinner, and an appropriate draft message to External Affairs on the subject was prepared. Kilgour was to review it the following morning, amend it if necessary and, after Norman's approval, dispatch it to Ottawa. After dinner they picked up two of the Normans' friends, and during the showing of the movie, the ambassador supplied some explanations about its contents. Entitled "Mask of Destiny," it dealt with the self-destruction of the leading character; although his fate had been decided, he was, nevertheless, unable to control the flow of events. During the movie and over drinks afterwards, Norman appeared to feel better, taking an active part in the conversation,[10] and even making arrangements to play croquet the following afternoon.[11]

It was not to be, for on the morning of April 4 he ended his life by jumping off the roof of an eight-storey apartment building. How much seeing the Japanese film the night before may have contributed toward the chemistry of his suicide is an imponderable, as his inspection of the chancery's roof had occurred several days before....

Mrs. Norman strongly denied that Herbert had ever discussed suicide either with her or with Dr. Doss. Indeed, in conversations with others he may have appeared depressed or uneasy, but had never spoken of taking his life. Mrs. Norman wanted this fact conveyed to Lester Pearson—which it was—and also to Prime Minister Louis St. Laurent. What Herbert had discussed with Dr. Doss, according to Mrs. Norman, were his vexations and disquiet over what had developed. She feared that anything said by Herbert's physician might be twisted and overstated.[12] Interestingly, Pearson never publicly discussed the information relayed to him by Mrs. Norman. To have spoken of it would have undercut the notion that Norman had been driven to his death solely by the activities of the Senate Subcommittee. Politically, it was wiser, even more advantageous, to ignore it and perpetuate the myth. America—specifically the Senate Subcommittee—would be the convenient whipping boy.

But what did Norman supposedly say before his death? According to the Senate Subcommittee report for 1957, the CIA had in its file an April dispatch from a highly reliable source in Cairo stating that on the night before he took his life, he had dined with a physician. He had informed him that he feared Prime Minister St. Laurent was not supporting him and that a Royal Commission of Inquiry would be established. If called to testify "he would have to implicate 60 to 70 Americans and Canadians and that he couldn't face up to it and that he was going to destroy himself."[13]

Before making a textual exegesis of this purported CIA dispatch it should be pointed out that the CIA never denied the existence of a dispatch resembling the text cited by the Senate Subcommittee. Moreover, no agency, no department of the American government, nor the White House have ever denied it. The Diefenbaker government subsequently refuted the existence of any record indicating that prior to Norman's suicide, the St. Laurent government had intended to establish a Royal Commission of Inquiry. The possibility that there may have been unofficial discussions within the government about such a commission was unfortunately never investigated.[14] Nevertheless, there was silence on the American side, especially by the CIA, which usually is quick to deny even the most far-fetched story that tangentially might concern it.

However, like any information conveyed through several sources, this CIA dispatch, assuming it exists and had not got its Egyptian events muddled, has obviously undergone some distortion. There is no evidence that Norman dined with any physician on the evening of April 3. He saw Kilgour before lunch and that evening he and his wife dined with him. Then, accompanied by friends, they went to see the Japanese movie. Apart from Norman's alleged observation that Prime Minister St. Laurent was not supporting him, the other comment credited to him in the purported conversation with a physician was about his fear that a "Royal Commission of Inquiry" would be struck and, if called as a witness, his testimony would implicate sixty to seventy Americans and Canadians. Supposing the intelligence and knowledge of the alleged physician with whom he was said to have dined were above average, that individual would have had to be very sophisticated to conjure up the phrase "Royal Commission of Inquiry." Without fear of contradiction, it therefore can be asserted that the nature of such a specialized government body would have been unknown to almost every American and, undoubtedly, to almost every Egyptian. In this instance, the words could only have been voiced by a Canadian or someone familiar with analogous British royal commissions. Only Norman himself could have made such a comment. In line with his remarks about St. Laurent, one can only conclude that the purported conversation had at least some basis in fact, and that some sort of conversation therefore may have taken place. Only a Royal Commission of Inquiry, with its draconian powers, could have posed questions and would have insisted on the kind of replies that no Senate Subcommittee would have been able to emulate because of lack of jurisdiction and in view of Norman's diplomatic immunity.

The reported conversation, undoubtedly, took place in Cairo between Norman and another individual. Whether he was a physician or someone else is unclear. We know that similar comments were made by him to Kilgour who then reported them to External Affairs: "he mentioned the possibility of being recalled to Ottawa for investigation—the result of which might be that he was not properly cleared."[15]

Ten years later a chronology of the events leading up to Norman's suicide was drafted. It seemingly included all the relevant telegrams sent to and received from Cairo. Nowhere is there a message, either from Louis St. Laurent or Lester Pearson, discussing such possibilities.[16]

The only message that we know came from Ottawa was Pearson's handwritten note, sent about a week before Norman's suicide.[17] He might have commented on St. Laurent's uneasiness or he may have made some remarks which, though innocent, may have sufficed to unnerve Norman.

Norman's scribbled suicide notes are so enigmatic that they offer no clear picture of why he actually took his own life. The prudent and reasonable person is placed in the unenviable position of having to weigh and judge jottings made only minutes before his self-destruction, in light of what we now know of his past record. These notes, therefore, must be dissected with the greatest of care.

In the longest, intended for External Affairs, he speaks about being "overwhelmed" by his "consciousness of sin." He asks for God's forgiveness and goes on to say that time and access to the record would show to anyone "impartial" that he was "innocent" of the main allegation, namely, of having conspired or acted against the security of Canada or that of any other state. Claiming never to have violated the secrecy oath as a member of External Affairs, he states that he felt the issue would be obfuscated and twisted. He was exhausted by all of it and, though innocent, was faced by formidable forces. He thought it was better to end it all now than to face further calumny. He then begs for his family's forgiveness.

External Affairs would naturally be upset by the implications of his suicide, the scribbled note continues, but he trusts that an impartial and thorough study would support his "innocence." At this very moment, and because he liked his work in External Affairs, he would, with alacrity, confess to any security breach he may have made. He observes that his weakness has been "illusion," and his chief flaw "naïveté." It had been naive of him to think that it was sufficient to be innocent of any act that contravened security. External Affairs, he contends, was aware of his "error," but he had committed no crime. He concludes the note by stating that he was unworthy of his wife, whose loyalty had sustained him throughout trials and disappointments.[18]

Then there is the note to his brother Howard, a man who had never lost his belief in Christianity and who, over the years, had been at odds with Herbert about his sequential views of life.[19] Although Norman never specifically mentions the Senate Subcommittee by name, he says that he had been "overwhelmed by circumstances and had lived under illusions too long." Stating that Christianity was the only true road, he asks for Howard's forgiveness because things were not as black as they appeared, though, God knows, they were bad enough.

For what should Howard have forgiven him? Was it for straying from the true Christian path or for planning to take his own life? The answer is unclear. Herbert again claims that he had never betrayed his oath of secrecy, observing that guilt by association had begun to crush him. He was praying to God for forgiveness if it was not too late ... Yet, why should guilt by association have necessitated God's forgiveness?

In a second note to his brother and sister-in-law, he again pleads innocence, and once more dwells on his own weak Christianity and how it had, nevertheless, helped to sustain him during the previous days.[20]

The fourth note is addressed to his wife. In it he contends that he could no longer live with himself and was unfit to live at all. The short note concludes that he lacked hope of meriting any sympathy.

That Herbert Norman was a sensitive and civilized human being who cared for his fellowmen is attested to in the fifth note addressed to the Swedish minister; it is the shortest and most macabre. He begs forgiveness for choosing his apartment building as the place from which to take the fatal plunge, explaining that it was the only one which would allow him to avoid endangering someone below.[21]

At this point it might be appropriate to examine the qualities potential candidates had to have in the 1930s after having been talent-spotted for recruitment by the Communist Party and the Russian intelligence services. The types of persons in whom they were interested were the well-meaning and those who were moved by idealism. The 1946 Royal Commission described them as people who had "a burning desire to reform and improve Canadian society according to their lights." If properly groomed and cultivated through "study groups" and the appropriate literature, such as the periodical *New Masses,* to which Norman had subscribed, they would gradually develop what the Royal Commission called "a sense of divided loyalties" or, in extreme cases, "a transferred loyalty." This process was assisted by whatever "sense of internationalism" would have motivated the potential recruit. He was encouraged to develop feelings of loyalty toward an "international ideal," rather than to any particular foreign state. "This subjective internationalism" was then linked through courses of indoctrination and by appropriate Russian propaganda "with the current conception of the national interests" of Soviet Russia and "the current doctrines and policies of Communist Parties throughout the world."[22]

As we have seen, Norman possessed all the right qualities, as even at the bitter end he made sure that no one else suffered. He also had succumbed, for various reasons—some peculiarly Canadian—to the ideological siren of secular optimism and human perfectibility. This probably was the "sin" to which he alluded in his suicide note to External Affairs. Unlike his brother Howard, he had believed in a false god for so long that that sin was partly redeemed by discovering—at the very end—the staying power of his weak Christianity. This may also, at least partially, explain why the Senate Subcommittee was not specifically mentioned in the notes, and was perhaps only hinted at in the remark that he faced formidable forces, although he was innocent. Was this omission due to his perception that the subcommittee was less at fault than he himself because of his prior activities?

He claims to have lived under an illusion and that he had shown naïveté, that he could not live with himself, was unfit to live, and lacked any hope of meriting sympathy. He says he is innocent of having violated Canada's security and his oath of secrecy, yet his silence about any association with the Communist Party is deafening. Surely, this would have been the time to categorically deny that he was or had ever been a member. He did not do so. Why? Because that part of the *mea culpa* curtain had to be kept tightly drawn. Knowing as we do that he was or had been a member, what are we to make of his denials of all the allegations made against him? Because, to admit even the remotest association with communist elements quickly would have placed in doubt all his other statements.

Norman believed in the great march of history which is part and parcel of communist scripture. No matter what he did, no matter how illegal it was, it could be justified ideologically and psychologically. The laws of communism's dialectical materialism were higher than those governing Canada, higher than any secrecy oath, and greater than thoughts of national security. Moreover, one should differentiate, as Norman had not done, between conveying to unauthorized individuals "secret information" covered by the secrecy oath and "privy information" not covered by that oath. If secret and/or privy material was conveyed by Norman to Moscow during the war, when Canada and Soviet Russia were allied, he could have rationalized that Canada's security was not being compromised. However, even if he had passed nothing that was either secret or privy, his denials would not have covered his actions as an agent of disinformation and/or of influence. As pointed out in Brian Crozier's book *Strategy for Survival,* in the United Kingdom and in some other Western states as well—and that would include Canada—"*it is not a punishable offence to be a Soviet agent of influence, even a conscious and paid one.*"[23] (Italics in the original.)

The question of whether or not Norman was an agent of influence must have bothered the mandarins at External Affairs because, almost two weeks after he had committed suicide, someone in its Middle East Division sent a report to Glazebrook's Defense Liaison II, stating that a selection of Norman's telegraphic reports on political matters had been examined and that a cursory check had been made of his Cairo dispatches. Their quality was considered "outstanding," and no trace had been found that showed any inclination on Norman's part "to sympathize with Communist ideology or practice." On the contrary, in contact with Egyptians and other Arabs, it appeared that he had gone to some trouble to warn them of the dangers which Russian penetration would, in the end, pose to their governments and the peoples of the Middle East. Norman consciously seemed to have developed wide-ranging sources among Egyptians, Arabs, and the diplomatic corps in Cairo, and he had close and friendly relations with the Indian ambassador. This, the report maintains, illustrated that he had not hesitated to pursue any "useful channel," even though he "must have realized that evidence of contact with and dependence on 'neutralist' sources increased his personal vulnerability to irresponsible charges." Of the materials examined only three telegrams had been dispatched after March 14, when the Senate Subcommittee released Emmerson's executive session testimony.[24]

The Middle East Division's analysis is somewhat naive. No agent of influence would have been foolish enough to reveal anything in a telegram or dispatch. Of value to his true masters would have been the type of advice he might have tendered to his government and perhaps to others who could have been influenced by it. What Norman supposedly had said to Egyptians and other Arabs is virtually non-verifiable. Therefore, the Middle East Division's contribution would have been far more significant if his advice to Ottawa on how to handle Middle East events had been juxtaposed with Russian objectives in the region, particularly in Egypt.

Thus, Norman's deep commitment to the cause may help explain his inability to acknowledge the enormity of the evil that had stalked the Russian landscape, especially during the Stalin era and, subsequently, other regions of the world.

One writer sympathetic to Herbert Norman said about him in 1977 that his "outright naivetè" was "linked to his lack of any strong sense of evil."[25] Three years earlier, almost the same comments were made many miles south of the 49th parallel by a stepson about his stepfather, who he considered to have been a "severely repressed and morally rigid person." The stepson recalled that he was "a man capable of inflicting great suffering on himself in order to protect others at all costs." Moreover, until his stepfather's conviction and imprisonment, the stepson asserted he " 'had no sense of evil.' " That man was Alger Hiss.[26] The same characteristics were also noted in the longtime Canadian KGB agent Hugh Hambleton, who was convicted in Great Britain under the Official Secrets Act. He, too, never seemed to have been "interested, and never would be, in making any moral judgement of the Soviet regime."[27]

This is not the time to examine the traits which appear to run like threads through the psyches of many who have served the Russian behemoth; let others who follow delve into the matter. If they wish to do so, they might consider the words of the Israeli novelist Amos Oz who said, " ' Whoever ignores varying degrees of evil is bound to become a servant of evil.' "[28]

What exactly were the "overwhelming circumstances" that had decided Herbert Norman to take his own life? Unexpectedly, after a long silence, the Senate Subcommittee on Internal Security again became interested in him, especially after Emmerson's testimony. Some days later, Patrick Walsh attempted to contact Pearson to present a brief dealing with Norman's communist background.[29] Is it possible that Walsh's overtures were mentioned in Pearson's handwritten note to him? Then Tsuru testified before the subcommittee, although Norman apparently was not aware of it. This is possible but not probable, considering the circles in which he moved in Cairo. Even if we discount his purported comments about the establishment of a Royal Commission of Inquiry, he had, after all, mentioned to Kilgour "the possibility of being recalled to Ottawa for investigation."

Although Arnold Heeney had been made Canadian Ambassador to Washington by this time, Pearson was still in harness directing External Affairs, and there were others in positions of influence who, in the past, had been sympathetic to Norman's plight. The relative immunity he had enjoyed in the past would probably continue into the future, as long as the Senate Subcommittee desisted from delving into his background and activities. Was it lining up a new surprise witness? Testimony by Jaffe would be damaging in the extreme. Norman undoubtedly knew that he had broken with the American Communist Party and the extreme Left in the late 1940s. Was someone else being groomed to testify against him? Who else was there, and what new evidence might surface, even without the subcommittee's initiatives? Other information it might uncover could again lead to interrogations by Messrs. Guernsey, McClellan, and Glazebrook. That had to be avoided at all costs.

As in Edgar Allan Poe's classic, *The Pit and the Pendulum,* Norman had escaped several brushes with the pit of destruction. But like on the narrator of Poe's tale of horror, the "walls" were closing in and forcing him inexorably toward the pit. The walls, in this case, were the mounting testimony against him and the fear of possible further revelations concerning his past activities, some of them suspicious. In line with information supplied by the RCMP, the FBI, and MI5, they might have led to a fuller and more vigorous interrogation than the one he had experienced in 1952. Buttressed by a full RCMP field investigation, the façade he had so carefully and cleverly constructed over the years would collapse. Aware of this distinct possibility and dreading, no doubt, that his unmasking would expose others, including perhaps influential friends, Norman decided to commit suicide. Of all the bleak options he may have had, taking his own life must have appeared the least objectionable. No doubt, he was well aware of E. M. Forster's 1930s credo, mouthed by Anthony Blunt and dear to the heart of the Left, "that betraying one's friend was worse than betraying one's country."[30]

Notes

1. See Chapter 7, p. 107.
2. Unless cited otherwise, what follows is based on a report by Norman's deputy Arthur Kilgour, about the events in Cairo before and after Norman's suicide. Kilgour to Léger, April 10, 1957, Norman File, RCMP (CSIS) Papers. Kilgour's subsequent version of these days is slightly inaccurate, based as it was on memory. Arthur Kilgour, "On Remembering Herbert Norman," in Roger W. Bowen (ed.), *E. H. Norman: His Life and Scholarship* (Toronto: University of Toronto Press, 1984), p. 77. See also Charles Taylor, *Six Journeys: A Canadian Pattern* (Toronto: Anansi, 1977), p. 147. As to the affidavit, see E[gerton] H[erbert] N[orman] to Glazebrook, March 12, 1952, and the attached documents especially the affidavit, Norman File, RCMP (CSIS) Papers.
3. See Chapter 4, p. 41.
4. Italics added. Kilgour to Léger, April 10, 1957, Norman File, RCMP (CSIS) Papers.
5. Kilgour to Léger, April 10, 1957, Norman File, RCMP CSIS Papers.
6. King Gordon to [Pearson], April 7, 1957, Vol. 44, Pearson Papers, MG 26, N1, PAC. On Holland's letter, see Hearings, *Institute of Pacific Relations,* Part 1 (July 25, 26, 31, August 2 and 7, 1951), pp. 320–321, and *ibid.,* Part 14 (May 2, June 20, 1952), pp. 5030–5031.
7. Italics added.
8. Italics added.
9. Italics in the original.
10. Kilgour to Léger, April 10, 1957, Norman File, RCMP (CSIS) Papers.
11. Taylor, p. 147.

12. Holmes to Pearson, July 18, 1957, Vol. 44, Pearson Papers, MG 26. N1, PAC.

13. Committee on the Judiciary, *Internal Security Annual Report for 1957,* p. 101 fn.

14. Canada, Parliament, House of Commons, *Debates, Official Report,* 24th Parliament, 1st Session, Vol. I (May 15-16, 1958) (Ottawa: Queen's Printer, 1958), pp. 92, 137–138.

15. This chapter, p. 592.

16. Chronology—Part II, February 23, 1967, Norman File, External Affairs Papers.

17. See Chapter 7, pp. 111–112.

18. Kilgour to External Affairs, No. 260, April 6, 1957, Norman File, External Affairs Papers.

19. H[oward] Norman to Pearson, April 13, 1957, Vol. 44, Pearson Papers, MG 26, N1, PAC.

20. Taylor, p. 149.

21. Kilgour to External Affairs, No. 259, April 6, 1957, Norman File, RCMP (CSIS) Papers.

22. Report of the 1946 Royal Commission on Espionage in Canada, pp. 72–73. On the *New Masses,* see Chapter 4, p. 36.

23. Italics in the original. Brian Crozier, *Strategy of Survival* (New Rochelle, New York: Arlington House, 1978), p. 136.

24. Middle East Division to D[efense] L[iaison] II, April 17, 1957, Norman File, External Affairs Papers.

25. Taylor, p. 119.

26. Allen Weinstein, *Perjury: the Hiss-Chambers Case* (New York: Knopf, 1978), pp. 526–527.

27. Leo Heaps, *Hugh Hambleton, Spy. Thirty Years with the KGB* (Toronto: Methuen, 1983), p. 53.

28. *The New York Times,* January 16, 1986, p. 17.

29. See Chapter 7, p. 111.

30. Andrew Boyle, *The Fourth Man* (New York: The Dial Press/James Wade, 1979), p. 384.

CHAPTER

14 MULTI-CULTURALISM

Initial encounters between native peoples and the European newcomer on the eastern seaboard first raised the issue of the place of the immigrant in North America. Subsequent waves of settlers renewed the quandary at regular intervals, not only for the native people but also for European transplants who embraced the continent as their own. While the geographic concentration of the French in Canada permitted them to survive the British and Loyalist invasions of the late eighteenth century, inter-cultural relationships were uneasy at best. In 1867 a French-English rapprochement resulted in Confederation and the notion that their often separate worlds would continue. For much of the next century, despite the arrival of millions of immigrants from diverse regions, it was assumed that the newcomers would integrate into the host society, especially the increasingly dominant Anglo-Canadian world. To be sure, in the twentieth century the term "mosaic" was popularized as a recognition of the growing diversity of Canada's population and a rejection of the American "melting pot" ideology. But while the notion of a "mosaic" had some validity, often in practice the idea had more form than substance, for as late as 1947 Prime Minister William Lyon Mackenzie King declared: "The people of Canada do not wish to make a fundamental alteration in the character of their population through mass immigration."

Despite that government policy, dramatic increases in immigration in the 1950s and 1960s led to ethnic diversification on an unprecedented scale. Officially the English-French dominance went unchallenged, although the final Report of the Royal Commission on Bilingualism and Biculturalism 1965 did enunciate a vision of Canada as an "equal partnership between the two founding races, taking into account the contribution made by other ethnic groups to the cultural enrichment of Canada." Perhaps the most unexpected result of the B and B Commission was the increased visibility of those "other ethnic groups" and their demands for a place at the national table. In 1971, a mere twenty-four years after King's policy statement, those pressures led Prime Minister Pierre Elliot Trudeau to announce: "A policy of multiculturalism within a bilingual framework commends itself to the Government as the most suitable means of assuring the cultural freedom of Canadians." This in turn led to the declaration that Canada was "officially" a multicultural nation and the appointment of a Minister of State responsible for Multiculturalism.

In general, academics have not been kind either to the concept of multiculturalism or to its implementation in Canada. The word itself is subject to a multitude of interpretations, and people choose the one that suits the purpose of the day or time. Supporters and critics also usually subscribe to one or more "myths" as justification for their respective positions. Various aspects of those myths are explored by the two excerpts reprinted in this chapter. In the first,'Ethnic Identity,' Jean Burnet and Howard Palmer sympathetically examine the changing character and composition of ethnic self-identification and its meaning for Canada. The unit concludes on a controversial note, with an anti-multiculturalism statement by writer Neil Bissoondath, excerpted from his *Selling Illusions: The Cult of Multiculturalism in Canada.*

Suggestions for Further Reading

Bibby, Reginald W., *Mosaic Madness: The Poverty and Potential of Life in Canada.* Toronto: Stoddart, 1990.

Bissoondath, Neil, *Selling Illusions: The Cult of Multiculturalism in Canada.* Toronto: Viking, 1994.

Burnet, Jean, "Myths and Multiculturalism,"*Canadian Journal of Education* 4,4 (1979), 43–58.

———, *Multiculturalism in Canada.* Ottawa: Department of the Secretary of State, 1988.

Careless, J.M.S., "'Limited Identities' in Canada," *Canadian Historical Review,* L, No. 1 (March 1969), 1–10.

———., "Limited Identities—Ten Years Later," *Manitoba History* (Spring, 1976), 3–9.

Fleras, Augie, and Jean L. Elliott, *Multiculturalism in Canada: The Challenge of Diversity.* Scarborough: Nelson, 1992.

Kallen, Evelyn, "Multiculturalism: Ideology, Policy and Reality," *Journal of Canadian Studies,* 17, 1, 1982.

Pal, Leslie A., *Interests of State: The Politics of Language, Multiculturalism and Feminism in Canada.* Montreal: McGill-Queen's Press, 1993.

Palmer, Howard, ed., *Immigration and the Rise of Multiculturalism.* Vancouver: Copp Clark, 1975.

Satzewich, Victor N., *Deconstructing a Nation: Immigration, Multiculturalism and Racism in 90s Canada.* Halifax: Fernwood Publishing, 1992.

ETHNIC IDENTITY

Jean Burnet with Howard Palmer

In Canada it is common to reply to the question "Who are you?" in ethnic terms. Immigrants in the past were sometimes not aware of an ethnic identity when they arrived, seeing themselves only as coming from a village or at most a province, or as adherents of a particular religion. They became ethnically conscious as they were thrust into association with others who shared their language and culture or their physical traits or both, and were accorded a common label and common treatment. But they usually knew of some people from whom they sharply distinguished themselves. More recently, with the salience of ethnicity throughout the world and with the sophistication of many immigrants, people have had an ethnic identity on arrival, and an attitude toward it, either as a burden to be cast off or as a treasure to be passed on to their children. With the passage of time and of generations, both the content and the meaning of immigrants' ethnic identities change. Whether they continue to consider themselves in the same way or begin to couple the word "Canadian" with the old label, or to call themselves simply "Canadian," the ethnic aspect of their selves and their lives is transformed. Their children and their children's children have a different sense of ethnic identity and manifest it in different ways.

The sense of ethnic identity is difficult to gauge. It is essentially subjective or internal, but it has external aspects that are frequently used as indices. It is for the external aspects that governmental aid is sought and recently has been frequently obtained. The relationship between the external and internal aspects of identity is extremely complex: the feelings of ethnic identity of individuals may or may not be in line with objective criteria defining ethnicity.

For white ethnic groups, among the most conspicuous external manifestations have been language, folklore, cuisine, and sports. Ancestral languages, however important or unimportant in the past, have recently been given primacy as ethnic symbols because of the salience of language in industrial and post-industrial societies and, in particular, the salience of language in Canada since it became officially bilingual in 1969. Languages have been considered to be inseparable from cultures, and linguistic transfer has been deemed to be loss of language and culture. Languages have played a crucial role in many of the white ethnic groups as vehicles for other elements of culture. They have served as means of unifying the groups: people who have spoken regional dialects have, through learning the standard version of their language, come not only to enlarge the number of those recognized as their ethnic fellows but also to identify with linguistically dependent aspects of the high culture of their homeland. Languages have been boundary markers, for unless they are world languages they are exclusive to the group.

From *"Coming Canadians": An Introduction to a History of Canada's Peoples* (Toronto: McClelland and Stewart, 1988), 212–222. Reproduced with the permission of the Minister of Supply and Services Canada, 1995.

The descendants of peasant immigrants with high rates of illiteracy, unaccustomed to give importance to linguistic matters, have become keenly interested in linguistic retention. Ukrainians are perhaps exceptional because of the perceived threat to their language in their homeland: their concern about their language in the schools and in the media has been unremitting. The abolition of bilingual schools in Manitoba and the punishment of children for speaking Ukrainian in Prairie schools have played a prominent part in the litany of grievances of Ukrainians against Canadian governments and society. The recent introduction of heritage languages into the curricula of the public schools and the introduction of bilingual Ukrainian-English education in the city of Edmonton have been viewed as triumphs.

Not only schools but families and churches have been crucial to the transmission of ancestral languages. The term "mother tongue" is often interpreted as indicative of the role of the family: the mother, because of her contact with the young child, is seen as having the duty to pass on the ancestral tongue. In an immigrant group, the myriad other duties devolving on the mother hamper her endeavours in regard to language teaching. One of the results of the mother's role in some groups, such as the Armenian and the Jewish, is that women have been allowed to teach language classes while being barred from many other occupations outside the home. In settled communities the old also play a role in transmitting language and culture, as storytellers to the young, but the absence of grandparents is another obstacle to the teaching of the ancestral language in many immigrant households.

The church has frequently regarded its well-being as tied to the traditional language. Sometimes this language is not in everyday use: through centuries, Hebrew was the language of Judaism, too holy for daily use, until it became the language of Israel; in some sects high German was the language of the religious texts and services while low German was used in other aspects of life; until the 1960s Latin was employed in many Catholic religious rituals. But churches have been among the most dedicated sponsors of language classes for children, and priests and pastors have been among the teachers of such classes.

However cherished the mother tongue is, among first-generation immigrants comprehension of one of the country's official languages and fluency in speaking it have been crucial for economic and social adjustment. Spokespeople for immigrants have been much concerned about opportunities to acquire knowledge of the official languages. They have pointed out that workers in segregated occupations and women in the home have often lacked such opportunities. It has been rare, though not unknown, that people have protested that the teaching of English and French has infringed on the rights of another language in Canada.

Knowledge of ancestral languages declines sharply from generation to generation. Research has shown that fluency in non-official languages is virtually confined to first-generation immigrants, and that in the third and succeeding generations the majority have no knowledge at all of the ancestral tongue. On the other hand, even in the third generation most people profess to be in favour of the retention of ancestral languages by their children. The chief reason all generations give for favouring retention is, however, not the keeping up of customs or traditions, nor communication with other members of one's ethnic group. Rather, it is the economic and cultural advantage of knowing more than one language.[1]

Linguistic transfer does not necessarily mean a renunciation of ethnic identity. The Canadian-born may claim the right to select their own symbols of identity and resist pressure from their elders to give primacy to language. How long and how intensely they retain identification with their ancestral group once they have adopted another language may vary greatly from group to group, but the linguistic versatility of Jews and the ethnic retention in spite of linguistic transfer of Scots and Irish indicate that language is not always essential.

One of the ways other than language that members of ethnic groups have had of displaying their ethnic identity has been by maintaining their folkloric heritage and transmitting it from one generation to another. Few belonged wholly to a folk culture or society before coming to Canada: even many eastern Europeans who came out during the Sifton era had been migrant labourers to industrial cities or had had contact with migrant labourers and thus with city ways. They often learned folk arts in Canada, as symbols of their heritage, rather than having retained them. So, among South Asians, music and folk dance have become important community phenomena; among Japanese, Kabuki dance, flower arranging, and paper folding are taught and practised; Ukrainians have bandura orchestras and teach embroidery and the painting of Easter eggs. The intellectuals of the group often profess to scorn "red boots multiculturalism" and "dancing in church basements" as trivial or frivolous. Nonetheless, folklore has proved to be extremely persistent.

Several explanations can be given for this persistence. Folklore has great symbolic value:

> Generally, the folklore symbolizes an era in which the people, now in danger and in too much contact with others, were alone and showed their traditional culture in a more pure form. The heroes of lore are thought to have possessed the true virtues, the virtues that distinguish this people from others. The true German of folklore was unspoiled by foreign influences, whether Roman or Jewish. He was set up as a model for the new, restored, true German. Something like this is happening in the Zionist movement, too, where a hardy, sometimes belligerent, athletic Jewish youth is set up both as the original and as the true model for the future.[2]

Folklore is also eminently suited to display before those who do not belong to the ethnic group. Ethnic dancing and instrumental music in particular have become the stock in trade of ethnic or multicultural festivals. A study sponsored by the Multicultural Directorate of the Department of the Secretary of State in 1982 found that in a representative sample of approximately 6,000 folkloric performing arts groups from across Canada, most performances, while they mark special occasions or holidays of the group's own ethnic community, are for general audiences rather than the ethnic community only, and substantial numbers of performances are also for other people's festivals or galas and for special Canadian events and national days.[3]

Certain forms of folklore, such as music, dance, and theatre, have appeal to the young. The Multiculturalism Directorate's study indicated that passing the culture on to children and youth ranked high among reasons for participating in the performing arts. It also showed that in fact the performers tended to be concentrated among those under thirty-five years old. The folkloric performing arts thus are a means of transmitting some of the cultural symbols of the group to new generations so that social networks are established on an ethnic basis and chances of endogamous marriage are increased.

That the folklore thus transmitted is symbolic rather than part of a functioning folk culture is shown by periodic attempts to "purify" it or "make it more authentic." A functioning culture changes and adapts. Weeding out Canadian variants in favour of old country forms indicates that the folklore reflects only a museum culture.

One frequent type of change not resisted is the transmutation of elements of folklore into "high culture." Many immigrants have not been familiar with the high culture of their homeland: to southern Italian peasants, for example, Leonardo da Vinci, Michelangelo, Dante, and Verdi have meant little. But they and their children have learned of the homage the world pays to such immortals and have come to take pride in them. Immigrant and native-born artists in various fields who contribute to high culture have been cherished by their ethnic groups, and have on occasion incorporated the folk symbols of those groups into their work. The symbols have thus become part of a more universal heritage.

The same might be said for ethnic foods, whether everyday dishes or *haute cuisine*. They also have become symbolic and, likewise, are suited to sharing and to becoming part of wider Canadian custom. In Canada in the 1980s ethnic bakeries, food stores, and restaurants multiply and flourish. Members of many ethnic groups have not been able to maintain their dietary patterns in their homes for lack of ingredients or lack of time for preparation. They have had to limit their ethnic dishes to ceremonial occasions, or to indulge in them only in restaurants. There the general public shares in the dishes, and the dishes are modified to meet the more general tastes.

Foods, ways of cooking and serving them, and meals have been important experiences in the lives of all immigrants. Food, of course, is intimately related to the family. Fasting and feasting are also religious rituals of great importance. The familial and religious connotations of ceremonial meals, such as Christmas and Easter dinners, and of fasting, in Judaism and Islam as well as Christianity, result in memories of eating and drinking and fasting as part of a social group being among the most poignant recollections of childhood.

Ethnic entrepreneurs have taken advantage of the situation to establish businesses. Markets serving a particular ethnic group or groups from a particular region; bakeries; butchers at which the religious prescriptions of a group and the customs concerning kinds and cuts of meats and seasoning of sausages can be maintained; fishmongers; restaurants—all these have contributed to the rise of businessmen in the occupational and income structure. Bread was a staple for many European peoples and came to be endowed with rich cultural and religious symbolism; hence, bakeries have sprung up in most immigrant areas. In Toronto, for example, by 1912 there were ten small Jewish bakeries producing bread and rolls in the Ward, the area bounded by Yonge, University, Queen, and Dundas. In the 1920s, as the community spread out, so did the bakeries; they began also to serve non-Jewish immigrants from eastern Europe. In the 1930s the dispersion continued, the bakeries began to show some specialization along class lines, a variety of cakes and pastries began to be offered, and the clientele was extended beyond Jewish and eastern European immigrants to include Canadians of all origins. The war accelerated and accentuated these trends, and the 1940s and 1950s were a time of prosperity. They also brought competition, as more recent arrivals began to set up their own small family-run bakeries.

The Estonians were among those who quickly saw that the influx of continental European immigrants offered an opportunity to suppliers of European-type breads. A number of them established small bakeries in Toronto and Hamilton, and some of the bakeries soon grew into sizeable enterprises. In the 1960s many new German and Italian bakeries were established, and these offered competition to the Estonian businesses; in the 1970s all the Estonian bakers retired except one.[4] Bakers often did not pass their businesses on to their children: in both the Jewish and the Estonian groups the children of bakers, though they worked in the shops in their youth, tended to go on to higher education and to enter professions.

Ethnic restaurants have ranged from "greasy spoons" to luxurious dining places. At one extreme are cafés and grills in which hamburgers, hotdogs, and sandwiches are served to the public but special soups and stews and sausages are prepared for the owner's family and acquaintances; at the other extreme are restaurants in expensive locations that advertise their exotic character in their service, menu, décor, and prices. In all cases the dishes on the menu have been modified, not simply by the unavailability of ingredients (in the 1970s and 1980s, transportation and refrigeration have made most foodstuffs accessible everywhere), but by the necessity of appealing to the tastes of the public as well as those of the appropriate ethnic group.

The Chinese were early in making the restaurant business an ethnic specialty. For them, at the turn of the century, it was an alternative to the laundry business; it required somewhat greater initial outlay than a laundry but offered a larger return. As the Chinese spread eastward from British Columbia they set up restaurants in small towns, where sometimes the restaurateur was the only Chinese, and in large cities. Usually they were inexpensive eating places serving Western-style foods, and their owners had to fight the discrimination visited upon Asians. For example, by-laws restricted them to certain areas and laws made it illegal for white women to work in Chinese restaurants. But they prospered nonetheless, and restaurants in Chinatowns serving Chinese-style food in the 1930s and 1940s began to enjoy a vogue that has continued to the present. Nowadays, not simply Chinese cookery but styles of cooking from various provinces of China are offered.

Macedonians also have made of restaurant-keeping something of an ethnic specialty in the Toronto area, where they have concentrated. It is said that during World War I a quarrel broke out between Canadian soldiers and a Greek restaurant owner, which led the soldiers to wreck a number of Greek-owned restaurants. After this incident many Greeks sold their restaurants, and large numbers of Macedonians who had been working in the restaurants bought them. A study of Macedonian restaurants in Toronto in the 1970s, while unable to establish the exact number of Macedonian-owned restaurants, refers to estimates ranging from 600 to two-thirds of all restaurants in Toronto.[5]

Before World War II, eating in restaurants was not a major aspect of Canadian life. With urbanization and industrialization, eating outside the home has become much more general. The burgeoning of ethnic restaurants in all large cities has led to emphasis on food as one of the prime areas of ethnic differentiation. French, Italian, Japanese, Korean, Vietnamese, Moroccan, and many other types of restaurants have come to enjoy great popularity. Sometimes a restaurant offers more than one ethnic cuisine, Chinese and Middle Eastern, for example, or Ukrainian, Polish, and German.

Although they are less often singled out as expressions of group identity than folklore or cuisine, sports and athletics have been important parts of the tradition of many ethnic groups and have been transplanted to Canada by early arrivals. Ethnic sports associations and athletic achievements for a long time attracted little notice because they lay outside the North American mainstream. Only a few outstanding individuals of non-British origin, such as Bobbie Rosenfeld, a Russian-born Jewish athlete whose many achievements included winning a silver medal at the 1928 Olympics, became household names. But sports were important within ethnic communities as means of holding the loyalty of the young, particularly the young men. Churches often recognized the role of sports and offered the use of their premises for gymnastics, or sponsored basketball, baseball, and hockey teams. Political movements also saw the utility of sports, and a workers' sports movement thrived in the 1920s and 1930s among Canadian Communists.[6]

Since World War II, the people who have emigrated from every corner of the earth have brought their sports traditions with them. Finns, Czechs, and Estonians have brought modern and rhythmic gymnastics, for example, the

West Indians have revivified cricket, originally brought to Canada by upper-class Britishers, and the East Asians have made karate and tai chi popular. Above all, soccer has won a place as a Canadian sport, not so well publicized and patronized as hockey, baseball, and football, perhaps, but taught in the schools and played in leagues at a number of levels. Harney describes the ethnic aspect of soccer in the Toronto region in the 1970s:

> ... in the Toronto and District Soccer League in the early 1970s, more than three-quarters of the seventy-eight teams had ethnic emblems, colours, and/or specifically national associations in their names. Among the teams were Panhellenic, First Portuguese, Croatia, Serbia White Eagle, Toronto Falcons, Hungaria and Heidelberg. Rivalries were along ethnic and sub-ethnic lines, and although sports should be either a substitute for or a mock and harmless form of warfare between nations, the National Soccer League had to stop its season prematurely in 1974 because of violence among players and fans of competing South Slav teams.[7]

In addition to supporting Canadian teams emblematic of their ethnic group, through television people are able to follow the soccer exploits of teams in their homelands. Italy's 1982 soccer victory in the World Cup occasioned an outburst of joy in the Italian community of Toronto, the largest in Canada, that has become legendary. It has been estimated that half a million people assembled on the streets to celebrate the victory.

However, sports and athletics are not simply expressions of group identity. Teams bearing ethnic designations have often selected players in terms of ability rather than ethnicity, so that matches that appear to be inter-ethnic actually pit polyethnic teams against one another. Similarly, in professional team sports, individuals of outstanding ability have been sources of pride for their ethnic group, but at the same time those individuals have been subject to de-ethnicization or ethnic transfer.

Most permanent external symbols of ethnic identity are physical traits. A person can change his or her behaviour, including linguistic behaviour; he or she cannot change skin colour, hair form, or other physical characteristics except by procedures that are often painful and costly. Thus it has been possible to single out members of the visible minorities for discrimination. Their numbers in the country were for long kept low by immigration regulations, and those who were admitted were denied full participation in Canadian society. Blacks, South Asians, Chinese, and Japanese developed their own communal structures and retained some of their distinctive behaviour patterns. They were given little opportunity to think of themselves as Canadians. Black Canadians whose ancestors came to Canada in the seventeenth and eighteenth centuries and Chinese, Japanese, and South Asian Canadians whose grandfathers or great-grandfathers immigrated in the late nineteenth century and early twentieth centuries complain of being asked where they came from.

However, visibility is not clear-cut. Sensitivity to physical differences and knowledge of the appearance of members of different ethnic groups vary. Some ethnic groups are considered at times to be and at other times not to be visibly distinguishable from the bulk of the population.[8] Individual members of some groups can "pass" as members of the dominant white groups. Further, intermarriage can decrease physical differences from the rest of the population: the high rates of intermarriage among Japanese Canadians have led to fears that, without renewal of immigration, they might disappear as a visible group. In addition, it is possible that in time the conception of a Canadian may be broadened and redefined so that black and Asian Canadians are not as frequently asked where they come from, as they now tend to be. As their numbers and their social and economic status increase they may become increasingly recognized as Canadians.

Ethnic self-identification is usually examined in terms of the survival of ethnic groups, and change of ethnic identity is seen as loss. It can instead be seen as transfer. In most cases, to cease to regard oneself as Polish or Greek or Danish is to begin to regard oneself as Canadian, or as both Canadian and a member of an ethnic group. In some cases, however, individuals may lose one identity without acquiring another: "I don't know what I am" is a complaint of some second-generation immigrants.

Efforts to probe the internal aspects of identity have usually centred on the question, "To what ethnic group do you feel you belong?" In a study of ancestral languages carried out in 1973, which included no one of British or French ethnic origin, people were asked how they usually thought of themselves and were given four options, ranging from an ethnic label to Canadian. In a sample, two-thirds of which was composed of immigrants and almost 20 per cent of which was composed of people who had been in Canada less than ten years, "17.3 per cent identified themselves with an ethnic label ('Chinese,' 'Dutch,' and so on), 44.5 per cent identified themselves with a dual label ('Chinese-Canadian', or 'Canadian of Chinese origin,' and so on), and the remaining 35.4 per cent identified themselves simply as 'Canadians.'"[9]

A more recent study, conducted in Metropolitan Toronto between 1977 and 1979, used a sample of men and women between the ages of eighteen and sixty-five who were in the labour force or were students. It employed an Ethnic Identity Index, based on "(1) the respondents' self-definition in terms of the hyphenated or unhyphenated ethnic or Canadian label, (2) the importance the respondents place on their ethnicity, (3) the respondents' perception of closeness of one's ethnic ties." The range of index scores was from 3, indicating high ethnic identity, to 8, indicating low ethnic identity. The scores do not, of course, show the degree to which a strong Canadian identity has emerged. Of the groups surveyed in the first generation, the West Indians had a score of 3.94, the Chinese 4.35, the Italians 4.37, the Jewish 4.44, the Ukrainians 4.61, the English 5.12, the Portuguese 5.26, and the Germans 5.73.[10]

Generation is usually considered to be the chief factor affecting ethnic identity. First-generation immigrants often have cultural and linguistic badges they cannot shed even if they wish to; second-generation immigrants may still have, or feel they have, distinctive marks, but even more commonly have a feeling of being divided or being in transition; members of the third and later generations, unless they have visible characteristics linking them to their ancestral group, have a choice of identifying themselves with that group or simply being Canadian. In a study carried out in 1969-71 in eighteen ethno-religious bloc settlements in north-central Saskatchewan, all Hutterites favoured preservation of ethnic identity, but among Doukhobors, Ukrainian Catholics, Ukrainian Orthodox, Mennonites, Scandinavians, French, and German Catholics there was a steady increase from the first through the second and third generations in the proportion not favouring identity preservation.[11] In the Metro Toronto study, the indices for the groups that included three generations in all cases but one increased regularly. For Germans, the index in the second generation dipped to 5.57 but in the third generation this rose to 7.69, the highest index attained by any group.[12]

The significance of generation is made most evident among the Japanese, where different terms are used for the different generations. The immigrants are Issei, their children are Nisei, their grandchildren are Sansei. Since most immigration of Japanese to Canada before 1967 occurred from 1904 to 1914, the generational names also indicate roughly the age of the person and the outstanding historical events experienced.

Important as it is, generation is not the sole factor influencing ethnic identity. Through the years, questions in the Canadian census have given prominence to ethnic origin. Periodically efforts were made to remove the questions, or to allow people to answer Canadian or American. However, spokespeople for various ethnic groups fought against such efforts: in 1961 members of the Legislative Assembly of Quebec threatened to call upon French Canadians to boycott the census or answer Negro to the question about ethnic origin if Canadian and American were accepted as answers.[13] The question has continued to be asked, with the difference that in 1981 it no longer specified that origin should be reckoned on the male side. Having to claim an ethnic origin, and knowing that it was entered in official records, has accentuated ethnic consciousness. It is ironic that immigration statistics ceased to be kept regarding ethnic origin in the late 1960s when the Royal Commission on Bilingualism and Biculturalism had brought ethnicity to the forefront in Canada.

Surnames also have an effect. The bearers of surnames that are not of British origin are often asked what the origin of the name is and are approached for support by ethnic organizations that make assumptions about origin based on names. In 1986 it was revealed that "foreign-sounding" names on court dockets were routinely checked by immigration officers looking for illegal aliens. Researchers sometimes propose surnames as found in telephone directories or on voters' lists or assessment rolls as the basis for sampling an ethnic group, or employ names as clues to the immigration and settlement of ethnic groups.

Names are, however, an uncertain guide to ethnic identity. They may be changed fairly easily. Sometimes in the past immigration officers simplified names or changed them completely for convenience; immigrants later also simplified or changed their surnames, especially (according to two studies of name-changing carried out in Ontario in the early 1960s[14]) Slavic immigrants. Such changes in many cases, but not all, reflect changes in ethnic identity; sometimes individuals or their descendants revert to the original family names.

Although the legal process of changing one's name by deed poll is easy, the psychological process may be extremely difficult. When attempts were made to Anglicize the names of the Armenian orphans known as the Georgetown boys in 1923, one boy said of another, "... do you see that boy sitting on the end of this row? He lost his father and mother, his home and country—everything that is dear to a boy's heart. All he has left of his past is his name. Please sir, you won't take that away from him, will you?" As a result the attempt at name-changing was abandoned.[15] In the case of one Italian immigrant, the Anglicizing of his name from Veltri to Welch has been blamed for his mental illness and early death.[16]

Discrimination based on name, appearance, or accent against members of various ethnic groups has heightened ethnic consciousness; it has also exerted pressure toward discarding an ancestral ethnic identity. The novelist John Marlyn has described how the protagonist of *Under the Ribs of Death,* Sandor Hunyadi, the Canadian-born son of a cultured Hungarian immigrant growing up in Winnipeg in the 1920s, was led by discrimination to turn away from the values of his father and to change his name to Alex Hunter so that nobody would be able to tell that he had ever been a foreigner.[17] The signal discrimination against enemy aliens, especially Germans during World War I and Japanese Canadians during World War II, appears to have led in the first instance to many denials of reprobated ethnic origins and in the second to avoidance of ethnic communities and institutions and to intermarriage.

The policy of multiculturalism also has contradictory effects. It has been interpreted as encouraging retention of ancestral ethnic identity, culture, and language, and has been criticized either for attempting to do so or for doing so inadequately. At the same time, it involves programs designed to remove barriers to full participation in Canadian society and to promote interchange between different ethnic groups: thus, to the degree that it succeeds, it facilitates development of a Canadian identity. The contradiction reflects a paradox in the aims of ethnic groups. They want both to remain distinctive and to have equality, as collectivities and as individuals, with others. However, the question must be posed whether more than marginal differentiation, or symbolic ethnicity, is possible in an egalitarian pluralism. Critics of the policy of multiculturalism accuse it of ignoring issues of economic and political power in favour of cultural issues. They assume that the two kinds of issues can be separated. The assumption is erroneous: "Cultures ... differ in nothing more than in the skill, work habits and goals which they instill into the individual."[18] Hard choices must be made as to whether stress will be put upon preservation of differences or equality; the choices will be made by individuals rather than by collectivities.

Notes

1. O'Bryan et al., *Non-Official Languages.*

2. Everett C. Hughes, *The Sociological Eye: Selected Papers* (Chicago and New York: Aldine Atherton, 1971), p. 186.

3. The Levy-Coughlin Partnership, "The National Survey of Folkloric Performing Arts Groups," Prepared for the Multiculturalism Program of the Government of Canada, 1982.

4. Aun, *The Political Refugees,* p. 58.

5. Harry Vjekoslav Herman, *Men in White Aprons: A Study of Ethnicity and Occupation* (Toronto: Peter Martin Associates, 1978), p. xiii.

6. Bruce Kidd, "The Workers' Sports Movement in Canada, 1924–40: The Radical Immigrants' Alternative," *Polyphony,* 7, 1 (1985), pp. 80–88.

7. Robert F. Harney, "Homo Ludens and Ethnicity," *Polyphony,* 7, 1 (1985), pp. 9–10.

8. Doug Daniels, "The White race is shrinking: perceptions of race in Canada and some speculations on the political economy of race classification," *Ethnic and Racial Studies,* 4, 3 (1981), pp. 353–56.

9. O'Bryan et al., *Non-Official Languages,* p. 97.

10. Wsevolod W. Isajiw, "Ethnic Identity Retention," Ethnic Pluralism Paper No. 5 (Toronto: Centre for Urban and Community Studies, University of Toronto, 1981), pp. 47–49.

11. Alan Anderson and Leo Driedger, "The Mennonite Family: Culture and Kin in Rural Saskatchewan," in Ishwaran, ed., *Canadian Families,* p. 166.

12. Isajiw, "Ethnic Identity Retention," p. 49.

13. *Globe and Mail,* 18 January 1961.

14. Canadian Institute of Cultural Research, *Ethnic Change of Name, Ontario—A Pilot Study* (Toronto: Canadian Institute of Cultural Research, 1965); Brenda Conway, "A Study of Factors Involved in Name Changing by Members of Ethnic Minorities," (M.A. thesis, University of Toronto, 1966).

15. Jack Apramian, "The Georgetown Boys," *Polyphony,* 4, 2 (1982), pp. 44–45.

16. John Potestio, "The Memoirs of Giovanni Veltri," *Polyphony,* 7, 2 (1985), p. 14.

17. John Marlyn, *Under the Ribs of Death* (Toronto: McClelland and Stewart, 1957).

18. Hughes, *The Sociological Eye,* p. 75.

THE SIMPLIFICATION OF CULTURE

Neil Bissoondath

> *In Canada, I don't think we've really explored how the immigration experience changes people, when they move from one country to another. It's easier just to comment on different foods and folkloric dances than to really understand what people go through when they emigrate .... In Canada, there has been a tendency to trivialize.*
>
> Nino Ricci quoted in *Profiles*, February 1994

It is at times strange to me that for my great-grandparents English was a second language. They were Brahmins, members of the learned caste, but poor. In Trinidad they led tenuous lives working the land, going about their daily tasks—cutting sugarcane stalks, tending rice paddies—mostly in Hindi. That I find this strange says much about the change that the years have brought. Both the lives they led and the language they spoke have now grown impossibly remote, their faces, even their names, long drifted, for my generation at least, into an irretrievable anonymity.

Change, made inevitable by time and space and Bible-toting missionaries from another British colony called Canada, marked itself on their children. In the schools that bartered education for religious conversion (the bargain not always kept, my paternal grandfather and one of his brothers remaining loyal to the old faith while two other brothers embraced the new), a greater facility in English was acquired. In an agrarian society, this could not have been easy—but forever after, my grandfather ritually read his daily English-language newspaper, lips soundlessly forming the words.

For both my grandfathers, the new language offered escape from the eviscerating labours of the field. My paternal grandfather found success in commerce, while my mother's father, less practical, more of a dreamer, engaged what little literary life the island had to offer by becoming a newspaper reporter who wrote short stories in his spare time.

Success, though, exacted a price. For my father's parents (my mother's father died before I was born), Hindi eventually became little more than a language of religion and secrets, spoken only in prayer and for privacy between themselves. In both families, English, the language of success, was the language of communication with the children, the result being that my parents spoke no Hindi save a word here and there, mostly terms of endearment or disparagement infrequently uttered.

Within three generations, then, the language of my great-grandparents had all but disappeared, and along with it had gone a way of life: dependence on the land, religious belief. We felt no sense of loss, no tincture of regret, no romantic attachment to a language that no longer served the purposes of our circumstance. And those of my parents' generation who still clung to the distant past—the few women who only wore saris, the few men who went to India in search of wives—came to be viewed as eccentric and foolish.

My own world was very different from the one in which my parents had grown up. While, for them, going abroad to study represented a grand and lengthy journey—farewells at the docks, the slow progression of the ship towards the horizon—for my generation it was one more step in a normal progression. Like my contemporaries, my mode of travel was jet-powered, the trip a few short hours. My only language was English, my popular cultural influences, in an island independent only ten years, less British or Indian than American: not Ravi Shankar or Laurence Olivier but the Temptations and Clint Eastwood. Through schooling, I acquired French, Spanish and the cultural influences they entailed, including an enduring love of the poetry of the Spanish poet Federico Garcia Lorca.

When, at the age of eighteen, I left Trinidad for Canada, the journey that had begun in India a century before—and here I mean not just the physical journey—was simply proceeding to its next logical step. (Members of my family now live not only here but in England and the United States as well.) After twenty years, this country now claims all of my loyalty, intellectual and emotional.

India and many things Indian have been left behind. Trinidad and many things Trinidadian have been left behind. Much else, though, has been assumed along the way.

In a way, then, time and circumstance have succeeded where the Canadian missionaries failed—not in terms of religion but in terms of culture. It is a change that can be viewed as a loss to be mourned, but there is, too, a less nostalgic way of looking at it.

In his novel *A Bend in the River*, V.S. Naipaul, my uncle, writes: "The world is what it is; men who are nothing, who allow themselves to become nothing, have no place in it."[1] Making a place for ourselves is what my families have long been good at: it is one of the effects of the fear of becoming nothing. Both families are now replete with doctors and lawyers, teachers and writers. All this has come, in great part, through a refusal to brood over the loss of one language and its cultural baggage and a willingness to fully embrace another. English, then, is not for us a borrowed language but an acquired one, as fully part of my families today as Hindi was a hundred years ago: the distinction is vital.

The languages I speak are central to me. My attachment to them is strong and passionate. They have made me what I am, have provided me with a way of looking at the world, of exploring and understanding it. Perhaps most important of all, they have given me the means of expressing what I see. For in being a writer, in engaging through my imagination the varied elements of familial experience, I am linked to my maternal grandfather and to all of those faceless, nameless people who came before.

Culture is life. It is a living, breathing, multi-faceted entity in constant evolution. It alters every day, is never the same thing from one day to the next. Stasis is not possible. A culture that failed to grow from within inevitably becomes untrue to itself, inevitably descends into folklore.

Culture is a complex entity shaped in ways small and large. A preference for coffee over tea or beer over wine. Movies over books or sitcoms over documentaries. Free-trade over managed trade or insularity over adventurism. Change through negotiation or change through arms. Nothing is inconsequential. Culture must be measured in its minutiae. The very breath of a people must be appreciated, or else that people and their history are trivialized, reduced to the most common of denominators: stereotype.

No consequence of multiculturalism policy is as ironic—or as unintended— as what I would call the simplification of culture.

The public face of Canadian multiculturalism is flashy and attractive; it emerges with verve and gaiety from the bland stereotype of traditional Canada at "ethnic" festivals around the country. At Toronto's "Caravan," for instance, various ethnic groups rent halls in churches or community centres to create "pavilions" to which access is gained through a purchased "passport." Once admitted—passport duly stamped at the door with a "visa"—you consume a plate of Old World food at distinctly New World prices, take a quick tour of the "craft" and "historical" displays and then find a seat for the "cultural" show: traditional songs (often about love in the wheat fields) and traditional dances (often about harvesting wheat) performed by youths resplendent in their traditional costumes. There is tradition in sufficient quantities in these pavilions to satisfy even Tevye, that glutton of tradition from *Fiddler on the Roof* (except that some national traditions never mentioned would see Tevye reduced to traditional pulp at the hands of mobs driven mad by traditional anti-Semitism).

After the show, positively glowing with your exposure to yet another tile of our multicultural mosaic, you make your way to the next pavilion, to the next line-up for food, the next display, the next bout of cultural edification. It is a kind of journey, not of the "If it's Tuesday this must be Belgium" kind but of the "If it's two o'clock it must be Kiev" kind: a world tour in an afternoon.

And at the end of the day, you may be forgiven if you feel, guiltily to be sure, that you have just sat through a folksy, Canadian-mosaic version of the Jungle Cruise at Walt Disney World in Florida.

It is a sad spectacle, the Jungle Cruise. The guide, in his big-white-hunter outfit, stands at the head of the boat spouting rehearsed wisecracks into a microphone. On shore and in the water—the Amazon, the Nile—mechanical creatures (hippos, pythons, a pride of lions, Indian and African elephants) nod and huff in sightless animation. The guide, cool as a cucumber, fires a cap pistol to "scare off" the threat of a curious hippo.

To accept the reality of these creatures, to be sufficiently taken with them not to feel cheated, requires not imagination but the failure of it. This is nature remade and sanitized, Jungle the Good. It is illusion—and, being from Disney, is not meant to be more. Anyone disembarking from the boat convinced that he has truly experienced the jungles of South America and Africa would be taken for a simpleton.

And so it is with the ethnic cultures offered at the pavilions of Caravan and other such festivals: all the colourful ethnics bowing and smiling in mechanical greeting at the tourists, themselves mostly other ethnics, passing by. They look like the real thing, but their smell is synthetic. They have no bite. They are safe. Culture Disneyfied.

Implicit in this approach is the peculiar notion of culture as commodity: a thing that can be displayed, performed, admired, bought, sold or forgotten. It represents a devaluation of culture, its reduction to bauble and kitsch. A traditional dance performed on a stage is not a people's cultural life but an aspect of it removed from context, shaped and packaged to give a voyeuristic pleasure. It is not without value, but value on par with the reproduced treasures of Tutankhamun sold in every sad store on the continent.

To attend an ethnic cultural festival, then, is to expose yourself not to culture but to theatre, not to history but to fantasy: enjoyable, no doubt, but of questionable significance. You come away having learnt nothing of the language and literature of these places, little of their past and their present—and what you have seen is usually shaped with blatant political ends in mind. You have acquired no sense of the everyday lives—the culture—of the people in these places, but there is no doubt that they are, each and every one, open, sincere and fun-loving.

Such displays, dependent as they are on superficialities, reduce cultures hundreds, sometimes thousands of years old to easily digested stereotypes. One's sense of Ukrainian culture is restricted to perogies and Cossack dancing; Greeks, we learn, are all jolly Zorbas, and Spaniards dance flamenco between shouts of "Viva España!" Germans gulp beer, sauerkraut and sausages while belting out Bavarian drinking songs; Italians make good ice cream, great coffee, and all have connections to shady godfathers. And the Chinese continue to be a people who form conga lines under dragon costumes and serve good, cheap food in slightly dingy restaurants.

There are Chinatowns, it seems, in just about every major city on this continent, benign ghettos (at least to the outsider not prey to gangland extortion) crowded with designer-clad youths and shrunken, combative grandparents. Restaurants, few of which are models of interior decoration or sanitation, jostle stores dense with wicker and plastic; evil-smelling supermarkets offer exotic foods and suspicious-looking herbs. Business establishments are often exquisitely named. I was always particularly fond of the "Happy Meat Market" and "Wing On Funeral Home," both once of Spadina Avenue in Toronto, and recall with delight the young Taiwanese man who, having decided that he must have an English name, chose Shark, because he admired the animal's tenacity, and when told this would not do, chose Ladder, because it symbolized his ambition. He finally settled on Jay, for its beauty and simplicity.

We are proud of our Chinatowns. We show them off to visitors. It is a sign of how far we have come. Once victims of xenophobia, prey to discriminatory head-tax, the Chinese, whether of Hong Kong, Taiwan, or the People's Republic of China, now find Canada, officially at least, a welcoming place. We even have a special immigration program to lure them (or at least their money) here.

But there are problems still, resentments that arise towards any burgeoning group of immigrants, visible or invisible. Some blame the Chinese for the cost of housing in Vancouver; some resent their successes in school, the fashionable clothes, the costly cars.

It was all so controllable before. The Chinese were seen as a silent, hardworking, dispassionate people. They kept mostly to themselves, procreating rather spectacularly, living in tiny, dark rooms, playing mah-jong, gambling in "dens." Now, though, they are going beyond their traditional enclaves, are even unblanding the Toronto suburb of Scarborough with a new Chinatown. And this is profoundly unsettling to those who would rather have their multiculturalism exoticism safely caged, costumed and staged. We are being forced by events, both here and abroad, to admit that these are people pushing the boundaries of their stereotype. We are being forced to confront their wholeness.

In the early 1980s, I earned my living teaching English as a Second Language. At one point, the school welcomed what were still at the time rather exotic creatures: three students, two young women and a man, from the People's Republic of China. They were good students of differing abilities, ready with smiles, as friendly as their command of the language would allow.

One day, as we all sat around having lunch, one of the women began talking about life in China. The words did not come easily to her. She wrestled with the language, passion in her voice, while her compatriots listened blankfaced, adding nothing. But when the words "cultural revolution" spilled with a striking bitterness from her tongue, the man's gaze suddenly bore down on her. In rapid Mandarin, he snapped her harshly into an instant silence—a silence that blanketed the room. Conversation was slow to return in the charged atmosphere.

Back in the classroom that afternoon, the young woman, to my surprise, again took up the theme. This time there was no one to stop her. Within minutes, she was raging about the Red Guard brutality visited upon her father, a doctor; about the destruction of her family; about the poverty in China that allowed children to run around ragged and barefoot, with little education and little food. Her eyes reddened, big tears slicked her cheeks. Her declaration of her intention never to return to China was choked off by sobs catching in her throat. I declared a break while a Venezuelan student offered comfort. When the class resumed a few minutes later, the talk was all of nouns, verbs and adjectives. The subject of life in China was never raised again, but in the quiet classroom in the heart of Toronto her display of rage was rare and, so, unforgettable.

When, some years later, in the spring of 1989, a million demonstrators defied the government in Tiananmen Square; when the brutality of the army was met by the brutality of the protesters; when a man, alone and unarmed, confronted tanks sent to crush his ideals, I heard the rage again, and I witnessed, as did millions of others around the world, the courage of that rage. I saw rage transform forever all notions of the silent and dispassionate Chinese: people seen with greater clarity, people seen in their wholeness. Suddenly, in their hunger for the freedoms we profess to cherish, they were more like us.

So who are they, then, these Chinese people? Their multicultural niche gives us no hint of their passions. If, before, the Dragon Dance evoked hazy background images of restaurants and laundries, it might now offer images of waving banners, excited faces, tanks, gunfire and pools of blood. It might help us to understand that there is more to these people than our exhibitionistic multiculturalism has ever allowed us to appreciate. An honest Chinese pavilion at future ethnic festivals should offer, along with the costumes and the dances and the food, photos and videos of the turmoil in Tiananmen Square—along with honest exposition of the startling economic reforms, instituted by the geriatric government, that are quickly transforming Communist China into Capitalist China. But would this ever happen? Or would such frankness prove too unsettling for Canadian appetites? Maybe the reality is too much. Illusion, after all, is much easier to bear. In the Canadian multicultural context, my former student would, I suspect, find another kind of betrayal, another kind of rage. It is, in the end, a question of respect.

Cultural heritage is not always a pretty thing. It involves the good and the bad, the attractive and the unattractive, reasons for pride and reasons for shame. The brutality of the Red Guards is a vital part of my former student's heritage. It informed, and deformed, her life. It is part of the baggage she brought to this country, an inherent part of herself. She will never forget, she will never forgive. But where do her passions fit in our political concept of multiculturalism? Ours is not a policy that accommodates blood and brutality. We seek only the light and choose to ignore the shadows.

Furthermore, how misleading it is to speak of "the Chinese," as if no radical differences of experience, of outlook, exist between the people of Hong Kong, so long a British protectorate, the people of authoritarian Taiwan and the people of the brutalized mainland. Only through misrepresentation can a place be made in the mosaic for "the Chinese community." Can multiculturalism accommodate the complex reality of these lives? Can it be unflinching multiculturalism? Or must it inevitably trivialize?

Our approach to multiculturalism encourages the devaluation of that which it claims to wish to protect and promote. Culture becomes an object for display rather than the heart and soul of the individuals formed by it. Culture, manipulated into social and political usefulness, becomes folklore—as René Lévesque said—lightened and simplified, stripped of the weight of the past. None of the cultures that make up our "mosaic" seems to have produced history worthy of exploration or philosophy worthy of consideration.

I am reminded of the man who once said to me that he would never move into an apartment building that housed any East Indian families because the building was sure to be infested with roaches: East Indians, he explained, view cockroaches as creatures of good luck, and they give live ones as gifts to each other. I had known the man for some time, was certain that he was in no way racist—a perception confirmed by the fact that he was admitting this to me, someone clearly of East Indian descent. His hesitation was not racial but cultural. So searching for an apartment, he perceived potential neighbours not as fellow Canadians, old or new, but as cockroach-lovers, a "cultural truth" that he accepted without question. I was not of India: he would not hesitate in having me for a neighbour. But what would he have done, I wondered later with some discomfort, had he not known me and seen me emerging from a building he was about to visit?

The vision that many of us have of each other is one of division. It is informed by misunderstanding and misconception: often what we know of each other is at best superficial, at worst malicious.

The "Mongolian blue spot" is a light birthmark common to children of Asian and black descent which often disappears as the child gets older. Three-year-old Joshua Ahn and his one-year-old sister Megan were born with Mongolian blue spots. On their first day in day-care in Surrey, B.C., their mother, Jinny Ahn, was informed that they were being detained by day-care personnel and that, furthermore, the RCMP had been called. The children, she was told, had bruises that appeared to be evidence of child abuse. "They told me they suspected me of beating my children," she said. While police contacted the children's doctor, Mrs. Ahn was not permitted to comfort her distraught toddlers.

This was not the first time that Mongolian blue spots had led to problems: in New Brunswick in 1992, three toddlers were abducted by a day-care worker who mistook their spots for bruises. These were certainly honest mistakes prompted by the urge to do good—but is ignorance ever a defence? Mrs. Ahn said, "I think people involved with child care shouldn't be so ignorant of racial differences." They should not be, but it is hardly surprising that they are: we are cognizant of the differences—the shape of the eyes, the colour of the skin—that do not count, but we remain uninformed concerning the ones that do.

Multiculturalism, with all of its festivals and its celebrations, has done—and can do—nothing to foster a factual and clear-minded vision of our neighbours. Depending on stereotype, ensuring that ethnic groups will preserve their distinctiveness in a gentle and insidious form of cultural apartheid, multiculturalism has done little more than lead an already divided country down the path to further social divisiveness.

The Excesses of Sensitivity

It was a case both banal and horrifying. Banal because one would wish such actions less common in our society, horrifying because of the sheer perversity of the act—and also because of the reaction it drew from the trial judge.

On January 13, 1994, Québec court Judge Raymonde Verreault sentenced a man, unidentified in order to protect the identity of his victim, to twenty-three months in prison for sexual assault. The crown prosecutor had asked for a term of four years. The victim was the man's eleven-year-old stepdaughter. In justifying her leniency, Judge Verreault explained that she had taken the man's religion—Islam—into consideration. The accused, she told the courtroom, had "in a certain manner" spared the victim. She based this conclusion on "the fact that the accused did not have normal and complete relations with the victim— that is to say, vaginal sexual relations, to be more precise—so that he could preserve her virginity, which seems to be a very important value in their religion."[2] The man had preserved the girl's virginity by repeatedly sodomizing her over a two-and-a-half-year period. In view of the man's continued denial of the abuse and his evident lack of remorse, Judge Verreault added, she saw no point in ordering any rehabilitation treatment for him. The defence attorney, while admitting that he found the comments on the lack of vaginal penetration "unbelievable," also lauded the judge's "very, very courageous" decision. "She did recognize that there's a value structure,"[3] he told *The Gazette*.

The defence lawyer was right. The judge did recognize the existence of a value structure—but both the defence lawyer and the judge failed to question not only the terms of that structure but its validity as well. Montréal's Muslim community was not alone in its outrage at the use of Islam to minimize what would be a crime in any society. Judge Verreault was subsequently ordered to appear before a hearing into her actions by the Québec Judicial Council, and so it should be when a judge's competence comes into question.

What is most interesting, however, is Judge Verreault's instinct in deciding on the sentence. Her appreciation of the situation was faulty, her knowledge of Islam inadequate to the task, but she also clearly believed she was being sensitive to the man, to his victim and to the larger ethnic and cultural context. How easily, though, the instinct of sensitivity leads to a loss of perspective. How easily it betrays the urge to do what's right.

It is a lesson the government of Ontario has had to learn.

In November 1993, the Ontario Public Service employment paper Job Mart advertised a senior management position for a director of information technology, a job that offered an annual salary of between $74,000 and $111,000. "The competition," the ad read, "is limited to the following employment equity designated groups: aboriginal peoples, francophones, persons with disabilities, racial minorities and women."[4] The ad's approach is positive; it is superbly worded to offer a vision of inclusion. And yet it might have been franker, more honest, had its true message been explicitly spelled out: "White, English-speaking males need not apply." This, of course, would have been too blatant; it would have re-called similar sentiments once directed against Jews and Blacks and Irishmen. So the writer of the ad chose instead to be verbose and circumlocutory, perhaps in the hope that no one would notice that, under the laudable banner of em-ployment equity, the Ontario government was implementing a hiring policy not of non-discrimination but of targeted discrimination—and that only one group in society could now acceptably be targeted.

The government of Ontario describes this approach to hiring as one of "pos-itive measures." It has, according to a Management Board memo obtained by *The Globe and Mail*, instituted a programme in its various ministries to modify the hiring and promotion process by "limiting competition to designated groups."[5] The programme is not limited to provincial government, however. The employ-ment-equity legislation, Bill 79, applies similar requirements to private companies in order to ensure that "[e]very employer's workforce, in all occupational categories and at all levels of employment, shall reflect the representation of aboriginal people, people with disabilities, members of racial minorities and women in the community."[6] The programme aims to establish "goals" and "timetables," but not "quotas," which has become a loaded word. But how is the desired repre-sentation to be achieved—how is it to be measured—without a head count? Without *quotas*? Like the writer of the *Job Mart* advertisement, the defenders of the legislation play linguistic gymnastics—a sleight of tongue, as it were—but no amount of twirling and tumbling can disguise the underlying artifice.

Discrimination is discrimination is discrimination. There is nothing wrong with the word. Life is at its best when there is choice, and choice implies dis-crimination. We discriminate every day when we choose this newspaper over that one, one lover over another, give to this beggar rather than the next. Sometimes we can verbalize the reasons for our discrimination; sometimes we just go on in-stinct. But discrimination is always a moral choice; it must be exercised with subtlety: Do I pull into this gas station because its price is better—or because the attendant at the next is black? Do I give change to this beggar because he is an old man battered by life—or to the next because she is a young woman bat-tered by life? I once met someone who left New York City because this moral choice, confronted daily and endlessly, proved overwhelming. But choice cannot be avoided, and in a multi-ethnic society such as ours, the issue must be con-fronted. The Ontario government cannot be blamed for trying, yet its approach appears to be yet another instance of sensitivity derailing perspective. The ad-vertisement, quickly mired in controversy, was withdrawn a few days later.

The problem is simple: Is the aim of a hiring program to construct as efficient a public work force as possible, or is it to construct a public service that is sta-tistically reflective of the make-up of the society? If almost one out of every three inhabitants of Metropolitan Toronto is of a visible minority, must one out of three members of the Ontario civil service in Toronto be "visible"? Such a goal, whatever it merits, is not incompatible with the goal of efficiency. What is important is where the stress is placed—on the performance or the appearance. The wording of the Job Mart advertisement would suggest that this program stresses the latter: it clearly calls not for the best person for the job but for the best person from the designated groups. The white, male English-speaker who might stand head and shoulders above everyone else in qualification is automatically excluded—and the efficiency of performance is automatically lowered.

Ontario citizenship minister Diane Ziemba said in a reaction to the designated-groups controversy, "You might want to do that after many years of failure at bringing people into a workplace. It is one of those temporary positive measures that you might use in an extreme case if everything else has failed."[7] Impatience is understandable. Progress in integrating traditionally excluded groups into the civil service has been slow. But it is now more than ever that patience is required—patience and a stern refusal to compromise on essentials.

Reaching for short-term results at the expense of long-term process serves the goals of ideology—but it serves no one's purposes, least of all the purposes of the designated groups. If it is hateful to be the victim of discrimination because your skin is brown or you must use a wheelchair, it seems to me to be equally hateful to profit from it—and the attitude of those who would make it so reminds me of those people who go in search of, say, a black lover "for the experience": it is only the skin that attracts, not the person. What may appear open-minded is in fact just another kind of marginalization. It is the attempt to present a restrictive label in the most attractive and respectable light.

It is not impossible to have employment equity—to actively search out and hire those who have been the historical victims of discrimination—without sacrificing the quality of work. A certain amount of discrimination is inevitable, but everything must be done to keep it to a minimum: to force all white, English-speaking males to pay for the wrongs committed by others of their colour, language and gender is like giving an entire class detention because one of its number scribbled a dirty word on the blackboard. It is juvenile and discriminatory.

The ideal in hiring policy, then, would be an initially blind approach, looking only at education, experience and ability: the best person gets the job. But, in the event of parity in those areas, other elements—colour, gender, ethnicity, disability—might justly be engaged in the name of social justice. It is likely that, initially at least, most of those hired will be white anglophone males, but in the long term, as the "designated groups" acquire the necessary tools and qualifications, this too will change. It is not dramatic; it will not purchase votes; but it will in the end serve the goals of ideological belief as well as the needs of the public service and the designated groups.

To adopt the approach of the Ontario government is to breed resentment and to run the risk of rewarding incompetence. It is to create the perception of preferential treatment in the public mind.

On a personal level, as a member of one of those targeted racial minorities, I can think of few things more demeaning to me than to be offered an advantage because of my skin colour. It is demeaning because, no matter what I have struggled to achieve, I am still being judged on the colour of my skin and not simply as a human being with strengths and weaknesses. I am still, even with the best intentions, being viewed racially—and that is offensive to me.

The same vision seems to have taken hold in education. Hard on the heels of the announcement of an Ontario government policy to encourage high school students to "affirm their racial identity," the University of Ottawa Law School designed an "Education Equity Program" to ensure fairness to "any and all students who feel that traditional examination arrangements are prejudicial to their optimum performance."[8] Since "the examination process with its systematic components may disadvantage some persons," such persons would be allowed to apply for "exam accommodation," meaning that they would be given twice the usual time—in one instance, six hours instead of three—to write their examinations.

While certain of the grounds—illness, religious holidays, physical disabilities—were laudable in their sensitivity, others were, to be generous, certainly creative. Single-parenthood was given by the Dean of Common Law as one instance justifying accommodation on the grounds of "family responsibility": single-parenthood is onerous; time, which childless students can put into studying, must be put into child-care. It is a valid argument, but one that must also be applied to the economically disadvantaged (once known as the poor) who must spend time at part-time jobs that the economically advantaged (still known as the rich) can put into studying.

But it is the grounds of "barriers related to race and culture" that I find both intriguing and creative. What in the world could this possibly mean? It may be a failure of imagination that prevents my understanding. I have searched for a scenario that would justify a student's being given twice the time to complete an examination because of the colour of his or her skin. A cultural scenario worthy of such consideration has also eluded me. But I am quite prepared to offer the benefit of the doubt. The university authorities must have sufficient cause for accepting such grounds.

It is also my imagination, though, that gives me reason for pause. I could imagine myself, sometime in the future, charged with some crime—assault of a literary critic, say—and in need of a lawyer. I make an appointment with a lawyer—of colour, naturally, since I am most comfortable with one of my own—and as I am ushered into his or her office my eye falls on the framed diploma and I read "University of Ottawa." And my first question for my potential lawyer is whether he or she took advantage of the exam accommodation. Should the answer be affirmative, I immediately take my leave. Lawyers charge $250 an hour. I would rather have an attorney who can deal with my case in half the time, unhampered by "barriers related to race and culture."

Such sensitivities and the policies they engender—whether those of the Ontario government or of the University of Ottawa Law School—serve the interests of no one. They are inimical not only to the society at large, by their possible institutionalization of incompetence, but also to the individuals they affect, by providing such ready excuses. Nothing is as seductive as special consideration: why make the intellectual effort when other factors will ensure success?

That there are problems to be addressed there is no doubt. But simply changing the focus of discrimination, treating members of visible minorities as if their skin colour were a handicap, is no answer. As notions of fairness, such policies are simplistic and disarming. They work against the righting of the wrongs they wish to address and, in doing so, clearly reveal the moral muddle in which we have gone about administering our multicultural society.

Notes

1. V.S. Naipaul, *A Bend in the River* (New York: Alfred A. Knopf, 1979), p. 3.

2. Irwin Block, "Women outraged by judge's remarks," *Montreal Gazette*, January 15, 1994.

3. Geoff Baker, "Stepdad gets 2 years in sex assault," *Montreal Gazette*, January 14, 1994.

4. *The Globe and Mail*, November 12, 1993.

5. *Ibid.*

6. *Ibid.*

7. Margot Gibb-Clark, "Ontario stage set for job equity," *The Globe and Mail*, November 24, 1993.

8. "Examination by disadvantage?" editorial, *The Globe and Mail,* February 19, 1994.

Index